EXECUTIVE SECRETARIAL PROCEDURES

fifTH Ed.

Irene Place, Ed.D.

Professor, Business Education
Portland State University
Portland, Oregon

Edward E. Byers, Ed.D.

Editor in Chief,
   Business/Management/Office Education
Gregg Division
McGraw-Hill Book Company

Elaine F. Uthe, Ph.D.

Head of Business Education
University of Kentucky
Lexington, Kentucky

Gregg Division / McGraw-Hill Book Company

New York   Atlanta   Dallas   St. Louis
San Francisco   Auckland   Bogotá   Düsseldorf
Johannesburg   London   Madrid   Mexico
Montreal   New Delhi   Panama   Paris
São Paulo   Singapore   Sydney   Tokyo   Toronto

Sponsoring Editor	Margaret Halmy
Editing Supervisor	Susan Goldfarb
Production Supervisor	Laurence Charnow
Design Supervisor	Caryl V. Spinka
Art Supervisor	Howard Brotman

Designer	Judy Grossman
Cover Designer	F. Ronald Fowler
Photographer	Martin Bough

Library of Congress Cataloging in Publication Data

Place, Irene, (date)
    Executive secretarial procedures.

    Fourth ed. by I. Place, C. B. Hicks, and E. E. Byers
published in 1972 under title: College secretarial
procedures.
    Includes bibliographical references and index.
    1. Office practice.   I. Byers, Edward Elmer, joint
author.   II. Uthe, Elaine F., (date), joint author.   III. Title.
HF5547.5.P55 1980   651'.3741'0202   79-9097
ISBN 0-07-050255-2

Executive Secretarial Procedures, Fifth Edition

234567890   DODO   87654321

Preface

Almost every aspect of secretarial performance is changing. The relentless demand for more information and more productive communication in business, industry, and government is producing new office procedures and technology for handling business transactions and the accompanying paperwork. The widespread movement for equal job opportunities for everyone, regardless of sex and ethnic background, is forging changed attitudes toward secretarial work. Affirmative action programs are broadening career paths and opportunities for secretaries. Newly trained secretaries are beginning to view themselves as "progressional," accepting secretarial assignments with the understanding that they are being apprenticed for higher-level administrative or supervisory jobs. This new upward mobility is dramatically altering the long-standing tradition that secretaries can advance only laterally into top management offices in support of successful executives.

Executive Secretarial Procedures, Fifth Edition, is written for students who will seek employment in business and government as contributing members of an administrative team and who will need office procedure skills. The program emphasizes the competencies that allow secretaries to assume responsibility without direct supervision, exercise initiative and judgment, and make decisions within the scope of their authority—the requisites for promotion.

Opportunities for those who want to be secretaries have never been better. The nationwide demand for secretaries is expected to increase faster than the average for all other occupations through 1985 because of the growing volume of paperwork as business and government continue to expand their operations. Working conditions for secretaries will continue to improve markedly. In an effort to attract competent secretarial candidates, employers are expected to offer generous fringe benefits—vacations, discounts, tuition plans, group insurance, pensions, and even options on company stock.

Executive Secretarial Procedures, Fifth Edition, contains 26 chapters grouped into seven parts. Part One deals with the multidisciplinary characteristics of secretarial positions, the office environment, and career self-fulfillment. Part Two discusses communication with people inside and outside the business office. Part Three outlines the secretary's role in handling office mail and storing and retrieving needed information. Part Four describes the new generation of office equipment and procedures for receiving dictation, transcribing from shorthand notes or from dictation equipment, editing and composing, and reproducing recorded information. Part Five introduces the technology used to read, record, classify, sort, calculate, store, and report business data. Secretarial responsibility for researching information and the skills required to prepare reports and graphic presentations are also explained in detail. Part Six stresses supervisory opportunities available to the secretary as well as responsibilities of assisting with travel plans and arranging meetings. Secretarial financial and banking duties are also discussed. Part Seven examines career options the secretary should consider in selecting the right entry-level position. Suggestions are given to help secretaries realize their potential as members of an executive team and to move into management positions.

There are four kinds of exercise material at the end of each text chapter. "Reviewing Your Reading" questions check the students' comprehension of the key procedures and practices introduced in each chapter. "Using Your Skills" problems give students a chance to pull together their knowledge and to apply their skills in simulated office tasks. "Exercising Your Judgment" presents hypothetical situations that test the students' knowledge of human relations. "Applying the Reference Section" exercises provide a valuable review of spelling, usage, and the chief aspects of style—the essentials for anyone who writes, transcribes, edits, or types.

Central to *Executive Secretarial Procedures*, Fifth Edition, is the set of secretarial in baskets that reinforce the objectives of the text. Each in basket represents a realistic office day. Priorities must be established, decisions must be made, and learned competencies must be put to use.

In developing the content of *Executive Secretarial Procedures*, Fifth Edition, the authors have avoided the kind of detail that could expand each chapter into a tome; the kind of superficiality that covers everything but teaches little; and the condensation that produces a reference book rather than a readable text. The resulting program for study and application is intended to spur students to a better understanding of their performance potential so that they will be able to progress and achieve success as secretaries.

IRENE PLACE ——————— **EDWARD E. BYERS** ——————— **ELAINE F. UTHE**

CONTENTS

PART ONE/The Professional Secretary

CHAPTER ONE / The Modern Office

The modern business office is the communication center of any company, large or small. It provides a connecting link between suppliers and manufacturing and distribution staffs. Most important, the business office is the link between the customer and the company.

Secretaries are needed in every type of office: in advertising and public relations, radio and television, government, law and medicine, public utilities, manufacturing and heavy industry, publishing and education, insurance and banking, airlines and travel. They work for board chairpersons, for presidents and vice presidents, for partners and owners, for controllers and general managers, for department heads and supervisors, for salespeople and purchasing agents, for deans and principals. They also work for celebrities, politicians, clergy, writers, and judges. Few other professions or careers offer a choice from among so many types of employers with such widely differing interests and objectives.

The Modern Office

A business firm represents an important segment of American economic life. Each company provides needed products or services. Furthermore, the products or services must be produced efficiently if the business is to continue to exist in a free enterprise system. Businesses that cannot operate efficiently or that fail to offer a needed product or service soon disappear.

Role of the Office
The office of a business firm makes a vital contribution to the success of the company. The office is the pulse of action, the heart of a complex communication system within the company, and between the company and its suppliers and customers. The office is a place in which people work with products, machines, paper, and words, a place in which manufacturing functions and a distribution system designed to produce and sell products and services are brought together.

The business office can be a challenging place. Data is collected and analyzed in report form; projections are made; policy is developed and carried out; budgets are prepared; financial records are maintained and audited; records of all types are managed; and profits (or losses) are determined.

The modern office functions as a communications center in many ways: (1) between manufacturers or suppliers and customers; (2) between internal groups such as advertising and accounting departments; (3) between top-level management (decision makers about policy), middle management, and general office workers; and (4) between the company and governmental agencies.

All these activities involve people. Each individual is a part of the team—from the typist and receptionist to the secretary, the accountant, the office manager, the vice president, and the president. Each has specific duties, tasks, and responsibilities according to job title and is expected to perform the assigned duties willingly and cooperate with others as an office team. Certain jobs require more education or skills than others; salaries vary according to qualifications and level of responsibility.

Technological Changes in the Office

The interaction of activities and people is enhanced by the variety of machines found in today's offices.

The telephone system involves more than traditional person-to-person communication; it now includes teledata transmission from computer to computer and the sending of facsimile copy from station to station. The telephone companies also provide their customers with many optional services.

Typewriters are constantly being improved and now include such features as correction keys, dual pitch capabilities (both elite and pica), changeable elements with different type styles, memory features, and variable horizontal and vertical spacing. Some memory typewriters type materials from left to right on one line and from right to left on the next line, which increases production speeds. Other memory typewriters have visual displays for editing and proofreading before hard copy is actually typed.

In just a few years the computer has become a vital tool in maintaining records, compiling reports, and storing information. When much of the work in a company depends on the computer, data processing specialists must be involved in developing their systems and in operating the equipment. Management determines what data is needed and the format in which it is wanted and interprets the computerized results. Many office workers may be involved in preparing data for the computer.

Minicomputers may be found on individual workers' desks to recall information from records instantaneously by means of electronic display screens. Many companies use computerized accounting systems.

Electronic word processing is an effort to increase efficiency in communication. Word processing centers use a systems approach (a combination of automatic typewriters and centralized dictation machines) to enable specialists to transcribe ideas into written form. Several new job titles have emerged, such as "correspondence specialist" and "supervisor of a word processing center." People interested in the word processing concept formed a professional association in 1972, called the International Word Processing Association.

Atmosphere of the Office

Office designers often work closely with company personnel to create attractive, efficient offices. A great deal of attention is placed on physical and psychological atmosphere. The physical atmosphere involves two aspects, space arrangement and physical environment. The office, as the hub of all business functions, must contribute to, rather than discourage, communications. Since space is expensive, it needs to be well used for efficiency. Businesses expand and change direction. Therefore, the design must be flexible enough to make changes possible. In planning a new office or remodeling an existing one, the designer needs to know the company objectives, its expansion plans, and its operational procedures. The office must be arranged so that work moves efficiently from one work station to the next, so that workers may communicate easily with others, and so that efficient traffic patterns (aisles) are provided.

For example, some offices use an "open-space" arrangement—that is, semipermanent but movable partitions and modular equipment. The self-contained work stations can be rearranged with little effort; thus, the open-space concept permits flexibility in moving work stations and adjusting aisle space without costly remodeling. The movable partitions are usually 4 to 5 feet high. When a worker is seated, the partitions provide privacy and eliminate distractions. However, when a worker is standing, the partitions permit a view of the entire office. The lack of doors and private offices for middle-management individuals promotes communication from worker to worker and from subordinate to superior.

In many companies only top management (or those who often conduct interviews and some types of creative work) have private offices. A small conference room is usually available for others who have only an occasional need for privacy. Work stations are often grouped by functions such as accounting, advertising, sales, and customer service, to name a few. In offices where several workers may be involved in processing the same form, the desks may be adjacent. This pattern makes it easy to move the work from one person to the next.

Rose Manufacturing Company

Movable partitions make this open-space office arrangement a good choice in areas where employees need privacy but have reason to communicate with one another frequently.

Modern Office Procedures

An alternate type of office layout positions the desks of these administrative secretaries in a row adjoining the offices of executives.

The secretary's work area is located near the person or persons served. The departmental secretary is located in an open area near the manager's office and may also be near the entrance to the department. An executive secretary is located in the reception area adjacent to the executive's office; this area may be a separate room or an open area a short distance from the general office.

The secretary's desk may be placed in such a way as to control access to the manager's office if greeting visitors is part of the job. However, some executives have an open-door policy for workers and clients. In that case the secretary's desk may be situated a little farther from the office door.

The Shaw-Walker Co.

Even in an open-space office arrangement, the secretary (*right foreground*) may be positioned to control access to the executive's office.

Regulating the physical environment of an office involves maintaining a comfortable temperature and humidity as well as controlling the noise and smoke level. Problems can sometimes arise in these areas because of the various degrees of comfort and tolerance levels of each human being in the office.

In creating a pleasing psychological atmosphere, the office designer works with color, style, texture, lighting, and decoration. Research shows that certain colors are depressing or induce fatigue, while other colors are warm or create excitement.

The modern office is often carpeted to create a pleasant atmosphere, to set off attractive office furniture, and to control the noise level. Movable partitions and the ceilings are made of soundproofing material. In some offices special areas are set aside for noisy machines. These areas are convenient to work stations but separate from them.

Furniture styles and colors are selected to enhance efficiency and atmosphere. Often, furniture styles are varied to indicate status within the company as well as to meet job specifications. For example, a secretarial chair is especially designed for flexible back support and for making adjustments to fit the individual. In contrast, the executive's chair has arms but no adjustable back support.

Various levels of lighting are employed according to the type of work done in the area. The office may have special decorations to aid in creating a positive psychological atmosphere, such as murals, representations of company symbols, and green plants, as well as paintings and other forms of artwork.

Whether an office uses a contemporary or traditional design, it should be an efficient communication center. However, the *human relations* atmosphere probably has more influence on efficient communication and service than the physical and psychological atmosphere. The secretary is a vital link in this communication chain; the secretary must be supportive and service-minded in carrying out duties and responsibilities.

Allied Chemical Corporation

Lighting, space, construction materials, and tasteful furnishings make this handsome reception room a reflection of the company's status.

Function of the Office

The major function of an office is to facilitate the production and distribution of its products or services to the user. Clerical work is required in every phase of a business operation. The office serves as a clearinghouse for records and generates new data.

The office must be well organized to achieve efficiency. There must be an orderly system or work flow for incoming and outgoing communications. For example, when an order arrives in the mail, the mail clerk needs to deliver it to the order department. Workers there must check the inventory to determine whether the goods are in stock. Also, the credit department must see whether the buyer's credit is good. If the goods are in stock and the buyer's credit is good, the shipping department must ship the goods, and the accounting department must prepare an invoice. The salesperson's commission is computed; the stock inventory is updated; and the buyer is billed for the purchase.

This simplified flow of work—and paper—must be handled quickly and efficiently. Also, a system must be developed for handling service calls and complaints as well as for seeking additional sales.

The modern office develops a work flow system so that each worker knows what tasks and duties are required for that particular position. The system is supervised so that it operates smoothly.

The responsible office worker also becomes aware of the *source* of each task by asking questions such as: Who developed this report or form? What is its purpose? How did it get to my desk? What did each person do or add to the report or form? What do I do with the form? If I have any questions about this data, whom can I ask for assistance?

Furthermore, the responsible office worker learns where to send the work next. By knowing the work flow system, the office worker gains a better understanding of the importance of each report or form as well as of the need for accuracy and efficiency in keeping the work flowing through the system.

The office functions, therefore, as a processing center for communications, both oral and written. Each office worker, regardless of job level or job title, is an important link in this work flow system.

The Secretarial Profession

The secretary has a vital role in office communications. In fact, the secretary serves as a channel for communications in several areas: (1) between management and subordinates, (2) between management and customers, clients, or suppliers, (3) between the secretary and office workers at other levels, and (4) between one manager and others at the same level.

The Challenge of Change Technology poses no threat to the secretary. Although technological developments may alter a secretary's duties, they certainly will not eliminate the secretarial function. In fact, as the economy expands, the demand for secretaries will steadily increase. Most company executives agree that the present shortage of competent secretaries, stenographers, and typists will continue.

Traditionally, a secretary has been a *confidante*—that is, one who is entrusted with important information. Secretaries continue to fill this role and, in addition, are expected to work shoulder-to-shoulder with, rather than for, an executive. The executive's job has become both more difficult and more challenging because of higher labor and production costs, automation, more sophisticated management education, more thorough forecasting techniques and market analyses, and tougher business competition. Secretaries' jobs, therefore, have also become more demanding. Secretaries must meet new challenges, accept more responsibility, and work with less direct supervision.

Most executives would like to turn large amounts of work over to their secretaries. They need freedom from as much routine work as possible so that they will have more time to concentrate on planning, forecasting, and carrying out special projects. Ideally, the secretary and the boss should work as a team, with the executive making most of the decisions and the secretary following through on details and the actual implementation of those decisions. As never before, the secretary and the executive must pull together, complementing each other's strengths and weaknesses, being tolerant of each other's moods, and trusting the other's ability to do the job. Each must, therefore, try to understand and accept the other's point of view.

Through the years secretaries have emerged as important members of management teams. They are vital links between the making and the implementing of business plans. For example, besides being custodians of office records, secretaries now play an expanded role in processing reports, schedules, and directives. They help to gather data for use in reports, keep mailing lists for their distribution, and develop filing systems for their maintenance and retrieval.

The smooth flow of activity in an executive's office often depends on the secretary's ability to set priorities as well as to take care of routine matters. In setting priorities, a secretary needs to exercise good judgment. When an executive is out of town, the secretary determines priorities for mail, callers, and items of business. At all times the secretary serves as a filter, handling some items, relaying some to other executives, and giving the boss only those that need special attention. The secretary also acts as an antenna, keeping eyes and ears open to spot ways to help the team be more effective. An alert secretary often sees many aspects of the business environment that the boss might fail to notice.

The Secretary's Environment

In the office, activities are carried on that are vital to both the overall objectives and the daily operations of a business. The secretary works within this world and needs to be at home in the environment.

When a company's operations are limited, its office staff is proportionately small. One or two employees may be enough to perform the whole range of office activities. In large companies, however, specialists pool their talents and energies to do the office work for such basic functions as sales, marketing, research, transportation, purchasing, production, personnel services, accounting, and office services. The following categories of office job titles indicate the degree of specialization in processing and maintaining the office records and reports needed to keep a large business going.

Secretarial/ Stenographic	Data Processing/ Accounting	General Office
administrative assistant	programmer	credit clerk
executive/ administrative secretary	tape librarian	duplicating machine operator
	computer operator	file clerk
	card-punch operator	information clerk
secretary	data-entry clerk	inventory clerk
stenographer	accountant/auditor	interviewing clerk
transcribing machine operator	accounting machine operator	mail clerk
	adding/calculating machine operator	messenger
clerk-typist		order clerk
typist	billing machine operator	photocopy machine operator
correspondence specialist	general accounting clerk	receiving clerk
word processor	cashier	receptionist
		shipping clerk
		statistical clerk
		stock clerk
		typist

The Secretary Defined

The role of a secretary is supportive. A secretary is usually defined as someone who, without direct responsibility, assists another person with communications and public relations in business, professional, and personal affairs. Not all who carry the title of secretary or perform aspects of secretarial work conform to this definition, however. To obtain some idea of the range of existing secretarial positions, it is helpful to consider several levels of secretarial activity.

Presecretarial Positions.   The secretary to a junior executive is likely to be a receptionist, a clerk-typist, or a stenographer rather than a full-fledged secretary. In any of these jobs, a person will probably be expected to answer the telephone and greet visitors. Such work is, of course, good training for a person who needs experience in meeting the public and who wants eventually to work into a secretarial position.

A receptionist is often a Jack-or-Jill-of-all-trades, especially in a small business or professional office. This person's main function is to help establish good public relations; the job requires pleasant personal characteristics and good communications skills. The receptionist may also be called upon to do some typing, filing, and mail processing and to handle the petty cash fund.

A clerk-typist's main duty usually is typing, often limited to typing final copy from someone else's rough drafts or to typing rough drafts from machine-dictated material. Another function of the job may be filing, as well as keeping office mailing lists up to date.

A stenographer's main function is to take dictation in shorthand and tran-scribe it on a typewriter. The job usually includes many of the same clerical tasks that are performed by the receptionist and clerk-typist. The stenographer may also make appointments for the employer. Stenographers may work for only one person, but many are assigned to two or more junior executives or middle-management people.

Secretarial Positions.   Secretaries combine the qualities and capabilities of the stenographer, clerk-typist, and receptionist. In addition, secretaries need a variety of other talents and skills. For example, they must know how to locate information and assist with research; how to write many types of business communications as well as their employers can—and, indeed, to use their language and style; how to behave like a diplomat, a politician, and a confidential adviser; and how to be businesslike and professional. As personal and confidential assistants, they can become invaluable members of an executive staff. As they move up through the secretarial hierarchy, it is increasingly important for secretaries to get along with co-workers, to be mature in personal relations, and to accept responsibility.

No two secretarial positions are alike. Each is molded and modified by five variables:

- The size and nature of the business or profession.
- The position and status of the executive.
- The personality of the executive and his or her willingness to delegate work and responsibility.
- The ability of the secretary to assume administrative duties for which the executive is responsible.
- The personality and intelligence of the secretary.

In a small operation, a secretary's work is varied so that there is a chance to gain a wide range of experience and to grow in the position. In a large enterprise, on the other hand, a secretary is often assigned to a specialized department such as marketing, production, personnel, or legal. There is less opportunity to gain companywide experience unless the executive and the secretary move up through various departments and levels of the firm. Each business firm has its own vocabulary, style, and preferred channels of internal and external communication.

The level at which an executive functions is affected by education, personality, and communication skills. Obviously, the executive's level affects the nature of the secretary's work. The attitude of an ambitious, enterprising young executive toward work and career opportunities in the company may be quite different from that of a well-established executive or of one who is looking forward to retirement.

Executives also differ widely in temperament. Some are good-natured, outgoing, and confident. Others may be more reserved and quiet in manner. Some prefer to handle many details of their jobs themselves, while others are thankful to have their secretaries become detail experts.

Secretaries, too, differ in ability as well as in readiness to assume responsibility. The most successful secretary is the one who studies the boss's work habits and attitudes, learns preferences and dislikes, and fills in where help is needed most.

Postsecretarial Opportunities.   More and more secretaries are qualifying as personnel directors, buyers, production coordinators, editors and advertising executives, office managers, programmers, and systems analysts. Although the route from secretarial to nonsecretarial management posts is not heavily traveled, there is a definite trend to select for management training and promotion those who are experienced within a company or a certain type of industry.

Young men and women entering secretarial work can, therefore, realistically aspire to good postsecretarial positions, provided that they acquire a few years' experience during which they learn about the total operations of their companies and prove their capabilities. However, secretaries who aspire to these careers may need additional education in order to qualify for different positions.

The Specialized Secretary

In setting career goals, consider the feasibility of matching your particular abilities and interests to specialized secretarial opportunities in different business, professional, and government organizations. For example, you might consider qualifying as a legal or a medical secretary, a technical secretary, or a bilingual secretary.

Specialization can be a practical way to command a higher salary. Special secretaries must have excellent basic skills, plus a knowledge of techniques and a special vocabulary. The reward for specialization is usually an interesting job and a good salary.

The professional secretary need never feel bored or in a rut, for secretarial skills can be used anywhere in business or the professions. Secretaries may work in a variety of departments within a large company, or they can test their capabilities in a number of different types of businesses. The ability to adapt to new situations and environments is a prime asset of the person pursuing a secretarial career, both for the secretary personally and for all prospective employers.

A secretary may achieve professional recognition and success through membership in the National Secretaries Association (NSA) and by becoming a Certified Professional Secretary (CPS). CPS status is achieved by passing a six-part examination (taking approximately 12 hours) and meeting other requirements set by the Institute for Certifying Secretaries of the NSA.

Responsibilities of the Secretary

There are many descriptions of the secretary's job. A prototype has been developed by the National Secretaries Association; it describes those skills that you as a student will need to develop in order to become a successful secretary, including the following:

A secretary relieves executive of various administrative details; coordinates and maintains effective office procedures and efficient work flows; implements policies and procedures set by employer; establishes and maintains harmonious working relationships with superiors, co-workers, subordinates, customers or clients, and suppliers.

Schedules appointments and maintains calendar. Receives and assists visitors and telephone callers and refers them to executive or other appropriate person as circumstances warrant. Arranges business itineraries and coordinates executive's travel requirements.

Takes action authorized during executive's absence and uses initiative and judgment to see that matters requiring attention are referred to delegated authority or handled in a manner so as to minimize effect of employer's absence.

Takes manual shorthand and transcribes from it or transcribes from machine dictation. Types material from longhand or rough copy.

Sorts, reads, and annotates incoming mail and documents and attaches appropriate file to facilitate necessary action; determines routing, signatures required, and maintains follow-up. Composes correspondence and reports for own or executive's signature. Prepares communication outlined by executive in oral or written directions.

Researches and abstracts information and supporting data in preparation for meetings, work projects, and reports. Correlates and edits materials submitted by others. Organizes material which may be presented to executive in draft format.

Maintains filing and records management systems and other office flow procedures.

Makes arrangements for and coordinates conferences and meetings. May serve as recorder of minutes with responsibility for transcription and distribution to participants.

May supervise or hire other employees; select and/or make recommendations for purchase of supplies and equipment; maintain budget and expense account records, financial records, and confidential files.

Maintains up-to-date procedures manual for the specific duties handled on the job.

Performs other duties as assigned or as judgment or necessity dictates.*

Educational and Professional Qualifications

Preparation for almost every worthwhile career is continual. Secretarial work is no exception. Employers look for applicants who are well informed. The broader your educational background, the better. Many of the best jobs go to those who have successfully completed secretarial or business administration programs in a junior college, a community college, or a business college. A four-year college degree program that combines liberal arts and business courses also provides a superior—and well-rewarded—secretarial foundation.

Those who go into office work immediately after high school should seek

---

*"NSA Prototype Secretarial Job Description," *The Secretary*, May 1978, p. 21.

additional training after they start working. They should take courses in English, speech, psychology, economics, accounting, law, and business administration at local business colleges or in adult education programs. Many companies sponsor tuition-refund programs for employees interested in continuing their education in approved courses. Some also offer a wide range of educational opportunities in the form of on-the-job training programs. Still others assume the entire expense of sending secretaries to special seminars or workshops sponsored by professional organizations.

General Education

Opportunities for high-level secretarial jobs and for promotion come most often to those who have combined a broad general education with vocational or professional business courses. General education subjects are divided into three categories—humanities, social sciences, and physical sciences. The humanities include languages, philosophy, history, literature, and fine arts. The social sciences include psychology, sociology, economics, and political science. The physical sciences include mathematics, biology, chemistry, physics, geology, and astronomy.

Through the study of humanities and our cultural heritage, a potential secretary gains insights that lead to better appreciation of the total environment and the ability to converse and work more intelligently with all types of people. Basic communication skills are imparted in English and literature courses. A good knowledge of one's own language is indispensable. In fact, the ability to express oneself clearly and forcibly is a genuine asset in all types of work.

Social science courses such as psychology and sociology acquaint you with the fundamentals of human behavior and the structure of society. They will help you to understand yourself as well as other people. Courses in economics and political science aid your understanding of current events and business.

By studying the physical sciences, you can come to understand and appreciate the world about you and many of its problems. You will gain a clearer understanding of how your future will be affected by modern technological developments, from data processing and telecommunications advances to space travel and oceanography.

Vocational Education

Many of the so-called general or academic courses have vocational values as well. A foreign language, for instance, is a distinct asset if you are working in an export department or in the international office of a corporation. Courses in the humanities help you function more effectively and make better decisions.

There are many special technical and professional courses that prepare people for specific occupations. The vocational skills needed by a secretary vary according to the position and the company. For example, to work as a legal or a medical secretary you will need special skills, knowledge, and vocabularies. However, there is a basic core of vocational training that every secretary needs. Important components of this training are shorthand, typewriting, communications, office procedures, accounting, data processing, business and management principles, and human relations.

As a secretarial trainee you should plan your program so as to obtain a balanced general education as well as the appropriate vocational training for the career you have in mind. An educational balance is achieved when your intellectual curiosity and interest are aroused, when you are poised in dealing with people, when you acquire skill in identifying problems and making proper value judgments, and when you master the necessary vocational skills.

Collegiate Secretarial Studies

Although businesspeople generally agree that typing and shorthand are the most important vocational tools of a beginning secretary, they are quick to point out that the secretary who wishes to advance also needs to be management-oriented. This means understanding business organization and terminology and being familiar with management and problem-solving techniques.

Criticism is frequently directed toward one-sided secretarial training programs that purportedly prepare top-level secretaries yet stress only basic vocational skills. Today it is increasingly evident that an important prerequisite to top-level secretarial performance is a balanced education.

The executive secretarial program found in most four-year colleges will include approximately 50 percent general education courses, 25 percent business courses, and 25 percent secretarial studies. The secretarial studies program in a two-year college has a greater proportion of study in the secretarial studies area and less in the general education areas. Each college organizes its secretarial curriculum as much as possible according to students' interests and the job market in the geographic area.

The secretarial studies portion of a college program includes typewriting, shorthand and transcription, business communications (oral and written), business machines, filing and records management, and secretarial procedures. The program may include data processing and may require an office internship.

The business portion includes accounting, economics, human relations and organizational behavior, finance, management principles, business law, and data processing. Some programs recommend statistics, marketing, and personnel administration as well as other courses.

The general education portion revolves around English, humanities, social science, mathematics, physical education, and science and may include sociology, speech, and other electives.

Your Future as a Secretary

As a secretary, you have a vital function to perform in an office as a member of its team. For that role you first need to acquire basic secretarial skills and a knowledge of office procedures. After that, to become a successful secretary with administrative capabilities, you will want to pursue broader aspects of the business world; develop greater interest in your company and explore its relationship to others in the community and nation; take courses related to the business; and participate in professional and community associations.

You will need to plan your secretarial career carefully, for there are many facets or specializations in the secretarial profession, and there are many types of business for which you may work. Try to discover your talents and interests as you pursue your study of secretarial procedures. The office is the hub of business—and you'll find it a challenging place.

1. Name at least four ways in which the office serves as a communication center.

2. Technological changes are affecting many types of office equipment. In what ways has the typewriter changed recently? Are there some changes you can think of that are not mentioned in this chapter?

3. What is meant by the term *psychological atmosphere* of an office? Identify some factors that influence it. What is meant by *physical atmosphere*?

4. Describe an office that has an open-space plan. What advantages or disadvantages does it have?

5. Where would you place your desk if you were responsible for controlling visitors' access to your employer's office?

6. A secretary must be *supportive* and *service-minded* and must also be a *confidante*. Define these three terms and list some actions that illustrate whether or not a secretary meets these criteria.

7. What is meant by the term *work flow*? *maintaining the work flow*?

8. What is the significance of the statement "Technology poses no threat to the secretary"?

9. Look up the meaning of the term *secretary* in an unabridged or a collegiate dictionary.
   a. What is its derivation?
   b. Give four common meanings for it.
   c. How is a secretary defined in this chapter?

10. Compare the functions of a stenographer and those of a secretary.

11. What five variables influence the character, scope, and responsibility of a secretary's job?

12. Explain why young people entering the business field can aspire to non-secretarial management jobs via the secretarial role.

13. Of the criteria for a competent secretary, which ones reflect character traits and attitudes rather than training and know-how?

14. a. Explain why a balanced general and vocational education is a prerequisite for top-level secretarial work.
    b. What are the three broad areas of instruction that comprise a secretarial-training program?

1. **Secretarial Responsibilities.** What do you believe to be the secretary's responsibilities in the areas of decision making, planning, data processing, teamwork, public relations, and the secretarial profession? In the area of decision making, for example, you might cite such activities as gathering data for an executive's decisions, making routine decisions in typing and filing by oneself, and being a sounding board for an executive's deliberations or tentative decisions. Think about each of the other responsibilities and cite at least three secretarial responsibilities for each. Present a written report.

2. **The Office Atmosphere.** Visit several companies that have recently re-modeled their offices. Type a description of your observations about their use of open-space or other space arrangements, the psychological use of color and design, and any control-of-noise features. Ask your instructor or a local office-equipment firm for names of companies that would be interesting to visit.

3. **Your Secretarial IQ.** Secretarial efficiency involves many other things besides typewriting, dictation, and transcription. What is your judgment about the importance of each of the following practices in secretarial work? On a separate sheet of paper list the practices you consider undesirable. Explain briefly why. Type your report as directed by your instructor.

   a. Arrive at the office each morning at least five minutes early.
   b. Keep your identity separate from general office personnel as much as possible.
   c. Check each day to see that mail you prepare is sent.
   d. Skip lunch to do the filing.
   e. Be ready for dictation at a moment's notice.
   f. Clean your typewriter before you leave each night.
   g. Review the day's appointment schedule carefully each morning.
   h. Come to work even when ill.
   i. Record appointments on the boss's calendar as well as on your own.
   j. Keep a message pad by the telephone.
   k. Systematize paper-handling procedures, such as filing and mail processing.
   l. Talk your methods over with the boss so that you can work together better.
   m. Ask the boss for a list of special words used in dictation.
   n. Help the boss handle rush items first.
   o. Take the initiative in reorganizing the files.
   p. Erase mistakes on carbon copies.
   q. Show enthusiasm for your work.
   r. Relieve the boss of as much detail as possible.
   s. Avoid making promises you can't keep.
   t. Anticipate the boss's needs.

4. **Your Secretarial Career.** Compose an article of 500 or more words entitled "How I Expect to Use My Secretarial Training." Indicate how you plan to use your training in conjunction with your other education and your major interest; why; the type of organization you want to work in; and where you want your career to be five years from now. Discuss the qualifications you need, both personal and technical. Work the following eight words into your article: (a) ambition, (b) initiative, (c) integrity, (d) stamina, (e) enthusiasm, (f) persistence, (g) courage, (h) confidence.

EXERCISING
YOUR
JUDGMENT

The human relations discussion cases at the end of each chapter of this book are designed to give you an opportunity to review and discuss human relations guidelines. Many people who are discharged from positions lose them because of human relations problems, not technical incompetence. The process of improving one's human relations skill is much like the process of improving one's vocabulary. It has to be worked on day after day and week after week. The cases presented at the end of each chapter are sharply focused on what may appear, at first glance, to be very simple situations. Prepare to discuss the pros and cons of these situations and to summarize the discussion by identifying a human relations guideline. The case entitled "Later" follows.

Later. You work for a very busy boss, yet you have little work to do yourself. Your boss reads everything, opens all mail, answers all telephone calls, and does many things that you know you could do yourself. Whenever you suggest doing certain jobs, the answer is always "Later."

What should you do?

APPLYING
THE
REFERENCE
SECTION

Vocabulary Building. Vocabulary is an important tool in speaking and thinking. To communicate effectively with others, you should look for opportunities to improve your vocabulary, working on it regularly. This does not mean learning unusual words to impress people. It does mean refining your understanding of words you already know so that you can use them more accurately, thus improving your ability to express your thoughts. One way to make progress in this kind of vocabulary building is to learn synonyms, homonyms, and antonyms for words you now use.

In the Reference Section at the back of this book is a list of words to watch. These words were selected because they are commonly used in business, because many of them are easy to misspell, and because their synonyms, homonyms, and antonyms provide a good start for vocabulary building.

You may want to review the spelling rules in the Reference Section as you compose your own letters and reports. Keep an unabridged dictionary available so that you get in the habit of consulting it. If you are in doubt about the spelling or meaning of any word, look it up. You will increase your vocabulary considerably and make it easier both to compose your own letters and to transcribe those your employer dictates.

CHAPTER TWO / The Office Team

Whether in sports or in business, a team is a group of people working for a common goal—to win the game, to make a profit. When each person plays the game well and cooperates with the others, there is good team spirit. When a team member plays for his or her own glory, the team suffers and the game may be lost.

The office team is exactly the same. There are a designated number of players with specific positions or roles to play; and each position requires certain skills or talents. Some positions involve more responsibility, some are more active, but each is important. Just as the visible team—the one on the field—is supported by coaches, managers, maintenance crews, ticket sellers, and so on, the business office needs the support of every individual member of the office team. Whatever the office position, the individual is important to the team and its success. As a secretary, you seldom work alone. And in order to work with people successfully, you need to learn the rules of teamwork. Begin by learning as much as you can about your company—how it is organized, how it conducts its affairs, and what the scope of your responsibilities is—so that you know as much as possible about the companywide team as well as about your immediate office team.

It is important for you to know the managerial chain of command within your office—those who are subordinates to your boss, those who are peers or on the same level, and those who are superiors or on a higher level. You should also know the secretarial chain of command and the way in which it interacts with the managerial chain.

Although a person's level within the company will sometimes affect the procedures and decisions you make, deal courteously with each individual, regardless of managerial or secretarial level. Your contribution to maintaining a smooth work flow through the managerial and secretarial team is consistently to process work accurately and efficiently.

Types of Business Organization

A business usually assumes the type and form of organization best suited to its objectives and resources. Knowing how your company is organized helps you to understand its objectives, its strengths, and its shortcomings. Such understanding will help you to do a better job and to see in what areas opportunities might arise for you.

Sole Proprietorship

A business owned by one person is called a sole proprietorship. A business person chooses the sole proprietorship in order to have complete control, make all the decisions, and receive all the profits.

Characteristics.   The sole proprietor of the business runs all the business affairs personally and does not have to consult or report to any stockholders or to a board of directors. There usually are few employees, and the owner handles all problems connected with personnel selection and supervision, operations, and management, rather than employing specialists in these areas.

Most sole proprietorships cater to a local consumer public. The money to operate the business is provided by the owner and may be augmented by funds borrowed from relatives, friends, or banks. The owner keeps the profits of the business after taxes and is also legally liable for all debts of the business. There are, of course, disadvantages to a sole proprietorship. The owner may not have enough money available to finance all aspects of the business. Moreover, the owner runs all the risks and has no one at the same level with whom to consult about business problems.

Peter Roth

Secretaries seldom work alone.

Advancement Opportunities.   An employee of a sole proprietorship needs to understand certain aspects of this form of business ownership. The owner is the boss and is solely responsible for the total operation of the business. This person may be well qualified to handle certain functions, but not so well qualified for others. This kind of management imbalance can have an adverse effect on employees as well as on the profitability of the business.

If you are a secretary to the sole proprietor of a small business, you are likely to have varied duties because you may be the entire office staff. Your dependability, resourcefulness, and judgment will be relied on. Since the owner's personal fortune is at stake, it will be particularly important for you to be knowledgeable about everything that is going on.

In some ways, a sole proprietorship offers limited opportunity for secretarial advancement, since there is no higher executive for whom you can work. However, it also offers an exceptional opportunity to learn firsthand how a business is run and to assume administrative and supervisory responsibilities as the office staff grows. A few secretaries have gone on to become partners with their bosses when the business expanded. Others have become branch office managers when new offices were opened. Still others have opened their own businesses as a result of the experience gained as secretary to a sole proprietor.

Partnership

When two or more persons decide to join in the ownership of a business, they usually form a partnership. This plan brings more capital and talents into the business than either partner would have in a sole proprietorship. Although any small- or medium-sized business can operate as a partnership, partnerships are most common in local wholesale and retail operations, brokerage firms, insurance agencies, and real estate brokerages.

Characteristics.   In a partnership the amount of capital available is not limited to the resources of one person. The combined judgment and specialized skills of the partners are distinct strengths of a partnership. Shared thinking usually produces wiser courses of action and increased profits. Since each partner is generally liable for the actions of the other, there is usually an intense involvement of both in every operation of the business. The death of one partner terminates the formal partnership.

Advancement Opportunities.   As a secretary working for a partnership, you may serve all of the partners, or you may work for only one. If you work for one partner, you will be concerned with the particular responsibilities of that person. For example, in a law firm your employer may be the lawyer who specializes in tax cases or corporate law. Your secretarial support will be focused only on those cases and the proceedings they generate. However, because partners consult each other and work in concert, you must also keep in mind your employer's role in the partnership.

If you work for several partners, you need to study each one's personality and methods so that you can complement them effectively. At the same time, you may enjoy considerable freedom in your own branch of general office operations.

A partnership pools talent
as well as capital.

Bauder Fashion College

Corporation   The corporation is the dominant form of business ownership in the United States, accounting for more than 80 percent of the sales of all business firms and approximately 60 percent of all net profits. By definition it is an artificial entity, created by law and endowed with the rights, duties, and powers of a person. These include the right to own, buy, sell, manage, mortgage, and dispose of property it possesses. By law it is permitted to use a common name, change its members and ownership, and have perpetual life.

Characteristics.   A charter, issued by a state official, authorizes the formation of a corporation. The owners are called stockholders. The stockholders exercise indirect control over the management of the business. Once a year they vote the shares of stock they own in order to elect a board of directors, who serve as their representatives. The directors elect the officers of the corporation, who are directly responsible for the management of the business. The president or the chairperson of the board is the chief executive of a corporation. Senior vice presidents, group vice presidents, vice presidents, and general managers are entrusted with specific management and financial authority.

One advantage of the corporate form of business ownership is that each stockholder risks only the amount of money invested. By dividing ownership into shares of stock, the corporation obtains working capital from many individuals. If the corporate affairs are well managed and the business prospers, it can remain in business indefinitely, even though ownership changes hands and officers and employees depart or become incapacitated. By and large, a corporation can afford to assemble the specialists and the experts it needs to achieve its full market potential.

Corporations do have their limitations. Large ones can sometimes become too impersonal in their dealings with customers and workers. Corporations are also subject to many legal restrictions and taxes. A high level of profits is expected, however, and the management is under constant pressure to achieve even higher goals.

Advancement Opportunities.   Corporations offer excellent opportunities for secretaries. As a well-educated secretary, you should have little difficulty in being assigned to a junior executive and then working up to greater responsibility. As you advance, you will become increasingly familiar with management practices and specialized procedures. Sometimes advancement means a transfer from one operational area to another. This is especially true in corporations that are large enough to justify the delegation of duties to specialists in marketing, production, accounting, law, research, personnel, advertising, and public relations. Since specialists are expected to perform efficiently, you will find much emphasis on improved methods and the use of time- and effort-saving office equipment.

Company Policies and Organizational Structure

Every company, regardless of its size or of the product or service it offers, must set up policies and procedures that answer fundamental questions, such as who is responsible for what functions. A complete organization plan states company objectives; describes company policy regarding lines of communication, administrative practices, planning and reporting requirements, and line-and-staff relationships; presents organizational structure; and indicates responsibilities and authorities.

Company Objectives   The results that a business must achieve year after year in order to remain successful are its objectives. For purposes of long-term thinking, five-year objectives are most common. These goals generally reflect the results that managers of the organization commit themselves to over a five-year period. The following objectives are illustrative of those that might be formulated in a large company:

- Increase sales by 60 percent.
- Generate $20 million in gross sales by the introduction of new products.

- Maintain a 23 percent operating profit.
- Reduce product-development costs, in terms of unit cost, each year.
- Reevaluate and reshape personnel services to meet increased responsibilities brought on by company diversification and expansion.
- Implement a new employee recruitment program to successfully cope with the tight labor market and attract qualified minority-group applicants.
- Provide resources and work jointly with other local community interests in dealing with problems of ecology.

Company Policies

As set forth in the company plan, company policies cover most aspects of the firm's relationships with its employees, its customers, other companies, the local community, and the nation. The range of topics covered may include working hours, paydays, and leave time; special privileges or restrictions; regulations affecting the employees' relationships with customers, suppliers, and competitors; and general policies concerning the firm's participation in community activities, politics, and other local or national affairs. In the area of company operation, the policies usually delineate the lines of communication, specific administrative practices, planning and reporting requirements, financial policies, and security regulations.

Organizational Structure

An organization chart blueprints the command structure and shows the relationships between operating units as well as the channels of communication. A number of formats are used for organization charts—line, concentric, scalar, functional, and line-and-staff.

Looking at the command structure portrayed in the organization charts that follow, you can establish the levels of management, the extent of management at each level, and the functional alignments. Also apparent are management's communication channels and organizational philosophy.

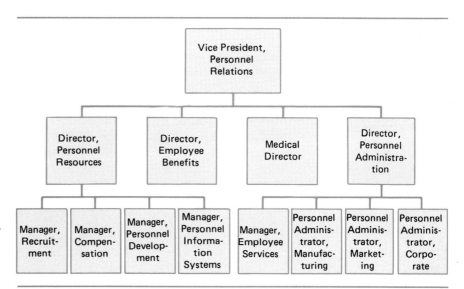

Line organization. Authority runs from top to bottom in this simplest and most common form of company command structure.

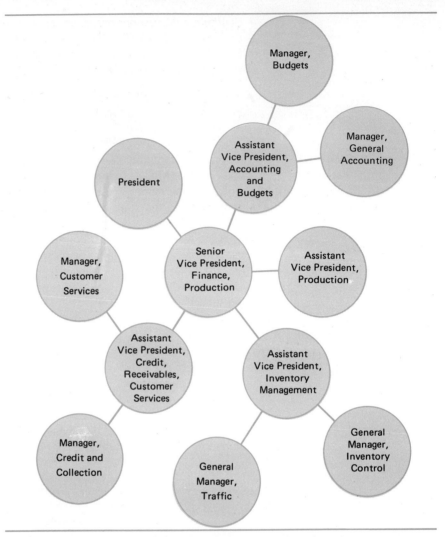

Concentric organization. Ten people report directly or indirectly to the senior vice president in charge of finance and production.

Line Organization. The small office where only two persons, the boss and the secretary, work is an example of the simplest type of business organization. The boss gives orders, instructions, and information to the secretary. The secretary carries out the orders and reports back to the boss. This straight-up-and-down organization, with authority running from top to bottom, is called line organization.

The line organization is by far the most common type in all kinds of firms. Orders originate at the top and are passed down through specified channels. Each person in the line of authority passes the order down to subordinates. The person receiving an order is responsible to the immediate superior for completing the assignment.

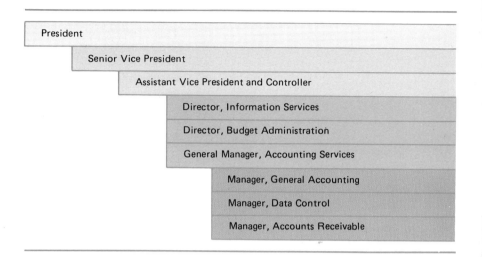

Scalar organization.

As a secretary in a line organization, you have just one boss to worry about. As long as you meet the boss's standards, your job is well done. You actually have no authority over others unless your boss gives it to you. Approval of all new ideas and procedural changes must come from the top. You work for other members of the organization only with the permission of your boss and within the limits your boss sets.

Functional Organization.   The functional plan of organization introduces the concept of specialization. The head of the sales department, for instance, is the sales specialist and runs the department in his or her own way. The head is responsible to superiors only for results, without having to explain how those results were achieved just as long as broad company policies are observed. In this type of organization, the top official becomes a coordinator, leaving specialized decisions to the specialists who know the most about them.

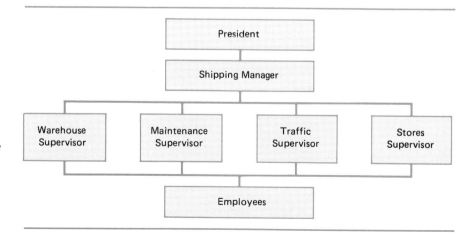

Functional organization. Department heads are free to function as specialists, making decisions independently, as long as company policies are observed and satisfactory results achieved.

Line-and-Staff Organization.   The line-and-staff plan is a modern compromise between the line organization and the functional organization. Operations are controlled by line-organization methods. Planning, research, and special projects are assigned to staff personnel. The staff personnel feed ideas to top management. If top management adopts an idea, the orders are issued down the line.

As a secretary working for the sales manager in a line-and-staff organization, for example, you will have a boss who has more freedom of action and decision than in the line plan. As a result, you will find that methods and procedures are more flexible, and changes are probably made more often. When line-and-staff organization is used, a department head is able to encourage self-expression. Unit managers get quicker answers because they know their problems firsthand and have expert advice from staff specialists.

Specialization can be overdone, however. Experience shows that people can become so engrossed in their specialties that they lose sight of broad objectives. The line-and-staff organization provides for balanced action.

The introduction of the staff element into an organization leads to variations in secretarial work. In this setup, you have the choice of working with operations managers or with planners. The line-and-staff plan results in a considerable amount of paper work in the form of bulletins, budgets, and instructions moving down from above, as well as performance records and reports moving up. In this environment, a competent secretary is indispensable to the boss.

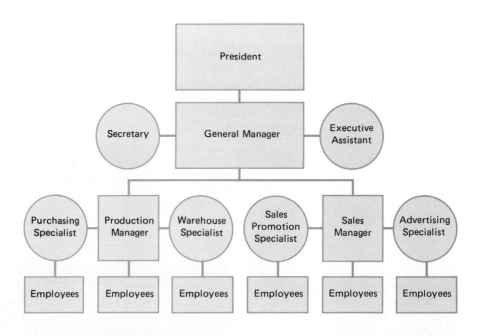

Line-and-staff organization. Staff specialists may advise the line organization but do not make decisions or formulate policy.

Responsibilities and Authorities

The responsibilities and authorities of company personnel can be defined in the company plan in several ways. The method adopted usually depends on the amount of detail desired.

Functional Diagram. A functional diagram provides a short description of the responsibilities and authorities involved in each position or department in the company, and these functions are shown within the framework of the total company structure. Such a diagram particularly emphasizes the flow of information and the delegation of function rather than the relationships between the parts of the company.

Chain of Command. As a top-level secretary you will always want to be aware of both the formal and informal chain of command in the office. Many secretarial decisions are made by following appropriate procedures up and down this chain. Following these procedures enhances the team spirit and fosters communication among all levels.

Communications going upward on the chain of command are usually polite requests, questions, or completed tasks or reports. Downward communications are usually polite demands, information, or assignments. Horizontal communications are usually cooperative discussions.

Job Description. When greater detail concerning responsibilities is desired in the company plan, job descriptions are used. A specific description is drawn up for each management position in the firm. For lower levels, one general description covers many individuals who hold similar jobs. All secretaries at a given level are usually covered by a single description.

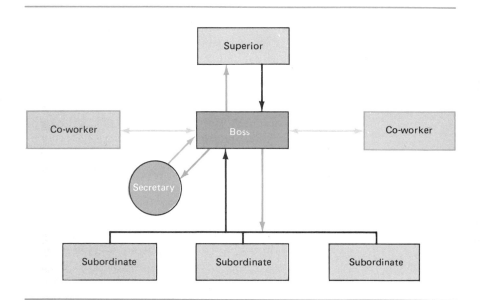

Communications on the chain of command.

No description can ever completely define what a person does or what the full scope of authority is. When written carefully, however, it does express a person's essential responsibilities. The estimated percentage of time spent in executing each duty is often included as well and can provide meaningful information about the relative importance of each duty performed.

Job descriptions vary from company to company, but most include a description of the specific duties, responsibilities, and authority. The job description that follows is for an executive secretary:

Secretary to General Manager

1. Take dictation in shorthand and transcribe a variety of letters, memorandums, and reports. (25 percent)
2. Read all incoming mail and attach related material from files; seek out requested data; retain routine correspondence for independent action. (15 percent)
3. Assist in analysis of budgeted and actual operating costs of the various operating units. (5 percent)
4. Maintain a correspondence file and a tickler file to record future work to be done. (10 percent)
5. Answer incoming telephone calls, giving and receiving information and expediting the flow of work. Make inquiries by telephone and locate information. Conduct library research. (20 percent)
6. Maintain an appointment book. Make travel arrangements and arrange for hotel reservations. Help arrange for meetings. (15 percent)
7. Prepare expense account statements from receipts and records provided. Keep a periodic check on telephone expense. (3 percent)
8. Exercise internal control of office supply expenses and petty cash expenditures. (5 percent)
9. Keep informed of the unit's medium- and long-range objectives and of areas of responsibility within the unit in particular and in the corporation in general. (2 percent)

Personal Efficiency

Becoming an indispensable team member of a business organization involves more than understanding a company and how it is organized to conduct business. Also important is a professional attitude toward your job requirements and a thorough understanding of your secretarial duties.

Getting the job under control is the first step. A big question for a new secretary is, "What does the boss expect of me?" Naturally you will take dictation, transcribe notes, handle incoming and outgoing mail, answer the telephone, greet callers, make appointments, and file. But you will want to learn your boss's preferences in regard to these duties and many others. What letter style is preferred? Do you edit dictation or type exactly what is dictated? Do you answer the telephone, or does your boss? Should you interrupt the boss for urgent matters? How should the files be organized? What is the best time for you to go to lunch? Which of your duties should be given top priority?

There is much to be learned and committed to memory during the first few weeks on a job. You will find it helpful to make notes of your boss's instructions and personal preferences. Most bosses will explain things once, but they may question your capability if they have to repeat instructions too many times.

Organize for Efficiency

You are responsible for properly completing the tasks assigned to you and for getting them done on time. Such responsibility can be simple to execute if you follow a few guidelines for maximum efficiency.

Efficiency Engineering. Decide the order in which you should perform various tasks. If you are uncertain, ask your boss. In a short time you will not only learn his or her preferences, but you will also understand your role so well that you will be able to rely on your own judgment in setting priorities.

Make certain you understand just what is to be done and how. Write down instructions when they are lengthy or involved. Follow them carefully and completely. If at any time you cannot figure out how to proceed, stop and ask. An executive would rather have you ask questions than have you do the job over.

Always complete priority jobs first. Give each task, no matter how small, your undivided attention. Divide complicated jobs into steps, and do one step at a time. If possible, finish one job before you begin another. Work carefully, and then check when you are finished to make sure that you have been thorough and accurate and that you have attended to all loose ends.

Work Area Efficiency. With a place for everything and everything in its place, your work will flow more smoothly and you will suffer less emotional wear and tear. Keep your desk uncluttered, your supplies conveniently available, and your working materials arranged for a minimum of waste motion. The things you use most often should be closest at hand. Nonessentials that crowd your work space should be moved to another area. This guideline applies to desk drawers, too.

Consider the use of timesaving services and office equipment in order to get tasks done more easily and quickly. Treat equipment with care so that it will serve you well. Report needed adjustments or repairs to the proper person promptly in order to avoid time-consuming breakdowns. Keep your desk, your equipment, and your work area clean.

Teamwork Considerations

Other considerations that contribute to a secretary's efficiency as a team member are the following:

Disclosing Information. As a secretary, you will have access to confidential information. Be closemouthed about the business of the office. Do not talk about matters under consideration or about agreements concluded. Never divulge salary information or recommended promotions. Remarks of this kind made to the person involved or to co-workers can cause embarrassment to your executive and to others as well. They may also cost you your job.

Undertaking the Peacemaker Role. The atmosphere of an office is the product of the personal relations existing among members of the office group.

Congenial exchanges among co-workers, as in this lunchtime group, can make a newcomer feel welcome and more secure.

Allied Chemical Corporation

Offices become unpleasant when the people in them are wrangling or jealous or take sides. Keep relations on a business basis and never be the cause of discord. You need to be a peacemaker, one who stops friction before it has a chance to start. Do not listen to or encourage gossip.

Assuming Social Responsibilities.　Part of the secretary's social role in the office is to welcome new employees to the department. You may be expected to see that the new employee meets fellow workers; has an inviting desk or other work area; knows where supplies are kept; and is shown the location of the restroom, coat rack, and water cooler. Equally important is your responsibility to see that someone accompanies the newcomer to lunch on the first day. First impressions are important in establishing good rapport and in helping the new employee to adjust easily to the new environment. The socially responsible secretary can do much to make this adjustment pleasant.

Reviewing Your Reading

1. **a.** What is the simplest form of business organization to establish, operate, and dissolve?
   b. In what two situations is it generally the preferred form?

2. Why should the secretary to the owner of a small business expect to have widely varied duties?

3. What three characteristics of a partnership form of business organization eliminate the weaknesses of the single proprietorship?

4. If you become the secretary to several business partners, what are some of the essential questions that must be answered concerning your responsibilities?

5. Who in the personnel hierarchy are responsible for day-to-day operations and decision making?

6. Describe the secretarial opportunities that a large corporation offers.

7. What is meant by "company objectives"?

8. What does an organization chart reveal?

9. Of the three formats used for organization charts—line, concentric, and scalar—which is most often seen?

10. Discuss the advantages and drawbacks of line organization from the secretary's viewpoint.

11. How does a functional diagram differ from an organization chart?

12. Explain how a job description tells the employee what is expected.

13. In addition to understanding a company's objectives and its organizational structure, what must a secretary do to become an indispensable member of a business organization?

14. Draft guidelines that will help you to keep work flowing smoothly.

15. Explain the terms *vertical* and *horizontal communications* through the chain of command. How are your secretarial duties affected?

Using Your Skills

1. **Qualifications for a Small Office.** You are about to apply for the job of secretary in a small professional office where you would be the entire office staff. List duties (in addition to shorthand and transcription) for which you are now prepared to assume full responsibility.

2. **Qualifications for a Large Office.** Select one of the departments of a corporation (sales, purchasing, personnel, production, market research, finance) and indicate specific secretarial knowledge and skills that might be needed to work in such a department. Helpful information for completing this assignment can be found in books and magazine articles, describing these areas of business administration and from observation of such departments. Type the report in good form.

3. **Secretarial Roles.** You have heard that one of the companies you are interested in working in asks the following questions of all secretarial applicants. Outline how you would answer them.
   a. What do you believe is the key role of a secretary?
   b. Is the role of the secretary in today's organizations changing? If not, why not? If so, how and why?
   c. How will your perception of secretarial roles affect your behavior?

Exercising Your Judgment

Favors. You have gone to the mail room a few minutes after closing time with some important letters that Mrs. Johnson, your employer, has just signed. You usually keep stamps at your desk for such an emergency, but you neglected to check your supply and do not have enough. The mail room employees are on their way out, the automatic stamping machine is locked, and the key has been put in the safe. You do not have access to the supply of stamps.

1. To whom will you turn in the mail room—someone you know or a new employee with whom you are not too well acquainted? Why?
2. Will you offer an explanation for not having enough stamps at your desk?
3. What reason will you give for coming after closing time?
4. Mrs. Johnson is a top executive. Will you allow the importance of your position to influence your actions?

Applying the Reference Section

Study the words in the subgroups below to determine whether they are correctly spelled. If necessary, refer to the spelling rules in the Reference Section and consult a dictionary.

1. Do the following words end with *sion* or *tion*?
   - **a.** communica—
   - **b.** illustra—
   - **c.** conclu—
   - **d.** persua—
   - **e.** appor—
   - **f.** repeti—
   - **g.** compul—
   - **h.** provi—
   - **i.** inten—
   - **j.** comple—

2. Should the italicized letters be doubled?
   - **a.** a*l*together
   - **b.** bu*l*etin
   - **c.** competitor
   - **d.** co*n*ection
   - **e.** im*i*tate
   - **f.** we*l*fare
   - **g.** po*s*esion
   - **h.** benefiting
   - **i.** a*p*arent
   - **j.** inte*l*igent

3. Supply the missing letters (*y*, *i*, or *ie*):
   - **a.** bus—ness
   - **b.** dr—ness
   - **c.** occup—ing
   - **d.** rel—ance
   - **e.** trolle—s
   - **f.** da—ly
   - **g.** pa—d
   - **h.** sla—n
   - **i.** enjo—ment
   - **j.** tr—s

4. Which of the following words are spelled incorrectly?
   - **a.** apologize
   - **b.** merchandize
   - **c.** supervize
   - **d.** characterize
   - **e.** analyse
   - **f.** realise
   - **g.** advertise
   - **h.** paralyze
   - **i.** exercise
   - **j.** compromise

5. Provide plurals for the following:
   - **a.** witness
   - **b.** century
   - **c.** journey
   - **d.** piano
   - **e.** 1980
   - **f.** foot
   - **g.** tomato
   - **h.** lb.
   - **i.** analysis
   - **j.** worry

CHAPTER THREE / Managing Responsibility

The secretary is a vital member of the office team and has a supportive role in relation to the employer. Some duties and responsibilities such as opening mail and answering the phone are common to all secretarial jobs. In other positions, however, there are unique duties and responsibilities that may involve a greater variety of tasks or more complex ones. These are assigned to the secretary who is thought to be capable of managing and carrying out more responsibilities.

Because you are a supportive member of the office team, you need to understand your duties and responsibilities and then perform them efficiently and with a minimum of supervision.

Concepts

Managing responsibility has a twofold meaning: first, that there are certain duties and responsibilities inherent in secretarial work beyond those specified on a job or in a job description; second, that secretaries are responsible for managing their time and their work. Managing, then, means organizing and planning as well as making decisions about work priorities and procedures.

Identifying Duties and Responsibilities

Explicit duties and responsibilities are those that are directly assigned either in writing or by oral directions. The explicit ones listed in your job description are usually major tasks; your immediate supervisor generally identifies these and explains any special procedures.

Some duties and responsibilities are implicit in nature—that is, they are a subpart of a major duty; you are simply expected to know that they are part of your responsibility. For example, if an explicit duty is typing correspondence and forms, the corresponding implicit responsibility is maintaining the typewriter in good working order—cleaning keys, changing ribbons, and calling for service when needed. A company handbook may describe the procedures for calling the service company, but you, the secretary, have the implicit or unstated responsibility for doing so.

Sources of Identification

Three sources of information are useful in identifying your duties and responsibilities and providing a variety of information about them: (a) a written job description and company handbook, (b) your employer's oral directions, and (c) the ethical standards of a professional business career.

Job Description.   When you are interviewed for a position, the interviewer will provide a general description of the job and may identify specific tasks. Your training and previous office experience will be assessed to determine whether you have the skills and abilities to perform these tasks. You may be asked to take one or more employment tests. In larger companies or businesses a written job description may be available, such as the one for the secretary to a general manager described in Chapter 2. It may include some duties peculiar to the particular position and company, such as "preparing Audit Form 156 weekly." A job description is an excellent source of information.

If a written job description is not provided, you will need to develop your own from the oral instructions given you by your employer or supervisor. That list of tasks, duties, and responsibilities will be of great help to your replacement should you leave your job.

Employer's Instructions.   In addition to a written job description, you are likely to receive additional instructions from your employer. When these are given orally, jot them down immediately. Procedures for accomplishing each task to be done will be given you by your employer or someone else. A company handbook explaining such procedures may be available.

After you have been on the job for some time and, with less direct supervision, are successfully completing the tasks first assigned you, your boss may assign more duties and responsibilities. These explicit or directly assigned duties and responsibilities make your job more supportive and enable your boss to accomplish more work. Such additions to the major duties and responsibilities listed on your job description make your position more interesting.

Ethical Standards.   The secretarial profession cherishes its reputation for high ethical standards. Honesty, dependability, loyalty, courtesy, and pride in doing good work are included in these standards. Summed up, they are labeled "attitude." Although the expectation is not listed in a job description, the person who hires expects that a secretary will have the right attitude.

Your employer may have expectations and preferences different from yours. The professional approach of a secretary should be to reconcile them with his or her own ethical standards and attitudes.

Directional Flow of Responsibility

As a secretary you will work closely with many people to achieve company objectives. The adjacent figure illustrates the directional flow of responsibility to four groups of people: (a) your employer and his or her superiors, (b) co-workers

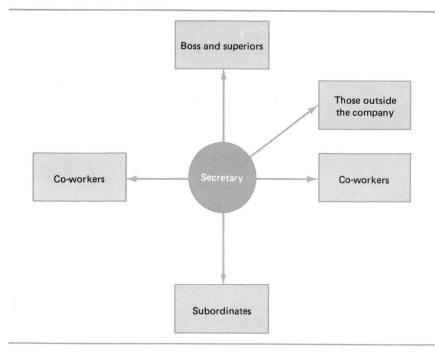

on your level, (c) subordinates, and (d) those outside your company. This directional flow of responsibilities has two major aspects: maintaining good interpersonal relationships, and maintaining a smooth, efficient work flow.

Your responsibilities flow upward to your superiors who assign duties to you. You assign and supervise work of your subordinates (if any) in a downward flow. You maintain a horizontal flow with your peer group as you share responsibility for various tasks. An additional outward flow of responsibility relates to your interpersonal relationships with suppliers, customers, and clients.

Amount of Supervision

The amount of responsibility and supervision you will have as a secretary generally are inversely related. That is, the more responsibilities you are capable of assuming, the less supervision you are likely to have.

There are three levels of supervision: (1) close supervision, (2) general overall supervision, and (3) little or no supervision. As a new employee or an inexperienced secretary, you may expect your boss to closely supervise your work. Tasks will be assigned daily; many decisions about work priorities will be made for you; your work will be checked carefully to see that it is accurate; and your procedures will be studied to determine whether they are correct.

If your work is satisfactory at this level, your boss may soon provide only general overall supervision. You will be expected to complete your daily tasks without any reminders. You will make your own decisions about the priorities of work in most cases. The work you complete will not be checked as carefully for details, nor will your work procedures be observed as closely. Your boss will be available to answer questions but you will be expected to begin tasks on your own, to complete your work on time, and to produce accurate work. Directions about new tasks will include fewer detailed instructions, since your boss will assume that you know the general procedures.

High-level secretaries (executive and administrative) work with little or no supervision. They have proved that they are self-starters and know their work. These secretaries are considered assistants to the boss.

In some offices, such as law firms, you may find that all of your work is supervised carefully because of the extreme need for accuracy. You may also find individual executives who prefer to make all decisions and check all work. In fact, they insist on it, and you must respect their preference.

Managing Your Responsibilities

Successful secretaries manage their many duties and responsibilities with relative ease. Why? They have learned to make decisions about the priority of each task; they plan and organize their work area; they simplify their work as much as possible; they develop clear-cut procedures for each task; they produce work efficiently and constantly strive to improve their office skills.

Managing is the key word to efficiency. It is the process of planning and organizing materials, supplies, and work space in order to simplify procedures and to complete tasks efficiently. The managing process involves identifying duties and responsibilities, determining alternative plans of action, following company procedures and policies, and making decisions.

Your managing skills may be utilized in four ways as a secretary: (1) managing the office, (2) managing your time, (3) managing the flow of work by deciding on work priorities, and (4) managing or supervising the work of subordinates.

Of course, a balance will exist between your preferences and those of the company and your employer. You may plan and organize the arrangement of supplies and materials in your own desk, but the location of your desk is likely to be the company's decision.

Managing the Office
Some employers expect you to manage their offices—that is, return folders to personal files, check to see that the maintenance personnel have cleaned properly, and post appointments on desk calendars.

You will usually be responsible for managing your boss's files. When the company has a centralized file room, you will be responsible for ordering and returning files.

In some offices you may be responsible for ordering supplies for yourself and others; in others, individual employees request supplies from a centralized supply room. If you are responsible for a supply cabinet or room, you will need to organize it for easy use and control. Supplies used in quantity should be placed where they are easy to reach. Each type of supply should have its place, and that place should be labeled. If a number of individuals need supplies from the same cabinet, a control procedure should be used so that one person (you or someone else) distributes them. This procedure ensures that the supplies are not wasted and that they are kept clean and in order. Also, the control person takes the responsibility for replenishing supplies when they run low.

The reception area near your boss's office may also require your management even though the maintenance personnel clean it. The furniture and magazines may need to be straightened occasionally. Old or worn magazines may need to be discarded. If brochures describing the company and its products or services are available, you should see that they are replaced when necessary.

If there is a conference room you may be given the explicit responsibility for scheduling meetings in it. Other implied responsibilities are to check to see that it is in good order before and after scheduled meetings and sometimes to lay out special materials before meetings.

Your own desk should be organized for efficiency and appearance. Keep only constantly used items on your desk top; supplies and other materials should be kept in the drawers. Place your telephone and a message pad within easy reach and on the side that permits you to pick up the receiver with your nonwriting hand. Keep all confidential papers in the drawers unless you are working on them. Lock your desk at night and when you are away from it.

Be aware of many other implied responsibilities in managing your work area. Your ability to recognize and act on these enhances your image as an efficient, successful secretary.

Managing Your Time

Secretaries have many duties and responsibilities to perform. They also have a large quantity of work to produce each day. Therefore, your time must be carefully planned. The management of time may be viewed in three ways: (1) scheduling of time in general, (2) deciding on work priorities, and (3) searching for ways to simplify work to save time.

Here are some procedures to help you manage and schedule your time.

Develop the Things-to-Do-Today Habit.   Before you leave the office at the end of the day and while the tasks are fresh in your mind, jot down in your notepad or on your calendar a list of tomorrow's tasks and the order in which they need to be done. When you arrive in the morning, you can simply start your

THINGS TO DO TODAY
1 Type agenda for Wednesday morning.
2 Call Mr. Patterson at 9 a.m.
3 Deposit money.
4 Make reservation for Mr. T's trip next
5   week.

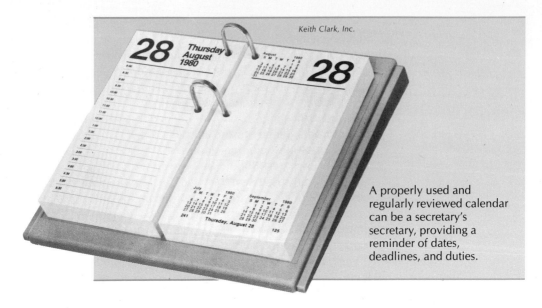

Keith Clark, Inc.

A properly used and regularly reviewed calendar can be a secretary's secretary, providing a reminder of dates, deadlines, and duties.

tasks without having to reread and make decisions. At the end of the day, and occasionally during the day, review this list and cross out completed tasks. The ones remaining and any new tasks should be scheduled for the next day. You may want to have a similar list of tasks for the week or month.

Plan for Infrequent Tasks.   Some duties and tasks are easy to forget because they occur only at infrequent intervals—a monthly report, for example. Use a calendar notation system. Jot down the task to be done on your calendar three or four days before it is due and also on the due date.

You can also use a tickler system of file folders alone or in combination with your calendar notations. In this system, you make up a file guide and one file

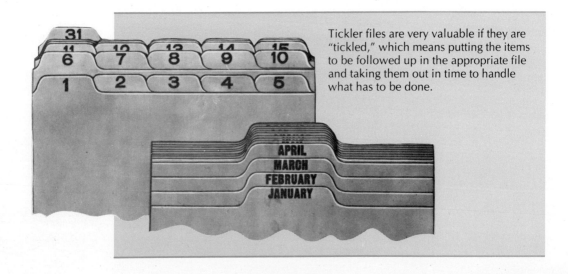

Tickler files are very valuable if they are "tickled," which means putting the items to be followed up in the appropriate file and taking them out in time to handle what has to be done.

folder for each month of the year. Number a second set of file folders from 1 to 31 and place it behind the current month's guide. Then, as you find tasks that need to be done on the twenty-fourth of the current month place them in the file folder labeled "24." If a report is due three months from now, say in June, place all materials pertaining to the report in the June file folder.

Each day check the file folders to determine if there are tasks that need attention. Then move the empty day of the month folder to its appropriate place behind next month's guide. It is also a good idea to check several days ahead, since some tasks require collection of data or more time to complete. An advantage of the folder system is that materials can be collected and stored until the day the work is produced.

Set Aside Time Daily or Weekly for Routine Tasks.   Routine tasks such as filing often have a relatively low priority and are, therefore, neglected. Some secretaries spend more time shuffling papers in the in basket hunting for a letter that has not yet been filed than it would have taken to file it in the first place. Develop the habit of doing the routine tasks at the scheduled time. If the end of the day is generally hectic with last-minute tasks, schedule the routine tasks earlier in the day.

Your boss may also have preferences about scheduling time, and your schedule should take this into consideration.

Batch Your Work to Save Time.   Work on similar tasks at the same time. For example, set your typewriter for typing letters and then do all you have to do at one time, or set up your typewriter for typing invoices and then type all the invoices. Batching your work this way saves time in making machine adjustments.

Use the same principle for filing, especially if you must leave your desk to file. Collect all the filing for the day and do it at one time. If you need to get a letter from the file during the day, take along any items waiting to be filed.

Use Special Tools and Accessories to Simplify Your Work.   Use a rubber finger in counting papers and cards, in collating papers, or in filing.

If your work includes collating large numbers of long reports, simplify the task by using expandable collating racks or electrically operated collators. When collating smaller quantities of short reports (three to four pages), lay out your materials so as to save motions.

Making Decisions About Work Priorities

Managing your work involves making decisions about what to do first. This decision-making process is often called "setting work priorities" or the "in basket technique," since it usually includes sorting the papers and tasks delivered to the in basket on your desk.

Six steps for determining work priorities follow. By applying these steps you will be able to make decisions about the priority of all your tasks at once. You can then proceed to do them without constantly shuffling through your tasks and losing valuable time trying to decide which one to do next.

1. Set priority categories.
2. Identify tasks to be done.
3. Examine each task for clues.
4. Decide on priority and sort into stacks.
5. Complete tasks in order of priority.
6. Reexamine priority of all tasks when a new task is received.

Develop a system of priority categories, such as 1, 2, 3, and 4 or *emergency, important, routine,* and *hold,* or categorize tasks by the time at which they must be done—*immediately, as soon as possible, today,* and *this week.*

Search for and identify all the tasks that need to be done. Check your calendar and tickler files, your boss's calendar, your memory, the mail, and your in basket.

The quality of the work desired contributes to the importance or priority of the task. Although an interoffice memo should be well typed, it may have less need for perfection than a special report your boss will present to the company president.

As you examine each task, estimate the time required to do the job, based on your skills. If you are asked at 9 a.m. to type a 20-page report for a three o'clock meeting the same day, how long will it take to do the job? Is this report an emergency item or an important one? If you type 50 words a minute, you can type five to six pages an hour, including proofreading time. If you type 70 words a minute, you may produce six to seven pages an hour. Be sure to consider how complex the report is, that is, the number of tables and figures in it and whether it is in longhand, in rough draft form, or in copy with few corrections.

As you make your decision about the 20-page report, also estimate the number of interruptions that are likely to occur. Although this is difficult to judge, you need to allow extra time to handle interruptions easily and tactfully.

Some decisions about priorities depend on whether the work is needed by someone else by a certain time. In such instances your decisions should be based on the need to maintain work flow from your desk to others.

At times a task requires the cooperation of others, such as a report that needs to be reproduced in quantity in the reprographics department. In such cases you need to plan sufficient *lead time* to obtain another department's services as a routine task. Sometimes you will be forced to request emergency service, but as much work as possible should be managed so that you do not repeatedly request emergency service.

Some decisions about work priority depend on the amount of money involved. For example, if you have two contracts to type and they have the same deadline, you would normally type the $500,000 one before the $5,000 one.

Although you work for your boss, you are, of course, employed by the company. Occasionally, you may receive tasks from your boss's superiors, and, with your boss's approval, they should take precedence over your regular work. At times you may also be requested to help out others in your department.

If you work for more than one person, you will occasionally have two tasks that need to be completed at the same time. If one person holds a higher rank than the other, you may decide to do that person's task first; if the individuals

Peter Roth

Sorting the morning mail is usually the first task in a busy secretary's day.

hold equal rank, your best decision may be to ask both of them to decide the priorities for you! If tasks for others constantly take up so much time that you cannot finish those for your immediate boss, you may need to request that the individuals involved reexamine your responsibilities and job description.

Tasks that are batched should be placed in the same priority category. Occasionally one such item may need rush treatment, in which case it should be classified as a separate item.

Offices often experience emergencies due to absenteeism or rush jobs and you may be asked to help out, or you may recognize the problem and volunteer to help. Cooperate when you can, but be sure to complete your own emergency and important tasks first.

Once your decisions about priorities are made, you will find it easy to work productively. Your uncluttered, well-organized desk, with all supplies available and in their place, will also contribute to your efficiency. In effectively managing the execution of tasks both important and routine, explicit and implicit, large and small, you increase your value and stature as a team member. In managing your own responsibilities well you develop the ability to manage other individuals.

Managing Others

The office team has members at various levels. As you mature in your role as a supportive secretary you may be asked to supervise or coordinate the work of others. To prepare yourself for such responsibilities, learn as much as possible about the operations and procedures of your company. Learn about good management principles if an office course is available. Read the chapter on motivation and job advancement that comes later in this book. Study the directional flow of responsibility that operates in every office.

<table>
<tr><td>Reviewing Your Reading</td><td></td></tr>
</table>

Reviewing Your Reading

1. What is meant by the term *managing responsibility*?

2. What is the difference between an explicit and an implicit responsibility? Give two examples not in this chapter.

3. Name three sources you may use to identify your duties and responsibilities. Which source may cause the most problems and misunderstandings? Why?

4. Give examples of ways to maintain good interpersonal relationships and to maintain a smooth work flow for each of the four directional flows of responsibility.

5. In what four areas do you need managing skills?

6. Name and describe two tickler systems. Which is best? Why?

7. Name and briefly describe each step in the process of making decisions about work priorities.

8. In what ways do your typing and transcription skills affect your decisions about work priorities? How many typewritten pages can you produce in an hour if the copy is in longhand? in rough draft form with many corrections? If your boss dictated ten medium-length letters, how much time should you schedule for transcribing them (with two carbons and an envelope for each)? How much additional time should be scheduled for interruptions?

9. Describe three ways in which a secretary can manage time.

10. What is the relationship between a job description and a company handbook? How do the two differ?

11. Explain in your own words what is meant by the statement "Managing is the key word to efficiency."

12. Explain what is meant by the term *in-basket technique*? How did it get its name?

Using Your Skills

1. **Things-to-Do List.** Develop the habit of managing your work by keeping a weekly and daily things-to-do list. Start by making a list of the major tasks you need to do this week. Then develop a list of those major and minor tasks, errands, and assignments you need to do tomorrow; assign a work priority to each one. At the end of each day review your list and cross off all those you completed. Make a new list for tomorrow. Save these daily lists for a week and then compare them with your weekly one. Analyze your progress and type a one-page report to hand in to your instructor. Attach your daily and weekly lists (in rough form).

2. Planning the Day. Assume that your new employer gives you dictation daily between 10 and 11 in the morning and between 2 and 3 in the afternoon. He has asked you to outline a plan of today's work with this in mind. You have the following things to do: prepare an itinerary for your employer's trip to a regional office ten days from now; write four letters to office furniture manufacturers asking for their catalogs; proofread the monthly report you typed for your employer yesterday; make out a request for supplies that are running low; file routine correspondence. Prepare a schedule for the day divided into half hours, starting at 9 and ending at 5. Explain the ordering of the tasks and the time allotted for them.

EXERCISING
YOUR
JUDGMENT

1. The Conference Room. You are responsible for scheduling meetings in the conference room. Your boss has reserved it from 9 to 10:30 on Thursday (today is Tuesday) for a meeting with three advertising executives from your department. Mrs. Anderson, head of the accounting department, is on the phone now about scheduling the conference room from 10 to 12 on Thursday for a special meeting with ten accountants from other companies. What alternatives do you have? Which one will you decide to use? Why?

2. A Rush Job. Mark and Susan are secretaries for Mr. Wilson, the other attorney in your office area. They are working frantically to mail out special notices for an emergency meeting he just scheduled for next Friday. Three hundred envelopes need to be addressed and then stuffed with the notices; it is now 3:30 on Friday and the notices must go in the mail today. Friday afternoon is always hectic in your office as there are usually quite a few phone calls and visitors. You work only for your boss, Mrs. Wicks, and you still have several tasks to complete today, including the typing of an agenda for Mrs. Wicks' 9 a.m. meeting on Monday.
a. Mark and Susan have not asked you for help. Should you volunteer?
b. If you volunteer, what should you offer to do?

3. An In Basket. You are secretary to Richard Hut, the head of the advertising department of a large company, and perform occasional secretarial duties for other people in the department as well. This morning, Wednesday, May 10, you had planned to resume typing an important 15-page report prepared by Gloria Johnson, but Mr. Hut, who is leaving for Chicago tomorrow, called you into his office and dictated six letters. You then made a short trip to the accounting department to check a figure mentioned in one of the letters.

When you returned to your desk, you found in your in basket a handwritten note from Mr. Hut saying "Urgent! Set up meeting with Weeks, Brown, Johnson, and Arkas for today at 4. Have Johnson report early." There is also a telephone message from a Mrs. Whitman of the local high school asking if Mr. Hut could speak to her marketing class on Monday, May 22, at 9:30 a.m. Another message reveals that Mr. Arkas has the flu and won't be in today or tomorrow. Finally, you find Mr. Hut's expense account with a note asking you to type it today and apologizing for not having given it to you earlier.

On a separate sheet of paper, list the order in which you would handle all these items and indicate what you would do in each case.

1. Which of the words in the parentheses correctly expresses the meaning required to complete the sentence? Type the letter of the item and the correct word or words on a separate sheet of paper.
   a. My, but this (current, currant) jelly is good.
   b. Be sure your lines are (straight, strait).
   c. The tools have (already, all ready) been bought.
   d. The scents of the different flowers (purveyed, pervade) the room.
   e. I received many (complements, compliments) on my new outfit.
   f. Yes, I (ought, aught) to open a savings account.
   g. Defacing this property is a misdemeanor; the fine (therefore, therefor) is $50.
   h. My notebook has lost (its, it's) cover.

2. In each of the following sentences, decide whether the single word or the pair of words in parentheses gives the meaning intended. Consult a dictionary when in doubt.
   a. The flood (maybe, may be) the cause of the delay.
   b. I am prepared to (enforce, in force) the decision.
   c. The circulars are (already, all ready) to be folded.
   d. I plan to take a vacation (some time, sometime) in March.
   e. The man made an (in direct, indirect) reference to the subject.
   f. (Any one, Anyone) of the methods is satisfactory.
   g. The blouse is (all most, almost) worn out.
   h. (Someone, Some one) failed to close the window.
   i. Miss Jones is (always, all ways) here promptly.
   j. I am proud of (everyone, every one) of you.

Chapter four / Career Opportunities

As you begin your career as a secretary, you should be aware that you have made a career choice that offers many opportunities. Various options are open to you; your horizons can expand depending on your interests, needs, and abilities.

You may decide to enhance your opportunities by continuing to improve your typewriting, shorthand, interpersonal relationship, and managing skills so that you advance from presecretarial to the highest secretarial levels.

Or you may decide to specialize in an area such as technical, medical, legal, or word processing—all of which offer interesting secretarial opportunities.

You may decide to gain experience and first-hand knowledge of the business world as a secretary while you study for a supervisory or management position, for an entirely different business career, or for starting your own business.

Regardless of your choice, your job can be interesting or dull depending on your own attitude, initiative, and creativeness. Working with people is never boring, and as a secretary, you work closely with many people—your boss, co-workers, and customers. Every job from selling to acting has its share of routine and uninteresting tasks. Such tasks must be done efficiently and as cheerfully as possible. As you progress in your career, there will probably be fewer routine tasks and more complex tasks and challenges to meet.

Now that you have chosen a secretarial career you need to develop a sound foundation of secretarial skills. With them and a desire to succeed, you can look optimistically to the future and your expanded horizons.

Job Opportunities

The labor market for secretaries will continue to grow. In fact, according to Bureau of Labor Statistics figures, the number of secretarial positions will expand by nearly 50 percent by 1985. There will also be a need for nearly 35 percent more typists by 1985. The need for employees who take only stenography will decrease, but this decrease is deceiving because most jobs making use of stenography are being changed from *stenographer* to *secretary*. The shift to the use of word processing equipment has also resulted in a drop in the strictly stenographic position.

Thus, the demand for secretaries will remain high, and the responsible, well-qualified secretary will have many career options.

The Career Ladder

Your career as a secretary can be compared to progression on a ladder. The first rung on the ladder corresponds to your first office job. That job might be as receptionist, stenographer, general office clerk, or secretary. Whatever the job, each has its place on the office team. In some offices the receptionist position is considered a beginning one, whereas in others, it is filled by an individual who knows the company and who is especially good at public relations.

Progression on your career ladder may be achieved in several ways: by increased responsibilities and pay on the same job, by a change in secretarial levels—from secretary to executive secretary to administrative assistant—or by a change in careers.

Your progression on the secretarial career ladder may occur within one company or may require that you move to another company. Or you may decide to add to your secretarial skills by specializing in some specific technical area or on some of the newer office machines such as the automatic text-editing typewriters.

Federal legislation has had some effect on secretarial opportunities. Employers may no longer discriminate in work and pay between the sexes. Sex stereotyping in the secretarial profession has existed for many years. Some of the

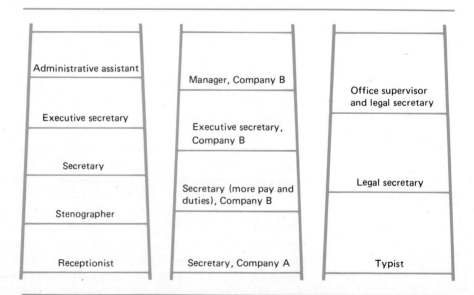

The secretarial career ladder can take you in many different directions.

more common misconceptions are that secretaries are always female; that executives are always men; and that women should not be offered jobs that involve moving to another location, especially if they are married.

Under the recent federal legislation employers must eliminate both sex bias and sex stereotyping in hiring and promoting all workers, including secretaries. Consequently, some career horizons may be expanded for both female and male secretaries. An executive may be either male or female. A secretary, male or female, may be working for a person of the opposite or the same sex. Either way, the interpersonal relationships in an office should proceed in a businesslike way with courtesy toward all.

Career Options

You can make your choice of a career within the secretarial area by considering either job by level according to experience and skills, job by specialty or technical area, or job by type of company.

Secretarial Jobs by Level   Secretarial job levels are not always fixed. Jobs will vary, and in some instances overlap, because of the particular nature of a business or the requirements of individual employers. The levels that follow are the more traditional ones.

Presecretarial.   The mail clerk, receptionist, and typist positions are examples of presecretarial positions. Individuals in these positions perform only specific office tasks in a limited range. The typist generally spends the majority of the day typing reports, business forms, and other materials and has little or no responsibility for answering the phone, greeting callers, or transcribing. The inexperienced person or one with little office training often finds employment in such presecretarial or entry-level positions.

Stenographer.   The position of stenographer involves mostly the taking of dictation and transcribing, with only a few other minor office duties and tasks. This position occurs in companies where an executive may have large quantities of correspondence to answer and prefers to work with a stenographer who has good dictation and transcription skills.

Secretary.   The secretarial position pulls together many skills, including those of the mail clerk, the receptionist, the transcriber, the typist, and the telephone operator. It is a combination of handling incoming and outgoing mail, answering the phone and placing calls, transcribing letters, typing reports and business forms, serving as receptionist, and many other responsibilities. For that reason many people find secretarial positions varied and interesting.

As a secretary you may progress by taking on additional complex duties and responsibilities and still keep the title of secretary. Such added assignments are rewarded with more pay and prestige as well as by your being accepted as a more valuable member of the office team. A beginning secretary is often assigned to a junior executive. In time, as both employer and employee gain experience, the beginner is rewarded with additional pay or a promotion.

Executive Secretary.   As an executive secretary you perform the regular functions of a general secretary, of course, but with greater finesse and skill. Other duties and responsibilities or more complex tasks may be assigned to you. Because an executive secretary has already demonstrated ability and dependability, the boss usually provides little or no supervision. Promotion to this level is usually based on demonstrated knowledge of good office procedures, efficiency in producing work, good managing skills, and most of all, good interpersonal relationships.

Administrative Assistant.   When an executive secretary is capable and has acquired additional training, another change in duties and responsibilities may occur—from executive secretary to administrative assistant. In that position you work *with and for* the boss rather than only *for* the boss as a secretary does. You generally work independently with little direction and supervision. An administrative assistant may develop special reports at the request of the boss, act in the boss's place at times, and often be considered to be in a quasi-managerial position.

Each secretarial level with its own requirements and qualifications is important. Many of the same tasks, duties, and responsibilities are present in each position, but the degree of skill and maturity needed increases as you climb the career ladder. Decision making, managing ability, and the ability to cope with emergencies are not skills acquired automatically. They are the result of experience, hard and persistent work, and in most cases additional study.

Secretarial Jobs by Specialty or Technical Area

Some secretarial positions require training in special technical areas or on special equipment. This training is in addition to what you need to be a general secretary and it may be obtained at a postsecondary school (vocational technical school, community college, or four-year college or university) or through the equipment manufacturer. Secretarial specializations are discussed in detail in Chapter 24, "Making Career Choices."

Secretarial Jobs by Type of Company

Although secretarial office positions in most companies are similar, some variations do exist depending on the type of company, the clientele, or the geographic location. You may be attracted to such a secretarial position precisely because of its special variations. For example, if you are interested in advertising, you may want to take a secretarial position with an advertising agency or the advertising department of a large company.

Similarly, you may want to work for a publishing firm, a public relations firm, an insurance company, an international company, the foreign service, a travel agency, a theatrical agency, a state or national legislative body, a financial institution, a stockbroker, or any one of many other businesses.

Basic office procedures will be similar in most of them but in all cases you will want to learn something about the product or service, the special vocabulary used in connection with it, and the nature and needs of the clientele with which the company deals. For example, if you worked for a gypsum processing plant that made cement, plaster, and dry wallboard you would need to be able to write terms concerning cement in shorthand. And it would certainly help in transcrib-

AT&T Co.

Good secretarial skills give you many career options, because there are few businesses anywhere that do not need secretarial support.

ing letters intelligently if you knew that "popping" meant "the breaking of air bubbles in poured cement that results in an uneven surface of sharp rings."

Expansion of Horizons

In addition to the secretarial options open to you, there are other horizons that you may want to explore. In some ways they are expanded variations of the commonly recognized secretarial job and may fall into one of these categories: word processing, management and supervision, self-employment, and career change.

Word Processing

The term *word processing* was coined to describe a system or process for improving the quality and speed of production of words from a dictator to a readable finished product through the use of personnel, equipment, and procedures. It evolved because of the great need for more rapid word production. That need is the result of business growth, increased governmental forms that must be completed, and computers that must be fed increasing amounts of data for rapid processing.

Interestingly enough, the steps involved in the processing of words have not changed much since the typewriter was installed in most offices. The procedures for handling office documents improved when the computer took over the processing of calculations and accounting and the printing of statistical reports, bills, and forms. Executives, however, continued to dictate to a secretary or a dictation machine, and secretaries continued to transcribe at 25 to 30 words a minute. Even though the demand for word output increased drastically, output was restricted to the limited capacity of the secretary to transcribe the words.

Careers in word processing are promising because of the expanding interest in systems that expedite the handling of written communications. Responsibilities are divided between an *administrative secretary*, whose work consists of traditional administrative secretarial tasks but only occasional typing, and a *correspondence specialist*, who processes all types of communications.

To be a correspondence specialist you have no need for shorthand, but you are expected to type proficiently and have a good command of English spelling and grammar. The career path from there can lead you to be a word processing supervisor, a position that requires a complete understanding of the capabilities of word processing equipment as well as the ability to efficiently manage a word processing center and supervise a staff of correspondence specialists.

Word processing is discussed in greater detail in Chapter 11, "Word Processing Equipment and Systems."

Management and Supervision

You may decide to try to expand your horizons by moving to a supervisory or management position in the office. Such positions require experience and knowledge of company policy and office procedures beyond that of the average secretary. Most of these positions also require additional training at the collegiate level. The career options include office manager, records manager, word processing supervisor, and others relating to office services.

Self-Employment

A well-qualified secretary with good management skills and a knowledge of the business world may start a secretarial services business or some other business.

Some self-employed individuals work in hotels that cater to executives who need secretarial services while traveling. Others offer secretarial services to a nearby college or university community where students need theses and dissertations typed. Others set up a business combining typewriting with fast printing. Another self-employed business has to do with providing temporary office personnel for local businesses.

If you plan to be self-employed or start a business, you must study local city and state laws about licensing and zoning, conduct market surveys to determine the need for the service and fair prices, contact suppliers, employ workers, buy equipment, and develop advertising campaigns. Accounting procedures necessary for local, state, and federal taxes must be developed. Loan applications may need to be made and a facility rented or purchased. If your business is to prosper, you must know enough, through study, to meet crises successfully.

Career Change

As you gain a greater knowledge of business procedures through your work as a secretary, you may find that you have developed interests in some other area, or that some new technological discovery has changed your horizons and your options. Whatever your decision, your experience as a secretary, working with people and coping with problems, will be a most valuable asset.

Reviewing Your Reading

1. Name at least four career options that are open to you as a secretary.
2. Will the job opportunities increase or decrease for secretaries? typists? stenographers?
3. What is meant by the term *career ladder*?
4. Name some of the common sex stereotyping misconceptions.
5. Identify three titles used to indicate career options by job level within the secretarial field.
6. There is no duplication of duties and tasks from one office job to another. True or false? Explain.
7. What is the difference between an executive secretary and an administrative assistant? Is it possible for an executive to have people employed in both positions in the same office?
8. Describe what is meant by the term *word processing*.
9. What are some options available to you if you want to be self-employed? What are some of the advantages and disadvantages of self-employment?

Using Your Skills

1. **Interview.** Select one secretarial job title (or your instructor will assign one) in which you are interested. Interview someone in that position to learn (a) the job duties and responsibilities, (b) qualifications needed, (c) different forms used, and (d) advancement possibilities. If possible, collect sample forms to show the class. Type a summary report about your interview.

2. **Self-Analysis.** What type of secretarial job do you want?
   a. Type a list of your interests, qualifications, and future goals.
   b. Check the want-ad section of a newspaper in your locale. Count the number of ads seeking receptionists, typists, and secretaries (any type). Then select four ads for secretaries—two you think you might consider and two in which you would not be interested. Discuss your reasons for choosing these four ads after mounting them on another sheet of paper.
   c. Add a paragraph in which you describe the secretarial job you would prefer—job title, location, setting, special features, and so on.

3. **Sex Discrimination.** Find an article or news story about sex discrimination in a business office and bring a copy of it to class. Be prepared to discuss it. You may want to check the *Business Education Index, Business Periodical Index,* or *Reader's Guide* for sources; perhaps your local newspaper carried a story or feature about this topic recently.

4. **The Text-Editing Typewriter.** Observe someone operating an automatic text-editing typewriter and ask him or her to explain its features. Does your school provide training on this equipment? If so, learn to operate it. If not, where can you go to learn these skills?

Exercising Your Judgment

1. **More Favors.** On Tuesday a close friend asks you as a personal favor to type a 20-page report by Friday noon. What will you decide to do? Why?
2. **Overtime.** Occasionally your boss asks you to work an hour or so later to complete some special project. Nothing has ever been said about pay. Today you were asked to stay until you could finish a special financial report needed for an 8:30 a.m. meeting tomorrow. You estimate you will finish about 7:30 tonight. What action would you take about these recurring overtime hours?

Applying the Reference Section

1. Decide which of the following possessives are incorrectly spelled, and type the correct spelling on a separate sheet of paper. If the correct form is shown, type it as it is shown here.
   - **a.** whose
   - **b.** ladie's
   - **c.** companys'
   - **d.** White and Co.'s
   - **e.** women's
   - **f.** two lawyer's
   - **g.** their's
   - **h.** misse's size
   - **i.** five customer's complaints
   - **j.** it's color
2. In the following phrases, apostrophes may be needed to indicate the possessive case. Type each phrase correctly on a separate sheet of paper.
   - **a.** the businesspersons luncheon
   - **b.** two weeks advance notice
   - **c.** no one elses responsibility
   - **d.** its reputation
   - **e.** boys shoe department
   - **f.** a ladys handbag
   - **g.** my son-in-laws car
   - **h.** my order at the butchers
3. Each of these sentences contains a frequently heard error in grammar or in word usage. Type the correct form on a separate sheet of paper.
   - **a.** If she don't improve her spelling she'll never become a good stenographer.
   - **b.** I had ought to be going.
   - **c.** She says to me, "Be sure to put an airmail stamp on that letter."
   - **d.** Do you want this here piece of fruit?
   - **e.** I'm going to order cream chicken on toast.
   - **f.** May I have the lend of your fountain pen?

PART
TWO / INTERPERSONAL
COMMUNICATIONS

CHAPTER five / COMMUNICATIONS With Others

The problem of creating goodwill in a community becomes increasingly difficult as society becomes more impersonal. To communicate with the public a company uses many tools, such as advertising, direct-mail letters, booklets, posters, billboards, meetings, and speakers' programs. When used in the right way and at the right time, each can be an effective public relations tool.

Secretaries are strategically placed to help their companies build good public relations. Through the friendly and efficient performance of their duties, they have an opportunity to temper the ill effects that bigness and depersonalization have on a business and on the public it reaches. Each time you type a letter, talk on the telephone, or receive an office caller, you have the opportunity to convey an impression that will help your company earn understanding and acceptance.

There are two aspects of communications for you to consider: the public relations function for the company as an entity, and the personal communications techniques needed.

COMMUNICATION

What is meant by communication? Communication is the process of exchanging information, ideas, and emotions. It is a two-way process. It may take place in person, by letter, or by telephone. There is even communication via body language.

Your communications follow the same patterns that were illustrated by the directional flow of responsibilities discussed in Chapter Two—vertically and horizontally within the company and outward to those outside the company.

Effective communication takes effort. The message must be stated clearly; it must be in a language that the receiver understands, and it should be communicated at a time when the receiver is paying attention. Once the message has been sent, the communicator should check to see that it was clearly received—a step that ensures that communicating is a two-way process.

Need for Public Relations

Since most United States citizens live in large cities or in the suburbs, their environment is an impersonal one. Most of them take little part in civic affairs. They vote, if at all, for people they do not know and are likely to consign the conduct of community affairs to people they have never seen. Similarly, many employees do not know the top executives of their company. Fellow workers usually live in widely scattered areas and see each other only at work. They receive information through mass media such as television, newspapers, and magazines, which are one-way communications; the viewers or readers do not know the people who are speaking or writing, and they rarely take time to react directly to what they see, hear, or read. As a result, they ignore or merely tolerate many messages. But businesses must overcome these difficulties in communication if they are to secure the public's cooperation and the goodwill they need to operate effectively.

Importance of Public Relations

Public relations-minded business people view their public as all those with whom their organization does business. This may include customers, stockholders, suppliers, dealers, employees, and government, financial, or community groups.

The ground rules under which business managers operate require that they take on new roles, such as equal-opportunity employer, participating com-

Business managers strive to maintain good relations with the public, as here at a stockholders' meeting.

Continental Can Company

munity citizen, supporter of education, and customer analyst. Success in these roles depends largely upon how well the public sectors are analyzed and how effective are the communications aimed toward these sectors.

Good public relations advances the interest of a business by straightening out misconceptions arising from lack of information or from incorrect information about the firm's products or services. It also generates trust in management decisions, improves employee morale and productivity, and stimulates enlightened labor and government relations. Ultimately it makes a favorable impact on sales—management's yardstick of success.

A company's public relations department performs a dual function. It keeps management informed of what the company's public image is and of how it changes. It also counsels management as to the impact certain actions are likely to have on public opinion. In other words, public relations works two ways: it measures the effect that groups of people have on the company and it measures the effect that the company has on groups of people.

Growth and Influence of Public Opinion

Public relations is a barometer of social conscience. The public usually reacts to a company's failure to live up to its claims. The business that claims to be enlightened thereby assumes obligations to live up to those claims and suffers when it fails to do so.

Over the years the public has become increasingly sensitive to half-truths, false appeals, concealed support, and lies. In addition, public opinion has acquired far-reaching influence as a result of improved and expanded mass communications. In a matter of minutes, the actions of a company or the performance of its products can be communicated to the eyes and ears of millions of people.

Principles of Effective Public Relations

Communication is accomplished with words and symbols, through discussions and observations, among friends and strangers. Communication is most effective when it reflects the following considerations.

Personalization

Since it is rather difficult to think in the abstract, people tend to be more comfortable when personalized characteristics—real or fictitious—are attached to impersonal things such as a business enterprise. For example, many large business corporations stand out in one's mind because they are identified with a colorful, recognizable personality or character such as Green Giant's Jolly Green Giant or Borden's Elsie the Cow.

Suiting the Message to the Audience

In general, people see what they want to see and hear what they want to hear. In all one-way communication, such as television, radio, newspapers, and magazines, there is a risk in assuming that communication has been achieved when, in fact, it may have been only partially received. One-way communication is likely to be absorbed only by those who are receptive to it. Thus, when you employ one-way communication you must tailor your message to your audience.

Using Clear Language   When the message received by the audience is not exactly what you intended, communication has failed. To convey information as intended, the speaker must use words that will stimulate the listener to respond.

Dramatizing Communication   Good communication can be nonverbal. Pantomimes, cartoons, and pictures, as well as body language, when used with intelligence and good taste, can make a lasting impression and communicate things that words alone cannot convey.

Using Repetition   Good ideas are sometimes abandoned before they take root because their sponsors become discouraged by public apathy. In trying to communicate with a preoccupied public, you often can get positive benefits with sustained repetition and some variety in presentation.

Timeliness   Events that are a part of common experience often command attention and offer a good opportunity to communicate. If people have been exposed to an event and are talking about it, they will absorb related topics.

Straight Talk   Honesty in facing a situation, even when unpleasant, is the best procedure if you want to communicate. The unvarnished truth can gain attention and help build the company's reputation for reliability.

Stressing Positive Benefits   The element of self-interest is inherent in most successful public relations communication. Properly used, positive-benefit appeals are more constructive than emotional or intellectual appeals.

Two-Way Communication   Both within and without a company, two-way communication is important. The effectiveness of communication in general, and of public relations messages in particular, is weakened when those who are supposed to receive the message feel they are not given the opportunity to make a response of some kind, verbal or non-verbal. That is, people tend to resent being talked at without having a chance to express their reactions. Customers or prospects can respond by buying or not buying the advertised product. They can also write letters or make telephone calls, of course, but few bother to do so.

Within a business organization, suggestion boxes offer limited two-way communication between employees and management. Small-group discussions and surveys of employee opinion are other ways to promote two-way communication. The most satisfactory method, of course, is to develop such a feeling of confidence between employees and their supervisors that problems can be freely discussed.

Joan Menschenfreund

Employee suggestions can result in improvement in a company's products and services, and for that reason they are welcomed and rewarded.

Areas of Public Relations

There are four broad areas of public relations: community relations, customer relations, employee relations, and legislative relations.

Despite its share of failures, public relations has been able to cope with numerous problems that make up a company's day-by-day existence. Examples of public relations accomplishments include the successful promotion of new products, increased customer confidence, improved labor-management relations, and greater prestige in the financial community.

A company that can secure the cooperation of its public greatly strengthens its operating activities. Disgruntled customers or community groups who criticize a company's policies or actions can hinder its operating efficiency. People often base their opinions of a business on what the people around them seem to think about the company and its products or services. A company's communication with its own employees is also an important aspect of its public relations effort.

Community Relations   An area in which every company needs to build good public relations is its sensitivity to community needs and its participation in community affairs. The battle for goodwill is often won or lost here. In some instances, building goodwill consists of taking advantage of an obvious opportunity to perform a public service in times of emergency or unusual need. Or it may be the fruition of a long-range plan to improve some aspect of community welfare.

Good community relations and a bonus of enjoyment are the products of a company employee's interaction with this group of children.

Customer Relations

Customer relations, which occupy a large place in any public relations program, take a long time to build but can be quickly destroyed. A human error, a malfunctioning product, or a labor-relations breakdown can trigger a chain reaction of adverse public opinion. Once started, the reaction can spread like a brush fire. People can be influenced, however, and one of the objectives of a company's public relations program is to exert such influence in a positive way.

A manufacturer of automatic washing machines was alarmed by declining sales in the face of an industrywide pickup. Investigation showed that many consumers were complaining that their washers needed too many costly repair calls in a year. Further investigation showed that the complaints were justified and that almost all the repairs were necessitated by manufacturing defects. This company saved its reputation and future sales by deciding to replace about 40,000 defective washers with new models, at a small additional cost to the owners of the unsatisfactory machines. The goodwill generated enabled the company to end the year profitably.

Legislative Relations

Local, state, and national governments comprise another public relations area that requires careful observation and planning. A public relations program should keep abreast of government and political developments as they influence public opinion. For example, economic conditions such as unemployment, foreign competition, surplus production, and inflation can prompt legislation that will adversely affect a business enterprise. An equally sensitive area is that of foreign relations, with which the general public—or large sections of it—may not be in sympathy. Companies that are involved in these conflicts can suffer from negative public reactions.

Employee Relations

One of the most sensitive areas of public relations, one directly related to productivity, is employee relations. To an employee, a company that loses its ability to communicate internally becomes distant and impersonal. Unless corrective steps are taken, policy and information trickle through unreliable grapevines and are often distorted. Public relations personnel must build rapport between employees, management, and labor organizations. Newspaper articles, pamphlets, brochures, company publications and newsletters, and forums may all be utilized to remind employees that their company is a fair and just employer, and that they are members of a progressive and enlightened business organization.

Public Relations on the Job

Secretaries are most effective when they generate enthusiastic cooperation among co-workers, keep customers satisfied, and help maintain an office atmosphere that enables the executives to perform at top efficiency. To accomplish all of these things, you need to be thoroughly familiar with, and practice, successful procedures for working with people. Several roles are involved: you may act as intermediary between the executive and other executives and subordinates; as office host or hostess; as expediter of tasks; as interpreter of authority; and as appeaser when misunderstandings arise.

Review your ability to communicate with others as an individual and as a company public relations representative. Determine first what good personal communications skills are. Then observe yourself carefully until you can pinpoint the areas in which you are effective and those in which you need to improve. Reviewing your skills occasionally keeps you from falling into poor habits without noticing it.

Your ability to communicate with others—your own public relations abilities—can be demonstrated in two ways: orally and kinesthetically (that is, with your body). Communicating in written form is discussed in other chapters.

Developing Your Public Relations Image

To perform your public relations duties satisfactorily, you need to set performance guidelines and follow them. Those discussed below will help you get started.

Behavior. Tact, poise, sincerity, enthusiasm, resourcefulness, and self-assurance are important traits that contribute to your ability to motivate others, command confidence, and earn acceptance.

Appearance. Good posture and a neat appearance can suggest desirable characteristics, such as capability, understanding, alertness, and dependability. A slouch can be interpreted as impatience, weariness, boredom, or lack of interest.

Receptiveness. When you receive a call or greet visitors, your warmth, coupled with the efficiency with which you handle their requests, will create a good public image for your company. Your knowledge of the company, its various divisions and operations, and the channels through which decisions are made, is a great asset in getting things done smoothly.

Perception.   Greeting callers successfully and deciding which ones your boss will see and which ones are to be seen by others places you in the role of chief of protocol. Your success or failure is often determined by knowing when to trust your judgment and when to ask for guidance in order to avoid embarrassing the executive by a wrong decision.

Etiquette.   To some extent, the atmosphere in an office may be improved by pleasant and thoughtful secretarial actions: greeting each caller pleasantly, getting names right, handling each caller's situation correctly and graciously, offering special courtesies, and saying a pleasant good-bye to a departing caller. By carefully observing social amenities, a thoughtful secretary can moderate the sometimes chilling effect of corporate size and impersonality.

Empathy.   Your manner should convey to callers that you are being as understanding and helpful as possible while carrying out your boss's wishes, even when a request must be rejected. You need to be sincere and convincing rather than glib or patronizing, even when a request is obviously impossible or inappropriate.

Frankness.   Good public relations requires an ability to acknowledge mistakes or oversights as unfortunate happenings that need to be rectified rather than denied or excused. Convey willingness to see what can be done to straighten out an error and to prevent a recurrence, and where a customer is involved, follow through to make sure that the customer is satisfied.

Cheerfulness.   A cheerful attitude and willingness to help puts other people at ease. Agreeableness, accompanied by a pleasant voice and a friendly manner, is usually returned in kind.

Attentiveness.   Like everyone else, you can learn by listening, but first you must learn to listen. To talk effectively about your company, first listen attentively to those who know its history, products, channels of responsibility, and management policies. Listen also to your boss's instructions, comments, suggestions, and criticisms in order to follow through. And listen to callers, customers, and other employees who have information to relay or problems to be solved.

Facility in Communication.   The ability to speak with simple but forceful directness is essential. It enables you to get things done and to persuade others to act. To be effective, speak reasonably slowly and clearly so that the listener can easily grasp what you are saying. Avoid repetition and irrelevant detail that would only confuse or tire the listener.

Avoiding Public Relations Pitfalls

Seemingly little things can be big things to a customer. A trucker, for example, may track in dirt when making a delivery to a customer's home; a salesperson may overstate the size of a customer's shoes; or a billing clerk may make an error on a customer's statement.

A secretary's list of little things to remember can be long. Here are a few things you can do to avoid offending the public.

- Spell names correctly and use correct addresses.
- Make sure that letters do not contain thoughtless remarks offending the reader's dignity or implying that the customer was wrong, careless, or at fault.
- Find information promptly when someone is waiting for it; if more time is needed, offer to call back—and keep your promise.
- Answer the telephone promptly and pleasantly.
- Transfer calls to the right person.
- Greet a caller cordially and correctly.
- Avoid keeping a visitor waiting without explaining the delay.
- Hang up the telephone only after the caller has hung up.
- Refrain from exchanging personal comments with a co-worker in the presence of a caller.
- Schedule appointments carefully to avoid conflicts.
- Give each caller accurate information.

COMMUNICATING ORALLY

Oral communication is a two-way process that involves speaking and listening. To be a successful secretary you must be effective in both processes. Three factors contribute to effective oral communications: voice quality, choice of language level, and listening skills.

Voice Quality

The quality of your voice depends upon its rate, pitch, resonance, and volume. Other essentials are proper enunciation, articulation, pronunciation, and the tone that you use in speaking—which should reflect sincerity and pleasantness.

Assuming you have healthy vocal organs, you can improve your speaking voice through proper exercises faithfully performed.

First, evaluate your own voice. Listen to yourself. Try to arrange to speak into a dictating machine or some other kind of recording equipment and then play back the recording to hear what your voice is really like. Or ask your family or friends to tell you how your voice sounds over the telephone. Once you have identified your voice problems, you can begin a voice improvement program. Some specific suggestions follow.

Rate. If people do not readily understand you, it may be that you speak too fast. Or you may speak so slowly that they lose interest. Your objective should be a moderate rate of speech; about 120 words a minute is a good rate for speaking. Of course, familiar phrases or thoughts may flow more rapidly while unfamiliar thoughts or technical vocabulary may be expressed more slowly or even be repeated.

If You Speak Too Fast.   Force yourself to slow down by practicing reading aloud. First, time yourself by reading at your normal rate. Then read the passage again, more slowly. Give each word its full sound. Pause at punctuation marks, pause between sentences, and pause between paragraphs. Practice deep breathing as you read, and good breath control. Try telling someone about an interesting experience, but at a deliberately slower rate than you usually speak.

Pitch or Tone.   A voice may be described as being either too high or low according to its pitch. The pitch or tone of your voice is determined largely by the way you breathe. When you are under stress or emotional strain, your rate of breathing increases, causing your pitch to rise.

If Your Voice Is Too High.   Try saying aloud in your normal voice, "Hello, how are you?" Say it again, putting your hand on your forehead and pitching your voice toward your hand. Then say it, placing your hand on your chest and pitching the words low to the chest. Notice the greater depth and richness. Although you have not actually lowered your voice, you have used your lower register by practicing sounds that can be resonated in the chest. You can develop these warm lower tones of your voice by breathing more deeply as you talk and by speaking softly when under stress.

If Your Voice Is a Monotone.   No matter how attractive, sincere, or alert you are, people will not know it if your speaking or telephone voice is a monotone. To bring warmth to a droning voice, practice laughing out loud up and down the musical scale. Another cause of a colorless voice is "talking through the nose." Use your mouth, throat, and chest to correct this defect. Richer, fuller, and lower tones result if you speak out.

Resonance.   Adequate resonance in your voice keeps it from being flat and thin in quality. Since resonance is produced by vibration, you need to use your mouth, throat, and chest in voice production.

If Your Voice Is Harsh.   Most shrill or brassy sounds originate from tension in the throat and jaw. Try relaxing your throat muscles by slumping forward in your chair. Let your head drop, your jaw sag, and your arms dangle. Then, slowly and gently roll your head in a circular motion for approximately three minutes. Yawn a few times, open your mouth wide, and say such words as "long," "song," "saw," and "brawl."

Volume.   The degree of loudness is called volume. Some people speak so softly that one must strain to hear them. Others speak so loudly they assault the ear. Neither extreme is desirable. Nor is a dreary sameness of volume. To achieve a good volume, learn to increase your volume for emphasis and then to decrease it. Never shout. And do not let your voice trail off at the ends of sentences.

If Your Voice Is Weak.   A thin, shy, uncertain voice is an indication that your diaphragm is weak and that your breath control and voice power are underdeveloped.

You can check your breath control by holding a lighted candle about three inches from your mouth and then reciting, "Peter Piper picked a peck of pickled peppers. . . ." If you manage to keep the flame alive, you have good breath control.

Better breath control can be developed by whispering-aloud exercises. Try whispering to someone standing across the room. Just as soon as you are heard clearly, have the person move farther away, and then as far away as your whisper can be heard.

You can help strengthen your diaphragm by taking walks during which you practice deep breathing. Following such exercise, see how long you can read aloud without taking a breath. Ability to read for 20 to 25 seconds in one breath is an indication of a vigorous diaphragm.

Enunciation and Pronunciation.   To deliver each separate sound clearly, you need to use your tongue, teeth, lips, and jaw. Closely related to *enunciation* is the process of articulating, or the combining of sounds into syllables. The combining of syllables into words is called *pronunciation*. Mastery of each of these processes is essential to good speech. Your enunciation may be faultless and your articulation clear, but you will still make a poor impression on your hearers if you pronounce words incorrectly. Learn to understand and follow the diacritical marks in your dictionary.

If Your Speech Is Slurred.   To attain clarity in your speech you must use your tongue, lips, and teeth. If you are misunderstood or asked to repeat statements, you probably need to enunciate more clearly. Practice aloud several times, "The rain in Spain stays mainly in the plain." If it makes you feel tongue-tied, you may be lip-lazy. You need to use your tongue and lips more energetically. Practice reading aloud to yourself with your teeth closed tightly. You will find it necessary to exert more power in your voice and your speech will be clearer.

Cultivating a Pleasant Voice.   A pleasant voice is definitely a business asset. Telephone callers are much more likely to respond favorably to "the voice with a smile." It is easier to speak pleasantly and to feel pleasant when you cultivate an attitude of genuine consideration of and interest in others. In professional terms, a pleasant voice makes you more valuable to your employer in promoting goodwill and makes you a better worker to have around.

Choosing Language Level

Everyone uses three levels of language in speaking: formal, informal, and casual.

The formal level is used in speeches, in important social events, and in job interviews, for example. At such times you call the other persons by their titles and names or, when the situation warrants it, address them as "sir" or "madam." You take special care to be courteous and to follow the best rules of etiquette.

The informal level serves in most business situations and in conversations with superiors, parents, and older persons. You are still courteous, call others by their titles and names, and follow the rules of etiquette. But you relax somewhat

AT&T Co.

The millions of business telephone calls made every day are most productive when the words spoken are enunciated so that they are clearly understood.

and tend to use a more informal type of language. The difference between the formal and informal level of language is more a matter of degree than an actual difference in language and action.

The casual level is usually reserved for close friends and those of your own age group; it includes slang, special shortened phrases, jokes, and idioms that have special meaning derived from common experiences and interests. You tend to speak in phrases rather than sentences and often use such expressions as "yep," "yeah," "okay," and "nope." In your position as secretary in a business office, you would always want to use the formal and informal levels of language.

When you communicate orally, give clear, precise directions and maintain a pleasant tone of voice. That is especially important when the listener is upset or angry or does not understand what is expected.

Language is very important in the business world. Do everything possible to increase your speaking and reading vocabulary.

Listening

Since communication is a two-way process that involves both speaking and listening, it is important to develop your listening skill. Some barriers to productive listening are (1) words that the listener does not understand, (2) lack of attention, (3) an undiagnosed hearing problem, (4) a long or complicated message, and (5) the speaker's voice, whether too soft or too loud.

Many of these barriers can be removed or minimized by either the speaker or the listener. Appropriate words can be spoken in a voice that is easily heard. Long, complicated messages can be broken down into steps and perhaps reinforced with a written message. You can test whether a message was received clearly by asking the listener to repeat it. A listener should be given the opportunity to ask questions.

Usually, the effect of a hearing handicap can be reduced somewhat. The telephone company has amplifying equipment that can be attached to telephones. As a secretary, you are likely at some time or other to encounter either co-workers or customers who have hearing problems. Recognizing the condition will help you to address them courteously.

Many of your functions as a secretary require that you use your own listening skills, for example, when using the phone, receiving instructions, and talking with callers and co-workers. Listening is an area in which most people need strengthening, particularly when it comes to paying attention.

Paying attention means giving the speaker your undivided interest, asking for clarification when necessary, and making mental note of the message. Writing down important points will train you to pay attention. Repeat instructions and messages to the speaker—particularly when they are long or very important—to be sure that you understand them. Repeating a telephone message and number should be routine.

The best way to develop good listening habits is to practice listening daily while at work, in school, and with friends and family. Remembering messages and details about your work is easier when you are concerned and take an interest.

Communicating Kinesthetically

There is another form of communication that does not involve words. Kinesthetic communication involves facial expressions and the stance of the body. In body language your muscles react according to your emotions, thoughts, and ideas. Kinesthetic expressions are difficult to describe because the observer sees a series of muscles reacting in minute ways. For example, if you observe a person sitting slumped in a chair, it's hard to tell whether the slump is due to sadness or fatigue. Your guides are the muscle arrangements, facial expression, and posture.

An alert secretary must be aware of kinesthetic communication and its effect. You may use the right words but communicate a contradictory message kinesthetically. (That message also has an effect on the tone of your voice. This is why telephone experts emphasize the importance of developing the "voice with a smile." Your expression is reflected in the tone of your voice and "seen" by the listener. If your face is set in a bored expression, it is reflected in your voice.)

At times you may find it necessary to control your kinesthetic expressions so that you do not communicate an inappropriate message, especially when you are angry or emotionally upset. Emotions cannot be eliminated completely, but they should be controlled or channeled into positive actions. Instead of becoming angry with a customer who has become upset, you need to remain calm and in control of the situation.

<table>
<tr><td>

**REViEWiNG
YOUR
REAdiNG**

</td><td>

1. What are the two primary segments of the public with which a business must deal? Give two or more examples of each segment.
2. Explain how good public relations benefit a business.
3. What are some of the internal and external means of communication that a company may use to reach its public?
4. Suggest some ways in which a business may lose goodwill.
5. Name five principles of effective public relations.
6. How can a company foster good community relations?
7. Name at least two ways in which public opinion may be adversely affected by a company's products or its personnel policies.
8. Why must a business enterprise keep abreast of government and political developments?
9. Suggest five ways in which a secretary can promote good public relations.
10. Name six qualities the secretary should have in order to set the public relations climate for the office, and state how they should be used.
11. Explain what is meant by the statement "Oral communication is a two-way process."
12. Name the three different levels of language commonly used in speaking and give examples to illustrate each level.
13. Name at least three barriers to good oral communications.

</td></tr>
</table>

<table>
<tr><td>

**USiNG
YOUR
Skills**

</td><td>

1. **a.** Identify a building some distance from the room in which this class is held. Be prepared to give oral directions to the class for reaching this building. Do not tell them what the goal is. How many of your classmates can name the goal after listening to your directions?
   b. Give oral directions to the class for inserting paper into the typewriter; do not demonstrate with your hands or with a typewriter.

2. **a.** Record your voice and then listen to it. Evaluate your enunciation, tone, and volume. First, record yourself while you read a paragraph or two from this book. Second, record yourself and a friend while talking about a topic that interests both of you. On a separate sheet of paper type a list of three areas in which you need to improve; suggest ways in which to make these improvements.
   b. While you are giving an oral demonstration, while you are talking to a friend, or as you sit in a restaurant, count the number of times the word *okay* is used. Were other words or phrases used excessively and without meaning (such as *you know* or *I mean*)? If so, make a list of them to turn in to your instructor.

3. Your instructor will read a short paragraph. Then some questions will be asked about it. Do not take notes, since this is an exercise in listening and retention.

</td></tr>
</table>

4. With increased public awareness and increased publicity, business managers must play many roles. Select at least two articles from your local newspaper dealing with such subjects as chemical pollution of waterways and explain how the issues highlighted in the articles affect the role of today's business managers.

EXERCISING YOUR JUDGMENT

Communicating Orally. Mr. Preston, your boss, has handed you a memorandum from the president of the company and asked you what you think should be done about the problem it raises. The memorandum says: "Recently several visitors to our offices have commented about the amount of time our staff spends talking about personal matters, often neglecting to greet visitors properly. They also commented on the excessive slang they heard. After hearing these comments, I visited several of the departments to observe our workers. We do need to improve oral communication skills."

What recommendations would you make?

APPLYING THE REFERENCE SECTION

Building Your Vocabulary.

1. From each of the following groups of words, choose the word that is nearest in meaning to the first word of the group and type it on a separate sheet of paper.
   a. formalize—stretch, shape, reduce, forget
   b. listless—weak, unorganized, rude, energetic
   c. profound—discovered, ancient, deep, metallic
   d. scrutinize—inspect, drill, seal, join
   e. whittle—whistle, pare, reply, shiver
   f. maneuver—manage, leap, assemble, correct
   g. diametric—round, shiny, tiny, opposite
   h. hobble—jump, duck, limp, complain
   i. specie—type, showy, classification, coin
   j. tort—whole, cake, wrongful act, claim
   k. waiver—abandoning of a right, faltering, hesitating, insisting
   l. duly—stupidly, sweetly, in due time, readily
   m. authority—jurisdiction, group of writers, genuineness, submission
   n. retroactive—full of energy, affecting prior acts, looking back, recurring
   o. coercion—guilt, force, punishment, sticking together

2. From the words in parentheses choose the one that correctly completes the meaning of the sentence and type the word and its letter on a sheet of paper.
   a. Her actions were rather (affected, effected).
   b. The (principals, principles) of accounting merit hard study.
   c. Please send your application to the (personal, personnel) director.
   d. What is the (capital, capitol) of New York?
   e. Please prepare a (memoranda, memorandum) to be sent to the treasurer of the class.
   f. The (expression, impression) she gave was favorable.

g. Did the lawyer (cite, site) a previous court decision covering a similar case?
h. The speaker was not (adverse, averse) to answering questions.
i. The story was printed in (serial, cereal) form.
j. A (duel, dual) highway ran close to the plant.
k. In this (instants, instance) the company decided to make an exception.
l. He insisted on (muddling, meddling) in the affair even though it was outside his authority.
m. The messenger was afraid that he would (lose, loose) the envelope.
n. May this be a (lesson, lessen) for the future.
o. Quality is more important (than, then) quantity.

CHAPTER SIX / HANDLING INCOMING Calls and Callers

A challenging secretarial responsibility with wide public relations implications is the management of incoming calls and callers. The more knowledge you have about your boss's performance goals, the people he or she works with, the meetings attended, and the organizations he or she belongs to, the more effective your efforts will be to help your boss meet the right people at the right place and the right time.

MANAGING AN EXECUTIVE'S APPOINTMENTS

Receiving callers in the office area itself and talking with people over the telephone involve many of the same procedures and techniques.

Record of Appointments

You need not have a marvelous memory or extrasensory perception in order to coordinate appointments made by telephone, by letter, and in person. All you need is an orderly and reliable system of reminder notations that both you and your boss observe.

Desk Calendar. It is your responsibility to keep your boss's desk calendar in order, as well as your own. Note on it events such as dates for professional meetings and appointments. The calendar should be large enough to record the names of persons attending a meeting and the purpose, location, and time of appointments. Make similar notations on your own calendar as a follow-up reminder.

Desk calendars come in a variety of sizes and styles. One popular style has loose-leaf sheets for each day, with half-hour subdivisions and enough space to record essential information.

Mobil Oil Corporation

Updating calendars daily so that both yours and your employer's match is the best way to make sure that all appointments are recorded.

Appointment Book or Yearbook.   The standard-style appointment book or yearbook is a bound book with pages that divide each day into hour, half-hour, or quarter-hour segments. Such a book can serve as a permanent record of an executive's appointments and expenses as well as a source from which to retrieve names, telephone numbers, and addresses.

Pocket Memo.   Most executives carry pocket date books. In them they record dates that are made while they are at meetings or on trips. Since these may conflict with appointments already made and marked on the office calendar, you will need to have a definite arrangement whereby you regularly check your executive's pocket date book against your calendar or appointment book. It is your responsibility to remind your boss of the need to check.

Appointment Procedures

The appointment duties of secretaries vary widely. Some secretaries spend much of their time taking care of appointments and callers, while others deal with relatively few appointments and callers. The procedures described here should be adapted to your situation and your boss's preferences.

Preparing a Calendar.   Before the beginning of each year, enter on a new calendar all notations for the entire year. Known events, such as company holidays, vacations, regularly scheduled meetings, and tax dates can be recorded at this time. Keep your own list of recurring events, and around November, as you begin to make engagements for the coming year, record these regular commitments on your boss's new calendar.

Coordinating Appointments.   Do not trust appointment arrangements to your memory. Whenever you or your boss make an appointment or promise to do something at a certain time, make a note of it in the appropriate place. If possible, review the calendar together to find out whether plans or commitments have been made that do not appear on your calendar. At the end of each day, review the list of events on both calendars, note incomplete or postponed items, and plan appropriate follow-ups. Then glance at the next day's events. It is a good idea to keep about one week ahead of items marked on the calendar or noted in any other tickler file so that you will have time to gather any information that will be needed.

Find out what your executive's preferences and work habits are before you attempt to schedule appointments. For instance, your boss may prefer not to see people on the morning or afternoon before leaving on a business trip. And the boss may prefer to avoid or limit appointments on the day after a trip, so as to catch up on events and correspondence. For similar reasons, Monday morning appointment schedules should be kept as light as possible.

Other considerations may affect the scheduling of appointments. Your boss may prefer to catch a commuter train or start to drive home before the five o'clock rush. In that case take care not to schedule appointments that may run beyond 4:30 or 5:00 p.m. Other bosses prefer early-morning appointments with clients or customers they can see on their way in to work so that they avoid coming into the office first and then backtracking to the customer's office half an hour later. Similarly, you can schedule late-afternoon appointments your boss can keep on the way home if you know their exact locations and the approximate time it takes to reach them from your office. Try to think always in terms of conserving both travel and appointment time for your boss.

Appointments are scheduled in several ways. A visitor may write or telephone for an appointment, or your boss may ask you to schedule an appointment with a customer or a colleague. There will also be the occasional caller who arrives unexpectedly only to find that the executive is out of the office or otherwise occupied. However the request is initiated, you should obtain certain essential information:

* The full and correctly spelled name of the person requesting the appointment, the business affiliation, and the telephone number.
* The date, time, and probable duration of the appointment.
* The place of meeting and, if the appointment is scheduled elsewhere than your boss's office, the full address, including floor or room number.
* The purpose of the appointment.
* The data or information your boss is to provide.
* The names and affiliations of other people attending.

Cancelling Appointments.   Occasionally an unexpected event or an emergency necessitates the cancelling of an executive's appointment. It is your responsibility to get in touch with the expected caller as soon as possible, explain the cancellation, and, if possible, reschedule the appointment. You need to exercise tact and good judgment so that the person does not feel slighted.

Cancellations are usually handled by telephone. Prepare for such a conversation carefully so that you handle it diplomatically. Apologize courteously and express sincere regret. Give a reason for the cancellation if you can do so without revealing confidential information. Try to reschedule the appointment at the caller's convenience. The conversation might go something like this:

"This is Ms. Hoffer, Mr. John Ritchey's secretary, of Commonwealth Products. I am calling about your appointment with him tomorrow at 2:30 p.m. Mr. Ritchey has unexpectedly been asked to attend a district manager's meeting. He is extremely sorry he can't see you at that time, but he would like to talk to you soon. Could we reschedule the appointment for 10 o'clock Thursday? Or would another time be more convenient for you?"

Sometimes the nature of the caller's business is such that it cannot wait. In that event, you should be prepared to arrange for the caller to see another executive at the time of the original appointment, if possible. Your boss will undoubtedly be aware of this urgency and will make the appropriate suggestion either through you or personally.

Receiving Office Callers

Your appearance and your behavior reflect the company. They promote or diminish goodwill. Therefore, you will want to receive visitors with the same consideration you would show a guest. Callers, whether unannounced strangers or familiar business associates, should leave the office feeling they were treated sincerely, courteously, and with efficiency. In the eyes of the caller, *you* are the company.

Preparing for Callers   Few things are more annoying than to be mistreated by a secretary, whose responsibility it is to see that appointments are managed efficiently. Before a caller arrives, therefore, make all the necessary arrangements so that both you and your boss are prepared for the appointment.

Daily Reminders.   A useful document to include with the morning mail is a typed schedule of your boss's appointments for the day. Since you have complete information on your boss's regular calendar or appointment book, you need not repeat the full date. A brief notation, such as, "9:30, Mr. Jones, Apex," should be sufficient. Attach to this note all the materials needed for the appointment.

Some secretaries keep a permanent record of all callers, for their own reference. Such a caller diary can be especially useful in an office where there is a continuity of business transactions with a client or customer and where time must be charged for each client, such as in a legal or an advertising office. Other secretaries keep a "who's who" card index in which they record pertinent data about each important caller. This information can be a lifesaver for a substitute secretary.

Visitor Comfort.   A caller should be made as comfortable as possible in the waiting area. Make sure the office is neat and orderly, with sufficient ventilation. Dusty tables, books, paintings, and lamps give a company an unattractive image.

Invite the caller to be seated. Provide a current magazine or newspaper. Invite the person to put a coat and umbrella on a rack or in an available cloak room.

Handling Callers

Most large companies employ a general receptionist to greet and assist all visitors to the company or the division. But even if there is a full-time receptionist, an executive's secretary is not relieved of the responsibility of receiving callers. The receptionist usually telephones to announce an arrival. You may ask that the visitor be directed to the office or you may go to meet the person and show the way to the executive's office.

Although receiving callers is only one of the many duties in a secretary's busy day, never be too busy to give each visitor—known or unknown, from within the company or from outside—your prompt and undivided attention. When the visitor arrives, interrupt whatever you are doing to help. It is extremely discourteous to keep a caller waiting while you finish some work.

There are patterns for coping with visitors in most offices; these patterns are a combination of the guidelines for coordinating and cancelling appointments and procedures for coping with scheduled and unscheduled callers to be discussed in the next section. As you continue to read, refer to the flow chart here of the decision-making process for handling callers; follow the lines through the various options available to the secretary when the boss is unavailable for either a scheduled or an unscheduled caller.

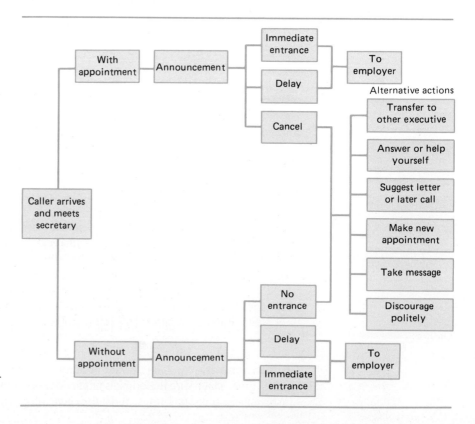

Flow chart of the decision-making process for handling callers.

Callers With Appointments.   Greet each scheduled visitor by name. The ability to remember names and faces is one of the hallmarks of a top-notch secretary, and your use of the caller's name (pronounced correctly) promotes good public relations.

Announce the visitor to your boss. If the visitor has not been in the office before, lead the way and introduce the caller to your boss if necessary. If you are busy on the telephone when the visitor arrives, excuse yourself to the telephone caller while you either take the visitor into the office or ask him or her to wait a moment.

Occasionally an expected caller cannot be seen immediately. Tell the person approximately how long the wait will be, explain the delay, and apologize. If the delay is longer than anticipated, use your judgment about calling to remind your boss that someone is waiting. During the waiting period, keep busy at your desk. If the visitor wants to chat, keep the conversation on non-confidential and noncontroversial subjects. If the caller is silent, don't attempt a monologue.

Callers Without Appointments.   Many office callers arrive without an appointment. It is a good idea to discuss with your boss the procedure for handling such unscheduled visitors. Superiors, other executives, and key staff members usually have free access without formal appointments. Friends and family may enjoy the same freedom, but this should be confirmed by your boss. In any event, you will need to ask unscheduled callers to wait if your boss is busy.

You may find it necessary to guard against an inclination to be overprotective of your boss's time by turning away visitors. Avoid snap judgments about callers on the basis of personal appearance, manner of speech, or behavior. Remember, too, that as far as the public is concerned, both you and your executive are there to serve them. Any impression that your boss is too busy or too important to be bothered with unexpected visitors should be avoided at all costs.

Try to learn who the unscheduled caller is and what the visit is about. Begin by greeting the caller with a genuine smile and a pleasant tone. If no name or business card is offered, you might begin by saying, "May I have your name, please?" or "Who shall I say is calling?" Write down the name, making sure you have the correct spelling. If the pronunciation is unfamiliar, write it phonetically or in shorthand. From then on, call the visitor by name.

Inquire about the purpose of the visit and the caller's business affiliation. Almost all callers are willing to give this information and usually offer it. By quickly determining the nature of the visit, you can save everyone's time, especially if the caller's business is not within the scope of your executive's responsibilities. When the caller should be referred to someone else in the company, you might handle the situation in the following manner.

To visitor: "Mr. Coburn is not currently involved with employee insurance. Would you like to talk to Mr. Rogers in the Personnel Department? If you would like me to do so, I'll see if he is in."

To Mr. Rogers: "Mr. Rogers, this is Miss Green, secretary to Mr. Coburn. Could you talk to Mr. Albert Shore of Consolidated Insurance Corporation, who

Peter Roth

Sometimes the secretary meets the caller and handles the introduction.

is here and would like to discuss aspects of the employee insurance program?"

To visitor: "Mr. Rogers can see you now. His office is on the sixth floor. Just tell the receptionist that Mr. Rogers is expecting you."

If you think your boss would not be interested in what an unscheduled caller has to present, you might say: "Mrs. Wyatt, I don't believe the company is planning to purchase any office equipment in the near future, but let me make sure." You can then check with your boss. You have already established a possible reason for your boss to refuse to see the caller.

If you believe your boss *would* be interested in meeting an unscheduled visitor but is unable to do so immediately, schedule a later appointment and ask the caller to leave a business card and any descriptive literature for your boss.

Introductions.   Each executive has individual preferences about receiving callers and handling introductions. Some go out to meet callers and accompany them to their offices. Others prefer to have their secretary meet the caller and handle the introduction.

When your boss receives a caller in person, he/she may introduce you: "Mrs. Wyatt, this is my secretary, Miss Green." A pleasant "How do you do, Mrs. Wyatt" is sufficient response on your part. You need not shake hands unless the caller makes the first move.

In most cases, you should present the caller to your boss. Either one of the following introductions is acceptable:

"Mr. Coburn, this is Mrs. Wyatt, who has an appointment with you."

"This is Mrs. Wyatt of Consolidated Insurance Corporation, Mr. Coburn."

Interruptions.   While your boss is in conference, you may receive urgent messages that make it necessary for you to interrupt. Type the message on a card or message form, and hand it to your boss. It usually is not necessary to knock or speak when entering the office during a conference. When a high-ranking executive telephones, it may be standard procedure to put the call through immediately.

When there is a telephone call for the visitor, ask the person calling if you can take a message. If so, type it on a slip of paper addressed to the visitor and note the time the message was received. If the caller insists on speaking to the visitor, enter the office. After getting the attention of your boss and the caller, apologize for the interruption: "I'm sorry to interrupt, Mr. Coburn. Mrs. Wyatt, your secretary is on the phone and wishes to speak to you. Would you prefer to take the call at my desk?" The visitor can then leave the room to take the call privately, can accept it on your boss's telephone, or can ask you to take the message.

Handling Atypical Callers

Some callers do not fit into the usual categories. A secretary may be called upon to talk with a difficult caller or one who has some special relationship to the executive.

Problem Callers. The unknown, unexpected, uncommunicative caller can present difficulties and test your ability to remain courteous and tactful. The caller may try to avoid giving you specific information or say that the business is personal or confidential or anything else to conceal the fact that he or she is selling something not related to the executive's business interests or is collecting funds. It is up to you to discover, in a polite but firm and businesslike manner, who the caller is and the purpose of the call.

Begin by asking for a business card. If that is not successful, tell the visitor, "Mr. Coburn is in a meeting right now and will be busy for some time. Please tell me what you want. Perhaps someone else can help you." Avoid inflammatory statements such as, "I am Mr. Coburn's private secretary and I must know your business before you can see him." Even if it is literally true, this is hardly the way to encourage a responsive attitude on the part of the recalcitrant visitor.

Some callers feel that a secretary is there to keep them away from company representatives; hence, their reluctance to discuss the purpose of the visit and their insistence on seeing someone immediately. The challenge to you is to change this resistance into cooperation by showing friendly concern and by giving a reasonable explanation of the necessity for your questions. Becoming curt or angry will only aggravate the situation.

If the difficult visitor persistently refuses to give a name or the reason for the visit, you might call your boss on the intercom with the following message: "Mr. Coburn, there is someone here to see you who would like to discuss personal business with you. I have said you are busy most of the day, but perhaps you would like to talk about a future appointment." If your boss agrees, hand the visitor the telephone. The caller will have to give a name to your boss over the telephone; jot it down and follow through if your boss agrees to see the caller later.

There are also charmers who try to win favors with flattery, overaggressive salespeople, and cranks. Handling them requires all your restraint and good judgment. For the caller who asks leading questions about the business or about your executive, "I really don't know" or "You might ask Mr. Coburn about that" should be sufficient.

Important Visitors. Some callers, such as top executives of the company and family members, receive preferential treatment. Never inquire about the purpose of their visits. You need not stand when a top official of the company or your boss's spouse enters your office, but it is a tactful and gracious thing to do in deference to their positions.

When an important caller arrives unexpectedly, and your boss is conferring with someone of lesser importance, greet and seat the caller, then go into the boss's office with a note providing the caller's name. Your boss then has the opportunity to terminate the meeting at once or to step into the outer office to greet the important caller in person.

Terminating Visits. Most callers manage to conclude their business without exceeding the time scheduled for them. Usually a visitor realizes that the meeting is over when the executive rises from the desk or makes a concluding statement. If hints of this kind are not sufficient, an executive often uses a prearranged signal to get your help. You may help in several ways:

- By handing your boss a message that gives him or her a chance to announce another engagement.
- By using the telephone to ask if an interruption is needed in order to terminate the meeting.
- By announcing quietly that the next appointment is waiting.

Such hints should be given as tactfully as possible. Usually, given a reminder, the visitor will realize that it is time to leave.

Office Personnel. Many executives keep an open door to office personnel. But you save your boss considerable time if you tactfully screen these callers for problems that you can handle. If the employee does not want to confide in you, however, do not insist.

When your boss asks you to call a subordinate or an associate to come for a conference, tell the person what it is about unless the matter is special or highly confidential. Thoughtfulness is a key to office etiquette. A summons to see one's superior can easily disturb an employee. A simple explanation, such as "Mr. Coburn would like to see you about your recommendation on controlling production costs," can allay unfounded fears and also suggest to the employee what material to bring to the meeting.

Receiving and Making Telephone Calls

Quick, effective action often spells the difference between success and failure. To get faster results, many companies prefer to telephone clients rather than to write them. In some offices, the major portion of the contacts are made by phone.

Here is where a secretary's telephone assets are in demand. Your knowledge of effective telephone techniques, the pleasant quality of your voice, and your familiarity with telephone services and equipment pay dividends not only to your employer but to yourself.

Many of the procedures for handling visitors to the office are also used in receiving telephone calls. Therefore, refer to the flow chart on page 74 occasionally as you read these sections.

Achieving a Good Voice

What you say and how you say it determines the mental image you project by telephone. Whenever you use an office telephone, you become the voice of that office. If you have any oral communications problems such as poor voice quality, wrong choice of language, or difficulty listening (as discussed in the last chapter), they will be magnified over the telephone. Practice your telephone techniques until you achieve a pleasant voice in receiving and placing telephone calls.

Handling Calls Efficiently

Knowing the capabilities of the phone systems to which you have access is a first step in handling calls efficiently. Make sure you are completely familiar with the instrument at your disposal or any you make use of.

Expressing Courtesy.   Telephone courtesy simply means making a caller feel welcome. It is an extension of the same type of thoughtfulness that should be practiced in daily living. Every caller should be greeted pleasantly. If your voice is friendly and generates enthusiasm and sincerity, your telephone callers will be attracted.

AT&T Co.

Answering the telephone with a voice that projects interest conveys to the listener that you are responsive to what is being said.

Try to use the caller's name. There is no sweeter music to a person than the sound of his or her name. Try to visualize the person to whom you are talking. To do this, speak to the person at the other end of the line, not at the telephone. Be attentive. Do not interrupt. Listen politely. You would not turn away in a face-to-face conversation; apply the same rules of courtesy in telephone conversation.

Take time to be helpful. It is better to spend minutes making a caller happy than hours trying to regain goodwill. If you make an error, apologize. Even though things don't always go smoothly, you can always be courteous. When you are sincere, your explanations will not sound artificial. If you observe courtesy always and say "Thank you" and "You're welcome" to your telephone callers, people will feel that courtesy is a consistent practice in your company's business dealings.

Receiving Calls.   When your telephone rings, get the conversation off on the right track by answering pleasantly and promptly, before the second ring if possible. If you delay, your caller may hang up and call a competitor. When you answer a telephone promptly, you give the impression of wanting to be of service and you help build a reputation of efficiency for yourself and your company.

In answering the telephone, identify yourself by giving either your name or that of the company, department, or employer. For example, say, "This is Miss Jackson," or "Purchasing department—Mr. Whiteman," or "Davis Manufacturing, Mr. Payne's office." Responses such as "hello" and "yes" are inadequate, time-wasting, and actually discourteous.

Speak distinctly over the telephone. Avoid any tendency to shout or whisper. A loud voice sounds gruff and unpleasant, while a whisper or a mumble is equally unpleasant because it is hard to understand. Keep pencils, candy, and gum out of your mouth. You cannot articulate distinctly when chewing.

Give the caller your undivided attention. When the phone rings, lay aside the task at hand so that you can be friendly and helpful to the telephone caller. Avoid giving the impression that the caller has intruded upon your privacy or has interrupted you. Instead, make the caller feel welcome. Whenever a delay is necessary, say, "Will you wait, or shall I call you back?" Everyone likes to be given a choice, even if it is limited to waiting on the line or having you call back later with the information.

When you promise to call back, by all means do so. A broken promise usually means a disappointed person, and a disappointed person may mean a lost customer. The goodwill of customers and the public is best maintained through a reputation for being reliable and trustworthy.

When you end a call, do it graciously with a pleasant closing remark, such as, "Thank you for calling, Mr. Dexter. Good-bye." It is courteous and good practice to wait for the caller to say good-bye and hang up because the caller's last words may be a valuable instruction or an order. Replace your receiver quietly.

If you must be away from your telephone, arrange to have someone else answer it. Tell the person who answers your phone where you can be reached and when you expect to return.

Answering Your Employer's Telephone

Answer with "Dr. Forrest's office, Pat Ballard" when your employer's telephone rings. These five words tell the caller that Dr. Forrest's office has been reached and that you are ready to help the caller. In identifying yourself by name you encourage the caller to volunteer a name.

Often your employer may not be in the office or may be otherwise occupied when a call comes in. Tell the caller when your boss will be back. If the call is important, tell the caller where your boss can be reached.

Offer to help by providing what information you can. Avoid giving the caller the impression that you are simply giving an excuse. It is better to say, "Dr. Forrest is at a meeting and is expected back at 3:30. May I help you?" than "Dr. Forrest is in conference." A caller may be suspicious of the words "in conference" and may also be offended by a terse "Who's calling?" The latter phrase implies that your employer is too busy to speak or might not be available to this particular caller. It is more tactful to say, "May I tell Dr. Forrest who is calling?" or "If you will give me your name and telephone number, I will ask Dr. Forrest to call you when he returns to the office."

To: **B.H.**

Here is a Message for You

Ann Pulaski

of **Melendez + Smith Adv.**

Phone No. **(212) 555-3600**   Ext. **283**

☑ Telephoned   ☐ Will Call Again
☐ Returned Your Call   ☐ Came To See You
☑ Please Phone   ☐ Wants To See You

She wouldn't give me a message, but it sounded urgent.

Taken By	Date	Time
M.H.	**10/8**	**12:45**

A telephone message form should be as complete as possible.

When you find that you cannot help the caller, offer to take a message. A form for telephone messages should be kept near the telephone. When taking a message, write down the caller's name, telephone number, plus area code if needed, the time of the call, and the purpose of the call if known.

When a person-to-person long distance call is received and your employer is not available, write down the operator's number, city and state, date, area code, telephone number, and the caller's name and extension number. Then, place the message near your boss's telephone.

Transferring Calls

If someone else is more qualified to handle an incoming call, offer to transfer the call. Transfers can be disturbing to a caller, however, especially if the caller must describe the problem several times. To avoid this irritation, observe the following step-by-step procedure when you transfer a call.

1. Explain why the call should be handled by someone else. You might say, "Mr. Cook handles service inquiries. I'll be glad to transfer you if you wish."
2. Be sure whether the caller wants to be transferred or prefers to call back. In the latter case provide Mr. Cook's extension number. Or offer to ask Mr. Cook to return the call. Before you hang up, get the caller's name and telephone number and some idea of the purpose of the call.
3. If the caller agrees to a transfer, signal the switchboard operator by slowly and firmly depressing the receiver button to the count of one-two-pause, one-two-pause. If you move the receiver button too quickly, the switchboard operator will not receive the signal.
4. Ask the operator to transfer the call to Mr. Cook in the Service department and give the extension if possible.
5. Wait for the operator to acknowledge your request and then hang up quietly.

Placing Calls for the Boss

Before lifting the receiver to place a call for the boss, make sure you know the number you wish to call. Eliminate guesswork by keeping at hand a list of frequently called numbers. A rotary desk-top card file is easier to keep up to date than a typed list, which may become unreadable after many changes and additions. If you look up a number in a directory, jot it down rather than trusting to memory. You may need it when you place the call later if you do not find the party in.

Find out in advance whether anyone else will do if the party is not available. Make sure your boss is ready to speak to the person you are calling.

Allow time for your call to be answered; the telephone companies suggest waiting for ten rings. If the called party is not available, find out when the person will be in. If you are placing the call yourself, perhaps to request information, always offer to call back if the person you are calling is not available.

Courtesy and efficiency are watchwords as much in placing calls as in receiving them. Be brief, be polite, be businesslike. End the call with a pleasant, "Thank you, Miss Jones, for the information."

Procedures for placing long-distance calls are discussed on pages 84 and 85. Arranging for conference calls is explained on page 90, and other types of calls are covered on page 91.

Using Directories

Telephone directories are actually reference books. Their primary purpose is to list subscribers and their telephone numbers and addresses. They also aid in locating certain types of businesses, provide useful information about community services, are a source for checking the spelling of names, and serve as a guide to the various types of telephone services. You should know how to use a directory quickly and accurately.

Alphabetic Directories

The white pages of a directory contain an alphabetic list of subscribers with addresses and telephone numbers. The introductory pages contain helpful information, such as emergency and service numbers, dialing instructions, area codes, time zone maps, long-distance rates, message-unit calling areas and charges, and ZIP Code numbers for nearby places.

In determining the alphabetic order of names listed in a directory, the filing rule "nothing before something" is used. For example, *Clow, Wm. E.*, comes before *Clowee's Beauty Salon*, and *Fox, A.*, before *Fox, Abe*. Titles, such as *M.D.* and *Mrs.*, are placed at the end of a listing and are not considered when alphabetizing unless all other parts of the names are identical.

The ampersand (&) and the apostrophe (') are also ignored. Hyphenated names are treated as one; a two-part surname, such as *von Amsberg,* is considered as if it were one word (*Vonamsberg*).

Classified Directories

The yellow pages of a directory list businesses by product or type of service. For large cities, a separate classified directory is available. To locate a lawyer, an accountant, or an electrical contractor, look under their respective headings. Many cross-references are also supplied; for example, no entries are listed under "Doctors," but cross-references are given to specific headings such as "Dentists" and "Physicians and Surgeons." If you have forgotten a name but remember the address of, say, a plastics products firm, simply turn to the heading, "Plastics— Products (Finished)" and scan the addresses of such firms until you find the name with the address you remember. Or suppose you want to arrange for your office phone to be answered when the office is closed. You can turn to "Telephone Answering Services" and select one.

Company Directories

Many large firms supply their employees with a company telephone directory, which not only lists the extension numbers for all departments and employees but may also list branch offices, tie-line service, and the like. You are responsible for keeping both your own and your boss's directory up to date. For quick reference, you may type a brief list of frequently called intracompany numbers and attach a copy near your employer's phone as well as your own.

Personal Directory

For your own and your employer's use, prepare a personal telephone directory, alphabetically arranged, of persons or firms frequently called, listing both telephone numbers and addresses. Since such information is subject to change, maintain it on a card file or a desk-top rotary file rather than in a booklet. To be truly useful, such a list must be kept up to date.

Basic Telephone Services

Every telephone subscriber is offered certain basic services by the telephone companies. Some services are free; for others there is a small charge. Charges are made, of course, for actual calls completed.

Information or Assistance

If you do not find a listing in the telephone directory for the person you wish to phone, call the information operator (usually 411). If the person is outside your calling area, call the desired area code followed by 555-1212 to contact the information operator there. You will find most area codes listed in the telephone directory. A limited number of information calls are free.

You may not find a directory listing if the person has an unlisted number. Nor is the information operator permitted to disclose such a number. In an emergency, however, the operator may be willing to call the party and report that someone is trying to get in touch. Once you have gotten an unlisted number, make a note of it and keep it confidential.

If you place calls through your company's switchboard operator, you may seldom need the outside operator's assistance. But if you place calls yourself, you may need to dial "0" for Operator and request help in any of the following situations.

* If the call does not go through, ask the operator to place it for you.
* If the connection is very poor, hang up, dial 0, and ask the operator to clear the line.
* If you are repeatedly cut off, ask the operator for help.
* If you get a wrong number on a toll call, tell the operator at once, so that the charge may be canceled.
* If the number you are trying to reach is continuously busy and your call is a genuine emergency, you may ask the operator to break into the busy line.

Long-Distance Calls

To call someone outside your calling area, you may call station to station or person to person. Choose a station-to-station call if you are willing to speak to anyone at that number. Charges begin the moment the called party answers and continue until one of you hangs up. Rates for station calls are lower than for person-to-person calls. But if you cannot be sure that the person you wish to reach will be available, choose a person-to-person call, since you are not charged if the person cannot be reached, even if the call is answered.

Direct Distance Dialing. If you wish to place a station-to-station call, dial the area code (preceded by 1 in some cities) + the seven-digit number. If you wish to place a person-to-person call, charge the call to another number, make a collect or credit card call, or place any other call needing operator assistance, dial 0 + area code (if outside your own area) + the seven-digit number. The operator will come on the line, ask you for specific information (your name and telephone number, the person being called, and so on), and complete the call for you. If the call is person-to-person, the operator will try to locate the person you are calling, even if it means tracing that person to another number or arranging to call back.

Area Codes.   The United States and Canada are divided into about 120 telephone areas, each identified by a three-digit area code number. The area code must be used preceding the telephone number when dialing direct from one area to another. Of course, the area code is not used for calls between telephones in the same area.

Even if you place a call through the operator, it goes through faster if you use the area code. Just say "Area code 412, 555-1939." You need not give the name of the city you are calling unless the operator asks for it.

You will find the area codes for many places listed in the front pages of the alphabetic telephone directory. To obtain the area code for other places, ask the long-distance operator.

Time Zones.   If the place you are calling is in a different time zone, you need to calculate the difference in time before you place the call. Unless there is an emergency, consider the convenience and availability of the person you are calling.

The United States and Canada are divided into five time zones: Atlantic, Eastern, Central, Mountain, and Pacific. From east to west, each time zone is one hour earlier (except where Daylight Saving Time must be considered). A time zone map is shown in the front pages of many alphabetic telephone directories and is reproduced below.

Mobile Calls   A mobile telephone enables a person to make and receive calls from a car or truck while traveling. Mobile numbers are listed in the telephone directory. In the

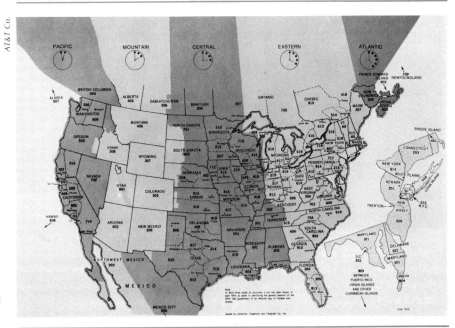

Time zone differences must be considered in making long-distance calls.

last few years mobile telephone service has been improved and expanded, so that it now provides all the features of regular telephone service.

Overseas Calls   If your firm has overseas business or foreign representatives, you may be asked to place overseas calls. It is a good idea to check with the long-distance operator first as to the rates for the call. You may also need to ascertain the time differential between your city and the country you are calling. Keep this information at hand if you often make overseas calls.

To make an overseas call, you can now dial directly (see your telephone book for dialing instructions), or you can ask the long-distance operator to place the call for you.

Ship-to-Shore Calls   Calls may be made to (or from) a person on a ship at sea if the ship is within calling range and is equipped to accept telephone communications. Such a call is placed through the long-distance operator and then the marine operator. Information as complete as possible should be given to the operator: name of ship, person being called, stateroom number, and telephone number if any.

Telephone Equipment and Services for Business

The size of the business office in which you work generally determines how much contact you have with phone systems other than the phone on your desk. It is useful to be familiar with the various systems in use. The most common ones are described here.

Touch-Tone Telephone   The Touch-Tone telephone with its 12-button keyboard arrangement is rapidly replacing rotary-dial equipment. Ten buttons are used for numbers; the other two buttons, labelled * and #, are available to signal special services.

Always listen for the dial tone (a steady hum) before you begin pressing the desired buttons for the number you are calling. As you press a button, a musical tone indicates that the number has been sent to the central office equipment.

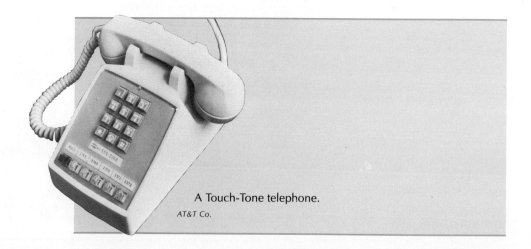

A Touch-Tone telephone.
AT&T Co.

Key Telephone By means of buttons, a key telephone is connected to several telephone lines through an intercommunication system. When the phone rings to signal an incoming call on a particular line, the button for that line lights up and remains lit as long as the line is in use. If more than one call comes in at the same time, you can answer one and ask the caller to hold the line a moment; then you can depress the "hold" button and answer the next call. The first line will be held open while you finish the second call.

Call Director To handle more calls than is possible with a key telephone you may select the Call Director, which can handle up to 29 lines at a single location. The desk-top Call Director can be connected to a switchboard (see below) and can also be connected with an intercom system. Since it can also be equipped with a plug-in headset, a Speakerphone, or a feature to permit conference calls, the Call Director is a versatile piece of equipment.

Larger Call Directors with visual displays are available and are operated electronically for faster service. They may include many of the special features listed above.

Switching Systems When telephone traffic is heavier than can be handled with the Call Director, switchboard equipment has to be installed. Many companies depend on PBX equipment. The telephone console is a newer development. Larger firms with heavy telephone volume select the Centrex system.

PBX Boards. A secretary may occasionally be asked to relieve a switchboard operator, so it would be useful to know how to operate a switchboard or, more technically, a private branch exchange (PBX). If that is likely in your office you would probably receive training from an experienced operator or as part of a training course.

The switchboard operator performs these basic functions:

- Screens all incoming calls and switches them to the proper extension.
- Either dials outgoing calls or connects the caller to an outside line.
- May complete interoffice connections.
- May also keep various telephone records.

PBX equipment is designed to channel calls throughout a firm. The two main types of boards are cord and cordless. Large companies usually have the cord type because of its larger capacity.

A PBX system may be either nondial or dial. On the nondial, the switchboard operator connects all calls. On a dial PBX, an extension user can dial directly to another extension in the company. Some boards are also equipped so that an outside number may be dialed by an extension user without going through the PBX operator.

Telephone Console. A company may prefer the convenience of the console-type switchboard. Since the console is cordless, a full-time operator is not needed and an attendant is easily trained for console duties along with other responsibilities. The console needs little personal attention since calls are automatically distributed in the order in which they are received.

Console models vary in size and can handle everything that a PBX can, including conference calls and tie-line service.

Centrex.   Direct inward dialing, or Centrex, is available for large-volume telephone users, with many telephone extensions within the company. Every telephone in a Centrex system has an extension number used for inside calls. The same number forms part of the outside number as well. Thus, an outside caller can dial direct to a person within the Centrex system without going through a PBX operator. For example, the company number may be 555-3000. All extension numbers within the company begin with 555 followed by a different four-digit number. Of course, if you are calling a company with a Centrex system and you do not know an individual's number, you call the general company number and ask the operator for the individual's extension. Keep a record of all such frequently called extensions.

Centrex calls are not only faster but cheaper, especially for long-distance calls, since a Centrex call is a station call.

Computerized Branch Exchange.   The new Computerized Branch Exchange or CBX system utilizes a compact minicomputer (rather than the older electromechanical ones). It is designed for offices having 120 to 800 stations. The CBX automatically selects the least costly circuit to use and permits the office worker to hold the call request until an outside circuit becomes available. Information about some or all outgoing calls can be recorded so that the company can control calls and allocate costs to the department making a call. Other features of the CBX include distributing systems, call pick-up, group pick-up, "do not disturb" (which means that the bell does not ring), and call forwarding, as well as others.

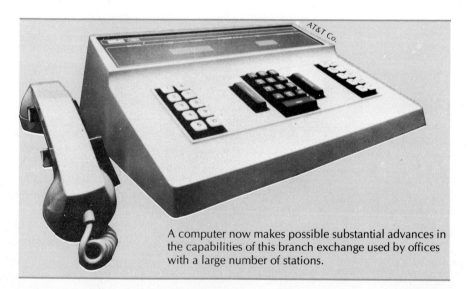

A computer now makes possible substantial advances in the capabilities of this branch exchange used by offices with a large number of stations.

Speakerphone

The Speakerphone is a regular telephone plus a microphone and a loudspeaker. If the receiver is lifted, the Speakerphone can be used as a regular telephone. To use it and keep the hands free, the user pushes a button to activate the microphone and loudspeaker. Voices are picked up by the microphone, which is sensitive enough to hear voices clearly anywhere in the room. The caller's voice is heard over the loudspeaker, which has adjustable volume.

The Speakerphone can also be used as a conference telephone, since it enables a group in one office to take part in telephone discussions with a group in another office. By means of a special feature, it is possible for one person to speak to another person in the room without being overheard in the other office.

Plug-in Headset

A plug-in headset can be attached to the telephone to free your hands for typing dictation coming in over the telephone.

Automatic Call Distributor

When the volume of telephone calls swamps switchboard facilities, as in hotel reservations offices or brokerage houses, the automatic call distributor switches incoming calls directly to the party called. When all the phones are busy, calls are held and then released as fast as phones are free. The greater number of calls handled in this way means economy, efficiency, and customer satisfaction. For a charge, the telephone company provides music during these periods.

Automatic Dialing Features

Several options are available for automatic dialing of frequently called numbers. The *Automatic Dialer* is easily programmed with 32 important numbers and four emergency ones (fire, doctor, police, or the like); each number is then automatically dialed by pressing one button only. *Custom Calling* systems enable you to dial only three digits to reach certain seven- or ten-digit telephone numbers. Other automatic dialing features are the *Card Dialer* telephone, which uses a prepunched plastic card inserted in a slot on the telephone; the *Magicall* or *Rapidial*, which stores numbers on a magnetic tape; and the *Call-A-Matic* dialer, which stores up to 500 telephone numbers on a motorized directory tape.

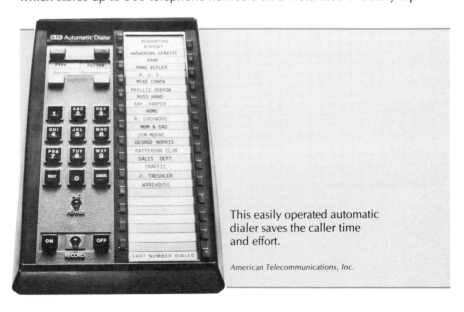

This easily operated automatic dialer saves the caller time and effort.

American Telecommunications, Inc.

Conference Calls

When an executive wishes to confer with several persons in different locations outside the firm, you may arrange a conference call. First get all essential information: what persons? where are they? what are their telephone numbers? when is the conference desired? Then call the conference operator (after first dialing 0 for Operator) and give the necessary numbers, names, time, and so on. The conference operator will call the participants and obtain from each a personal acceptance of the conference time. The operator will then reserve the conference equipment for the time requested and will place the call then.

Conference calls are charged at the same rate as person-to-person calls. A call to three people, for example, would be charged as three person-to-person calls. If the conference is not lengthy, it can be a great saving over the costs of a face-to-face meeting involving travel time and expense for all the participants.

Independent Answering Services

An independent answering service involves an arrangement with a trained operator to cover your telephone in your absence. Let the operator know when you will be out and whether and where you can be reached for urgent calls. The operator answers all your calls and takes messages that the callers may give. At the end of the day, or whenever you return to your office, you call the operator for your messages.

An answering service may also include a mobile service so that the boss can be signaled by a special beep when there is an urgent call. Mobilfone service operates within a 50-mile radius to subscribers with pocket radio message receivers, from car to car or from car to office.

Automatic Answering Services

Automatic answering services use a tape to receive and transmit messages in your absence. If a caller phones your number when you are not there, a recorded instruction asks the caller to leave a message at the sound of a bell or a beep. The caller then dictates the message into the phone, and it is recorded on the tape. When you return, you play back the tape to hear the messages. It is also possible for you to call your own number while you are out, setting off the playback by a signal tone so that you can listen to messages without returning to the office.

Tie Line

As the name implies, a tie line "ties" telephones together. An office may have a special tie line to a branch office in another city or to an office in another part of the same city. The connection is direct; the tie line is reserved entirely for the subscriber at a fixed monthly charge. The service may also be extended to cover transmission of business machine data, including facsimile, teletypewriter, and Data-Phone.

Wide-Area Telephone Service

Business firms that make many long-distance calls often use wide-area telephone service, or WATS. A business firm may acquire an access line that connects with a national network, a regional network, or a state network. The choice of access line depends upon the area the business wishes to cover through a direct connection. The charge for this service is based on the time the service is in operation, not on the individual telephone calls.

Your telephone book contains many numbers with an 800 prefix; these numbers are part of a WATS line and you may call them without charge.

Examples are car rental agencies, airline reservation desks, and chain motels or hotels.

Additional Services   With electronic equipment, telephone companies are providing faster, more efficient service. Other capabilities of present equipment include:

- Transferring incoming calls automatically to another number (at night or when you are away from your desk).
- Arranging a three-way conference without assistance.
- Signalling the user of a busy telephone that another call is waiting.
- Automatic redialing through an automatic call-back feature when the busy telephone is finally free.
- Automatically preventing predetermined telephones from making calls by means of a call-restriction feature.
- Programming a telephone not to receive calls with a "Do-Not-Disturb" feature.

ELECTRONIC COMMUNICATION

Executives may choose to send a communication electronically when they wish to achieve a dramatic effect or convey urgency, or when speed is necessary but a written record of the message is desired.

Telegraph Services   **Telegram.**   Western Union offers two traditional basic services: the regular fast-service telegram and the more economical overnight telegram. The regular telegram is usually delivered within two hours; the minimum rate is based on 15 words. The overnight telegram, with a minimum rate based on 100 words, is used for complicated proposals, reports, and instructions.

The telegram seems to be on the way out as the Mailgram and teledata communication services are expanding.

Mailgram.   The Mailgram, one of Western Union's newest electronic mail services, can be sent 24 hours a day; it is flashed via microwave and satellite networks to a United States post office near the addressee and is delivered by letter carrier. If the Mailgram message is received by Western Union before 7 p.m., it will generally be delivered the next postal delivery day.

Cablegram.   When an urgent message needs to be sent to someone in a foreign country other than Canada or Mexico and you want it delivered quickly to the person you wish to reach, a Western Union International telegram, usually called a cablegram, can be used. Like telegrams, however, cablegrams should be used only when less expensive forms of communication will not accomplish the objective. Classes of service offered include full-rate cablegrams, night letters, international Telex service, and radiograms. A cabled money order is a quick, safe way to send money to someone abroad.

Other Telegraph Services.   You can indicate that your telegram is to be sent regularly or in any of several special ways, among them collect and personal

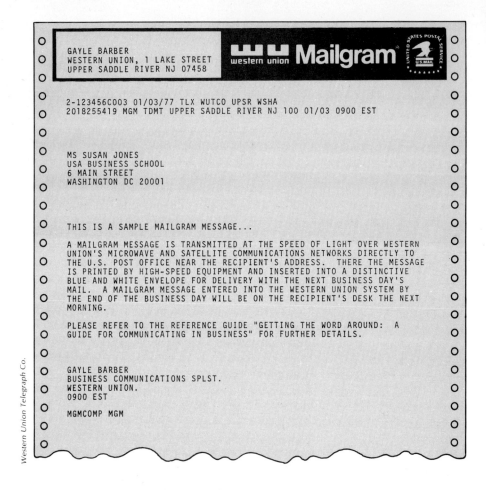

Western Union Telegraph Co.

```
GAYLE BARBER
WESTERN UNION, 1 LAKE STREET          western union  Mailgram
UPPER SADDLE RIVER NJ 07458

2-123456C003 01/03/77 TLX WUTCO UPSR WSHA
2018255419 MGM TDMT UPPER SADDLE RIVER NJ 100 01/03 0900 EST


MS SUSAN JONES
USA BUSINESS SCHOOL
6 MAIN STREET
WASHINGTON DC 20001


THIS IS A SAMPLE MAILGRAM MESSAGE...

A MAILGRAM MESSAGE IS TRANSMITTED AT THE SPEED OF LIGHT OVER WESTERN
UNION'S MICROWAVE AND SATELLITE COMMUNICATIONS NETWORKS DIRECTLY TO
THE U.S. POST OFFICE NEAR THE RECIPIENT'S ADDRESS.  THERE THE MESSAGE
IS PRINTED BY HIGH-SPEED EQUIPMENT AND INSERTED INTO A DISTINCTIVE
BLUE AND WHITE ENVELOPE FOR DELIVERY WITH THE NEXT BUSINESS DAY'S
MAIL.  A MAILGRAM MESSAGE ENTERED INTO THE WESTERN UNION SYSTEM BY
THE END OF THE BUSINESS DAY WILL BE ON THE RECIPIENT'S DESK THE NEXT
MORNING.

PLEASE REFER TO THE REFERENCE GUIDE "GETTING THE WORD AROUND:  A
GUIDE FOR COMMUNICATING IN BUSINESS" FOR FURTHER DETAILS.


GAYLE BARBER
BUSINESS COMMUNICATIONS SPLST.
WESTERN UNION.
0900 EST

MGMCOMP MGM
```

delivery only. You can request a confirmation copy. You can also wire money orders, flowers, personal opinions to elected officials, and even Braillegrams and large-print messages.

Some special services are available for cables and mailgrams, but not all of the above.

Sending Telegraph Messages

To send a telegram or a Mailgram, you can telephone Western Union and dictate the message to the operator; write or type it out and take it to a telegraph office or your company communications center; or send it via a teletypewriter communication system such as Telex or TWX. Overseas telegraph communications may be phoned in or brought directly to Western Union International (different from Western Union), RCA Corporation, or French Cable.

When you are requested to send a message by telegraph or cable, verify any special services and determine the projected time of delivery as well as the urgency of the message. Consider not only the time of day (because of time zones) but the day of the week and upcoming holidays in selecting the appropriate kind of telegraph service.

Facsimile Transmission

The *graphic transceiver*, or *facsimile*, makes possible the sending and receiving of documents and pictures. By means of this portable equipment, a full page of type can be transmitted, line for line, in three to six minutes. The equipment scans the message with a light-sensing device and transmits an exact image electronically. Facsimile transmission is becoming a common form of electronic mail. It is relatively expensive, as it requires a sending as well as a receiving machine.

Teletypewriter Service

The telephone company provides a special service to facilitate rapid communication between two or more business concerns—the teletypewriter. This instrument resembles an ordinary typewriter and is operated like one. It transmits written messages between two points almost instantaneously. Messages can be sent at 100 words a minute and more.

Three types of teletypewriter service are available: private line (TWPL), central exchange (TWX), and Data-Phone. With TWPL, two or more machines are directly connected. TWX, on the other hand, is a central exchange where any office that is registered can be connected with any other listed in the directory. Teletypewriters can also be used on Data-Phone service.

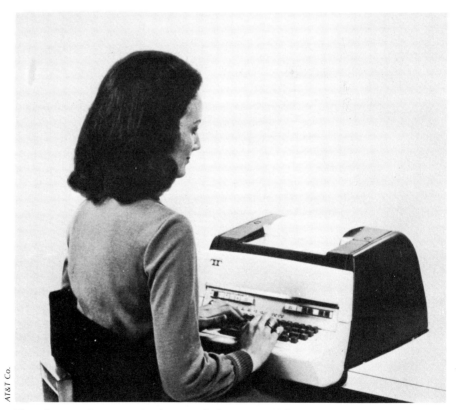

AT&T Co.

The teletypewriter transmits data rapidly between widely separated offices. At the receiving end the data is duplicated as sent, sometimes in two colors.

Data-Phone   Data-Phone service makes it possible for two machines to "talk" to each other. Information in any form—photographs, drawings, maps, punched tapes, or cards—can be transmitted by business machines using this service. Business machines at sending and receiving locations are connected to the telephone network via Data-Phone. Information is transmitted after establishing a normal telephone call between the locations involved. Rather than handle human language, the equipment converts machine language (punched cards, punched tape, or magnetic tape) to electronic tones for transmittal and converts them back to machine language at the receiving end. With such equipment, information can be sent across the country at speeds around 2,500 words a minute.

Data-Phone service is a giant step forward in meeting the growing need for faster communication of information across long distances. The following are a few examples of how the service is used:

- A supermarket can order merchandise from its supply centers daily so that limited shelf space is kept filled.
- An insurance company's home office can immediately answer inquiries from thousands of branch offices.
- A doctor can get immediate and continuous information at the office or at home about patients in several hospitals scattered throughout a large, congested population center.

REVIEWING
YOUR
READING

1. What are the three kinds of appointment records that the secretary is likely to use? What is the purpose of each?

2. What essential information should you obtain before making an appointment for an executive?

3. Describe the proper way to cancel an appointment; to cope with conflicting appointments. What options are available in coping with cancellations?

4. Describe how you should handle a scheduled caller; an unscheduled caller.

5. What courtesy should be shown a waiting caller? How should the visitor be presented to your boss?

6. What should you do with incoming phone calls when your boss has a caller? when a visitor overstays the scheduled time?

7. Name at least four things you can do when receiving calls to show your mastery of telephone techniques.

8. What essential data should you write on a message form when you answer your employer's telephone?

9. In what circumstances would you send a telegram rather than using other means of communication to transmit business information?

10. How does time affect the selection of the most appropriate type of telegraph service?

11. Describe the procedure for arranging conference calls through the telephone operator.

12. Of what benefit to a secretary might a key telephone be? a Call Director?

13. How does an automatic answering service work?

14. Describe the procedures you would use for each of these visitors to the office: a job applicant who arrives when there is no opening, a salesperson who sits on your desk and asks you personal questions, a well-dressed young woman carrying a briefcase who refuses to give her name.

Using Your Skills

1. Telephone Manners. Discuss ways to improve these telephone conversations. Keep in mind the pointers on telephone manners given in this chapter.

a. The telephone rings in an office and Miss Adams, the secretary, answers.

> Miss Adams: Hello. (*Short and abrupt.*)
> Caller: Is this Mr. Richards' office?
> Miss A: Yes.
> Caller: May I speak to him?
> Miss A: Yes, but you'll have to wait a minute. He's talking on another phone.
> Caller: How long will it be?
> Miss A: I don't know. It's hard to say.
> Caller: I'll wait.
> Miss A: Okay.

About five minutes later Mr. Richards finishes his previous call and is told another call is waiting.

> Mr. Richards: Richards speaking. (*Pause.*) Hello, hello . . . Miss Adams, who was calling?
> Miss A: Oh, is he gone? He must have hung up.
> Mr. Richards: Who was it?
> Miss A: He didn't say.

b. A call comes for Mr. Richards, who is not at his desk, and Miss Adams does not know where to find him. She answers his telephone after it has rung a few times.

> Miss A: Mr. Richards' desk, Miss Adams speaking.
> Caller: Is Richards there?
> Miss A: He hasn't been here all afternoon. I really don't know whether he is coming back today.
> Caller: Do you know where I can reach him? It's quite important.
> Miss A: No, I do not. Just a minute, maybe some of the others know. (*Aside to those at neighboring desks.*) Do any of you know where Mr. Richards is this afternoon? Where? Pontiac? Are you sure? Oh, Pontiac or Flint, he didn't say for sure? (*To caller.*) Well, we aren't sure; he may be in Flint or in Pontiac.
> Caller: All right. I'll try another time. Thank you.
> Miss A: You're welcome. Good-bye.

2. **Personal Index of Telephone Numbers.** Look up telephone numbers for the following organizations and agencies in a telephone directory, and type the list on a sheet of 8½ by 11-inch paper, putting the names in alphabetic order.
   a. Police department.
   b. Fire department.
   c. Local school board.
   d. Local chamber of commerce.
   e. Typewriter repair service.
   f. Office service bureau for temporary help.
   g. State employment agency.
   h. Railroad or bus station.
   i. Airport.
   j. Better Business Bureau.
   k. Post office.
   l. Public library.
   m. Long-distance directory assistance.

3. **Telephone Situations.** Select the best suggestion for each telephone situation below by writing the number of the answer on a separate sheet of paper. Then, on an 8½-by-11 sheet, 60-space line, state briefly why you think the answer you chose for each situation is best. Single-space your material, but leave a double space between answers.
   a. You are a typist in the sales department of the James Manufacturing Company, Fort Wayne, Illinois. At 8:30 a.m., just as you enter the office, the telephone rings. (Your company has a private switchboard operator.) In which of the following ways would you answer the telephone?
      (1) "James Manufacturing Company."
      (2) "Sales Department."
      (3) "Sales Department. (*Your name*) speaking."
      (4) "Good morning."
      (5) Other.
   b. You are an employee in the personnel department of the James Manufacturing Company. Someone has called and asked for information that will require some time to find. In which of the following ways would you handle the situation?
      (1) Excuse yourself and get the necessary information.
      (2) Ask whether you can call back or whether the person calling would care to wait while you get the information.
      (3) Tell the caller you will have the information in about half an hour and ask the person to call back.
      (4) Simply leave the telephone to get the information.
      (5) Other.
   c. A telephone call from the president's office comes for your employer, a lawyer in the legal department of the James Manufacturing Company. Your employer, Mr. Johnson, is working on an important case that is to be heard in court tomorrow. He has asked to be disturbed only when it is very

important. In which of the following ways would you handle the situation?

(1) Tell the caller Mr. Johnson cannot be reached this afternoon.

(2) Take the message and the number to be called. Leave the message on Mr. Johnson's desk just before you leave at five, if he is still there.

(3) Take the message and number to him at once and place it quietly on his desk where he can see it.

(4) Ring Mr. Johnson. Since the call is from the president's office, it is probably important.

(5) Other.

EXERCISING
YOUR
JUDGMENT

1. Delayed Attention. The receptionist telephones that Mr. Howard Byrnes, the salesman who represents a manufacturer from whom your company buys many items, is in the reception room to see Mr. Ward, your employer. Mr. Ward is extremely busy on a report he is trying to finish. He says to you, "I don't need anything right now. Tell Mr. Byrnes that I'll call him when I'm ready to see him." When you talk to Mr. Byrnes, you discover that he intended to tell Mr. Ward about some special offerings he is presenting in advance to a few valued customers. The matter really seems to demand Mr. Ward's immediate attention. What should you do?

2. "Just a Minute, Please." As secretary to Mrs. Anderson, economic adviser to the president of the company, you have a busy telephone. You have four lines on a key-type desk telephone and are responsible for screening all calls to Mrs. Anderson. Sometimes while you are talking on one line, two other lines flash for incoming calls. When your boss is out, you have even had calls on all four lines; then you get really frustrated. You're getting so nervous that you hate to hear the phone ring or see the lights flash. When you discuss the situation with Mrs. Anderson, she asks you how often you have had four calls at one time. You remember then that it very rarely happens, but you know it could happen at any time. Afterward, thinking it over, you realize that you have very seldom had even three calls at one time. What should you do?

APPLYING
THE
REFERENCE
SECTION

Word Choice. This exercise requires reviewing some homonyms to help you further develop your vocabulary and the ability to use words precisely.

Consult the discussion of homonyms in the Reference Section and a dictionary for help in completing this assignment.

1. In some of the following sentences, a word similar to the correct word has been incorrectly substituted. Type the correct word on a separate sheet. If the sentence is correct, place an x beside the letter on your answer sheet.

a. Grace has expected Mrs. Stanton's invitation.

b. No one eluded to his accident.

c. Begin every sentence with a capital letter.

d. I find history more interesting than mathematics.

e. The new oil company has an impressive suit of offices.

f. Please make another appointment latter in the week.

2. The pairs of brief definitions below describe words that sound alike but are spelled differently. Type the proper spelling of the word on a separate sheet of paper.
   a. the pathway to the altar
   a small island
   b. to cure
   the hind part of the foot
   c. a part in a play
   to move by turning over and over
   d. to take unlawfully
   a form of processed iron
   e. a fragment
   freedom from war
   f. audibly
   permitted

3. The following pairs of words and phrases define words that are spelled exactly alike but are accented differently. Type the proper word on a separate sheet and show where the accent falls. For example, "an official document" defines the noun *'rec ord*; "to set down" defines the verb *re 'cord*.
   a. sixty seconds; very small
   b. behavior; to carry on or lead
   c. a struggle for superiority; to make a subject of dispute
   d. an aim; to disapprove
   e. an arid region; to abandon

4. Select from the pair of words in parentheses the one that correctly matches each definition, and type it on your answer sheet.
   a. to vary (defer, differ)
   b. a law (statue, statute)
   c. as a result (therefore, therefor)
   d. aid (assistants, assistance)
   e. consent (assent, ascent)
   f. before (formally, formerly)

PART THREE/Channeling Information

CHAPTER SEVEN

PROCESSING INCOMING MAIL

Every day countless sheets of paper flow through a company's offices. Your boss needs to receive this mail early so that it can be handled as soon as possible. You have an important supporting role to play in handling the incoming mail whether it comes through the postal service, by interoffice mail, by private carrier, or is transmitted electronically. You may also receive parcels from commercial delivery trucks or from suppliers.

Your function is to process the incoming mail so that your boss can assimilate facts and opinions easily and then react promptly and effectively. The responsibility for handling some incoming correspondence may be yours.

Initial Handling

In large business organizations mail is received in such quantities that special staff in the mail department must first sort it by departments or other organizational classifications. Any mail that is not addressed to an individual or to a department is routinely opened, date-stamped, and inspected in order to determine its disposition. All the mail is then delivered to various departments or placed in containers to be picked up by authorized department personnel.

In small offices the secretary or the receptionist receives the mail directly from the letter carrier. The mail is then sorted and delivered to various receiving stations in the office or placed in some kind of receptacle for pickup. Whether or not you sort *all* the mail, you will, of course, sort and process the mail for your own boss.

Sorting Mail

There is a way to deal with each of the types of mail that arrive in an office. The importance of the mail determines its priority.

Preliminary Sorting. First sort the unopened mail into several piles. The categories you use will depend somewhat on your boss's preferences, but five piles ordinarily suffice:

B. D. Unsworth

Sorting incoming mail before presenting it not only enables you to become familiar with its contents, it also helps the executive establish priorities for responding to it.

- Personal mail, which is not to be opened.
- Priority mail, which is to be opened immediately.
- General business mail relating to office operations, which is to be opened as soon as possible.
- Circulars, packages, newspapers and periodicals, and other less urgent material, which are ordinarily processed only after all other mail has been opened.
- Mail to be forwarded later today.

Priority Mail.   Give prompt attention to priority mail, which is any communication that requires immediate handling. The type of service used by the sender is one clue to priority mail. Place telegrams, special delivery, registered, insured, and certified mail on top of the mail pile, so that they receive your boss's immediate attention. Other items that are usually considered priority mail are those marked "Rush," "Personal," or "Confidential." Any telephone messages or mail that you know your boss is eager to see should be treated as priority mail. You will learn about other priority items from experience and from conversations with and instructions from your boss. Don't be misled by third-class advertising and promotional mail that uses such attention-getting devices as "Rush reply" on the envelope.

General Business Mail.   Much of each mail delivery is first-class mail and other communications that relate to day-to-day business operations. General business mail includes letters, orders, inquiries, invoices, remittances, and interoffice memorandums and reports. For the most part these are important communications that require prompt attention. They determine many of your employer's daily tasks and the pace that must be maintained in order to complete these tasks.

Bulk Matter.   Other mail consists of second-, third-, and fourth-class items. In the bulk-matter category are newspapers, magazines, professional journals, books, circulars, catalogs, packages, and miscellaneous printed matter. Although you open this material last, do not assume that it is unimportant. A certain periodical, a package holding film, or a circular advertising a new or competing product may be of great interest to your employer. Use your judgment to determine the priority of bulk-matter items; some, including advertisements, may be important enough to add to the general-business category.

Mixed-Class Mail.   A first-class letter may be attached to the address side of mail of another class, or it may be enclosed with other items in a larger envelope or parcel. When a letter is enclosed with other material, the words FIRST-CLASS MAIL ENCLOSED are written or stamped below the postage and above the address. The first-class portion may be removed and added to the general business or priority categories; the rest of the material should be placed where your employer can readily locate it after reading the letter.

Forwarding Mail

As you sort the incoming mail, you may find some items that need to be forwarded. Either readdress them immediately and put them in your outgoing mail box or put them in a separate pile and deal with them later. Your decision depends on the quantity of such items, your need to deliver incoming mail to your boss quickly, and whether you know the forwarding address or need to take time to locate it.

If you do not know the forwarding address for a letter mistakenly sent to your office, write on the envelope "Not at this address" or "Addressee unknown" and return it to the post office. If you know the forwarding address, cross out the old address and write the correct one on the envelope. First-class mail is forwarded without additional postage. To forward second-, third-, and fourth-class mail, the regular postage must be paid again.

If the mail to be forwarded is registered, certified, insured, c.o.d., or special-handling mail, no extra fees for these services are charged, although ordinary postage charges, if any, must be paid. Special delivery mail will not receive this service at a second address unless a change-of-address card has been filed with the post office.

You may occasionally have mail returned to you as undeliverable. Check the stamped explanation on the envelope, put the contents in a fresh, correctly addressed envelope, and mail again with the correct postage.

Sometimes mail is received for an individual who has left the company. If the address includes a job title, the letter is usually given to the person presently holding that position unless the envelope is marked "Personal" or "Confidential." Often the return address will give a clue as to whether the piece of mail should be opened or forwarded.

If a magazine comes addressed to a former employee, consider who paid for the subscription. If the company paid for or receives free copies of the magazine, then deliver it to the person holding the former employee's position and notify the publisher of the change. If the former employee paid for the subscription, the current issue should be forwarded and a reminder sent to the former employee to inform the publisher of the change of address.

Opening Mail

A secretary usually opens the boss's mail with a hand-held letter opener. However, if you are required to open a large volume of incoming mail, you may use the office letter-opening machine.

Opening Envelopes by Hand. Opening envelopes by hand can be speeded up by stacking the envelopes face down so that the flaps are on the right (or the left if you are left-handed). Slip the letter opener under each flap, and cut with a quick forward motion. Slit all the envelopes at one time before you begin removing the contents.

As envelopes are opened, there is some danger of cutting papers inside them. As a precaution before slitting envelopes, tap a fair-sized batch of them on the desk to move the contents toward the edge opposite the flap.

Opening Envelopes by Machine. Offices with a large volume of mail usually use machines to open it, since the faster mail is opened, the sooner it can be processed. For a relatively light volume of mail, using a hand-operated machine is three to five times faster than performing the task manually. For a medium volume of mail, hand-fed, electrically powered machines are available. These openers cut three sides of an envelope in one operation. They can feed, open, and stack five hundred or more letters a minute. Another advantage of mechanized openers is that they minimize the likelihood of slicing or otherwise damaging enclosures.

Handling Mail Opened by Mistake. To guard against the possibility of opening other people's mail by mistake, check the addresses on the envelopes as you stack them for opening. If you do happen to open a letter by mistake, reseal it with cellophane tape, mark it "Opened by mistake," and sign your name. Forward it immediately.

Opening Packages. Open packages with scissors, a heavy-duty razor, or a knife. Take care to avoid hurting yourself or damaging the contents. If a letter is enclosed with a package, place it with the general business mail. In order to identify the contents of a package, cut the mailing label from the outside wrapping and attach it to the contents.

When packages containing merchandise or supplies are delivered, check to see that you actually did order the materials before accepting delivery. Also, check the quantity and condition of each item in the shipment against your purchase order; note any differences on the invoice before paying the account.

When merchandise arrives, the deliverer may request that you sign a "delivery received" form. This form may simply state "two boxes" from XYZ

Company or may provide more detail such as "two typewriters with serial numbers — and —." In either case, check to see that the items delivered match those on the form.

Handling Personal Mail.   Do not open personal mail unless you are authorized to do so. Although it may be difficult to tell whether mail is personal, such mail is usually identified by the word "Personal" or "Confidential" on the typed envelope. A handwritten envelope with a return address that is obviously a residence usually signals personal mail and should be treated as such. If you open a personal letter in error, seal it with tape, mark it "Opened by mistake," and sign your initials. Be sure to treat the information as confidential. The nature of your employer's business also helps determine whether you open personal mail. For example, in a doctor's office or an insurance agency, such mail usually contains checks and is therefore opened by a secretary.

Handling Interoffice Mail.   Interoffice mail is generally received in reusable envelopes called chain envelopes. They are seldom sealed unless the contents are confidential or valuable. If one is sealed, open it carefully so that the envelope can be reused. If the enclosed item is a letter or a memorandum, place it with the first-class mail. If it is a routine report or general information, place it with similar material, unless you know it is something your boss is waiting for.

Removing Contents   Special care must be taken when removing the contents from envelopes. It is easy to overlook something and throw it away in a supposedly empty envelope. If you slit three sides of the envelope and spread it out flat in front of you, you will avoid the possibility of overlooking enclosures.

Enclosures.   An enclosure should be attached immediately to the letter it accompanies. Large enclosures should be fastened to the back of the letter. Small enclosures, such as cards or folded brochures, may be attached to the front.

Take special care when envelopes contain checks, money orders, or cash. If your boss prefers to have you include the remittance with the letter, attach it to the front of the letter. If the remittance is to be separated from the letter, place it in a cash box or send it to the cashier. In either instance, note the fact that the remittance was enclosed by making an entry opposite the enclosure notation— or somewhere else on the letter if there is no enclosure notation—and then initial the entry. The entry should read: "Received: $15 check; deposited cash box, 1/26/—. AGB."

Check every letter for enclosures. As you unfold each letter, glance at the lower left corner for an enclosure notation. If the enclosures indicated are not present, note this fact on the letter. You may wish to write a note to the sender calling attention to the omission or your boss may do this in a reply.

Disposition of Envelopes.   There are a number of reasons for keeping envelopes until you are sure the information they contain is no longer useful. For example, when a customer seeks a discount even though the discount period has expired, the cancellation date on the envelope shows when the customer's letter was received at the post office. Thus it is tangible evidence to support a decision on whether to allow the discount. If a problem arises because a letter was not received in time to take appropriate action, a discrepancy between the date on the envelope and the date on the letter may explain the delay. If the return address of the writer is not on the letter, it may be on the envelope.

In some offices, the policy is to attach all envelopes to the back of incoming mail. When such a policy is not stated, do not discard envelopes until you check to see that the return address given in the letter is the same as that on the envelope and that the writer's name is signed legibly on the letter. If there is any question about receiving letters or bids by a specified deadline, keep the envelopes as a record of postmark.

Stamping Mail

All incoming mail should show the date of receipt. Such a record can be important.

Date Stamp.   If there was a delay between the time the item was mailed and the time it was delivered, the date stamp will show this discrepancy. The date record also serves as a reminder to whoever is processing the mail that time is passing and prompt action is desirable.

An efficient method of stamping mail is to use a rubber date stamp that prints the word *Received* and the month, day, and year. When a stamp is not available, write this information in longhand in abbreviated form. When possible, stamp every letter in the same place, usually in the upper right-hand corner or in the space between the letterhead and the body of the letter. Magazines, circulars, catalogs, and booklets should also be stamped in one place, usually on the front or the back cover.

Time Stamp.   The exact time that mail is received is sometimes important in processing orders or in maintaining customer credit records. Automatic time stamps contain a clock and a printing mechanism that stamps the hour and exact minute as well as the date. The stamp may also include space for other information, such as *Received by*, *Attention of*, or *Answered by*.

Stromberg Products

With an automatic stamper, the date and time incoming mail is received can be recorded in a matter of seconds.

Mail Registers   Any items that are sent registered, insured, certified, or special delivery are usually valuable or contain material that must be handled with care. For this reason many secretaries keep a separate record of such incoming mail as well as of letters that contain remittances.

Parcel-Receipt Register.   If you receive frequent parcel post, air freight, or truck deliveries, you may find you cannot depend on memory for answers to questions about them. A parcel-receipt register in which all essential information is recorded can be a useful memory aid. In such a register allow ample space for a description of the material received, the name of the sender, the identity of the shipper, the name of the addressee, the date of delivery, and the charges, if any.

Negotiables Register.   When incoming mail regularly contains remittances, negotiable instruments, stocks, bonds, legal documents, contracts, and other such valuable items, keep an accurate record of their receipt. A register similar to the ruled form shown here can be used:

Date & Time Received	Description of Item	Sender and Address	Delivered By

Separate-Cover Register.   Letters often refer to material being sent separately. In watching for such material, you may find it helpful to keep a register of expected mail. The register should include space for an entry date, a brief description of the expected material, the name of the sender, the date sent, and finally the date received. Check the register at least once a week so that you can follow up on any items not yet received.

Keeping Registers Handy.   A loose-leaf notebook or file folder in your tickler system may be used for keeping your mail registers readily available.
The headings below are suggested:

SEPARATE-COVER REGISTER					
Date	Article	From Whom	Date Sent	For Whom	Date Received

REMITTANCE REGISTER

Date	Sender	For	Form	Amount

SPECIAL DELIVERY, REGISTERED, AND INSURED MAIL

Date	From Whom	For Whom	Type of Mail

Digesting Mail

Many executives are hard-pressed for time to read, comprehend, and react to everything that finds its way to their desks. They therefore depend on their secretaries to preview and digest some of it for them. How much mail you digest depends, of course, on your ability and on the executive's preferences.

Reviewing Mail   A competent secretary can help the boss digest material by highlighting important facts. To do this, you need to develop the ability to scan, underline meaningfully, annotate, and preview.

Scanning.   Scanning means reading something quickly in order to grasp the important points. When you scan, give full attention to what you read, keeping in mind these questions: What is the subject of this message? What are the facts? What problems are raised? What action is desired?

Underlining.   After you have scanned an item and have grasped its major ideas, underline the important points—the who, when, what, where, and why of the communication. Underline only key words and phrases—probably two to four words or places in an average letter.

Annotating.   Once you have scanned a letter and underlined the important points, you are ready to annotate it. Begin by verifying all computations and price quotations. Next, assemble previous correspondence and any other related material. Make marginal notations on the letter about possible action or reactions to the writer's ideas or requests. For example, if the writer asks for a report or brochure, attach the material and note on the letter that the requested item is attached.

When annotating, be brief and record any actions taken.

Previewing Special-Interest Mail

Even though your boss deals with each day's letters, there often is still a problem in keeping up with business and professional magazines, house organs, and newspapers. You can help your boss keep abreast of this literature by marking, clipping, annotating, and sometimes summarizing articles of special interest.

To handle such material it is best to glance through it first, noting articles or items that relate to your employer's interests and business responsibilities. If you find an item of interest, place the publication on your boss's desk with a note clipped to the front cover. For example, you might say, "Article on page 75 discusses impact that current films have had on toy market. Might contain useful data for your presentation to marketing staff next month."

You might also start a resource file of articles related to your employer's professional field. Into the file you can put copies of articles, clippings, and illustrations, classifying them by topics. This material could come in handy for a report or speech.

In previewing material, exercise special care not to overlook important features. It is time-consuming work and should be done only if your employer wishes it.

Peter Roth

You can help your employer keep informed about business developments by summarizing articles and other correspondence of special interest.

Suggestions for previewing and summarizing items are:

1. Scan items first for a broad understanding.
2. Read items a second time, underlining only key words and phrases, including the fewest possible words that still retain the original meaning of the statement.
3. Organize the main ideas into a logical summary. Be sure to include purpose, facts, conclusions, and recommendations.
4. Be sure to indicate the original title, author, and publication source on the summary, if it is to be separated from the original article.
5. Type a rough draft.
6. Polish and tighten the language.
7. Prepare the final draft.

Presenting Mail

When presenting mail for action, try to anticipate what information your employer will need. Place the incoming mail on your boss's desk with personal mail on top, priority mail next, and general business mail last. Bulk mail may be placed under this stack or to one side. If the executive's desk is in an open area in the office, you may want to slip the open mail in a file folder first for privacy.

Previous Correspondence

If a letter contains a reference to previous correspondence, get the correspondence from the files and attach it. If you do not have time to get the related material before your boss starts to read the mail, make a note of what is needed and find it after presenting the mail.

Background Information

Often, an inquiry cannot be answered until certain information has been gathered. Anticipate such situations, and try to get the necessary information before your boss requests it. This type of preparation often requires no more effort than a telephone call to another department and a few questions or requests for data.

Routine Requests

Your boss may receive routine requests to send a catalog, brochure, or other printed information. Some of these requests may be referred to another department, but they might just as easily be handled from your desk. You might suggest that a routine form letter be developed that you could type individually and send with the materials. It may be that your boss will prefer to see these requests, either before or after you send the materials, and may occasionally dictate an individual letter about them.

Circulating Mail

Mail received by one executive is often of interest to other employees in the organization. Bulletins, reports, quotations, inquiries, trade magazines, and announcements, for example, sometimes need to be circulated among several people. There are several ways to circulate this type of mail.

```
PLEASE ROUTE TO:        Date    Initial

Robert Mandelkern     _____  _____

Susan Nicholson       _____  _____

Stan Leighton         _____  _____

Debra Werner          _____  _____

                      _____  _____

                      _____  _____

                      _____  _____


Return to:  Charles Harper  _____
```

A routing slip.

Routing Slip

A small slip of paper, perhaps 3 by 4 inches, is often used as a circulation or distribution list. Names of those to receive the item are typed in a column. The item is sent to the first person on the list, with the slip attached. After reading it, that person crosses off his or her name and sends the item to the next person on the list. A routing slip may also list various possible actions on the item being circulated (such as "For signature," "For approval," "Note and return"). The router merely checks the box opposite the action requested. Routing slips may be printed in pad form, prepared from a rubber stamp, or typed and duplicated by the secretary.

Transfer Form

Another way to circulate information is by using a transfer form. For example, if a letter contains information of interest to one or several individuals or departments, the part which is of particular interest is transferred to a special printed

```
              TRANSFER FORM
                      Date  1/20
The attached papers are referred

TO  Ralph Newton

for the purpose indicated by the check mark:
____  Please note and file.
____  Please note and return to me.
____  Please note and see me about this ___ a.m./___ p.m.
  ✓   Please answer, sending me one copy of your letter.
____  Please prepare reply for my signature.
____  Please take charge of this.
____  To be signed.
____  For your information.
____  Please make comments.
____  For your approval.
____  RUSH--take immediate action.
Remarks:


Signed  SJW
```

form or an interoffice memorandum that identifies the source and states that you are passing on pertinent information. The information is then typed or a copy of it may be attached.

Copy Machines

Most offices are now equipped with copying equipment. These versatile machines can reproduce almost everything. Relatively inexpensive, errorproof reproductions, comparable in quality to the originals, can thus be made available for immediate distribution to a number of people. A secretary can save time and increase efficiency in circulating mail by using a copying machine to make copies of items that can be forwarded to several persons, departments, branches, or regions at the same time rather than routing them from one to another.

Carbon Copies

It is the preferred practice in some offices to make enough carbon copies of letters and memorandum reports for distribution to the persons or departments involved. One-time, snap-out carbon packs permit the production of the same information on five or six separate sheets of paper with a single typing and eliminate the chore of assembling a carbon pack. Corrections should be made on all copies.

Protecting the Employer's Mail

After you prepare the boss's mail, you may place it in an in basket on his or her desk. You may also put it in a folder and place it in a conspicuous spot on the desk. Or you may use a pocket organizer for presenting mail, with separate pockets for the various categories. When a folder or a pocket organizer is not used, protect mail from the eyes of others by reversing the top letter.

Handling Mail During the Employer's Absence

When your boss is on a business trip, you are expected to exercise judgment in handling the mail. Responsibility of this kind requires that you read and digest the incoming mail and take appropriate action when possible.

Writing Acknowledgments

A substantial number of letters that arrive during your employer's business trip, vacation, or sick leave may not require immediate action. In many instances, you may want simply to acknowledge receipt. If it is likely that your boss will answer the letter, indicate that an answer may be expected soon after the boss returns to the office. Ordinarily, it is preferable not to explain to a correspondent why your employer is absent from the office. Here is an example of such an acknowledgment:

> Dear Mr. Havemann:
>   Thank you for your letter of January 10 seeking advice about your refinished floors.
>   Mrs. Harris is on an extended business trip. Your letter will be brought to her attention as soon as she returns.
>   Sincerely yours,

Handling by Others
Urgent letters that should be acted upon immediately during an executive's absence should be given to an associate or a superior. Make a copy and note on it to whom you referred the letter so that your employer may inquire later about the action taken.

Taking Independent Action
A few letters will require action that you can take yourself. In this case, do what needs to be done and then write a memo to your boss explaining what you did. Attach this to the original letter before placing it in a mail-received folder to await your employer's return.

Forwarding Copies
An employer going on a trip may say exactly what mail you should forward to him or her. Use judgment about what other mail you should forward. Send copies of letters of interest or importance, retaining the originals for follow-up review when your employer returns.

Keeping a Correspondence Digest
You may prepare a digest of all important communications during your employer's absence. This should include a chronological summary, by the day, of correspondence, telephone calls, and visitors. A summary form like the one shown here is recommended; however, summary forms may also be in outline or tabular form.

Whatever the form, these are the essentials:

- Date of each item.
- Name of correspondent.
- Concise but complete summary of message.
- Explanation of any action taken.

```
                    DIGEST OF IMPORTANT CORRESPONDENCE
                            March 11, 19--


          1.  (3/5)  Johnson Studios, Chicago, says Lake Michigan photos,
                     including four extras, will arrive by this Wednesday.
                     Acknowledged and sent copy to J. C. Miller, Public
                     Relations, for his information.

          2.  (3/6)  Marguerite Mackay, Boston, acknowledged receipt of
                     check for advance royalties on her manuscript,
                     Where Do You Stand?

          3.  (3/7)  Frank Guardi, Salt Lake City, wants you to speak--
                     humorously!--at University Father's Day Banquet,
                     May 2.  Acknowledged; said you would respond in
                     near future.

          4.  (3/8)  James Longstaff, Philadelphia, sent another market
                     information survey.  Publication deadline for mar-
                     ket analysis data is March 21.  Referred question-
                     naire to Dave Weinstein, Marketing; asked him to
                     complete and return to you by March 15.
```

A digest of important correspondence received during an executive's absence.

Reviewing
Your
Reading

1. Why is the secretary's efficiency in processing incoming communications vital to an executive?

2. What is priority mail? Besides telegrams and special delivery letters, what other priority mail should you be aware of?

3. Identify the categories of business mail requiring prompt attention.

4. Explain how mail is handled when it is addressed by title to an individual who is no longer with the company.

5. Outline the procedure for opening mail by hand.

6. How should enclosures such as checks, money orders, or cash be handled?

7. Why is using a time stamp to designate the exact time that mail is received of value to both you and your boss?

8. Summarize the three techniques you may use to help your executive read, comprehend, and react to all incoming mail.

9. How can you help a busy executive keep up with the volumes of business magazines, trade journals, house organs, and newspapers that should be read?

10. Besides the name of the sender and a description of the material received, what information should you include in a parcel-receipt register?

11. When mail received by an executive is of interest or concern to other employees in the organization, what methods of distribution can you use?

12. Describe what you would do about letters that arrive during your executive's business trip, vacation, or sick leave that do not require immediate action.

13. Describe what you would do about letters that arrive during your executive's absence that should be acted upon immediately.

14. In what three ways may a correspondence digest be arranged? Outline the essentials to be included when preparing a digest.

15. When opening a package to present the contents to your employer, what precaution should you take regarding identification of the sender?

Using
Your
Skills

1. **Mail Records.** Prepare a mail register and on it record the following incoming mail:

APRIL 2. A letter from Sperry Rand Inc. stating that filing information is being sent separately. The letter mentioned that the package was sent April 1 and was addressed to the filing department.

4. A check for $25.10 from J. R. Smith to apply on account.

5. A money order for $51.10 from R. C. Downs for goods sent him on March 15.

8. A letter from M. N. Owens stating that some merchandise is being returned for replacement.

10. The package was received from Sperry Rand Inc.

15. A $10 check from Sally Bruce to apply on account.

20. *Office Systems* magazine arrived. Type a routing slip for this magazine to be sent to Mr. Bowers, Mrs. Hayes, Miss Martin, and Mr. Smith. Make a pencil notation telling Mr. Smith to see page 15.
21. A letter from Jane Wyman asking for a bid on a certain job.
21. A registered letter from A. B. Vann. You may sign for it.
22. A special delivery letter was received by your employer from the M. & T. Office Supply Co.
23. A check for $50 from Frank A. Matthews, representing the amount due on a note.
24. Merchandise received from M. N. Owens.
27. The sum of 25 cents in stamps from Alan Long, for postage we paid.
28. An insured parcel-post package from Bates Corporation. The package is addressed to your employer.
29. A letter from M. N. Owens asking whether the merchandise he returned had been received.
30. A subscription renewal notice from the publisher of *Office Systems* magazine.

2. **Digesting Correspondence.** Read the following three letters. Using plain paper, prepare a digest of correspondence for the three letters, following the form in this chapter.

BRAWNELL'S BUSINESS COLLEGE
492 Holsom Avenue
Pittsburgh, Pennsylvania 15208

February 17, 19—

Roberts & Jones, Inc.
270 Madison Avenue
New York, New York 10016

Ladies and Gentlemen:

Dr. Edward T. Randall, of our Department of Personnel Methods, informs me that you are conducting a study involving management. Since I plan to do my doctorate work in this field, I am deeply interested in any current developments affecting that area.

I should like very much to receive any information concerning this work that is available and any other current material that you may have contributed to this field.

I shall appreciate very much any assistance you can give me in this matter.

Sincerely yours,
John B. Duke
Instructor

CABOT, BREWSTER & WINTHROP
12 Milk Street
Boston, Massachusetts 02117

February 17, 19—

Roberts & Jones, Inc.
270 Madison Avenue
New York, New York 10016

Ladies and Gentlemen:

Thank you for mailing to us the card requesting a prospectus of DIVIDEND SHARES, INC. I am enclosing a prospectus as well as some other literature.

At the request of any stockholder, the company is required to repurchase shares at the full net asset value under terms specified in the charter.

I hope that you will find the enclosed literature both interesting and informative. Please feel free to call on me for any information regarding any security in which you are interested.

Very truly yours,
Frank N. Cole
Vice President

RAYMOND & WIGENT, INC.
489 Madison Avenue
Plainfield, New Jersey 07060

February 17, 19—

Roberts & Jones, Inc.
270 Madison Avenue
New York, New York 10016

Ladies and Gentlemen:

In an article in the November 19 issue of *Personnel Journal*, we noted that you have carried on an extensive personnel research program. We should be particularly interested in knowing the results of research in the following:

1. Evaluation of interviewing and counseling.
2. Worker attitudes.
3. Organization and executive leadership.
4. Reduction of absenteeism.
5. Personnel practices in small businesses.

If any papers have been written in connection with these research projects, we should appreciate information as to how the papers may be obtained and at what cost.

Very truly yours,
RAYMOND & WIGENT
Warren J. Locke
Personnel Director

3. **Techniques Review.** On another sheet of paper type the responses needed to complete these statements:
   a. Special _____, _____, and certified mail are examples of _____ mail.
   b. _____ mail means to arrange it according to the importance of each piece.
   c. If a first-class letter is enclosed in a package, you should place it with _____ _____ _____ if the package is large.
   d. If money is enclosed in a piece of mail, you should make an entry opposite the enclosure notation, such as _____.
   e. You should discard envelopes as soon as you open the mail. Is this statement true or false? _____
   f. Most interoffice mail is received in reusable envelopes called _____ envelopes.
   g. All incoming mail should show the _____ of receipt.
   h. Since most executives' time for digesting mail is limited, they often depend on their secretaries to do some _____ for them.
   i. In underlining, you should look for the _____, _____, _____, _____, and _____ of the communication.
   j. The secretary might help the boss by _____ or _____ professional reading matter.
   k. A secretary should keep a _____ of important mail that is received.
   l. Generally speaking, it is preferable to arrange mail in order of _____ and _____.
   m. A letter opened by mistake should be resealed and marked _____ _____ _____ followed by your name.
   n. A _____ _____ is often used to circulate mail among several people.
   o. You should acknowledge _____ of mail in your employer's absence.

4. **Situational Analysis.** On a sheet of paper describe what action you would take in each of the following situations:
   a. Your employer is away. An important letter arrives, stating that action on a contract that your employer is holding must be taken before the following day.
   b. A letter marked "Personal" and "Rush" arrives addressed to your employer. Your employer is in a meeting that will last all day.
   c. The mail carrier brings a letter to you marked "Insufficient Postage" and asks for the money to cover the additional postage required.
   d. A registered letter for your employer arrives. Someone must sign for it.
   e. Opening the heavy volume of mail that comes in takes up time that you feel you could better spend on other work.

EXERCISING YOUR JUDGMENT

Orders. Your boss, Miss Richards, the general sales manager, is out of town negotiating an important contract. You have just received a telegram from her asking you to wire certain cost figures to her immediately. The assistant sales manager, Mr. Gordon, who is in charge during Miss Richards' absence, was standing at your desk when the telegram arrived. He took the telegram out of your hands and said that he would take care of the request. When you made a discreet inquiry through Mr. Gordon's secretary about an hour later, you were told that he had not yet had time to reply. When you checked again a few hours later, you were told that Mr. Gordon had left for the day without dispatching the information. A few minutes before closing time you receive a long-distance call from your boss. She is very impatient and wants to know why you didn't follow her orders. What should you say?

Applying
the
Reference
Section

1. Type the two-letter abbreviations recommended by the post office for each of these states:

   a. Kentucky   **f.** Connecticut   **k.** Alaska
   b. Maine   **g.** Delaware   **l.** Maryland
   c. Missouri   **h.** Wisconsin   **m.** Hawaii
   d. Montana   **i.** Iowa   **n.** Nevada
   e. Louisiana   **j.** Arizona   **o.** Nebraska

2. Type the correct abbreviations for the following, using appropriate spacing:

   a. American Automobile Association
   b. United States of America
   c. Cash on delivery
   d. Federal Communications Commission
   e. Young Women's Christian Association
   f. National Organization of Women
   g. 9 (ante meridian) in the morning
   h. et cetera

CHAPTER EIGHT / PROCESSING OUTGOING MAIL

A secretary's responsibilities for preparing outgoing mail vary according to the size of the company. In large offices a secretary is usually relieved of the actual work of mailing out routine correspondence. Mail clerks collect letters and weigh and stamp them. In smaller offices, however, a secretary usually attends to all mailing and shipping duties. Whether you handle some or all of your employer's outgoing mail, it is your responsibility to see that it is correctly prepared and ready to mail.

Assembling the Mail

Correspondence should be mailed as soon as possible after it has been signed. Although this sounds quite simple, mistakes are made and trouble and expense incurred when a secretary does not know how to assemble and dispatch mail properly.

Checking and Arranging

Check each letter to be sure it is signed and that all enclosures are present. Carelessness here has sent untold letters to their destination without accompanying checks or other important papers. A busy executive may be signing letters while receiving telephone calls or visitors and may easily miss signing a letter or may misplace enclosures. It is up to you to see that everything to be signed is signed and that all enclosures are sent to their proper destinations.

Check each letter carefully for notations of corrections or revisions. This requires a keen eye, especially when an executive is considerate enough to make corrections with a light pencil so that the letter need not be completely retyped. Lay such letters aside and make the corrections as soon as possible, on both the original and the carbon copies. Failure to correct carbon copies sends to the files many copies that are not true copies of the letters mailed. If an executive adds a postscript in ink, especially on a letter to a friend, note the addition on the file copy, unless it is purely personal.

Letters that are to be completely retyped should also be laid aside for the time being. Unless they are important and the executive is waiting to sign them, they should not delay your attending to other mail that is ready to go out.

Verifying Agreement of Envelope and Letter Addresses

Making sure that the envelope address agrees with the inside address on the letter is important for two reasons: to be sure that the address is correct, and to be sure that the right letter is inserted in the right envelope. Mailing one person's letter in another person's envelope is embarrassing to say the least. The results may be humorous, or serious, or only inconvenient; but in any case, they reflect unfavorably on the person who sent the letter.

The return address should appear on all envelopes; often the department or the individual's name is typed above it.

Meeting OCR Address Requirements

Not only is ZIP Coding now routine on all business mail, but OCR sorting of mail in post offices is becoming widespread. The Optical Character Reader (OCR) requires that the envelope address be surrounded by white space so that the OCR can focus on the address. For guidelines to follow in addressing envelopes, and for the recommended two-letter state abbreviations to use for OCR sorting, see the Reference Section.

Sending Enclosures

A reference in dictation to an enclosure signals you not only to type the enclosure notation at the end of the transcript but also to gather the appropriate enclosures and place them with the transcript when presenting it for signature.

Enclosures may be folded together, and stapled or not stapled, before being inserted in the envelope. They should not, however, be stapled to the letter they accompany. It is good practice to fold enclosures and slip them inside the last fold of the letter, so that when the letter is removed from the envelope, the enclosures come out with it. Do not use a file copy of an original as an enclosure. Instead, prepare a photocopy or a typewritten copy of the original material.

An enclosure larger than the letter it accompanies, such as a brochure, a contract, a price list, a prospectus, or a catalog, should be mailed in a large manila envelope clearly marked "First Class" or in a special green diamond-bordered envelope. When a letter accompanies such an enclosure, the letter may be sent with first-class postage and the enclosure with third-class, provided that a combination mailer is used and the enclosure qualifies as third-class mail (see page 126). A combination mailer is simply a large envelope with a standard No. 6 or No. 10 envelope attached to the front of it.

Another way to mail oversized or bulky enclosures is to mail the enclosure as third-class matter in an unsealed envelope and to mail the letter separately in a sealed envelope. If this is done, a "Separate Cover" notation should be added to the letter.

Enclosures smaller than the letter they accompany are usually clipped to its face. However, coins should be taped to a card and stapled to the face of the letter; stamps may be enclosed in a small cellophane envelope and attached similarly.

Applying Work-Simplification Procedures

When special mailing equipment is not used you can simplify manual procedures by applying motion-saving principles. The following three practices should save you considerable time and effort:

1. Specialize. That is, divide a job into parts or operations, and perform each operation on all the pieces at one time. This eliminates unnecessary make-ready and put-away motions. For example, fold five or six like items (such as a printed letter) at one time. Then shake them apart, pick up one at a time, and sharpen the creases.
2. Assign a definite place to each article. Avoid loss of time and unnecessary fatigue from unplanned, haphazard arrangements.
3. Arrange materials for the best sequence of motions. Develop a work pattern that uses a logical sequence of activities and avoids unnecessary motions.

Work simplification and economy of motion are timesaving when applied to inserting enclosures, sealing and stamping envelopes, and the like as described below. How many other illustrations of motion economy can you think of?

Folding and Inserting

The neat and exact folding of a letter contributes to the recipient's good first impression when opening the letter. The correct way to fold letters for both No. 6 and No. 10 envelopes is detailed in the illustration below.

When you have a quantity of like items to insert, first open and flatten the flaps of a quantity of envelopes by using one hand to slide each envelope under the flap of the one beneath it as you hold the envelopes with the other hand. Then hold a batch of envelopes in one hand and a batch of folded enclosures in the other. Insert the top enclosure into the top envelope, drop the item to the desk,

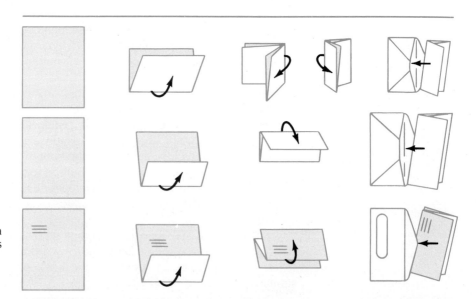

The size and style of the envelope determine how a letterhead is folded. Letters going into window envelopes are accordion-folded so that the address appears in the window.

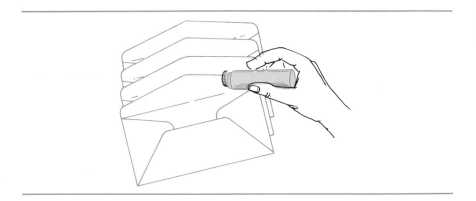

Envelopes lined up for fast, efficient sealing.

insert the next enclosure into the next envelope, and continue until the batch is finished.

Several letters for the same address can be sent in the same envelope, preferably a No. 10 or even larger if there are many enclosures.

Interoffice mail within an organization is usually sent in special printed envelopes that are ruled so that the envelope can be addressed repeatedly. Each time the envelope is used, you simply draw a line through the previously written name and location and write your addressee's name and location on the next ruled line. Interoffice envelopes usually have a string closing and need not be sealed unless the enclosed material is confidential.

Sealing

For a heavy volume of outgoing mail, you may need an envelope-sealing machine. Otherwise, you can seal letters with a sponge or a sealing device, such as a ceramic wheel moistener. Flaps should not be licked, not only because it is unsanitary, but also because you may cut your mouth or tongue.

Once a batch of letters has been placed in envelopes, stack the envelopes with the open flaps facing you. Next, fan the stack so as to expose only the gummed flap of each envelope. Then sweep a moistening device across the flaps and quickly seal each one.

Stamping

Whether you stamp your outgoing correspondence by hand or use a postage meter is determined usually by the size of the office in which you work. The larger the company, the more likely it is to provide a centralized mailing service with mechanized equipment.

Using a Postage Meter. Many secretaries need to know how to use the simpler types of postage meters. Whatever its size, the machine itself is purchased; the meter portion is rented from the manufacturer and licensed (free) by the post office. With the license, you receive a meter record book. You take the meter to the post office and buy a specified amount of postage. The meter is then set so that this amount is recorded on the meter dials. In your meter record book, you record the total postage used each day and the amount left on the dials. When the unused balance runs low, you take the meter to the post office again, purchase more postage, and have the meter reset to show the new balance.

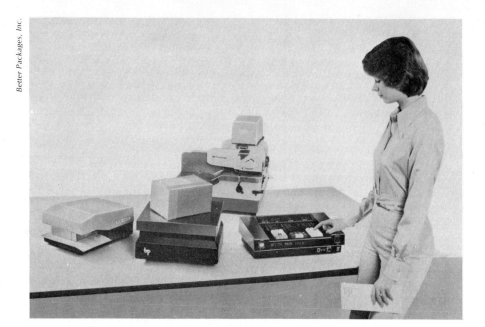

Better Packages, Inc.

Considerable savings can be effected in mailing if a postage meter is used.

There are several precautions to take when using the postage meter:

- Check dials to make sure the amount to be printed is correct.
- When you finish metering a batch of mail, set dials to zero to be ready for next use.
- Check the weight of any unusually heavy items and meter them separately. Don't guess. (See page 132 for the use of a postal scale.)
- Make sure postage is printed in upper right corner of envelope.
- Arrange metered mail face up and bundle it by class of mail service.
- If any adjustments are needed, take meter to post office or request a call by the manufacturer's maintenance service. (Upon application to the post office, you may obtain refunds of up to 90 percent of postage value for misprints.)

Stamping by Hand.   To stamp a relatively small quantity of mail, fan the envelopes so that about an inch of each shows. Moisten a strip of stamps and place one on the exposed right-hand corner of each envelope. Stamps can be purchased in sheets of 100 and torn into strips. Or you can buy stamps in roll form and use a hand stamp-affixer.

Practice motion-saving procedures, especially if you have many envelopes to stamp. For example, with the stamps in strips and the envelopes stacked, hold the stamps in your right hand (unless you are left-handed). Press a stamp on the sponge or moistener and affix it to the envelope at the same time that you tear the stamp from the strip. Then as your left hand lifts the stamped envelope off the pile, your right hand moistens the second stamp, and so on.

Make sure that you use the correct stamp for each envelope. Avoid plastering a heavy envelope with a whole row of stamps; keep a supply of larger denominations for such purposes.

After you have stamped a batch of envelopes, go over your work, double-checking the following:

- Envelopes all sealed?
- No envelopes stuck together?
- Proper postage on each envelope?
- Overweight items weighed and proper postage affixed?
- Needed postage affixed for special delivery?
- Special-service letters separated, such as for registered or certified mail?

Economies in Mail Handling

Your image as management's "right arm" is considerably improved when you practice efficiency and economy in dispatching the mail. Here are some useful guidelines.

Use Only Minimum Service Needed

Do not pay for special delivery service to cities that can be reached overnight, since ordinary mail delivered by a regular carrier may get there at the same time or even sooner. Find out by making a test mailing. Also, check train and plane schedules at your local post office. You may also be able to check schedules at the city of delivery by inquiring at your post office. Do not send Mailgrams on Friday to businesses that are closed on Saturday.

Keep Postage Scale Accurate

"Penny wise, pound foolish" describes an office in which the postal scale is hard to read, difficult to keep in balance, or faulty in any way. If, however, a reading is truly borderline, affix an extra stamp to mail. Any mail on which postage is due is returned to the sender, causing unnecessary delay. (See page 132 for postal scale equipment.)

Pay Exact Postage

Keep a supply of the various denominations of stamps you ordinarily use. (And, of course, check the weight of any heavy item by using a postage scale.) Then you won't use two 15-cent stamps when a 28-cent stamp is required.

Send printed letters, statements, notices, and the like as third-class instead of first-class mail, unless the attention you want the addressee to give it is of prime importance. For this reason, printed sales-promotion letters are often sent first-class.

Third-class envelopes may be sealed only if "Third Class" is printed on the envelope. A "pennysaver" envelope or an open-end-flap envelope may be used without these words.

Get Maximum Value

If you normally use promotional leaflets, fill each envelope up to the weight limit. Include some order blanks, reply envelopes and the like.

If during the day you have more than one piece of correspondence going to the same addressee, combine all such mail into one envelope, saving postage, envelopes, and addressing time. Mail to branch offices, suppliers, and traveling staff members can be economically handled in this manner.

If the contents of an envelope are just over the weight limit, trim the inserts, if practical. Before you prepare a large batch of identical mail, weigh a sample envelope with all the inserts. You may save postage by switching to lightweight stationery or even omitting a less-essential insert.

Mark Each Piece Properly

Clearly label large first-class envelopes as "First Class," to avoid their being mistaken for third-class mail. Special green-diamond-bordered envelopes are available that identify oversized "flats" as first-class mail.

Mark third-class mail as such and seal it for safer and easier handling. Mark it "Return Requested" so that if it is undeliverable it will be returned to you. Such returns often are stamped with the reason for nondelivery, or even a forwarding address. The small fee charged for returned items is well worth paying as a means of keeping your mailing list up-to-date. Fourth-class mail may also be marked "Return Requested"; you should also expect to pay duplicate postage when it is returned.

Place only one address label on a package. It is a good idea, however, to place a duplicate label inside a parcel in case the outer label comes off or the parcel becomes undone. You may also wish to place in the package an invoice or a list of the contents.

Before taking mail to the post office, separate local from out-of-town mail to expedite handling in the post office.

Mail at the Best Time of Day

Since mail deposited at peak periods (especially the close of the day) means slower handling at the post office, deposit mail as early in the day as you can and as often as possible. An hour's delay in mailing can mean the difference between mail catching an early train or plane so as to be received next morning—and not being received until the following day.

Any mail that needs to be forwarded should be returned to the post office the same day it is received.

In companies that budget by department, records are kept of each department's mail.

STATEMENT OF MAIL TO BE STAMPED		DATE PROCESSED	STATEMENT NO.	CORRECTION OR ADJUSTMENT

Charge To: __Promotion Dept.__
Department or Office

Account Number: 4 2 0 - 1 1 - 6

	MAIL CODE	PIECE COUNT	PIECE RATE
BR-BULK RATE			
CM-CERTIFIED			
FA-FOREIGN AIRMAIL			
IN-INSURED			
PC-POSTCARD			
PP-PARCEL POST			
RM-REGISTERED			
SD-SPEC. DEL.			
1C-1ST CLASS			
3C-3D CLASS			
4C-4TH CLASS			

32 PIECES FOREIGN AIRMAIL   22 PIECES LIBRARY RATE

260 PIECES 1ST CLASS   _____ PIECES PARCEL POST

_____ PIECES 3D CLASS   _____ POSTCARDS

_____ PIECES 4TH CLASS   _____ PIECES PRIORITY

_____ OTHER _____
(Specify: insured, spec. delivery, etc.)

MAILED BY __N.O.__   DATE __3/3/--__

FOR MAILROOM USE ONLY

Maintain Postage Records   In companies that budget by department, you may have to keep records for the postage used. Two ways are to attach a special punched card with your account number on it as you deposit the mail, and to fill in a form that identifies the number of pieces in each category. At the end of the month the department account is adjusted for the total amount of postage used.

Mailing Money, Stocks, or Bonds

When your employer entrusts you with sending money, stocks, or bonds through the mail, use the safest and, when necessary, the most expeditious method.

Checks   Business firms usually send money through the mail in the form of ordinary checks. Most regular bills are paid in this manner. Checks are considered routine enclosures and may be clipped to the front of the letter they accompany or, preferably, inserted within a fold of the letter when it is placed in the envelope. If the check is certified by a bank, it should be sent first-class mail registered (see pages 129–130). The same is true for cashier's checks, bank drafts, postal money orders, and express money orders.

Bills or Coins   It is best to avoid sending currency through the mail. If, however, a small amount must be sent, observe these precautions. Fold the money inside a letter or order blank in such a way that it cannot be detected by casual inspection from outside. Tape coins to a card and staple the card to the top of the letter.

Stock Certificates and Bonds   Use registered first-class mail to send stock certificates and bonds that are negotiable. Nonnegotiable stocks and bonds can be sent certified first-class mail or simply first class.

Classes of Domestic Mail

In handling mail, you should be familiar with the classifications of domestic and international mail service and know which class to use for which type of matter. You will find it worthwhile to become acquainted with the local post office and to obtain copies (free) of various reprints from the *Postal Manual*, according to your needs. Sample titles indicate the range of information available: *Domestic Postage Rates and Fees*, and *How to Prepare Second and Third Class Mailings*. Since all booklets are dated, see that the information you have is current.

First-Class Mail   First-class mail includes all matter sealed against postal inspection and included in the following categories:

- Typewritten or handwritten matter and copies of such matter (with certain exceptions detailed under second and third class).
- Checks, invoices, and other documents partly printed and partly written or typed.
- Postal cards.
- Business reply mail.

Second-Class Mail   Second-class rates apply only to newspapers and other regularly issued publications for which permits are obtained from the United States Postal Service. A printed *notice of entry*, such as "Entered at the Post Office at Davenport, Iowa, as second-class matter," or simply "Second-class postage paid at Dayton, Ohio, and additional mailing offices," is required on each copy of the publication.

The frequency of issue of the publication, the number mailed, the percentage of advertising the issue carries, and the distance mailed all influence the rates charged. These rates are for bulk mailing by the publisher. All bulk-rate pieces must indicate the ZIP Code in the addresses.

Copies of second-class publications not mailed in bulk may be sent either at the "transient" rate, marked "Second Class," or at the fourth-class rate, marked "Parcel Post"—whichever is cheaper, depending on the weight of the package. All rates are subject to change and should be checked periodically.

Third-Class Mail   Mailable matter not covered by the first- or second-class descriptions and weighing less than 16 ounces per item is third-class mail. Such matter includes books and catalogs containing 24 or more printed pages, merchandise, photographs, drawings, manuscripts, recordings, films, and such printed matter as calendars, pamphlets, brochures, and the like. For items mailed separately the single-piece rate applies.

For identical items mailed at one time the bulk rate applies, which is less for material mailed by authorized nonprofit organizations than for all others. For bulk-rate mailings a permit must be obtained from the local post office and a bulk-rate mailing statement submitted with each mailing.

Bulk-rate mail must be sorted by the mailer, tied in bundles according to destination, and properly labeled before being taken to the post office. Since it does not go through the cancelling machine, such mail has either precancelled stamps affixed by the mailer or imprinted "bulk permit" postage.

Third-class rates also apply to keys and identification cards or tags with instructions to return and a statement guaranteeing payment of postage due on delivery.

Third-class mail must be so prepared by the mailer that it can be easily examined at the post office. It may be sealed but must be clearly marked "Third Class."

ZIP Codes are essential in preparing bulk mailings. They must be shown for all addresses.

Fourth-Class Mail   All mailable matter not eligible for first-, second-, or third-class rates is classified as fourth-class mail, commonly called parcel post. Parcel-post rates increase according to the postal zone (there are eight), which have to do with the distance the item must travel to its destination.

Rates are based on weight of item as well as zone. A maximum weight and a maximum girth for each item varies according to whether it is being sent to a first-, second-, third-, or fourth-class post office, which has to do with the size of the city in which the post office is located.

ZIP Code National Areas

Puerto Rico and Virgin Islands **0**

Alaska and Hawaii **9**

What Is ZIP Code?

ZIP Code is a five-digit geographic code that identifies areas within the United States and its possessions for purposes of simplifying the distribution of mail by the U.S. Postal Service.

In devising the ZIP Code, the United States and its possessions were divided into 10 large geographic areas. Each area consists of three or more states or possessions and is given a number between 0 and 9.

Because of favorable transportation facilities, key post offices in each area are designated as Sectional Centers. Each Sectional Center post office receives and transmits mail moving *between post offices within its section.* It also receives and transmits all mail moving *into or out of the section.*

Together, the *first three digits* of any ZIP Code number stand for either a particular Sectional Center *or* a metropolitan city.

The *last two digits* of a Sectional Center ZIP Code number stand for one of the *associated post offices* served by the Sectional Center.

The *last two digits* of a metropolitan city ZIP Code stand for one of the *delivery areas* served by the city post office, its branches and stations.

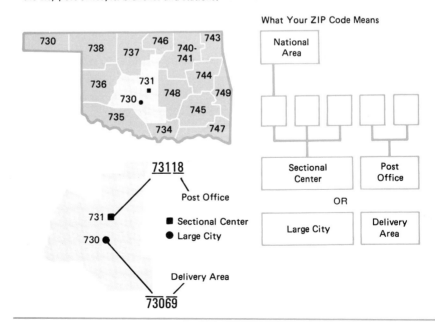

What Your ZIP Code Means

National Area	
Sectional Center	Post Office
OR	
Large City	Delivery Area

73118

731 ■ Post Office

■ Sectional Center
● Large City

731 ■
730 ●

Delivery Area

73069

FOURTH-CLASS MAIL		
Material	Special Fourth-Class Rate	Library Rate
Books—24 pages or more	Yes	Yes
16-millimeter film	Yes	Yes
Sound recordings	Yes	Yes
Filmstrips, slides, microfilm	No	Yes
Transparencies	No	Yes
Printed sheet music	Yes	Yes
Printed objective tests	Yes	No
Manuscript for books and articles	Yes	No
Duplicated or photographed library material	No	Yes
Printed educational reference charts	Yes	No
Pages and binders of medical information	Yes	No
Bound academic theses	No	Yes
Periodicals	No	Yes

Fourth-class items must be so wrapped that they can be easily examined. Most parcel-post labels include the words, "May be opened for postal inspection if necessary."

Letters may be enclosed in third- or fourth-class parcels if postage for them at the first-class rate is added to the postage for the parcel and if the parcel is marked "First-Class Mail Enclosed" below the postage and above the address. Or a combination mailer may be used (see page 119).

Special fourth-class rates are available for books, films, printed music, recordings, manuscripts, certain educational and medical materials, and items eligible for the special library rate.

When in doubt about whether an item is eligible for the fourth-class or library rate, find out by consulting your post office or the current applicable *Postal Manual* booklets. The table above will help you.

Priority Mail   Almost any mailable matter may be sent priority mail so long as it does not exceed the weight limitation of 70 pounds and the length and girth restriction of 100 inches. The rates are not only by weight but also by postal zone. Matter not acceptable includes anything that can be damaged or can become harmful after changes in temperature or atmospheric pressure, permanent magnetic materials with unconfined fields, and matter specifically excluded by federal agencies.

Priority mail items should be prominently labeled "Priority Mail" on all sides (below the postage on the address side). Priority mail is the fastest small-package air service available and costs less than air express or air freight. For items of high value and low weight, such as jewelry or precision machine-tool parts, priority mail is worthwhile.

Special Services

Upon payment of a specified fee, a mail user may obtain additional postal service to speed the delivery of mail or to ensure its safe receipt. Such a fee is added to the regular postage charges. Special postal services include special delivery, special handling, registering, insuring or certifying mail, c.o.d. service, and Express Mail.

Special Delivery

Special-delivery mail is delivered on a special fixed schedule during prescribed hours to addresses, rural or urban, within specified delivery areas. Any class of mail may be sent special delivery, and special-delivery mail is delivered 365 days a year.

Special-delivery fees should be reserved for urgent mail that is likely to reach the delivering post office after the last regular mail for the day has left. For example, do not use special delivery for a letter likely to arrive in the delivering post office on Saturday morning if the letter is addressed to a business firm whose offices are closed for the weekend. Nor should a special-delivery letter be sent to a post office box number, since it must wait until it is picked up by the box holder.

Special Handling

Special-handling service provides the most expeditious handling and transportation of third- and fourth-class mail but it does not provide special delivery. Special-handling parcels are delivered as parcel post is delivered. Fees are according to weight. The words "Special Handling" should be marked on the parcel below the stamps and above the addressee's name.

Especially urgent third- or fourth-class mail may be sent both special handling and special delivery, upon payment of the proper fees.

Certified Mail

Certified mail provides for a receipt to the sender and a record of delivery to the office of address, for a fee; it is available for first-class mail only. Such evidence of delivery may be desired for important mail that is without intrinsic value, such as contracts, specifications, medical records, and the like.

For an additional fee, restricted delivery may be specified and/or a return receipt requested. A further fee is charged if the return receipt is requested after the item has been mailed.

Registered Mail

Valuable first-class mail or priority mail of intrinsic value may be sent by registered mail, which provides added protection and insurance liability. The sender must declare the full value of an item presented for registration. Such items as negotiable instruments, money, precious metals, and valuable merchandise are best sent by registered mail.

Upon payment of extra fees, additional services may be obtained, including restricted delivery and various types of return receipts. The envelope should be plainly marked for the service desired, above the address, such as "Deliver to Addressee Only" or "Return Receipt Requested."

Envelopes of registered mail must be securely sealed by the sender. Sealing tape may be used but should not cover the entire flap of the envelope.

Insured Mail   Since registering is available only for first-class mail or priority mail, a similar service provides for insuring of mailable third- and fourth-class mail against loss, rifling, or damage. Insurance is not available for mail to foreign countries. The fees charged are based on value claimed up to $200 maximum. Extremely fragile articles and items not adequately packaged are not accepted. For small additional fees, on mail insured for over $15, restricted delivery may be specified and return receipt requested.

C.O.D. Mail   Collect-on-delivery (c.o.d.) service is available to a person who wishes to mail an article for which the buyer has not paid and have the price and the cost of the postage collected from the addressee when the article is delivered. The amount collected is returned to the sender by means of a postal money order, with a $200 maximum. This service is not available to overseas military addresses, nor can it be used for the collection of debts.

The fees for c.o.d. include insurance against loss, rifling, or damage to the article, as well as failure to receive the amount collected from the addressee. For slight additional fees, the sender may specify restricted delivery or notice of nondelivery.

Express Mail Programmed Service   Companies and people who need fast delivery to specific locations may use the post office's custom-tailored Express Mail program that delivers mail in 24 hours. Banks use Express Mail daily to speed checks and financial data quickly to and from branches and other banks. Manufacturers and other businesses may use Express Mail to deliver payrolls to branches.

There are four system options: door to door, door to destination airport, originating airport to addressee, or airport to airport.

International Mail

Mail to other countries is divided into postal union mail and parcel post. If your secretarial responsibilities include the dispatching of much international mail, you should become familiar with Chapter 2 of the *Postal Manual* and the *Directory of International Mail*, available at your local post office or from the Superintendent of Documents, Government Printing Office, Washington, D.C. 20402. A condensed statement, "International Mail," is also available. Be sure to keep all such information up-to-date by checking with your local post office.

Postal Union Mail

The two categories of postal union mail, LC and AO, consist of the following:

LC (Letters and Cards)	**AO (Other Articles)**
Letters	Printed matter
Letter packages	Samples of merchandise
Air letters (aerogrammes)	Matter for the blind
Post cards	Small packets

Parcel Post

Parcels sent to other countries are subject to weight and size limits that vary from country to country. Moreover, certain articles are prohibited entirely; other articles are prohibited to certain countries. For such restrictions and for rates and weights, consult the post office. Check also as to what may be sealed and what must not be sealed.

You can also obtain from the post office the customs declaration forms (free) required to be attached to overseas parcels.

Mailing Guidelines

In addressing any piece of international mail, you should observe the following guidelines:

- Place address on right half of address side of piece.
- Write legibly and completely, using roman letters and arabic figures.
- Use capital letters for names of post office and country.
- Use English for name of post office, province, and country.
- Place sender's name and address in upper left corner of address side.

Upon payment of additional fees, international mail may be sent airmail, registered, special delivery, special handling, return receipt, or priority mail to practically all countries. Check with the post office for details.

Mailing Equipment

Just as your responsibilities for processing outgoing mail vary with the size of the company you work for, so will your responsibility with regard to mailing equipment. Such equipment may be simple and compact and located near your desk, or it may be large and automatic, located in a centralized mailroom where incoming and outgoing mail activities are coordinated.

As a company expands its operations, its mail activities increase. Even the smallest business has a mail department, whether or not it is so labeled. In any event, the forward-looking secretary learns about the kinds of mailing equipment available in order to relate it to the mail service that management wants provided. You should realize that in today's increasingly automated offices, communications ranging from monthly customer statements to financial analyses and periodic reports are mass-produced. And mailing them requires the selection and use of postal scales, postage meters, folding and inserting machines, collators, and automatic stuffing and packaging machines.

Friden Mailing Equipment Corporation

An electronic postal scale.

Postal Scales

A spring, beam, pendulum, or electronic postal scale should be used to weigh any piece of mail for which the amount of postage required is questionable. Such scales show weights in ounces and pounds. The correct amount of postage is then determined by the class of mail service used.

Postage Meters   Procedures for using postage meters have already been discussed. The use of metered mail for both large and relatively small mailings provides the following benefits:

- Saving of time and effort.
- Elimination of office drudgery.
- Flexibility and convenience.
- Security and accurate accounting.
- More expeditious movement of mail through post office.
- Ease in stamping parcel-post packages.
- Added prestige of metered mail.
- Advertising benefit through use of imprinted slogan.

Folding and Inserting Machines   It takes a capable secretary at least an hour to hand-fold and insert a single enclosure in 500 envelopes. A folding and inserting machine can do the job in about 10 minutes. These versatile machines insert bills, letters, notices, flyers, leaflets, booklets, statements, price lists, bulletins, tabulating cards, reply envelopes—practically anything, in fact—into regular or window envelopes.

Collators The three basic types of collators are manual, semiautomatic, and automatic. Collators are available in desk-top models or floor models, with capacities from 4 to over 100 stations (pockets, hoppers, or bins). A manual collator, which is relatively inexpensive, consists of rows of trays or racks. You do the actual gathering and collecting. Semiautomatic collators push the sheets out of the stations, but you still must gather them by hand. Automatic models assemble sets of papers completely automatically. They need only to be fed and unloaded.

Shipping Services

A secretary is sometimes responsible for making arrangements for shipping articles by other than postal services. Although you would probably not be expected to be familiar with all the details that differentiate one shipping service from another, you should know what services are available and where to turn for more information. Articles may be sent either by express or by freight.

Arranging for Parcel Delivery In some metropolitan areas, private companies offer delivery service for packages—and letters, too—for a fee. These firms may be located through the Yellow Pages of the telephone directory.

Other companies, such as United Parcel Service, operate a delivery service throughout a number of states and connect with other delivery services to provide a nationwide system. Rates are determined by weight and distance. Check with the delivery service for restrictions as well as services available.

Mailing Lists

Mailing lists are the lifeblood of many companies, particularly those that do direct-mail selling or mail out catalogs or any other type of periodic mailing. A resourceful secretary may have occasion to take the initiative in maintaining a mailing list.

Maintaining a Mailing List **On Cards.** The conventional 5- by 3-inch index cards provide a convenient and flexible way to type names and addresses and to file them. A mailing list on cards is easy to separate and sort as desired. Different colored cards can be used to key various sections of the list.

On Sheets. Standard 8½- by 11-inch sheets are satisfactory for a list that is used infrequently. A disadvantage of a sheet list is that corrections are difficult to insert. Also, many additions and deletions soon make the list unreadable.

On Labels. Lists can be typed on perforated sheets of address labels; carbon copies may be made at the same time.

Lists can also be typed on master sheets from which duplicates can be made with various photocopy machines. The names and addresses are reproduced on sheets of pressure-sensitive labels that are then transferred one by one. To make a correction on the master sheet, type a new label and paste it over the old address.

By Automatic Addressing Systems.   Addressing machines are capable of great speed and can select certain names from a list, according to a predetermined keying system. The initial expense and upkeep of such systems are justified only when the list is used frequently for mailings.

Keeping a Mailing List Current

The increased mobility of people today makes it more important than ever to keep a mailing list up-to-date. Doing so may be a weekly or monthly chore.

To "clean" a mailing list you must delete old names, add new ones, and enter all changes of address. One method of removing the deadwood in a list is to write (using a double postal card) to all the people on the list, asking if they wish to continue to receive your mailings and whether they can suggest others who might wish to do so. The wording of the questions on the card should be carefully considered so as to make it easy for the person to respond. For example, you might want to say, "If you wish to continue to receive our mailings, please check the box at the left. If your address is not correct as shown on the reverse of this card, please write your current address below."

When pieces are returned from a mailing as undeliverable, they should be checked against the list and changes or deletions made as needed. If directories of names in your company's line of business are published periodically, use these to check your list.

Another way to keep your mailing list current is to submit it, for a fee, to the post office for correction. To do this, you must type each name and address on a card the size of a postal card with your company's name and address in the upper left corner. Where possible, new addresses will be furnished and names will be crossed off if mail cannot be delivered or forwarded.

Postal Considerations

When planning a mailing, always consult the current postal regulations regarding mailing rates, classes of mail, and envelopes.

If the budget permits, a mailing can be sent at the first-class rate, but normally, third class is used for printed matter such as circulars and catalogs. For many third-class mailings, a bulk rate is used to mail separately addressed pieces in quantities of not less than 50 pounds or of not less than 200 pieces. All pieces mailed under the bulk rate must be identical in size, weight, and number of enclosures. They must have the correct ZIP Codes and be presorted in accordance with bulk-mailing ZIP Code requirements.

Reviewing Your Reading

1. What three things about a letter should you check before you fold and insert it in an envelope?

2. How should enclosures be folded when they accompany a letter? How should you send an enclosure larger than a letter?

3. Why should you verify that the envelope address and the letter address agree?

4. Explain how to handle an enclosure instruction that calls for your file copy or the original.

5. Describe three work-simplification procedures that can be applied to the manual processing of mail.

6. After you have stamped the envelopes, what questions should you ask yourself?

7. Name several procedures you can adopt in order to get maximum value out of each piece of outgoing mail.

8. Describe four ways of marking mail properly so that it receives prompt handling in the post office.

9. Give four examples of the kind of matter that is classifiable as first-class mail.

10. What does fourth-class mail, or parcel post, include? On what are charges based?

11. What are the seven special services the post office provides (for additional fees) to speed up or ensure the safe delivery of mail?

12. For what class of mail is registering available? What comparable service is available for what other classes of mail?

13. Indicate several ways in which a mailing list can be kept current.

Using Your Skills

1. **Effecting Economies in Mail Handling.** Because your employer is concerned about utilizing mail services efficiently, you have been asked to provide specific examples of each of the principles for mail handling discussed on pages 123–125. You have also been asked to suggest similar principles worth considering. Decide what type of business your employer has; then type your examples and your suggestions.

2. **Checklist for Assembling Outgoing Mail.** Prepare a checklist of questions that you might ask yourself to make sure you have exercised proper care and judgment in assembling outgoing mail. Type your final list in acceptable form.

3. **Preparing a Mailing List.** Arrange the following addresses alphabetically by states. In each state group, arrange items alphabetically by cities, and in each city, alphabetically by firms. If two or more persons are listed for the same firm, alphabetize according to individual names. Then type a list, two columns to the page, single-spaced, with a double space between each address. Use the two-letter state abbreviations and open punctuation. Proofread your list with someone else in the class.

Miss Alice C. Frey
Acme, Incorporated
Winston-Salem, North Carolina 27106

Three Best Grocers
Grand Island, Nebraska 68801

Mr. C. Handley Barton
Barlow, Barton & Barnes
Athens, Ohio 45701

Barstow-Burdett Company
715 Arthur Avenue
Oakland, California 94615

Rural Hills Center 1
R.F.D. 1
Bismarck, North Dakota 58501

Mrs. L. R. Harris, President
Harris & Green
Fond du Lac, Wisconsin 54935

Curtis Dayton & Sons
Camden, New Jersey 08100

Five-Mile Lodge
R.F.D. 2
Denver, Colorado 80210

Mr. H. Donald Towle
J. C. Tomkins & Company
Park Highway
Hartford, Connecticut 06103

Mr. G. R. Williams
Carr Chemical Company
Claremore, Oklahoma 74017

Mrs. June Hays
C. W. Lyons, Inc.
Bemidji, Minnesota 56601

Mr. E. H. Raymond
Ball-Delton Company
Zanesville, Ohio 43701

Mr. L. Larry Dryden
Brewster, Bennett & Burns, Inc.
West Liberty, West Virginia 26074

Johnson & Johnson, Inc.
Rhinelander, Wisconsin 54501

General Community Store
Choteau, Montana 59422

Pioneer Chemical Company
Pierre, South Dakota 57502

Miss C. R. Parks
Endicott & Jones Company
Altoona, Pennsylvania 16601

Mr. George G. Coxwell
Barrett & Company
Asbury Lane
Lowell, Massachusetts 01850

Adams Company
Las Vegas, Nevada 89100

Kansas City Mills
Kansas City, Kansas 66110

Miss Naomi M. McKenzie
Standard Products Company
17–42 Raleigh Avenue
Biloxi, Mississippi 39530

Parkeville & Dalton, Inc.
Kansas City, Missouri 64105

Mr. J. C. Tomkins, President
J. C. Tomkins & Company
Park Highway
Hartford, Connecticut 06103

Mr. George Bond
Bond & Company
72 Springfield Drive
Holyoke, Massachusetts 01040

4. Labeling Outgoing Mail. The items below must be mailed today, Friday. On a sheet of paper indicate what class of mail should be used and what special service or markings are necessary. Your goal is to send the items with the best service and the least cost.
   a. Textbook.
   b. Magazine to be forwarded.
   c. Merchandise needed by next Friday (4 lbs.).
   d. Carbon copy of a letter.
   e. Mimeographed report.

f. Letter needed on Monday.

g. Diamond ring valued at $500.

h. Legal paper to be delivered only to Mr. Sam Davis.

EXERCISING YOUR JUDGMENT

Eager Beaver? Mary has been on her first job three months. One of ten people in the office, Mary was an excellent worker, having come well recommended by her former teacher. But Mary was cool and distant to the others and, consequently, soon earned their dislike. They resented her not joining them on coffee breaks and for lunch and her rushing back to work after lunch. Her production was noticeably higher than theirs, and they felt she was trying to show them up. As a result of their resentment and declining morale, their own production decreased and they were wasting even more time. The office manager began to realize that the staff members were acting as they were because they resented Mary, but she did not see how she could get them to change their attitude. Nor did she feel she could ask Mary to work less. Since she could not dismiss everyone, she decided to let Mary go on the basis of incompatibility. However, she told Mary she would give her an excellent recommendation to any prospective employer.

a. Can you account for Mary's attitude and her inability to be friendly with the other workers?

b. Should she have been dismissed?

c. What would you have done if you had been Mary? the office manager?

APPLYING THE REFERENCE SECTION

Word Division. Maintaining a fairly even right-hand margin in typewritten communications requires that a secretary know how to divide words correctly at the ends of lines. Accepted guidelines for hyphenating end-of-line words are reviewed in the Reference Section. See how well you can apply these guidelines in the items below:

1. Which syllable is the preferred point of division when these words come at the end of a line of typing? On a separate paper write just the syllable that will begin the next line.

a. crit-i-cize

b. time-wast-ing

c. pre-par-a-to-ry

d. val-u-able

e. sev-er-al

f. a-bout

g. a-bil-i-ty

h. by-prod-uct

i. an-a-lyze

j. sep-a-rate

2. For each of the words below that is divided incorrectly, type the correct form on your answer sheet.
   a. access-ible
   b. adviso-ry
   c. bul-letin
   d. nor-mal
   e. know-ledge
   f. a-lone
   g. solv-ing
   h. prod-uct
   i. fi-nal
   j. tech-nique
   k. particu-lar
   l. near-ly

3. Type the following words, dividing them as you would if you were nearing the end of a line of typing.
   a. planned
   b. necessary
   c. begin
   d. businesswoman
   e. amount
   f. convertible
   g. self-operated
   h. beneficial
   i. S. L. Harley
   j. Henry Thorpe

CHAPTER NINE / Filing Systems

No matter how simple or how complex an office filing system is, basically it is an orderly means of placing information where it can be found when needed. The measure of your filing know-how is often how promptly you can find a communication or a record when it is needed, but knowing what should be filed and what can be discarded is also important.

Function of Filing

The purpose of filing is the safekeeping of business papers, either originals or copies, in an orderly manner and a predetermined sequence until they are wanted.

To realize how vital is the filing function in any business one has only to consider the cost of filing malfunction. Time is money and it is wasted when a customer is kept waiting while a document is hunted for or an executive decision is delayed because essential information is buried somewhere in the files.

The filing cost for one letter is approximately 22 cents; the average 25-inch file drawer contains 4,000 items. Therefore, each file drawer represents an $880 expense. The estimated cost of a misfiled paper ranges from $60 to $80. It is evident that the filing investment must be justified; not only must materials contained in the files be easily retrievable, but they must also be worth retaining.

If the goal of filing is that a paper be found when needed, it follows that you must be a successful finder. Each item must be filed accurately and systematically.

To play your part in the filing activities of your company, you need to look at the whole picture of filing. You need to understand the nature of office records and the management of those records.

The worth of any filing system depends upon the ease and speed with which documents can be retrieved.

Peter Roth

Office Records

Ease of access to facts and figures on file is an essential ingredient in the profitable operation of any business. Its files are its memory, where the countless papers, documents, records, agreements, correspondence, pieces of information, and other data are kept so that they can be referred to frequently.

The content of the records of any particular business is largely determined by the nature of its operation. Common to almost all businesses, however, are correspondence, personnel records, financial reports, and other information required by managers as they carry out their responsibilities and come to grips with performance objectives. Budgets, progress reports, market analyses, and profit studies must be prepared periodically and retained for quick reference.

Other material that must be kept includes legal documents, such as contracts, whose provisions must be complied with. Special items include blueprints, punched cards, film and photographs, catalogs, clippings, tax data, microfiche, and computer printouts.

The paper explosion in office records in the last few years has many causes. The marked increase in regulatory laws and contracts has necessitated additional records, such as those for social security, workers' compensation, income tax, health, and employee retirement benefits. The rapid growth of computer technology and the corresponding enlargement of business operations by merger and by expansion into new domestic and international markets have introduced a new generation of forecasting techniques and investment strategies. Research and development programs have been introduced in practically every corporation. In most offices, the resultant increase in the processing and filing of data has severely strained existing recordkeeping facilities.

Records Management

As a company's operations expand and funds become available, its filing and retrieval activities may become mechanized or automated. In fact, the closer a business gets to the concept of a total information system, the closer it gets to the integration and centralization of its filing functions. For example, a company may use a computer (often on a time-sharing basis) as a means of storing, interrelating, and retrieving a mass of information with a speed and precision impossible through manual or semiautomatic processes.

Procedures for the creation, retention, and discarding of records vary from office to office. It has been estimated that fifteen hundred trillion pieces of paper are on file in our offices and storerooms. Each year the contents of 62 million file drawers are added to this total. Studies show that of the total, 35 percent could be destroyed today and not be missed. Another 20 percent is equally useless. Of the remaining papers 95 percent are useful for five years or less. About 50 percent of this bulk can be kept in low-cost storage rather than in high-cost office space. Only 1 percent must be kept permanently.

Controlling ever-growing paperwork requires management decisions on exactly what is to be kept, where, for how long, and when and how it is to be disposed of. Equally important is the implementing of such decisions by the appropriate office workers. One key person is the secretary, who conscientiously follows company guidelines in what is stored or is not stored in the employer's files and in the office, and what system is used to file what is kept.

A two-way control is urgently needed. First, measures must be taken to stop the production and retention of useless papers. This is filing management. Second, specific procedures must be formulated to identify the most efficient and economical ways to file and make accessible those papers that are found to be useful. This is filing operation.

Basic Filing Systems

Although there are many combinations of classification systems, filing hardware, and filing methods, for practical purposes there are four basic filing methods: alphabetic (by name), geographic (by location), subject, and numeric. Strictly speaking, alphabetic filing is used for names, subjects, or locations. Traditional usage, however, restricts the term *alphabetic* to name files. Geographic and subject files are referred to as such. Although items and folders in a numeric system are arranged numerically, a cross-index, often called a related index, must be used to indicate what the numbers stand for. The related index is alphabetic.

Alphabetic Filing Classifying material according to name and filing it alphabetically is a simple and quick way to store certain types of business records, especially correspondence. Because of its simplicity compared with other methods, alphabetic filing is recommended for all files where it can possibly be used. Sometimes filing systems are overly complicated when a plain alphabetic file, perhaps with a few subject folders added, would serve the purpose.

Indexing Procedures. Indexing is the mental process of selecting the name or word under which a paper is to be filed and the priority or sequence in which the units within that name are to be considered.

Since there are problems in alphabetizing names that do not occur in alphabetizing dictionary words, rules have been developed for alphabetic name files. The rules are not standardized, so those a secretary or an office adopts should be followed as consistently as possible. However, the rules that follow are widely accepted. A general guide to follow when in doubt is the telephone directory.

Rule 1. Alphabetic order is determined by comparing the first unit in each name, letter by letter. The second unit is considered only when first units are identical; third units, when both the first and second are identical. If two names are identical, consider addresses (see Rule 18).

Name	Unit 1	Unit 2	Unit 3
Manning	Manning		
Nelson	Nelson		
Newport Books	Newport	Books	
Newport Chemical	Newport	Chemical	
Rath Insurance Company	Rath	Insurance	Company
Rath Insurance Corp.	Rath	Insurance	Corp.

Rule 2. A name consisting of a single letter or word follows the rule "Nothing comes before something." For example, a name consisting of a single letter precedes a name consisting of a word, a one-word name precedes a name that consists of the same word plus one or more other words, and so on.

Name	Unit 1	Unit 2	Unit 3
B	B		
Barden	Barden		
Barden Printing	Barden	Printing	
Barden Printing Company	Barden	Printing	Company

Rule 3. Names of individuals are transposed and alphabetized with the surname or last name first, the given or first name second, and the middle name or initial, if any, third. Each part of the name is treated as a separate unit.

Name	Unit 1	Unit 2	Unit 3
Nelson	Nelson		
C. Nelson	Nelson	C.	
C. Harry Nelson	Nelson	C.	Harry
Charles Nelson	Nelson	Charles	
Charles H. Nelson	Nelson	Charles	H.

Rule 4. A surname prefix is not a separate indexing unit. It is considered part of the surname. Ignore any variations in spacing, punctuation, or capitalization in names with prefixes such as *d', D', Da, de, De, Del, Des, Di, Du, Fitz, La, Le, M', Mac, Mc, O', St., Van, Van der, Von, Von der,* and others. The prefixes *Mac, M',* and *Mc* are indexed exactly as they are spelled. The prefix *St.* is indexed and filed as though fully spelled as *Saint.*

Name	Unit 1	Unit 2	Unit 3
Victor J. D'Ercole	D'Ercole	Victor	J.
Robert H. DeRiemer	DeRiemer	Robert	H.
David C. MacCarthy	MacCarthy	David	C.
Richard R. McCarthy	McCarthy	Richard	R.
Robert E. Ober	Ober	Robert	E.
Frederick O'Brien	O'Brien	Frederick	
Mildred St. Paul	Saint Paul	Mildred	
Earl von der Haus	von der Haus	Earl	
Richard Von der Haus	Von der Haus	Richard	

Rule 5. If any part of an individual's name contains a hyphen, ignore the hyphen and consider the hyphenated part as one indexing unit.

Name	Unit 1	Unit 2	Unit 3
J. H. Scott-Paine	Scott-Paine	J.	H.
Earl Scottsfield	Scottsfield	Earl	
Betty Sim-Ron	Sim-Ron	Betty	
Ethel Simron	Simron	Ethel	
Jerry Sims	Sims	Jerry	
Betty Ann Smith	Smith	Betty	Ann
Betty-Ann Smith	Smith	Betty-Ann	
Betty Smythe	Smythe	Betty	

Rule 6. If a title is used with only one part of an individual's name, consider the title as the first unit.

Ignore a title when it is used with an individual's last name plus one or more other parts of the individual's name. However, consider the title *Mrs.* as an indexing unit if a woman uses her husband's name and you do not know her first name; treat *Mrs.* as it is spelled.

Name	Unit 1	Unit 2	Unit 3
Prince Edward	Prince	Edward	
Frank F. Prince	Prince	Frank	F.
Dr. Larry Richards	Richards	Larry	
Mrs. Larry Richards (whose own first name is not known)	Richards	Larry	Mrs.
Mrs. Hank Townsend (Betty)	Townsend	Betty	
Mr. Hank Townsend	Townsend	Hank	

Rule 7. Professional titles and degrees (such as *CPA*, *Ed.D.*, *M.D.*, and *Ph.D.*) and seniority terms (such as *Sr.*, *Jr.*, and *III*) or any other designation following a name are ignored.

If two names are considered identical, they are arranged according to address (see Rule 18).

Name	Unit 1	Unit 2	Unit 3	Unit 4
Earl Chambers, CPA	Chambers	Earl		
Henry Chambers, Ph.D.	Chambers	Henry		
Dr. Mary Chambers	Chambers	Mary		
Mrs. Susan Checkers	Checkers	Susan		
Ray C. Clark III (Chicago)	Clark	Ray	C.	Chicago
Ray C. Clark III (Detroit)	Clark	Ray	C.	Detroit

Rule 8. Consider any abbreviated part of a name (such as *Robt.* for *Robert*) as if it were written in full. Consider a name such as *Kate* for *Katherine* only if it is the true name or if the true name is not known.

Name	Unit 1	Unit 2	Unit 3
Al (Alfred) Smith	Smith	Alfred	
Wm. B. Smith	Smith	William	B.
William C. Smith	Smith	William	C.
Ed Towers	Towers	Ed	
Edwin Towers	Towers	Edwin	
Jas. Towers	Towers	James	
Kate Towers	Towers	Kate	
Katherine (Kate) Towers	Towers	Katherine	

Rule 9.   In names of business firms, treat each word as a separate unit and index the units in the same order as they are written. However, when the name of the firm includes the complete name of an individual (that is, the surname plus one or more parts of that person's other names) transpose the individual's name according to Rule 3 and maintain the indexing order of the other units.

Name	Unit 1	Unit 2	Unit 3	Unit 4
Chappell Answering Service	Chappell	Answering	Service	
C. Chappell Foods	Chappell	C.	Foods	
Chas. Chappell Catering Service	Chappell	Charles	Catering	Service
Chappell Cleaners	Chappell	Cleaners		
Chappell Television Repairs Company	Chappell	Television	Repairs	Company

Note that a title in a firm name is considered a separate unit. Treat abbreviated titles as though they were written in full, except for *Mr., Mrs.,* and *Ms.*

Name	Unit 1	Unit 2	Unit 3	Unit 4
Captain Ray Shop	Captain	Ray	Shop	
Dr. Scholl Shoes	Doctor	Scholl	Shoes	
Mr. J Formal Wear	Mr.	J	Formal	Wear
Ms. Francine Dress Shop	Ms.	Francine	Dress	Shop

Rule 10. Articles, conjunctions, and prepositions (such as *a*, *an*, *and*, *for*, *in*, *of*, or *the*) are ignored in indexing the name of a business firm unless they are a distinctive part of the name. In the examples below, note that the article *the* is not an indexing unit.

Name	Unit 1	Unit 2	Unit 3
Cafe in the Round	Cafe	Round	
For Fun Bowling	For	Fun	Bowling
Jack in the Box Togs	Jack	Box	Togs
Joseph the Hairdresser	Joseph	Hairdresser	
The Modern Shop	Modern	Shop	
Under Six Shop	Under	Six	Shop

Rule 11. Abbreviations appearing in a firm name are indexed as though the word were written in full.

Name	Unit 1	Unit 2	Unit 3	Unit 4
Natl. Food Carrier Co.	National	Food	Carrier	Company
National Mfg. Company	National	Manufacturing	Company	
Nissely & Beamer, Inc.	Nissely	Beamer	Incorporated	
Northcutt Bros. Importers, Ltd.	Northcutt	Brothers	Importers	Limited

Rule 12. Single letters that are not abbreviations are considered as separate units, whether separated by spaces or not. Note, however, that hyphenated single letters are treated as one unit (see Rule 13).

Name	Unit 1	Unit 2	Unit 3	Unit 4
B & W Canning Corp.	B	W	Canning	Corporation
BWT Farms	B	W	T	Farms
B-W Bakery	B-W	Bakery		
N W Pottery Shop	N	W	Pottery	Shop
WKLX Radio	W	K	L	X

Rule 13. Hyphenated names in a company's (as in an individual's) name are indexed as one unit.

Name	Unit 1	Unit 2	Unit 3
J. H. Scott-Paine	Scott-Paine	J.	H.
Scott-Paine Marine-Corp.	Scott-Paine	Marine	Corp.
Max Scott-Paine Co.	Scott-Paine	Max	Company

Rule 14. One- or two-word names that may be spelled as either one or two words or with a hyphen should be indexed as one unit.

Name	Unit 1	Unit 2	Unit 3
Mid-Way Restaurants	Mid-Way	Restaurants	
Midway Ski Club	Midway	Ski	Club
National Air Lines	National	Air Lines	
Northwest Airlines	Northwest	Airlines	
North West Mills	North West	Mills	

Rule 15. In words with possessives and contractions, ignore the apostrophe and consider all letters as part of the indexing unit.

Name	Unit 1	Unit 2	Unit 3
Can't Lose Shop	Can't	Lose	Shop
John Cantrell	Cantrell	John	
Perrys' Delivery	Perrys'	Delivery	
Perry's Fur Storage	Perry's	Fur	Storage

Rule 16. Numbers in the name of a business firm are considered as though written in words and are indexed as *one* unit. Express the number in as few words as possible; for example, *1,823* should be indexed as *eighteen hundred twenty-three* and not as *one thousand eight hundred twenty-three*.

Name	Unit 1	Unit 2	Unit 3	Unit 4
The Six Camels	Six	Camels		
610 Novelty Shop	Six hundred ten	Novelty	Shop	
16th Street Grocers	Sixteenth	Street	Grocers	
6300 Club	Sixty-three hundred	Club		
Tom's 84th Street Cafe	Tom's	Eighty-fourth	Street	Cafe

Rule 17. Treat each part of a geographic name as a separate indexing unit. Note, however, that hyphenated parts of a geographic name are treated as one unit. Variations of *Saint* (*San*, *Santa*) are considered as spelled.

Name	Unit 1	Unit 2	Unit 3	Unit 4
Des Moines Engineering Works	Des	Moines	Engineering	Works
New England Millwork	New	England	Millwork	
North American Vans	North	American	Vans	
San Francisco Steel	San	Francisco	Steel	
Santa Barbara Mills	Santa	Barbara	Mills	
Wilkes-Barre Mills	Wilkes-Barre	Mills		

Rule 18. Addresses are considered as indexing units only when the same name appears. Consider the parts of the address for indexing in this order: city or town, state, street name, and then direction (if it is part of the address—*North*, *South*, *Northwest*, *Southwest*). If all these units are identical, consider the house or building numbers by arranging them in numeric order from lowest to highest.

Name	Unit 1	Unit 2	Unit 3	Unit 4	Unit 5
Gerber Bros. 5 Inwood Drive Dover, DE	Gerber	Brothers	Dover	Delaware	Inwood
Gerber Bros. Jackson Street Dover, DE	Gerber	Brothers	Dover	Delaware	Jackson
Gerber Bros. 18 West Jackson St. Dover, DE	Gerber	Brothers	Dover	Delaware	Jackson West
Gerber Bros. Lincoln, NE	Gerber	Brothers	Lincoln	Nebraska	
Gerber Bros. Lincoln, NC	Gerber	Brothers	Lincoln	North	Carolina
Gerber Bros. Lincoln, ND	Gerber	Brothers	Lincoln	North	Dakota

Rule 19. Index each part of the name of a bank or other financial institution in the same order as it is written.

Name	Unit 1	Unit 2	Unit 3	Unit 4
Bank of Lexington (KY)	Bank	Lexington	Kentucky	
Bank of Lexington (VA)	Bank	Lexington	Virginia	
First Security Bank of Lexington	First	Security	Bank	Lexington
Lexington Bank and Trust Company	Lexington	Bank	Trust	Company
Lexington Finance Co.	Lexington	Finance	Company	

Rule 20.   Index the name of a hotel or a motel in the same order in which it is written. However, if the word *Hotel* or *Motel* appears at the beginning of the name, consider the distinctive parts of the name first.

Name	Unit 1	Unit 2	Unit 3
Motel Shady Lane	Shady	Lane	Motel
Sunset Motel	Sunset	Motel	
Hotel Wilson	Wilson	Hotel	
Wilson House Hotel	Wilson	House	Hotel

Rule 21.   The name of a hospital or a religious institution should be indexed in the same order as it is written.

Name	Unit 1	Unit 2	Unit 3	Unit 4
Good Samaritan Hospital	Good	Samaritan	Hospital	
Hospital of the Good Shepherd	Hospital	Good	Shepherd	
House of God Church	House	God	Church	
Houston Street Baptist Church	Houston	Street	Baptist	Church

Rule 22.   Names of universities, colleges, high schools, elementary schools, and libraries are indexed in the same order as written. If a word such as *University* or *College* appears at the beginning of the name, consider the distinctive parts of the name first. Transpose names of individuals as indicated in Rule 3.

Name	Unit 1	Unit 2	Unit 3	Unit 4
Hillcrest Baptist Elementary School	Hillcrest	Baptist	Elementary	School
High School of the Holy Rosary	Holy	Rosary	High	School
Houston Public Library	Houston	Public	Library	
University of Iowa	Iowa	University		
Julius Martin Elementary School	Martin	Julius	Elementary	School
College of St. Thomas	Saint	Thomas	College	

Rule 23. The first three indexing units for any name that pertains to the federal government are *United States Government*. Then consider the name of the department, and finally the name of the bureau, division, commission, board, or other subdivision. Words such as *department, bureau, division, commission, office,* and *board* are used in indexing and follow the distinctive name of the department, bureau, or board.

Remember, for the following examples, the first three units are *United States Government*.

Name	Unit 4	Unit 5	Unit 6	Unit 7	Unit 8
U.S. Department of Justice	Justice	Depart- ment			
U.S. Labor Department, Bureau of Labor Statistics	Labor	Depart- ment	Labor	Statistics	Bureau
U.S. Treasury Department, Internal Revenue Service	Treasury	Depart- ment	Internal	Revenue	Service

Rule 24. Other political subdivision names are indexed under the name of the political division followed by the classification, such as *state, county,* or *city* (the classification is considered even when it does not appear in the name as written), and then subdivided by the title of the department, bureau, division, commission, or board.

Name	Unit 1	Unit 2	Unit 3	Unit 4	Unit 5
Health Department of the Town of Brookline	Brookline	Town	Health	Department	
Labor Department of the State of Michigan	Michigan	State	Labor	Department	
Traffic Department of Michigan City	Michigan	City	Traffic	Department	
Traffic Department of the City of St. Louis	Saint	Louis	City	Traffic	Department
Board of Education, City of Woodstock	Woodstock	City	Education	Board	
Board of Education, Woodstock County	Woodstock	County	Education	Board	
Probate Court of Worcester County	Worcester	County	Probate	Court	

Rule 25.   A name pertaining to a foreign government is indexed first under the distinctive name of the country and then by the classification *dominion*, *republic*, *kingdom*, or other designation. Then the name of the governmental department or other subdivision is considered. Note, however, that committees without governmental status are indexed as written.

Name	Unit 1	Unit 2	Unit 3	Unit 4
Dominion of Canada, Department of State	Canada	Dominion	State	Department
Ministry of Defense, Kingdom of Denmark	Denmark	Kingdom	Defense	Ministry
Committee for Economic Stability	Committee	Economic	Stability	

When to File Alphabetically.   The most common way to classify or organize papers in a systematic manner is alphabetically in the A–Z sequence. Refer to and file items by name whenever you can. If names are few, a subject or a chronological breakdown may become necessary and simplify retrieval. When some of the papers in a file cannot conveniently be associated with name headings, other filing systems must, of course, be considered.

Where subject filing seems necessary, correspondence is probably only a part of the material to be filed. In such instances an alphabetic name file may still be preferred with clearly identified subject folders interspersed. Make a separate folder for each subject.

Parts of an Alphabetic File.   In order to quickly retrieve materials from the file, the contents must be organized in logical sequence. There are three parts of the file that help in this organization: guides, miscellaneous folders, and individual folders.

Guides.   Guides are signaling devices installed in file drawers and other types of file containers that help you find and file papers quickly and easily.

Notations on the guide tabs may be either *open* or *closed*. The former indicate only the beginning letters of a particular alphabetic division; the latter indicate both the beginning and the end. For example, open notations for the first five guides might be: *A, Ah, Am, Ap,* and *Ar.* Closed notations for the same guides would be *Aa–Ag, Ah–Al, Am–Ao, Ap–Aq,* and *Ar–As*. Open notations are recommended, for they permit easy expansion of a system by the simple insertion of new guides as the system grows.

Miscellaneous Folders.   Labeled to correspond to each alphabetic guide in a filing system is a folder for miscellaneous items. The miscellaneous folder is usually the last one before the next primary guide. Papers filed in miscellaneous folders are arranged alphabetically. Papers with the same name are arranged by date, with the most recent on top. As soon as there are five or six papers for the same correspondent, an individual folder should be made up for them.

Individual Folders.   Individual folders usually come immediately after a primary guide so that when looking for an item, you reach first for the correct primary guide and, drawing it forward, run rapidly over the individual folder labels. If the name you want is not there, you proceed to the miscellaneous folder, where the paper in question should be found. Letters in individual folders are arranged by date with the most recent at the front, since it is most likely to be needed.

For each correspondent with five or more papers in the file, make up a separate folder labeled with the name of the individual or company. The name placed on the folder is called a *caption*. Professional titles and degrees, seniority terms, and other designations following a name are ignored in indexing but must be included in the caption. They are enclosed in parentheses and placed at the end of a name. For example, the caption for *Peter F. Valdez Jr.* would read *Valdez, Peter F. (Jr.)*.

Articles, conjunctions, and prepositions, which are ignored in indexing, must also appear in the caption. These words should be placed in parentheses in the order in which they occur. However, if the word *The* appears at the beginning of a name, place it in parentheses at the end. For example, the caption for *The Restaurant in the Park* would read *Restaurant (in the) Park (The)*.

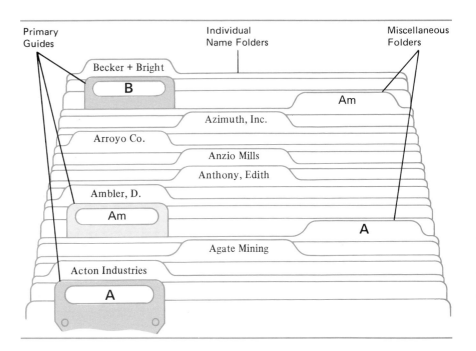

An alphabetic file. Note open notation on tab.

Subject Filing

Subject filing is used when it is more desirable to assemble information by topic than by name. Thus, all available information about a given subject is accumulated in one folder. For this reason, a manager may prefer subject filing for budgets, forecasts, statements of income, performance goals, and monthly sales reports.

Certain records, such as files of clippings, do not lend themselves to name filing. They are better filed under subject headings. Secretaries are often responsible for subject filing. Some file without understanding the criteria for a good subject file or without appreciating the complexities inherent in maintaining a subject system. In such instances, filing and finding depend heavily on memory.

Subjects should be chosen according to the specific needs of an executive and the nature of the business. Titles (subjects or key words), especially those used for primary guides, should be brief—rarely more than three words. When the scope of a subject is broad, it should be broken into smaller divisions on secondary guides.

A subject filing system is one of the most difficult to plan and maintain. Choosing key words under which to file and centrally accumulate related documents can be quite difficult. Success in initiating a subject file requires extensive study of and practical experience in an organization's activities, operational policies, and objectives. There are no miscellaneous folders in subject files.

Fundamental Principles. For a subject file where a variety of related documents may be called for under one key word, it is helpful to keep a comprehensive list of subjects in a notebook or a card index. When cards are used, the name of a correspondent may be typed on a card with all subjects under which that correspondence is filed listed beneath.

Since indexing items for a subject file frequently involves a choice of topics (for example, a quotation on typewriter ribbons might be indexed under *Typewriters*, *Office Machines*, *Supplies*, or *Ribbons*), a secretary should not incorporate or change headings in an established subject file without consulting the executive. Since few people think alike about any one subject or item, conflicting points of view about a subject may cause problems.

One problem when filing by subject is thinking of an item by one topic when filing but by another topic when finding. To lessen this problem, cross-reference carefully and keep a complete list of subjects in a convenient form so that everyone connected with the file has access to it. Following is a sample of a subject classification, in outline form on standard 8½-by-11-inch sheets inserted in a binder. The format permits the insertion of headings in proper alphabetic sequence, with cross-references following them, in parentheses.

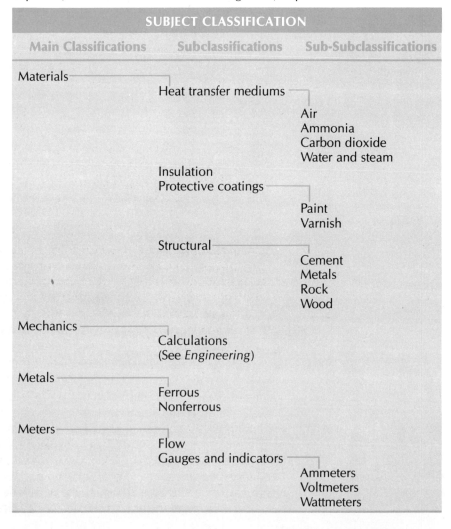

SUBJECT CLASSIFICATION		
Main Classifications	**Subclassifications**	**Sub-Subclassifications**
Materials		
	Heat transfer mediums	
		Air
		Ammonia
		Carbon dioxide
		Water and steam
	Insulation	
	Protective coatings	
		Paint
		Varnish
	Structural	
		Cement
		Metals
		Rock
		Wood
Mechanics		
	Calculations	
	(See *Engineering*)	
Metals		
	Ferrous	
	Nonferrous	
Meters		
	Flow	
	Gauges and indicators	
		Ammeters
		Voltmeters
		Wattmeters

Subject-Dictionary.   The simplest subject file consists of a set of alphabetic guides with key words written on tab folders that are arranged alphabetically behind the guides. Coding is accomplished by writing the subject in an upper corner of each paper, or by encircling it when it has already appeared in the body of the document. Read each paper carefully to determine the proper subject for filing or for cross-referencing.

Subject-Classified.   Some subject files are particularly valuable to an executive because they bring related subjects together under a central title rather than scattering them alphabetically as in the subject-dictionary method. This type of subject filing is sometimes referred to as encyclopedic subject filing. For example, the following encyclopedic-subject system provides a folder for each key topic yet, at the same time, keeps together folders related to one project:

> *Project Intercom*
>   Art
>   Design
>   Manufacturing
>   Cost estimates
>   Invoices
>   Marketing
>   Market analysis
>   Market plan
>   Promotion

Subject-Duplex.   The subject-duplex is a numeric system in which subjects are further identified by numbers. Main headings are numbered in sequence; subdivisions are designated by auxiliary numbers or letters or both: 1.1, 1.1a, 1.2, 1.2a. For example, when we apply the subject-duplex system to the illustration above, if *Project Intercom* is 15, then *Cost estimates* would be 15.3a or 15.c1.

For a rapidly growing file with numerous subdivisions, this system has advantages over the subject-dictionary system. Numbers on frequently used folders are easy to memorize and faster for the eye to scan than subject subdivisions. There is also less danger of misfiling a folder since a number out of place shows up readily. Coding and cross-referencing a subject-duplex system are similar to the way a straight alphabetic file is done except that numeric as well as alphabetic references should be used. In finding, the index for a subject-duplex system must be consulted unless the number has been memorized or has special significance.

Subject-Decimal.   The decimal system is an adaptation of the subject-duplex system. Neither the number of main divisions nor the number of subdivisions under any heading may exceed nine. The first step in developing such a system is to divide everything into nine general categories, then subdivide each category into nine subdivisions, and so on. For example, in the list of subjects just presented, if *Project Intercom* were assigned 400, *Art* would be 410, *Invoices* 432, and *Promotion* 443.

An alphabetic card file by subject or name is also essential in a subject-decimal system. Such a related index facilitates cross-reference, control, and finding an item called for by name. The subject-decimal system can become quite complicated and should not be attempted until a completely formulated plan based on a thorough study of the filing problem has been developed.

Geographic Filing

Geographic filing is used when *location* is an important factor in using and controlling records. Direct mail advertisers, for instance, find it useful to organize customer records by state and city. Sales offices frequently arrange files by sales territories or regions.

Arrangement.   A geographic system classifies papers by location, first by state, county, city, or town and then by company and individual name, or by subject. In such a system, state names appear on primary guides and city or town names on secondary guides. Prepare a folder with appropriate labels for each primary and secondary guide. These serve as miscellaneous folders in which items for low-volume correspondents may be accumulated alphabetically by state and city. Individual name folders, when used in a geographic system, are arranged alphabetically by names of correspondents in their appropriate geographic sections.

Operation.   Coding for a geographic system is handled similarly to coding for other systems. Each document is marked to show the captions under which it will be filed. The name of a correspondent is usually underlined, and the location under which the record is to be filed is circled. Some documents may need to be cross-referenced between individual names and geographic locations. Such items may also need to be cross-referenced in a relative card index so that papers may be found when called for by name and not location. The relative index can be an alphabetic list of names and addresses, which might then also be used as a mailing list.

Material in individual folders is filed chronologically with the most recent in front. When there is no individual folder for an item, file it alphabetically by name in the miscellaneous folder for the appropriate city or state until enough material has accumulated for an individual folder.

Other Geographic Arrangements.   There are many variations of geographic filing. Instead of filing by state, city, and individual name, for example, some offices file by county or region. In other instances states are disregarded and sales territories are used as primary divisions. When correspondents are located primarily in large cities, the primary guide may be city, then state and individual name.

Numeric Filing

Numeric filing systems use numbers as captions on both guide and folder tabs. They are useful when records already bear identifying numbers; for example, invoices, contracts, requisitions, licenses, certificates, vouchers, checks, and purchase orders.

Although numeric filing is a simple method for arranging records, it is not a complete system of filing in itself. A numeric filing system must always be backed by an alphabetic index that refers the user to the numbers. Thus, if a manager asked for the letter in which Mr. Rollins explained why he canceled his order, you would first consult the relative alphabetic index to find the number that was assigned to the Rollins file. For this reason, numeric filing is impractical for correspondence files. On the other hand, a numeric system is useful for filing confidential information, such as medical or legal cases, so that unauthorized persons cannot find a file as readily as when an alphabetic name system is used. Since there is less chance of error in filing numbers than names, a numeric system is sometimes preferred for operations that require a high degree of accuracy. Then too, numeric files are easy to expand. They are easy to check for missing numbers, thus automatically providing a system for inventory auditing and accounting control.

In large companies with computer centers, some alphabetic files are being converted to numeric systems because computers handle numeric data faster than alphabetic characters. For this reason, a secretary working with computerized records may be asked to file them in a numeric system.

Numeric Files.   In a numeric file, each topic or correspondent is assigned a number. Usually the tab of an individual's folder carries the name as well as the number assigned to it. Guide tabs are marked with numbers only. Numbered guides and folders are arranged in ascending order from 1 on. Within folders, papers are arranged chronologically, with the latest on top. When subjects as well as names are used, a complete list of them should be made so that it can be referenced when coding—or even when finding.

Numeric coding involves three steps when the number cannot be derived from the item to be filed: select the name or word under which the paper is to be filed; search the related, alphabetic card index for the number; write the number on the paper.

When the numbers for items filed in numeric systems are not printed on them or when the numbers cannot be derived as part of a known code, an index is an indispensable part of such a system. Here again, 5- by 3-inch index cards are probably most suitable because they are easy to arrange and to update. Also, odd bits of related information can be accumulated on them in addition to names, addresses, cross-references, or whether an item is in a miscellaneous folder, although numeric filing systems rarely include miscellaneous folders.

An advantage of numeric filing is easy cross-referencing. The index cards are used for cross-referencing, so that cross-reference sheets such as those used in alphabetic name correspondence files are not used. The method is simple. Merely make a card for each name under which a particular paper might be filed. The number on the card will lead you to the proper file. For example, if a company changed its name, the card for the new name would contain the file number as well as the old name.

Whatever the method used to assign numbers, it should be followed consistently. It may be handy to number a supply of index cards or folders ahead. As new items are added to the file, each is assigned the next number in order. A numeric list showing to whom or what each number was assigned may also be helpful. For example, it can be used to identify folders that may be missing from the files.

When items have not been added to or taken from a folder for a year or so, it can probably be declared inactive. It is not desirable to reassign inactive numbers.

Numeric Systems.   The way a numeric file functions depends considerably upon which numeric filing system is used: the *consecutive-number* system, the *serial-number* system, or the *terminal-digit* system. In the consecutive-number system, numbers are assigned in strict sequence (1, 2, 3, 4, 5, 6, on up). The most recent records have the highest numbers and are filed at the open end of the system. A weakness of this method is that, as the file matures, the main activity will be among the high-numbered items, since they deal with current transactions. Thus, problems of gaps in the numbering system and of uneven distribution of records delay filing and finding.

Terminal-digit filing copes with the distribution problem that usually occurs when files are put into a normal ascending sequence. In a terminal-digit system, the last unit of a number is referred to first. For example, 123456 would ordinarily be read from left to right. A folder so marked would be filed before 124456 and after 122456. In terminal-digit filing, the number is divided into units and reversed. For example, 123456 becomes 56-34-12. Items numbered 456, 3456, and 123456 would all be filed behind the same guide, and in that order, because all the numbers end with 56. The first pair of terminal digits is used on the primary guide, the next pair to the left on the secondary guide, and the last digits to the left on the final guide.

A terminal-digit file usually staggers the guides, as shown here. In the illustration, the cabinet number is the primary guide, the raised tabs are secondary guides, and the numbered papers in the file serve as final guides.

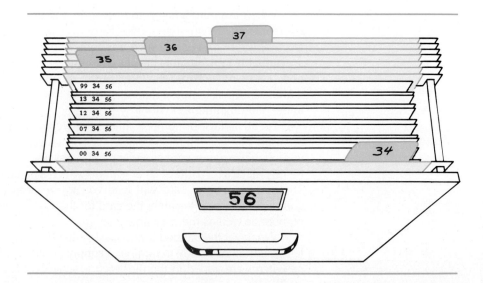

A terminal-digit file.

Chronological Filing

In every office many things have to be done at certain times. Each thing has its own due date. For example, salary reviews, performance evaluations, expense statements, sales reports, and schedule reviews must each be performed at a certain time. Since no one can depend entirely on memory to recall such due dates, a reminder system is necessary. Reminder systems are known variously as follow-up files, tickler files, suspense files, and pending files. Even though such systems may vary somewhat in operation, they are all essentially chronological files.

Calendar Pad Follow-Up
The simplest follow-up or reminder system is a desk calendar. Activities are merely recorded on appropriate date pages. Where numerous notations have to be made, however, a calendar pad may be too small. Moreover, a desk calendar pad is primarily an appointment book and to some extent personal so that it is not a satisfactory follow-up system, especially if several people use it.

Single-Folder Follow-Up
A follow-up system may be merely a single folder labeled *Follow-Up* and kept in a desk file drawer. Memorandums about all kinds of things—budget due dates, meetings, insurance, and reports are accumulated in it. The memorandums are arranged chronologically, with the earliest date in front. The folder should be checked every day. On Fridays it should be checked especially thoroughly for things that must be handled the following week so that related papers can be collected and other preparations may be made in plenty of time. In fact, it is a good practice when using this type of tickler system to check a month ahead now and then so as not to overlook anything.

Card Follow-Up
Some secretaries prefer to use a card follow-up system (5-by-3 or 6-by-4 cards) on which they note pertinent reminder information. They choose it because a card system can be expanded and handled easily. A set of monthly guides and one or more sets of daily guides in a card box make up the primary equipment. A desk tray or folder may also be needed to hold copies of essential papers referred to on the follow-up cards, since the system is for memorandums and does not include a self-contained folder for copies of related letters, forms, and other documents.

Folder Follow-Up
A more elaborate reminder system, one that does provide for accumulating related copies and documents, consists of twelve monthly folders and sets of daily folders, usually three, numbered from 1 to 31. A reminder for more than three months ahead is placed in the daily folder for that month. As the reminders for each current day are processed, the folder is moved back three months. For example, assume that today is April 12; after processing the reminders, put the folder marked *12* behind folder No. 11 behind the *July* folder. By the end of the month, all the daily folders used in April will have been moved behind July where they will accumulate July reminders. Only memorandums, extra carbon copies, and photocopies should be used in a follow-up system. Original papers belong in their regular files because they may be needed at any time.

Reviewing
Your
Reading

1. What are the two urgently needed controls to achieve effective records management?

2. Of the four basic filing systems (a) which can be based on names, on subjects, or on locations, and (b) which is an indirect method?

3. Explain what is meant by *indexing* and its relation to alphabetic order.

4. Explain and illustrate the indexing rule suggested by the statement "Nothing comes before something."

5. What are the three primary rules for indexing and filing firm names?

6. How would you index and file each of the following: abbreviations, conjunctions, titles or degrees, seniority designations, and numbers?

7. What is the correct procedure for indexing names of banks, universities, and hotels?

8. What is the correct indexing order for federal, state, and county names? foreign countries?

9. How are papers arranged in a *miscellaneous* folder in an alphabetic file?

10. In a subject file, how can you solve the problem of thinking of one topic when filing and any number of others when finding?

11. How would you arrange and code a geographic file?

12. What are the advantages of a numeric file?

13. What are the three steps in coding material for a numeric file?

14. What problem is likely to arise with consecutive-number filing, and how does terminal-digit filing avoid it?

Using
Your
Skills

Classification Aptitude. Accuracy in filing is essential. In the six exercises that follow, check your aptitude for finding errors, coding, comparing, alphabetic filing and listing, and geographic filing.

1. **Error Checking.** List the letters from *a* to *i* on a separate sheet of paper. Compare the two columns of figures and type correctly items where the check column number does not match the number in the guide column.

	Guide Column	Check Column
a.	424518	424158
b.	26987663	26987663
c.	39810214	39810214
d.	31280772	32180772
e.	89402145	89420145
f.	21793316	21793316
g.	33265948	33265948
h.	57020463	50720436
i.	19626835	19626835

2. **Coding.** Letter from *a* to *i* on a sheet of paper and put on it the figures and letters in each item below into correct sequence, starting with the lowest number or first letter and continuing to the subsequent ones. Letters should precede numbers. If a digit or letter is used more than once, repeat it. Alphabetic O's are underlined.

a.	942ACA53	**f.**	14XA224GT
b.	50617802	**g.**	54102498
c.	42004S<u>O</u>P	**h.**	6133R9S8
d.	SPA6221S	**i.**	84956323
e.	7N20M37A		

3. **Comparing.** Letter from *a* to *h* on a separate sheet of paper. Opposite each letter list the items in the check column that do not agree with those in the guide column.

Guide Column	Check Column
a. Paul Timberlaine	Paula Timberline
b. John Goetz, St. Claire, Mich.	John Hertz, St. Claire, Wisc.
c. Johathan C. Wilson, Marble Head, Mass.	Jonathan G. Wilson, Marble Head, Mass.
d. Ruby Stacey, 14 Hooker Road, Helena, Montana	Ruby Stacey, 14 Hooker Drive, Helena, Montana
e. Robert Ferdig, Birminghan, Alabama	Robert Frisby, Birmingham, Michigan
f. Martha Ann Baker, Grosse Ile, Michigan	Martha Anne Baker, Grosse Ile, Michigan
g. Genevieve R. Barkume, Lighthouse Pointe, Maine	Genevieve R. Barkume, Lighthouse Pointe, Maryland
h. Cel-u-los Products, Jackson, Tenn.	Cel-u-los Products, Jackson, Tenn

4. **Alphabetic Filing.** On a separate sheet of paper type the names in each item in alphabetic order. Underline the first indexing unit in each name.

Example: <u>Fielding</u>, Anna W.
 <u>Fielding</u>, Irving F.
 <u>Fien</u>, Frederick

a. James A. Farmer, Family Department Store, Russell Farncett.

b. M. H. Faupel, Robert C. Fashbaugh, N. R. Faupel Insurance Agency.

c. M. Burleson Fitz, Otis Fitzharris, Five Point Service.

d. Fingerle-Hollister-Wood Lumber Company, R. N. Fingerle, H. W. Fingerle.

e. Perry's Building Company, Perry's Garage, Elmer Perry.

f. Arthur Elvidge, Elvidge & Adams Heating Company, Mrs. Harry B. Emaus.

g. R. L. Evidge, Ernie's Ice Cream, The Ernest Insurance Agency.

h. The Mayflower Transit Company, A. V. Mayflower, P. McCollough.

i. The Kenneth Marsh Agency, Marsh & Son, Marsh Office Supply, Inc.

j. McPherson Oil Company, Robert E. McCleery, Herman Mayo.

5. **Alphabetic Listing.** Arrange the following names in alphabetic sequence. Type an alphabetic list with the first filing unit in all capitals.

Vera A. Wallace
Art Craft Doll Co.
United States Cutlery Co.
Artbook Imports
Ralph B. Vanderveer
Southall Bros.
Carpenter & Paula
Mack's Valetorium
Adam Dowds Co.
City Hall Hardware Co.
Thos. M. Mackintosh
John-Raider Associates
Ernest R. Foy
A. J. Howse Corp.
Sarah D. Walker
Artcraft Clothes
U.S. Bureau of Census
Cora L. Destefano
Peter Baier Inc.
Michel of Paris Inc.
Alfred V. Dowd
Walk-Over Shoe Co.
Law Dept., State of South Dakota
Pamela A. Michl
Paul G. Carpinter
401 Beauty Shop
Louis G. De Stasio
S. Alex Dowd
House of Beauty

6. **Geographic Filing.** On a separate sheet of paper arrange the following items alphabetically by state first, then by city or town, and finally by the name of the correspondent. Type the correctly arranged list on a plain sheet of paper, insert the correct two-letter abbreviation in parentheses immediately following the state's name, and add the appropriate ZIP Code for each item.

Leonard Saltzer Bros., Water Valley, Miss.
David I. George, Kings, Ill.
Helena M. Cain, Coyville, Kans.
Walter B. Upson, Portland, N.Y.
Ada T. Kaiser, Long Pond, Maine
Hay's Market, Akron, N. Dak.
Anne A. Porte, De Witt, Mich.
Frances L'Abbate Bros., Bluffs, Ill.
Warren E. Taylor, Rockaway, Mo.

V. James Forte, Sandford, Ind.
Carl Edelman & Co., North Liberty, Iowa
Charlotte E. MacAdam, Westfield, Mass.
Rudolph J. O'Neil, Dexter, Minn.
Adele Durant, Leonia, Idaho
Vincent U. Fortuna, Sandborn, Ind.
Kane & Sons, Courtland, Kans.
Emma J. Maccare, West Newton, Mass.
Emily I. MacCarthy, West Newton, Mass.
Maria S. Hayden, Albany, N. Dak.
Harriet L. Hoffmann, Glendale, Ill.
Lewis N. Woods, Plainfield, N.J.
Carrie G. Adelman, Northboro, Iowa
Upson-Walton Co., Pt. Leyden, N.Y.
Joseph N. Hays, Bell Farm, Ky.
Adelia C. Kaire, Longcove, Maine
Emile McCarthy Inc., West Newton, Mass.
Martha R. Hayes, Akron, N. Dak.
Lester W. Salzman, West, Miss.
Adeline Durante, Lenore, Idaho
Georgia Dairy, Kingston, Ill.
Helen O. Caine, Covert, Kans.
A. M. Speirs' Sons, Dallas, N.C.
John P. Hay, Bell City, La.
Anna B. Porter, Dexter, Mich.

Exercising Your Judgment

Overworked? Sally is one of several secretaries in a large office. She does her work accurately and enjoys it, but she cannot keep up with it. She is spending so much of her time on details that she never seems to have enough time for more important things. She comes to work early, takes a short lunch period, and stays every night.

Sally's predecessor did not seem to have so much difficulty. She completed her assignments easily during the normal workday by planning her work carefully and delegating nonconfidential tasks to others. As a good friend, how can you tell Sally what her trouble is without hurting her feelings or arousing her resentment? Should you try?

Applying the Reference Section

1. In some of the words below the italicized letter should be doubled. On a separate sheet of paper write the correctly spelled word. If the word is correct as it appears, write "C" on your paper.
   a. cliente*l*e
   b. a*s*essment
   c. plainti*f*
   d. proce*d*s
   e. reconci*l*e

2. Rewrite the following words, supplying the missing vowels (a, e, i, o, u):
  a. cl___nt
  b. interl___c___tory
  c. min___r
  d. cav___at empt___r
  e. a posteri___r___

3. Rewrite correctly on your paper any of the following words that are misspelled. If a word is correct, write "C."
  a. escheat
  b. deponant
  c. dependent
  d. brokerage
  e. colatteral

4. Write the plurals for these words:
  a. proxy
  b. security
  c. client
  d. lease
  e. alias

5. Rewrite correctly the following misspelled words:
  a. acommodate
  b. fullfill
  c. resistence
  d. embarass

CHAPTER TEN / Filing Operations

As a secretary, you are not likely to be responsible for the records management program of your employer, but you should be aware of that program so as to observe its requirements. To fulfill your daily filing responsibilities, you need to be familiar with the filing system you work with. Equally important, you must know how to find material once it is filed—and even when it may have been misfiled. If central files are maintained within the company, you need also to develop a pleasant working relationship with those who work in the files and to observe proper chargeout procedures. To store and retrieve inactive material, you must be familiar with your company's transfer and retention systems.

A secretary moving up the employment ladder may be consulted on the choice of filing equipment and, eventually, on the planning of a filing system. You will find suggestions at the end of this chapter.

Preparing Materials to Be Filed

The prompt and successful finding of already filed material depends partly on how accurately the material was prepared for filing. For that reason, using established filing procedures ensures quick retrieval of each item filed. There are five steps in preparing an item, especially correspondence, to be filed: inspecting, indexing, cross-referencing, coding, and sorting.

Inspecting   The first step in preparing an item for filing is to inspect it to make sure it has been released for filing. The release signal may be the initials of the person releasing it, a line drawn across the face of the item, the word *File*, or some other special mark. An item not marked for release should be returned to the person who handled it.

Indexing   Indexing is the determination of the name, subject, or other caption under which an item is to be filed. In selecting an indexing caption, determine the most likely heading under which the paper to be filed will be recalled and what the

A cross-reference sheet and a letter marked for cross-referencing.

important elements are by skimming each item. Your knowledge of the business, its objectives, its personnel, and its operational patterns will aid you when making indexing decisions. Your choice of an indexing caption will be one of several possibilities:

1. Name on the letterhead (incoming mail).
2. Name addressed (outgoing mail).
3. Name in the signature (incoming mail).
4. Name or subject included in the content of the paper (either incoming or outgoing).
5. Location (either incoming or outgoing).
6. File or contract number (either incoming or outgoing).

Cross-Referencing
When indexing it is often difficult to know which of two or more names is the more important. How is the paper most likely to be recalled? You can make sure it can be found regardless of how it is recalled by filing the original under one name and preparing cross-reference sheets under the others.

Printed forms may be used for cross-reference sheets, or plain sheets of colored paper. The important thing is to refer from one name to the other, as *Anson, Charles R.—See First Investors Corp.*

Consider using a cross-reference in the following situations:

1. When some word other than the first in a company or institution name clearly identifies the organization. For example, *University of Connecticut* would be filed as *Connecticut, University of*, and then cross-referenced as *University of Connecticut*.

2. When it is difficult to decide which part of an individual's name is the surname. In the case of *Daniel Herbert* you might index the name as normally written and use a cross-reference under a transposition of the name.

3. When an organization is better known by initials than by its complete name. File under the complete name and then cross-reference to the abbreviation. *Trans World Airlines, Inc.*, might be cross-referenced *TWA*.

4. When a paper is likely to be called for most often by subject. File under the subject caption but cross-reference to individual or company names.

Coding   Coding is the marking of an indexing caption on an item to be filed. With highlighted captions, items can be handled quickly and efficiently. Coding also helps one to replace papers recalled from the files. The indexing caption may be checked, circled, or underlined on the record being coded for an alphabetic system. When the name under which the record is to be filed does not appear on the record, it is written in the upper right corner.

Numeric coding involves three steps: selecting the name under which a paper is to be filed, referring to the card index to determine the number to be assigned, and marking the number in the upper margin of the paper.

Subject files are coded by writing the subject in the upper margin of each record, unless it already appears in a subject position. Each record is carefully examined in order to determine the most appropriate subject to be coded.

Sorting   Sorting is arranging items to be filed in alphabetic order according to the indexing captions. If sorting is done prior to taking the material to the file cabinets, much valuable time and energy can be saved. File drawers and folders need only be opened once, as the materials to be filed are in alphabetic sequence.

If many records are to be filed, special collating racks may be used to expedite the sorting process. When such equipment is unavailable, papers can be rough-sorted on a table or desk top according to the following routine:

1. When alphabetizing, sort items into convenient divisions such as A—D, E—H, I—L, M—R, and S—Z.

2. Sort each category again for more exact sequence.

3. Assemble all the material in proper sequence.

Placing Material in Files

The final step in manual filing is to place the papers in appropriate containers, usually file folders.

Regardless of size, papers are placed in folders with the top of the page to the left as you face a file. To insert material, lift the folder out of the file drawer in order to (1) make sure you have the correct folder, (2) insert the papers evenly, and (3) insure that material you are inserting is in correct sequence.

Avoid overcrowding a folder. Although standard folders have a capacity of 100 items, a maximum of 50 pieces in one folder usually gives greatest efficiency. Overcrowding extends records beyond the top edge of the folder, causing frayed edges; it also pulls the back of the folder down and hides the caption.

Folders have creases across the bottom of the front flap to accommodate increasing bulk. By creasing along these lines as the volume requires it, you can expand a manila folder to take a stack of papers as much as three-quarters of an inch high without bulging or buckling. When the scored capacity is reached, it is time to use a second folder.

Removing Attachments

Good housekeeping and simplified procedures are as important in filing as in other office operations. Paper clips, rubber bands, and other such attachments should be removed from papers before they are filed. Torn pages should be repaired with transparent tape.

Arranging Drawer Space

Provide enough working space in each file drawer of active records to permit easy access to the folders. It takes twice as much time and energy to insert papers into folders when drawers are jammed to capacity.

Guides and folders should not be pulled out of the files by their tabs. The tabs are not handles and will soon be worn out if so used.

When folders in a file drawer begin to sag, they may need to be replaced, or the "follow block," which supports folders and keeps them erect, may need to be adjusted. Proper positioning of the drawer compressor helps to keep folders upright in a drawer.

Filing Clippings

Clippings that need to be interfiled with related materials, such as correspondence, should be marked with the name of the publication and the date of the issue from which they were taken. Small clippings should be mounted on plain paper (preferably with rubber cement rather than transparent tape), but clippings larger than 8 by 10 inches may be filed loose and folded as needed to fit the folder.

Filing Bulky Material

Bulky material should be filed separately in appropriate storage lockers or on suitable shelves. Such material should be arranged by a classification system, either numeric or alphabetic. Items may need to be cross-referenced to related correspondence files. If not, they should be controlled by a card index. They should be neatly arranged, clearly marked, and kept clean and dusted.

Retrieving Material From Files

If papers have been properly prepared for filing and if they have been carefully placed in the correct file folders and in the right drawers, finding them when they are needed should be a simple matter. Removing papers from the files, however, requires leaving some record of their removal, especially if the files are used by many different people. Chargeout procedures should, therefore, be carefully followed.

Chargeout Procedures

A chargeout system tells you where a record can be located after it has been taken from the files. An elaborate chargeout system is not necessary unless you maintain a file for a number of individuals. If you must often conduct an office search to find records that should be in the files, you need a chargeout system.

Oxford Pendaflex Corporation

An out guide with a pocket to hold a copy of the borrower's requisition slip.

Two types of charge records are desirable: one to account for complete folders removed from a file, and the other to account for papers taken from a folder. Their function is the same: to ensure that the records that were removed will be returned. Both must provide the name of the borrower, a description of the material borrowed, and the date.

A folder chargeout may be either an *out folder* or an *out guide*. The out folder is a manila folder with a tab marked "Out" and ruled spaces on the front for recording chargeout information. It replaces a removed folder; incoming items are filed in it until the regular folder is returned. The out guide (pressboard) has a pocket into which a copy of the requisition slip made out by the borrower can be inserted. When out guides are used, incoming items are accumulated in a tray or special folder until the regular folder is returned.

A good way to control requests for files is to use a special form known as a requisition slip. Preparing the slip in triplicate saves time and controls returns. The original slip is put into the pocket of the out guide, the first copy goes into a follow-up file box where it is filed by date, and the second copy is clipped to the items that were taken from the files to identify them and to remind the user of the due date.

Searching for Misfiled Items

Filing errors are costly and frustrating. Their cost includes executive time lost while waiting for missing records as well as extra secretarial time spent searching for that needle in a haystack. The following clues help to uncover many misfiled papers.

On Someone's Desk? When tracking a misplaced record, look first through your own desk, then the executive's. Not there? Look through the material to be filed next.

The Folder Before or Behind the Right Folder?   Have you looked in the folder immediately ahead of or immediately behind the folder in which the paper belongs? This type of filing error is easy to make.

Between or Under Folders?   Look between the folders on either side of the folder in which the missing paper should be. Not there? Then look *under* the folders. Single papers and even folders have been known to slip gradually under the other folders when the guides are not attached by a rod.

Transposition of Names?   Some names, such as Francis James, are easily transposed. A letter to the Francis James Company may turn up in the *Francis* folder. Hyphenated or compounded names, such as the Jones-Smith Corp. or Allen, Wharton-Bickford, Inc., may produce this type of error.

Similar Names?   Look under similarly spelled names. There are many different ways to spell names like Baer and Snyder. All such variations are potential candidates for misfiled material. The Jones paper may be in a Joans, Johns, Joens, or even Janes or Janis folder.

Cross-References?   Look under the cross-references. Originals sometimes get filed with cross-reference sheets. Check previous correspondence for cross-reference clues. For example, the Francis James Company correspondence may mention a Maxwell and Kent subsidiary. Check under both Maxwell and Kent. Who usually signs letters from this company? Could the letter you are tracking have been filed under the name of the person who signed it?

Characteristics of the Filing System Used.   When the item you are tracking is out of a subject file, look under related subjects. If the filing system is numeric, look under transposed numbers. If the file began with 74, look under 47.

Paper Clips.   Paper clips have a way of picking up neighboring papers. This is one of the reasons secretaries are advised not to use paper clips in files. To locate a record that may have hitchhiked on a paper clip, start at the beginning of the file and look for paper clips.

Transfer and Retention Methods

Since records are being constantly added to files, they would increase beyond bounds if nothing were ever removed. Moreover, many papers are of limited usefulness and are not kept for very long.

In general, secretaries and executives file too much. Many nonessential items go into files because it is easier to file them than to decide to destroy them. As a result, all who use such files must flip through irrelevant material before they find what they need. One way to keep files free of nonessential items is to throw the items away before they get into the files. The executive who releases items for a file should be encouraged to throw away routine and easily replaceable items.

Bankers Box, Records Storage Systems

Files that are no longer active but need to be retained are stored in warehouses that are usually located in areas where space is less expensive.

Transferring files is the process of removing old and inactive items from the files. However, transferred materials are not automatically destroyed. They may be retained for years, but in a less active work area. Some secretaries prefer to transfer files at regular times, once or twice a year. Others do it during free times when the boss is away. This type of continual weeding is probably most effective. In fact, a folder can be examined quickly for nonessential items almost any time it is removed from the file.

Most large companies transfer records to a warehouse or a branch-office storage area, where space is less expensive than at the main office. Theoretically, there are two general transfer methods: *perpetual* and *periodic*.

Perpetual Transfer   The perpetual transfer method moves records to the inactive area as they become inactive. This method is effective when the nature of the business makes it impractical to set definite transfer periods. For example, case records of an attorney, doctor, contractor, or architect are ready to be transferred when the case is closed.

Periodic Transfer   When a periodic transfer method is used, files are moved at stated intervals, once or twice a year. Technically, there are three periodic transfer plans: one-period, two-period, and maximum-minimum period.

One-Period Plan.   In the one-period plan, *all* file contents are removed from active files to a transfer file at one time. The guides usually remain in the active files. The transferred miscellaneous folders are used as guides in the transfer files. New individual and miscellaneous folders are made for the active files. Although this transfer plan seems simple to execute, it becomes cumbersome to use if there is frequent reference to items that have just been transferred.

Two-Period Plan.   When the two-period transfer plan is used, active files are divided into two classes—current records and those left from the previous transfer filing period. For example, if a 6-month transfer period is used, the active file contains papers from the current 6-month period, and semiactive papers from the previous 6-month period are kept close by (but not in a warehouse). Thus, files for both periods are easily reached although separated. The older period may be kept in less accessible file drawers, such as the top and bottom ones of five-drawer cabinets.

At the end of each transfer period, the old files are moved to storage and the files of the period just completed are moved to the less accessible drawers. The two-period plan overcomes the disadvantage of the one-period plan, even though it requires two sets of active guides and folders—one for current files and one for files for the previous 6 months.

Maximum-Minimum Period Plan.   When the maximum-minimum period plan is used, records are moved directly from active to transfer files. They are never held in inactive files. Maximum and minimum periods are decided on. If, for example, the minimum period is 6 months and the maximum period is 18 months, files are held for 6 months plus one year and considered active. At the end of that time, files for the first 12 months of that 18-month period are removed and put into transfer files. Files for the remaining 6 months are held for an additional year, at which time (as before) the files for the first 12 months are removed and put into transfer files.

Retention Schedules

Most companies have a policy and a schedule specifying the amount of time records should be kept. Such schedules are formulated only after careful consideration (usually by a committee) about the types of information that are derived from them, how they are used, and legal and auditing requirements. Such an analysis usually reveals the following four categories.

Records Kept Permanently.   Two broad classes of business records are generally retained permanently: those that provide evidence of corporate and individual rights and those with historic implications. Such records are generally irreplaceable and are considered essential to the existence of the business. Photocopy duplicates of them should be stored in several locations as a precaution against destruction. Old documents may require special restorative or preservative methods to protect them against deterioration.

Some records that should be kept permanently are:

- Capital stock and bond ledgers and registers.
- Partnership papers.
- Stockholder and director minutes.
- Deeds and other title papers and mortgages.
- General ledgers, journals, and cashbooks.
- Records of cost and inventory value of plant equipment and fixtures.
- Tax backup records.
- Audit reports.

- Records relating to bills and accounts payable.
- Paid drafts, checks, and cash receipts.
- Correspondence about stop-payment orders and duplicate checks.
- Payrolls, paychecks, and other evidences of payments for services.
- Employee applications.

Records Kept Six or Seven Years.   Records kept for six or seven years facilitate routine business operations and are replaceable only at considerable cost and delay. They should be transferred when inactive to secure storage. They include the following:

- Lists of security holders present at meetings.
- Records of interest coupons, paid and unpaid.
- Contracts, leases, and agreements (seven years after expiration).
- Accounts receivable ledgers.
- Schedules of fire and other insurance and papers substantiating claims.
- Deposit books and record stubs.
- Inventories of materials with adjustment records.
- Sales records.
- Collection records.
- Record of uncollectible accounts.

Records Kept Three or Four Years.   Many business papers are temporarily useful and replaceable at slight cost. They may be safely destroyed after three or four years. The following illustrate this category:

- Proxies of holders of voting securities.
- Employee fidelity bond records.
- Insurance records—changes and cancellations of policies.
- Records about employee salary garnishments and assignments.
- Purchase orders.
- Credit ratings of customers.
- Expired insurance policies against which unreported or pending claims might arise.
- General correspondence.

Records Kept One Year or Less.   Some records are destroyed after they have served their purpose. According to the National Records Management Council, about 35 percent of all records used in business offices can be destroyed in a year or less. Examples of this type of record include copies of bank deposits, statements of interest due on daily balances, and bank statements. Memorandums, announcements, form letters, congratulations, and condolences can often be disposed of soon after they have been written.

Regulations Affecting Retention Schedules.   State and federal laws prescribing the retention of records for taxes and civil actions must be considered in setting up a retention schedule. In many states limitations on civil action require that contracts and promissory notes be retained for as long as 20 years. Such records need not, however, be in correspondence files. They may be kept in separate "do not transfer" folders and cross-referenced to related correspondence files.

Legal counsel should be sought regarding state and federal retention requirements. A good reference for an in-depth treatment of the topic of records retention and destruction schedules is the *Federal Register*, National Archives of the U.S. in Washington, DC.

Microfilming

Microfilming is a process of photographing records and reducing the film copy to a miniature of the original. Microfilms can be maintained in rolls, in strips, or as individual chips and save 95 to 98 percent of the space needed for storing original records. Microfilmed material can be viewed on a projector and, when needed, can be reproduced as paper copy in regular size.

Savings in Storage Space
Microphotography is one of the answers to saving space in high-rent office areas. It can reduce letter-size documents at a ratio of 170 to 1. One microfilm file cabinet can hold the equivalent of the contents of about 160 four-drawer, letter-size files. A 100-foot roll of 16mm film, for example, will photograph 3,000 letters, 5,800 6-by-4-inch cards, or 13,000 bank checks.

Economics of Microfilming
Although microphotography saves filing space, the costs for filming, proofreading, refilming, indexing, and preparing film "targets" generally are greater than anticipated. Microfilming the contents of one four-drawer file cabinet costs approximately $80 on continuous-roll film and $200 on microfiche, although the subsequent storage cost of the film is negligible.

Studies that compare microfilming costs with the cost of retaining originals

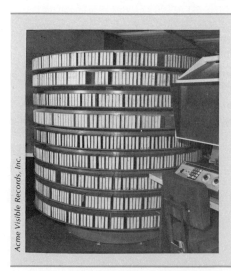

Acme Visible Records, Inc.

A visible and accessible rotary microfilm storage file cabinet.

conclude that unless the records have to be kept for at least 7 to 12 years, it is not economical to microfilm. Microfilming is recommended for providing copies of permanent records and as a way to protect against the possible loss of originals. The federal government and most states accept microfilm or photographic copies of most business records as legal evidence.

Microfilming Limitations

In addition to cost, microfilming poses a few other problems. When microfilming, all paper clips and staples must be removed. Colored, mimeographed, and fluid- (spirit-) copied materials and carbon copies do not film well. When referencing or finding materials, it is sometimes awkward to find all the papers from different sources that relate to the same subject. Also, microfilm is useless without film-reading equipment.

Microfiche

Microfiche is the name given to a sheet or card full of microimages. Dozens of pages of a file can be microfilmed and stored on one card that can in turn be kept in a convenient numeric or alphabetic card file system. Microfiche can be handled manually, examined on a viewer, or reproduced as hard copies by a high-speed photocopier. Microfilm has become an important part of both manual and computer filing systems. The process of generating computer printout as microfilms is called COM (computer originated microfilms). Some computer equipment generates 1,800 microfilm images a minute.

Image-Retrieval Systems

Technological developments in indexing and retrieving records are extensive. More than 25,000 legal-size papers can be stored and code-indexed on one reel of phototape. Another development is a file that replaces file folders with television recordings. The system can store 250,000 pages on a 14-inch reel of video tape, with index notations for each page. Locating and reproducing records is accomplished at push-button speeds. The user can read the material on a visual display screen or have a paper copy printed in seconds.

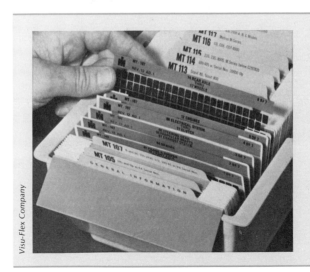

Visu-Flex Company

Hundreds of microimages can be assembled on a single microfiche card and filed in a fraction of the space the documents would otherwise occupy.

Filing Equipment and Supplies

Good filing equipment and supplies not only speed up filing and finding, but they pay for themselves in cash savings. Replacements are less often needed. Quality materials also enable you to handle more filing with greater accuracy.

Cabinets   A letter-size file drawer usually carries a load of 60 to 70 pounds and should have strong telescoping slides that give support when the drawer is fully extended. In addition, drawers operate on ball-bearing rollers so that they can open and close with ease.

Standard Cabinet Sizes.   Filing cabinets are available in various sizes to take care of different sizes of cards and papers. The most common sizes for papers are correspondence (8 by 11 inches) and legal (8½ by 13 inches). Files may be obtained in two-, three-, four- or five-drawer combinations or in one-drawer units with separate bases and top sections. A popular style provides a two-drawer unit of desk height (30 inches) so that it can be placed beside a desk. Three-drawer sections are called counter-height units. Most offices still use the more traditional four-drawer cabinet. The newer standard five-drawer cabinet has 25 percent greater filing space, yet is only 5½ inches higher. Its top is less accessible as work space. Either four- or five-drawer cabinets may be lined up in a row to form partitions for work alcoves or departments.

Use of Filing Cabinets.   Try to use the middle cabinet drawers for the most active material, saving the bottom or top drawers for less active files. Do not waste cabinet drawers by storing stocks of blank forms, office supplies, or publications. It is usually more economical to house such material in transfer drawers or supply cabinets or on shelves. More than one drawer at the top of a cabinet cannot be opened at a time without risk of tipping the cabinet forward. Safety requires all drawers to be closed when you have finished.

Card Files   Many records, such as sales, inventory, purchases, and accounts receivable and payable ledgers, are kept on cards. Card files are also efficient for storing names, addresses, telephone numbers, and special human relations data. *Vertical* card records in which cards are stored on edge and *visible* card records where information on the edge of each card can be seen without handling can be organized on an alphabetic, numeric, geographic, or subject basis—just as correspondence records are.

Card files are generally one of three standard sizes: 8 by 5 inches, 6 by 4 inches, or 5 by 3 inches. The cards, guides, and filing equipment should all be the same size. The size, weight, and grade of the cards you use are determined by the use to which the cards will be put. It is not economical to select a lightweight card for a permanent record or a heavy one for a temporary record.

Cards.   Filing cards are available in various weights and in several grades of durability. Rough to smooth finishes are available for hand or machine posting. Plastic coverings can be purchased for index cards that are subject to fre-

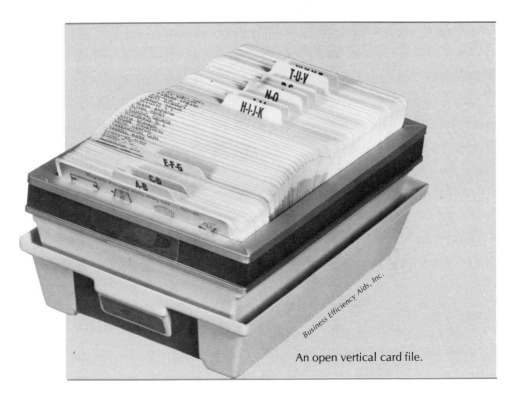

An open vertical card file.

quent handling. Cards can also be purchased in several colors for special classifications.

Card Guides.   Card guides are available with as few as ten or as many as several hundred alphabetic divisions. They can also be obtained with divisions by days, months, states, or other useful categories.

Vertical Card File.   Vertical card files are organized in drawers or open cabinets with guides, in much the same way as correspondence files but without folders. Each card contains separate data. In addition to the standard card sizes already mentioned, there are 7⅜- by 3¼-inch tabulating or punched cards.

When preparing cards for vertical filing, type the caption on the second line from the top of the card. Keep additional information as near the caption as possible so that it can be read without removing the card from the file.

Visible Card File.   Visible card files store cards horizontally (with overlapping edges) in drawers, on vertical rotary racks, in large tubs, on rotary wheels, or in looseleaf visible books. Regardless of how they are stored, an edge of each is visible at all times, thus speeding up the finding or signaling of information they contain.

Separate guides are unnecessary in most visible files because each card, being partly visible, acts as its own guide. Colored signals and protruding tabs may be inserted to highlight important facts and to ensure appropriate action.

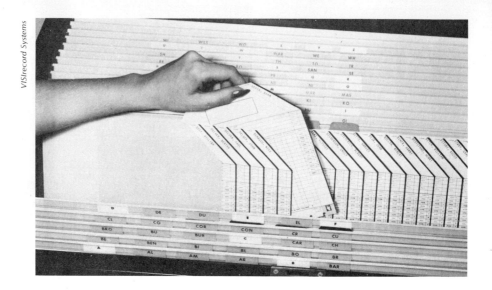

VISIrecord Systems

A visible card file.

Shelf Files   The use of open-shelf filing has increased and is influenced by the need to save space and equipment cost. It is most practical when the volume of records is large enough to result in significant and recoverable space savings. Open-shelf filing is not appropriate, however, in an executive suite or a reception area where appearance is a primary consideration. Numeric filing is especially suited for shelving because numbers can be read easily on the vertical guides that are characteristic of open-shelf filing. On the other hand, names written in this way are not easy to read. Name files on open shelves usually require special tabbing devices. Folders tend to sag, and loose papers spill unless adequate compression supports or hanging folders are used. Fewer papers can be filed loose in standard folders in open-shelf filing than in cabinet filing.

Some shelf files are on motorized shelves—that is, the shelves are stored adjacent to each other without aisle space. When you need access to a specific file shelf, you push buttons to move the shelves forward or back until an aisle space is cleared at the appropriate shelf.

Guides   Using a series of well-organized guides speeds up filing and retrieval procedures.

Guide Functions.   Guide cards are signposts because they help to organize and locate needed files. Since they are usually made of pressboard, they also help to keep folders erect. In open-shelf systems, guides have protruding metal tabs with windows that are angled to make inserted label captions easy to read. Guides can be purchased with a bottom metal eyelet through which a guide rod runs to hold them securely in a file drawer.

Guide Tabs.   Guides are available with tabs in different positions, staggered by threes or by fives. Third-cut guide tabs are preferred for captions composed of

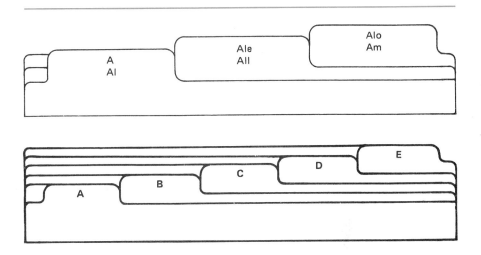

Third-cut guide tabs are used here for double-letter captions and fifth-cut guide tabs for single-letter captions.

several letters, and fifth-cut tabs for captions composed of single letters. Guide tabs can, by location, show the relationship of subdivisions to main headings. For example, a subject file might use first-position guide tabs for primary headings, second-position tabs for first-level subtopics, and third-position tabs for further breakdowns of subtopics. The same idea can be used to signal the subdivisions of geographic files. Color coding can also be added.

Guide Labels.   Guide labels should be typed or printed and should identify the contents of the folders that follow. Labels can be made in colors or coded with color bands to further aid filing and finding control.

File Folders   Folders protect file contents and keep related papers together. The durability of a folder depends on the thickness of the material of which it is made. This thickness is gauged by a point system, one point being 1/1000 inch. In determining folder durability, each side is measured separately. Thus, 20-point stock is 10 points thick on each side. An 11-point folder meets the normal needs of most offices. A light color tab is best for handwritten notations.

Folders can be reinforced along the top edge, along the tab, or both. On straight-edge folders, the rear side projects about ½ inch above the front side. Most folders, however, are tabbed instead of straight-edge. A caption may be typed or written directly on a tab or on a label that is placed on the tab. Tabs may be reinforced with celluloid, acetate, or a laminating synthetic. Folder tabs can be purchased in various cuts and positions. Planning the position of folder tabs in relation to guide tabs is a first step toward successful file maintenance. Be consistent. Have a system. Make tab locations meaningful.

Some file folders are available in a sturdy plastic for greater durability; these folders can be ordered in one color or a variety of colors for easy coding.

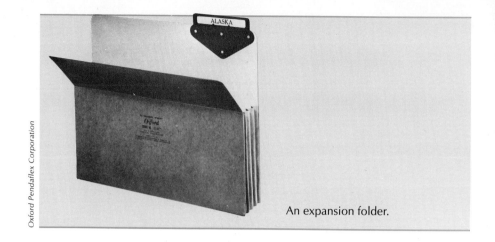

Oxford Pendaflex Corporation

An expansion folder.

Special-Purpose Folders. Binder or fastener folders should be used when valuable papers are moved to different locations while out of the files. These folders are equipped with metal or plastic fasteners that hold the material securely. The fasteners can be attached in any of several positions. Expansion folders of all sorts can also be purchased with an expanding base. Such folders are usually scored three times along the bottom of the front flap, and folds can be made in them as materials are added and they grow bulky. Expansion folders are also available with enclosed sides and a flap and cord for tying.

Oxford Pendaflex Corporation

Hanging folders.

Hanging Folders.   Hanging or suspension folders have been widely adopted as an improvement over regular drawer folders. Hanging folders are suspended on a metal frame placed inside the regular file drawer so that they do not rest on the bottom of the drawer. Folders sliding along the rails can be distributed evenly, thus keeping the records neat and straight. The follow block used to keep traditional file folders upright is not needed. Plastic tabs, purchased separately, are inserted into slots at the top of the folders.

Word Processing Files.   Magnetic cards (mag cards) and floppy discs used in word processing areas require special storage facilities. Some companies prefer the card file with guides similar to those in a regular card file but of a size suitable for the mag cards. Other firms prefer to use special file folders for storing in drawers or folders punched for ring binders.

Folders With Signal Flags.   Some people use signal flags (colored metal tabs or plastic film) to remind them that action needs to be taken. For example, salespeople need to plan lead follow-ups. The customer's file folder is flagged with different colored tabs to mean such things as "date of original call," "week customer should make decision," "time to make return call," and "date for next call." When the salesperson opens the file drawer, the colored signal flags make it easy to identify those customers who need to be contacted. The same signal flag procedures may be used in any office in which there is need for follow-up at specific times.

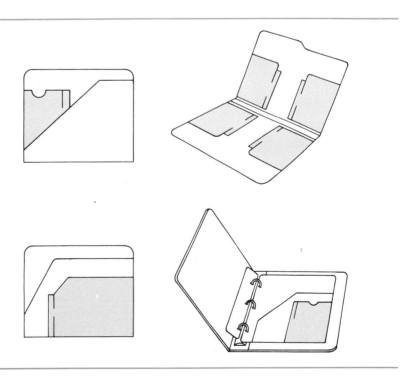

Mag card storage folders.

Planning a Filing System

A good filing system is distinguished by simplicity, efficiency, and usefulness. It is simple when it is orderly and easy to understand. It is efficient when it works quickly with few errors. It is useful when it is relatively free of useless papers.

Design Layout
The larger the filing operation, the greater the need for properly arranged files and work space. With some careful thinking, a little hard work, and a bit of interest and enthusiasm, a secretary can design (or help design) a model filing system. The simplest is an alphabetic system. If a 26-letter subdivision is not big enough, use the telephone or city directory for ideas for expanding. Guide cards and folders imprinted with alphabet divisions can be purchased to handle almost any size file.

The percentage of names beginning with each letter of the alphabet varies widely. It has been estimated that 51 percent of all names in large alphabetic filing systems begin with *B, C, H, M, S,* and *W*; 45 percent with *A, D, E, F, G, J, K, L, N, O, P, R,* and *T*; and 4 percent with *I, Q, U, V, X, Y,* and *Z*.

Once you know how much drawer space you can give a file, deciding on the number of index divisions is simple. For example, 3 three-drawer filing cabinets give you a total of nine drawers of available space. If you plan to put 20 primary guides in a drawer, you will need a total of 180 guides (9 × 20). By using the Index-Name-Frequency Guide here, you can determine how many divisions to provide for each letter of the alphabet. The letter *D*, for example, with 4 percent frequency, should have seven alphabetic divisions (180 × .04 = 7.20).

INDEX-NAME-FREQUENCY GUIDE

Alphabet	Frequency Percentage	Alphabet	Frequency Percentage	Alphabet	Frequency Percentage
A	3	J	2	S	11
B	9	K	5	T	2
C	7	L	5	U	1
D	4	M	9	V	½
E	2	N	2	W	7
F	4	O	1	X	
G	5	P	5	Y	1
H	8	Q	½	Z	
I	1	R	5		

Work Flow
To avoid unnecessary backtracking and lost effort, keep files that you use regularly near your work station. Where possible, store regularly used files within arm's reach. Plan to have adequate work space on the desk or at a nearby table for processing papers to be filed.

Space Standards   Allow 36 inches of aisle space between file cabinets. Place small clusters of filing cabinets against walls or railings. An empty standard five-drawer file cabinet weighs about 195 pounds, while each linear foot of letter-size record matter weighs about 30 pounds. If there is a weight problem due to floor load limitations, you may have to place filing cabinets along the walls or over sustaining supports. Arrange file cabinets so that they are in consecutive order from left to right, in short rather than long rows.

Reviewing Your Reading

1. What are the five operating steps to prepare papers to be filed?
2. When you are selecting an indexing caption, what five heading choices should you consider?
3. In what four situations would it be logical to file an original paper under one name and make cross-reference sheets under others?
4. Describe the methods of coding papers for alphabetic, numeric, and subject filing systems.
5. What three-step procedure should you follow when placing a paper in a file folder?
6. What four clues can help you uncover most misfiled papers?
7. Which drawers of a four- or five-drawer filing cabinet should you use for the most active materials?
8. When is it more appropriate to use shelf filing rather than cabinet filing?
9. Explain the basic functions of primary guide cards and of file folders.
10. What is the objective of a chargeout system? Describe two desirable types.
11. What are two considerations that support a retention schedule outlining how long filed records are to be kept in any business organization?
12. Describe the two general methods of transfer of filed material.
13. What factors should you consider when comparing the cost of microfilming to the cost of retaining the originals?
14. Identify three limitations of microphotography.
15. In planning a filing layout, where should you place your most-used files? Should the file cabinets be in consecutive order from right to left, or from left to right? Are long rows of file cabinets more efficient than shorter rows? Why?

Using Your Skills

1. **Occupational Challenge—Clerking or Managing?** The concept of secretarial filing responsibility in modern offices has evolved from one of being a *file clerk* to one of being a *records manager*. List in two columns what you see as the characteristics of each point of view. The contrast between the two should then become very apparent. Prepare a final typed copy of the two columns and summarize the differences.

2. **Developing a Subject Index.** Prepare a subject classification covering the items below, received in your office today. Use no more than five main headings, each with two to four subheadings (*miscellaneous* not permitted). You need not use all the subheadings. Type your classification in correct outline form. Then type the letters from a to o on a sheet of paper. Opposite each letter write the number of the heading and subheading under which you would file each item below.

   a. An announcement about dates and program for a midwinter American Engineering Society program. Your boss is an engineer.

   b. A letter from a former employee asking your boss for a letter of recommendation.

   c. A reprint of an article the boss wanted, entitled "Grinding a Part from Start to Finish."

   d. A notice about a rate change in the hospitalization program.

   e. Some specification sheets about a new airbrake design.

   f. A letter from a customer asking about new grinding tools.

   g. A monthly gas bill from Standard Oil. The boss uses a credit card.

   h. A program announcement for the next monthly dinner meeting of the Economics Club. The boss is a member.

   i. Reports from unit heads who report to your boss, containing annual budget information.

   j. A memo from the company treasurer's office reminding the boss of the due date for final divisional budget reports.

   k. A reminder from a local university that the boss is to speak before one of its student engineering groups.

   l. A memo from the president's office about a meeting on the fourteenth of the month.

   m. A notice that a subscription to an engineering magazine is expiring.

   n. An outline of an in-company training program the boss has prepared for unit heads in the department.

   o. A brochure about a text for selecting supervisors.

3. **Ordering Filing Folders.** Mrs. Holden has asked you to set up a file based on the 12,500 names in your local telephone book. How many file drawers are needed if you determine that each one would hold 25 folders? How many file folders do you need to order? How many folders should you plan for each of the 26 letters of the alphabet? Present the information as a one-page report.

4. **Retention Decisions.** Using the following retention classification, decide the retention period for each of the documents listed below. On a separate sheet of paper, list the letters of the items and write the retention period you have chosen. When in doubt, be conservative.

   Wastebasket.
   Retain 1 to 3 months.
   Retain 2 to 3 years.
   Retain according to the Statute of Limitations.
   Retain permanently.

a. A stationery stock-withdrawal form.
b. A letter asking for a catalog, which was sent.
c. Tax records.
d. Union contracts.
e. Announcement of a departmental committee meeting.
f. Copy of a letter asking for a hotel reservation.
g. Duplicate deposit tickets.
h. Expired insurance policies.
i. A form letter about a new magazine.
j. A purchase requisition for five boxes of carbon paper and a dozen carbon typewriter ribbons.
k. Punched cards for routine data-processing systems.
l. A departmental report about personal telephone usage.
m. A shipment receiving ticket.
n. An announcement of a convention which the boss will attend.
o. Auditor's reports.
p. Air schedules.

EXERCISING YOUR JUDGMENT

Who Will File? You are a secretary in a company and have three junior assistants. No one wants to file, and consequently the filing stacks up. Several times in the last two days Mrs. Irving has asked you to bring specific files while she was talking to a client on the telephone and you have not been able to locate the file in time. The last time it happened, she told you in no uncertain terms that the filing must be done on time.

What should you do? Tell one of the assistants to do it? Do it yourself? Find a new job? Or find another alternative?

APPLYING THE REFERENCE SECTION

1. Each sentence below contains a common error in English. Type the sentences on a separate sheet of paper, making the necessary corrections.
   a. The experience surely learned me a lesson.
   b. Place these envelopes with them others.
   c. I wish I could draw like she does.
   d. The cleaning tasks are divided among Mary and me.
   e. Each salesperson must submit their expense account.
   f. Dan is a person whom I think will go far.

2. Improve these sentences by rewriting them to say what the writer means. Type your version on a separate sheet of paper.
   a. To succeed as a secretary, many skills are required.
   b. Entering the office, the disorder astonished me.
   c. While traveling in Europe, the weather was good.
   d. When in the fourth grade, my teacher aroused my interest in biology.
   e. Once relaxed, her shorthand was well written.
   f. He was well prepared in mathematics, thus enabling him to pass the examination.

3. Type these sentences on a separate sheet of paper so that similar elements are arranged in parallel form.
   a. I neither saw the messenger nor his car.
   b. We expect our employees not only to be courteous but helpful.
   c. Often telephoning is more satisfactory than to write.
   d. I both need more time and more money.
   e. It would be better to return the imperfect goods than trying to repair them.
   f. Our competitor carries radios of better quality and having higher prices.

4. List the letters from a to f on your answer sheet. In each of the following sentences, select the correct verb in parentheses and type it opposite the appropriate number.
   a. Not one of the letters (is, are) mailable.
   b. She is one of the most promising beginners who (has, have) come to our company.
   c. Some one of the boxes surely (is, are) empty.
   d. I bought one of those fountain pens that (does, do) not require refilling.
   e. Someone in this room (was, were) to blame for the accident.
   f. Every one of these letters (is, are) overweight.

PART FOUR / PROCESSING WRITTEN COMMUNICATIONS

CHAPTER ELEVEN

WORD PROCESSING EQUIPMENT AND SYSTEMS

Information processing has grown at an increasing rate in both volume and cost. Over 75 percent of a manager's time is spent in communicating day-to-day business transactions. The resulting flood of paper and the costs of workers' salaries, benefits, office space, and equipment have prompted the search for more effective word processing methods and equipment. It is commonly recognized that the difference between profitability and loss is often the cost of preparing a single business communication. Recent studies show that the traditional process of dictating a one-page letter or memo that someone types, changes, retypes, copies, distributes, and files costs from $3.25 to $5.25. This cost is expected to increase to $6.75 or more by 1985.

New devices for processing office work are already in use in business offices. These are designed to expedite the handling of the increased volumes of business transactions and accompanying paperwork. The word processing center is one such development. In these centers, correspondence secretaries handle the typing of letters, memos, manuscripts, and statistical reports. Much of what they process is received mechanically from dictation equipment and typed on automatic repetitive, mechanical text-editing, or electronic typewriters. Another new technology for processing information is the cathode-ray tube (CRT), which permits the secretary to edit copy on a screen before it is reproduced as final copy. The most sophisticated pieces of word processing equipment are the shared-logic or minicomputer-based systems and time-shared services. Shared-logic systems use a number of terminal stations and a small computer located in the office. Time-shared systems provide users with part-time use of a large computer located in some remote location. The hook-ups between input and output terminals and the computer location are made by telephone lines.

The differences in the capabilities of text-editing machines and regular electric typewriters have to do with technology. With both types of machine, the typewriter keyboard serves as both input terminal and output terminal for converting dictated thoughts and data into typewritten or printed copy. Every secretary must, therefore, view the typewriter as the primary word processing tool. Employers expect their secretaries to be skillful in the operation of their typewriters. They also expect their secretaries to be familiar with the typewriter's automatic capabilities for the editing, revision, and storage of text.

Standard Typewriters

The typewriter is an office staple. It continues to undergo improvement to yield quicker and cleaner copy and fewer operating complexities.

Manual Typewriters

Manual typewriters are still found in a declining number of business offices where usage demands are light and where the amount and quality of the end product are not critical concerns.

Electric Typewriters

The office electric typewriter—standard, single-element, and proportional spacing—is a mainstay of business. A number of features are common to virtually every electric typewriter. The *impression control* regulates how hard the element or typebar strikes the paper. The *touch regulator* matches your keyboarding touch with key or element sensitivity. *Repeat keys* or *functions* (x, underline, dash, and space) will operate repeatedly until you release the key.

Other features are obtainable as options on the more sophisticated models. A *partial carriage return* lets you stop midline when the carriage return key is depressed. A *reverse underscoring key* allows underlining from right to left. A *selection switch* permits you to fully utilize the top, middle, and bottom of a ribbon. *Incremental spacing* allows you to create super- and subscripts (like CO_2), control half-line vertical spacing, and allow room for omitted letters.

Single-Element Typewriters. IBM's single-element Selectric has special operational advantages that typebar machines cannot match. A spherical element with the alphabet and special symbols on its surface replaces conventional typebars and the movable carriage. The element moves from left to right across the surface of the inserted paper, free of key jamming and without distracting noise and machine vibration.

In addition to speed, the ability to change type size quickly is a special single-element feature. Over thirty elements with different type styles and special symbols are available, including lightface, boldface, italics, and all capital letters.

The Selectric II permits you to change the pitch (number of characters per inch) from 10 to 12 by simply moving a lever and changing the element.

This is the IBM "Executive" Secretarial Type ideally suited for typing clean, legible stencils. This type brings quality, ease, and speed to today's typing.

This is the IBM "Executive" Bold Face Italic Type. It provides unusual emphasis in a wide range of typing applications.

This is the IBM "Selectric" Pica 72 Type. It is similar to the Pica type styles offered with the IBM Model D Typewriter.

THIS IS THE IBM "SELECTRIC" ORATOR TYPE. IT IS A LARGE, SANS-SERIF TYPE STYLE RECOMMENDED ESPECIALLY FOR SPEECHES AND OTHER APPLICATIONS REQUIRING UTMOST LEGIBILITY.

This is the IBM "Selectric" Script Type. It is a special-purpose type style that simulates handwriting. It provides a pleasing change of pace and emphasis for a wide range of typing jobs.

This is the IBM "Selectric" Elite Type. It is similar to the Elite type styles offered with the IBM Model D **Type-**writer. It is well suited for a wide range of typing applications.

Some typewriter type styles.

iiiii	iiiii
ooooo	ooooo
wwwww	wwwww
mmmmm	mmmmm
Regular Spacing	Proportional Spacing

To show various spacing between words
(2-unit space bar, backspace one)

To show various spacing between words
(2-unit space bar)

To show various spacing between words
(3-unit space bar)

Proportional spacing.

Although *elite type*, with 12 characters per inch, is usually preferred for office communications, *pica type*, with 10 characters per inch, is more popular for statistical typing.

Proportional Spacing Typewriters.   In proportionally spaced typing, each character is assigned a space appropriate to its width. Proportional spacing machines have four or five different character sizes. An *I*, for example, might be two units wide, an *e* three units, and an *M* five units. As a result, the wide characters typed next to each other do not seem crowded, and the gaps between narrow letters are eliminated.

Copy produced on proportionally spaced machines looks like typeset printing. It is pleasing to the eye and easy to read. Proportionally spaced copy (with even right-hand margins) is produced in a two-step process. You make a first draft of the copy, typing as close to a ruled right-hand margin as possible. Then you calculate how many character units must be added to fill out the line or subtracted to fit the line. These adjustments are made by shortening or lengthening the spaces between words. The material is then retyped with the calculated adjustments incorporated into each line. The Olympia typewriter has a unique one-step automatic justification feature that does not require retyping.

Proportional spacing can be a problem when it is necessary to make corrections. Filling in letters missed in the original typing or correcting misspelled words can necessitate a retyping of an entire line, the entire paragraph if margins have been justified.

Proportional spacing typewriters are well suited to executive correspondence, reports, and other areas where a high-quality image is desired. They also offer a lower copy-preparation cost than most composing equipment when preparing page copy for company or technical publications.

Another feature of proportional spacing typewriters is *expanded spacing*. This feature adds a one-unit space after each letter and also makes the two-unit space bar into a three-unit bar, and the three-unit space bar into a four-unit bar. This feature is used either in headings for emphasis or for ease in reading when preparing copy for a speech.

Proportional spacing typewriters also permit *variable spacing*. The spacing control is divided into two-unit and three-unit spacing bars. The two-unit bar is used for normal correspondence typing. The three-unit bar permits ease in statistical typing since arabic figures, the dollar sign, and periods and commas are three units wide. Also available is a *repositioning indicator* that allows you to find typing position by aligning a slender vertical wire pointer. The pointer is activated by a lever and returns to its invisible position when a character is typed. The feature is convenient when realigning for correction is required and proportional spacing characters of varying widths are being used.

Keyboard Controls

All electric typewriters offer spacing controls that can aid in the preparation of typed copy.

Half-Space.   The half-space key allows you to advance horizontally by half-spaces and to squeeze in missed letters or unite two or more letters or characters.

```
        Justifying copy when typing is/
not difficult to do if you know how/
to follow directions.  Simply go step
by step and you will not have any///
problems.



        Justifying copy when  typing is
not difficult  to  do if you know how
to follow directions.  Simply go step
by  step  and  you  will  not  have  any
problems.
```

Typed copy before and after justification by half-spacing.

The half-space key also permits you to produce a justified right margin. As when using proportional typewriters, you prepare a draft with each line ending as close as possible to the desired margin. Calculate the number of half-spaces that need to be added to or subtracted from each line. The half-space key is then used to type a final copy with a justified right-hand margin.

Vertical Spacing.   All electric typewriters have a mechanism to regulate the vertical distance advanced when the carriage return key is depressed. Depending upon the make and model of typewriter, the spacing can include single-, double-, and triple-space advances as well as adjustments that include 1½- and 2½-space advances. The vertical half-spacing options are useful in typing envelopes and drafts as well as subscripts and superscripts.

Index Key.   The index key allows you to space vertically down the page without returning to the left-hand margin.

Multiple-Copy Control.   A multiple-copy lever on the typewriter platen moves the platen out. This allows extra space between the platen and its casing for the insertion of extra pages and carbons. An impression control adjustment allows the type keys or element to strike the paper harder so that all copies of a multiple copy pack will be legible.

Page-End Indicator.   A page-end indicator lets you know when to insert a fresh piece of paper so that you do not spoil a typed page with an uneven bottom line due to paper slippage in the carriage. The indicator is also convenient when you wish to allow space for page numbering or footnotes. The most common device is located on the platen. When set at the beginning of a typed page it will signal the remaining inches from the bottom of the sheet.

Line Finder.   The line finder is a lever that allows the platen to be moved vertically to an off-line position. When the lever is reengaged the page is returned to the established typing line without loss of alignment. This feature allows you to make off-line insertions such as double underlinings, subscripts, and superscripts.

Variable Left Margin.   On some electric typewriters the variable left margin allows you to set a new, temporary left-hand margin for typing indented copy. When the lever is in position, a touch on the carriage return brings the carriage to the indented position. This results in a time saving over the carriage return–tab procedure used on most electric typewriters.

Decimal Tabulations.   Some typewriter manufacturers offer an optional set of keys above the regular keyboard that allows you to index to the right column position without using the tab or backspace key. Combined with the regular number keys, the extra keys permit the rapid typing of numerical tabulations and statistical data.

Sound Reduction.   Sound reduction features are available by special typewriter construction and by a hood placed over the type mechanism. This option is appropriate where a premium is placed on low noise levels; in hospitals and recording studios, for example.

Dead Key–Dead Key Disconnect.   The IBM Correcting Selectric offers a dead key and a dead key disconnect that allows you to type a character and accent it without backspacing because the element does not advance. This feature is especially convenient when you are using a foreign language element. The dead key disconnect is used for regular IBM elements.

Velocity Control.   Interchangeable element typewriters such as the Selectric offer a velocity control dial that can be adjusted for the printing of unusual characters. This feature is useful for typing with technical typing elements that have very small or very large characters. Without a velocity control such characters would differ in density from the rest when typed.

Removable Cylinders and Interchangeable Carriages.   Some typewriters have release locks on their cylinders so that special cylinders can be interchanged for such applications as multicarbon typing and stencil cutting. Other typewriters allow you to interchange the carriage with another of greater length, accommodating such large forms as financial statements.

Typewriter Ribbons

There are two kinds of typewriter ribbons—carbon film and fabric. Carbon film ribbons, which give a clear, precise print, are made of either Mylar or polyethylene and are coated with carbon on one side. These ribbons generate top-quality final copy, good enough for photo-offset printing or optical character recognition (OCR) uses. Carbon film ribbons are preferred by secretaries who process executive correspondence and reports. Previously, the problem with carbon ribbons has been their short lives. These ribbons could be used only once—one stroke per space on the ribbon. Multiuse carbon ribbons are now available. They cost more, but repetitive use compensates for the additional cost. The multiuse carbon ribbon also provides confidentiality. With the one space–one stroke ribbon, typed material can be read from the imprinted ribbon. With the multiple-use carbon ribbon, however, the imprinted ribbon cannot be read.

Although the ribbon moves from spool to spool once, the type heads or element strike the same spot on the ribbon repeatedly (six to nine times) before advancing. It is thus impossible for anyone to read the ribbon.

Fabric ribbons—cotton, nylon, or silk—are inexpensive and can be used repeatedly before a replacement is required. Their principal drawback is the quality of final copy they produce, which can be blotchy. They are perfectly adequate for routine typing, however. Nylon is the strongest of the fabrics. Although the ink dries out faster on nylon than on other fabric ribbons, nylon is most popular in offices using electric typewriters.

Manufacturers are now turning to cartridges and automatic threading techniques. SCM's Coronamatic features a ribbon cartridge that plugs into the side of the typewriter. The system permits both fabric and carbon ribbon cartridges as well as different colors, blue, green, and brown, in addition to the traditional black and red. The Hermes 705 permits you to thread carbon film ribbons automatically. A tape leader is inserted into an intake slot located just in front of the platen, on the left-hand side of the machine. You press a key-shaped lever that threads the tape to the take-up spool. When the tape is used up, you eject the full take-up spool directly into a waste receptacle. No handling of the tape is required.

Correcting Procedures.   Various means have been devised to permit you to correct mistakes directly from the keyboard. Errors can be covered over or lifted from the page. To enable you to cover incorrect characters, a white strip is added to the lower part of the ribbon. By backspacing to the error, pushing a correction lever, and hitting the incorrect character again, you mask the mistake. You then retype a new character in the space. Manually applied correction fluids such as Liquid Paper and Wite-Out are also used frequently.

To lift mistakes made with carbon ribbons from the page with electric typewriters such as the Correcting Selectric, you use a special correcting key and a reel of correcting tape. When the error is made the key is depressed, backing up the element one space. The error is struck again and this time erased. The element remains in the same position, allowing you to strike the correct character key. If the correctable film ribbon is used, the appropriate correcting tape actually lifts the error off the page, making a clean, detection-proof correction. If a Tech III ribbon is used, a special, self-contained coverup correction tape covers the error with a white substance and allows you to type the correct letter over the error. Such corrections are detectable on off-white stock.

Word Processing Hardware and Media

Word processing eliminates the present duplication of typing and proofreading by capturing keystrokes on a magnetic medium such as tape, card, or disc. The stored information is simply revised and corrected rather than retyped whenever revisions are necessary. At present the market is dominated by specialized devices that range from simple automatic typewriters to cathode-ray tubes (television-type display units) and shared-logic systems.

Xerox Corporation

One of the many stand-alone word processing units that make use of some form of magnetic medium.

Stand-Alone Word Processing Systems

Stand-alone systems (systems that are not connected to other computer systems or system components) combine recording capabilities with machine play-back and storage. These systems act as self-sufficient units and contain all the required operational components. Included in this category of text editors are the word processing magnetic (mag) keyboard or typewriter systems used for repetitive typing and text editing as well as stand-alone video display systems with cathode-ray tube (CRT) display screens. The latter frequently include more sophisticated editing features than the classic mag keyboard stand-alones.

Mechanical Text Editors.   The basic stand-alone word processor consists of a keyboard printer that is coupled with a logic element that manages the operations, an internal memory, and a magnetic medium recorder (card, cassette, tape cartridge, or diskette). With such mag keyboard word processors, the printer is used to produce text for editing operations and for final copy output.

Display Editing Devices.   Another type of stand-alone word processor re-places the keyboard printer with a keyboard video or CRT display terminal and adds a separate printing element that looks like a flattened daisy. Text is keyed, edited, and changed on the display before printout.

Screen size is a primary consideration. When as much copy as can be fitted on the screen is entered, the limit is reached, and copy must be either recorded or cleared. Full-page CRTs offer the ability to view an entire page of text exactly as it will appear in print. A full page is defined as the number of characters that fit on an 8½- by 11-inch sheet of paper. Most manufacturers claim that a display that accommodates 52 single-spaced lines of 80 characters each is a full page. Partial-page CRTs offer a thin window that moves over an entire document, allowing you to see the text as it is created or edited. While the partial-page CRTs do not allow an entire page of text to be viewed at one time, they do offer text

Martin Bough

The CRT screen enables the operator to see what has been typed and to make any corrections necessary before the copy is transferred to a magnetic medium.

manipulation features that are beneficial when frequent and extensive editing requirements are the rule. If you require the CRT as a tool for page layout, however, as in printing applications or for executive-level documents when perfect presentation is crucial, the full-page CRT is superior.

With a CRT, once you are satisfied with the copy, it can be transferred off the screen onto the mag medium. This capability permits corrections to be made to the copy as it is being typed without a waste of paper or any sort of record that has to be corrected. It eliminates the difficulties of correcting errors in the typewriter. CRTs also help you to locate material. Copy can be placed on the screen for viewing from the magnetic medium at a faster rate than it can be printed out.

Shared-Logic Word Processors

Shared-logic systems combine a central processing unit with video display or keyboard editing-input stations. As many as twelve and sometimes more editing-input stations may be supported by the central minicomputer. There are variations on the makes of equipment contained in shared-logic systems, especially in text-editing software that makes these systems operate and that should reflect work needs. Newer shared-logic systems feature stand-alone work stations with their own capabilities, but some components are shared by all the work stations.

Shared-logic, multiterminal word processing systems save money. Because these systems share the use of the minicomputer logic and output printers, their costs can be spread over a number of work stations. They are attractive to users who produce a high volume of papers and extra long documents. With their greater control logic, editing capabilities, and larger on-line memory and storage capacities, word processing systems can store, search, and retrieve text as multipage documents throughout updates and revisions.

Time-Shared Word Processing Services

Time-shared word processing services provide the business office with part-time use of a large computer or backup for user-owned word processing equipment. To have access to a large computer located elsewhere, users buying time must have their own computer display or printing terminals as well as communicating word processors. Subscribers to time-shared services call the remote computer from on-site terminals (typewriter keyboards) using ordinary telephone lines. Users pay telephone charges, computer time charges, storage charges, and charges associated with output such as printing and photocomposition.

The advantage of time-sharing is that it does not require the user to make long-term financial commitments. The user who sporadically requires copy for specifications, contract writing, and reports may find time-sharing services best to get the job done economically.

Magnetic Media

All word processing systems have some internal memory that permits a segment of text to be held on magnetic media and manipulated. Media may be internal and nonremovable for about 100 pages or up to several thousand pages in a fixed disc system. Removable media allow you to store any amount of material offline. Major types include reusable, page-recording MC/ST mag cards, cassettes (standard, mini, and micro), magnetic tape cartridges for MT/STs, and shared-logic systems, belts, and floppy discs. Applications of magnetic media in word processing are limited by their internal memory capacity.

MAGNETIC MEDIA		
Type	Memory Capacity	Best Applications
Internal	1 line to about 125 pages	Short documents with short-term storage requirements
Mag Card	5,000 to 10,000 characters (about 2 to 4 pages)	Short documents with limited revisions
Mag Tape	3 to 12 pages	Short to medium documents with limited revisions
Cassette	30 to 40 pages	Short to medium documents with limited revisions
Minidiskette	60,000 to 100,000 characters (about 24 to 40 pages)	Documents of any length, extensive revisions
3M Data Cartridge	50 to 100 pages	Short to medium documents (some systems can handle more extensive revisions)
Diskette	250,000 characters and up (about 100 pages)	Documents of any length; extensive revisions
Disc	1 million characters and up (400 pages and up)	Long documents with extensive revisions; data base applications

The medium most often used is the magnetic card, which can be stored with pages of hard copy in conventional files for subsequent revision or printing. As many as 5,000 characters of text and coding can go on a card. Several vendors offer cards with up to 10,000 characters (four or five pages). Cards that permit recording on both sides are also available. They require additional logging but reduce storage space needs by half.

The IBM MT/ST uses tape cartridges with 50, 100, or 120 feet of medium for from 3 to 12 pages of text and codes. The 3M data cartridge with 300 feet of tape has the capacity for 50 to 100 pages of text. Cassettes usually hold about 40 pages of text. Cassette systems such as Redactron and Xerox offer high-capacity cassettes for up to a million characters or about 400 pages.

Diskettes give the word processing operator flexibility in document length (full-size diskettes hold about 100 pages, minidiskettes about 25 to 30 pages), and no limit to revision length. Access is afforded to either side of the diskette directly from the keyboard.

Word Processing Support Systems

Word processing is a management support system by which ideas and information are committed to readable form. The system makes use of people, procedures, and equipment.

Word Processing and Administrative Support

The word processing concept divides the generalized functions of the traditional secretary into two specialized areas. In this style of organization, typing and everything else a secretary does are carried out in separate centers and independently supervised. Two kinds of workers are employed: *correspondence specialists* (also called *word processing specialists*) and *administrative secretaries*.

Correspondence (Word Processing) Specialists.   The correspondence or word processing specialist is concerned with typing, transcription, proofreading, and editing. To qualify, the person must be a combination machine technician, style specialist, and grammarian and must be highly efficient and productive in typing letters, memos, reports, and statistical data on automated text-editing equipment. Word processing specialists do not report to the principals for whom they produce correspondence and other forms of information. However, whenever dictation is difficult to understand or an assignment is unclear, they query the principal by telephone.

The International Word Processing Association identifies several job titles and levels of advancement in a word processing center:

A. Word Processing Trainee

Entry-level position for those having 0–12 months' word processing experience. Must have adequate typing skills; good knowledge of grammar, punctuation, spelling, and formatting; the ability to use dictionaries, handbooks, and other reference materials; and be oriented toward teamwork and the use of machines. A trainee's functions include routine transcription and manipulation of text from various types of source information (dictation, handwritten, etc.). Maintains own production records, and may be required to proofread own work.

B. Word Processing Operator

The next level up from Word Processing Trainee, for those having 6–24 months' word processing experience. In addition to having all the qualifications and functions of Position A, a word processing operator handles special documents, meets established quality standards, uses all of a machine's text-editing functions, and is familiar with department terminology and company practices.

C. Word Processing Specialist I

A word processing operator with a minimum of 18 months' experience who can format, produce, and revise complicated documents such as lengthy technical and statistical reports from complex source information, including the retrieval of text and data from electronic files. Exercises independent action when interpreting instructions to produce a quality document, understands proofreader's marks, and assumes full responsibility for document accuracy and completeness. Has a thorough knowledge of center procedures and maintenance of records. May operate word processing equipment in the telecommunication mode.

D. Word Processing Specialist II/Assistant Supervisor

A person at this level exercises all of the competencies of Position C and may act as assistant supervisor. A Word Processing Specialist II is able to operate all the information-processing functions within the installation. Responsibilities include coordinating and assigning work, analyzing requirements for specific projects, communicating with users, compiling production statistics, and recommending changes in center procedures. May also assist in training personnel.

E. Phototypesetting Specialist

A word processing operator who enters special codes while keyboarding and revising text that is to be output on a photocomposition system. Has knowledge of points, picas, typefaces, leading, and other aspects of typesetting and printing.

F. Word Processing Trainer

Someone with a minimum of 24 months' experience operating word processing systems who spends the majority of time training new operators. May also be responsible for instructing users in dictation methods and other procedures to insure maximum utilization of a word processing center. Should make recommendations to management with regard to new equipment purchases from the standpoint of ease of use.

G. Proofreader

Proofreads typed copy for text content, spelling, punctuation, grammar, and typographical errors. May be responsible for setting grammar and format standards, guidance and/or training of secretaries and principals.

H. Word Processing Supervisor

With all the competencies of a Word Processing Specialist II, a supervisor is responsible for the operation of a center (or section within a large center). Schedules and coordinates work flow, assists word processing personnel in document production and in establishing and maintaining quality standards. Also analyzes production data and procedures, identifies potential improvements, and may be responsible partially for budgets and equipment recommendations. Reports to word processing manager.

I. Word Processing Manager

Exempt (salaried). Responsible for the overall operation of a word processing center, including the guidance of supervisors, personnel administration, staff requirements, user liaison, and evaluation, design, and implementation of future word processing systems. Also is responsible for budgets, overall production reports, and coordination of services with administrative support. May also manage the operation of photocopying, printing, mailing, or graphics services. In larger organizations, the word processing manager reports to Director of Secretarial Support Systems.*

Administrative Secretaries.   Administrative secretaries are responsible for the basic nontyping secretarial tasks, such as processing the mail, managing the telephone, and filing. They also provide paraprofessional assistance in such areas as corresponding, recordkeeping, and research. Administrative secretaries are located close to the executives, managers, and staff they assist.

This form of administrative secretarial organization establishes a vertical career path based on the capabilities of the secretary. The job levels identified by the International Word Processing Association are as follows:

AA. Administrative Secretary

Someone who works for a group of principals as part of a team under the direction of an Administrative Support Supervisor or Manager. Responsibilities include the support functions, such as filing; photocopying; maintaining calendars, records and lists; and providing special secretarial services.

BB. Senior Administrative Secretary

Has a record of exceptional performance. At times may act as assistant to supervisor of an administrative team, and is qualified to compose and edit documents for principals, provide research support, and perform other paraprofessional duties. Handles special projects and is fully aware of company standards and practices.

---

*Reprinted with permission of the International Word Processing Association, from their "1979 Salary Survey Results."

CC. Administrative Support Supervisor

May have the responsibilities of Position BB in addition to scheduling and administering work flow to a team of administrative secretaries. Responsible for liaison with and training of users who benefit from administrative support. Evaluates staffing requirements, prepares management reports, recommends new methods of handling administrative secretaries. Reports to Administrative Support Manager.

DD. Administrative Support Manager

Exempt (salaried). Has full responsibility for developing, maintaining, and evaluating all service structures under administrative support within an organization, such as filing, telephone, mail, and paraprofessional support. Monitors the success of the administrative support group and is familiar with the company's goals and objectives. Works closely with the word processing manager to insure cooperation of the two functions. May manage other major administrative duties such as records and retention, microfilm, print shop, purchasing, etc. Reports to Director of Secretarial Support Systems (in large organizations).

EE. Staff Analyst

Exempt (salaried). Responsible for consulting and assisting Word Processing and Administrative Support Supervisors and Managers. Conducts studies, reviews operations, and determines and recommends appropriate staffing, procedures, and equipment. Reports to Director of Secretarial Support Systems or Word Processing Manager or Administrative Support Manager.

J. Director of Secretarial Support Systems

Exempt (salaried). May be vice president or assistant to vice president in some organizations. Has total responsibility for all aspects of an organization's office system, including word processing, administrative support, and other information processing. Insures the collaboration of all support functions. Reports to a chief executive officer.*

Administrative Support Alternatives

In a word processing system, administrative support can be provided in various ways, although typing is almost always separated from all other administrative duties. In designing such a system, the needs of the organization it supports must be met. There are a number of administrative configurations.

Secretary-Principal. Common in upper management levels is an administrative support arrangement that permits the personal secretary to serve the executive on a one-to-one basis. In this capacity the secretary fulfills both typing and administrative needs. The least supervised arrangement, it is preferred by most

---

*Reprinted with permission of the International Word Processing Association, from their "1979 Salary Survey Results."

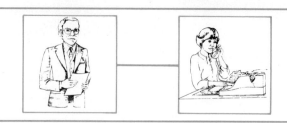

Secretarial assignments vary, depending upon the size and needs of different offices. This secretary works for just one boss.

executives who regard their own personal secretaries as paraprofessionals. This arrangement can be costly but usually yields the highest quality of work. Since one-to-one support secretaries are supervised by their principals, whose time is expensive, a secretarial supervisor is sometimes assigned to oversee the quality and amount of the secretarial output.

Secretary–Multiple Principals. When one secretary serves several executives, he or she fulfills both the administrative and typing functions. In this arrangement, as is the case with the one-to-one configuration, there is little or no professional supervision. Work distribution, quality control, and productivity standards are difficult to maintain. Neither this nor the one-to-one mode differentiates the administrative functions from the correspondence functions.

Augmented Arrangement. Secretaries achieve the role of administrative secretaries with an augmented arrangement. A separate typing facility is provided. This may be a typist at a text-editing machine or a correspondence center that processes most correspondence for administrative secretaries or word originators. Secretaries can devote most of their time to administrative functions. Administrative secretaries may do some typing, but high-volume, time-consuming typing jobs are sent to the correspondence facility.

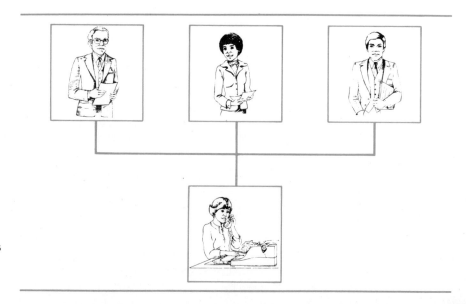

Here one secretary handles both administrative tasks and correspondence for three executives.

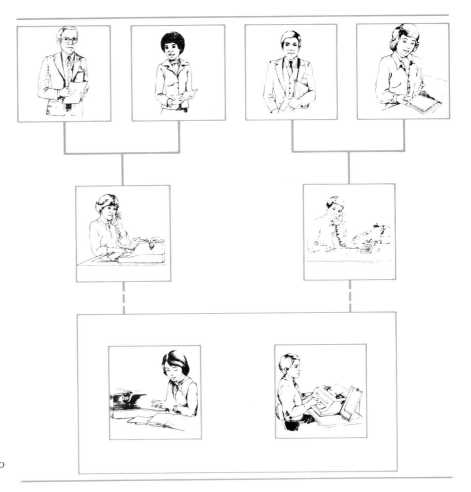

A separate typing facility frees secretaries to devote most of their working day to administrative duties.

Work Group. The work-group concept is related to the augmented mode. It is a complete administrative support and correspondence facility that utilizes a division of labor but serves only one department or functional group. Secretaries within the groups are assigned to either administrative or correspondence sections. The administrative secretaries answer the telephone, take messages, make appointments, and file. The correspondence specialists process correspondence and related assignments. Since all work is done for one particular group, secretaries are familiar with procedures, principals, and terminology.

Centralized Support. The centralized mode features separate sources of administrative and correspondence services. In this arrangement, administrative secretaries do not deal with typewriters at all. They work directly with executives, often with the added responsibility of submitting and proofreading material going to and coming from the centralized correspondence center. Additional duties such as researching and drafting letters, memos, and reports are often assigned.

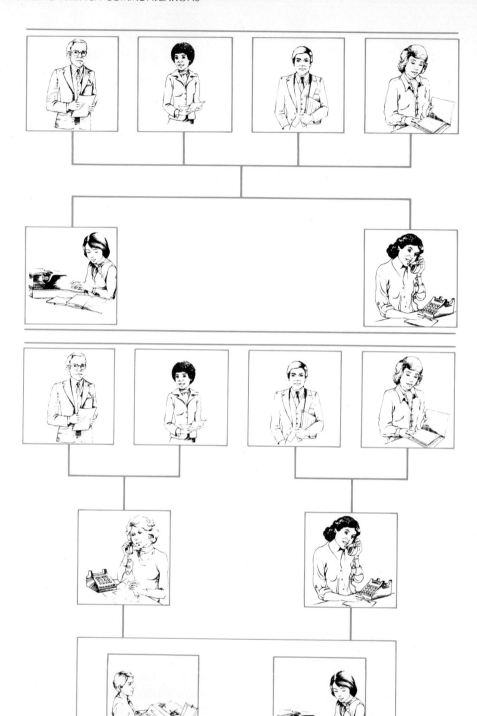

A work group handles correspondence and administrative duties for one department or functional group.

The ultimate in secretarial task division: the administrative assistants never touch a typewriter.

Reviewing Your Reading

1. Explain why each of the following conditions will have an impact upon every secretary and necessitate change in the offices of the future: (a) increasing costs of processing office work; (b) increasing volumes of business transactions and paperwork; (c) increasing numbers of technical developments; and (d) increasing need for accurate, timely information for making decisions.

2. Identify the three basic changes that mark the switch from the traditional office to the word processing–administrative support concept of office operations.

3. Identify and describe the two kinds of specialized secretaries that support executives, managers, and staff in a word processing–administrative support system.

4. Describe three main benefits of a word processing–administrative support system.

5. Identify the individual components of a stand-alone word processing system and the types of storage media it can use.

6. Describe the function of the cathode-ray tube (CRT) display screen in a stand-alone word processing system and identify its primary advantage over a keyboard printer.

7. Explain the communicating capabilities of a shared-logic word processing system terminal.

8. Compare a time-shared word processing service to a shared-logic system, highlighting their notable differences and the primary advantage of time sharing.

9. Compare the capacity and best application of mag cards, mag tape, and diskettes.

10. When faced with a variety of options in organizing administrative support, how does one go about judging which is best suited to the needs of a business organization?

Using Your Skills

1. Concerns about job descriptions and career paths have become an important issue in business offices. Titles, required skills, and business practices vary. Most employers have strong feelings concerning these issues. Interview one business manager or executive and obtain answers to the following questions:
   a. What is the policy of your company concerning the career paths of secretaries?
   b. Are secretarial positions well defined within your company?
   c. Do you feel possessive about your secretary's time?
   d. Are you able to function effectively without your secretary?
   e. Is your secretary more of a correspondence processor or an administrative assistant?
   f. Do you feel that, in general, a secretary either makes or breaks an executive?

2. What are the essential factors to be considered if an administrative support system is to operate successfully?

3. You have been asked to prepare the specifications for an IBM Correcting Selectric your department will purchase. Refer to the manufacturer's literature for specifications that cover such characteristics as:
   a. Configuration.
   b. Page size.
   c. Format.
   d. Ribbon.
   e. Repeating keys.
   f. Keyboard controls.
   g. Spacing controls.

4. Prepare the following article with the right-hand margin justified. Set marginal stops for a 60-space line. Type the article double-spaced with paragraph indentations. Accompany your retyped, justified copy with the first draft containing right margin penciled guide rule, oblique line fillers, and check marks indicating the distribution of spaces.

Word Processing–Administrative Support Systems

There are three main reasons for the slow progress in the implementation of total word processing–administrative support systems. First is the increase in the number of word processing equipment manufacturers, who are primarily interested in the installation of text-editing and dictating equipment. Since the administrative support portion requires virtually no equipment at present but requires substantial analysis as well as implementation effort, vendors cannot be expected to expend effort in these areas.

Second, management's reluctance to give up exclusive secretaries, as well as intermediate and senior secretaries' reluctance to give up their status, have meant that word processing is implemented by general staff and junior-to-intermediate secretaries. Word processing has, in many cases, been implemented without senior management support, while the senior staff members retain their secretaries.

Finally, since the implementation of a total word processing–administrative support system requires selling the concept, the task has been very difficult to achieve by in-house staff. The number of management consultants, analysts, and manufacturers capable of convincing senior management of the benefits of such systems is relatively small, and progress has been slow.

EXERCISING YOUR JUDGMENT

Productivity. The office in which you are employed as a secretary has a number of long-time employees who are not doing their jobs well. Many of them would be overpaid even if they were doing what they were supposed to do. The office manager to whom you report has discussed the need to encourage higher productivity and has asked you to submit a plan of action. At the same time, the manager wants to give recognition to those employees who are loyal supporters of the company but who can't perform as well as the younger workers. What would you recommend?

Applying
the
Reference
Section

Study the words in each subgroup to determine whether they are correctly spelled. Each subgroup emphasizes one or more spelling aids in the Reference Section. Type your answers on a separate sheet.

1. What is the correct spelling when the ending shown is added to the word?
   a. re + occur
   b. acknowledge + ment
   c. use + ing
   d. profit + ed
   e. guide + ance
   f. arrange + ment
   g. true + ly
   h. transfer + ed
   i. nine + th
   j. confirm + ing

2. What are the missing letters?
   a. perc__late
   b. attend__nce
   c. sep__rate
   d. controver__y
   e. p__rsuade
   f. leg__cy
   g. spec__men
   h. advis__ry
   i. reno__n
   j. industr__al

3. What happens when you add *ed* to the end of each word?
   a. transfer
   b. plan
   c. benefit
   d. specify
   e. interrupt
   f. believe
   g. ship
   h. remit
   i. occur
   j. differ

4. Which of these words are misspelled?
   a. cancellation
   b. cancelled
   c. traveler
   d. installment
   e. marvellous
   f. skilful
   g. enrolment
   h. equaling
   i. jewelled
   j. labeled

CHAPTER TWELVE / DICTATION

Two basic secretarial skills are the ability to take dictation accurately and rapidly and the ability to produce mailable transcripts of the dictation. You should also know how to give dictation to others, for a good secretary often processes communication by dictating material to the word processing center or by dictating to another secretary. These three skills must be fully developed for the secretary to do a complete job of assisting the busy executive in the processing of communicating with customers, suppliers, management, subordinates, and others who are part of the business environment.

The most common ways of taking dictation are by shorthand or by machine recording. Correspondence might also be dictated to you at the typewriter as the material is typed in rough draft or finished form, or the dictation may be received by telephone hook-up from a central dictation unit.

Since you may use shorthand in performing a number of job responsibilities, the skills and procedures involved in handling dictated information are stressed in this chapter. Transcription techniques are discussed in Chapter 13.

PREREQUISITES FOR DICTATION

Both dictation and transcription require not only well-developed shorthand skills but also competence in English usage and thorough knowledge of your company's policies and procedures.

Language Facility

The basic tool of word processing is language. Recording dictation with ease and transcribing it with confidence is possible only if you are familiar with English usage, sentence structure, paragraphing, and general editorial style.

With the right word at your command, you can communicate with clarity and precision. In fact, the value of your service to your employer may well be measured by your ability to handle language; to catch omissions, errors, or ambiguities in the dictation; and to correct them or call attention to them.

Knowledge of the Company

Your employer will not expect you to work at peak efficiency when you first begin. You will have time to learn to know your company, to pick up specialized terms, and to adjust to new routines. To speed this adjustment process, you will need to make conscientious efforts to orient yourself to the job. Here are some suggestions that can help simplify your daily routines as well as save your time and energy:

- Familiarize yourself with the names and addresses of people with whom your employer often corresponds. If a card file of such information is not available to you, start one.
- Study any procedure or style manuals that your company provides. Inform yourself about recommended styles for letters, memorandums, and reports. Follow your company's preferences even if they sometimes differ from what you have learned previously. Perhaps some day when you are a seasoned employee, you may be asked for suggestions. But for the present, adapt yourself quickly to new ways of doing things.
- Begin building a list of special terms your employer uses in dictation. Cultivate the habit of using a dictionary to verify their spelling, pronunciation, and meaning. Learn shorthand forms for these special terms and practice them until they are familiar.
- Read copies of previous correspondence and reports. Try to get the feel of the business.
- Become acquainted with professional, trade, and industry magazines in your company's field. You will find it an asset to be able to recognize names of products, persons, organizations, and places that recur in dictation.

Shorthand Fluency

Shorthand continues to be a basic tool in secretarial work. Top-level secretaries depend on their shorthand ability as they work closely with executives who dictate on the run, need instant transcripts, or expect quick notes to be taken of matters under discussion. With notebook and pen always ready, secretaries find shorthand not only an irreplaceable tool but a significant advantage when responding to and meeting communication needs.

Research shows that most employers are satisfied if a secretary can write shorthand at 90 words a minute for five minutes and at 110 words a minute for three minutes, as detailed in the table shown here:

DICTATION SPEEDS			
5-Minute Dictation Speed (words a minute)	3-Minute Dictation Speed (words a minute)	Qualification Level	Percentage of Dictators Served Adequately at Each Level
60	80	Minimum	10
70	90	Minimum-Average	20
80	100	Average	40
90	110	Average-Rapid	60
100	120	Rapid	75
110	130	Rapid-Expert	85
120	140	Expert	95

To manage your employer's dictation with confidence, you should measure up to the following performance requirements:

- Good basic knowledge of the shorthand alphabet, word formations, word beginnings and endings, and brief forms.
- Ability to take shorthand at least as fast as the majority of employers require. Accuracy of outline must be the first consideration, of course, with speed secondary.
- A memory trained to retain and recall what the employer says during sudden spurts of dictation. When the person dictating knows what must be said, the words may flow at a fast rate. You can catch up during lulls when thoughts are being organized by the dictator.
- The writing of an outline for every word. Your notes need not be letter-perfect, but they must be readable. Occasionally you will need to create an outline or to write part of a word in longhand in order to get it down at once. Use a shorthand dictionary to check the outlines for doubtful or unfamiliar words.
- Regular dictation practice. Use tapes and records for your practice, and use shorthand in all reminders you write to yourself.

Readiness for Dictation

You should always be ready to take dictation. The only supplies you need are a notebook, pen, and perhaps a file of pending material.

Dictation includes instructions as well as correspondence. Experienced secretaries answer every summons with an open notebook and pen in hand. You may wish to keep a separate notebook by your telephone.

Preparing Your Notebook

- Make sure that a rubber band holds the used pages of the notebook against the cover so that you can open immediately to the proper page.
- Keep two pens under the rubber band. If you leave your desk, you only have to remember to pick up your notebook.
- Start each day's dictation on a fresh page. Write the date on the bottom of each page as you use it. This makes it easy to find previous notes.
- If your current notebook is nearly filled, carry a new one with the old.

Planning for Dictation Sessions

Develop a sense of anticipation about dictation so that you plan ahead for a dictation period.

Let's see, will he need the Carter proposal? . . . He'll probably dictate the answer to Ferguson; I'd better get out his last letter. . . . That memo this morning from the marketing manager mentioned something about a regional sales meeting in San Francisco next month. What does the boss's calendar look like? . . . The letter from O'Donahue asked for cost information about our computer operations; I think there's a report about that in the files.

Arrange for someone to cover your telephone while you are taking dictation, so as to eliminate interruptions. If this is not possible, handle incoming calls as expeditiously as possible.

If your employer calls you for dictation while you are talking to someone on the telephone or in person, terminate the conversation promptly and courteously so you can begin the dictation session.

Dictation

If at all possible, sit directly opposite the dictator. Some secretaries prefer to rest their notebooks on their laps as they take dictation. A more secure position is to rest the notebook on the desk.

Be careful not to distract the dictator's attention by such nervous habits as tapping a pen or a foot. Refrain from looking around the room or staring out the window while you wait for your boss to dictate. Instead, keep your eyes on your notes, inserting punctuation and the like.

Handling Interruptions If your employer must be interrupted to take a telephone call or to see a visitor, and if the interruption is likely to be lengthy or of a personal nature, it may be understood that you will return to your desk. But if it is preferred that you remain, use the time to go over your notes. When the dictator is ready to resume dictating, read the last sentence dictated before the interruption.

Interrupting the Dictator. Most executives prefer their secretaries to signal them if for any reason a word or phrase is not clear. Of course, such an interruption should never result from lack of shorthand skill or unfamiliarity with the basic vocabulary of the business.

If you must interrupt the dictator, learn whether the preference is to be interrupted at once or when the piece of dictation is finished. Some executives may lose the sequence of thought if interrupted midway; others may prefer to clarify everything as the dictation is given.

You may be able to hear the troublesome part again without breaking the flow of thought by repeating questioningly the last word or phrase you heard distinctly or an approximation of the part you did not understand. The dictator can then repeat the word or phrase without a complete break.

It is even more essential to interrupt if the dictator speaks increasingly softly, mumbles, or otherwise makes it difficult for you to understand. No one should dictate while biting on a pipe or while facing away from you.

Taking Advantage of Dictation Interruptions. During long pauses or when you are waiting for the executive to resume dictation, insert and circle punctuation marks in your shorthand notes and repair hastily written words and phrases. You will probably not have time to complete this task until you return to your desk after dictation.

As you reread your notes during dictation pauses, identify doubtful items by a symbol such as a circled question mark. Use the same symbol for points to be verified later or for ambiguous expressions you may need to have clarified.

Signal Priorities. During the dictation, be alert to your employer's preferences about items that must be transcribed first. A letter that must reach the recipient before a certain meeting, for instance, might be your first priority in transcription. Even interoffice communications may be of top priority if time is important. Consider all telegrams as rush items.

Flag each piece of rush dictation by marking the item with a colored pencil that you reserve just for rush items. Or fold that notebook page diagonally so that part of it extends beyond the edge of the notebook.

Deletions.   To indicate a deletion in your notes, use a heavy diagonal line. If several words are to be deleted, use a wavy line to cover the entire area.

> *Example:* "You will receive as basic salary for your services the sum of $593.75 a month. (Take out *basic*.)"

This would appear in your notebook as:

Substitutions.   To indicate a substitution of one word or phrase for another, place a line through the deleted word or a wavy line through the deleted phrase and write the substituted word or phrase next to or above it.

> *Example:* "You are hereby authorized to proceed with final production plans. (No, *to expedite preliminary production specifications*.)"

You would record this in your notes as:

Restorations.   To restore an original outline after it has been struck out and changed, rewrite the word or phrase as though it were a completely new form.

> *Example:* "Our production manager would like to visit your plant (No, *meet with you*; oh, leave it *visit your plant*) on July 24."

Your notes should look like this:

Instructions.   To provide space to record special instructions during or after the dictation of a letter, separate each item of dictation from the next by several blank lines. To ensure that such instructions stand out prominently, some secretaries use a colored pencil to write them in the notebook.

>   *Example:* "Send a carbon copy to Johnson, Personnel; a blind carbon copy to Martin, Sales."

You would record this as:

Transpositions.   To indicate a transposed word or phrase, use the proofreader's transposition mark.

>   *Example:* "We had, in addition, replacement-part expenses amounting to $10,000. (No, make that *In addition, we had . . .*)"

In your notes, this would appear as:

To transpose an entire sentence or even a paragraph to another part of a letter, circle the material to be transposed and indicate the new position by an arrow.

>   *Example:* "You will read in all local papers a notice of acquisition. Stock prices will rise. The time for action is near. (Let's put this last sentence at the beginning of the paragraph.)"

In your notebook, this would appear as:

Insertions.   To indicate a long insertion, first write and circle a large *A* at the point where the new material is to be inserted. Draw two heavy horizontal lines after the last item dictated in order to separate it from the insert. Write and circle "Insert A" under the two heavy lines. Write the insert. Finally, draw two heavy horizontal lines in order to indicate the end of the insert.

Example: "Congratulations on the success of your research team. I am asking our attorneys to prepare the application for a company patent on the process finally adopted. (After the word *team,* add this sentence: *Project 72 has now been approved for production.*)"

In your notebook, this would appear as:

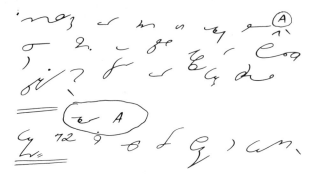

Questions.   To indicate missing information, such as a date, price, or name, leave a blank space and put a question mark in a circle at the end of that line in the margin. (Some secretaries prefer to use a large X in the margin.) This is also a handy symbol to use if you did not understand an instruction and will need further clarification later.

Adjusting to Dictation Patterns

Most executives prefer to dictate in the morning after the incoming mail has been read and preliminary matters have been handled. Then the dictation is usually transcribed by midafternoon. This pattern provides sufficient time for signing and mailing correspondence.

Some executives, however, prefer to dictate in the afternoon. This makes it necessary for you to decide which items to transcribe the same day and which to put off until the next morning.

The dictation pattern followed will be the choice of your executive. Executive secretaries agree that a secretary can try to change a boss's dictation pattern only when it is a habitual all-day, off-and-on pattern. Even then, be sure that changing the pattern will best serve your employer's interests and working environment.

Telephone Dictation

An executive who is away from the office for several days at a time will often use the telephone to dictate letters and memos. Since you and the person dictating cannot see each other, signal periodically to indicate that you are hearing and recording the message. An occasional "Okay" or "Got it" will suffice. Always read back your notes before the call is terminated. Verify names, addresses, and figures.

Occasionally you will be asked to monitor a conference call or an important telephone conversation between your employer and another person. If your employer has not done so, inform the other person that you are on the line and taking notes. If the conversation is too rapid, take down the main aspects of the conversation as one takes lecture notes. Always transcribe such notes promptly while the exchange of words is fresh in your mind.

Telephone conversations may be recorded on a cassette, belt, or disc. Each person participating in the conversation must be advised that the conversation is being recorded electronically. The tape can be transcribed completely, summarized, or simply filed for reference. The other person(s) may request a transcribed copy of the conversation or a copy of the tape.

Dictation at the Typewriter

You should be prepared to take your employer's dictation or that of an office visitor at the typewriter. Since the length of the dictated data will influence margin and vertical placement decisions, ask if the letter or memo will be short, long, or more than one page. Because the person dictating often asks for corrections, a retyping is usually necessary. When this is the case, do not stop to correct typing errors. Before retyping, give the dictator an opportunity to read your typewritten draft and to make further insertions or corrections.

After Dictation

Make a Quick Check of Notes

Before you leave the dictator's office, try to resolve any questions in your notes. Should the letter to Myers be sent by registered or certified mail? When will the date for the Denver meeting be definitely settled? It is a good practice to write all names carefully in longhand. If they are not ones you can easily check in files or other reference sources, ask the dictator for help.

Be sure to take back to your desk all items referred to in the dictation so that you can verify names, addresses, and the like. Such items should be released to you by the dictator after the communication in which they are referred to is dictated. As you get them, number each in the upper right corner to correspond with the number given the dictation in your notebook. Not only do the supporting papers serve as a check on names and addresses, but they also provide background material to enable you to transcribe more intelligently.

Be sure also to take back to your desk all your notes and personal possessions.

Complete Notes Promptly

When the dictation session is over, fill in any blanks and research missing information. It is best to verify doubtful matters right away while pertinent instructions are still fresh in your mind.

Make sure you have flagged any priority items from this dictation session.

Machine Dictation

Dictating and receiving equipment is being used in many business offices to supplement or replace the taking of shorthand. There are advocates of both approaches. Those who endorse the use of machine dictation and transcription point out that the system expedites the dictation process, even though it eliminates immediate and direct contact with the transcriber. Material can be dictated whenever and wherever it comes to the dictator's mind. The dictator is alone and does not require the services of a second person to record the dictation. It is also argued that machine dictation ensures a steady flow of work and a better distribution of work among transcribers. This factor frequently minimizes the number of transcribers needed in a business office or department. Many executives carry a portable dictating device when commuting to and from their homes and when on business trips. Others use them to dictate when working at home. Recorded dictation of this kind can be mailed in special envelopes so that the material can be transcribed during the dictator's absence from the office.

Word Processing Equipment

Dictation can be recorded on plastic discs and belts and on magnetic belts and tapes. The first two are inexpensive. Although not reusable, they can be sent through the mail and can be filed conveniently. Magnetic tapes and belts can be erased electronically and reused many times. They can also be mailed and filed easily. Magnetic tapes (cassettes) can be erased accidentally, however, if someone pushes the wrong button on the machine. The length of dictation contained on the tape is difficult to judge. You may find it necessary to process the material in rough draft when placement of the material is a major concern.

Most of the nonportable dictation systems are operated through the telephone. By pushing the designated button on the telephone you make contact with the dictation unit. You can play back your dictation and make corrections as often as the need arises. Endless loop or tank access systems use independent

IBM

By using an indicator slip, it is easy to judge the length of dictation on magnetic belts. The belts are reusable.

transmission lines to connect each dictator to the transcription center. Only one person can dictate at a time into a magnetic-tape loop. Transcription can go on uninterrupted at any time. The most popular dictating machine units, however, are those that fit on the dictator's desk. The dictation is recorded on tapes, belts, or discs and is either transcribed by the secretary or sent to a central word processing center.

Dictation to Others

At some point in your business office career, after you have become familiar with your employer's responsibilities and preferred practices, you may be asked to handle some correspondence on your own. The need to dictate to a junior secretary or to a word processing center usually occurs when additional administrative tasks are assigned and it becomes necessary to turn over routine work to others.

The prospect of giving dictation to another need not worry you. The skill can be easily mastered if you have carefully noted, as you take dictation from various executives, those practices that make one person a better dictator than another. The following principles and practices of good dictation apply when you dictate to a junior secretary who takes down your statements in shorthand and when you use a voice recorder.

Preliminary Planning Organize your time, materials, and thoughts. Plan to dictate when interruptions can be kept to a minimum. Since you need a quiet span of time in which to convey your thoughts, ask the receptionist or someone else to screen unex-

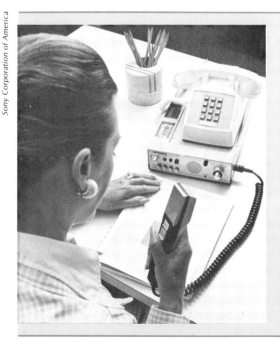

Sony Corporation of America

Good dictation technique is a matter of speaking distinctly and giving clear instructions.

pected callers. Before calling in a junior secretary or beginning to use a voice recorder, thoroughly digest the communication to which you are replying and think about the letter or memo you are originating. By reading correspondence carefully before beginning to dictate, you gain an opportunity to find in advance any background materials or files you need to respond completely and accurately. Think through what you are going to say before you say it. The recommended procedure is to outline the reply in advance. The outline may be jotted down in the margins of the incoming letter or on a scratch pad. Reminder notes of this kind can help you to avoid overlooking anything in your reply that could result in needless additional correspondence.

Authority and Responsibility

All correspondence you dictate for your employer's signature should be free of statements or actions that would conflict with the position your employer would take in replying. If there is the slightest chance you are exceeding your delegated authority or that of your employer when planning a reply to a letter or memo, obtain a confirmation of your proposed statement before you dictate. Discuss the point with your employer or refer the matter to someone at a higher level of management who is responsibile for the appropriate action.

Writing Style

Pattern your writing style after that of your employer when you are dictating a reply for his or her signature. Ideally, the communication should sound as though the person signing it had written it. Develop an awareness of the employer's preferred words, expressions, and sentence structure.

Dictating Procedures

You will experience less difficulty in dictating efficiently by avoiding the faults of others who make it difficult to transcribe dictated material properly.

- When dictating by machine, study the operation manual for the machine until you can operate all the controls.
- Speak clearly. Don't talk too fast or mumble. Avoid chewing gum, smoking, chewing a pencil, or eating while dictating. When using a machine, talk directly into the mouthpiece (two to three inches from your mouth) or toward the dictation unit or receiver. Enunciate word endings and dictate at a natural pace. Avoid dropping your voice at the end of a sentence.
- Give instructions. Identify the nature of the communication you are dictating—letter, memo, report, or telegram. State whether it is to be rough draft or final copy. List special requirements such as double spacing, specific margins, kind of paper, number of copies, and who should get each copy.
- Spell the name and address of each recipient.
- Dictate special or unusual punctuation and indicate new paragraphs; for example, say, "Comma, close quote," or "Period, new paragraph."
- Dictate figures carefully and spell out words that might be confusing such as *counsel* or *council* and *stationery* or *stationary*. Also spell unusual words, technical terms, and foreign language expressions.
- Provide an instruction when a title or word is to be underlined and when columns of data are to be centered.
- If there are attachments or enclosures, furnish them or explain where they can be located.

REVIEWING
YOUR
READING

1. When you are taking dictation and transcribing, what skills are needed?
2. Why is language skill the basic tool of word processing?
3. Identify the four requirements for secretarial competence in taking short-hand.
4. Of the two basic elements in writing shorthand—speed and accuracy—which is more important?
5. Describe the procedure for finding the place in your shorthand notebook to begin new dictation; for referring to old notes.
6. When your employer pauses for thought during dictation, what should you do? What should you avoid doing?
7. If your employer is interrupted by a phone call or a visitor while dictating, what should you do?
8. Name two ways to indicate in your shorthand notebook that certain items require prompt transcription.
9. In taking dictation, how would you handle these problems: (a) deleting several words, (b) restoring an original outline after it has been struck out, (c) noting a blind carbon copy instruction, (d) handling a transposed phrase, (e) marking a transposed sentence or paragraph, (f) putting in a long insertion, and (g) indicating a question for later clarification.
10. Describe the correct procedure for handling all related letters, files, and other items as you receive them when taking dictation.
11. After a dictation session, when should you check over your notes?
12. Why is it helpful to listen to a recording of your voice?
13. What are nine principles of good dictation to follow when you are the person originating the message?

USING
YOUR
Skills

1. **Building Your Vocabulary.** From each of the following groups of words, choose the word that is nearest in meaning to the first word of the group. Type on a sheet of paper just the letter and the answer.
   a. Caption—army officer, title, development, almanac.
   b. Porter—redcap, conductor, messenger, professional.
   c. Statute—order, law, waybill, invoice.
   d. Illuminate—paint, light, cut, place.
   e. Requisition—list, note, order, quitclaim deed.
   f. Affix—handle, mail, depart, attach.
   g. Facilitate—help, hinder, execute, effort.
   h. Obsolete—new, produce, out-of-date, recall.
   i. Participating—going, sharing, perishing, deciding.
   j. Humility—cheerfulness, damage, modesty, distress.
   k. Equity—authority, position, fairness, horsemanship.
   l. Option—eye doctor, choice, view, persuasion.

2. **Similar Words.** From the words in parentheses choose the one that correctly completes the meaning of the sentence and type the letter and word on a sheet of paper.
   a. The (extract, abstract) of title was mailed Saturday.
   b. Her actions were rather (affected, effected).
   c. Joan will (precede, proceed) June in the procession.
   d. To master the (principals, principles) of accounting, one must study hard.
   e. Please send your application to the (personal, personnel) director.
   f. The president of the company I work for receives a $60,000 (salary, wage) yearly.
   g. What is the (capital, capitol) of New York?
   h. A (confirmation, conformation) of the telegram will follow.
   i. Please prepare a (memoranda, memorandum) to be sent to the treasurer of the class.
   j. The (expression, impression) she gave was favorable.
   k. The man (knew, new) about the mistake.
   l. He (past, passed) the bill for payment.
   m. She found herself in dire (straights, straits).
   n. The book (lay, laid) on the chair.
   o. He had chocolate mousse for (desert, dessert).
   p. The river has (raised, risen); the tide has turned.

3. **Rationale for Standardized Methods.** You have reviewed in this chapter a number of techniques for taking dictation effectively. Understanding the reasons for using such techniques should facilitate your making them part of your permanent dictation capability. Type brief reasons why each technique below should be used.
   a. Gain a good working knowledge of punctuation, spelling, and hyphenation.
   b. Train your memory to retain and recall whole phrases and sentences.
   c. Write an outline for every word dictated.
   d. Always have a notebook handy and ready for use.
   e. Date each day's work.
   f. Leave several blank lines between items dictated.
   g. Know standard proofreader's marks.
   h. Write proper names in longhand.
   i. Insert punctuation during pauses in dictation.

EXERCISING
YOUR
JUDGMENT

Tracking the Boss. You work for two partners who both have the same annoying habit. They leave the office without telling you where they are going or when they will be back. You hesitate to ask them any questions about their plans for fear of annoying them. However, you are constantly embarrassed because when other persons ask for them you are unable to say where they are or when they will return. You decide to take the matter up with both partners. What approach could you use?

Capitalization. To capitalize a word draws attention to it. Generally accepted business usage sanctions the use of capitals for a proper noun, the title of a published work, and the like. But some words may or may not be capitalized, depending on a given situation. For example, in the sentence, "The credit department of Barnes & Adams has reported an increase in overdue accounts receivable," there is no need to capitalize "credit department." But in this sentence from a company directive, "Refer all telephone complaints about customers' statements to the Credit Department," the capitals are justified for the name of that particular department within the company. Too much capitalization, however, may defeat its purpose of singling out special words. When everything is made to stand out, nothing stands out. The trend today, therefore, is toward less capitalization.

Retype the following paragraphs on a plain sheet of paper, with correct capitalization. Use double spacing and provide a suitable heading.

Our state highway department has sent you a bulletin about this matter. Refer to bulletin no. 412 of that organization to obtain a direct reference. The bulletin indicates that several million dollars is due from the federal government for the old-age pension fund. Tomorrow the revenue and taxation committee will consider this problem. Last tuesday at a meeting of this committee, action was postponed until may 12.

A similar problem was presented to the illinois state highway commission by j. k. allen, president of the acme corporation. The problem referred to rentals under a lease with the excell corporation. Their agent, mr. john applegate, reported that lease no. 470 was in dispute and presented as evidence a copy of general letter no. 3, dated february 12. Additional information may be obtained from the tax collector of cook county.

Chapter Thirteen / Transcription

Transcription is the process of converting dictated communications into acceptable hard copy. The specialized techniques you use when working from shorthand notes or using dictation media apply here. The finished product is a transcript that displays the dictator's words correctly and attractively. An acceptable level of performance depends upon such interrelated skills as the correct use of grammar, keyboarding, transcription and typing, and the ability to use reference works.

Transcription Prerequisites

The basics of grammar, usage, and style are prerequisites to high-quality transcription. The chief aspects of style are punctuation, capitalization, numbers, abbreviations, spelling, and word division. In all aspects of grammar, usage, or style, you are assumed to be the expert and are held responsible for applying the rules governing them with intelligence and taste.

Additional transcription prerequisites are work station organization, good judgment, and high performance standards.

Work Station Organization

Most secretaries are assigned to an existing work station and to a previously purchased typewriter. Although such equipment is expensive and not frequently exchanged or replaced, you control the manner in which it is utilized. Discover efficient ways of performing your tasks—from the elimination of wasted motions in manual operations to the rearrangement of the work station.

First decide on the most efficient organization of your desk and supplies. Your desk drawers should be organized for productive operation. Store frequently used supplies such as felt pens, pencils, erasers, elastics, paper clips, scissors, staples, ruler, Scotch tape, and rubber stamps and pad in the center drawer. Use the top side drawer with sloping dividers for letterheads, plain bond second sheets, carbon sheets, and dictation notebooks. Stack envelopes on edge at the front. The middle side drawer is a convenient storage space for work in progress and such occasionally used supplies as correction fluid, extra typeface elements, and replacement typewriter ribbons. The bottom side drawer can hold personal articles and infrequently used records.

An analysis of the flow of materials and the pattern of work movement in relationship to machines, equipment, and other office personnel is an essential part of an operation study. You might begin by experimenting with the organization of the immediate work station and supplies to see whether operations or elements can be eliminated, combined, changed in sequence, or improved. Also analyze the method, motion pattern, materials, and equipment used in an individual operation to determine the best way to organize.

Look for opportunities to eliminate unnecessary motions. What kinds of reaches do you make? Do you waste energy? Improvements, even small ones, are measures of progress. For example, when typing, consider the location of supplies, use of a copyholder, and your motions of inserting, typing, and removing material.

Grammar and Usage

A thorough knowledge of the English language is indispensable. With the right word at your command, you can communicate with clarity and precision. When an executive makes an occasional grammatical slip during dictation, you can quietly make the necessary correction. Your job is to handle language; catch omissions, errors, or ambiguities; and correct them before they show up in hard copy.

If you are unsure of the basic rules governing subject and verb agreement, verb tenses, agreement of pronouns with antecedents, adjectives and adverbs, prepositions, and sentence structure, learn how to look things up in a handy style manual. Increase your vocabulary through reading and the use of a dictionary. Add new words to your speaking and writing vocabulary by using them. Give

Al Green

Using a dictionary to verify spelling assures accuracy, and at the same time expands one's vocabulary.

special attention to words that are often misused or confused, such as the ones below:

above, foregoing	farther, further
aggravate, irritate	if, whether
amount, number	imply, infer
between, among	leave, let
can, may	shall, will

Spelling Most people agree that a business letter, memo, or report is not acceptable if it contains a spelling error. When a spelling error slips by undetected, the business communication in which it appears reflects unfavorably on the person who wrote it. Keep a reliable reference, such as *Webster's New Collegiate Dictionary*, within arm's reach. "When in doubt, look it up" is a maxim worth adopting. Mastery of the key spelling guides will help you keep your dictionary references to a minimum.

A source such as *20,000 Words, Spelled and Divided for Quick Reference*, 7th ed., compiled by Louis A. Leslie (Gregg Division, McGraw-Hill Book Company), is an exceptionally useful secretarial tool. Such references give you the spelling and word division for an extensive list of words.

With a little effort, you can develop a spelling-improvement program. One practical procedure is to keep a list of troublesome words that you misspell or have to look up in the dictionary. Use a small notebook, with two pages allotted for each letter of the alphabet except *q*, *x*, *y*, and *z*. Whenever you add a new word, quickly review the other words on the page, with their pronunciation and meaning. Thus, if a page contains seven words, you will have studied the first one seven times. As soon as a word becomes a permanent part of your vocabulary, cross it off the list and continue reviewing the others. Another list of words worth keeping contains words that sound alike but are spelled differently. The shorthand outlines for these words are either identical or similar. For example:

accept (to take; to receive)	capital (chief; foremost)
except (to exclude)	capitol (building in which legislature meets)
affect (to influence)	coarse (rough, common)
effect (a result; to bring about)	course (action; a way)

Other words that sound the same or have similar shorthand outlines are *advice* and *advise*, *allude* and *elude*, *anyone* and *any one*, *appraise* and *apprise*, *complement* and *compliment*, *loose* and *lose*, *principal* and *principle*, and *than* and *then*.

Punctuation Correct use of the marks used to indicate relationships between words, phrases, and clauses and give more precise meaning to a sentence are your responsibility. The standard terminal or end-of-sentence marks are the period, question mark, and exclamation point. Internal punctuation includes the comma, semicolon, colon, dash, parenthesis, quotation mark, underscore, apostrophe, ellipsis, asterisk, diagonal, and bracket.

Most dictators do not dictate punctuation. The competent secretary soon learns that voice inflection is usually a good clue to where to insert punctuation in the transcript. But to do this quickly and correctly, you need to be familiar with good punctuation practices. You also need to have a style manual at hand—and use it.

Punctuation practices tend to change over the years. The current tendency is a compromise between the overpunctuation of an earlier day and recent attempts to reduce traditional rules of punctuation to the simple guideline "Use punctuation only when it is essential for clearness." The difficulty with the latter rule is that what is clear to the writer may not be clear to the reader. You must learn, therefore, to exercise good judgment in using whatever punctuation is appropriate and essential to prevent misreading.

The Reference Section at the back of this book provides a helpful review of current rules for punctuation.

Capitalization

Capitalizing a word gives it distinction, importance, and emphasis. Current practice is to use capitalization sparingly. In addition to the first word of every sentence, the names of particular persons, places, or things are capitalized. Commercial products, headings, titles of literary works (except for the articles, conjunctions, and prepositions of fewer than four letters), names of organizations, days, months, and holidays are capitalized. Common nouns are not capitalized.

Abbreviations

In executive or professional writing, where a more formal style prevails, use abbreviations sparingly or not at all. In routine memos and letters, business forms, and catalogs, abbreviations may be used more freely. In statistical matter, footnotes, and technical writing, where the emphasis is on conveying information in the briefest manner, abbreviations occur frequently. Avoid abbreviating a term in one place and then spelling it out in another.

Names of well-known business organizations, government agencies, acronyms, and standard time zones, when abbreviated, are usually written in all capitals and without periods.

AT&T	American Telephone and Telegraph
YMCA	Young Men's Christian Association
ZIP Code	Zone Improvement Plan Code
PERT	Program Evaluation and Review Technique
PDT	Pacific Daylight Time
FCC	Federal Communications Commission

Transcription Procedures

Before you begin to transcribe dictation, you need to make some preliminary decisions about how to proceed.

Priorities   From your shorthand notes or instructions given by the dictator, determine the order in which the items dictated are to be transcribed. Give matters of importance or urgency the highest priority. Process them immediately, present them for signature, and mail them before less urgent items are transcribed. The remaining items can be processed and presented for signature by the end of the day. Some items can be carried over until the following day. Keep them in a special place where they can be transcribed the next day along with any new dictation.

Editing   Read your shorthand notes carefully before you begin to transcribe them. As you read, insert needed punctuation. Indicate where paragraphs begin. Write out unfamiliar or difficult words. Eliminate ambiguities, errors in grammar, and repetitious words. Where necessary, rewrite awkwardly worded sentences. Verify all dates, names, quantities, and the like. Make special note of any enclosures or attachments. If these were not given to you, retrieve them from the files or from the appropriate source. Find and insert additional information when instructed to do so. If some portion of your notes is not complete or does not make sense to you, check back with the dictator in person or by telephone.

Letter Length   By means of a simple procedure, you can estimate from your shorthand notes the number of words contained in the body of a dictated letter. First, count the number of words contained in ten complete lines of your shorthand notes. Then calculate the average number of words you get on a line of your shorthand notes by dividing the total number of words by ten. Record this number on the front cover of your shorthand notebook. Use it to estimate the length of any dictated letter by simply counting the total number of complete lines of shorthand notes and multiplying this total by your estimated number. After a while, you will be able to estimate the length of a letter merely by looking at your shorthand notes.

Letter Placement   The secretary is responsible for seeing that each letter transcribed is positioned on the page so that it is pleasing to look at and easy to read. A letter should be placed so that the margins appear as a white frame around the message. The frame should be in proportion to the size of the paper, with the bottom margin slightly deeper than the width of the side margins.

A number of letter-placement guides have been developed, but none is comprehensive enough to fit all letters and letterheads. A standard procedure is to locate the date on line 15 and the address on line 20. The guide here provides variable placement specifications for three letter-length estimates:

LETTER PLACEMENT GUIDE				
Content Estimate	Type Spaces Pica	Elite	Date Position	Address Position
Short (under 100 words)	40	50	line 16	line 24
Average (100–200 words)	50	60	line 15	line 20
Long (over 200 words)	60	70	line 14	line 18

There are two basic "expansion joints" in most placement plans: the space between the date and the inside address, and the length of the typing line (the width of the margins). As a general guideline, make the width of the side margins just about equal to the space between the date and the inside address.

Some business offices prefer a uniform 60-space line for all letters regardless of the number of words in the letter. An adjustment is made in the number of lines to be left between the date and the inside address. For a short- to average-length letter, 9 to 12 blank spaces are left between the date and the inside address; for long letters, 3 to 6 blank spaces are left.

Most secretaries, however, learn to rely on their own placement estimates. They know that most business letters contain between 100 and 200 words. Using this knowledge, they visualize specifications that will, for a given letterhead, fit letters in the 100- to 200-word span. For a shorter letter, they expand the letter vertically by allowing more space after the date, allowing more space for the signature and lowering the reference initials. For longer letters, they reverse the procedure. By allowing less space after the date, edging the lines a little farther to the right, allowing less space for the signature, and raising the reference initials, you can condense a longer letter.

Copy Requirements

After your shorthand notes have been completely edited, check for instructions as to the number of copies needed and the names of the persons to whom copies are to be distributed. Also determine whether additional information is to be added on certain copies. When enclosures are specified, make sure the appropriate persons on the distribution list receive copies.

Many business offices retain two copies of every transcribed communication. One is kept in the correspondence file and the other in a handy chronological file of communications processed and dispatched each day. This short-term, quick reference file can be helpful when you are trying to locate a hard-to-find item.

Stationery

Most business offices use several kinds of letterheads. An official one is designated for all routine business transactions. In addition, there is an interoffice memorandum that people at all levels of management and staff use when communicating with each other. Key executives usually have special letterhead that differs from official letterhead in the size and quality of the paper. Such special letterhead usually displays the company's name and address and the executive's name and title. Occasionally, within a company, there are operations or projects that require additional letterheads; these may display the company's trademark or a special product.

For letters requiring more than one page, plain paper of the same quality, weight, and color as the letterhead is provided.

Paper Standards.   For correspondence, a good-quality paper is essential. Although 100 percent rag paper is the most expensive and is used primarily for such permanent documents as wills and minutes of meetings, it is also used for executive letterheads. For ordinary correspondence a 25 percent rag paper is commonly used. Sulphite papers, which are made from wood pulp, are not so

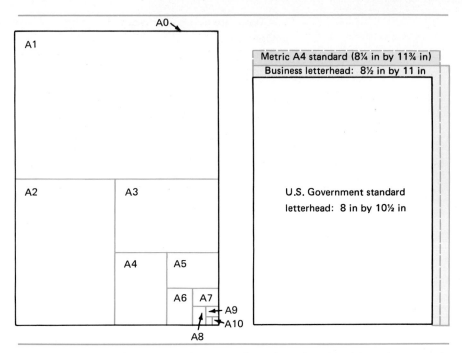

ISO standard metric paper sizes.

strong as rag-content papers and not usually so long-lasting, although a recently developed sulphite sheet is unusually durable.

Some offices use stationery in International Standards Organization (ISO) recommended paper sizes. The use of ISO paper sizes limits the number of sizes used. Since the papers stack more neatly, a better use of storage facilities results. The use of ISO sizes also results in easier filing with fewer sizes and shapes to handle. Microfilming is simplified because all sizes in the ISO paper series can be reduced to film of the same proportions.

ISO paper comes in A, B, and C series. The main A series is formed by halving a rectangle of paper (AO size) measuring 841 x 1,189 millimeters, which is about 33.1 x 46.8 inches. The number following the A or B designation indicates how many times the AO or BO size was halved. The ISO letterhead size is A4 and measures 210 x 297 millimeters, which is about 8¼ x 11¾ inches.

An ISO standard exists for paper substance weight. The measurement of paper in grams per square meter allows easy comparison of different sheets. Thickness of paper is measured in micrometers.

The standard typewriter accommodates A4 letterhead size, and machines with longer carriages can receive the larger A3 size. Minor changes in markings for centering paper are needed.

The A4 letterhead fits easily into legal-size file cabinets. Care must be exercised in placing the A4 paper in letter-size file drawers, because A4 paper is close to the length of the letter-size file folder.

Envelope, Postcard, Poster, and Folder Standards.   The ISO B series is used for posters, large envelopes, wall charts, and similar items. The C series accommodates smaller envelopes, folders, and postcards. The DL size envelope is

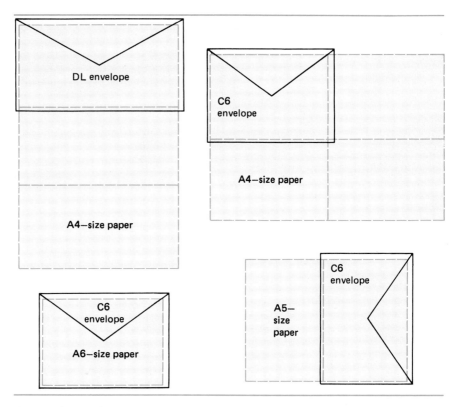

ISO standard metric envelope sizes. A6-size paper fits into the C6 envelope without folding.

designed to replace the No. 10 envelope currently in use. International agreement was reached on using only ISO standard envelopes of certain sizes for regular international mail. Other size envelopes would require a surcharge of about 50 percent over regular postal rates to compensate for special handling.

Second Sheets.   Lightweight stationery, called "second sheets" or onionskin, may be used for file copies and carbon copies sent to people other than the addressee. The stationery may be plain or imprinted with the company name and address. The word "copy" may be imprinted at the top or diagonally across the sheet. Such sheets vary in weight from 7 to 13 pounds, with either a smooth or a rippled finish. Of course, the thinner the sheet, the less space it will occupy in the files and the lower the mailing cost. Use the following table as a guide in selecting the appropriate paper weight for second sheets:

CARBON COPY CAPABILITIES			
Electric Typewriters		Manual Typewriters	
Paper Weight	No. of Copies	Paper Weight	No. of Copies
13 pounds	1–8	13 pounds	1–5
9 pounds	9–12	9 pounds	6–8
7 pounds	12–14	7 pounds	8–10

Second sheets are available in an assortment of colors, but legibility is highest with white, pink, or yellow sheets. Some offices use prepared carbonless paper packs for typing file copies and copies of correspondence and forms that are to be distributed. Although carbonless paper packs are convenient and time-saving, they are more expensive than paper-and-carbon packs or assembling carbons manually.

Special-Finish Paper.   Some bond papers permit erasing of typed and written impressions with an ordinary soft pencil eraser. These papers have a coating that slows the absorption of ink into the paper. When erased promptly, errors can be corrected without evidence that an erasure has been made. Although time can be saved and paper waste reduced, easy-to-erase finishes smudge easily. When erasing, be careful not to smudge the surrounding typing.

Carbon Paper

A secretary should know how to select the right kind of carbon paper for each copying assignment. To exercise such judgment, you should be familiar with the basic variations in weights and finishes.

Weights.   A standard weight of carbon paper is the easiest to handle and should be used when one to four copies are required. But when you need more than four copies, you can get much better results with a medium- or light-weight carbon sheet. The table below can serve as a guide for selecting the right weight and finish.

Finishes.   Most carbon paper is coated on the top side with a finish that makes the sheet curl-free. High-quality top-coated carbon paper is also smudge-free. For top-quality work, a plastic-base carbon sheet is available that comes in one weight and finish, makes from 1 to 10 copies in one writing, and can be reused 50 to 60 times.

Various carbon finishes are available to help you cope with such factors as whether the typewriter is electric or manual, condition of the typewriter cylinder, size of the type face, and desired color intensity of the copy. A soft finish is recommended when the typewriter has a soft cylinder, when the type is pica size or larger, or when the typist has a light typing touch. A hard finish is appropriate when the typewriter has a hard cylinder, when the type is elite size or smaller, or when the typist has a heavy typing touch. A medium finish is best for all normal typing situations.

Copies	Weight of Carbon Sheet	Finish of Carbon Sheet
1–4	Standard	Hard
5–9	Medium	Medium*
10+	Light	Soft*

*Use a hard finish in place of medium and a medium finish in place of soft on electric typewriters.

Carbon Packs. Since making corrections on multiple carbons is slow and costly, secretaries often prefer to type only an original and then reproduce the required copies with a photocopy machine. These time-saving copy machines do not totally eliminate the justified use of the carbon pack, especially in situations where one to four copies are required. Although prepared carbon packs are supplied in some offices, you may have to assemble a carbon pack for insertion into the typewriter or to build the carbon pack right in the machine.

To assemble a carbon pack, place the glossy side of the carbon sheet against the paper on which the copy is to be made. Add another sheet of paper and carbon for each copy desired. The top sheet is the letterhead or plain sheet that is to be the original copy. Once the pack has been assembled, straighten the sides and top of the pack and insert it into the typewriter with a quick turn of the cylinder. To keep the sheets straight when inserting, try placing the pack in the fold of an envelope or in the fold of a piece of paper.

Another way to assemble a carbon pack is to roll a sheet of typing paper around the platen. Insert the carbon pack between the end of the paper and the platen. The pack can then be fed into the typewriter easily and evenly.

Letter Styles

Many companies furnish their secretaries with a company correspondence manual covering authorized letter styles. Secretaries are then responsible for adhering to company preferences.

In the absence of specific company directives, executives are usually free to follow their own preferences. Their secretaries are expected to endorse them.

Some executives leave the choice of letter format entirely to their secretaries' judgment. The letter style chosen should convey the company's type of business and the image it wishes to convey to its correspondents. For example, a conservative law firm would be more appropriately identified by one of the more traditional letter styles, such as the semiblocked, than would a manufacturer of hang gliders.

Dates

Date every item you transcribe: notes, outlines, rough drafts, reports, letters, and memos. Date a letter the day you transcribe it. If you cannot transcribe it the day it is dictated, remember to alter such references as "today" or "this afternoon."

Transcription by Phrases

Glance ahead in your notes so that you can transcribe a whole phrase at a time, rather than transcribing word by word. You will not only improve the accuracy of your work as you transcribe according to meaning, but you will also get the job done faster. The ability to read ahead as you transcribe will enable you to foresee such problems as errors in grammar and changes in dictation.

Rough Drafts

The purpose of a rough draft is to allow the dictator to revise, rewrite, and reorganize dictated material. A rough draft should be typed on inexpensive paper. Allow generous 1-inch margins and triple space between each line. Correct typing errors by crossing out incorrect copy with consecutive Xs. Speed of transcription is important at this stage. Style and accuracy count only in the final transcription.

Confidential Information

When transcribing or otherwise working with confidential material, be careful to protect it from inquisitive eyes while it is on your desk. Cover it if someone is near your desk. Put it away if you must leave your desk. Word processing centers usually assign confidential work to controlled-access areas.

Remember that rough drafts, carbon paper, and one-use carbon ribbons can be as informative as the final copy.

Proofreading

The accuracy of hard copy is your primary responsibility. Before removing it from the typewriter, proofread the copy carefully. Compare the transcript with your notes sentence by sentence to be sure nothing has been omitted. Only a close check will uncover a word substitution such as "than" for "that" or "not" for "now." Try proofreading the following newspaper paragraph by scanning it.

In 1947, the prime interest rate, the very lowest rate that big banks quote to their very best customers, was 1.5%. As recently as January 1972 it was only 4.75%. But not it is around 10%.

Use the file copy for proofreading once the original has been removed from the typewriter. Mark required corrections in ink on the file copy before reinserting and aligning the original in the typewriter.

When proofreading technical or tabulated data or contracts, it is a good practice to enlist the help of another person to read transcribed copy while you read aloud from original shorthand notes.

Corrections

A mailable transcript contains no strikeovers or smudges. Corrections must be so skillfully executed that they are almost undetectable. If there are any smudges visible after you remove the transcript from the typewriter, use an artist's gum eraser to remove them. Gum erasers are not abrasive enough to erase typewritten characters. Make sure that any corrections you make on the original are made on the distribution copies also. Retype the complete transcript when lengthy changes are required.

Canceling Notes

As soon as you have transcribed a piece of dictation, draw a diagonal line entirely through your shorthand notes. You can then see at a glance what remains to be transcribed. Since you may be interrupted during transcription and since you seldom transcribe items in the exact order in which they were dictated, you will find that the visual signal provided by the canceled notes will help you avoid transcription omissions.

After Transcription

Your transcription responsibilities are not yet finished when you remove an error-free, well-positioned transcript from your typewriter. Several things must be done before you submit your transcribed material to the dictator for signature.

Enclosures

If enclosures are noted in a letter, check to be sure you made the appropriate notation following the reference initials. This notation is needed as a reference on your file copy and as a reminder to the receiver. If an enclosure is to be mailed separately or does not accompany the letter being presented for signature, advise the dictator by note. It will serve as a reminder to obtain the enclosure before the covering letter is mailed.

It is not a safe practice to use as an enclosure a file copy of a letter or document or the original copy of a letter received. Take the time to prepare a photocopy.

Carbon Copy Recipients Check to see that copies are provided for each person indicated by the dictator. When a letter is addressed to more than one person, carbon copies are used as originals. Place a check mark beside the name of the person to whom each individual copy is being sent. Address an envelope for each recipient and accompany the letters with the appropriate envelope when presenting them for signature.

Type the reference notation *bc* and the names of the recipients of blind copies on all copies except the original. Use a strip of paper to block the notation on the original when typing it on the carbon copies.

Envelopes Prepare an addressed envelope for each of your transcribed letters. A time-saving technique is to insert an envelope between the letter and the typewriter platen. As you remove the letter, the envelope will be positioned for addressing. After you remove the envelope from the typewriter compare the envelope and the letter name and address for agreement.

Presenting Transcripts for Signature

The time of day that you present finished transcripts to your employer for signature is usually determined by a schedule of mail pickups or the urgency of a communication. Present rush items as soon as they are ready; present all other items (in batches) sufficiently early in the day for expeditious handling. Presenting transcripts for signature at the end of the day can result in needless delay.

Assembling the Pieces The following procedure is recommended when submitting transcripts for signature:

1. On top of the letter, place the addressed envelope, address up, with the flap tucked over the top edge of the letter.
2. Place small enclosures in the envelope to prevent their being lost. Clip full-size enclosures in back of the letter.
3. Under the letter to be mailed, place any extra copies, with their accompanying envelopes, that are to be sent to other departments or persons.
4. Staple the file copy onto the original correspondence. On the file copy make notations about enclosures, extra copies, arrangements for material to be sent separately, and follow-up requirements.
5. Put the transcripts and accompanying papers in a labeled signature folder and place it on your employer's desk, in a specified spot.

The form in which you present the transcripts may depend on the dictator's preferences. Discuss with your boss whether or not you are to include carbon copies of the transcription or retain them. The boss may wish to have them so that minor corrections or notes can be made on the copies. Such details, however, are usually taken care of by the secretary. If your employer prefers to sign or initial information copies being sent to other persons inside or outside the company, these should then accompany the original transcript.

Signing the Dictator's Name

If you are given permission to sign the dictator's name to certain letters, write your initials directly below and close to the end of the signature. On some routine letters, you may be authorized to sign the dictator's name without adding your initials.

The practice of including a "dictated but not signed" notation on a letter is obsolete. It is poor public relations, for it gives readers the impression that the writer is indifferent to them.

Machine Transcription

Your transcription equipment may be an individual or a centralized unit. Individual units consist of a headset, a foot pedal, and a playback unit that accepts recorded media such as magnetic tapes, belts, discs, or cassettes. Playback units have various controls for volume, clarity, and speed and an index-scanning lever. The foot pedal permits you to control the forward and reverse action of playback and usually controls the repeat of the last few words dictated following a stop and resumption of playback. You must load and unload most individual transcription units.

Centralized dictation units have the capability of distributing dictation to

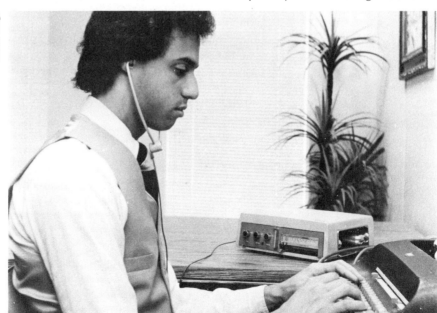

Martin Bough

With an individual transcription unit, the operator can control volume, clarity, and speed.

one or more secretaries through a program console. Gauges on the program console indicate the amount of untranscribed dictation remaining in the recorder. The supervisor can switch a secretary from one tape tank (as tape containers are called) to another. An intercom system connects each dictator with the program console operator. Urgent communications can be transferred to a priority tank and processed before other dictation. The system also monitors the total amount of dictation recorded on each tank during a given period, the total amount of dictation recorded by the entire system, and the duration of each item of dictation.

Steps in Machine Transcription

Machine dictation may be transcribed on a standard typewriter, a typewriter equipped with correcting tape or ribbon, one with an internal memory, or one equipped with paper or magnetic tape. In each instance, you keyboard the material dictated without stopping for the correction of errors. The copy is then edited and corrected. The corrected copy is typed into final hard copy or as an updated computerized tape file.

With typewriters equipped with correction tapes or ribbons, you can make corrections to the initial draft, but the carbon copies must be corrected manually. Retyping is necessary, however, when significant changes in copy are required. Memory typewriters allow you to record copy quickly and to correct typing errors by striking over them as the copy is recorded in the memory. Copy is then given to the dictator for approval. Any subsequent changes noted on the copy are simply typed manually from the keyboard during the final typing. Magnetic tape or card media permit you to make corrections directly on the tape or card, which may be retained for future use.

Operation of Equipment.   Machine transcription is the processing of communication that has been recorded on such media as tapes, cassettes, discs, and belts. The producers of transcribing machines provide instruction manuals that introduce the machine's operations and the functions of the foot pedal and headset. Instructions are also provided on how to get power to the unit, how to place the recorded medium into the machine, and how to start, stop, and repeat the dictated words.

Proofreading.   Proofread transcribed letters, memos, or reports while they are still in the typewriter. Reposition the scanner at the beginning of the dictation. Keep the foot pedal depressed as you proofread the copy. Make any required corrections, remove the transcript from the typewriter, and remove the recorded medium from the unit.

Reviewing Your Reading

1. Explain the relationship between dictation and transcription.
2. Name three prerequisites for managing dictation that are just as essential for transcription.
3. List some work station items that should be readily accessible.

4. Why do most business executives agree that a letter is not mailable if it contains even one misspelled word?

5. What is meant by the statement "Although a secretary may augment the effectiveness of the dictator's communications, the dictator is responsible for the meaning they convey"?

6. Of the several transcription preliminaries, which ones should be completed as soon as possible after a dictation session?

7. Since no single letter-placement guide is comprehensive enough to fit all letters, what procedure must a secretary employ in order to position transcripts attractively?

8. What are two ways of making carbon copies? What are the advantages of each?

9. Why is transcribing by phrases a good idea?

10. What is the proper format for typing rough drafts?

11. Describe the recommended procedure to follow if material is removed from the typewriter before it has been completely proofread.

12. Why is it considered to be good practice to draw a line through dictation that has been transcribed?

13. Before you present an error-free transcript to an employer for signature, what three additional transcription responsibilities remain?

14. Describe the procedure you may safely follow when assembling the parts of a transcript for an employer's signature.

USING
YOUR
Skills

1. In each of the following pairs of words, one word is correctly spelled. Prepare a typewritten list of the correctly spelled words. Indicate where you might divide each word if it appeared at the end of a typewritten line and word division was unavoidable.

   a. accommodations
      accomodations

   b. calander
      calendar

   c. consistent
      consistant

   d. convinience
      convenience

   e. withholding
      witholding

   f. mispelled
      misspelled

   g. accessable
      accessible

2. For each of the following words, find a word that sounds the same but has a different spelling and meaning. Provide brief definitions.

    a. complement

    b. disburse

    c. preceding

    d. stationary

    e. waive

3. Edit this draft of a letter, and then transcribe a final copy:

To all Member of Camera America:

~~As you know~~ May 21st is the day for the annual meeting of Camera America, the fastest-growing amateur photographer's club in the country. The meeting will be held in the ballroom of the ~~National~~ [Marriott] Hotel in Denver.

The a.m. session will begin promptly at 10:00 o'clock. We shall first hear reports of the years' activities from each of the regions ~~branches~~, and ~~several branches will~~ [will be] exhibited photos taken by members. also, the nominating committee will present it's slate of officers for next year.

Lunch will be served at one in the Gold Room at the hotel. ~~Tickets to~~ [The charge to] members will be 5.50, to guests, six dollars. ~~Dont you~~ [Please] send your reservations for lunch to our secretary, Paul Capsis, before May 10.

At the afternoon session we will discuss whether the annual dues should be increased also, we will vote on whether we should merge with the National Camera Club.

Try to attend and [to] bring at least one interested guest.

Yours for the best meeting yet,

Chairman

---

4. Transcribe these two letters, as they appeared in a shorthand notebook, on separate sheets of paper and type mailable versions of each. Observe insertions, corrections, and the like.

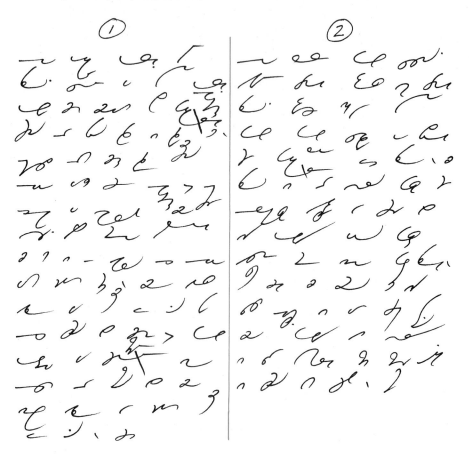

EXERCISING
YOUR
JUDGMENT

Moonlighting. Your employer has learned that you are working as a singer in a private club from 5 p.m. until 1 a.m., six days a week. She indicates to you that it is not wise for you to continue double employment because it will have an adverse effect on your health. You enjoy singing in the club very much indeed and are not willing to give it up. However, your pay as a singer is extremely low, and you need to continue working in the daytime as well in order to meet your expenses.

Since company policy does not prohibit "moonlighting," does your employer have the right to tell you that she does not feel that you can hold two full-time jobs and do justice to both? Under what conditions can your employer tell you that you cannot continue with the extra job while still in the company employment?

<table>
<tr><td>Applying
the
Reference
Section</td><td>

Consult the Reference Section of your text or a standard reference manual in completing this assignment.

1. On a separate sheet of paper, type the recognized abbreviations for the following words:
   a. Square inch
   b. United States of America
   c. Enclosure
   d. Doctor
   e. Doctor of Philosophy

2. Identify the words represented by the following abbreviations:
   a. acct.
   b. distr.
   c. i.e.
   d. e.g.
   e. dtd.

</td></tr>
</table>

CHAPTER fOURTEEN

Editing and Composing Techniques

One of the most important secretarial responsibilities is the processing of dictated letters and memorandums for the employer's signature. Initially, your goal is to transcribe accurate communications that are attractively displayed. These letters and memos must reflect good typewriting skills and the ability to proofread, punctuate, spell, capitalize, and recognize correct grammar. Eventually, after you have become familiar with your employer's responsibilities and writing style, you will find opportunities to edit and rewrite dictated information and to handle writing assignments from basic research and draft all the way to final copy. In doing this you must demonstrate your ability to produce written communications that mirror your employer's reasoning patterns, vocabulary, and style of expression.

Proofreading and Editing

Check dictated copy with particular care, since spontaneous dictation rarely lends itself to polished prose. Read through your notes before you type. You may need to type a rough draft of the copy first to pick out confusing wording and inconsistencies in style. Be on the watch for dangling modifiers, ambiguous pronouns, faulty subject-verb agreement, and redundant expressions.

Proofreading   Proofreading means more than checking for typographical and mechanical errors. It also includes checking for spelling, grammar, punctuation, hyphenation, format, and meaning.

Whether a word is genuinely misspelled or just mistyped, it looks like a spelling error and produces the same result—distraction and sometimes confusion and misunderstanding. One wrong letter or two transposed letters can create an entirely new word and thus alter meaning. Keep a dictionary within reach when you proofread, and use it whenever you have the slightest doubt about spelling.

Examine each punctuation mark critically. Since punctuation serves to clarify meaning and the grammatical relationship of words, also be alert for missing but necessary punctuation. Check hyphenated words at the ends of lines. Divide words as the preferred office dictionary divides them.

You may become involved in proofreading in several different ways. One way is to check your own work for errors of any kind. You may also proof the work of others, or make changes and corrections on a rough draft for others to type. In addition, you may type the final draft of copy proofed and marked up by someone else. Therefore, you must not only be able to recognize errors, but also be able to mark them so that others will understand what changes and corrections are to be made.

The most commonly used proofreading marks are presented in the Reference Section.

Proofreading Guidelines.   When proofreading by yourself, read aloud when you can. This technique will slow you down, direct your eyes, and help you concentrate on listening. If the material to be proofread is long, involved, or technical, team up with someone else. One person can read aloud from the typed copy while the other follows silently on the original. To relieve fatigue and monotony, trade jobs occasionally. Sound out all punctuation marks and hyphens. Spell out all proper nouns, technical words, and homonyms like *your* and *you're* and *affect* and *effect*.

If possible, proofread early in the day when you are fresh rather than just before quitting time, after lunch, or when you are in a hurry. If you have a tendency to skim over material that is familiar to you from previous reading or typing, hold a straight-edged ruler below each line as you read. This device will aid you in concentrating and ensure that you check every word and line.

Letter and Memo Formats

Even before a letter is read, the reader gets an impression of the writer. Smudges, obvious erasures, errors, unequal margins, and the like create a negative impression. Conversely, a centered letter that looks clean and crisp is an inviting introduction to the message it contains.

Letters.   Many large business offices have their own style manuals, but the majority allow secretaries to use their own judgment in selecting the letter style to be used for correspondence.

The Reference Section illustrates the basic business letter styles and the recommended positioning of the standard heading, opening, body, and closing, as well as such variables as personal or confidential notation, reference notations, attention line, subject line, company signature line, enclosure notation, mailing notation, carbon copy notation, and postscript.

Punctuation Patterns.   Although standard punctuation is always used in the body of a business letter, the other parts may be punctuated according to one of three patterns—standard (mixed), open, or close (full). The standard pattern, which is the most commonly used, makes use of a colon after the salutation and a comma after the complimentary closing. In open punctuation, no punctuation is used at the end of any line outside the body of the letter unless that line ends with an abbreviation. In the full pattern, which is rarely used nowadays, each line outside the body of the letter ends with a comma or a period. The open and standard patterns are illustrated in the Reference Section.

Interoffice Memorandums

For communications within a company, an interoffice memorandum is used, which is often typed on a preprinted form. Both the style and the tone are less formal than in outgoing correspondence. The tone, of course, may be somewhat more formal if the writer is addressing a superior. In any case, both the salutation and the complimentary closing are omitted.

The printed headings indicate essential information to be supplied. The arrangement of these guide words may vary slightly; one standard form is shown below. To type the information for each guide word, follow this procedure:

1. Align the typewritten line with the bottom of the guide words.
2. Set the left margin stop or tab to align the information two spaces after the longest guide word in the left part of the heading.
3. Set a tab stop two spaces after the longest guide word in the right part of the heading.
4. Type in the information for each guide word.

Allow equal left and right margins. Begin the message no less than two blank lines below the last guide word in the heading. Use single spacing, with a blank line between paragraphs. Paragraphs are not usually indented. Use outline form and enumerated listings for summarizing data as succinctly as possible.

Interoffice Memorandum

To:	Sales Staff	From:	W. J. Scott
Subject:	Sales Conference	Date:	January 6, 19--

The weekly sales conference will be held this Thursday, January 9, in my office at 11:30. Lunch will be sent in; plan to stay until 2:30.

Come prepared to discuss the following topics:

1. New products--selling points.
2. Spring promotion campaign.
3. Advertising appropriations for next quarter.

                                        W.J.S.

WJS:cvf
cc: Lewens
     Kalt
     Yates
     Jensen

Not only is the complimentary closing omitted, but the handwritten signature is also left out. Some dictators prefer to initial their memos, but usually the dictator's initials are typed. For more formal messages, the dictator's name and title may be typed in the signature position. Reference initials and enclosure and carbon-copy notations are used as in letters.

Good Writing Standards

The effective use of words is the key factor in writing letters, memos, and reports that are easy to read and understand. When written communications are complete, concise, clear, correct, and appropriate in tone, they get ideas across and help win favorable reader response.

Make It Complete.   Check the completeness of the things you write. Give all the information necessary and answer all the questions the reader may have in mind. A common kind of incompleteness is illustrated by a memo that asked for a further report, declaring that "the memo submitted did not include all the data required." The nature of the missing data was not specified. To supply it required further correspondence and expensive delay.

Do not hesitate to take a positive position, to give a clear-cut *yes* or *no*, or to commit yourself unequivocally. Too many letter writers hide what they should say with overcautious words and phrases such as *it is reported*, *it might appear*, *it is not too clear*, and *it may be observed*. The reader gets the impression that the writer is hedging or avoiding taking a position.

Completeness should not be sacrificed for brevity. A message that is not complete is not clear; it fails to say all that needs to be said. A letter may be several pages long and still be concise, or it may be one paragraph long and still be wordy.

Make It Concise.   Long-windedness is the bane of effective writing. Many reports, letters, and memos can be shortened from 20 to 50 percent and made more effective by omitting unessential ideas and words. If you want to get a message across, you must get others to read what you write. The longer it is, the less likely they are to read it. Too often, long memos or reports are merely scanned and put aside.

You also have an obligation to the reader. People in responsible positions spend much of their working time reading through an endless flow of written material. Many hours can be saved for productive work by avoiding the tendency to tell everything you know about a subject, rather than just what the reader needs to know. For example:

We are wondering if sufficient time has passed so that you are in a position to indicate to us whether favorable action may now be taken on our recommendation to employ Rudolph Willoughby.

Is the statement concise? Obviously not. It is stiff and wordy. The reader need not be told about the writer's wonderment. The idea that needs to be expressed can be written briefly:

Have you had sufficient time to consider our recommendation to employ Rudolph Willoughby?

Sometimes an effort to be concise may result in a curt tone or in a concentrated style that is difficult to understand. Most writers, however, need to look critically at their writing to see whether they include only essential words and phrases. Many windy phrases are used unnecessarily in place of single words. Note how the simple and more direct words or phrases at the right get the point across more effectively than the wordy phrases at the left.

Wordy	Concise
in view of the fact that	because, since
confirming our telephone conversation	as agreed by telephone
all that is necessary for you to do is	(just say what the reader is to do)
in connection with	by, in (give the connection)
we have discontinued the policy of	we no longer
we ask that you remit	please send
will you please arrange to send	please send
in the most careful manner	carefully
prior to	before
reduce to a minimum	minimize
under date of	on (give the date)
in the event that	if
due to the fact that	because
at a later date	later
at all times	always
in regard to	about, in
with reference to	about
in the amount of	for
despite the fact that	though, although

Try to avoid using a group of words for a simple verb. For example:

give instruction to	instruct
she is of the opinion	she believes
have need for	need
give consideration to	consider
make an adjustment in	adjust

Sometimes a word can do the work of a whole phrase or even a clause; "is due *in large measure* to" can be stated as "is due *largely* to."

Make It Clear. The primary aim of any written communication is to convey ideas so that they will be understood by the reader without unnecessary time and thought. Problems often arise, however, when you use complex or unusual words. The person who wrote, "After a comprehensive appraisal of all the circumstances pertaining to the issue" could simply have said, "After a careful review of the facts."

The best business letters use words that are unaffected and are comfortable to the reader. To establish understanding with your reader, choose the simplest words you can think of that convey your meaning. These are the short, easy words that enable you to say what you want without using professional jargon and stilted phrases.

The words and phrases in the left column are likely to cloud meaning. Use the simpler equivalent for each as shown at the right.

High-Sounding Words	Simpler Words
enlighten us	let us know
ascertain	find out
procure	get, obtain
render	give or send
consummate	end, complete, finish
inquire	ask
forward	send
interpose an objection	object
encounter difficulty in	find it hard
initiate or institute	start
it is requested that	please

Note how the simple and more direct words or phrases get the point across more effectively.

Make It Correct.   Statements that are not accurate cause no end of trouble. To avoid this problem, have your facts and figures straight to the last detail before you begin to write. You cannot afford to fall back on the excuse of lack of time for failing to research the facts. You will save time in the end by checking every statement for accuracy whenever there is the slightest doubt.

Review grammar, spelling, and punctuation for correctness. Grammatical errors lessen the respect of the reader and divert attention from the message. More important, they may cause actual misstatements. Observe the difference in meaning that results from misplacing one word:

These job vacancies *only* will be filled through the personnel department.

These job vacancies will be filled *only* through the personnel department.

Make the Tone Appropriate.   Tone refers not to what you say but to *how* you say it. Your tone may make friends, or it may make enemies who can damage your customer relations efforts.

There are times when a formal style is entirely appropriate. A common error, however, is the use of a formal tone when the situation does not call for it. Many writers become stiff and unnatural when they begin to write or dictate. They choose pretentious, impersonal words that they would never use in talking. In this kind of writing, *before* and *after* become *prior to* and *subsequent to*, and people never *get jobs*; they *secure employment*. As a result, the writing sounds dull and stuffy.

Avoid stock phrases like, "In reply to your letter," "Under separate cover," and "Enclosed please find." Such expressions are old-fashioned and slow down both writer and reader. Contrast the stilted expressions at the left with the crisp expressions at the right.

Stilted	Better
acknowledge receipt of . . .	thank you for . . .
as per . . .	according to . . .
at an early date	soon or on (specific date)
attached hereto	attached or enclosed, or here is
due to the fact that	because, since
in re	regarding, concerning, about
the writer	I, me
trust	hope, believe
under separate cover	I am sending

Use Personal Pronouns.   Humanize your business correspondence by using personal rather than impersonal pronouns. *You, we,* and *I* add warmth to a business letter and give it conversational tone. Using personal pronouns can help you to avoid the passive voice.

Impersonal: It is unfortunate that there was a delay in filling your order.

Personal: You were very patient while waiting for us to fill your order, and we appreciate it.

Impersonal: The beneficiary form C-902 is being returned because it has not been signed.

Personal: Please sign the enclosed beneficiary form and return it to me.

Accentuate the Positive.   A positive statement is one that stresses the favorable. Words like *might, may, think, hope,* and *if* undermine the forcefulness of a positive expression. Practice changing negative and indecisive phrases to positive ones, as shown here.

Negative	Positive
don't forget to let us know . . .	let us know; we want to help . . .
thank you for your trouble . . .	thank you for your help . . .
you won't be sorry . . .	you will be pleased . . .
to avoid further delay . . .	to hasten delivery . . .
we cannot quote you a firm price without first seeing the specifications . . .	as soon as we see the specifications, we will be able to quote you a firm price . . .

When you must convey negative action or unpleasant news, be as tactful with the reader as you can. You can often imply the negative rather than state it directly.

Blunt	**Tactful**
You failed to enclose your check.	We did not receive your check.
You claim we made a mistake.	There is a difference between your figures and ours, but . . .
You forgot to pay the sales tax.	You will see that we have added the sales tax to the invoice.

Sentence and Paragraph Structure

To be effective, a written communication must hold together. Each sentence should flow smoothly into the next, and each paragraph should connect with the following one. You can help the reader get the message clearly and quickly by constructing complete thought units and arranging them in logical order, placing important ideas in important positions.

Sentences. A long sentence often contains too many ideas. This confuses the reader. Keep sentences short by limiting them to one thought, or no more than two very closely related ones. By keeping your sentences to twelve or fifteen words, you can avoid the impression of choppiness, which is distracting. Connecting or linking words such as *besides, however, accordingly, therefore, of course, for example, nevertheless, furthermore,* and *in the second place* lead the reader from one thought relationship to another by indicating that the subject is being continued.

Paragraphs. The number of paragraphs used in a written communication varies. No matter how short the message, however, at least two paragraphs should be used if possible.

A paragraph should convey one principal thought, and all its sentences should bear on that thought. Try to limit each paragraph to six or eight typewritten lines. Longer paragraphs make a message difficult to read. Too many short paragraphs make for a choppy look and are frequently an indication of disconnected, rambling thinking. If possible, keep the number of paragraphs in a letter to three or four.

The indicator of transition between two paragraphs usually appears at the beginning of the second paragraph. When paragraphs are short, the linking words or phrases may be the same as those used to connect sentences. Linking words, however, do not resolve the problem of disconnected thoughts.

Mental or Written Outlines. Make a mental plan before you attempt to write a letter, memo, or report. Know the major ideas to be included and the order in which they should be arranged. Better yet, write down all the important ideas, using a word or phrase for each, and arrange them in their most effective order. For example, in replying to a request for approval to change an established procedure, you might begin with the following outline:

Acknowledge initiative.
The merits of change.
Disadvantage.
Endorse revision.

Each point in the outline can become a separate paragraph. You are then free to concentrate your thoughts on developing one idea at a time. Equally important, the outline reveals logical relationships and helps you avoid repetition.

For long reports, a written outline reduces the chance of omitting essential facts. It also eliminates the tendency to include material not relevant to the subject and purpose of the report.

Getting the Reader's Attention

From the moment a communication is in the hands of the reader, it must command attention. It must also accomplish its purpose or answer all questions the reader may have in mind. To achieve such goals, your message must get off to a fast start and have an effective ending.

The Opening Statement. The first sentence of a business letter should be short, to the point, and, when possible, provocative. If you succeed in piquing the reader's curiosity or interest, the person will probably read on to the end of the letter. Say something that will stimulate immediate interest. Avoid such time-wasting expressions as "We have your letter . . . in which you ask," "This will acknowledge receipt of your letter," or "In reply to your letter."

The first words of a letter should do one or more of these things:

- Tell the reader something interesting.

  Yes, we carry the spare parts you . . .
  The date for the next meeting is . . .

- Get the reader on your side.

  Thank you for writing about . . .
  We are pleased you brought up the question . . .

- Ask a meaningful question.

  Can you provide samples . . .?
  Are you in the market for a new car?

- Give a reason for writing.

  We are writing about . . .

- Command attention.

  No, it is not necessary for you to provide security for a loan.

- Get to the point.

  We have not received your January payment.

An Effective Ending.   End a letter with a statement or restatement of the action you expect of your reader. Clearly stated, it will not only leave the reader with exactly the impression you intended, but it will also satisfy the feeling of having reached the end. You will therefore need to edit the last paragraph carefully.

A letter that is necessarily long may end with a brief summary. Or, you might end with a reassuring statement about action to come. This type of ending is especially desirable if you think the reader's confidence in your company has been weakened. For example, when making an adjustment you might conclude, "We are sure that the new part will give you years of dependable service."

LETTERS SECRETARIES COMPOSE

The routine messages that make up a sizable portion of the letters written in business offices are the first that you may write for an executive's signature. Included in this broad category is a potpourri of easy-to-write messages, including request, acknowledgment, covering, referral, follow-up, and business-social

---

Rawlings Paper Products Company
63 Forest Hill Drive, Providence, Rhode Island 02915

August 9, 19--

Miss Angela Hoffman
Forms Incorporated
111-19 Hawthorne Place
Tulsa, Oklahoma 74116

Dear Miss Hoffman:

Carol — Take care of this please. A. H.

I was fortunate enough to attend a session of the industry study group at which you spoke on the subject of simplifying forms. Your talk was interesting and instructive.

You mentioned that you had assembled a set of simplified applications which listeners were welcome to review. I shall be in your area all next week and would like to look the forms over. Perhaps you would be good enough to let me know the day and *any* time this would be convenient.

Thank you for your generous offer. I am sure my company will *Tuesday* benefit from this timely project.

                          Cordially,

                          Matthew Kim

                          Matthew Kim

MK:pr

The secretary may be called upon to write routine letters for an executive's signature.

letters. Another category of business letter you may be called upon to write may contain a message your reader does not want to hear. Such letters take several forms—complaints, adjustment and credit refusals, and collection requests.

Requests and   Request and inquiry letters are either asking or answering letters in which you
Inquiries   convey simple facts. Make your statements specific and to the point. The objective is to write so that you cannot be misunderstood. For example, when requesting hotel reservations, state the name of your employer, the date and anticipated time of arrival, the accommodations desired, and the expected date of departure. Also request a confirmation.

Note the brevity and completeness of the following request letters:

Ms. Janice R. Kavaler, Marketing Director of C. R. Gibson, Inc., would like to subscribe to *Publishers Weekly*. Her check for $33 for a year's subscription is enclosed. Please send the magazine to her home address, 210 Sims Road, Edison, New Jersey 08817.

Please send me a copy of the booklet "Investment Hints," which was advertised in this week's *Time* (Nov. 11). I wish to use the information it contains in the consumer education course I teach in Oakdale High School.

Enclosed is 50 cents to cover the cost of mailing and handling. Send the booklet to 541 W. Oakdale Avenue, Chicago, Illinois 60657.

Replies to routine request letters should be made promptly, accurately, and courteously. The following writing guidelines apply:

* State only essential facts.
* Give all necessary information.
* Be accurate and truthful.
* Use a friendly and considerate tone.
* Consider sending additional information that might be useful.

Observe how these hints apply in replying to the following request for information:

I should like to have 50 copies of a booklet released by your organization, "Charting Work Procedures," for use in a training course for office supervisors. This course will start February 16.

Is this booklet available in quantity? If so, what will the cost be for 50 copies? How do I order?

Your reply might read like this:

We can send you 50 copies of the booklet "Charting Work Procedures," plus additional copies if you need them.

The cost for 50 copies is $13.75—$12.50 for the booklets plus $1.25 to cover handling and shipping expenses. Please return the

enclosed order blank with your check. The booklets should arrive
in plenty of time for your training program.

Acknowledgments An acknowledgment letter is one that tells the sender that a letter or some material has been received. It is sent when the matter presented cannot be completely dealt with the same day by means of an answering communication. Note in the following illustration of a routine acknowledgment how the criteria of completeness and courtesy have been observed.

We received the contracts relating to the Schmidt account this
morning. They will be returned just as soon as Mrs. Mindell finishes
reading them. Thank you for sending them so promptly.

Letters received in your employer's absence are either acknowledged but not answered, or acknowledged and also answered. Those that are acknowledged without an answer follow this simple pattern:

* Mention the date of the incoming letter and the subject matter.
* Give a brief and reasonable explanation of the delay in your employer's reply.
* Assure the writer that the letter will be answered as soon as your employer returns.
* Do not give detailed or confidential information about your employer's absence. Avoid referring to an illness.

Your letter of July 12 about your service contract arrived today.
Mr. Brown is on a business trip and will return Monday, July 19. Your
letter is being held for his immediate attention.

During your employer's absence, if you acknowledge a letter in which you give information that has been requested, be certain of your facts. The following pointers can be helpful.

* Identify the subject of the incoming letter.
* Explain that your employer is away.
* State the facts that answer the letter.
* When appropriate, indicate that your employer will respond in greater detail when he or she returns.

Covering and Transmittal Letters Covering letters inform the person who receives them that material is being forwarded separately:

You will soon receive our holiday catalog. We are confident that you
will find many gift-giving ideas in its 256 illustrated pages.

Transmittal letters accompany material being sent. They confirm the fact that material was enclosed and provide the sender with a record of when and how you sent what to whom:

Here is your automobile lease for the next 12 months. Please sign both copies. Keep the original for your records and return the other copy to us.

Referrals   Occasionally an executive receives a letter or memo about a transaction or problem that should be referred to someone else in the organization for handling. In your reply, inform the originator of the communication that the matter has been referred to another person who is responsible for all such matters. Give the person the full name and title of the person who will handle the matter. Avoid committing the associate to a specific course of action or time limit. Before you mail a referral letter, it's a good practice to alert by telephone or memo the person to whom you're referring the matter.

In the following referral letter, the secretary handles the assignment tactfully.

Your April 7 letter, in which you ask about a dealership in Boston, Massachusetts, was sent to Mr. Arthur C. Burgett, our eastern regional manager. Since all our dealerships are handled on a regional basis, Mr. Burgett is the person authorized to take the appropriate action. I am confident you will hear from him before long.

Of course, when you forward the letter to Mr. Burgett, you'll want to attach a covering memo.

Art,

Here is the letter from Ms. Jeanne Bianco about which I spoke to you today, along with my reply. Please let me know if I can be of further help in handling this inquiry.

When you refer the writer of a letter to an organization other than your own, be sure to include the complete company name and address.

The *World Almanac* is published by the Newspaper Enterprise Association, Inc., New York, New York 10017. If you write them at 230 Park Avenue, I am sure they will be able to take care of your request.

Follow-Ups   It is good procedure to maintain a follow-up system (tickler file) to keep track of anticipated action on matters of concern to your employer. This memory aid allows you to record and keep track of assignments that are pending or which have specific due dates. When something is due or overdue, you will be expected to send a reminder message to the appropriate person. These communications should be tactfully worded to encourage the person to complete an assignment or take a necessary action.

Note that the following reminder does not stress the other person's negligence or failure to be prompt.

When you were in the office last month, you mentioned that you would send Mrs. Shue a copy of the expense report form used by your company.

The committee working on forms revision will meet next Thursday, July 21, and Mrs. Shue would like to use your report form to illustrate her recommended changes. Would it be possible for you to send a copy before that time?

Business-Social Letters

Secretaries are asked to write various types of business-social letters to extend such messages as congratulations, acceptances or rejections of invitations, consolations, and expressions of appreciation. All such personal messages are appropriately written on an executive's personal stationery or on plain bond paper. The inside address may be typed at the bottom of the letter, at the left margin approximately 4 to 6 lines below the signature. The salutation and complimentary closing are usually informal and followed by commas or by no punctuation. Details such as the writer's typewritten signature, reference initials, and enclosure notations are generally omitted.

Congratulations. Your employer will expect you to remain alert to the accomplishments and honors earned by business associates. Whenever a promotion, anniversary, or retirement occurs, you can expect to assist in drafting the appropriate message.

Congratulatory messages should be brief but friendly. Begin by referring to the reason for the congratulations. Stress any known characteristics of the recipient that contributed to the accomplishment. Convey the likelihood of bigger future accomplishments if appropriate and your employer's interest in maintaining close association.

> Congratulations! The announcement of your promotion to group vice president has been warmly received by your many friends in the production department.
>
> Your spectacular progress since joining the company 10 years ago is a real inspiration to all the ambitious young men and women in the company.
>
> My sincere wishes for success in your new responsibilities.

Letters of congratulation should be sent as soon as possible. They can lose their impact when they arrive too long after the event has occurred. They should be written in a style that approximates the tone your employer would use, and they should be signed by him or her.

Invitations, Acceptances, and Regrets. Secretaries have many opportunities to draft or write acceptances and refusals to business-social functions their employers are invited to attend. Most of these invitations call for an informal response typed on executive or personal business stationery. The formality of the tone in your reply depends upon the nature of the relationship that exists between your employer and the person or organization extending the invitation. You can safely use a friendly but respectful tone.

Imagine that your employer has received the following invitation:

Dear Margaret:

I should like very much to have you as my guest at dinner on Monday, November 15, at the Jolly Ox Restaurant, 290 Long Ridge Road, Greenwich, Connecticut.

The reservation calls for a six-thirty serving.

Please let me know whether or not you will be available to join me and other committee members in what we anticipate will be an informative dinner get-together.

Cordially yours,
Philip

Your typed reply for your executive's signature might approximate the following acceptance or refusal:

Dear Philip:

I accept with pleasure the kind invitation to join you and other committee members for dinner on Monday, November 15. I will meet you at the Jolly Ox at six-thirty.

Needless to say, I shall be looking forward to an enjoyable dinner and discussion.

Sincerely yours,
Margaret

Dear Philip,

I am sincerely sorry that I cannot accept the kind invitation to join you and other committee members for dinner on November 15.

Unfortunately, I am committed to attend a management training seminar on that date.

I sincerely wish I could join the group in what will surely be a pleasant and productive dinner-discussion.

Sincerely yours,
Margaret

A secretary is usually responsible for composing, supervising the engraving of, and sending formal invitations, as well as sending handwritten acknowledgments of their receipt. Current and correct forms for invitations may be obtained from a book of etiquette or from any reliable printer or stationer.

Formal invitations are written in the third person, whether printed, engraved, or handwritten. The full name of the sender appears on the invitation, but only the last name of the guest. In the acceptance or regret, however, the reverse of this rule applies. The words *request the pleasure of* or *invite you to attend* follow the name of the sender. In an acceptance the words *kind invitation* are used; in a regret response, *very kind invitation*. The date and hour are used in an acceptance, but only the date is mentioned in a regret. The reason for declining an invitation is not required.

Formal invitations written in the third person require a response in the third person, written by hand on personal writing paper. The message requires no more than a paragraph with each line centered vertically and horizontally.

Above, formal invitation; *below left*, formal acceptance; *below right*, formal regret.

Appreciation. It is your responsibility to recognize when a letter of appreciation should be written by an executive and to see that it is written. Although the content of such messages cannot follow any set pattern because of varying personal circumstances (assistance, patronage, cooperation, services), there are several guidelines to follow. Letters of appreciation should reflect the executive's personal feelings. Tact and timing are important ingredients. An effective way to give an appreciation letter a tone of sincerity is to mention the specific thing that is being acknowledged and to recall something outstanding about it. Avoid using trite, brusque words that suggest that the recipient merely performed a routine task. You might compose a message like the following to acknowledge the contribution of a speaker who addressed a management training group sponsored by your employer:

Thank you for taking time from your busy day to address our sales managers last Tuesday afternoon.

Your explanation of the techniques involved in conducting a direct-mail sales campaign was especially timely and stimulated much discussion. Many of the managers present indicated that they intended to share your many good recommendations with their sales representatives.

I feel confident that your guidance and direction will enable us to increase our sales.

Consolation.   A number of circumstances in business require a consolation letter that a secretary may draft for an employer. Typical are expressions of sympathy for losses, reverses, or failures, and for the illness or death of an associate.

The purpose of consolation letters is to express concern about the grief experienced by a business friend and to offer whatever help is possible. Avoid insincere phrases such as "Please feel free to call on me at any time." Make any offer of assistance as specific as possible.

All messages of consolation should be written in longhand and signed by the sending executive.

Dear Frank,

All of us at General Appliance Company were deeply saddened by the news of the death of your daughter Margaret.

At a time like this, words are small consolation. Nevertheless, we want you to know that our thoughts and our sympathy are with you in your sorrow.

Sincerely,
Lawrence

Letter of consolation.

Complaint and Adjustment Letters

The true test of your letter-writing skill is whether you can say *no* nicely. Both complaint letters and adjustment letters herald unpleasant news. Your challenge is to compose a message that will minimize the anxiety and disappointment of the reader. Keep the following goodwill guidelines in mind:

- Make your opening statement friendly and as closely directed to the reader as possible.
- Present the reasons for your negative response, framing them in terms of the reader's benefits.
- Introduce the refusal as tactfully as you can, ideally by implication rather than by direct statement.
- Introduce a positive statement or counterproposal, avoiding any further reference to the negative statement.
- Close your letter cordially, by inviting a desired action, if appropriate, or by making an effort to indicate your desire to serve whenever there is an opportunity for you to do so.

Suppose it is your assignment to reply to the following complaint letter:

I fail to understand why I have not received the garden tool set offered in your ad in the July issue of *American Homemaker* magazine.
I sent you the coupon and a money order for $9.75 two weeks ago. If you cannot send the set within a week, I want my money back.

Upon investigation you find that an unexpectedly heavy response to the garden-tool ad exhausted the entire stock of the sets. A new supply was ordered and is expected within the next few days. Your reply might be this:

Your order for our popular garden tool set is appreciated. Unfortunately, so many readers sent in the coupon that our entire stock was exhausted before we received your order. A new supply is expected within a week and your set will be shipped promptly.
If, after you receive your set, you are not completely satisfied, return it and we shall promptly refund your money.

Here is a typical adjustment request letter:

On August 1, I paid $927.33 to Global Storage Warehouse, Inc., for the movement of my household goods from Weston, Massachusetts, to Greenwich, Connecticut.
This total contains a $40 overcharge. You show a $20 charge for two wardrobe cartons I did not receive and a $20 charge for insurance coverage I did not contract for. Copies of the Standard Household Goods bill of lading and freight bill 68790 were marked to specify these discrepancies.
Please refund this $40 overcharge.

Observe whether the reply to this letter follows the goodwill guidelines previously stated:

We sincerely regret the overcharge on the bill of lading for your recent move from Massachusetts to Connecticut. A quick check has revealed that both errors were made in our clerical department.

Enclosed is our check for $40 to reimburse you. Please accept our sincere apology for any inconvenience we have caused you. We want you to think favorably of Global Storage Warehouse, Inc., should you need packing and moving services in the future.

Credit and Collection Letters

Writing credit and collection letters is challenging and requires considerable insight into people's motivations. The extending of credit is based on the understanding and assurance that others will abide by the promises they have given. Credit collection, on the other hand, is the process of seeing that these promises are honored and kept.

Credit Letters.   When granting credit, express pleasure in welcoming the new customer. If credit cannot be granted, indicate that you are pleased that the applicant wishes to establish a credit account with your company. Then tactfully review the reason why such an arrangement would be unwise at this time. Be honest. In closing a credit refusal letter, suggest doing current business on a cash basis, offering special cash terms as an inducement. Make the central theme of your message the necessity of sound business practice.

Dear Ms. Serrano:

Your new Rent Anything Service will provide a much-needed service in this area, and we wish you success in this venture. We appreciate your thinking of State National Bank in planning your money requirements for the coming year.

After your service business has operated on a sound financial basis for 12 months or more, we will consider your request for a line of credit. This minimum period is necessary in order to protect the interests of our depositors.

In the meantime, we invite you to consult our competent staff of professionals regarding your day-to-day cash flow problems.

Sincerely,
Jane W. Boynton
Credit Manager

Collection Letters.   The objective of a collection letter is to collect a debt and, equally important, to educate customers to accept their credit responsibilities. To accomplish both, you must (1) convey concern that the customer's good credit standing is threatened, (2) not scold or preach, (3) use forceful and positive language, and (4) end the message with a request for action and a resumption of a sound business relationship.

Keeping a sales viewpoint is important. Although the objective is to collect what is owed, you do not want to drive away business. Collection letters are usually written in a series, with the pressure increasing from the first to the final letter. In the initial letters, assume that the customer intends to pay the bills and emphasize your belief in the customer's sense of responsibility. State the amount due, and be specific about what is expected. Avoid vague threats. Emphasize the importance of immediate action. The two examples below are a first reminder and a second reminder.

> Anyone can overlook a past-due bill. Perhaps this has happened to you. The amount of $88.50 is now subject to a late-payment finance charge that is computed at the rate of 1½ percent per month, which corresponds to an annual percentage rate of 18 percent.
>
> Please send us your check for $89.81 and avoid additional late-payment charges.

> The adage "No news is good news" is not always economical. We have been awaiting word from you and also your check to cover the $88.50 plus $1.31 late-payment charge that is owed us. Your account is now two months past due, and we must reluctantly add an additional $1.35 late-payment charge to your account.
>
> Please let us know if there is some reason why you have not taken care of this outstanding balance. Or just drop your check for $91.16 in the mail to us today.

Request Letters   Secretaries receive considerable practice in writing a wide assortment of request letters. You can expect frequent opportunities to write for your employer asking for information, action, and appointments and to order merchandise or service.

Request letters should be direct, concise, and easy to answer. Provide the background or reason for the request. Describe completely what you expect the reader to do. Point out the potential advantage the reader may gain by complying with the request. Whenever possible, write to a person rather than to a company.

Ordering Goods or Services.   In place of a purchase order form, a letter is often used to order merchandise or service. The chief requirements of such letters are clear arrangement of facts and accuracy of specifications. Give attention to such details as catalog numbers, quantity requirements, descriptions of items, unit prices, and price totals. The method of payment, desired delivery date, and destination of the shipment must also be clearly specified.

The following letter is typical:

> Please charge the account of J. H. Farrior and Sons, 2516 Boulder Street, Denver, Colorado 80217, for the following items selected from your catalog. These items should be shipped express.

Quantity	Item No.	Item	Unit Price	Total
5	950	Executive desk, wood	$249.95	$1,249.75
5	645	Executive swivel chair	198.95	994.75
4	152	File, 4-drawer, steel	94.95	379.80
2	630	Swivel side chair	92.95	185.90
2	528	Cabinet, 4-shelf, steel	87.95	175.90
				$2,986.10

This is our Order No. 250. If there have been price changes on any of these items or if you cannot deliver by Friday, January 5, please notify us before filling the order.

REVIEWING YOUR READING

1. What kind of errors does a secretary check for when proofreading?

2. What skills are needed to become a good proofreader?

3. What elements are included in writing style?

4. About how long should a paragraph be? How many paragraphs are there in the average letter?

5. For each of the following expressions, give a simpler, less affected word or phrase: *forward, procure, ascertain, it is requested that, enlighten us.*

6. In each of the following pairs of expressions, indicate which is more effective in a business letter and tell why:

I believe	It is believed
Will you kindly	Please
In the amount of	For

7. Make each of the following wordy expressions more concise: *due to the fact that, your check in the amount of $100, we ask that you remit, in regard to.*

8. Change these old-fashioned phrases to more up-to-date language: *acknowledge receipt of, in due course, due to the fact that, in a position to, under separate cover, attached hereto.*

9. How will an outline help you compose better letters?

10. How does the use of personal pronouns improve your message?

11. Change the following phrases to make them more positive or tactful in tone: *don't forget to let us know, to avoid further delay, we don't think you will regret, you say we're wrong.*

12. What three things do you need to keep in mind when you are composing letters for someone else's signature?

13. What is the purpose of a covering or transmittal letter?

14. Which of the following outlines would you use in writing a letter in which you must refuse a customer's claim?
   a. A frank statement of *no.*
      Reasons for saying *no.*
      Apology for the refusal.
      Plea for understanding from the customer.
   b. Expression of appreciation for opportunity to consider the claim.
      Review of the facts shown by the records.
      Conclusion based on the facts relating to the claim.
      Offer of an alternate solution, if applicable.
      Expression of desire to keep the customer's goodwill.

1. Shorten and simplify the following sentences:
   a. If you want a refund, please complete the enclosed application form, "Request for Refund," and return it signed to this office at the above address.
   b. The general manager spoke to us in regard to your proposal to reduce the clerical cost in connection with processing the backlog of accounts receivable.
   c. Please read the instructions on the form carefully so that you will get all the facts.
   d. She spoke in a manner that was courteous, and that was extremely appealing as well.
   e. Your attention is called to the fact that you must have your report in this office by October 1 to meet the deadline.
   f. The question that is in doubt is whether your company can meet the production schedule in the time you suggest.

2. Restate these wordy and stiff opening statements so that they are more natural and to the point:
   a. Reference is made to your letter of June 3 to Ross Trimboli, which has been referred to this office for attention and reply in connection with your interest in a position as a data analyst.
   b. In accordance with the instructions contained in your letter of January 26, the records of this office have been amended to show your name as Harold B. Levine instead of Harry B. Levine.
   c. This is in reference to your letter of August 11, in which you express concern about your account because of the difficulties you are encountering due to prevailing economic conditions.
   d. Reference is made to your letter of October 19, enclosing the receipt for the quarterly payment which was requested by a letter from this office dated October 11.
   e. An examination of the files of this office reveals a pamphlet entitled "Word Teasers," which appears to be the work to which you make reference in your communication of July 21.

3. Rewrite the following letter to make it more effective:

   Mr. Arthur N. Ponti, Ponti's Book Nook, 816 Puget Avenue, Pullman, Washington 99163. Dear Sir: Acknowledging yours of April 12 in regard to purchasing books from our firm on a credit basis and thank you for same. Our records do not show that we have ever done business with you on a credit basis in the past. We cannot honor your request for credit until we have ascertained certain credit information about your business. Attached hereto is an application form that we would advise you to complete in its entirety before a decision can be reached regarding granting credit to you. Trusting that we may hear from you at an early date and hoping that we can see our way clear to do business with you in the future, we remain, Ace Publishing Company, F. A. Ayres, Credit Manager.

EXERCISING
YOUR
JUDGMENT

Whose Mistake? Lori, a recent college graduate, has just become a steno-graphic assistant in your office. Your boss is the senior member of the corporation's legal department, and the work is very demanding. Accuracy is all-important. In filing some carbons of letters that Lori has typed for you, you are horrified to discover that she sent a memo to half a dozen officers in the corporation (it did not require a signature) with the word *shown* spelled *shone*. How will you explain this to your boss? What should you say to Lori? What should you do about the memo? Whose fault is it that the error was not detected before the memo was released?

APPLYING
THE
REFERENCE
SECTION

Hyphenation at the ends of lines and within sentences is covered in the following exercise. Refer to the Reference Section or a grammar, usage, and style manual if you need help.

1. Retype the following sentences and insert hyphens where needed:
    a. Your right hand margin is uneven.
    b. Is that an up to date newspaper you are carrying?
    c. She said she felt out of date.
    d. This is a never to be forgotten experience.
    e. His self conscious manner bothered his friends.

2. Supply hyphens where needed in the following words and phrases. Delete or retain hyphens as required.
    a. poorly-written book
    b. a step up in production
    c. twenty-nine
    d. a two-inch margin
    e. income tax form

3. Hyphenate the following words as though the end-of-margin bell rang on the first letter of each. Assume there are four spaces after the bell rings before the carriage locks.
    a. rearrange
    b. knowledge
    c. livable
    d. scientific
    e. limitless

Chapter fifteen / Reprographics

There are many makes and models of reprographic equipment available that contribute to both the speed and the scope of communications and records maintenance. They range from the simple to the sophisticated and complex in both operation and mechanics. Secretaries are usually not expected to understand how all of them operate, but you should be familiar with the commonly used processes, the kinds of work they are capable of handling, and the factors to consider in selecting appropriate equipment.

There are three basic forms of reprographic equipment: copiers, duplicators, and combinations of the two.

Copiers

Copying machines, frequently called photocopiers, produce exact images of original documents by taking pictures of them. Photocopying equipment is available in a variety of models, from desk-top units to those that automatically feed, reproduce, and collate lengthy business reports. For exact copies of complex documents such as contracts and financial statements, as well as artwork and graphic illustrations, a photocopier is an indispensable office machine.

Three processes of photocopying are used: electrostatic, thermographic, and diazo.

Electrostatic Copiers　In the electrostatic process, copies are created by means of an electrically charged image and the development of that image. The process is based on the principle that opposite electrical charges attract and similar electrical charges repel. The main classes of electrostatic copiers employ either a *plain-paper process* or a *coated-paper process*.

Plain-Paper Copiers.　Plain-paper copiers use a photoconductive drum to transfer the image. Toner adheres to an invisible image formed on the drum or belt. The toner image is then transferred to the charged surface of ordinary paper and fused with heat. Plain-paper copiers are more complex than coated-paper varieties. They require more maintenance and service, and drums or belts must be replaced after a specified number of copies has been made.

Xerox Corporation

This plain-paper copier can make reduced-size copies as well as same-size copies of documents.

Coated-Paper Copiers.   Coated-paper or electrofax machines project the image of the document being copied directly onto the coated and electrostatically charged paper surface. The charge is erased from those areas exposed to light, leaving a latent charged image of the dark areas of the original. This image is then developed by passing the paper through a bath of toner. The toner adheres to the charged latent image and forms a permanent image upon drying.

Coated-paper copiers require special paper stock that is costlier and heavier than plain paper. The paper surface is also subject to marking from metal objects. Both liquid and dry toner copies can smear immediately after processing if drying is not complete or fusing is inadequate.

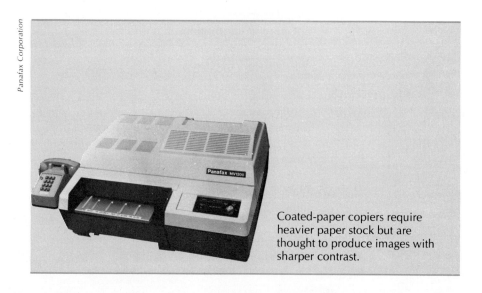

Panafax Corporation

Coated-paper copiers require heavier paper stock but are thought to produce images with sharper contrast.

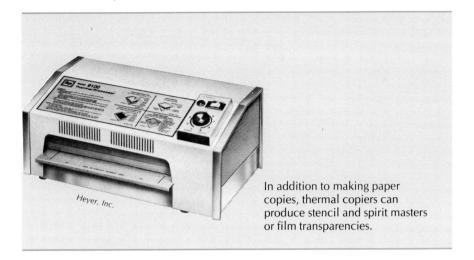

In addition to making paper copies, thermal copiers can produce stencil and spirit masters or film transparencies.

Heyer, Inc.

Thermographic Copiers

Thermal copiers use heat- or infrared-sensitive paper in making copies. The document to be copied and the copy paper are inserted into the machine facing each other. Light passes through the treated sheet and is absorbed by the image areas on the original. Heat is generated in the image areas and transmitted to the heat-sensitive treated sheet. The copy is produced by the chemical reaction of the heat in the image area.

Thermal copiers are best in offices requiring occasional copies (fewer than 500 per month), or for making stencil and spirit masters or film transparencies. They are also used to laminate an original document with a clear plastic coating.

Service and maintenance of thermal copiers are generally minimal, but the machines have some disadvantages:

- The need to insert sets of copy paper and original into the machine together.
- High cost of copy paper (6 cents to 10 cents per sheet).
- Slow speed for multicopy runs.
- Inability to copy images that lack metallic content or colors through which infrared light can pass.
- Drying and darkening of the copy paper with age.

Dual-Spectrum Copiers. Classified as thermal models, dual-spectrum copiers require two separate types of paper. Light creates a latent image on an intermediate paper. The intermediate paper is then used to produce an image on a final copy paper by means of heat. The transfer from original to intermediate and from intermediate to final copy is done either manually or automatically within the copier. Costs range from 4 cents to 8 cents per copy.

Film Transparency Preparation

Transparencies frequently add visual interest to an oral presentation. They can be made by placing a sheet of special acetate over prepared copy and passing the set through a thermal copier.

Transparencies can also be prepared by drawing directly on acetate sheets

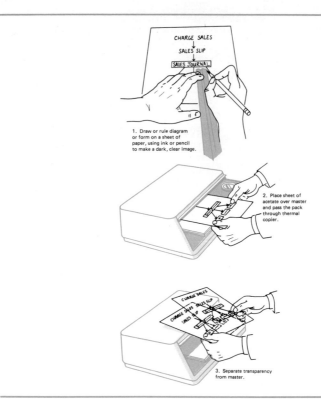

Preparation of a film transparency.

with special inks. Simply attach an acetate sheet securely with masking tape over the material that is to be copied. Then trace the image from the original to the acetate, using a pen and special ink. You can then mount the completed visual on a projection frame for viewing.

Visual Layout Principles.   Visual materials require careful design. Both their subject matter and their purpose should be immediately clear to viewers. Visuals that are hard to understand or take too long to read lose their effectiveness. The principles described here can help you to obtain the necessary clarity and effectiveness when preparing visual materials for your employer.

- Organize a visual for relationships rather than for details. The details are important in establishing a clear statement, but they should never outweigh or obscure the points contained in the statement. Once the layout is firm, there is usually room for necessary details. Organize the visual to lead the viewer logically to the conclusion stated in the headline. The reader might read only the concluding statement or the headline and still receive the visual's basic message.
- Strive for visual simplicity. Aim for visuals that allow viewers to grasp information at a glance. Avoid the temptation to qualify terms unnecessarily or to make the visual ornate.

- Develop an arrangement that helps viewers move their eyes over the visual smoothly. Viewers understand the content more clearly when they don't have to struggle to organize it by finding their way among the elements or by trying to understand the syntax of the statements. Make use of familiar conventions, such as reading from left to right and top to bottom. Use boxes around key words or phrases to help link groups of information.

Even the fluid or chemical duplicator can be used to prepare transparencies. Type, write, or draw on the master for a chemical or fluid duplicator. Place the master on the duplicator and run several good copies on regular duplicating paper. Then hand-feed a sheet of frosted acetate, frosted side up. Spray the frosted side of the acetate with clear plastic spray to coat the inked surface. Mount the transparency on a cardboard frame.

Diazo Duplicators

Diazo duplicators or whiteprinters are primarily used to make copies of large originals. Copy sheet sizes can range to cover 36 by 48 inches. Larger print copy sizes are possible on machines that have a roll-feed mechanism. Used by construction, engineering, and architectural offices, diazo duplicators produce copies of one-sided translucent drawings on specially coated paper, card, film, or cloth stocks.

Finished diazo copy may be altered or highlighted. When used as a workprint in the process of completing drawings and schematics, any type of diazo copy will accept ink or pencil additions. Deletions or erasures can be made with special liquid eradicators or erasure pens. For color highlighting, tinted paper stock and a variety of basic line colors are available.

Copy Quality

A copy is not, of course, an identical twin of the original document. The quality of the copy will vary with the copying operation. An office staff using a copier primarily to produce reproductions of memos and informal reports for interoffice communication should be interested primarily in readability. A large reproduction center that generates lengthy reports and documents for wide distribution should be concerned with copier power and more perfect copies. Those who produce and circulate policy statements and public relations communications to company managers, customers, and clients should demand machines capable of producing copies of the highest quality.

Copy quality is often the factor in choosing plain-paper copiers rather than coated-paper (dielectric, zinc oxide) counterparts. Newer coated-paper copiers that use dry toner methods have narrowed copy quality differences, although coated paper still feels and looks different from ordinary bond.

Copying Restrictions

Office copiers can produce copies of original documents that closely match the quality of the original. This capability should not be misused. For example, it is illegal to copy postage stamps, automobile registrations, drivers' licenses, passports, citizenship or naturalization papers, United States paper currency or bonds, and copyrighted material without permission.

Copier Misuses Controlling the degree and extent of misuse is an important factor in the management of copiers. Even an economical copier can become expensive when it is used for the wrong reasons. The common forms of copier misuse are:

- Using the copier for items unrelated to business operations—family records, personal data sheets, and so on.
- Copying typed text, memos, and business forms instead of using carbons, carbon sets, and multipart forms.
- Copying magazine, newspaper, or book items instead of using tearsheets or requesting reprints from the publishers.
- Generating more copies than required for a desired distribution instead of routing a few copies.
- Using the copier as a duplicator for forms.
- Rejecting less-than-perfect copies and rerunning originals.
- Operating the copier improperly by incorrect control setting and careless loading of copy paper.

Controlling Misuse of the Copier Establishing copying procedures can greatly reduce misuse and help minimize unauthorized copier usage. The following procedures can be followed.

Inform all users and management personnel about copying guidelines, the correct way to operate the copier, and the cost of copies. Stress the time spent walking to and from the copier, extra file space required by excess copies, and time lost reading extraneous copies.

Maintain a copier log book listing who made the copies, the number of copies made, the nature of the original copied, and the final disposition of the copies. A requisition slip for copies left at the copier can be used in place of a log book.

Limit access to the copier through the use of card or key counters that both activate the copier and maintain a cumulative total of all copies produced by each operator. Counters can be assigned to specified users. In addition to monitoring all copy activity, these counters function as a central recordkeeping system capable of recording copier expenses by department or group. Card or key systems are effective only if the devices are secure and the system carefully managed.

Duplicators

Duplicators, though more complicated to operate than copiers, offer the advantage of more copying power per dollar invested. They are available in a variety of models that use different reproduction processes. Impressions may be made by spirit, stencil, direct lithography, or offset lithographic techniques.

Duplicators use an intermediate or master in the image-forming or printing stage. Masters range from typed, direct-impression masters to photolithographic offset plates. Operator expertise is required. Involved are the preparation and mounting of a master and several start-up procedures. Duplicators function at high-run levels, making from tens to thousands of impressions per master.

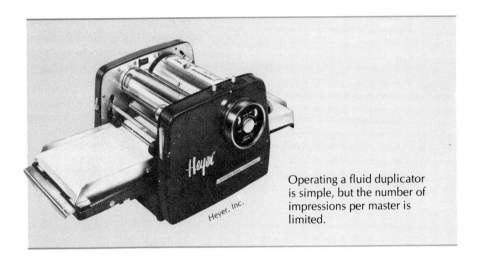

Operating a fluid duplicator is simple, but the number of impressions per master is limited.

Spirit Duplicators

The spirit or fluid process uses a negative image master and moistening solution technique to produce copies. The solution moistens blank sheets of paper before they come into contact with the master. The moistened sheets absorb the carbon dye from the master and transfer it to the paper. Colors may be reproduced by using multicolor masters, which come in purple, black, blue, red, and green.

Master Preparation. The most common method of preparing spirit masters is to use a typewriter, ball-point pen, pencil, or stylus device. A duplicating carbon sheet is placed face-up against the back of a master. Direct impressions transfer carbon images to the back of the master.

Errors. You can make corrections on a master by removing the carbon image from the master with a correction fluid that dissolves the carbon deposit, or with a special pencil, or by scraping off the carbon deposit with a sharp knife. If the latter process is used, rub a wax pencil over the scraped area to replace the glazed finish.

After the carbon deposit has been removed, type in the correction, using a new patch of carbon paper. This procedure is necessary since all of the original carbon was deposited onto the master during the initial impression. Keep portions of unused carbon for use in making corrections.

Graphics. Drawings and diagrams may be prepared on the master by using lettering guides, templates, shading plates, or shading wheels. These devices allow you to prepare oversized letters and numbers, special symbols, and shaded textures on carbon spirit masters.

Operation. Operating a spirit duplicator is simple. The machine is first primed by making the drum rotate four or five times with paper feeding into it. This allows the wick to become adequately moistened. You then adjust the pressure, and place and clamp the master with the carbon side up into position on the cylinder of the machine. (Specific directions for operating different models accompany the equipment.) As the cylinder revolves, a wick moistens the copy paper and the paper is fed into the machine. The pressure of the master against the moistened copy paper causes the image to be transferred from the master to the copy paper. Each time a copy is made, a small amount of the aniline dye is taken from the master. Because of this transferral process, only a few hundred copies of one master can be made on the spirit duplicator.

Image Quality.   Image carbon on a master is depleted as each copy is made. Thus, each copy becomes lighter until the master is used up. You will find pressure controls on most spirit duplicators to adjust image tone and maintain uniform copies during a run.

The maximum number of impressions per master is, however, limited. Long-run purple masters can produce from 200 to 500 copies, medium-run masters 100 to 200 copies, and short-run masters 50 to 100 copies. Color masters yield somewhat shorter runs. Legibility, however, ultimately determines the number of duplicates each master can produce. Light copies may be readable but not be acceptable because of poor appearance.

Azography Process.   The Azograph process is an optional direct method of spirit duplicating. The master copy is made with a brown wax-based substance rather than with an aniline-based carbon. When the brown wax-based image comes into contact with a special fluid, a chemical reaction causes the image to transfer onto the copy paper in blue. An advantage of this process is that you don't smear or stain your hands since dye is not formed until the master comes into contact with the special fluid as the copies are being duplicated. The use of the Azograph process is somewhat limited, however, since the master produces a maximum of 100 copies in blue only.

Stencil Duplicators   Stencil or mimeograph duplicators make use of stencil masters and an inking system to produce reproductions. The stencil masters consist of a fibrous backing through which ink can pass and an overcoating of plastic that does not permit ink

This electric stencil duplicator can produce up to 200 copies in one minute.

Bohn Business Products

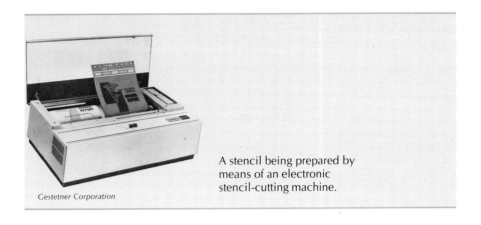

A stencil being prepared by means of an electronic stencil-cutting machine.

Gestetner Corporation

to pass through. Impressions on the stencil displace the plastic coating, leaving images backed by fibrous, ink-transmitting backing.

Stencil Preparation.   You can make stencil masters by direct impressions of the typewriter keyboard or by using ball-point pen, pencil, or a special stylus. Before you type a stencil, clean the keys or element of your typewriter thoroughly and place the ribbon indicator on the no-ribbon position. Move the paper bail rolls aside so that they will not roll on the typed stencil surface. Determine the correct typing pressure by first setting the indicator at the lowest pressure point. Then, to test, outside the printing area type sequences of periods and commas as you slowly raise the pressure until these marks are being reproduced evenly. Check periodically as you cut the stencil to verify that the typewriter impressions are even.

Insert a cushion sheet between the backing sheet and the stencil before typing a stencil. Some cushion sheets are color coated so that a readable impression of the typewritten message is made either on the backing sheet or the stencil itself, thus making it easy to proofread a stencil before it is run. For a sharper impression, use a typing plate instead of a cushion sheet.

Stencil masters of preprinted text and graphics may also be prepared directly on thermal or electronic platemakers. Thermal masters can only image carbon or metallic based impressions, and most ball-point inks will not reproduce. Electronic stencil cutting machines reproduce an original document by scanning it photoelectronically on a rotating cylinder. Electric signals create tiny sparks that burn holes through the master to form the stencil image.

Errors.   You can make corrections on a stencil simply by coating an error with a special correcting fluid and then retyping or writing. You can also patch stencil master segments together by using special cements.

Proofread a stencil before removing it from the typewriter so that any corrections can be properly aligned. If the insides of letters such as o, p, b, d, or q have fallen out, replace them; otherwise, the circle will fill in with ink. To replace the missing part, type the letter with a sharp stroke at the bottom of the stencil, in

A. B. Dick Co., Inc.

Stencil corrections are made by first burnishing the error and then applying correction fluid.

an area that will not receive ink. Remove the inside of the letter with a straight pin and carefully place it in the imperfect letter *after* the stencil has been inked on the machine, or stick it on the stencil with a speck of correction fluid.

Graphics.   You can trace, letter, or draw on a stencil. Clamp the stencil to a light table (an illuminated, glass-topped drawing board). If something is to be traced, place it between the stencil and the backing sheet. The light table lets you see what you are tracing and helps you make sure you have completely displaced the wax surface. Tools needed for art work include lettering guides, screen plates, curved rules, and styli. If a stylus is not available, you can use a dried-up ball-point pen.

Operation.   After preparation, the stencil master is mounted on a cylinder containing a fabric inking pad or an inking screen belt supported by inking cylinders. Ink is passed from the pad or belt through the stencil and onto the paper surface as sheets are pressed against the master.

A rough-textured paper is required for the stencil process, for it will absorb the ink. If a harder, smooth-finished paper is used, the ink is likely to smear unless the excess is absorbed by a process known as slip-sheeting. Slip-sheeting is also used to prevent ink ruboff on the backs of copies.

Cleaning and Storage of Stencils.   Stencils may be used many times if they are properly cleaned and stored. One method of cleaning a stencil is to put it between sheets of newspaper until all the ink is absorbed. Another cleaning method uses specially manufactured absorbent stencil covers that are made like folders the size of the stencil. Simply place the stencil in this folder.

Stencils should be stored on edge and away from heat. Avoid damage to the stencils; do not place any weight on top of them. Stencils may be stored in the boxes in which they came originally. To identify a stored stencil, file it with a copy of the message. The copy may be attached to the stencil or the folder with a paper clip or staple.

Offset Duplicators   Offset lithography is the fastest-growing form of duplication used in office reproduction centers. The offset printing and duplicating process is based on the principle that grease and water do not mix. Impressions are offset from a master

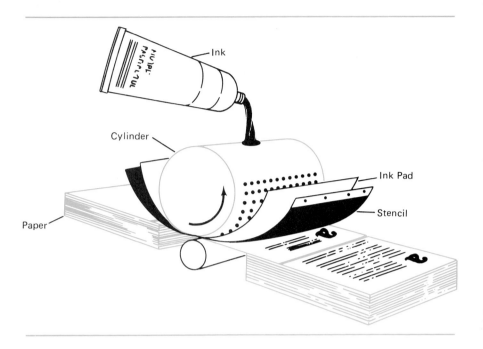

Ink

Cylinder

Ink Pad

Stencil

Paper

The stencil-duplicating process.

to an intermediate, and then onto a page. An image on an aluminum master is inked on a plate cylinder by a number of ink and water solution rollers. That image is then transferred from the plate onto an intermediate rubber blanket cylinder. The image is finally transferred (offset) from the blanket to a blank page that is backed up by an impression cylinder.

Masters or Plate Materials.   For office applications, presensitized aluminum plates are available for high-quality reproduction of 10,000 to 50,000 copies. Photo-direct masters, produced by integrated camera-processor platemakers, are best for up to 10,000 copies. Xerographic copier masters, generated on electrostatic copiers such as the Xerox 2400, can produce up to 5,000 copies per

Bohn Business Products

An office model offset duplicator.

master, and direct impression masters, produced by typewriter, pen, or pencil, accommodate runs of up to 2,500 copies.

Copy for photo-direct masters may be typewritten, drawn, or traced, as in the direct impression process. Photographs, detailed charts and diagrams, captions, and special effects may be pasted on a layout sheet. Copy can also be taken from almost any previously printed material. When the layout is complete, it is photographed. The image is then reproduced on an offset plate or master, in the same size or enlarged or reduced.

Copy and Duplicating Systems

New systems are now available that combine the simple operating methods of copiers with the quality of offset duplicating. These systems use one of three basic processes: offset lithography, direct lithography, and electrostatic copying.

Offset Lithography

Offset lithography is easy to use. After setting and inking the machine, merely place the original copy in the machine, dial the number of copies needed, and turn on the machine. The system generates a master and the required number of copies without further handling.

Direct Lithography

In direct lithography, the image from the master is made directly on the copy paper; the intermediate blanket cylinder is eliminated. In other respects, however, this process is much the same as offset. Skilled maintenance people and extensive operator training are required, however.

Electrostatic Copiers

Electrostatic copiers are perhaps the most promising of the copy and duplicating systems. These machines use the same basic method as the copier, except that a statically charged photoconductor belt is used instead of a master or plate. Electrostatic machines are less complicated to maintain than other systems and do not require a highly skilled operator. In addition, extensive preparation and clean-up procedures are eliminated.

Off-Line Reprographic Equipment

Reprographic technology is capable of producing large numbers of copies in a short time. To avoid problems at the output end, auxiliary equipment is needed to put the leaflets, booklets, or multipage sets in order, join pages together, and fold them if required.

Headliners and Composers

Type that is available with such strike-on units as the Addressograph Multigraph Varityper and IBM Composer closely resembles professional typefaces. Typefaces of 12-point size or larger are instantly interchangeable.

Headliners. Letter compositor systems are available that enable you to dial a letter and print it with a press of a lever. Large display type and special styles are delivered on sensitized strips of tape that are pasted on the layout that is being prepared for conversion to a master for duplication.

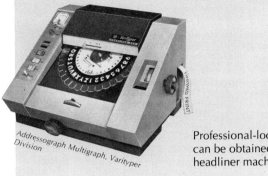

Addressograph Multigraph, Varityper Division

Professional-looking type can be obtained by using headliner machines.

Composers. Strike-on composing units such as the Varityper and IBM Composer function much as a typewriter does. They provide a variety of type sizes and styles, as well as even right-side margins for textual copy. Composers are especially appropriate for pieces that require a professional look, such as graphic displays, charts, graphs, booklets, reports, sales memos, product announcements, slides, and posters.

Automatic Typewriters. A popular reprographic device is the automatic typewriter. With it, many perfect copies of a typed letter can be reproduced automatically, each looking as if it were individually typed. The typewriter can be stopped when necessary for insertion of special data such as names, dates, and figures. The automatic typewriter is recommended for specialized mailings where high quality is important and expense is not a primary consideration.

With a composing unit and elements having different type styles, attractive graphic presentations can be prepared in-house.

Martin Bough

3M Company

With a facsimile transmitter, a 250-word letter can be sent across the country in 20 seconds.

Facsimile Equipment. The facsimile (fax) transmitter acts much as a photocopier does. It transmits exact copies of handwritten memos, typed documents, drawings, and photos over long distances. The document is inserted into the machine in one location, and a copy is printed out within seconds at an output terminal in another location.

Fax machines make it possible for branch offices to submit reports to a main or corporate headquarters located many miles away. The rental charge for facsimile machines is little more than for conventional photocopiers.

The facsimile process is also employed to produce offset masters and stencils. The copy to be produced is positioned on one cylinder of a two-cylinder machine. An electronic offset plate or stencil to which the image is to be transferred is installed on the second cylinder. A photoelectric scanner picks up the image from the copy as the first cylinder revolves and transmits it to the other revolving cylinder, where it is reproduced by stylus on the offset master or stencil.

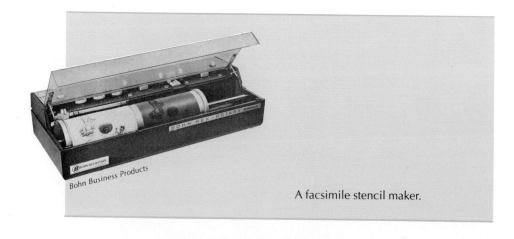

Bohn Business Products

A facsimile stencil maker.

A simple but effective collating device.

Michael Business Machines

Collating, Binding, and Folding Equipment

A wide range of equipment is available to speed up the final stages of processing copier and duplicator output. Even the simplest equipment can aid the office staff in collating material.

Collators. Some copier manufacturers provide sorters for their machines. Completed copies from the copier are distributed into a number of bins without operator intervention. When the copying cycle is complete, each bin will contain a complete set ready for stapling or binding. Other sorters are operated as independent units, detached from the copier or duplicator. The simplest commercial collating device has the paper stacked on end between dividers that slope at an angle and keep them in place.

Fasteners and Binders. The most common method of holding sets of paper together is stapling them. Edge stapling (two or more staples a half-inch from the left-hand edge of the paper) and upper left-corner stapling can be easily managed with an ordinary office stapler. The Swingline heavy-duty manual stapler can fasten 100 or more pages. Other models are designed for saddle-stitching or for long reaches up to 16 inches. Electric staplers can staple as rapidly as the work is fed into the unit.

An alternative to stapling is *spiral-comb binding*, which is similar to the binding of the ordinary ring notebook. Spiral binding machines operate in two steps. Rectangular holes (about 19 on an 11-inch-long sheet) are first punched along the left edge of the papers to be bound. The punched sheets and their covers are then placed on an assembly of metal fingers over which a spiral plastic comb has been placed. The binding machine combines or threads the comb with the sheets to form the bound document. Spiral binding machines come in both manual and electric models. The main advantage of a spiral comb is that it is easily removed: pages can be added or removed, then reused.

Flat-comb binding is a more permanent form of the spiral variety. A series of round or square holes (about one per inch) is punched along the left-hand

A binding machine.

Ibico Inc.

margin of the document. A two-part plastic comb strip (one with spikes and the other with holes) is then threaded and combined with the punched sheets and heat-sealed to form a strong bind. A special tool must be used to remove the plastic comb strip if pages are to be added, removed, or revised.

Hotmelt-glue binding employs a hotmelt or glue technique. The document is loaded into the machine spine edge down, and hot glue is automatically spread across the spine to bind the pages together. After several minutes the bound document is removed from the binding machine and placed on a holding rack until the glue sets.

Thermal tape machines apply a fabric-and-glue tape strip along the spine of the document and then pressure-heat it to create the bond. A portion of the tape extends over the edge of both front and back cover sheets, completely enclosing the document's spine.

Folding and Inserting Machines.   Folding and inserting machines can fold copied and duplicated sheets and insert them into mailers at a rapid rate. Booklets, reports, bulletins, letters, and leaflets can be folded in various ways. The more elaborate folding systems insert, seal, and stamp large mailings in one operation.

A folding machine and some of the various ways paper can be folded by machine.

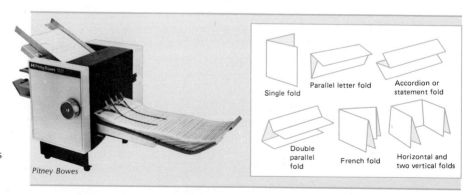

Pitney Bowes

Single fold

Parallel letter fold

Accordion or statement fold

Double parallel fold

French fold

Horizontal and two vertical folds

Choosing a Reprographic Process

Deciding which one of the reprographic processes to use for a specific job requires careful thought. First ask yourself which process is most economical. Then weigh other considerations: the number of copies needed, the desired copy quality, the nature of the copy, and the accessibility of the copier or duplicating equipment.

Copies Needed When just a few copies are needed, make carbon copies or use a copier. If expense is not a concern and you want a personal touch, use an automatic typewriter. For short-length runs of medium quality, consider a copier or duplicator or a fluid process. For medium-length runs of good quality, use the stencil process. When long runs of excellent quality are called for, use an offset process.

Copy Quality Copy quality is a prime factor in choosing bond copies in preference to those reproduced on coated paper. Copy quality should be rated on image sharpness, copy uniformity across the page, background whiteness, and the resistance to smudging of the final copy.

Nature of Copy When photographs (or halftones), solid areas, colors, and text boxed by solid colors are to be duplicated, a photographically prepared offset master is best. If only a few copies are needed, a facsimile process can reproduce photographs and make reductions and enlargements. Spirit and stencil processes are satisfactory when copy to be duplicated can be typewritten and involves no more than simple line drawings or tables.

Accessibility of Equipment A copy of a document needed immediately must be processed on a copier. Spirit and duplicator processes require preparation of a master or stencil and sometimes much planning, and an offset master that must be laid out and photographed usually takes a day or two.

Cost Copying costs are based on the method of reproduction used and the paper stock that method requires, the number of copies needed, the size of both the original document and the copy, and the cost of the masters. The decision which method of reproduction to use generally is determined by the quality and quantity required.

Reviewing Your Reading

1. Identify the two most commonly used electrostatic copiers.
2. Discuss the best use for thermal copiers.
3. Describe how to prepare a film transparency.
4. Discuss three examples of copier misuse.
5. What are the advantages of the copy and duplicating systems?
6. Explain the essential difference between office copiers and office duplicators.

7. Of two duplicating methods—spirit and stencil—which is best for intra-company memos and reports? What are its major limitations?

8. Describe the preparation of a master for insertion on the cylinder of a spirit duplicating machine.

9. What are the three manual processes used in the preparation of a stencil? Which requires the use of a stylus?

10. What is the best way to proofread a stencil if it has been removed from the typewriter?

11. Explain how you can replace the insides of letters such as o, p, b, d, or q that have fallen off the wax-coated stencil.

12. What is slip-sheeting and when is it required in stencil duplicating work?

13. Describe how stencils should be cleaned and stored.

14. What are the three ways to prepare a master for offset duplication?

15. Identify the six factors to consider when choosing a duplicating process for a specific job.

Using Your Skills

1. Prepare the following reprographic process comparison data in table format for facsimile reproduction.

REPROGRAPHIC PROCESSES

Characteristics	Copiers	Spirit or Fluid	Stencil	Offset
Recommended number of copies	1 to 10	10 to 300	30 to 3,000	11 to 10,000
Can two or more colors be used?	yes	yes	yes	yes
Can drawings be reproduced?	yes	yes	yes	yes
Can photographs be reproduced?	yes	no	no	yes
Can hand lettering be reproduced?	yes	yes	yes	yes
Can printer's type be reproduced?	yes	no	no	yes
Can the original be run again later?	yes	yes	yes	yes
Maximum size of copies	11" x 17"	11" x 17"	8½" x 14"	11" x 17"
Copy quality	Excellent	Fair	Good	Excellent

2. The form that follows is to be typed and positioned, four forms to a page, on a spirit duplicator master. All copies of the form are to be identical in size and arrangement when they are cut apart. To avoid waste, arrange the material first on a plain sheet of paper.

INSTALLATION AND SERVICE RECORD

Date _____

Firm _____

Street _____

City _____

Installation made in (describe)

_____

_____

_____

By _____Mechanic

Checked by _____Date _____

Checked by _____Date _____

Checked by _____Date _____

3. With layout guidelines in mind, design a visual to be used in a seminar presentation. Arrange the following information so that its purpose is obvious and it is easy to read and effective as a guide for discussion. Draw boxes around subheads and use arrows to link them to the descriptive phrases.

Main heading: *Treatment Objectives*

Subheads: Medical Care, Psychotherapy, Drug Therapy, Rehabilitation

Descriptive Phrases: Restoration of Physical Well-Being, Restoration of Mental Well-Being, Physical and Mental Support, Restoration to Society

4. The following duplicating jobs have been scheduled:

Order 718. An outline map of California, with highways indicated in a second color, 45 copies.

Order 719. An advertising letter on the company's best letterhead, 750 copies. The salutation is: To Our Customers. There is to be no personalized fill-in. Must be a finished, professional-looking job, resembling typewriting.

Order 720. Identical letters for 112 different names, each letter to have an individually typed inside address and salutation.

Order 721. A rush order for 225 copies of a price list that will have to be run again in a few weeks.

Order 722. An advertising piece showing a photograph of a machine, 2,500 copies.

Order 723. A factory form containing many ruled lines, 500 copies. Rush job. Form to be run in black. At the top, in large letters, "Factory Rush" in red.

Order 724. A notice to be sent to salespeople, 25 copies.

Order 725. A report that contains charts and tables with many figures, 12 copies, with several colors desirable for comparisons.

Order 726. The minutes of a meeting, 3 copies.

You are to choose the best duplicating process for the above orders. Using plain paper, tabulate your recommendations under the following headings: "Order Number," "Preferred Process," "Remarks." Under "Remarks" explain why you chose the particular process. In a few cases, you may wish to recommend more than one possible method; if so, indicate which method would be best. Be sure to date your report and to supply a heading on the subject line.

Exercising Your Judgment

Time or Money. Although your boss is a vice president of the company, she is a mild and conscientious person. She never throws her weight around. For some time the company has been trying to control the number of duplicating machines and get rid of the "private office" ones. You had a small hand-operated duplicating machine in a little storeroom off your office, but when the policy statement about private duplicators came out, your boss turned the machine over to the company's central duplicating department. After the machine was gone, you found you needed it very much. There is another copying machine two floors down in the building, but it is often in use, and you find yourself waiting for it while your office and telephone go unattended. Now you have learned that the secretary in the office next to you kept a hand-operated duplicating machine, having moved it to a place behind the door in the storeroom nearby (after the policy statement was distributed). What do you do? Why?

Applying the Reference Section

Develop word awareness by completing the following vocabulary teasers on a separate sheet of paper:

1. Type the word that is most nearly opposite in meaning to the first word:
   a. *lenient:* abundant, scarce, weak, strict
   b. *remote:* fictitious, close, real, unnecessary
   c. *superior:* defective, minor, inferior, worthless
   d. *ignorance:* knowledge, ability, truthfulness, familiarity
   e. *approximately:* almost, exactly, gracefully, incorrectly

2. Type a word that has the same meaning as each of the following phrases:
   a. not very often
   b. cannot be seen
   c. impossible to understand
   d. without fault
   e. in the order indicated
   f. fraudulent imitation
   g. all the people in the world
   h. do away with
   i. extremely valuable

PART
FIVE / Data
Processing

Electronic Data Processing

Electronic data processing (EDP) is fast becoming a necessary, basic function in many offices. The small business computer, no longer unaffordable, is becoming a common sight as business managers search for new ways to cut their labor costs and gain tighter control over their operations. The advent of the computer is bringing about changes in the secretary's job. Instead of serving as a compiler of routine data, the secretary is becoming a screener of data. Increasingly, the secretary's job responsibilities include more decision making and supervision.

In most data processing-supported offices, secretaries do not work directly with computers. More often they work with information that computers process. For example, computer printouts of sales and inventory are finding their way to the secretary's in basket. In some offices a computer access terminal is a part of the secretary's work station, providing a direct link to a computer. Entries are made in ordinary language through a keyboard much like that of a typewriter.

Data processing is the handling of information. The secretary performs data processing operations when reading, recording, classifying, sorting, calculating, summarizing, storing, reporting, and retrieving data. Electronic data processing is simply the accomplishment of these operations by means of electrical impulses through circuits at faster speeds than are possible with manual or mechanical impulses. A computer, for example, completes operations in billionths of a second. When properly instructed, the computer has the capacity to answer complex problems and store and retrieve large volumes of data quickly and accurately.

Input Units

To begin computer operation, gather all the necessary information. As a secretary in a payroll department, for example, you might receive weekly information from all cost centers in the company indicating how many hours each employee worked and how much overtime, and which employees were on vacation, sick, or absent without authorization. You would summarize that data and send it to

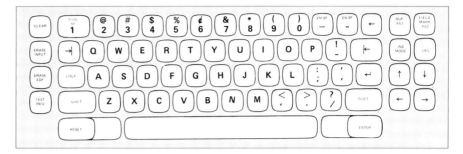

An alphanumeric keyboard.

the data processing center. There a programmer would define and analyze the problem to be solved and prepare it for the computer. That is, the computer would be told precisely how to arrange the information, what calculations to perform, and what to do with the answer. When applicable, the computer would be told where to find previously filed data to be used or updated. Several categories of input devices and media are used in communicating with the computer.

Keyboard Input

The data input to most small business computers is keyed in by an operator on an alphanumeric (typewriter) keyboard.

It is arranged in the conventional typewriter format and permits direct entry of both alphabetic and numeric information. Optional ten-key adding machine-style keyboards permit all-numeric data to be entered at much higher speeds than with a typewriter-style keyboard. Numeric keyboards are usually accompanied by control keys that activate various machine functions.

Punched Cards and Punched Tapes

One widely used method of feeding information into the computer is by means of holes punched in cards or in tapes. The card-punch operator depresses keys on a keyboard as the input data is read. The information appears on a card or tape as different numbers and letters. The cards or tapes are read by the machines through which they pass. With cards containing rectangular holes this is accomplished electrically; with cards containing round holes it is done mechanically

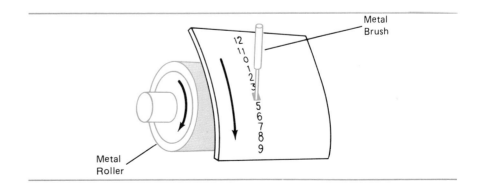

Electrical punched-card reading.

or photoelectrically. In the mechanical process, metal pins pass through the holes in the card and activate mechanical devices to perform a desired function. In the photoelectric process, the cards pass over a bank of photoelectric cells (above which is positioned a bank of lights), light passes through holes in the cards, and the machine is activated. In the electrical process, which is used with IBM 80-column cards, the card passes over a metal roller and under a series of metal brushes. As a metal brush meets a hole, it makes contact with the roller, thus completing an electric circuit. The resulting pulse tells the machine what function to perform. Thickness of the card is important in all processes, because a machine must be able to separate one card from the next card rapidly. For this reason, all card stock is of a uniform thickness.

The columns of the 80-column card illustrated below are numbered 1 through 80. Each column contains 12 possible punching positions or locations for holes. The first ten punching positions are numbered, starting from the bottom of the card with 9 and proceeding back through 0 at the top. The eleventh punching position, known as the 11 or X position, is located above 0. The twelfth punching position, known as the 12 or Y position, is located above the eleventh. Positions 1 through 9 are known as digit positions; X, Y, and 0 are zone positions.

A number is represented by punching a single hole in the appropriate digit position in a column of the card. A letter of the alphabet is represented by punching a hole in a zone position and another in a digit position in a single column of the card.

Magnetic Tape

A common medium in computer data processing is magnetic tape. It is made of a plastic and coated with metallic oxide, and it is rolled in reels, usually ½ inch to 1 inch wide. Magnetic tape, like paper tape, is divided lengthwise into channels. In these channels, data is recorded in the form of magnetized spots. There are as many as 1,600 recording positions to the inch on tapes having seven or ten channels along the length of tape.

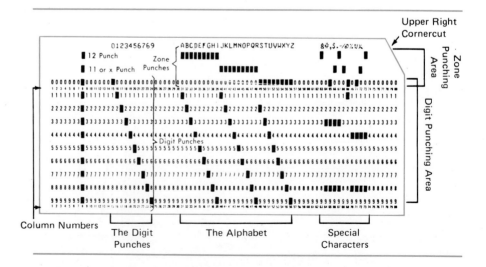

An 80-column punched card.

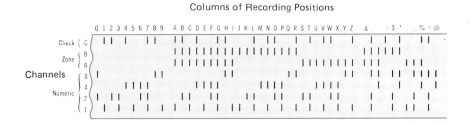

Coded seven-channel
magnetic tape.

Certain combinations of the invisible spots in a column represent the code designation of numbers and letters. The illustration here shows the code on a half-inch-wide seven-channel magnetic tape.

The primary advantages of magnetic tape are fast processing, erasability, and compact recording and storage. The complete file of 1 million customer accounts, for example, has been recorded on about 20 reels of tape. New technology now permits the direct recording of data on magnetic tape. Keyboards similar to those found on electric typewriters are used. However, it is somewhat difficult to identify errors when recording on magnetic tape. For this reason, data is often recorded first on punched cards or paper tape that can be checked for accuracy. It is then transferred to magnetic tape.

Magnetic discs are also used to record data in the form of magnetized spots. These are thin, circular, metal plates, coated on both sides with ferrous oxide. Approximately 484,000 numeric or 242,000 alphabetic characters may be stored on the two recording surfaces of each disc. Usually there are four to six discs in a pack. Whereas magnetic tape requires that the computer search from the beginning of the tape for needed information, magnetic discs permit the computer to go directly to any disc in a pack to find data for recording or reading.

Machine Scanning of Documents

Scanning machines (called character readers) are widely used to facilitate the input of data into computers. Two types are described below.

Magnetic-Ink Character Recognition.   Magnetic-ink character recognition (MICR) machines are used largely by banks to record data on checks and deposit slips. These machines read numbers designed in a special typeface and printed in a magnetic (iron oxide) ink.

The American Bankers Association has adopted the typeface shown on page 288 for use on checks issued checking-account customers. The account number is printed in magnetic ink on the lower edge of each check.

Because of its special properties, the magnetic ink can be given small charges of electricity, and the data transmitted to a computer through electrical impulses. Each character creates an impulse that distinguishes it from the other characters so that it can be read by the computer.

Besides recording check data for the updating of the balances of customer accounts, magnetic-scanning equipment sorts the checks themselves so that they can be returned to customers along with statements of their accounts.

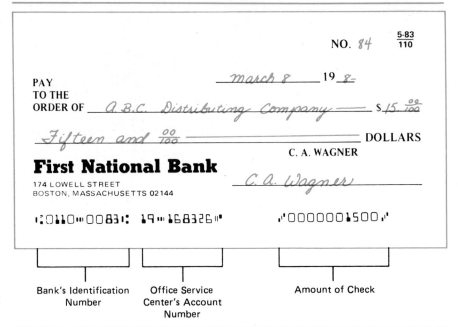

The identifying numbers on the bottom of the check are printed in magnetic ink that is read by the bank's computer.

Bank's Identification Number

Office Service Center's Account Number

Amount of Check

Optical Scanners. More flexible than magnetic-ink character readers are optical character recognition (OCR) scanners. These machines can scan documents and read numbers or letters printed on source documents and records created on adding machines, cash registers, and accounting machines. Scanners also read distinctive type styles directly from source documents into a computer. This eliminates the necessity in processing of having to transfer the data contained on the original document onto punched cards, paper tape, or magnetic tape.

Generally, the characters to be read must be positioned in a predetermined area of the document. The equipment has become quite versatile. Department stores use optical scanners to read price tickets and register tapes for billing and inventory control. Credit cards are scanned for the user's account number and the amount of each transaction. Schools are using OCR machines to grade tests and analyze test results.

Cathode-Ray Tubes

A cathode-ray tube (CRT) is becoming increasingly important to the small business computer. Many systems now include a CRT display and its associated keyboard as the principal means of entering data into the computer's memory. Data is directly entered by writing on the screen itself with an electronic marker, or by a typewriter keyboard.

Optical characters must be of a size and shape that permits accurate machine recognition.

9643210457

Wang Laboratories, Inc.

Central Processing Unit

The chief center of an electronic computer system is its central processing unit (CPU). This unit receives, processes, and stores data and directs the action of the input and output units. Its basic components are a storage or memory unit, an arithmetic logic unit, and a control unit. The computer storage holds data until needed for processing. The arithmetic and logic unit performs additions, subtractions, multiplications, and divisions as well as logical functions on the data. The control unit coordinates the operations of the memory and arithmetic units, including the input device and the output device that records the data processed by the computer.

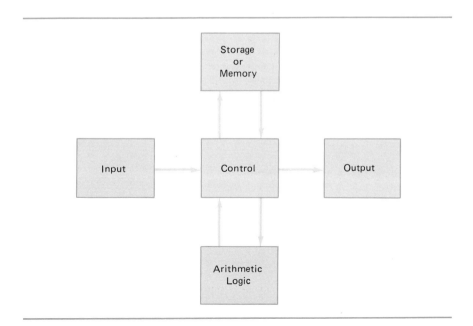

The five components of an electronic data processing system. The central processing unit is highlighted.

Storage or Memory Unit

One of the principal characteristics that distinguishes computers from adding machines and conventional calculators is an internal storage unit capable of holding and selectively retrieving quantities of data and instructions. The three devices most commonly used for storing data in computers are magnetic cores, magnetic discs, and magnetic drums. Because of its short retrieval time, flexibility, and reliability, *magnetic-core* storage is used to hold program instructions and items of data to be processed immediately. *Magnetic discs*, which are stacked like records in a jukebox, permit random-access storage. This allows the computer rapidly to select only the data needed for processing. *Magnetic drums* are the slowest method and are generally used as supplementary storage units for data awaiting processing or for storage of information to which quick or frequent access is required. Semiconductor storage is rapidly replacing core storage as the principal storage medium for large computers and is becoming popular in business minicomputers as well.

Access Time. The length of time it takes computers to store data or to retrieve data from storage is called *access time*. Measured in microseconds, access time is the time between the central processing unit's request for data and receipt of that data.

The two types of access are random (direct) and serial (indirect). *Random access* locates a specific address in a storage device and retrieves the data at that location with no intermediate searching. *Serial access*, on the other hand, makes it necessary to start at the very beginning of a storage device and search the entire memory until the desired data is located. Random-access storage devices are much faster than serial-access devices but are more expensive. Internal memory units such as magnetic cores generally provide random access to data. Auxiliary units such as magnetic tape are completely serial in access. Magnetic drums and discs provide random access in that a particular drum, channel, track, or side can be selected, but then data on that channel, track, or side must be searched serially from beginning to end.

Arithmetic-Logic Unit

To perform the basic functions of calculating and decision making, the computer must have a central processing or arithmetic-logic unit. The arithmetic section computes the data it receives from storage, and the logic section makes a decision when there is a choice of steps to be taken in processing the data.

Arithmetic Computations. Addition, subtraction, division, multiplication, and the comparison of numbers in a computer are accomplished through the use of binary arithmetic. This is a number system of only two digits, 0 and 1, rather than the ten of the decimal system (base 2 instead of base 10). This is necessary since data is represented in computers by combinations of the *presence* and *absence* of electronic signals. Since there are only these two conditions in a computer, a system of numbering is needed that can represent data with combinations of just two symbols. The symbol 1 in the binary system corresponds to the presence of an electronic signal; the 0 corresponds to the absence of a signal.

Decisions of Logic.   The central processing unit of the computer can also be programmed to make "yes" or "no" decisions about the data being processed. The results of the decisions determine the sequence of operations to be followed by the computer. This decision capability includes both conditional and unconditional operations. *Conditional* branching permits the testing of data being processed for specific conditions. For example, data being processed may be compared with data already in memory. If the comparison reveals that the data matches, a specified action is taken; if the comparison reveals a mismatch, an alternate action is taken. *Unconditional* branching causes the computer to breach the sequential order of a program in order to introduce new steps into the program and directs the computer back to the original program sequence after the new steps have been carried out.

Control Unit   To tell the input, arithmetic-logic, storage, and output devices when and how they should operate is the function of the *control unit*. This unit contains the electric circuitry and counters for accumulating or holding data. Both are necessary in order to select program instructions in proper sequence, to interpret these instructions, and to initiate the performance of each instruction.

The control panel is an important part of the control mechanism. It contains the switches for turning power on and off, for entering data, and for checking out the steps of a program. The flashing lights indicate whether or not the computer is functioning as it should. The console typewriter prints input and output information, including messages signaling data errors detected by the computer.

Output Devices

The output phase of electronic data processing is the recording of information from the input and manipulation phases. The recording may be in data storage for subsequent retrieval, or it may be a printed report that provides information for immediate distribution.

The printer is the most frequently used output device. It produces data processed by the computer in a form that can be read by business executives and staff. A carriage-control system permits flexibility in positioning data on continu-

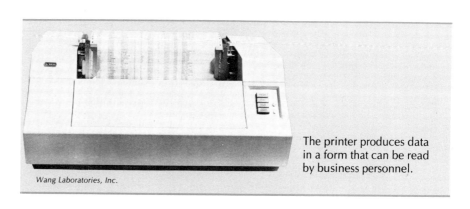

The printer produces data in a form that can be read by business personnel.

Wang Laboratories, Inc.

ous forms, so that the printer can prepare widely different business documents. Printers are capable of completing a full line at one time, using type bars as printing mechanisms. Printing speeds vary with the model of printer. Some can produce over 1,000 lines a minute. Those that print photographically can produce as many as 6,000 lines a minute.

The cathode-ray tube is being used effectively as an output device in business organizations that require persons at remote locations to look at records in a file.

Output devices also produce soft copy in coded form on punched paper tape, magnetic tape, and punched cards. This is translated into readable language by printers not connected directly to the main processing units of the computer.

EDP Approaches

The electronic data processing (EDP) service best suited for a business organization is generally determined by the costs, effectiveness, and dependability of the information the system can deliver. There are three basic categories of computer power that first-time EDP users consider—in-house computers, computer service centers, and remote computing services. An *in-house computer* is located on the business premises and is fully controlled by company personnel. A *computer service center* is located elsewhere and is operated by an independent service company such as a bank or accounting firm. A *remote computer service* is located on the premises of an independent service company but is directly connected by a telephone line to a terminal or teletypewriter in the user's office. Understanding the pros and cons of each of the three basic approaches to EDP and deciding which is best for a given business organization call for a careful consideration of the following factors:

- Availability of the system.
- Equipment reliability.
- Security.
- Turnaround time (elapsed time from input to printout).
- Programming services.
- Technical support by supplier.
- Suitability of equipment or service for certain classes of problems.
- Expandability of the equipment or service.
- Ease of physical installation.
- Ease of using the system.
- Need for specially trained people.
- Fixed, variable, and overall costs.

In-House Computer The most complete approach to EDP for a business organization is to install and operate its own computer. There is then no need to share it with other organizations or to worry about conflicting priorities. Reliability of the electronic portions of the system is high, but failures of the input and output devices must be tolerated. Security is also high, since none of the organization's records ever need to leave the premises. Turnaround time will depend upon the mode of operation selected—*on-line* or *demand mode*, in which each transaction is processed immediately, or *batch mode*, in which all transactions of a given type are accumulated, sorted, and processed in sequence on a daily or weekly basis. Packaged programs to handle common business data processing applications are readily available. Vendors usually assume full responsibility for writing and testing the programs and for turning a fully operational system over to the user. Many vendors, though by no means all, provide less technical assistance than users would like to receive. Many small business computers have small main memories and low computational speeds. For these reasons they are not suitable for large business problems. Expandability varies greatly among small business computers. Therefore, if the user's business is a dynamic one, the possibility of future expansion is an important factor to consider when making a choice about EDP service.

Since many small business computers are compact and require no special air-conditioning, flooring, or power supplies, they can be installed without incurring large costs for site preparation and physical installation. Once the programs have been written and tested, in-house computers can easily be operated by reasonably competent clerk-typists. If the user assumes responsibility for the computer's programming and installation, an experienced computer programmer and analyst is essential.

The fixed costs for an in-house computer installation are comparatively high and include purchase price or monthly rental charge, wages of the data processing staff, and cost of the space the facilities and personnel occupy. On the other hand, variable costs for supplies (cards, printer forms, and disc packs) and power are low.

Computer Service Center

The simplest way to make use of EDP facilities is to turn the job over to a computer service center. Available in every major city and many small ones as well, centers can be found listed under Data Processing Service in the Yellow Pages of your telephone directory. Computer service centers offer a wide range of services, ranging from computer time rental (where users supply their own programs, data, and operators) to packaged services that include everything from the pickup of raw data to the delivery of finished reports.

The decision to use such service requires careful consideration. Some centers have been known to give preferential service to important customers and miss deadlines on or handle sloppily the work of small accounts. Security is a factor that can cause concern, since some confidential records will necessarily have to leave the user's premises. Turnaround time is relatively long—data is picked up one day and reports delivered several days later. The key strengths of most service centers are their packaged programs to handle common business applications. Centers also modify existing packaged programs and prepare customized programs. The costs and ownership of such programs should be clearly resolved by the user.

Computer service center managers generally understand the importance of providing prompt, competent assistance to users who need help in preparing their input data, interpreting results, or planning new applications. All or most of the problems of operation are taken out of the user's hands, and there is no need to have specially trained people on staff. Fixed costs are very low since the user makes little or no investment in data processing equipment or in staff to operate it. Variable costs, on the other hand, may be high and should be carefully considered. The user is charged a fixed fee for each card punched, each transaction processed, and each report printed. The overall cost of having data processed at a computer service center, however, is generally lower than it would be if processed with an in-house computer. As the processing volume grows, however, in-house computers become less expensive.

Remote Computing Service

The benefits of EDP can be enjoyed quickly by making use of a remote computing service. This is accomplished by installing in a business office a teletypewriter or other data terminal connected by telephone lines to a powerful computer located miles away. Remote services offer either interactive time sharing or remote batch processing. *Interactive time sharing* allows many companies to use the computer's facilities at the same time and to get back data immediately. *Remote batch processing* operates in much the same manner as a conventional service center, but it speeds the entry of data and delivery of the results.

A potential strength of remote computing service is its availability. Most often, the user can dial and use the services needed whenever they are needed. Occasionally, however, the system may be unavailable when it is needed most, either due to equipment failure or because the system is already serving the maximum number of users simultaneously. Users can count on a high degree of reliable service from most commercial remote computing companies. Reliability is more of a problem with the telephone facilities that link the user with the computer. Since multiple users share a single computer system, careful planning is important to ensure that the confidentiality and integrity of each user's data and programs are safeguarded.

At their best, the interactive time-sharing networks provide instant responses to commands and inquiries. Remote batch processing can return processed results within hours, or even within minutes, after data has been entered. Programming services are available from nearly all the remote services. Many deal with computer service companies in order to gain access to their libraries of packaged programs.

Expandability is a strength of remote service. As a user's workload expands or contracts, more or less computer time is used and paid for. Operating the computer service, of course, is the supplier's problem. The user need only learn how to operate a simple data terminal, and the need for specially trained people on the user's payroll is minimal. The supplier provides all the required technical assistance to place computer applications in operation. Fixed costs are low, since the user need only rent or purchase one or more data terminals, pay the service charges for the communications link, and pay the cost of any custom programming. Variable costs involve fixed fees for each hour of terminal connect time and each minute or second of central processor time used. Many service companies charge additionally for the use of memory space, disc storage space, magnetic tape reels, and central-site input and output devices. Other companies charge primarily on a fixed-fee basis for each transaction processed. In addition, users must pay the telephone company for its facilities. The overall cost of remote computing services is still likely to be lower than that for an in-house computer center, however, as long as the workload is small.

The Implications of EDP

Computers have emerged as a key element in the processing and communication of data in the business community. Some people argue that computers will ultimately reduce the office work force. Others feel that the net effect of computers on employment will be negligible. There is agreement on certain aspects of computer developments. For example, computers now perform jobs involving both mental and physical effort that were formerly done by people. Therefore, the possibility of automating some jobs does exist.

In actual practice, however, automation has not resulted in many office workers being laid off. Those employees whose jobs are outmoded by computer operations are generally retained by their companies. They are either assigned new, more exciting jobs or given other responsibilities that are not economical to automate.

What are some of the advantages and disadvantages of EDP for the office worker affected by it? Generally, humdrum assignments are eliminated and working conditions are improved. The office environment tends to be uncluttered, efficient, and pleasant to work in. Freed of the need to perform tedious tasks, secretaries have more time to use their intelligence and become involved in supervisory management functions that require initiative and decision making. The secretary's challenge is to keep up with computer technology as well as to sharpen talents in human relations. Success requires competence in both, and those secretaries who work to perfect skills in both areas will find their jobs more rewarding.

The computer terminal is fast becoming just another office machine to many secretaries. It serves as an electronic filing clerk and a resourceful office assistant. As the computer continues to free managers' time for more planning and controlling, secretaries are assuming administrative functions their employers previously handled.

Eventually desk-top terminals will enable secretaries to retrieve documents from a central computer file and restore them to their original form. Minicomputers may be used by secretaries to maintain appointment schedules and to manage incoming and outgoing telephone calls.

The secretary, unencumbered by clerical duties, can become the middle manager of the office, assuming the executive's administrative responsibilities. The outlook for the future is one of more interesting and diversified involvement in office operations and of much greater job satisfaction.

1. Briefly define data processing.

2. Describe the primary purpose of data in the business office.

3. Identify the basic processing operations secretaries perform that are accomplished by electronic data processing (EDP) with electrical impulses.

4. What is the principal facility for on-line data entry to most business computers?

5. Explain how letters and numbers are identified on an IBM 80-column punched card.

6. Discuss the primary advantages of magnetic tape over punched tape or cards when you are introducing data into an electronic data processing system; its disadvantages.

7. Explain why the time needed to retrieve desired data is much shorter when magnetic discs are used as input medium than when magnetic tape is used.

8. Describe the unique processing feature of optical scanners that makes them increasingly attractive to business users of EDP systems.

9. What is the function of the EDP system's central processing unit? Identify its three components.

10. Discuss the two most common types of internal storage units that are linked directly to the main processing units of the computer.

11. Compare the two types of access that characterize storage devices and the way data is organized or processed for use in a computer—random-direct and serial-indirect.

12. Explain why the binary system of numbering, consisting of combinations of the two symbols 1 and 0, is used in computers to represent information instead of conventional numbers and letters.

13. Discuss the types of output devices used to produce hard copy in readable form and soft copy in coded form.

14. Identify the three approaches to computer power that first-time EDP users make use of.

15. What are the three basic considerations when deciding the approach to electronic data processing service best suited for a business organization?

1. To see how a computing machine operates, perform the following exactly according to instructions. First copy the strip of boxes on the next page, marking the "Start" box as shown. This represents a tape. Then write in the boxes, beginning with the third block from the left, the following numbers and symbols: 4, 3, +, 5, 2, =. Starting at the "Start" box, follow the arrows and perform each operation in the flow-charted instructions below the strip. (Continue through the circled A's, which represent connectors.) Where there are alternate paths, take the one determined by your answer to the question.

When you've come to "Stop" on the instructions, what you have in the boxes should be the answer to the problem you started with.

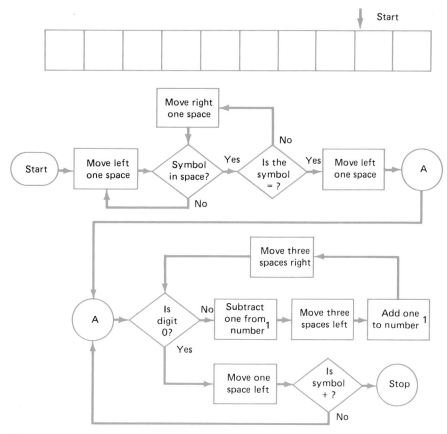

[1] Substitute new number

2. List the strengths and weaknesses of in-house computers, computer service centers, and remote computing services in terms of equipment, security, technical support, and expandability.

3. The shortest method of converting a binary number to a conventional number is to use a simple doubling and adding operation. Starting from the extreme right, the value of a binary digit, or bit, is 1. Moving left, the next column has a value of 2; the column to the left of that one has a value of 4; the column to the left of that has a value of 8; and so on. The sum of the value of each column yields the total value of the binary number. For example, the binary number 1011 is converted in the following manner:

Bit Value	8	4	2	1	
Binary Number	1	0	1	1	
Conversion	$8 + 0 + 2 + 1 = 11$				

Use the doubling and adding method to convert the following binary numbers to conventional numbers and write your results on a separate sheet of paper.

a. 10111
b. 10010
c. 110011
d. 100110
e. 111101

Something New. You have just learned that your employer is going to install an electronic computer. Your boss, the corporate economic adviser, will not be directly involved with the operation of the new computer, but you have heard rumors that many office employees will lose their jobs. You talk the matter over with several other secretaries. One plans to take a course at the local college to learn about computers. Another has decided to look for a new job. You begin to worry about the situation. You like your job and your boss, and you do not want to change jobs. You are reluctant to bring the subject up with your boss since what you have heard is really gossip, not facts. What should you do?

Type the following sentences correctly, consulting the Reference Section at the end of the text for guidelines on how to style numbers. Watch for typos and other errors.

1. There are antique shops along Spruce Street, between 2nd and seventeenth streets.

2. In the accident at the corner of 9th and Market streets 5 cars were damamged.

3. In the advertisement the boat was described as thiry by fifteen feet with a speed of about eleven knots.

4. The capacity of that parking lot is a hundred and seventeen cars.

5. The article, "business correspondence," is in the March issue, volume two, issue number 3.

6. A hundred fifteen-cent stamps were requisitioned for the proposed mailing.

7. You can earn more than 9% by investing your money in six-month savings certificates.

8. The speaker recited the first 2 stanzas of the poem on page eight.

9. Economic conditions in the U.S. during the 17th century was the subject of the report.

10. The Treasury announced plans to auction 2.69 billion dollars of two-year notes next Tuesday.

11. They left the City at seven o'clock on the morning flight to Denver.

12. July 1 begins the State's fiscal year.

CHAPTER SEVENTEEN / RESEARCHING INFORMATION

Executives rely on their secretaries to obtain or verify many types of information. No secretary knows the answer to every question. However, competent secretaries know where information is available and where to turn for help.

Your initiative and skill in researching information will enable you to cope with such inquiries and requests as:

- "What kind of federal approval is required for the marketing of a new drug?"
- "Where do I apply for a passport for the business trip I'm planning to Germany and Japan?"
- "Gather appropriate background material I can read relating to the speech I have been asked to present on corporation reorganization."
- "Please compile a scoreboard of sales and profits by quarters for the major airlines."

Sources of Information

Knowing where to find needed information is a basic skill for an information gatherer. The type of facts needed, of course, will help determine the source.

A selection of general and specific reference books may be close at hand on an office reference shelf. Your employer may have a file of current books, reports, and published documents that reflect his or her field of interest.

Many corporations maintain their own libraries, some staffed by trained librarians. These libraries usually subscribe to the leading business and trade magazines and to many government and trade association publications. They also purchase the latest books in company-related areas of interest and subscribe to major newspapers, both general and specialized. If you need current information about incentive compensation plans, for example, you can telephone the librarian and describe your needs. In a matter of hours, rarely more than a day, you will have in your possession everything available in the library on the topic.

A number of business firms also maintain a special research unit or office that will locate information, within specified areas, that is requested by company personnel.

When company information-gathering facilities are not available, you can make use of the reference section of a local public library. In many cities, there are also special libraries, each of which concentrates on a specialized field of endeavor such as law, engineering, business, or medicine. *The Directory of Special Libraries and Information Centers*, published by Gale Research Company, lists over 10,000 libraries by subject specialization.

Do not overlook the local chamber of commerce as a valuable source of information on business subjects. Business and professional associations such as the American Marketing Association or the Sales Management Association usually maintain information centers for their members.

Colleges, universities, hospitals, museums, newspapers, and courts maintain reference collections, usually more complete than a public library's. The extent to which you are able to make use of these sources of information is often determined by your ingenuity.

Library Facilities

It is a waste of time to wander through library materials hit-or-miss before you have thought through what you are looking for. If the subject you are interested in is broad, breaking it down into subtopics can be helpful. The best time to do your preliminary planning is before you approach the library information or reference desk. It is a good practice to organize the subject to be investigated into a list of topical headings. Think of synonyms for topics to be researched. If you wanted to learn about how to conduct a market survey, for example, you would surely look under "Survey," but you might also look under "Questionnaire," and "Marketing."

Finding Factual Information A library classification system establishes a uniform way of identifying published information, and it provides for the logical arrangement of such resources in the library.

Card Catalog. The library card catalog is a card file containing identification and location information about every book in the library. Each book in the card catalog is listed by author, by title, and by one or more subject classifications. This cross-reference method makes it easy for you to find a book even if you know only the author's name, the title of the publication, or the subject. Prominently displayed in the upper left corner of each card is the classification and book number, which directs you to the place where the book is located on the library shelves (stacks). Classification numbers are also posted on the library stacks, making it easy to locate the books you are seeking.

Catalog cards are printed by and available to libraries from the Library of Congress. A typical card is shown on the opposite page. In addition to (1) classification and book number, each card shows (2) author's name; (3) book title, coauthor(s), edition, publisher, and publication date and place; (4) text

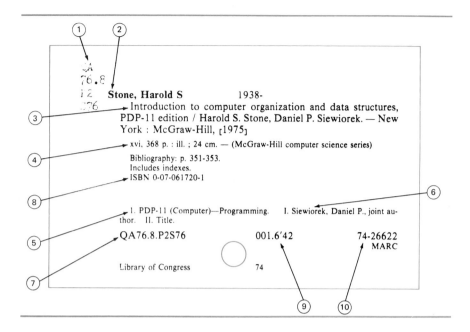

A Library of Congress catalog card.

pages and size of book; (5) subject classification; (6) joint-author entry; (7) Library of Congress call number; (8) International Standard Book Number (ISBN); (9) Dewey decimal classification number; and (10) serial number of the card.

Vertical File Service.   For nonbook printed materials, the *Vertical File Service Catalog* is a valuable library reference resource. It lists by subject such miscellaneous sources of information as pamphlets, booklets, and leaflets, which are easily overlooked because they are not indexed in the card catalog. Because of their miscellaneous sizes and bindings, these materials are usually held in vertical file drawers.

Classification Systems.   Libraries use one of two standardized classification systems. They are the Dewey decimal classification system and the Library of Congress classification system.

The Dewey decimal classification system is based on the logic that knowledge can be classified by ten primary groupings. Main subjects are identified by the hundreds, 000 to 900; subsubjects by the tens, 00 to 99; and sub-subsubjects by the units, 0 to 9. Additional breakdowns use additional numbers following a decimal point. For example:

300	Social Science
340	Law
347	Treatises
347.9	Judicial Branch of Government
347.97	Courts
347.972	Supreme Court

The Library of Congress classification system provides a great number of major classifications. This system employs the letters of the alphabet as a basis and supplements them with Arabic numerals. The letters *KF* in the example KF889.3.R68 classify this work as "Law, American." The letter following the second decimal point is always the same as the first letter of the last name of the author. The numbers that follow represent a short numerical equivalent for the rest of the author's name.

Using Indexes to Books, Pamphlets, Magazines, and Newspapers

Frequently the best way to begin a search for information in a library is to consult an appropriate guide or index. There are so many that only a select few can be described in this chapter. Familiarity with these, however, will help you to extend your research further if necessary, especially into particular fields where many specialized references are available.

Books.   *Books in Print* (R. R. Bowker Company, New York) is an annual author-title-subject index. It lists the books contained in over 2,000 publishers' catalogs. Volume 1 lists books by authors; Volume 2, by titles. The *Subject Guide to Books in Print* is a companion volume with listing according to subjects.

The *Cumulative Book Index* (CBI) (The H. W. Wilson Company, New York) provides a listing of currently published books in the English language. It is printed monthly, and cumulative editions appear quarterly and annually. The author, editor, publisher, binding, paging, edition, date of publication, price, and Library of Congress catalog number are given for each book indexed in the CBI. Government publications and pamphlets, however, are not included in this index.

The H. W. Wilson Company publishes a number of other bibliographic tools that provide the information gatherer with a quick reference to written material on a wide range of subjects. Indexes in special subject fields include: *Applied Science and Technology Index, Biography Index, Business Periodicals Index, General Science Index, Index to Legal Periodicals*, and *Social Sciences Index*.

Pamphlets.   Much of the information that business managers need must be current and is available only in pamphlets and booklets. Finding such materials is possible in the *Vertical File Index* of the library. This subject and title index to selected material gives title, descriptive notes, author, total pages, publication date, and publisher.

Of special interest to business executives is the *Bulletin*, published by the Public Affairs Information Service, New York. Published weekly and updated annually, the *Bulletin* lists by subject current books, pamphlets, periodical articles, government documents, and other useful reference materials in the fields of economics and public affairs. Articles from over 1,000 periodicals are also listed. Most of the material indexed is factual and statistical.

Magazines.   The *Reader's Guide to Periodical Literature* is an index to information in 180 magazines considered most generally useful. Entries are arranged alphabetically by author, title, and subject. When you find an article you would like to use, be sure to copy the name of the magazine, volume number, pages on which the article may be found, and the month and year in which the magazine was published. The full names of all magazines and explanations for abbreviations used in the index may be found at the front of each volume.

To look for current information about a topic or simply to track down an article, the subject approach is most commonly used. Suppose you want a recent article on employment. The best procedure is to take the most recent issue of the *Reader's Guide* and, looking in alphabetical order, locate the subject. Here is a sample entry under that heading:

EMPLOYMENT
Employment, how full is full? il *Progressive* 41:6–7 N '77

The subject heading is printed in boldface (heavy type). Beneath it is the title of the article, usually followed by the author's name, if it appears in the magazine. If the article is illustrated, that information is represented by the abbreviation "il." The next parts of the entry are very important and always appear in the same order. First is the name of the magazine (*Progressive*), the volume number of the magazine (41), a colon (:), the pages on which the article appears (6–7), and the date of the magazine (N '77 for November 1977).

The *Reader's Guide* is published twice a month, except in February, July, and August, when it appears once a month. During the year there are update issues that contain entries for a three-month period. At the end of the indexing year a bound volume is issued. Always check the cover of the *Reader's Guide* for the period covered. The date is important since it will guide you to the issue or volume of the magazine you need.

The *Business Periodicals Index* is published monthly, except in August, and bound into quarterly and annual volumes. It is a subject index to selected English language periodicals in the fields of accounting, advertising and public relations, automation, banking, communications, economics, finance and investments, insurance, labor, management, public administration, taxation, and specific businesses.

Newspapers.   A number of newspaper indexes are usually available in a library to assist you in locating newspaper articles that deal with the subject you are researching. Some of the more common indexes include the *New York Times Index*, *Christian Science Monitor Index*, and the *Newspaper Index* (including the *Chicago Tribune*, *Los Angeles Times*, *New Orleans Times-Picayune*, and *Washington Post*). Always check the name of the newspaper in the card catalog to see whether it is on microfilm and whether there is an index for it. If you are working on a national or international topic, the *New York Times Index* may be used as a general index to gauge approximately when the event occurred.

The *New York Times Index* is a subject index to articles that have been published in that newspaper. The entry for each article contains a brief summary statement and exact reference to the month, day, section (for Sunday editions), page, and column where the article can be found. Note that the entry does not give the year in which the article appeared. It is essential that you note this information from the top of the page for the years 1851–1906, and from the title page (or spine of the book) for the years 1907 to the present. Personal and organization names are included in the same alphabetical index as subjects.

Newspaper indexes usually take four to six months to be published, so current information is not available through them. More up-to-date information is available in *Facts on File*, a weekly summary of world news. It is usually received a week or two after the week it documents and has a subject index.

Making Research Notes

After you select a satisfactory reference work, use it correctly and intelligently. Read the title page for the affiliations and credits of the authors. Check the copyright page for the publication date. A five-year-old work, for example, may be of limited value if current information is needed. Read the preface and table of contents to get an overview of the coverage. Look for lists of illustrations and tables, for a bibliography, and for appendixes. Scan the index, for it is the key to the text.

Bibliography Cards.   For each reference you consult, prepare a 5- by 3-inch card that contains the following information:

1. Classification number (Dewey decimal or Library of Congress) and ISBN, if any.
2. Author's name.
3. Title of book, or article.
4. Publisher.
5. Place and date of publication.
6. Page reference.

Number each bibliography card at the top right corner and use these control numbers to identify subsequent notes taken from each source.

A bibliography card with a control number at the upper right corner.

⑯

Straight Commission Plan

Advantages: Offers considerable incentive in that rep's income depends entirely on performance. Some prefer this — no ceiling on earnings and very limited supervision. (Employee is "own boss.")

Weaknesses: Employee never knows how much earnings will be from month to month. "Feast or famine." This is chief objection to plan.

Since reps are virtually self-employed — difficult to demand and get consistently high performance. Also, "team effort" virtually nonexistent.

Ferguson: Salary Administration, p. 281

A note card.

Note Taking.   Take extensive notes, since you can't be sure until the project is drafted how much material you can use. For flexibility in organizing your notes into a workable outline, and for ease in adding or deleting, record your notes on uniformly sized cards (9 by 6 inches). Be sure to identify the source of the material on each card by recording in the upper right corner the control number you assigned to each bibliography card.

Use only one side of a note card, and limit each card to one subject. See the example shown here. Note the lines "Straight Commission Plan," "Advantages," and "Weaknesses." These lines should catch your attention later when you are organizing the material you have gathered.

Abstracting.   In contrast to note taking, abstracting is a summary of an entire article or longer work. Involved is your ability to extract the main ideas and to record them succinctly. If well executed, an abstract of a lengthy article or report is of great use to the executive who wants to obtain the substance of the complete work in the most condensed form possible.

Copying Equipment.   Most libraries provide copiers so that you may take with you an accurate copy of, say, a complicated table, diagram, or flow chart. A nominal charge is made for such services.

Microfilm.   Today many libraries are able to maintain a large backlist of magazines since these can be stored on microfilm and microfiche. Special equipment such as the microfiche reader is required for researching information that is stored micrographically.

Basic Information Sources

There are other references you will need in carrying out your secretarial responsibilities. The most helpful of these are described in the following paragraphs.

Dictionaries and Wordbooks

An up-to-date, desk-size dictionary should be within your reach. Between its covers lies more information than word meanings and spellings.

Dictionaries vary, but they usually include the following: vocabulary entry (the word being defined), including spelling, accent, syllable division, variant forms, hyphenation, and capitalization; pronunciation; part of speech; etymology (history); definition; examples of usage; cross-references (to further information); synonyms; derivatives; and lists of combinations and phrases.

Consult your dictionary's table of contents for such special items as biographical listings, abbreviations, table of chemical elements, list of geographic names, maps, list of proofreader's marks, spelling rules, grammar and usage notes, roman numerals, table of signs and symbols, synonyms, and table of weights and measures.

There are a number of unabridged and abridged, bilingual, and technical dictionaries and wordbooks, some of which are ideal quick-reference tools. The more popular ones are *The American Heritage Dictionary of the English Language*, *Webster's Third New International Dictionary* (Unabridged), *Roget's International Thesaurus*, *Dorland's Medical Dictionary*, *Black's Law Dictionary*, *20,000 Words* by Leslie, *10,000 Medical Words* by Byers, *10,000 Legal Words* by Kurtz, and the *Dictionary of Business, Finance, and Investment*.

Classified Directories

A directory lists persons or organizations in alphabetical order, giving addresses and affiliations of persons and addresses, officers, functions, and similar data for organizations. A familiar example is a classified telephone directory. In biographical directories you can find birth dates, education, affiliations, family data, and the like. The *Guide to American Directories* lists over 5,000 directories in over 300 fields of public and private endeavor.

For information about living persons, the British volumes entitled *Who's Who* are the most commonly used references. For citizens of the United States, *Who's Who in America* is the best source of information. Individuals are included in this publication either because of special prominence in their profession or because of official position. *Who's Who of American Women* is a biographical listing of notable living U.S. women. In addition to the volumes containing the names of living persons, *Who Was Who* and *Who Was Who in America* list notable persons deceased. *Who's Who in Finance and Industry* is a listing of top business executives throughout the world.

Thomas Register of American Manufacturers gives products and services alphabetically. Included in each entry are the company name, address, telephone number, branch offices, capital rating, and company officials.

Poor's Register of Corporations, Directors and Executives lists executives and directors of U.S. and Canadian manufacturing and mining companies, utilities, railroads, banks, savings and loan associations, engineering and insurance companies, and partners in financial institutions and law firms.

The American Medical Directory, published by the American Medical Association, lists the name of and professional information concerning every licensed medical doctor in the United States and in Canada. Various lists of hospitals are included, as well as lists of medical societies, medical boards, medical colleges, medical journals, and medical libraries.

City Directories

While directories differ from city to city, the general patterns are fairly similar, so that familiarity with one makes possible ready reference to another. City directories serve as encyclopedias of the economic and other activities of most large cities.

The miscellaneous section is the first of the several parts into which city directories are divided. Usually included in this division are government officials and offices, public schools and the board of education, private schools, public agencies and controlling boards for libraries and museums, parks, public buildings, incorporated companies, and cemeteries.

The buyer's guide is the second major section of a city directory. It is a section of classified advertisements that are indexed according to type of business but grouped alphabetically according to the size of the advertisement. That is, within a business category, businesses that purchased full-page ads come first, arranged alphabetically; then the half-pages; and so on.

The alphabetic list of names is the third and most important of the general sections of the directory. Most current directories include all residents over eighteen or a specified age limit. All business and professional concerns are listed, with names of proprietor, partners, or officers, and an indication of the type of business and the location.

The fourth major section of a city directory is the street directory or the directory of householders. The simplest street directory is an alphabetic list of the streets with a description of each, including origin, direction, and possibly place of ending. The house and building numbers are listed in numeric order, with the name of the householder or business firm that occupies each building.

Almanacs

An almanac is a compendium of facts, giving both current and past data. It usually includes a chronological record of recent events and statistics on government, labor, medicine, aviation, sports, education, literature, demographics, science, religion, and other areas.

A popular almanac is *The World Almanac and Book of Facts* (Newspaper Enterprise Association Inc.). This annual publication is a compilation of facts on many of the economic, social, educational, and political activities of the world.

Other annual almanacs are the *Information Please Almanac, Atlas, and Yearbook* (Simon and Schuster), *The Official Associated Press Almanac* (Hammond Almanac Inc.), and *Reader's Digest Almanac and Yearbook* (W. W. Norton & Company Inc.).

Encyclopedias

Encyclopedias are probably the best place to find a concise discussion of any subject. General encyclopedias are designed to cover the broad range of knowledge to date. There are also many encyclopedias specializing in a particular subject field. Most of these works are continually revised to keep pace with subject developments. Topical or alphabetic access is by index within separate volumes or by a separate index volume.

World Book Encyclopedia is one of the best known and most frequently used encyclopedias. *Encyclopedia Americana* is a more advanced work with more specialized information. *Encyclopaedia Britannica* is the most detailed and scholarly, with extensive coverage of literature, science, art, geography, and history.

The *McGraw-Hill Encyclopedia of Science and Technology* and the *International Encyclopedia of the Social Sciences* are two examples of the many specialized encyclopedias that are available in many libraries.

Government Publications

Every secretary at one time or another needs help in ferreting out a particular government agency, program, or regulation. Government covers such a wide range of programs and services that it is easy to become confused.

Information Centers.   The U.S. General Services Administration and the U.S. Civil Service Commission have together set up Federal Information Centers (FICs) in key cities across the country, with additional tie lines to nearby centers in other metropolitan areas. By calling, visiting, or writing to your local FIC, you will either get the answer you need or be put directly in touch with an expert who can give it to you. Often the FICs can help answer your questions about state and local governments as well. To obtain information about these centers and their locations, write to: General Services Administration, Washington, DC 20405.

Reference Books.   There are a number of reference books that may be helpful for tracking down information relating to government activities. Some government publications are free; others may be purchased or subscribed to at a nominal price. You will usually find most of them in the reference section of a public library or in the reference library of a city hall. The following sources are just a few you might keep in mind.

The *Congressional Directory* is published annually. It includes biographies by state of senators and representatives, delegations by state with names of senators and representatives, and alphabetical lists of Senate and House members with addresses of their homes and Washington offices. Also listed are committees and members, administrative assistants, and secretaries; statistical information about sessions of Congress; officers of the Senate and House; officers in executive departments and independent agencies; biographies of members of the Supreme Court; lists of international organizations and officials, foreign diplomatic representatives in the United States, and United States diplomatic offices.

The *Congressional Staff Directory* is published annually. It lists job titles, room locations, and telephone extensions of staff personnel in the offices of senators and representatives; members of Senate and House committees and subcommittees; district and state offices of senators and representatives with names of staff personnel; and key personnel of the executive departments and agencies, with liaison and information officers, room numbers, and extensions.

The *Federal Register* is published annually. It is a daily publication of rules and proposed rules from the federal and administrative agencies. The rules actually in force, first published in the *Federal Register*, then appear in the *Code of Federal Regulations*.

The *United States Government Manual* is published annually. This volume is the official handbook of the federal government. In it is a description of the purposes and programs of government agencies and a list of top personnel.

The *Book of the States* is published biennially by the Council of State Governments. It covers constitutions and elections, legislatures and legislation, the judiciary, administrative organization, finance, intergovernmental relations, major state services, and an informational alphabetic listing of states.

The *Congressional Record* is published daily by the Government Printing Office when Congress is in session. It contains the proceedings and debates of Congress and is revised and issued in bound form at the end of each session.

Taylor's Encyclopedia of Government Officials: Federal and State provides names, political parties, and terms of office for the governor, members of Congress, state senators, assembly members, and the attorney general and judiciary of each state. It also includes a listing of U.S. ambassadors; the members of the Senate, House, and Joint Congressional Committees; the Supreme Court; the federal judiciary; national political committees; and state political chairpersons.

All large libraries have catalogs and indexes of government publications, together with price lists. The *U.S. Government Printing Office Price Lists* are free and give current government offerings on specific subjects. *Selected U.S. Government Publications* can be obtained free. Listed in it are selected government publications, including prices and descriptions. The *Monthly Catalog of U.S. Government Publications* is a subscription service that offers a comprehensive listing of all publications issued by the departments and agencies of the government each month. An index of the references for the entire year is contained in the December issue.

Specialized Business Information Sources

There are services and sources for business information other than the general works mentioned earlier in this chapter. The general information sources do include business references; the specialized business information sources we will now discuss contain little else, and they are much more compact.

Learn what subscription information services pertain directly to the field with which your employer is concerned and whether these materials are available in local public libraries or in the company library. Since specific business information subscription services are relatively inexpensive, many business executives gladly purchase them when they learn about them.

Business Data Analysis
The *Conference Board* collects and analyzes business data and supplies factual information through its publications and information service. The Board publishes *Business Scoreboard* and *Road Maps of Industry*. Also published by the Board is *Focus*, containing a review of current research, conferences, and

activities; research on business policy, personnel policy, business economics, and public affairs; studies and reports; and a cumulative index. The *Conference Board Record* reports to management on business affairs.

Babson's Reports Inc. issues two weekly letters, *Investment and Barometer Letter* and the *Washington Forecast Letter*.

The Research Institute of America publishes *Research Institute Recommendations*, which is an analysis of economic, tax, and legislative developments.

Financial and Credit Information

Dun & Bradstreet Credit Service aims to evaluate every business enterprise in terms of its credit standing. The rating book is lent as part of a service to which the user subscribes on an annual basis.

Moody's Investors Service publishes *Moody's Handbook of Common Stocks*, *Moody's Bond Survey*, *Moody's Bond Record*, and *Moody's Dividend Record*. Moody's services are intended primarily for investors, providing them with a corporation's capitalization and various stock and bond issues, names of officers and directors, statement of assets and liabilities, and whether or not dividends have been declared with regularity.

Standard & Poor's Corporation provides data on balance sheets, earnings, and market prices for major United States and Canadian corporations and smaller businesses. Standard & Poor's publications include *Bond Guide*; *Stock Guide*; *Current Market Perspectives*; *Industry Surveys*; *Review of Securities Regulations*; *Register of Corporations, Directors, and Executives*; and *Daily Stock Price Records*.

The Kiplinger Washington Letter, published by Kiplinger Washington Editors, Inc., provides a weekly advisory letter service that digests developments and trends in the fields of business and government.

Business Periodicals

Become familiar with the trade journals and magazines that your employer reads regularly. To be as knowledgeable as possible, try to read or at least skim one or more of the following business-oriented magazines.

Business Week, published by McGraw-Hill, Inc., covers general business, business abroad, companies, finance, industries, labor, management, marketing, markets, names and faces, production, research, and transportation.

Changing Times, published by Kiplinger Washington Editors, Inc., contains information about business activities, political trends, and new developments in science, medicine, and the arts.

Forbes, published by Forbes, Inc., features company and industry profiles, articles of interest to investors, and statements by well-known investment analysts.

Harvard Business Review, published by Harvard University Graduate School of Business Administration, presents timely articles on management, labor, and specific industries.

The *Wall Street Journal*, published by Dow Jones & Co., Inc., is a daily newspaper covering current business news. Featured are new products; personnel changes; price changes; dividend news; and stock, bond, and commodity market reports with commentary.

Clipping Services. From trade journals, newspapers, and business-oriented magazines, you can build a resource file on the most pertinent and requested subjects. If your employer asks for articles appearing in out-of-town periodicals, consider a news-clipping service such as Burrelle's or Luce. These bureaus will clip articles on topics you indicate and forward them to you once a week.

Abstracting Services. Another specialized reference source is an abstracting service that publishes and distributes to subscribers a summary of the key points of articles in many specialized areas. It is often easier to work from abstracts than from complete works published in many different reference sources.

Secretarial Bookshelf

In addition to a dictionary, thesaurus, telephone directory, annual book of statistics, manual of grammar and word usage, and a copy of Murphy's *How and Where to Look It Up*, there are other references you may need to consult.

Postage and Shipping
Depending on the nature of your responsibilities, one or more of the following references should be no farther away than arm's reach:

- *Address Abbreviations*, U.S. Postal Service Publication No. 59, Washington, DC.
- *Bullinger's Postal and Shippers Guide for the United States and Canada*, Bullinger's Guides, Inc., New Jersey.
- *Dun & Bradstreet Exporters' Encyclopedia*, Dun & Bradstreet, Inc., New York.
- *National ZIP Code Directory*, Postal Service, Washington, DC.
- *Postal Service Manual*, U.S. Government Printing Office, Washington, DC.

Travel
If you are responsible for making travel arrangements you will find the following references invaluable:

- *Hotel & Motel Red Book*, American Hotel Association Directory Corporation, New York.
- *Commercial Atlas & Marketing Guide*, Rand McNally & Company, Chicago.
- Road maps obtained from various automobile associations and oil companies.

Etiquette and Parliamentary Order
Questions of etiquette in business relationships are best answered by consulting standard guides. The same is true for parliamentary procedures governing the conduct of business meetings. Useful references include the following:

- *Amy Vanderbilt's New Complete Book of Etiquette*, Doubleday & Company, Inc., New York.
- *The New Emily Post's Etiquette* by Elizabeth L. Post, Funk & Wagnalls, New York.
- *Robert's Rules of Order Newly Revised*, Scott, Foresman and Company, Illinois.

1. Explain why knowing where to find needed information is a basic skill.

2. List the kinds of information, other than word meanings and spellings, generally found in dictionaries.

3. Explain why library catalog cards are filed by author, by title, and by one or more subject classifications.

4. Explain how one can locate nonbook printed materials that are not indexed in the library's card catalog.

5. Suggest actions you might take if your employer suggests that a better file and record of office reference materials be devised.

6. Where would you look to find the name of the publisher and the price of a book published last month if you know the author and title?

7. Where would you look to find current information about benefits under the Social Security Administration, which your employer needs to prepare a speech?

8. What is the most appropriate reference to turn to if you are asked to check the accuracy of your company's mailing list of directors and executives of American and Canadian businesses?

9. Discuss the reasons a secretary should try to read or skim at least one newspaper and a business-oriented magazine that the employer reads.

10. Identify the essential information a secretary should record about each reference from which notes are taken.

11. Explain each part and abbreviation in the following entry in the *Reader's Guide to Periodical Literature*:

    ALLEN, Woody
       Kugelmass episode. il New Yorker 53:34–9 My 2 '77

12. Indicate how you would handle a research assignment for an employer who is preparing a company's history and needs to know the address of the original plant and what buildings were adjacent to it.

13. Indicate the appropriate newspaper index to use as a general index for gauging the approximate date of a national or international event and when other newspapers would have carried the story.

14. Explain why a reference such as *Facts on File* is more appropriate than a newspaper index when up-to-date information is required.

15. Identify the major sections of most city directories.

1. As secretary to the marketing manager, you receive a memo from the company president asking for a list of the presidents of banks in the greater Dallas–Fort Worth and Houston areas. The president is considering the feasibility of branching into a delivery service for banks in these cities. How do you handle this?

2. Identify the best source for obtaining the following items of information:
   a. Population of Kansas City, Missouri.
   b. Directors of the U.S. Steel Corporation.
   c. Credit rating of Gilmore Bros., Cleveland, Ohio.
   d. Newspapers published in Chicago, Illinois.
   e. Another word for *excellent*.
   f. Who said "To be or not to be."
   g. Room rates at the Drake Hotel, Chicago.
   h. Articles on employee testing programs.
   i. Exact name of an electronics manufacturer.
   j. Name of a new government agency.
   k. First-quarter dividends paid by IBM.
   l. Biography of Henry Ford.
   m. Author of a new book whose title you know.

3. Referring to a good dictionary such as *Webster's New Collegiate Dictionary* or the *American Heritage Dictionary of the English Language*, answer the following questions:
   a. Where is the superlative of *strong* divided?
   b. Give two brief definitions of *strong*.
   c. Give three synonyms for strong and indicate differences in meaning.
   d. What is the etymology of the word *strong*?
   e. What is the meaning of "a strong color"?
   f. What part of speech is *strong*?

4. Study the entries on the following library catalog card and identify (a) edition, (b) total number of pages, (c) subject entries, (d) Library of Congress call number, (e) International Standard Book Number, (f) Dewey decimal classification number, and (g) classification and book number.

```
PN
4193
W7        Stone, Janet, 1947-
S7             Speaking up : a book for every woman who wants to speak
           effectively / Janet Stone, Jane Bachner ; ill. by Catherine Tvir-
           butas. — New York : McGraw-Hill, c1977.

              xv, 199 p. : ill. ; 22 cm.

              Bibliography: p. 197-199.
              ISBN 0-07-061673-6




              1. Public speaking for women.    I. Bachner, Jane.   II. Title.

           PN4193.W7S7                    808.5'1'024042           77-7134
                                                                   MARC

           Library of Congress            77
```

Hurt Feelings. For some years you have been administrative assistant to the president of the corporation. You began working for her when she was only a branch manager. She is a good speaker and is much in demand for conventions, commencements, and the like. You laid the groundwork for quite a few of her speeches by preparing about a dozen 8- by 5-inch cards of notes that you take at the library about the topic she plans to discuss. You have enjoyed this aspect of your work because you were not only helping your boss but also learning a great deal yourself from reference sources. You took pride in this work because you knew that not many secretaries research their bosses' speeches.

But now you are more than a little disturbed. Your boss has told you that she is employing an additional assistant (a man) to take some of the extra work "off your shoulders, especially all that library work you've had to do for me." Your first reaction is to feel hurt; you think she must not have liked the material you have been preparing for her after all. You wonder why she has never said so to you. Your first impulse is to look for another job; your second is not to cooperate with the new assistant. What should you do? Why?

Identify the punctuation errors in the following sentences and type the sentences correctly on a separate sheet of paper:

1. The Johnson Corporation in Santa Fe, New Mexico sent its customers a copy of an article called Be Ready for Progress.
2. Mr Carpenter the new supervisor will arrive Thursday May 21.
3. They did'nt expect perfection, everyone makes mistakes.
4. If an employee stays with this company five years he or she gets a two-week vacation.
5. An interesting chapter in his new book is entitled *Make a Friend Today*.
6. The work is exciting see for yourself and well worth the time.
7. Only one thing is needed your check in full.
8. Mr. Timmons who just arrived is ready to leave now.
9. She said I'll join you at three pm sharp.
10. She read the May 15 report Investments in the Journal of Accounting.

Chapter Eighteen

Preparing Reports and Manuscripts

The expanding role of secretaries has created new tasks, among them gathering information from sources outside as well as within the company. Executives are happy to find secretarial support in this area, especially when they discover that the information collected is consistently accurate, well documented, clearly presented, and attractively produced.

Information Gathering

To gather accurate information in writing for use by business managers, you need to know where to find the data for the report. You should be aware of which computer printouts, which files, and which persons are the best sources of appropriate information. You should have a smooth working relationship with co-workers and executives from whom you will be getting needed information. Needless to say, it takes a lot of diplomacy to get someone to search through records for information you need. There is also the matter of tact and credibility. Quite properly, few co-workers will release sensitive information until they are reasonably sure it will be interpreted properly. The cooperation you get from others often reflects your reputation for being even-handed in presenting facts and figures with clarity, completeness, and accuracy.

Many business reports are intended to prevent problems from occurring and are prepared on a weekly or monthly basis. They serve to keep managers informed about such business controls as schedules, expenses, and income. Managers must analyze these in order to plan, organize, direct, and control business operations.

In one form or another, budget, expense, income, sales, production, and promotion reports are common to all organizations. Many of them contain row upon row of tabulated figures. Some reports are short and informal. They read like a memorandum, and their preparation requires good grammar and punctuation skills. Other reports are elaborate and formal. They include special introductory parts and appendixes and follow a specified typing format and strict content rules.

Planning and Writing the Report

Whatever type of report is involved, your preparation generally entails the same steps.

Finding Out Exactly What Is Wanted.   Ask your employer questions so that you understand clearly the purpose and scope of the report. Find out who will receive the report and what it will be used for. Prepare a flow chart of the work involved and the time you think it will take to complete each step or phase.

Obtaining the Facts Needed.   Contact the people who have the data needed for the report. Give them as much advance notice as possible that you need their assistance. Abstract or photocopy information from outside sources, such as library reference books and periodicals. If you get conflicting data or are not sure of a point of information, take time to check further.

Preparing an Outline.   Most experienced report writers prepare topic outlines to organize their material. Some find an informal kind of outline or the use of single-word topics to be a more flexible method. Although a few report writers argue that a written outline is time-consuming and a hindrance to creativity, most agree that extemporaneous writing presents the same hazard as extemporaneous speaking. Whatever the approach, an outline should not be rigid; it should be modified when appropriate as the actual writing progresses.

The two forms of outlines shown here are widely used. Each can identify omissions, redundancies, nonparallel topics, and incorrect sequence of data.

Two-Level Division

1. _____
   - a. _____
   - b. _____
2. _____
   - a. _____
   - b. _____
   - c. _____

or

A. _____
   1. _____
   2. _____
B. _____
   1. _____
   2. _____

Multiple-Level Division

I. _____
   - A. _____
   - B. _____
      1. _____
      2. _____
         - a. _____
         - b. _____
II. _____
   - A. _____
      1. _____
      2. _____
         - a. _____
         - b. _____
   - B. _____

Main headings and subheadings should not stand alone. Have at least a II for every I; a *B* for every *A*; a 2 for every 1; and a *b* for every *a*. If two or more parallel head levels are not feasible, the organization of the topic is probably faulty.

Two spaces are used after the period that follows each guide number or letter. Each additional heading guide begins flush at the left with the first letter of the first word of the preceding higher-value head. Double space between major heads and the first two subhead levels, and single space between third subhead levels. This spacing highlights the rank of each head and facilitates faster reading.

Preparing a Rough Draft.   Few people write so expertly that their first draft of a report is satisfactory as final or hard copy. Most are concerned mainly with getting their thoughts down in words first, so they do not pause to polish each sentence or to check spellings and mechanics. They expect to rework the copy one or more times.

To permit changes to be made easily on a rough draft, type it with generous spacing between lines (triple-spaced text) and wide margins. Use inexpensive paper and do not make carbon copies. If the draft is to be distributed to others for review, make a sufficient number of photocopies.

The extent to which you are involved in each step of report preparation will vary. In many situations you are involved in the processing of reports from start to finish. In some organizations, however, correspondence specialists type reports. Whether or not executive or administrative secretaries type, they remain accountable for the editing of reports; that is, for correct grammar, usage, spelling, punctuation, capitalization, and accuracy of numbers.

Revising and Editing.   Good report writing is generally the result of careful revising or reworking. The person who prepares the rough draft may be too familiar with the subject and inclined to omit necessary details the less-informed reader probably needs. It is in checking for readability that you can make a meaningful contribution. As the report is read, question whether the statements made are complete enough for the purpose specified. Examine each statement for clarity and accuracy. Note the need for additional examples, illustrations, or details. Review opinions and interpretations carefully for their reasonableness and see that they are qualified by words like *probably* when there are uncertainties. Determine whether the conclusions are stated crisply and emphasize the key points.

Look closely at word usage and the integrity of sentences and paragraphs. Question words that fail to add anything to the meaning or that do not express what the writer is trying to say. Break overly complicated long sentences into two shorter statements.

Use standard proofreader's marks, shown in the Reference Section, to make changes, corrections, and improvements in the draft. Place changes and insertions above the line of copy to which they refer or in the margin. Avoid placing them below the line, where they can be overlooked or incorrectly positioned in retyping.

Date each successive revision of a report and number its pages sequentially. The writer of the report may decide to refer to an earlier draft in order to retrieve deleted copy.

Asking for Permission to Quote.   Before material that is copyrighted can be used in a written report that is to be printed or duplicated and circulated, permission must be obtained from the copyright owner. Either call such instances to the writer's attention or assume the responsibility of writing for permission. Such letters of permission should be filed as evidence that permission was requested.

A letter requesting permission to quote should give the following information:

- Name and title of the writer.
- Title of the report being written.
- Purpose of the report.
- Specific reference to quotation, length, source, and page number.
- Probable date of release of the report.
- Probable distribution of the report.

The letter that follows is an example of an acceptable permission request letter:

Mr. David C. Bianco, marketing manager for Electronic Systems, Inc., is preparing a report on the use of direct mail in advertising our products. When completed next month, the report will be distributed to company executives.

Mr. Bianco would like to quote as follows from Daniel Melcher and Nancy Larrick, *Printing and Promotion Handbook*, Fifth Edition, 1976, on which you hold the copyright:

Three paragraphs from page 79, beginning with "Success in a direct mail campaign . . . ," and ending with ". . . envelopes, art work, postal regulations, etc."

Full credit will be given to the authors and the publisher. Please indicate in the space below that Mr. Bianco has your permission to quote.

Sincerely yours,

John Garcia
Secretary to Mr. Bianco

You have our permission to quote as requested in this letter.

_____
(Signed)

_____
(Title)

The Form of the Report

Some business reports are condensations of information in memorandum form, for quick distribution to people in an organization who need it for their work. Such memorandum reports usually consist of one or two typewritten pages and an attachment or two. They need to be written clearly and concisely in order to present progress, observations, recommendations, and statistical data in distilled form.

Lengthier, formal reports generally have—in addition to the body—a number of preliminary and supplementary parts as follows:

Preliminary Parts
    Cover and title page.
    Letter of transmittal or introduction.
    Table of contents.
    List of tables, charts, and illustrations.
    Summary or synopsis.
Body of Report
    Objectives of report.
    Procedures and techniques.
    Conclusions and recommendations.
Supplementary Parts
    Appendix or reference.
    Bibliography.
    Index.

The Body of the Report

The body of a formal business report is drafted, edited, and typed before the preliminary and supplementary parts are processed. Each page of the body is typed to conform with the page layout you adopt.

By carefully using marginal space, line spacing, indentation and underlining, and by placing illustrations artistically as well as logically, you can give a business report visual impact. And the more attractive a report is, the more effective it is likely to be.

Spacing and Paragraph Indentions

Memorandum and letter reports are usually single-spaced. Reports longer than three pages and formal reports are generally double-spaced. Paragraphs are either indented 5 or 10 (or occasionally 15) spaces or else they are typed flush with the left margin.

Margins

Uniform margins are maintained throughout a report. Whether the report is to be side-bound, top-bound, or unbound will influence the choice of margins. The table on the following page shows acceptable margins for unbound, side-bound, and top-bound reports:

MARGINS FOR REPORTS			
	Unbound	Side-Bound	Top-Bound
Top margin			
First page	12 blank lines	12 blank lines	12 blank lines
Page number on other pages	6 blank lines	6 blank lines	
Manuscript on following pages	9 blank lines	9 blank lines	9 blank lines
Bottom margin	6 blank lines	6 blank lines	9 blank lines (page number 6 blank lines from the bottom)
Side margins			
Left	12 pica spaces 15 elite spaces	15 pica spaces 18 elite spaces	12 pica spaces 15 elite spaces
Right	12 pica spaces 15 elite spaces	10 pica spaces 12 elite spaces	12 pica spaces 15 elite spaces

Prepare a backing sheet as a guide to keep margins uniform on all pages of the report. The guide illustrated on the opposite page should be ruled on a sheet of serviceable paper. Use a black ink that can be seen through the page of the report being typed.

The horizontal lines at the top of the guide designate the top margins of the report. The first page of the report and the initial page of all major parts of the body begin on line 13. All other pages of the body begin on line 10.

Note that top-bound reports are numbered up from the bottom of the page. Copy for such pages ends 2 blank lines above the page number.

Use the vertical line on the right side of the guide to keep the unjustified right margin of the report as uniform as possible. Do not type more than two or three letters beyond the guide line. Divided words at the end of a line slow you down and confuse the reader, so avoid them. When you must divide a word, do so at a point that will not hinder the reader's quick recognition of the word. Never end a page with a hyphenated word, and avoid hyphenated words at the ends of three or more consecutive lines.

The four short lines in the lower left corner are 8, 6, 4, and 2 spaces respectively from the last line of copy. These lines alert the typist in time to prevent an overlong page. The horizontal line at the bottom designates the last available line for typing. Avoid typing fewer than two lines of a paragraph on a page and carrying fewer than two lines of a paragraph to a new page.

The two vertical rules at the left of the guide indicate the left margin of the report. A wider space is needed when the report is to be bound at the left.

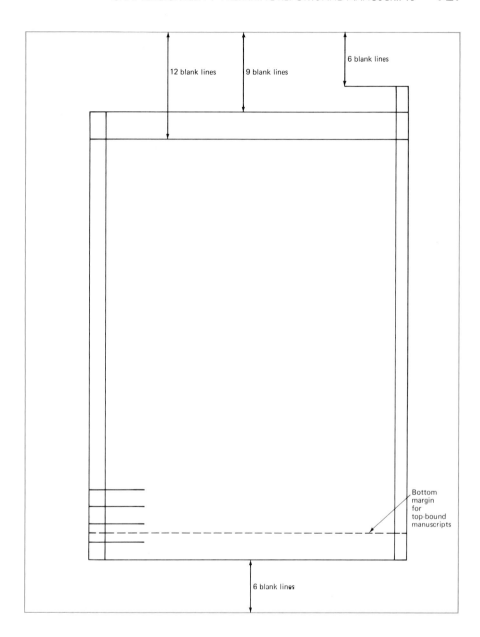

12 blank lines

9 blank lines

6 blank lines

Bottom margin for top-bound manuscripts

6 blank lines

A backing sheet.

| Headings and Subheadings | In general, headings and subheadings parallel the outline of the report. They guide the reader through the report by clarifying the content and increasing readability. Their form and position should tell the reader the degree to which the topic being introduced is being detailed in the report. |

Style Sheet.   Headings can be varied by their placement, by indentation, by underlining, and by the use of capital and lowercase letters. The plan you adopt to do this, known as a *style sheet*, must be used consistently throughout the report. If the report is to be typed in a word processing center, a style sheet such as the one here should accompany the drafted report.

Report Style Sheet

Heading Weights	Style and Placement
Title of Report	Two inches from top edge of paper. Centered horizontally. All capital letters. Four vertical line spaces to first line of report.
Main Headings	Flush with left margin, on separate lines. All capital letters. Two vertical line spaces to the five-space indented text that follows.
First Subheadings	Flush with left margin, on separate lines. Initial letters of main words capitalized. Underscored. Two vertical line spaces to the five-space indented text that follows.
Second Subheadings	Indented five spaces. Initial letters of main words capitalized. Underscored and followed by a period. Text follows on the same line.

Parallel Phrasing.   Headings of the same rank should reflect parallel construction. That is, the headings in one category or level should be all nouns or all adjectives or all phrases. If phrases are used, all the verbs should be in the same form. Compare the faulty construction in the list on the left with the parallel construction in the list on the right.

Faulty Construction	**Parallel Construction**
Steps for Basic Stitches	Steps for Basic Stitches
1. Making a Loop	1. Making Loops
2. The Left Hand	2. Using the Left Hand
3. Using the Right Hand	3. Using the Right Hand
4. Chain Stitching	4. Practicing the Chain Stitch
5. Rows of Single Crochet	5. Combining Rows of Stitches
6. How to Turn Your Work	6. Turning the Work
7. Using a Slip Stitch	7. Using a Slip Stitch

Quoted Matter   Use quotation marks to enclose the exact words of a speaker or a writer and give appropriate credit in a footnote reference or in the text. If the quotation consists of two or three sentences without interrupting words or phrases, use quotation marks at the beginning and end of the quotation rather than around each sentence within the quotation.

Single-space a long quotation consisting of four or more typewritten lines on a shorter line length than you use for the main body of the report. For example, indent all lines of the quoted matter five spaces from each margin. Quotation marks need not be used to enclose quoted matter indented in this manner. In copying quoted matter, follow the punctuation, spelling, hyphenation, and number style exactly. In the event the original wording contains an error, insert the term *sic* (meaning "this is the way it was") in brackets to indicate that the error existed in the original material. If you are omitting words within a quoted statement, use *ellipsis marks* (three spaced periods) to note the omission. If you are omitting words at the end of a quoted statement, use three spaced periods followed by the terminal punctuation required for the statement as a whole. A quotation within another quotation is enclosed in single quotation marks (the apostrophe key on a typewriter).

FOOTNOTES

Footnotes identify the source of statements quoted or cited in a report. They also convey subordinate ideas that the writer feels might be distracting within the text of a report. They are generally keyed by number to a word, phrase, or sentence.

Indicating a Footnote Reference.   Type a superior (raised) number following the statement cited. If a punctuation mark follows the statement, position the raised number immediately after the punctuation mark.

The numbering of footnotes should run consecutively throughout the report. Where there are only a few footnotes in a report, they may be keyed by a symbol (such as an asterisk) rather than by number.

Placement.   Although footnote references traditionally appear on the same page as the matter to which they refer, positioning all of them in a section at the end of the report is a popular practice.

When footnotes appear at the foot of the page, estimate the number of lines to be reserved at the bottom of the page as the page is being typed. Your estimate will be reasonably close if you allow three to four lines for each footnote reference. Footnotes are separated from the text on the page by an underscore line (about 20 to 24 strokes) below the last line of the text, starting at the left margin. The first footnote is typed on the second line below the underscore line. Each footnote is single-spaced; consecutive footnotes are separated by a blank line. The first line of each footnote is indented five spaces. All additional footnote lines begin flush with the left margin. (There is a trend toward blocking footnotes instead of indenting the first line as a result of the move toward work simplification.)

When footnotes are grouped in a special section at the end of a report or manuscript, center the appropriate title twelve vertical spaces from the top edge of the sheet. Use the same margins as on the other pages of the report. Indent the first line of each footnote five spaces and type the identifying number in alignment with the remaining elements of the footnote. Single-space each footnote with one blank space between footnotes.

Basic Pattern of Footnotes.   Although the following pattern for displaying footnotes in a report is recommended, you can modify the pattern as necessary to fit varying needs.

- Footnote number.
- Names of authors.
- Titles of complete works or parts of complete works.
- Publisher's name.
- Place of publication.
- Date of publication.
- Page numbers.

Note the following example:

> [1] William A. Sabin, *The Gregg Reference Manual*, 5th ed., McGraw-Hill Book Company, New York, 1977, pp. 276–286.

Subsequent Footnote References.   When a footnote refers to a reference that was fully identified in the footnote *immediately preceding*, it may be shortened by use of the abbreviation *ibid*. *Ibid*. replaces as much of the immediately preceding footnote as is the same.

> [1] Harry Shaw, *McGraw-Hill Handbook of English*, 3d ed., McGraw-Hill Book Company, New York, 1969, p. 170.
>
> [2] Ibid., pp. 400–409.

When a footnote refers to a reference already cited in an earlier but not immediately preceding footnote, it may be shortened as follows: [1]Author's surname, page number. A more formal style uses the abbreviation *loc. cit.* when reference is made to the very same page in the work previously cited, or *op. cit.* when reference is made to a different page in the work previously cited.

> [1] William Strunk, Jr., and E. B. White, *The Elements of Style*, The Macmillan Company, New York, 1959, p. 58.
>
> [2] Porter G. Perrin, *Writer's Guide and Index to English*, Scott, Foresman and Company, Chicago, 1959, p. 374.
>
> [3] Strunk, loc. cit.
>
> [4] Perrin, op. cit., p. 372.

Styles for typing and information about specific elements within footnotes may be reviewed in the appropriate part of the Reference Section of this text.

Page Numbering   The body of a report is usually typed and approved before the page numbers are permanently added. This procedure makes changes easier. Unpaged copy can be kept in order by numbering the unapproved pages lightly in pencil. Then, after the front and back sections have been typed and the report is approved and ready to be bound, the page numbers are added on the typewriter.

Page numbers for side-bound and unbound reports are typed flush right, on the fourth line from the top. The page numbers for top-bound reports are usually centered at the bottom of report pages on the sixth line up from the bottom edge of each page.

Numbering the first page of a report is optional. When it is numbered, the number is always centered at the bottom of the page. The preliminary pages, those that precede the body of a report, are numbered in small Roman numerals on the fourth line space from the bottom edge, centered horizontally.

Preliminary Parts

The preliminary parts of a business report are prepared after the body of the report has been completed. Items often found in the preliminary pages are the title page, letter of transmittal (preface), table of contents, and lists of tables and illustrations.

Title Page   The title page is the first page in a formal report. It displays the essential information that identifies the report, that is, the title, for whom the report was prepared, the person responsible for the report, the date, and the place of preparation.

The arrangement of these details requires some ingenuity and a feeling for design. If display space is limited, minimize the number of words used while still conveying the meaning.

The title of the report looks best centered horizontally in the upper third of the page. Unless the title is brief enough to permit a single-line display, it should be broken into several lines, according to sense. Short connecting words, such as *for*, *of*, or *by*, may be placed on separate lines.

MAGNETIC MEDIA
FOR
WORD PROCESSING

You can highlight a title page by using such devices as extra spacing, underlining, or capitals; by typing over key words to emphasize them; or by typing decorative borders or lines, using the *m*, *x*, *,), (*, or " keys. Do not use too much ornamentation, however. A title page should meet the criteria of simplicity, legibility, balance, good taste, and appropriateness to the subject matter of the report.

Center all other subsidiary details on the title page horizontally and type them in capitals and lowercase letters. Center the name of the writer, the location, and the date in the bottom third of the page. The identity of the person or organization for whom the report is prepared is appropriately displayed in the horizontal and vertical center of the page.

```
                        ANALYSIS

                           OF

                   TEN BUSINESS LETTERS











                       Prepared for
                       Dorothy Kovacs
                    Stimson & Hoyt, Inc.
                 Philadelphia, Pennsylvania
```
```
                        Submitted by
                        David Nakano
                       Columbus, Ohio
                     December 12, 19--
```

The title page of a report.

Letter of Transmittal When a formal report is completed, a letter of transmittal accompanies it. Placed after the title page, it represents the report as a whole in a highly condensed form. It explains the objectives and scope of the formal report, methods of treatment, sources of information, and the like. In short reports, the letter of transmittal or synopsis is unnecessary.

The letter of transmittal is generally typed on regular business letterhead and signed in ink.

```
                                           801 Canfield Hall
                                           Columbus, Ohio 43200
                                           December 12, 19--

           Mrs. Dorothy Kovacs
           Stimson & Hoyt, Inc.
           2510 Market Street
           Philadelphia, Pennsylvania 19100

           Dear Mrs. Kovacs:

           According to your recent request, I am enclosing a
           report analyzing ten business letters.

           The main purpose of this report was to consider the
           importance of various elements--tone, emphasis, unity,
           and coherence--in writing effective business letters.
           I call your attention to the recommendations in the
           final section.

                                           Sincerely yours,

                                           David Nakano

                                           David Nakano
```

A letter of transmittal.

Table of Contents

The table of contents for a report is prepared after it has been paged. The contents page provides easy reference to any part of the report. It lists the titles of the main divisions or topics of the report and their page numbers as well as the front and back matter, with page numbers. Subheadings and their page numbers can also be listed. When tables and charts are used in the report, you can list them, with page numbers, following the back-matter listings.

Consider the suggestions that follow when preparing a table of contents:

- Center *Table of Contents* or *Contents* horizontally 12 blank lines from the top of the page.

- Type the word *Page* at the extreme right margin, three spaces below *Table of Contents*. It can be typed in capital letters or underlined to set it off as a column heading.

- Type the first entry, beginning at the left margin, two spaces below the *Page* heading.

- Leaders (a series of periods) may be used to fill out the short lines of entries in a table of contents. Leaders are easier to follow visually when a space is used after each period. If you begin each line of leaders consistently on either an odd or even number on the space indicator of your typewriter, the periods will align vertically. The leaders should stop one or two white spaces short of the page numbers, for ease in reading.

CONTENTS

A table of contents.

- Use single- or double-spacing for each major head, depending on which arrangement looks best. Usually the table of contents is roughed out to get an idea of its length and width before the final form is decided upon. If you choose single-spacing, then double-space between the major heads.

Summary   The summary is a concluding statement in which the writer helps the reader to identify and retain the central ideas presented in the report and the reason for presenting them. Because the summary often reinforces the pattern of the report, it should provide the reader with a ready means of remembering the details by providing a framework on which to hang them.

There are several requirements to keep in mind when writing a summary. The summary should add to the value of the report. It should not contain new material, except to reinforce conclusions drawn or recommendations made. It should give the impression of a completed performance. The letter of transmittal (introduction) raised a question; the summary is the final answer.

Whatever the purpose of the report, the summary should convey the realization of that purpose. If the business report is a factual account of research or an investigation, a summary of findings, results, or conclusions is appropriate. Many reports are written for the purpose of giving a critical judgment or advising

SUMMARY

To be effective, business letters must have appropriate tone and emphasis. They must also have unity and coherence.

Of the business letters discussed in this report, several were found to be lacking in these qualities. The best letters were form sales letters.

Some of the letters could have been improved considerably if more time and effort had been spent on them.

A report summary.

another person what to do. The summary in all such reports should indicate a position based on a summary of arguments developed in detail in the body of the report. In advisory reports, the summary may take the form of argument, advice, or a sales presentation.

Supplementary Parts

The appendix, bibliography, and index (when necessary) both supplement and support the information presented in the body of the business report. These components come at the very end of the report.

Appendix   The appendix usually precedes the bibliography, and its pages are numbered consecutively with those of the body of the report. It presents pertinent information too detailed or specialized to be given in the body of the report—supporting data, computations, tables, or graphs that the reader can use in confirming the soundness of the report. All such supplementary material should be referred to in the body of the report.

Center the heading *Appendix* or *Appendixes* vertically on a fresh page or start on line 13 of the first appendix page, two blank lines above the first entry. If the appendix contains several items, begin each on a new page with an identifying heading that should be listed in the table of contents.

Bibliography   The bibliography at the end of a business report lists the works referred to in the preparation of the report as well as the works cited in the footnotes.

Begin the bibliography on a fresh page with the centered heading *Bibliography* typed on line 13, separated from the first bibliographic entry by two blank spaces. Use the same left and right margins as those used in the body of the report. Single-space each entry, leaving one blank line between entries. Begin each entry flush with the left margin and use a uniform 10-space indentation for additional lines within each entry.

Entries in a bibliography are not numbered and are listed alphabetically by author. They contain the same elements and follow the same style as footnotes with these exceptions.

- The name of the author is in inverted order.

  Phillips, David C., *Oral Communication in Business*, McGraw-Hill Book Company, New York, 1955.

- Page numbers are given only when the material cited is part of a larger work.
- Entries lacking an author are alphabetized by title, disregarding the words *The* or *A* at the beginning of a title.

  The Challenge of Change, The American Textbook Publishers Institute, New York, 1962.

- When more than one work by the same author is cited, replace his or her name with a dash (six hyphens in length) in each entry after the first. List works alphabetically by title.

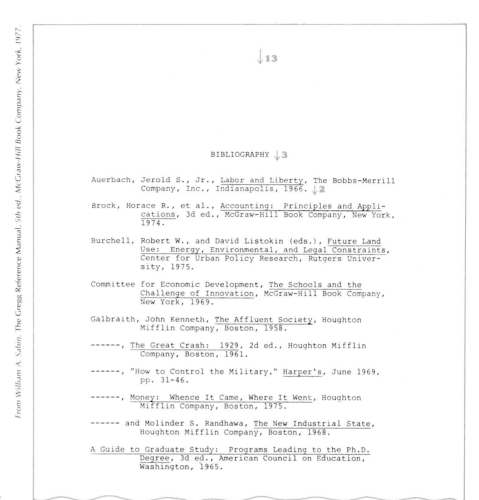

From William A. Sabin, The Gregg Reference Manual, 5th ed., McGraw-Hill Book Company, New York, 1977.

↓13

BIBLIOGRAPHY ↓3

Auerbach, Jerold S., Jr., <u>Labor and Liberty</u>, The Bobbs-Merrill Company, Inc., Indianapolis, 1966. ↓2

Brock, Horace R., et al., <u>Accounting: Principles and Applications</u>, 3d ed., McGraw-Hill Book Company, New York, 1974.

Burchell, Robert W., and David Listokin (eds.), <u>Future Land Use: Energy, Environmental, and Legal Constraints</u>, Center for Urban Policy Research, Rutgers University, 1975.

Committee for Economic Development, <u>The Schools and the Challenge of Innovation</u>, McGraw-Hill Book Company, New York, 1969.

Galbraith, John Kenneth, <u>The Affluent Society</u>, Houghton Mifflin Company, Boston, 1958.

------, <u>The Great Crash: 1929</u>, 2d ed., Houghton Mifflin Company, Boston, 1961.

------, "How to Control the Military," <u>Harper's</u>, June 1969, pp. 31-46.

------, <u>Money: Whence It Came, Where It Went</u>, Houghton Mifflin Company, Boston, 1975.

------ and Molinder S. Randhawa, <u>The New Industrial State</u>, Houghton Mifflin Company, Boston, 1968.

<u>A Guide to Graduate Study: Programs Leading to the Ph.D. Degree</u>, 3d ed., American Council on Education, Washington, 1965.

Bibliography for a report.

Rosenberg, Robert R., *College Mathematics*, McGraw-Hill Book Company, New York, 1971.

———, *College Mathematics for Accounting and Business Administration*, McGraw-Hill Book Company, New York, 1967.

Index   A long, detailed business report may include an index to make the contents more accessible to the reader. When making an index, begin by underlining the main ideas on every page of a copy of the report.

Preparing the Index Cards.   Write every entry for the index, with its page number, on a separate 5- x 3-inch card for convenience in alphabetizing. Show the most significant word first on the index card. When an entry contains two key words, either of which might be looked for in the index, make two cards. An entry should be a noun or a substantive phrase. An adjective, for example, would not be used alone.

Footnotes, patterns for, in a report

279

An index card. The check indicates that there is a cross-reference under "Reports, patterns for footnotes in."

It is easier to prepare an index if you alphabetize the cards as you make them. In this way you can see the structure of the index as a whole and solve problems as you encounter them. For example, if you find a second reference to a subject you have used before, you need only add another page number to the card.

Typing the Index.   After you have alphabetized and edited the entries and verified all cross-references, type the index on 8½- by 11-inch paper, double-spaced in single or in double columns. Show indention of subentries by using two typewriter spaces. Indent five spaces or more any entries that run longer than one line so that they will not be mistaken for subentries. A portion of a typewritten index is shown at the top of page 333.

Presentation of Data

Tables and graphic figures (charts and graphs) are excellent devices for presenting statistical facts that may be hard to understand at first glance in a form that is easy to read and easy to refer to. You may be responsible for deciding which format tables, charts, and graphs are prepared in for use in business reports.

Tables   Before typing a table, first study the statistical data to be tabulated and plan the column headings and their orderly arrangement. Prepare a rough draft showing all of the components to be used in the table.

Tables that appear on the same page with text copy should be centered horizontally within the margins of the text page and set off from the text by three blank lines above or below. When there are more tables than can be appropriately displayed in the text, they may be assembled on separate pages in the appendix of the report.

```
Measurements, 29-32

    abbreviation of, 31-32, 34, 35,

        37-38

    metric, 37-38

    plurals, 65

    spelled out, 34, 36, 38

Memos, 9; illus., 17

Metrication, 37-38

Money, 13-20

    amounts of, as subjects, 19

    in tables, 22

    in words, 13-14, 18, 20
```

A portion of a
typewritten index.

Table Title and Subtitles

Word the title of a table carefully so that the reader can quickly grasp what the table is about. Type the title in capital letters, centered over the table. If more than one or two tables are presented in a report, you may number them consecutively.

Type table subtitles in capital and lowercase letters and center them horizontally within the text-page margins. If the table is unruled, allow one blank line between the main table title and the subtitle and two blank lines between the subtitle and the column heads. If the table is ruled, allow one blank line between each rule and the title, subtitle, or column head above or below it.

Type the column heads in capital and lowercase letters and center them over the entries in their respective columns. If the table is unruled, underscore each line of the column head. Column heads show relationships among the items in a table. Spanner heads are used to cover related and adjacent column heads to indicate more than one level of classification. Column heads should be as short as is consistent with clarity; *a*, *an*, and *the* may be omitted. When space is limited, abbreviations may be used. If nonstandard abbreviations are used, explain them in a footnote below the table. Try to keep each heading no more than two lines deep and no more than two spaces wider than the widest item in the column. When horizontal headings must be lengthy, type them vertically so that they read up, not down.

If the title, subtitle, or column heads require more than one line, use single spacing for each additional line.

Alignment

Leaders are used in the stub column to help carry the reader's eyes across to the columns of data that follow. In typing, run them over to where the first vertically

ACCESSIBILITY OF AFTER-HOURS COURSES TO EMPLOYEES BY COMPANY SIZE AND TYPE							
		Percent of Employees at Facilities Having After-Hours Courses					
Categories	None	Less Than 10%	10%-49%	50%-89%	90%-100%	No Answer	Totals
Company Size							
10,000 or more	44%	19%	17%	10%	5%	5%	100%
5,000-9,999	46%	13%	10%	17%	12%	2%	100%
2,500-4,999	46%	12%	12%	14%	13%	3%	100%
1,000-2,999	54%	9%	14%	9%	13%	1%	100%
500-999	75%	1%	2%	11%	11%	-	100%
All companies	60%	7%	9%	11%	12%	1%	100%
Company Type							
Manufacturing	63%	8%	8%	10%	10%	1%	100%
Transportation	46%	10%	24%	10%	10%	1%	100%*
Wholesale/Retail . . .	72%	6%	5%	10%	3%	3%	100%*
Insurance	52%	4%	8%	13%	23%	-	100%
Other	55%	7%	7%	13%	18%	-	100%
All companies	60%	7%	9%	11%	12%	1%	100%

*Details do not total 100 percent because of rounding.

A ruled table.

ruled line is drawn. To align leaders vertically, start consistently on either the even or odd numbers of the typewriter scale.

In a properly constructed table, words and phrases are typed in columns with a uniform left margin. Figures are tabulated with the right margin in vertical alignment. In columns of dollar amounts, align the dollar signs in the first space to the left of the longest amount in the column. Insert a dollar sign only before the first entry in the column and before any total amount.

Item Order. The order of items within a table can be chronological, logical, alphabetic, geographic, by size, or by importance. Where time relationships are important, chronological order should be used. Logical order is best where categories or close relationships among items are to be stressed. When the table is to be used primarily for reference—for example, when it contains information about personnel or products—alphabetic order can be used. Geographic order is appropriate to show comparisons among sales territories or the sequence of cities on a particular travel route. Ranking by size in terms of dimension, volume, or dollars is often of significance. If no other rank is apparent, order of importance is generally used. In the table shown above, items are ordered both by size and by type.

In tables showing figures, statisticians recommend that four or five digits should be the maximum in a column (6,759; 67.59; 6.759). Notice how much more easily the figures that follow can be compared in terms of thousands and millions:

Absolute Figures	In Terms of Thousands	In Terms of Millions
19,320,584	19,321	19.32
13,357,478	13,357	13.36

Rulings.   Tables may be ruled or unruled. If the table is to be ruled, either of two methods may be used:

1. Insert all rules on the typewriter, using the underscore. Place a horizontal rule above and below the column heads and at the bottom of the table. The bottom line serves to close a table. These rules should extend to the full width of the table. Type each rule on the line immediately following the preceding copy. This creates the appearance of a blank space above the underscore. Leave one blank space between an internal rule and the table copy that follows; three blank lines between the bottom rule and any text copy that follows. Type vertical rules to separate columns by inserting the page sideways into the typewriter. Do not type rules to indicate side margins—they should be left open.
2. Draw all rules with a black ball-point pen and a ruler. Be sure to provide needed space for these rules when typing the table.

   Usually tables that are narrow enough to be centered horizontally look better without ruling, while those that are typed to the full width of the text line look better with lines separating them from the text.

Table Footnotes.   A footnote to an item in a table is usually noted by a letter of the alphabet. The footnote itself is placed two spaces below the table. Single-space the footnote if it occupies more than one line and double-space between footnotes if two or more are used.

Graphic Figures   Graphs, charts, diagrams, and pictorial representations of various kinds are routinely used in business reports. Thus, if you have acquired even the basic principles of graphic representation, you are in possession of a highly useful tool. In addition to organizing the presentation of information in an effective manner, you are often entrusted with the responsibility for making freehand drawings, sufficiently outlined to enable a commercial artist to prepare the finished figure.

Line Graphs.   The line graph is frequently used in a report to show trends or changes over a period of time. A changing series of values is plotted on a ruled background called the grid. The points are connected by straight lines. The higher the line is at any given point, the greater the quantity represented. The lower the line, the smaller the quantity. A sudden rise or drop in the line indicates a sudden rise or fall in the quantity.

   The simplest type of line graph presents the changes for only one factor over a period of time. In a *correlation graph*, the changes in two or more factors may

Birth and Death Rates per 1,000 Population, 1900–1980

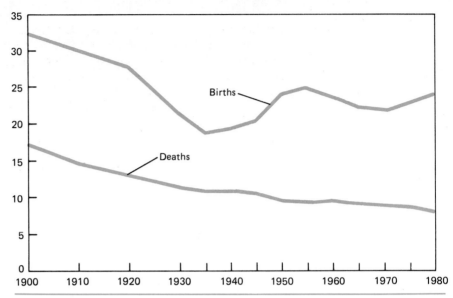

A line graph.

be plotted on the same graph by using different colors or different types of lines, such as a continuous line, a dotted line, a line of dashes, and a line of dots and dashes.

In constructing a line graph, consider each of the following pointers:

1. Use printed graph paper or draw a grid on plain paper.
2. Lay out two scales, one along the bottom line with values increasing from left to right, and the other along the left side with values increasing from bottom to top. The first is called the X or horizontal axis and the second the Y or vertical axis.
3. Put units of time on the X axis and units of changing quantity on the Y axis.
4. Always make your starting point zero. In the event that the curve occurs too high on the chart, use two wavy lines to designate an omission in the field. Omitting the zero produces a distorted impression with reference to the values represented on the graph.
5. Assign a value to each major division in the graph by dividing the largest amount to be represented by the number of lines or spaces available.
6. Avoid distortion in line graphs by maintaining a width that is at least one and one-fourth and not more than one and three-fourths times the height. If the values on the X axis are crowded together and those on the Y axis are spread apart, the resulting lines will be abnormally steep. If the values on the X axis are spread out and those on the Y axis are crowded together, the graph resulting from the same figures will show gently sloping lines suggesting very mild fluctuations.
7. Plot each statistical factor on the graph by placing a dot at the place where a line from each of the appropriate units on the axes would intersect. When the

dots for all the data have been positioned on the graph, connect the points together in one continuous line or curve.

Bar Graphs.   The bar graph represents different quantities by means of bars of the same width but of varying length according to the quantities involved. The bars may run either horizontally or vertically. The vertical bar is most common when the X axis represents units of time.

(a)

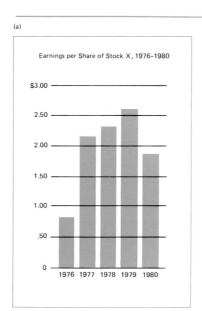

(b)

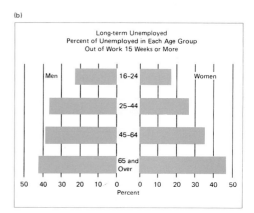

(c)

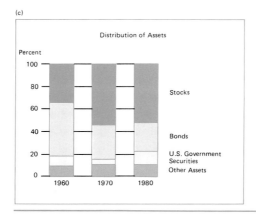

Three types of bar graph: *above left,* simple bar graph; *center right,* subdivided bar graph; *below left,* percentage bar graph.

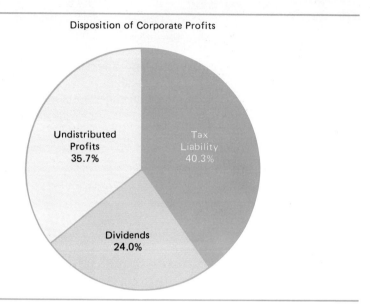

Disposition of Corporate Profits

Undistributed
Profits
35.7%

Tax
Liability
40.3%

Dividends
24.0%

A circle or pie graph.

A simple bar graph corresponds to the simple line chart in that only two related sets of facts or quantities are involved. One of these is shown on the X axis and one on the Y axis. Usually this type of bar graph makes comparisons of several periods of time, several geographic units, several products, several sets of data. In a subdivided bar graph an additional factor is involved. Each bar is divided into two or more parts so that the total is really a long bar made up of several shorter ones. This type compares not only the total quantities but also the parts of which they are composed. The percentage bar graph is closely related to the subdivided type. The bars are divided to show the relationship among component parts in terms of percentages.

A bar graph may be constructed on the typewriter by means of a heavy strikeover of capital Xs and Os or combinations of letters and characters.

Circle or Pie Graphs.   The circle or pie graph is an effective way to display the way any given quantity is divided into parts. It shows clearly not only the relationship of each part to the whole but also the relationship of each part to every other part.

The circle or pie graph is one of the simplest to construct:

1. Draw a circle of any desired size on a piece of plain paper.
2. Rank the segments to be plotted in percentage form, according to size.
3. Divide proportionally the 360 degrees that compose the circle. Thus a segment representing 20 percent will occupy 20 percent of 360, or 72 degrees of the circle.
4. Starting at "twelve o'clock" on the circle, use a protractor to mark off each segment of the whole in degrees, beginning with the largest segment and working clockwise around the graph.

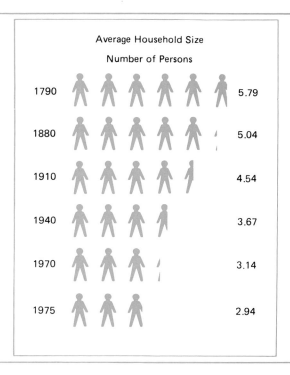

A pictorial graph.

5. Identify each segment by positioning a caption horizontally inside the segment, or outside it if the space is too small.

Pictorial Graphs. Area and solid diagrams are commonly pictorial; that is, the chart itself is made up of pictures. Bar charts are sometimes made in the same way, like a stack of coins that increases in only one dimension. Distortion in pictorial bar charts can be prevented by constructing the bars of conventionalized figures of the same size. The bars are increased in length by adding more figures. Illustrations may constitute the background of graph or be superimposed on the face of it. Any of these techniques serve to accentuate and enliven the facts being presented. Pictorial graphs are most valuable when reader attention is the primary consideration.

Flow Charts. A flow chart is a pictorial outline of a sequence of steps to be performed to solve a problem. The technique of flow charting consists of making a diagram using a standard symbol for each step and a brief text alongside or inside the symbol to clarify the step.

Flow chart symbols have been standardized for communication with machines, and templates for drawing them can be purchased.

The preparation of a flow chart involves three steps:

1. Defining the operation to be performed.

Standard Flow Chart Symbols

Terminal Interrupt: Used to show the start, stop, halt, delay, or end in a series of steps.

Flow: Used to show direction to the next step:

START (Terminal) — (Flow) → END (Terminal)

Operation or Process: Used to show a step, a specific operation, or a function that causes a change in value or form.

Manual Operation: Used to show any input/output function or any process without mechanical aid.

Decision: Used to show which of a number of alternate paths is followed.

Connector: Used to identify exit from or entry into different parts of a flow chart. A number inside the exit connector should match the number inside the entry connector.

Input/Output: Used to designate information available for processing or recording of processed information.

2. Determining where the operation begins and ends and arranging each intermediate step in sequence.
3. Identifying each step by its standard symbol and a brief clarifying statement.

The flow chart that follows illustrates the logic involved in operating an adding machine to solve an addition problem.

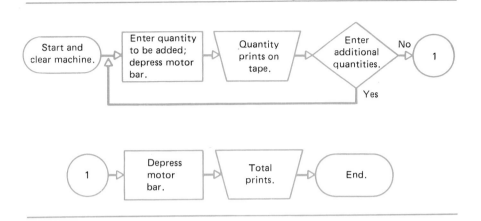

REViewiNG
YouR
REAdiNG

1. Identify the skills you can put to good use when gathering and assembling accurate information for your employer's use in business reports.

2. Describe a topical outline and explain what is meant by the statement "Main heads or subheads should not stand alone."

3. Discuss the space allowances you should provide when typing a rough draft of a business report.

4. Describe your role in assisting the writer in reviewing, revising, and editing the rough draft of a business report.

5. Identify the information needed in a letter requesting permission to quote from copyrighted material.

6. Describe the preferred procedure for numbering the pages of a typed report before its final approval and binding.

7. Indicate the preferred order of the items of information that should be given in a reference footnote.

8. Explain how a reference footnote may be shortened when it refers to a reference cited in the immediately preceding footnote.

9. List the ways you may differentiate headings when typing a business report.

10. Compare the elements of a bibliography to those of a reference footnote, indicating the differences.

11. Specify the best order of items within a table when (a) time relationships are important, (b) categories or close relationships among items are to be stressed, and (c) comparisons among sales territories are to be shown.

12. Describe a flow chart and identify the three steps involved in its preparation.

13. Outline a set of guidelines to be followed when constructing circular graphs.

14. Explain why pictorial graphs are frequently employed to present information in business reports rather than other, more precise graphic figures.

15. Discuss the purpose of headings and subheadings in a business report and explain what is meant by parallel phrasing within headings of the same rank.

USING
YOUR
Skills

1. Produce a guide sheet for use directly behind pages of a report being typed. Use ordinary bond ruled with dark ink or colored pencil that is visible through the top sheet.

2. Type the following outline on plain white paper. Make appropriate changes if any items lack parallel construction or could be improved in other ways.

Insurance

I. Nature of Insurance
   A. Protection against loss
      1. Distributing loss over a group
      2. Through the raising of a common fund for the payment of losses incurred
   B. To reimburse Losses
      1. Resulting from the happening of a certain event or some other contingency
      2. That involve a valid risk
   C. Types of Insurance
      A. How to protect property
      1. Fire insurance
         a. Ordinary fire insurance
         b. Coinsurance clause
         c. 80% average clause
      2. Marine insurance
      3. Automobile insurance
         a. Collision
         b. Property damage
      4. Burglary Insurance
      5. Casualty insurance
      B. Protection of persons
      1. Life insurance
         a. Ordinary, or straight life
         b. Limited payment
         c. Endowment
         d. Annuity
      2. Health
      3. Accident
      4. Employer's liability
      5. Automobile liability
      6. Title
      7. Fidelity
      8. Credit

III. Principles Affecting Insurance
   A. Fire
      1. Insurable interest
      2. Alienation clause
      3. Assignment before loss occurs
      4. Lightning clause
      5. Vacancy clause
      6. Double insurance
      7. Hostile fires
   B. Life insurance
      1. Change of beneficiary
      2. Incontestability clause
      3. Misrepresentation of age
      4. Suicide of insured
IV. Kinds of Insurance Policies
   A. The open policy
   B. The valued policy
V. Classes of Insurance Companies
   A. Mutual
   B. Stock

3. The following portions of a report, "Reducing Fluctuations in Workload," were drafted by Lorenzo J. Comiskey, Kagel Associates, Greenwich, Connecticut, for Graphics Concepts, Inc., 26 Turn of River Road, Stamford, Connecticut.

Prepare a style sheet to accompany the drafted report. Weigh the treatment of heads and subheads and add new ones if you think them necessary.

Proper planning and division of the flow of office work will result in a relatively stable workload. However, management must not overlook the factors outside the office that may produce fluctuations in work volume.

To the extent that such remaining fluctuations can be reduced or counteracted, it becomes easier to (1) staff the organization so that the work can be handled regularly without bottlenecks, (2) staff on the basis of average workload rather than peak requirements, (3) work out such timetables for the completion of work as are necessary, (4) increase the rate of production by giving regular assignments to the workers, and (5) provide more dependable service.

Fluctuations in workload frequently can be minimized or offset by instituting the following procedures:

1. Regulating the timing of work coming into the office,
2. Regulating the backlog in the office, and
3. Regulating the sequence of processing steps.

Regulating the Timing of Work Coming Into the Office

There are two commonly used methods of regulating the time-pattern of incoming work: (1) rearrangement of due dates and (2) promotional efforts to change "customer" habits.

Rearrangement of due dates is often practiced in both business and government. A large manufacturer, for example, maintained a staggered schedule for receiving reports from its overseas divisions. Similarly, a major oil company has established different reporting dates for different filling stations. One leading paper company staggers its mailing of checks to salespeople because the salespeople tend to send in their orders and commission sheets just before their checks are due. Stores, utilities, insurance companies, and other businesses frequently use staggered billings to level out the flow of work (incoming payments).

The federal government applies staggered working hours in the District of Columbia to even the load on the transportation system, and the federal government also applies staggered paydays to help stabilize the work of Treasury Disbursement and the work of the local banks. Although this method is relatively simple, considerable experimentation sometimes is necessary to determine the right intervals.

Common examples of promotional efforts to influence the inflow of work include attempts to get letters signed when written in order to avoid mailroom peaks at the end of the day, and attempts to get cassette tapes to stenographic pools before a certain hour for same-day service. Reduced long-distance telephone rates, off-peak power rates, campaigns to get housewives to do their shopping in off hours, and month-end sales are other examples of the same technique. Similarly, a major mail-order house times the mailing of its catalogs and of special "flyers" to bring in orders during slack periods indicated by previous experience.

The idea of regulating the work that comes into an office is a simple one, but it is very often overlooked. . . .

Changing the Step Sequence for Part of the Workload

The following highly simplified illustration demonstrates how fluctuations can be reduced by changing the sequence of steps for a portion of the work. Assume that two of the steps required in the adjudication of a certain type of claim are (1) recording data from the claim for research purposes and (2) obtaining medical data to be entered on a claim for purposes of adjudication. Assume also that Step 1 is now completed first (although it does not matter what order is used), that each step is performed by a different organization unit, and that the incoming work is received in quantities of 50 and 100 on alternate days. If each organization unit is staffed to handle the peak load (100 cases) per day, the work handled by each unit each day would be as follows:

	Mon.	Tues.	Wed.	Thur.	Fri.
Step 1	50	100	50	100	50
Step 2	100	50	100	50	100

The amount of work performed at Step 1 each day is the work received that day; the amount of work performed at Step 2 is that received the previous day, and on which Step 1 has been completed.

If, however, when the work was received each day it had been divided evenly with Step 1 performed first on half of the cases and Step 2 performed first on the other half, the workload would have been evened out like this:

	Mon.	Tues.	Wed.	Thur.	Fri.
Step 1	75	75	75	75	75
Step 2	75	75	75	75	75

4. Appropriately display the following data according to the suggestions made in this chapter.

a. Prepare a table showing clerks' salaries in five of a company's branch stores for last year.

Warren No. 1 store paid out in clerks' salaries $34,215.00, while No. 2 store at Warren paid out only $21,009.00. The highest amount paid, however, was at Upper Crossing, where salaries were $48,172.20. The Rand store figure was $10,141.00. The figure $3,157.10 for Southport is not really comparable, since that store began operations only three months before the end of the year.

Give the table a suitable heading, and indicate in a footnote that the Southport store was operated only for three months. Use leaders, but do not insert vertical rules. Find the total, and show it at the end of the table. Use a full sheet or a half sheet of plain paper. Make one carbon copy.

b. Make a bar chart of the same data.

EXERCISING YOUR JUDGMENT

You Don't Agree. Helen Gambrel, who had worked in your department ten years before you came and functions as a supervisor (but is not so designated; you both report to the same boss, Mrs. Pellatt), has several table style features she has developed over the years. For example, she always types a decorated border of asterisks on the cover, and she color-codes. She uses green paper for budget reports, pink paper for special reports, and yellow paper for personnel reports. She describes her special style to you and suggests that you follow it in the reports you prepare.

You like Helen, but you happen to dislike ornamentation on report covers, and you do not see much point to the color coding since these colors are also used randomly for memos and office bulletins. What should you do? Why?

APPLYING THE REFERENCE SECTION

1. Write on a sheet of paper the word in each set of parentheses that correctly completes the sentence.

a. The (biannual, biennial) meeting was always held in May.

b. Market conditions were (adverse, averse) all last year.

c. Although danger was (eminent, imminent), he was not able to leave the building.

d. The politician reaffirmed her (new, recent) decision.

e. We have several (empty, vacant) rooms for rent in our office building.

f. (Fewer, Less) employees than usual reported for work due to the flu epidemic.

g. She had an (inane, innate) sense of tact.

h. They nodded approvingly, agreeing that her decision was (equitable, equivocal).

2. Write on a separate sheet of paper the word in parentheses that correctly completes each of the sentences below. Following each word you list, write its definition (you may refer to a dictionary). Then write a new sentence using each word.

   a. Because this flower is a (biannual, biennial), it must be replanted every two years.

   b. The manager tried to help each employee discover and develop (inane, innate) talents.

   c. We sent boxes with food and clothing to help the (indigenous, indigent) people of that country.

   d. The committee chairperson was (adverse, averse) to holding weekly committee meetings.

   e. Bay trees are (indigenous, indigent) to Oregon.

   f. He sometimes makes (inane, innate) remarks.

   g. Accuracy in recording minutes is of (paramount, tantamount) importance.

   h. The food served in our company cafeteria is usually (palatable, palpable).

PART SIX / Administrative Responsibilities

CHAPTER NINETEEN / Supervisory Techniques

Employers no longer try to keep efficient assistants in secretarial positions by denying them opportunities to upgrade their status. Personnel directors point out that secretaries who have had training in business subjects can expect advancement into other operations of the business, if this is their goal. Opportunities for advancement are usually encountered within a two-year period following initial employment.

Secretaries have the opportunity to learn a great deal about the management and operations of a business. Since plans, policies, and decisions of top managers filter down through the several levels of management and their assistants, secretaries are in a strategic position to get others to do the work management wants done.

Obviously, the secretary who wishes to become a supervisor and to advance to the ranks of middle management must be ready for the opportunities and know how to take advantage of them.

Supervisory Qualities

Your readiness for supervisory responsibilities must be recognized by others in the organization. Unfortunately, there is no prescribed way to attain this recognition. It becomes apparent that you can handle supervisory responsibilities in many ways. You can show by your actions that you have the qualities that enable a supervisor to recognize problems, discover their real causes, and take corrective actions. You also demonstrate that you know how to motivate people. Supervisory qualities include the following:

- Ambition—the willingness to develop new skills and to accept assignments that broaden the scope of your job.
- Clear communication—the ability to present directions and ideas orally or in writing so that they are easily understood by your subordinates, peers, and superiors.
- Concentration—the ability to think through a problem or action without being distracted by noises or interruptions.

- Leadership—the knack of inspiring others to follow your direction and to work with you.
- Organization—the capacity to organize your work as well as the efforts of others in order to meet productivity standards.
- Initiative—the self-confidence and courage to take independent action without being told to do something.
- Perceptiveness—an awareness of the strengths and weaknesses in others when scheduling what needs to be done.
- Even-handedness—impartiality to all when resolving difficult problems.

These qualities should help you to realize that you cannot move from the general secretarial ranks to a position of supervision by simply deciding that is where you wish to be. It should be obvious, too, that as a secretary on the move you must be approachable and open-minded, maintain high expectations, provide ready access to needed information, display initiative, help subordinates learn from mistakes, and give credit for competent performance. The candidate unqualified for supervisory responsibilities, on the other hand, is usually authority-oriented, not receptive to new or different ideas, impatient with people who make mistakes, prone to look for scapegoats to blame for mistakes, and not likely to display initiative, or take risks.

AuthoriTy aNd RespoNsibiliTy

Secretaries need to clearly understand their responsibilities before they can effectively supervise the work of others. Read and familiarize yourself with the description of your job that has been prepared by your boss or by the personnel department of your company. If a job description has not been prepared for your position, draft one. The objective of the exercise is an accurate description of the primary duties of your position. As illustrated on pages 350 and 351, a job description usually includes the following information:

- Title of job.
- Summary description of job.
- Description of specific duties performed.
- Percentage of time allotted for each duty.
- Equipment used on job.
- Minimum qualifications for job.

Hand in hand with the responsibilities of the job goes the authority needed to carry out those responsibilities. It is inefficient and counterproductive to separate authority and responsibility. The executive secretary who lacks power to rate performance, to recommend merit increases, or to discipline office subordinates probably lacks authority equal in measure to delegated responsibility. Authority is the power to make decisions, to take appropriate action, and to discipline subordinates.

As a secretary with supervisory responsibilities, you also need to know how far your authority permits you to go before overlapping another person's responsibility. Your boss remains accountable to higher management even though

Job Description

(PLEASE TYPE ALL INFORMATION)

Job Title ___Secretary to Editor in Chief___ Department or Publication _Publishing Division_

Reports to ___Bernard Beitz___ ___Editor in Chief___ Section __Editorial__
  Name   Position

Prepared by   Reviewed and Approved by

_____Bernard Beitz_____
                  Name
__Editor in Chief__   __10/12/--__
    Position   Date   Department Head   Date

PLEASE READ INSTRUCTION SHEET BEFORE LISTING JOB DUTIES

FUNCTION (Briefly summarize the main function of job)
Transcribes rough drafted and dictated letters, memos, and reports. Receives and helps to answer all incoming oral and written communications. Helps maintain the flow, processing and follow-up of manuscript. Assists other sponsoring editors assigned to the publishing unit.

DUTIES (List duties by numbered statements)

1. Transcribes a variety of rough drafted and dictated letters, memos, and reports. Writes routine letters to authors, reviewers, and others relating to manuscript development, contracts, payments, and general instructions and guidance. Prepares reimbursement vouchers and transmits checks to reviewers and authors. (30%)

2. Answers all incoming telephone inquiries, giving and receiving information and expediting communication between the employer and other editors, authors, reviewers, and consultants as well as production and marketing specialists. Makes inquiries by telephone, seeking information and making needed arrangements. (10%)

3. Types manuscript from corrected and rewritten typed or longhand copy. Detects and corrects ommissions and errors in punctuation and grammar in organization of rough draft manuscript. Proofreads retyped manuscript. Surveys manuscript for completeness. (20%)

4. Files correspondence, records, and reports. Maintains an appointment calendar. Makes travel arrangements through Transportation Department and reserves hotel accommodations. Assists in arranging meetings with authors and agents. (10%)

5. Assists employer in reporting the biweekly editorial status of each program being processed for authorization and transmittal and the monthly status of authorized programs in respect to manuscript completion dates, manuscript-release-to-editing dates, and manuscript-release-to-compositor dates. Maintains a project control file for each of the publishing unit's authorized programs. (15%)

6. Performs a variety of miscellaneous duties. Prepares a monthly expense account statement for employer. Gathers book sales records. In consultation with employer, prepares contracts, manuscript evaluation and transmittal forms, and cost-profit studies. Makes photocopies. (5%)

7. Prepares letters and memos and does miscellaneous tasks for other members of the publishing unit. (10%)

certain responsibilities were delegated to you along with the authority to take appropriate action in carrying them out. Should you misuse this authority and fail to discharge your responsibility, your boss remains accountable to higher management for the way in which you handled the matter.

Supervisory Skills

Those who exercise supervisory responsibilities serve as a channel of communication—a funnel through which the functions of planning, organizing, staffing,

PLEASE ANSWER THE FOLLOWING QUESTIONS ABOUT THE JOB:

1. What *minimum* knowledge of specific subjects, normally learned in school, is *essential* to perform this job? Do *not* state a level of school.

   Take dictation at 90 words a minute. Typewrite accurately at 60 words a minute.
   Alphabetic indexing and filing ability. Ability to compose a routine letter.
   Above-average command of English grammar. Poise in dealing with people.

2. a. What job features, if any, *require* previous experience before an employee can *begin* work on this job?

   None.

   b. What job features, if any, require on-the-job training? Estimate length of time to learn each feature.

   Help with the styling and editing of first drafts of manuscript.

3. a. What kind of instructions (verbal, written procedures, previous correspondence, and the like) are furnished by the employer?

   Personal guidance and direction by editor in chief, to whom secretary reports.

   b. If the job requires judgment or planning, give examples of decisions required, factors to be considered, and guidance provided.

   Independent action in acknowledging receipt of and logging in manuscript and manuscript proposals. Collection of manuscript development, editing, and production
   information from editors for use in regular weekly and monthly status reports.

4. a. Is the employee required to supervise or otherwise direct other employees on a regular basis? No.
   If so, list job titles and number of employees on each job and describe the *nature and frequency* of such supervision.

   b. Is contact with others required in the performance of the employee's duties? If yes, identify contact, purpose and method (telephone, personal or correspondence). Include internal and external contacts.

   Yes. Oral and written contact with authors and with reviewers of publishing proposals.
   Personal communication with sponsoring and basic editors reporting to the editor in
   chief.

5. a. Does the employee work in a private office or share one with one or two other employees? No.
   b. Does the employee work in a general office area? Yes.
   c. Describe any disagreeable working conditions or unusual physical requirements in the job and give the percentage of time exposed to such conditions.

   None.

REMARKS:

directing, and controlling are relayed from one organizational level to another. Planning is setting the course of action needed to accomplish the company's objectives. Organizing is determining the activities needed to get work accomplished in the most productive manner. Staffing involves the activities needed to recruit, hire, and care for all needed employees. Directing is the guiding and direct supervision of subordinates in the performance of their assigned tasks. Controlling is the process of seeing that goals and objectives are being met. To support these functions, and to exercise supervisory responsibilities, you must possess a range of leadership and job knowledge skills.

Hiring Competent Subordinates

One of the important supervisory responsibilities is the building of a competent staff of subordinates. The process of selecting and assigning the best possible people is challenging. The goal, of course, is to select qualified persons who fit job descriptions so that employee dissatisfaction and turnover are held to a minimum. A variety of supervisory skills and considerations are involved when facts about job applicants are being gathered.

Job Discrimination and Affirmative Action.   In establishing employment procedures, the provisions of the Civil Rights Act of 1964 and the Equal Employment Opportunity Act of 1972, which prohibit job discrimination in any way on the basis of race, color, religion, sex, age, or national origin, must be satisfied. Any company engaged in interstate commerce comes under the law. All such employers must have an affirmative action plan to encourage the employment of minority workers. These plans detail employment conditions and specify what management intends to do about hiring and promoting women, blacks, Hispanics, and members of other minority groups.

Employment Application Forms.   To prevent haphazard hiring and possible conflict with job discrimination legislation, job applicants should be asked to fill out a job application form. On such a form, candidates should be asked to give information directly related to job qualifications and the applicant's welfare. For instance, applicants should be asked to furnish personal data. Other areas of information that relate directly to the job for which an applicant is applying include educational data, participation in activities (other than those that indicate sex, race, color, religion, or national origin), and skills. The previous work experience of an applicant is a useful part of every employment application form. This should show the duties performed for previous employers, the periods of employment, and reasons for making employment changes. A typical job application form is shown on pages 354 and 355.

As a rule, employment application forms should not contain questions that would yield prejudicial information unless such information relates directly to the job. It is illegal to ask the applicant to supply the following:

- Race or color of skin.
- Religion; name of pastor, parish, or church.
- Whether applicant is a naturalized or native-born citizen.
- Applicant's first language.
- Applicant's place of birth or birthplace of spouse, parents, or relatives.
- Organizations, clubs, lodges, and societies to which applicant belongs.
- Applicant's service in the armed forces of the United States.

Employment Tests.   Employment tests should be used to screen job applicants only if such tests have been proven to measure ability to perform or learn the job in question. They should not discriminate in some subtle manner and should not be devised so that it is easier for a member of one group to answer than a member of another. Employment tests should have a clear and obvious relationship to the requirements of the jobs in question (as typing tests generally do).

In any event, tests are just one selection tool and should not be the sole basis for accepting or rejecting any candidate. The best indicator of future performance has been found to be past work or school experience. The probing of past experiences—successes, strengths, weaknesses—can provide valuable clues to the readiness of the candidate for the job assignment under consideration.

Employment Interviews.   The interview is the most valuable tool for gathering facts and assessing whether the candidate is sufficiently motivated and has the desire to succeed.

The objectives of the employment interview are threefold:

- To gather information about the candidate that will supplement the factual information already available.
- To determine whether there is a good match between the candidate's interest in and ability to perform the job and the available position.
- To communicate information about the position that will provide the candidate with an opportunity to relate past experience or education.

In conducting the interview, you must show understanding in handling concerns or questions posed by applicants, even if they seem naive. Many candidates simply lack experience in dealing with potential employers. Needless to say, you should be familiar with legal restrictions about what can be asked in the interview (ask a woman only what can be asked of a man, for example). Above all else, you need to understand the techniques of interpreting facts collected during the interviewing process and developing personal reactions concerning the interviewee. Consider the following when conducting an employment interview:

- Base your evaluation of an interviewee on all the information available. If you allow one factor about a person to influence your thinking about all the other factors, you are displaying a lack of objectivity that does not augur well for your future as a supervisor. For example, you may be unfavorably impressed by the style of an interviewee's hair and then arbitrarily find everything else equally objectionable.
- Recognize strengths in a person more readily than weaknesses. A person's weak points are usually more apparent under the pressure of an interview. Any tendency to reject an interviewee even though the weaknesses are adequately compensated for by other qualifications or unrelated to the position may result in overlooking someone with desirable strengths. If the strengths outweigh the weaknesses, an interviewee should be favorably considered.
- The best person is not necessarily the best for the position. A person who is overqualified may soon become restless and frustrated on the job. Unless the overqualified person is promoted quickly, he or she will either leave the group or stay on to become a problem.
- Strive for a good mix of personalities, backgrounds, and abilities in your group. Avoid the temptation to surround yourself with people who meet

GIBBS CORPORATION

An Equal Opportunity Employer   Employment Application

Gibbs Corporation policy and federal law forbid discrimination because of race, color, religion, age, sex, or national origin.

Date _H/28/__

Personal Data

Applying for position as _Secretary_   Salary required $_185_   Date available _5/12/__

Name _Anderson_ _____ _Lars_ _____
     (Last)   (First)   (Middle)

Present address _1624_ _Darcia Pl.,_ _Encino,_ _CA_ _91316_ _2 years_
     (Street)   (City)   (State)   (ZIP Code) (How long at this address)

Permanent address _same_ _____
     (Street)   (City)   (State)   (ZIP Code) (How long at this address)

Telephone number _(213)_ _555-4704_   Social Security number _057-03-0000_
     (Area code)

Are you a U.S. citizen? ☑ Yes ☐ No   If noncitizen, give Alien Registration No. _____

Check appropriate box for age: Under 16 ☐, 16 or 17 ☐, 18 through 64 ☑, 65 or over ☐

Person to be notified in case of emergency:

   Name _Lloyd Anderson_   Relationship _Father_   Telephone _(213)555-4704_

   Address _1624 Darcia Pl., Encino, CA 91316_

In your own handwriting, please write a short statement explaining why you believe that you will be successful as an employee of the Gibbs Corporation.

I am interested in working as a secretary for a company
that recognizes ability and enthusiasm.

Activities

Do not name organizations that will reveal race, religion, age, sex, or national origin.

School and college activities _Sports editor of school paper_

Special interests outside   1. _Hiking_
of business   2. _Playing the guitar_
                            3. _____

Skills

List any special skills you may have _Proofread for school paper_

                          ☑ Speak   ☐ Speak   ☐ Speak
What foreign languages do you: ☐ Read _Norwegian_   ☐ Read _____   ☐ Read _____
                          ☐ Write   ☐ Write   ☐ Write

Business machines you can operate _____

                          ☑ Electric
Typing speed _72_ words per minute ☐ Manual Steno speed _110_ words per minute Method _Gregg_

narrow standards of conformity or who satisfy your preconceived personal standards.

- Reserve judgment about an interviewee until the end of the interview after you have gathered all of your facts. This precaution will enable you to make a better evaluation of the interviewee's character and avoid any tendency during the interview to generalize that a person who behaves a certain way in a certain situation will behave the same way in all situations.

Educational Data

Schools	Print name, number and street, city, state and ZIP Code for each school listing	Dates	Type of course or major	Graduated?	Degree received
Grade School	Willow Glen Elementary School, 98 Pico Boulevard, Los Angeles, CA	From 1966 To 1974		yes	
High School	Darcia High School, 82 South Alameda, Los Angeles, CA 91316	From 1974 To 1978	Business Ed.	yes	
Trade, Bus., Night, or Corres.	Los Angeles Community Center, 4520 Natick Pl., Los Angeles, CA 90066	From 1978 To 1980	Word Processing	yes	
College		From To			

Employment Data

Begin with most recent employer. List all full-time, part-time, temporary, or self-employment.

Company name	Western Life Insurance Co.		Employed from Mo-Yr 6/78 To Mo-Yr 6/80

Street address 509 South 7th Street   Salary or Earnings Start ____ Finish ____

City Los Angeles   State CA   ZIP Code 90014   Telephone (Area Code) (213) 555-1886

Name and title of immediate supervisor Harriet Sims   Your title Stenographer

Reason for terminating or considering a change   I would like to assume some administrative duties.

Company name ____   Employed from Mo-Yr ____ To Mo-Yr ____

Street address ____   Salary or earnings Start ____ Finish ____

City ____   State ____   ZIP Code ____   Telephone (Area Code) ____

Name and title of immediate supervisor ____   Your title ____

Reason for terminating ____

Company name ____   Employed from Mo-Yr ____ To Mo-Yr ____

Street address ____   Salary or earnings Start ____ Finish ____

City ____   State ____   ZIP Code ____   Telephone (Area Code) ____

Name and title of immediate supervisor ____   Your title ____

Reason for terminating ____

Permission is granted to the Gibbs Corporation to verify all statements contained in this application. I understand that my employment will be contingent upon the accuracy and acceptability of such information. My present employer will not be checked until after I accept an offer of employment with the Gibbs Corporation.

I have read the above paragraph and accept the terms as condition of my employment by the Gibbs Corporation.

Date April 28, 19--   Lars Anderson
                              (Signature of applicant)

Personnel Relations interviewer ____

- Weigh your personal attitudes and determine whether your personal preferences for appearance, dress, or personality are not influencing your judgment.

- Make certain you are evaluating the *candidate* and not using stereotyped concepts.

- Have another person independently interview qualified candidates after the initial screening interview.

Training Subordinates

After you select the best subordinates available, remember to carry out another of your primary supervisory responsibilities and provide for their training so that they develop their potential. Training is vital and goes on continually. Employees learn by making mistakes, by observing, and by imitating. Or they learn because someone makes an intentional effort to teach them—a far more effective way of enriching a subordinate's contribution.

The place to begin is with an assessment of what a subordinate presently knows and can do, and a determination of what needs to be known and done for a specific work assignment. Any disparity between what is known and what is needed is the gap that training seeks to bridge. Since learning is a gradual process, this gap is reduced gradually. Whatever the type or amount of training, the following four-step procedure will help shorten the learning period.

- Find out exactly what the trainee knows about the job he or she is about to be taught. Then you can establish the scope of the training as well as its starting and stopping points. You should also know something about the trainee's personality and temperament. Interest can be stimulated and rapport developed if you explain why the training is important, how it relates to the work, and how it contributes to the overall operation of the department.
- Teach by demonstration or by using sight-sound tutorial instructional materials. Merely describing a task to a trainee omits the greatest means of comprehension—the eyes—and makes the task of achieving performance objectives very much harder. You can use transparencies, slides, filmstrips, drawings, posters, or photographs and correlate them with taped or recorded instructions. You can also sit down and do a job yourself while the trainee watches.
- Let the trainee try doing what has been taught. Observe the performance closely and stop it, if possible, before it is performed incorrectly. Once the trainee performs correctly, have him or her repeat the procedure several times for practice, with few interruptions, to build self-confidence.
- Have the trainee proceed independently through several trial runs. Offer reassurance that help will be available if any difficulty is encountered. Check progress at specific intervals. With proper training, less and less supervision is needed, and both the supervisor and the trainee are headed in the right direction.

Motivating Subordinates

Knowing how to motivate subordinates is a vital supervisory skill. Practically all that is known about motivation indicates that encouraging others to engage in productive and satisfying teamwork is easier when there are opportunities to satisfy personal needs. Subordinates are more likely to do what is wanted because they want to do it, once they realize that by doing it they satisfy one or more of the five basic needs outlined by Dr. Abraham H. Maslow in his psychological research. These are the need for *survival* (to breathe, eat, sleep, reproduce, see, hear, and feel); the need for *safety* (economic security and protection from physical danger); the need for *social acceptance* (belonging to and being accepted by a group); the need for *esteem* (both self-esteem and the esteem of others); and the need for *self-realization* (living up to one's potential).

There is no formula that serves to motivate people to work. The best approach is to remember that those you supervise are people who bring their

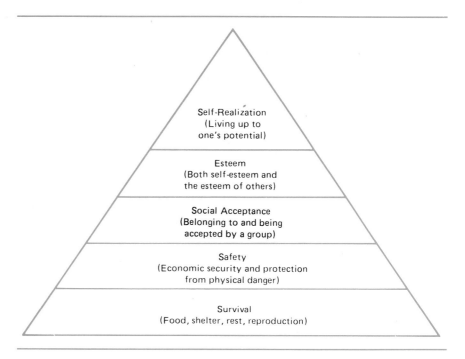

Maslow's hierarchy of
basic needs.

own individual emotions, goals, feelings, and values to their work. Each supervised person is a different personality. By respecting this difference and allowing individual expression, you can generate enthusiasm, devotion, and high regard for the goals of the group. By being sensitive to people and their needs and employing many of the following practices, you can get others to work for you.

Maintain Self-Control.   People do not like to be dominated, pushed, or intimidated. Control your emotions, vanity, likes, and dislikes. Few people respond productively to pressure and threats. On the other hand, practically everyone is willing to concede that someone has to be the supervisor. People will, therefore, carry out a supervisor's reasonable requests.

Encourage Others to Contribute.   Encourage subordinates to accept additional responsibilities and special assignments. Although many people have neither opportunity nor capacity to make spectacular contributions, everyone should be helped to gain personal satisfaction from a job. Look for unused skills and abilities in subordinates and try to make use of them. Recognize those who perform unusually well and who may be candidates for promotion.

Keep Communication Lines Open.   People should be informed in advance about things that affect them. Policies or happenings that relate to a subordinate's position or to his or her compensation are of vital interest. When any change is made in an organization, the workers are immediately concerned about how the change will affect their positions and their job security.

Recognize Effort.   Give recognition for work when it is well done. A word of praise spoken at the right time can motivate a subordinate or rekindle morale. Let those you supervise know how they stand. Keep them informed about how they are getting along. Give criticism tactfully and as soon as possible after an error is made.

Encourage Self-Expression.   See that everyone has opportunity to speak up. Be a good listener. Listen without interrupting, contradicting, or imposing your thoughts. Most workers realize that the supervisor will make the final decision. But that decision is easier to accept if divergent ideas have been weighed before a decision is made.

Treat People Fairly.   People respond favorably to fair treatment. When they put forth their best effort, they have a right to their share of resulting benefits. Accept responsibility for your own mistakes. You cannot hold the respect of subordinates if you refuse to admit to mistakes or inadequate planning.

Encourage Self-Development.   Explain to subordinates what you expect of them. Let them know the ways in which they can improve their work and more nearly accomplish their performance goals.

Giving Directions and Orders

Giving directions and orders is the act of putting your ideas and decisions into action through subordinates. How well you manage this skill determines in large measure your ability to get desired results. Since directing others is so important, you need to be aware of the words you use and how you say them. Commands, for example, may be appropriate in emergency situations where wrong actions could be costly. In most other situations, however, try to generate a feeling of understanding and voluntary cooperation in the subordinate when giving a direction or order. Initiative, creativity, and willing acceptance thrive where a spirit of mutual understanding and cooperation exists.

People often derive different meanings from the same words. Try to be sure your directions and orders are understood. Don't hesitate to repeat what you want done and when it is to be done. Give subordinates a chance to ask questions or to explain to you what they understand you want done.

Try to share with a subordinate the reason why something must be done. Understanding why a direction or order is given can stimulate enthusiasm. A failure to see or understand why something must be done usually results in a half-hearted effort and sometimes in hostility.

Delegating Responsibility

Delegation is the process of establishing productive working arrangements between yourself and a subordinate. It is achieved when a specific assignment is entrusted to someone else and the desired results are mutually understood. The skill of delegating authority is not easily acquired. The more common practice is to do work yourself when you are responsible for its execution. Unfortunately, failure to delegate keeps you from getting ahead. To your subordinate, the person dependent on you for career growth, your inability or unwillingness to delegate is an indication of personal dislike or a lack of qualification for more responsible work. There are several principles to be followed when practicing the art of delegation. Their application will heighten your supervisory skills and hasten your advancement as a manager.

Organize the Assignments.   Identify the routine tasks you are handling personally. Even though a task requires a degree of judgment, delegate the routine work to a subordinate. A good way to determine what should be delegated is to rank all your duties in the order of their importance. Identify the lesser duties that, when delegated, would free you for more important undertakings. Before delegating a duty, write down the steps involved in carrying it out.

Select the Best Subordinate.   Try to delegate to a subordinate who has enough competence to handle the additional duties. The best candidates are those who want to take on new duties because they view them as advancement stepping-stones.

Prepare the Subordinate.   When you delegate a job, be sure to tell the person why he or she was picked. Don't allow the subordinate to wonder, "Why was I given another job when I already have more to do than I can handle?" Exploit the opportunity to build self-confidence by expressing confidence in the subordinate and by emphasizing the importance of the delegated job.

Properly Explain the Work.   Use every means at your disposal to explain the delegated job. The subordinate needs to know what is to be done, how to do it, and when and where to do it. Explain how important the job is and what standards the subordinate's performance will be judged by. Let the subordinate know what to do when the assignment has been completed.

Encourage Independent Action.   Let the subordinate know you have enough confidence in his or her ability to carry out the assignment without your involvement. Let the person know that you will be available if problems arise.

Maintain Control.   When a subordinate fails to carry out a delegated assignment, you must accept responsibility. The probability of failure on the part of a subordinate is reduced if you establish deadlines and standards and ask for periodic reports of the status of the assigned project. Reviews that reveal problems before they become serious enough to delay completion of the project can serve to instruct the subordinate and eliminate the threat of failure. Adequate control by you leads to proper control by the subordinate.

**Disciplining
Subordinates**   Practically everyone encounters some form of discipline at one time or another. Corrective action is usually necessary when rules or regulations are broken, policy ignored, or assignments mishandled. Office workers, like all other employees, must willingly abide by established rules in order to reach desirable goals. Where discipline is lax, employees lose their drive and efficiency and become unhappy. Properly administered discipline, on the other hand, helps to kindle the spark of initiative in a subordinate.

Good discipline exists where there is self-discipline and self-control. It is encouraged by words and actions that convince others that they serve their interests best when they discipline themselves.

Self-Discipline.   If you wish to develop a productive and disciplined subordinate, you must first learn how to discipline yourself. Be prepared to set an example for a subordinate to follow. The person who looks to you for leadership will be less inclined to get to work on time when you are regularly late in arriving, for example.

Disciplinary Action.   Corrective action—a formal warning, reprimand, or penalty—is taken to restore order and efficiency by bringing an undisciplined employee back into line. The discipline should not be administered with a heavy hand unless the person is a chronic offender. A disciplinary action should serve to demonstrate that the best interests of everyone are served when there is compliance with established rules and regulations. That is, discipline should be used to improve the morale of those who have become unhappy at work and have lost their drive and efficiency.

There is no one right way to administer discipline. Certain steps are useful in changing behavior and in promoting employee self-discipline.

- Make certain employees are informed of and understand office rules and why they were established. Try to keep everyone informed about company and departmental goals and problems. Explain the reasons for policy changes. Encourage suggestions, recognize accomplishment, and give credit where it is deserved.
- Obtain all the facts before taking any disciplinary action. Learn what happened and the reason for the disregard of discipline.
- Control your temper. No matter how upsetting the employee's violation, keep control of your emotions. Few persons act rationally after they have lost their tempers. Invite the employee to walk with you to your office, or another private area, or to meet with you at a later time. The delay will give you a chance to regain your composure and to consult with others. Above all, do not touch an employee when angry; it can be viewed as assault and battery. (In the eyes of the law, an assault and battery conviction does not depend upon actual intent or actual present ability to inflict the injury that is threatened; it is sufficient if the person threatened reasonably believes the injury will be done.)
- Privacy is the rule when taking disciplinary action. Reprimands given in private, with helpful suggestions for improvement offered, can achieve good results. Public reprimands and ridicule injure the employee's ego, bring resentment, and result in bad attitudes and lowered morale.
- Be consistent in the application of discipline. Never turn your back on a breach of discipline because it is an unpleasant task or because you like the rule breaker. Being consistent, however, doesn't mean treating everyone in exactly the same way. It means basing punishment on the seriousness of the offense and the past record of the offender. Mitigating factors should be considered and every effort should be made to learn the reason for the disregard of discipline. For example, when Janice Yoder was late reporting to work it was because her car battery was dead. When Roger Grimes was late it was because he stayed in the cafeteria for an extra cup

of coffee. The first was an unintentional late arrival; the second was a voluntary violation. Different reprimands should be used in dealing with the two rule breakers.

- Be firm, fair, and impartial in dealing with rule infractions. Being firm means taking decisive action in dealing with infractions without getting tough or flaunting your authority. Fairness means showing consideration of the employee's feelings. When administering a disciplinary action, explain why the rule is necessary, why the action is being taken, and what the action is expected to accomplish. Avoid favoring any subordinates.
- End a disciplinary action on a positive note. Since the objective of a reprimand is training and not punishment, always indicate your confidence in the employee's ability to change his or her behavior.

Controlling Costs

The office supervisor must strive through cost control and cost reduction to keep a group's operating expenses within assigned limits. There are many effective ways to reduce operating costs. Foremost on the list are efforts to control wastefulness, save time, and use space efficiently.

Controlling Wastefulness. An important part of your supervisory responsibilities is to keep wastefulness under control. The attack on inefficiency must be continuous. Study the causes of wastefulness, then formulate a plan to reduce them. If inadequate instruction is the problem, strengthen your training procedures. If sloppy work practices or careless use of supplies is causing waste, better on-the-job guidance should be provided. If inefficient or incorrect use of equipment is reducing efficiency, demonstrations of proper methods may be needed.

The cooperation of employees must be won if a waste-reduction effort is to succeed. Let employees know how they will materially benefit from self-improvement practices and cost-consciousness. You can encourage participation by asking for suggestions and by making it clear that you are counting on each person to do his or her part. Follow up by keeping everyone informed of progress and by giving recognition to good performance.

Using Time Efficiently. Time is wasted in many ways. The more obvious ones include arriving late for work, quitting early, extending comfort breaks, socializing, waiting for someone to tell you what to do, and out-and-out loafing. These problems indicate low performance standards, low morale, and weak leadership.

The less visible time-wasting factors are more difficult to control. They are frequently concealed in inefficient working practices and resistance to change. Sometimes people may appear busy, yet they do not accomplish much. They must be shown how to work more productively and how to improve their efficiency. Poor planning may be the culprit. Look for evidence of improper scheduling, lack of equipment, or failure to anticipate operational problems. Work may not be correctly organized. Determine whether people know exactly who is to do what, and by when. A half-trained or poorly trained person takes twice as long to do an assignment as one who knows the most efficient way to proceed.

Managing Space. Space costs money. The money spent on providing space for office work is an overhead expense that is incurred whether productivity is high or low. If you can figure out how to better use the same space or achieve comparable efficiency with less space, you can reduce costs.

Solving Problems

All supervisors encounter problems. Technical problems are the easiest to solve. Most problems, however, concern people, and solving them is not easy. Still, by differentiating facts from emotions when a problem arises, you can use the following four-step procedure, common to many fields of endeavor, to solve a problem:

1. *Define the Problem.* The biggest part of solving a problem is clearly defining it. Everyone with supervisory responsibilities is constantly confronted with conditions, attitudes, actions, and developments that could be at the root of a problem. These are symptoms that must be analyzed before you decide what the problem is. You must be careful not to deal with symptoms instead of causes.

2. *Obtain All the Facts.* Once a problem has been defined, start collecting the information you will need in order to make a decision. Make an analysis of the problem and estimate the time it will take to seek out important data with a significant bearing on the problem. Without the facts, which are basic to good decisions, you will be making snap judgments.

3. *Find the Best Answer.* There is more than one solution to a problem. Avoid any tendency to favor a preferred solution or a preconceived idea about how the problem should be resolved. Always consider as many alternative solutions to the problem as you can assemble without too much delay and expense. Then think through each solution to determine the one that will work best for you and that involves the least risk.

4. *Make a Final Decision.* Plan carefully how your decision is to be carried out. Promptly inform the people who will be affected by the decision, and seek their support. Make periodic checks to be sure that your decision is being carried out according to your plan. Later, determine whether your decision achieved the desired results. This gives you an opportunity to study your mistakes. When a decision is successful, your evaluation of results will reveal what made it succeed, and the plan of action can be used again.

Reviewing Your Reading

1. How do secretaries reach the supervisory management level?

2. What performance qualities must a secretary display that will indicate a readiness for supervisory responsibilities?

3. Identify and explain the practices that allow for individual expression and that motivate people to work.

4. Where can the secretary get a clear understanding of those things he or she is held accountable for?

5. Explain the communication link that exists between the secretary with supervisory responsibilities and other organizational levels that plan, organize, staff, direct, and control.

6. When you are building a competent staff, what are the common interviewing objectives that will aid you in interpreting facts presented by the interviewee and in forming your judgment?

7. To prevent possible conflict with job discrimination legislation, what prejudicial questions should you avoid asking a job applicant, unless you can prove that they relate in some way to job qualification?

8. What is the primary consideration when determining whether to use an employment test in screening job applicants?

9. Outline a four-step instructional strategy a supervisor can use to help subordinates develop their potential.

10. Describe four basic principles a supervisor should apply in order to gain cooperation from subordinates.

11. Describe three aspects of an instruction that need to be communicated in order to improve a supervisor's order-giving techniques.

12. What are the four steps of the problem-solving procedure that is commonly used in many fields of endeavor?

13. What are the five basic needs, identified by Dr. Abraham Maslow, that give us the motivation to work?

14. Explain the principles to follow when practicing the art of delegation.

Using Your Skills

1. Which basic need in Maslow's hierarchy is indicated by the following drives?
   a. The desire to reach your highest potential, to make use of all your talents, to make the most of all your skills.
   b. The desire for the esteem of others, self-esteem, and recognition of your abilities and contributions.
   c. The need to be accepted by others and to be capable of honest relationships.
   d. The need to feel that your job is secure and that you will have an income until you retire.

2. Assume that, after being a secretary in a firm for some time, you are offered a supervisory position that you are capable of handling in technical, human, and managerial terms. Analyze the opportunity by fully answering the following three questions:
   a. Why might a person want to accept this offer? Cite many reasons but indicate those having most relevance to you.
   b. Why might someone *not* want to accept the offer? Follow the same procedure as for question *a*.
   c. What do you see as the key challenges in such a position? Cite several, but emphasize those you believe you are most capable of meeting.

3. The boss has asked you to supervise the dispatch of a special sales letter to a mailing list of 20,000 names. The operations involved are as follows:

Operation	Production Rate
Envelope addressing	1 per minute
Address checking	20 per minute
Letter folding	15 per minute
Envelope stuffing	12 per minute
Envelope sealing	100 per minute (machine)
Envelope stamping	100 per minute (machine)

EMPLOYEE EVALUATION FORM

NAME _____ *Steve Jacobs* _____ JOB TITLE *Asst. Cashier* DEPT. *Time, Payroll*

How long under your supervision? *Four Years* _____ Date of Employment? *March 10, 19—*

1. Knowledge of Job: Consider knowledge essential to person's job.	Has an exceptionally thorough knowledge of work ☐	Has good knowledge of work ☑	Requires considerable coaching ☐	Has inadequate knowledge of work ☐
2. Quality of Work: Consider the ability to turn out work which meets quality standards.	Highest quality ☐	Well done ☑	Passable ☐	Poor ☐
3. Quantity of Work: Consider the volume of work produced under normal conditions.	Large volume ☑	Good volume ☐	Slightly below-average volume ☐	Unsatisfactory volume ☐
4. Attendance and Punctuality: Consider frequency of absences as well as lateness.	Record is excellent ☑	Occasionally absent or late ☐	Frequently absent or late ☐	Undependable; absent or late without notice ☐
5. Attitude: Consider attitude toward work, company, and associates and willingness to work with and for others.	Unusually fine attitude ☐	Good attitude ☑	Passable ☐	Poor attitude ☐
6. Judgment: Consider ability to make decisions and to utilize working time to best advantage.	Justifies utmost confidence ☐	Needs little supervision ☑	Needs frequent checking ☐	Cannot be relied upon; needs constant supervision ☐
7. Reliability: Consider the ability of the person to get the work out under pressure, and to follow job through to completion.	Can always be counted upon ☐	Generally can be counted on ☑	Unpredictable under pressure ☐	"Cracks up" under pressure ☐
8. Flexibility — Adaptability: Consider the speed with which employee learns and the amount of instruction required to teach employee new duties.	Learns fast ☐	Learns reasonably fast ☑	Slow to learn ☐	Unable to learn ☐
9. Personal Characteristics: Consider appearance, personality, integrity, neatness.	Decidedly favorable ☐	Good ☑	Passable ☐	Generally unsatisfactory ☐

Appraised by *Herb Trout* Date *11/20/—* Reviewed by *HS* Date *12/14/—*

How many helpers would you need? How would you plan the work over a six-hour day? Assume that the boss would like the job done within three days and that mailing would take place only when the last piece is finished.

4. Shown below are merit-rating profiles of two candidates under consideration for promotion to a supervisory vacancy.

    Which candidate would you promote? Analyze the apparent strengths and weaknesses of each of the candidates to show how you reached your decision about which to promote.

EMPLOYEE EVALUATION FORM

NAME _June Lopez_   JOB TITLE _Asst. Cashier_   DEPT. _Time, Payroll_

How long under your supervision? _Two Years_   Date of Employment? _April 26, 19—_

1. **Knowledge of Job:** Consider knowledge essential to person's job.	Has an exceptionally thorough knowledge of work ☑	Has good knowledge of work ☐	Requires considerable coaching ☐	Has inadequate knowledge of work ☐
2. **Quality of Work:** Consider the ability to turn out work which meets quality standards.	Highest quality ☐	Well done ☑	Passable ☐	Poor ☐
3. **Quantity of Work:** Consider the volume of work produced under normal conditions.	Large volume ☐	Good volume ☐	Slightly below-average volume ☑	Unsatisfactory volume ☐
4. **Attendance and Punctuality:** Consider frequency of absences as well as lateness.	Record is excellent ☑	Occasionally absent or late ☐	Frequently absent or late ☐	Undependable; absent or late without notice ☐
5. **Attitude:** Consider attitude toward work, company, and associates and willingness to work with and for others.	Unusually fine attitude ☑	Good attitude ☐	Passable ☐	Poor attitude ☐
6. **Judgment:** Consider ability to make decisions and to utilize working time to best advantage.	Justifies utmost confidence ☐	Needs little supervision ☑	Needs frequent checking ☐	Cannot be relied upon; needs constant supervision ☐
7. **Reliability:** Consider the ability of the person to get the work out under pressure, and to follow job through to completion.	Can always be counted upon ☑	Generally can be counted on ☐	Unpredictable under pressure ☐	"Cracks up" under pressure ☐
8. **Flexibility — Adaptability:** Consider the speed with which employee learns and the amount of instruction required to teach employee new duties.	Learns fast ☑	Learns reasonably fast ☐	Slow to learn ☐	Unable to learn ☐
9. **Personal Characteristics:** Consider appearance, personality, integrity, neatness.	Decidedly favorable ☑	Good ☐	Passable ☐	Generally unsatisfactory ☐

Appraised by _Herb Trout_   Date _11/18/—_   Reviewed by _MS_   Date _12/14/—_

EXERCISING
YOUR
JUDGMENT

Emergencies. You are an administrative support secretary in your company's word processing center. Executives transmit their dictation by telephone to recorders located in the center. Correspondence specialists keyboard the material dictated using high-speed typewriters equipped with mag-tape recording and playback units.

Near the end of the working day, you hear a crash and a cry of "Oh, no!" A table supporting an electronic typewriter that a secretary was operating has given way, and the typewriter and a recording and playback unit have fallen to the floor. The secretary working at the station is in pain and says, "I think the typewriter hit my foot." What should you do immediately? What follow-up action is necessary?

Applying
the
Reference
Section

Correct errors in grammar, punctuation, usage, capitalization, and spelling in the following sentences:

1. July 1st is the start of the company's Fiscal year.
2. The product manager said we cant promise delivery on that order for 12 cases of two inch glass rods.
3. The credit manager ofered the customer an eleven per cent trade discount.
4. The employees celabrated there twnetyfifth employment annaversary and gifts were received.
5. A senior citizens home was built in Portland Maine.
6. There were three 68s in the list checked their should have been only 2.
7. It is only a five minute walk to the companys Laboratory.
8. The secretarys report was read at the stockholders meeting.
9. In service training included exercises in grammer, spelling and punctuation and the participating trainees appreciated the review.
10. The chairpersons remarks were not only complementary to the audience, but they were also relevant to the adgenda of the meeting.

CHAPTER TWENTY / Meetings and Conferences

Business executives spend considerable amounts of time in meetings, where problems are analyzed, experts are consulted, points of view are weighed, and decisions are made. Arranging meetings is an important part of a secretary's job. Smoothly run meetings generally accomplish their objectives. If meetings are not organized well in advance, with every detail planned, the valuable time of those attending can be needlessly wasted.

Executives participate in various kinds of company meetings, outside professional or community sessions, and special-purpose workshops and conventions. Company meetings can be held either by *standing committees*, which are scheduled to meet regularly, or by *ad hoc committees*, which are established to achieve a specified goal and are dissolved when the goal is achieved. Many such meetings, however, are simply informal office or conference room discussions your employer attends as an invited participant or as the group or team leader who has scheduled the meeting. In either case, your involvement as a secretary is a limited but important one. Some of your duties include:

- Talking to the secretaries of the other participants and agreeing upon a mutually convenient time and place for the meeting.
- Making sure the meeting is recorded on your employer's appointment calendar well in advance of the scheduled time.
- Reminding your employer of the time and place of the meeting at least an hour or two before it is scheduled to begin.
- Collecting and presenting your employer with any materials needed at the meeting, such as the agenda (if it is available) and any papers that may be referred to during the course of the discussion.
- Arranging for the comfort of those attending, when the meeting takes place in your employer's office.

COMPANY COMMITTEE MEETINGS

When your employer is the leader or chairperson of a company committee or meeting, you are normally given responsibility for making preliminary arrange-

---

Interoffice Memorandum

To: Richard Ginsberg
Greta Donaghy
Donald Bauer

From: Marie LeVander

Subject: Quarterly Budget Review

Date: July 7, 19--

A second-quarter budget review is scheduled for 9:30 a.m. on July 21
in the second-floor conference room.

Bring your year-to-date expense summaries so that we can analyze the
status of our current budget and project third- and fourth-quarter
adjustments.

MLV

SB

Notice of a meeting.

ments, helping your employer to summarize the proceedings, and distributing summaries to each participant.

Notifying Participants

One of the first steps in connection with most business meetings is to give telephone or written notice to those entitled to attend. Early notification is critical since executives have many demands on their time. If one or more participants already have commitments on the date set for a meeting and cannot attend, you may be instructed to set the meeting for another day when everyone can be present.

Make sure that the notice specifies the date, time, place, and purpose of the meeting. If a separate agenda of items to be discussed at a meeting is required, send it along with the notice of the meeting.

Preparing the Agenda

It is recommended practice to prepare an agenda (program of events) for standing committee meetings. Duplicate copies can be provided for each participant, with supplementary or support material if applicable. In some cases, a complete folder is prepared for each committee member in advance.

An agenda may be the result of an earlier meeting of the chairperson and other committee members. In any event, it should be approved by the chairperson several days in advance of the scheduled meeting (if possible) and distributed to each member.

Preparing the Meeting Room

As soon as the date and time of the meeting are final, check to determine whether the room in which the meeting is to be held is available and reserve it. A telephone call to the person who keeps track of conference room usage is usually necessary. When reserving the room for the period of time required for the

```
              Regular Meeting of the Advertising Committee
                     Friday, March 14, Room 1214

                              AGENDA

        1.  Fall campaign:  Ethel Ackerman.

        2.  Advertising media:  Dominick Loparco.

                              Earl
                              Earl Binin
                              Chair

     Distribution:

        E. Ackerman  J. Dugdale  T. Ottaviano  E. Towle
        B. Bidwell   D. Loparco  H. Salit      R. Voigt
```

An agenda.

meeting, add 15 to 30 minutes as a precaution. It can be an embarrassment if the discussion runs a bit longer than anticipated and another scheduled group tries to gain access to the room.

If the meeting room is unoccupied shortly before the meeting is to begin, quickly check to see that it is arranged appropriately, adequately heated or cooled, and in order. Any material left by a previous group should be collected and properly disposed of.

Other preparations will depend upon the chairperson's wishes. Pads and pencils may be required for each participant. If the meeting includes a coffee break, the chairperson may want coffee brought into the room at a specified time. Sometimes an informal meeting will include a delivered lunch. When this is the case, provide menus.

If special equipment such as an overhead transparency projector, blackboard, or portable easel is to be used, you may be asked to see that the specified equipment is in the room and ready to use. Sometimes the person who plans to make an audio or visual presentation will make the necessary arrangements for it. Be prepared to offer whatever assistance may be needed. This would include a preliminary check to see that the room is equipped with required electrical outlets. In short, try to evaluate the general setup and see that everything is done that will add to the comfort and convenience of the participants.

During the Meeting

When a meeting is in progress, screen all telephone calls to participants and exercise good judgment about making interruptions. If an interruption is necessary, enter the meeting room unobtrusively and hand a note to the appropriate person.

Sometimes the chairperson or another participant takes notes and summarizes the results of the discussion. Another common practice is to record the proceedings, which you or a word processor subsequently transcribes. However, you may be asked to attend a meeting for the primary purpose of recording the discussion that takes place.

When you are asked to sit in on a meeting and to take notes of the discussion, be sure you know everyone in attendance so that you can record the contributions each person makes. Pay particular attention to the different opinions and key points that are presented. Never become so engrossed in the discussion that you neglect your note-taking functions. If you don't hear something because the speaker is talking too fast or your attention is distracted, ask the speaker to repeat his or her comment. It is the prerogative of the recorder to interrupt the discussion when necessary in order to ensure an accurate summary of the proceedings. If a phone in the meeting room should ring, answer it. Of course, you will have arranged for your extension and your boss's to be covered during the meeting.

Following Up

The adjournment of the meeting does not end your involvement. See that the meeting room is left in good order, ready for immediate use. Since a conference room is usually occupied throughout most of the working day, be sure it is cleared of any materials brought into the room by the participants.

Summary of Proceedings.   Make your summary of the proceedings brief and concise. In most instances, only the remarks that serve as a record of what the participants decided and what needs to be done and by whom are recorded. In a few instances, where more detailed notes were requested, a tape can be used to supplement your notes. In any event, prepare a rough draft of the summary as soon as possible after the meeting is adjourned, while the proceedings are still fresh in your mind. Triple-space the typed draft so that there will be enough space for additions and deletions.

Before the summary of proceedings is typed in final form, you may wish to submit the draft to the chairperson for approval. This procedure is important if the chairperson signs the summary, but it is usually not necessary if you are authorized to sign it.

There are a number of acceptable formats for summaries of committee meetings. In the illustration on the opposite page, the chairperson's secretary signed the summary.

If you draft the summary, you are usually responsible for distributing copies to all participants. It is considered good practice to call attention to any action required of a participant by underscoring or otherwise highlighting the pertinent reference. A felt-tip highlighting pen could be used to call attention to Sandra Nilsson's topic on her copy of the summary. The same procedure would be used to highlight Burt Jonas's copy.

THE ALPHABET TOY & NOVELTY COMPANY

Meeting of the Advertising Committee

The regular monthly meeting of the Advertising Committee was held at 10:30 a.m. on Friday, March 12, 19--, in the Conference Room. William Fenley presided.

Those present included Lawrence Delbert, Burt Jonas, Richard Morris, Adele Perez, Sandra Nilsson, and Louis Weinberg. They constituted a quorum. John Sacco and Anthony Vincent were absent.

Copies of the February 12 meeting were distributed by Miss Perez. No corrections were made.

Fall Campaign. Mr. Jonas distributed copies of the tentative plans for the fall campaign to publicize the new line of back-to-school merchandise. He asked for reactions and suggestions on the theme and the sample photos and sketches. He noted that he needs such responses no later than next week.

Advertising Media. There was considerable discussion about the relative merits of television and radio commercials. Mr. Weinberg pointed out that 30- and 60-second commercials on children's Saturday programs have proved very successful in the past, but he also noted the trend of growing parental opposition to such commercials. Mr. Delbert suggested that it might be wise to expand the advertising placed in magazines and other printed media.

There being no further business, the meeting adjourned at 11:30 a.m.

Next Meeting. The next meeting of the Advertising Committee will be held on April 11, 19--. At this meeting the following topics will receive special attention:

        Promotional Giveaways (Sandra Nilsson)
        Budget for Convention Exhibits (Burt Jonas)

                                Adele Perez
                        Adele Perez, Secretary

A summary of a committee meeting.

Outside Meetings

Business executives are often active in business-related organizations such as professional and civic organizations and trade associations. If the executive is merely a member of these groups, your responsibility for the meetings will be minimal. It is when the executive is elected president or appointed chairperson that your involvement becomes extensive and time-consuming. In these situations, follow the procedures below.

Arranging the Date, Time, and Place

Arranging the date, time, and place of a regional or state meeting can be somewhat frustrating. The members are usually widely scattered geographically, and getting their agreement on a satisfactory meeting date, time, and place poses some difficulties. Here your communication skills are fully tested. There will be many letters written and telephone calls placed. Schedules and meeting sites may be proposed and rejected several times before final agreement is reached. You can expect this kind of duty if your boss is president of a professional or community organization. If the executive is appointed chairperson of a standing or special committee, setting up meetings can also be a necessary and difficult job. You will find that tact and persuasiveness are the most effective instruments in getting agreement.

"Where shall we meet?" is likely to be the first question asked after the date and time for a meeting are established. The chairperson has a good deal of say in the choice of a meeting site. A prime consideration will be how easy it is for all the members of the group to get to the meeting place. For groups whose members are scattered over a wide geographic area, a hotel, motel, or convention center within five or ten minutes of a large airport is often chosen as the site of the meeting. The reason is obvious. Participants can easily fly in, travel by car to the meeting site, return by car to the airport when the meeting is over, and board a plane to go back home.

Reserving Special Facilities

Another important consideration is whether the contemplated site has the desired facilities. If you are arranging a group meeting that will last two days or more, plan for lodging and meals as well as meeting rooms. Although the chairperson may not be responsible for reserving rooms for the individual participants, the required number of rooms must be reserved, and reasonable rates must be agreed upon. Special room rates are usually available to groups.

Arrangements for special functions must be made. At most meetings, there are scheduled luncheons, dinners, and breakfasts that participants attend (usually followed by a meeting). For these, menus must be selected, serving arrangements agreed upon, method of payment (including tips) decided, and so on.

Meeting room facilities are enormously important. Space, acoustics, furnishings, cleanliness, ventilation, accessibility, and lighting must be carefully examined. The effectiveness of a meeting or conference can be reduced by inadequate room facilities.

When discussing meeting rooms with the hotel management, it is a good idea to mention the need for audiovisual equipment, which you should confirm with the chairperson or committee participants in advance. Most hotels and motels that accommodate meetings and conventions either own or have access to all types of audiovisual equipment. Arrangements must be made well in advance of the meeting, since union employees may be delivering and setting up the required equipment.

At some conventions, members of the participants' families may accompany them. In this case the person in charge of convention arrangements must see to it that these people are provided for. Special arrangements might be made for recreation facilities, tours, and transportation to places of interest.

Confirming Meeting Place Arrangements

All the matters mentioned above can often be arranged and confirmed by telephone calls and letters. However, you may be asked to visit the proposed meeting site in person to make the final arrangements. There is no substitute for a personal visit to the meeting site, if it can be arranged, and a face-to-face meeting with the management to discuss what will and will not be provided. In such instances, your job is to talk to the sales manager of the hotel or motel (sometimes called the banquet manager) for confirmation of every service you expect. Usually the agreement is put in writing so that there can be no misunderstanding about requested services and facilities and their costs. Regardless of the size of the meeting, you should be meticulous about details. A meeting that is left to chance can be a disaster.

Contacting Invited Speakers

When someone is invited to address those attending a meeting or convention, it will be your job to see that travel and hotel arrangements are made and the speaker notified. You will want to keep in close touch with the speaker by letter or telephone to make sure there is no misunderstanding about the meeting place, time, reservations, and other details. There is no greater fiasco than a meeting the scheduled speaker fails to attend (usually because of a misunderstanding)!

If the speaker is to be paid an honorarium (fee), the amount and method of payment should be stated in writing. When the speaker is to be reimbursed for travel and other expenses, he or she should be told how the expense statement is to be submitted.

Making Preliminary Plans

When you are asked to assist an employer in setting up and managing an outside meeting, make sure you are familiar with the function of the group and its methods of operation. Read the minutes and reports of previous meetings. These records can give you a good idea of the way the group accomplishes its purposes and give you clues about your role as the chairperson's assistant. Also inquire about the availability of the organization's bylaws.

Bylaws. The specific regulations and procedures that govern the meetings of many organizations are contained in a set of published bylaws. Here are spelled out such matters as the composition of the organization, the qualifications of officers, the method of electing officers, the time and place of regular meetings, the definition of a quorum, the order of business, the rules of order, and many other vital matters.

A typical table of contents of a set of bylaws will include most of the following topics:

- Name of the organization.
- Purposes of the organization.
- Membership qualifications, election, and termination.
- Dues.
- Meetings.
- Order of business.
- Board of directors election, duties, and recall.

- Officers' election, duties, and term of office.
- Executive committee duties.
- Other committees and their duties.
- Compensation and expenses of officers and chairperson.
- Amendments, repeal, or alteration of bylaws.
- Rules of order governing proceedings.

If you are expected to assist at a formal meeting you should become fully acquainted with the bylaws and read over at least the significant sections before each meeting.

Meeting Folders.   As soon as the meeting is decided on and your role in it is defined, set up a file for all the notes, letters, and various other papers pertaining to it. You may need several folders—one for the program, one for hotel or motel arrangements, one for membership, and so on. Make notes of all the telephone conversations and conferences pertaining to the meeting, and place them in your file.

Notifying Participants   The invited participants of outside meetings are given notice of the date, time, and place by means of a typewritten note. The notice may be printed or reproduced by a duplication process for large groups. Postcards are acceptable for brief notices.

When meetings are scheduled regularly, a form notice may be printed so that only the time and date or other specific information need be supplied to complete the form. When the number of participants is small, the names of all those to receive a notice may be listed in place of a single name, address, and salutation. In such a tabular listing of names, the salutation should either be "Dear Member" or be omitted entirely. Individual letters may be used to notify members when the meeting is very important.

Take particular care that the announcements for a meeting contain notifications required by the bylaws and any others that may be desired. For example, amendments to the bylaws themselves can seldom be adopted unless the notice of the meeting contains information of the fact that such amendments have been proposed. Sometimes a list of nominees for office must be included in the notice. As a general rule, any important or unusual business to be transacted should be mentioned.

Usually the notices for special meetings must contain a statement of the purpose for which the meeting has been called, and a notation that other business is not to be transacted.

You are the logical person to keep track of the names of those who will attend the scheduled meeting. If double postcard notices are used, you can easily accomplish the task by sorting the "yes" or "no" responses on the returned portions of the postcards. Or you may follow up by telephone to determine who will attend and who will not. Another follow-up technique is to send a second notice a week to ten days before the scheduled meeting, as a reminder to those who have not yet indicated their attendance.

FORMAL MEETINGS

Formal meetings ordinarily follow a definite order of business that specifies the general topics under which matters come up, such as committee reports, unfinished business, and new business. If the meeting is conducted in accordance with the principles of parliamentary procedure, you need some familiarity with those principles to write up a proper set of minutes.

Preparing the Agenda

Many times the order of business is in accordance with *Robert's Rules of Order Newly Revised*. If this is the case, the following order is applicable:

- Call to order.
- Roll call.
- Determination of quorum.
- Reading and correction of minutes of previous meeting.
- Approval of minutes.
- Reports of officers.
- Reports of standing committees.
- Reports of special committees.
- Unfinished business.
- New business.
- Appointments of committees.
- Nominations and elections.
- Announcements.
- Program.
- Adjournment.

Frequently, however, there are meetings for which the order of business alone is not sufficient. If considerable business is to be transacted or if a number of matters are to be brought up, it will help considerably if you prepare a list, called the agenda, prior to the meeting. For meetings that are part of conventions, this may take the form of a printed program prepared in advance and adopted at the beginning of the meeting as the official agenda.

Reporting the Procedures

When making notes for a set of minutes, take down more information than will actually appear. Sometimes reference is made later to the original notes in case of a dispute as to what happened at the meeting. It is especially important that you record all motions accurately, although you are usually given considerable freedom in phrasing them later. Important discussions should be summarized. Motions or resolutions may have to be reported verbatim. It is good practice to make use of a recording device when word-for-word coverage is required.

Following Parliamentary Procedure

Any matter of business to be acted upon must be brought up in a formal meeting by means of a motion made by a participant who has secured the floor. The matter must then be seconded by another participant, after which it must be stated by the chairperson. It is then open for discussion and action.

In small meetings the chairperson sometimes does not require that a member make a motion to bring something up for discussion. Much of the business may be introduced by the chairperson, who merely states that a matter should be decided. If the resulting discussion produces complete agreement, the chairperson simply states, "If there is no objection, we will . . ." In the minutes, you might record, "After considerable discussion of . . ., it was unanimously agreed to do . . ."

After a motion on a particular subject is made in the prescribed way, it is considered to be a *main motion*. A main motion may be followed by a *subsidiary motion*. Following are some of the more common subsidiary motions that may be made before a main motion is voted on. Any of them must be decided upon before the main motion itself is voted on.

To Amend. To amend is one of the most common subsidiary motions and means that the mover wishes to change the wording of the pending motion. The amendment itself may be amended by a second motion.

To Refer to a Committee. A simple way to dispose of a question that needs further study or consideration is to move to refer it to either a standing or a special committee.

To Postpone Indefinitely. When it is evident that the consensus about a motion is unfavorable, the appropriate procedure is for someone to move to postpone it indefinitely instead of waiting for a vote on the motion itself and then voting against it. This motion serves to "kill" the matter.

To Postpone to a Certain Time. If a group is not ready to take immediate action and yet does not wish to kill the question, a motion may be made to postpone the main motion to the next meeting or to some other specified date. It then becomes your duty to see that the chairperson brings it up at that time, usually as unfinished business.

To Lay on the Table. Sometimes consideration of a question is deferred for a short period of time so that a more pressing matter can be disposed of first. A motion is made to "lay the first question on the table." It can then be "taken from the table" at any later time by a majority vote. Since the motion to lay on the table is undebatable, it can be used unfairly as a device to kill a motion.

To Vote on the Previous Question. To vote on the previous question means merely to close debate and take a vote on the pending question. It is made, as is any other motion, by someone who has the floor; it must be seconded; and it must be passed by a two-thirds vote. If it is passed, the chairperson allows no further discussion on the pending question but puts it to a vote.

To Limit Debate. Another way of preventing prolonged discussion of a question is to move that debate be limited to a specified number of minutes for each participant. This motion also requires a two-thirds vote in order to protect the right of a sizable minority to free discussion and at the same time to protect the group from obstructionist tactics.

To Reconsider.   Any vote taken by a group (unless action has already been taken because of it) may be brought up again at the same meeting by a motion to reconsider, made by a person who voted with the prevailing side. This cancels the previous vote and reopens the question as if it had just been introduced.

To Rescind.   Actions taken at preceding meetings may not be reconsidered, but they may be canceled by a motion to rescind. This motion requires a two-thirds vote unless prior notice of the planned action is given to the participants.

To Rise to a Point of Order.   A participant may interrupt a meeting at any time to "rise to a point of order." If a participant is not satisfied with the decision of the chairperson, an appeal from the decision of the chair can be made. The chairperson then puts to a vote the question, "Shall the decision of the chair be sustained?" A majority vote or a tie vote sustains the chairperson. All questions of order and appeals should be entered in the minutes, whether sustained or lost, since there might be controversy later.

Maintaining Order of Precedence of Motions

Some motions carry a definite ranking. A motion is out of order if it is made while a motion of higher rank is pending. It will then be rejected by the chairperson. The task of keeping straight the status of a number of motions pending at the same time is sometimes too much for the unaided memory, and the chairperson must rely on you for an accurate record of what has happened. When the chairperson announces the vote on the pending question and says, "The secretary will now state the pending question," you are expected to respond accurately.

The following list displays the most common motions arranged in their order of precedence. When any one of them is immediately pending, the motions above it on the list are in order, and those below it are out of order.

- Fix the Time at Which to Adjourn
- Adjourn
- Take a Recess
- Raise a Question of Privilege
- Call for the Orders of the Day
- Lay on the Table
- Vote on the Previous Question
- Limit or Extend Limits of Debate
- Postpone to a Certain Time
- Commit or Refer
- Amend
- Postpone Indefinitely
- Make a Main Motion

Determining a Quorum

The number of voting members required to transact business at a meeting is sometimes specified in the bylaws of the organization or in the minutes of past meetings. When this is the case, you generally make a count. When a quorum is not present, the only action that can be taken is to take steps to get a quorum or to adjourn.

In many large company meetings, such as sales meetings and planning meetings, quorum requirements are not specified. Nevertheless, as a matter of record it is important for you to make a note of those present at the start of the meeting. It is also good practice to keep track of those who arrive late and those who depart early. A membership list makes a useful attendance roll.

Handling Resolutions and Petitions

Motions to express appreciation, congratulations, or sympathy or to request an action are usually expressed as a resolution or petition. A *resolution* is an expression of the organization; a *petition* is an expression of only the individuals who sign it.

Such expressions are generally prepared in advance by a committee and presented by the committee chairperson, who moves their adoption. Occasionally you are instructed to write a resolution or a petition and you should be familiar with the language and the general format of each.

Both are entered in the minutes in the following manner:

> On behalf of the Committee on Policy, Mr. Burgess presented the following resolution, which, after brief discussion, was adopted unanimously: (*The resolution would follow.*)

Resolutions may be expressed in any one of many ways, varying from a simple letter to a legalistic document. A common type of formal resolution is shown here:

RESOLUTION
Adopted September 7, 19—

WHEREAS William C. Swain has, for the past ten years, been President of International Industries, Inc.; and

WHEREAS he declines to be candidate for reelection: Therefore be it

RESOLVED, That this Board of Directors recognizes the excellent, energetic, and intelligent service that William C. Swain has rendered the Corporation during his incumbency. We feel that the growth and success the Corporation has enjoyed has been due in large measure to his earnest efforts and untiring devotion; and be it

RESOLVED further, That in recognition of William C. Swain's service to the Corporation, he be elected Chairman to preside at the meetings of the Board for the coming year.

Secretary	Chairman

In formal resolutions, the reasons for the resolution are introduced by the word *whereas* in all capitals; the word following it is not capitalized unless it is a proper name. A comma is not necessary after *whereas*. The final paragraphs that state the action to be taken are introduced by the word *resolved*, also in all capitals and followed by a comma and a capital letter. The words *therefore be it* are placed on the line above *resolved*. Informal resolutions dispense with *whereas* and *therefore be it* and simply state the facts or events leading up to the resolution.

A petition is a written request supported by the signatures of those interested in the granting of the request. A petition may be expressed formally with the reasons for it introduced by *whereas* and the action to be granted introduced by *we* set in caps and followed by a comma and a capital letter. Informal petitions either omit the considerations leading up to the request or state them without an introductory *whereas*. Lines should be typed for the signatures as shown below:

PETITION

September 7, 19—

WHEREAS the employees of Davis Management Company are without adequate food service; and

WHEREAS the cost of food in restaurants in the area is prohibitive; and

WHEREAS other companies of similar size in the area now provide their employees with food service;

WE, the undersigned employees of Davis Management Company, do hereby petition said company to appoint a committee composed of two management representatives and two employees for the purpose of studying the food service needs of the company and submitting a feasible plan.

_____	_____	_____
_____	_____	_____
_____	_____	_____
_____	_____	_____
_____	_____	_____
_____	_____	_____
_____	_____	_____

Following Up After the Meeting

Although the responsibilities of those present may end with the adjournment of a meeting, yours do not.

As soon after the meeting as possible, make certain you have copies of all reports and resolutions presented during the meeting. If necessary, obtain copies of missing papers, since they may form a part of the permanent minutes. If time permits, it is also a good idea to verify the spelling of names or other doubtful points in the minutes. And before they can be mislaid, refile the various organization records that were taken to the meeting. In addition, make appropriate notations on your employer's calendar of the matters discussed during the meeting that require further attention.

You may often be instructed to write letters of notification when someone has been elected to an office or assigned a duty. Formal notification by letter of action taken at a meeting is necessary even when the person involved was present.

Help the executive make sure that assignments given to various members of the organization are carried out. Put a note in the tickler file concerning actions needed and the names of those assigned to perform them. Then follow up at an appropriate time.

Preparing the Minutes

Composing a Rough Draft.   The first step in the preparation of minutes of formal meetings is to type a rough draft of the notes taken during the meeting. Prepare and submit a rough draft of the proceedings of the meeting to your employer for approval before attempting a final draft. Rough-draft minutes should be double- or triple-spaced so that corrections can be made easily and clearly. Copies of the draft or specific portions of it are sometimes distributed for approval to the officers of the organization and to those who made resolutions.

Typing Minutes in Final Form.   The final form of the minutes as approved must be accurately typed, since special numbered pages are often used. Minutes may be either single- or double-spaced. Paragraphs are indented five or ten spaces, and each item of business is reported in a separate paragraph. Use a generous left margin in order to allow for marginal subject captions for the various sections. This feature will make the minutes more readable and will make it easier to locate specific information in them.

The following guidelines should be used when retyping the draft minutes in final form:

- Center in all capitals the name of the company and the name of the group. The date may also be centered.
- Use marginal and subject captions for the various sections. These captions can be typed with the first letter of each major word capitalized and each word underscored or in all capitals.
- Record the type of meeting; the day, date, and hour; the place; and the name of the presiding officer and secretary in the first paragraph.
- Indicate whether a quorum was present.
- Capitalize group words, such as Board, Company, and Corporation, when they stand alone, and the name of the group for which the minutes are written. Also capitalize the titles of key officers in the organization, such as President and Treasurer.
- List alphabetically the names of members present and those absent, in a paragraph or in a column indented five spaces from the left margin.
- Indent resolutions five extra spaces on both sides and single-space them.
- Type motions in all capitals.
- Present amounts of money mentioned in resolutions in the legal pattern—first as words and then as numbers in parentheses.
- Prepare an index of the minutes by subject. Because the personnel of organizations is constantly changing, an index represents the only practical way of keeping track of motions previously passed. Use the marginal captions to facilitate the preparation of the index.

Correcting the Minutes.   Minutes are read and approved by motion at the next meeting of the group. If there are any corrections, you make them at that meeting.

BURTON-HILL CONSTRUCTION CO.
BOARD OF DIRECTORS
REGULAR DIRECTORS' MEETING
FEBRUARY 20, 19--

February 20,
19--

The regular monthly meeting of the Board of Directors of the Burton-Hill Construction Co. was held at 10:30 a.m. Thursday, February 20, 19--, in the Board Room at 1236 Davis Avenue. The meeting was called to order by the Chairman, David C. Marshall. Helen Cain was the recording secretary.

Members present and comprising a quorum were:

Present
and Absent

Elmer A. Apple   James C. Lee
Frank S. Carver   George T. Nelson
Clem T. Cordman   Edward G. Thomas

Members absent were: Harold R. Boyd and Carl F. Pilsner.

Minutes
Approved

The minutes of the last regular meeting were read and approved, with the motion of Mr. Nelson regarding the expansion of the equipment yard to read as follows: "Mr. Nelson moved that the question regarding the expansion of the present site of the heavy equipment yard be referred to the Planning Committee for further consideration. Carried unanimously."

Treasurer's
Report and
Common Stock
Dividend

The Treasurer submitted a general profit and loss statement for the first half of the year, showing a net profit for the period of $----- ($-----). This report was accepted and is attached.

On motion made by the Treasurer and seconded by Mr. Lee, the following resolution was unanimously adopted:

WHEREAS it appears from the report of the Treasurer that the net profits of Burton-Hill Construction Co. for the first half ending June 30 amounted to the sum of $-----($-----), and

WHEREAS the surplus available for dividends has not diminished since that date: Therefore be it

RESOLVED, That for the purpose of paying a quarterly dividend of sixty cents ($0.60) per share on ----- shares of common stock of Burton-Hill Construction Co. now outstanding, there is hereby set apart out of the surplus net profits, the sum of $-----($-----), and from such sum the Treasurer is authorized and

directed to pay the said quarterly dividend of sixty cents ($0.60) per share on September 1, to the common stockholders of record at the close of business on August 9.

Planning
Committee
Reports

Mr. Apple reported that the Planning Committee was not yet ready to make final recommendations regarding the expansion of the present site of the heavy equipment yard. Several members wanted to investigate an alternate location on the corner of Lakewood Avenue and Merritt Boulevard, two blocks away from the new limited-access freeway.

Accounting
and Budgets
Committee
Report

On behalf of the Accounting and Budgets Committee, Mr. Thomas stated that all four revenue departments have submitted preliminary budgets for the next fiscal year.

Wage Study

The question of whether the present wage study should be continued was brought up for further discussion. It was moved, seconded, and passed THAT THE WAGE STUDY SHOULD BE CONCLUDED IN TIME FOR THE ANNUAL MANAGEMENT-LABOR CONTRACT NEGOTIATION MEETING.

Personnel
Policies

After a discussion about personnel policies, a committee consisting of Clem T. Cordman, Chairman, Harold R. Boyd, and James C. Lee was appointed to study ways by which all employees could be encourage to train for advancement through participation in both in-company and outside training programs.

Adjournment

On motion made by Mr. Carver and seconded by Mr. Apple, the meeting was adjourned at 12:30 p.m.

Helen Cain
———————————
Secretary

David C. Marshall
———————————
Chairman

Minutes of a formal meeting.

Errors in the minutes are not erased. Instead, corrections are made in a manner that will enable the reader to recognize them as such. Simple corrections are made by drawing a line in ink through the incorrect statement and then writing the correction in ink above the error. Major errors are frequently corrected by typing revised minutes on a separate page that is added at the end of the minutes. The erroneous material is crossed out in ink and a marginal note is used to refer the reader to the corrected statement.

REVIEWING YOUR READING

1. Explain the difference between a *standing committee* and an *ad hoc committee*.

2. If the executive for whom you are working is chairperson of a committee, what are your duties before the meeting? during the meeting?

3. When taking notes at a meeting, what kind of information should you write down?

4. Discuss the duties you are likely to have as the chairperson's secretary after a meeting has ended.

5. If you are making arrangements for a group that will be meeting outside your company's building, what is the best way to make sure that all details have been taken care of?

6. What are the main elements of a carefully prepared agenda for a meeting? How can an agenda serve as a helpful guide when you are reporting a meeting?

7. If the number constituting a quorum is not specified, should the secretary omit a record of those attending the meeting?

8. If you are taking notes at a meeting, what part of the proceedings must you record word for word?

9. When preparing minutes, what specific information would you generally include in the first paragraph?

10. Explain how the minutes of a meeting are corrected.

11. Describe a main motion and indicate its primary characteristic.

12. Describe a subsidiary motion and explain its relationship to a main motion.

13. Name the four subsidiary motions that require a two-thirds vote for adoption and that are not debatable.

USING YOUR SKILLS

1. Rank the following motions on a separate sheet, positioning the lowest in rank at the bottom of the list and the highest at the top. Also indicate with check marks the two motions that require a two-thirds vote for their adoption.
   a. Lay on the table.
   b. Amend.
   c. Adjourn.

   d. Main motion.
   e. Previous question.
   f. Raise a question of privilege.
   g. Limit or extend limits of debate.
   h. Postpone to a certain time.

2. Following is an example of a motion as it might appear in the transcript of a recorded meeting:

> *Grasso:* It is obvious that this issue cannot be settled now. I think it should be referred to a committee.
>
> *Horst:* Do you wish to make that as a motion?
>
> *Grasso:* I so move.
>
> *Horst:* Do you wish to include the number of members and the method of appointment?
>
> *Grasso:* I suggest three members and that they be appointed by the chairperson.
>
> *Horst:* Is there any objection to this being included in the motion? (*Pause*) There being none, it is so ordered. The question is: Shall the pending motion be referred to a committee of three to be appointed by the chairperson? Are there any remarks? (*Pause*) Those in favor say *aye*. (*Ayes*) Those opposed say *no*. (*None*) The motion is carried.

Show how the final minutes might read.

3. Given the following statement, draft a resolution on behalf of the committee on community improvement:

> The youth of this community are without adequate recreational facilities. During the past three months, two accidents involving games played in the street have demonstrated the danger of the prevailing conditions. Available property on Spring Street is appropriately located for a community recreational area. The present condition of this property is a threat to the health and safety of the residents of this community. This committee goes on record as favoring the purchase of the specified property by the city, by condemnation proceedings if necessary, and its conversion into a neighborhood recreational area with appropriate facilities. We propose that a copy of this resolution be submitted by the secretary to the president of City Council for presentation to that body.

4. Provide brief answers to the questions that follow:
   a. How large a vote is required to adjourn a meeting?
   b. Does a motion to recess have precedence over a motion to adjourn?
   c. May a member interrupt a meeting to ask that guests withdraw during a certain discussion?
   d. When an amendment is made to a motion, is the motion voted on first and then the amendment?

e. May a motion to refer a matter to a committee be amended?

f. Can an amendment be amended?

g. What subsidiary motion has highest precedence?

h. Does a motion to postpone definitely have precedence over a motion to postpone indefinitely?

i. How large a vote is required on a motion to vote on the previous question?

j. Must a member be recognized by the chairperson to make a main or a subsidiary motion?

k. Is the motion to lay a motion on the table debatable?

l. Is it a motion to say, "I suggest that . . . "

m. Do all main motions require a two-thirds vote?

n. Are privileged motions related to a main motion?

o. May any participant initiate a motion to reconsider any vote taken by a group?

EXERCISING YOUR JUDGMENT

Fitting In. You are a male secretary recently hired to work in a department with four other secretaries, all women. While they are polite to you, they do not include you in their casual banter or ask you to join them in the company lunchroom. You feel it is important to be accepted by them, not only because you would be more comfortable at work but also because you think that you could do a better job as a secretary if you felt free to exchange information informally with the other secretaries in the department. What steps can you take to get them to accept you as a member of the secretarial group?

APPLYING THE REFERENCE SECTION

Whether the following are one or two words depends on their meanings. From the choices in the right-hand column select the one that matches the meaning in the left-hand column.

1. Routine.   everyday, every day

2. Entirely prepared.   already, all ready

3. Anybody at all.   anyone, any one

4. An amount of time.   sometime, some time

5. Might be.   maybe, may be

6. At all times.   always, all ways

7. Not any.   none, no one

8. Oblique.   indirect, in direct

Travel Arrangements

Executives whose business takes them away from the office for periods of time depend on sound travel plans to help them accomplish their objectives with a maximum of efficiency and a minimum of stress. Transportation and room reservations can be arranged beforehand by a competent secretary directing operations from the office. Whether the plans call for a short day trip to a nearby city or travel to a distant destination, the travel arrangements you make can mean the difference between success and failure of a business trip.

Company Policy and Employer Preferences

Before attempting to arrange for an executive's travel or overnight accommodations, you should be familiar with company policy. Are there preferred practices regarding the making of travel reservations, the use of private cars and car rental services, the selection of hotel or motel accommodations, and the obtaining of travel advances? Policy sometimes sets limits on daily travel allowances and specifies that economy flight accommodations be used.

Sometimes an executive prefers certain hotels or kinds of travel (nonstop flights or a particular type of aircraft, for example). Special room accommodations may be required when business with clients is to be conducted in the room. You also need to know who is responsible for handling travel arrangements.

Transportation Department

Large business organizations generally have transportation departments or services that maintain close contact with all major carriers and car rental agencies. These offices have on hand the official guides for airlines and railroads. Making use of such service is by far the handiest way for you to manage travel arrangements. Simply let the service know the desired itinerary, and you will receive schedule options for the executive's approval. Once the decision has been made, the department either obtains or issues the necessary tickets.

Commercial Travel Agencies If there is no company travel service available, you can turn with confidence to a commercial travel agency. The agent there plans the complete itinerary, handling the ticketing, hotel reservations, car rentals, and special discounts. Agents can also be a reliable source of information on international travel documents such as passports, visas, and health certificates.

In order to get the most satisfactory travel arrangements for an executive, you must provide the agent with the names of cities to be visited, preferred mode and class of travel, cost limitations, date and time of arrival in each city, time of departure from each city, hotel or motel preferences, and the name and business and home addresses and telephone numbers of the traveler. Travel agencies do not charge the customer a fee for their services; they receive a percentage of the cost of tickets and room rates from transportation lines and hotels or motels.

Secretarial Arrangements If the executive for whom you work represents a small company or rarely travels, you may wish to make the travel arrangements personally. You will need to be aware of details when undertaking this responsibility, since you will deal directly with the carriers' representatives and with hotel reservation personnel.

Whether reservations are handled by the company travel office, by a commercial travel service, or by you, it remains your responsibility to verify that the arrangements and accommodations made are in accordance with the executive's needs. When the tickets are delivered, for example, check the dates and times of departures and class of travel to make certain that errors have not been made. Call to the boss's attention such considerations as allowing time to get from one scheduled flight to another. Request and be sure you receive hotel and motel reservation confirmations before the executive's departure.

Domestic Air Travel

Flying is the method of travel preferred by most business executives. Conveniently scheduled flights allow them to conduct out-of-town business transactions without being away from their base of operations for too long. An executive in Miami, for example, can take a plane to St. Louis in the morning, conduct a business conference, and be back in Miami in time for an early-evening engagement. Even a coast-to-coast trip—say, from Philadelphia to Los Angeles—takes only about four hours.

Flight Information You can make flight reservations by contacting the airline ticket office of the preferred airline directly. All connecting flight reservations, even if they are with other airlines, can be made with the airline through which the trip is initiated.

Airline Guides.   Many business offices subscribe to one of the airline guides published by Reuben H. Donnelly Publications, 2000 Clearwater Drive, Oak Brook, IL 60521. Subscribers to the *Official Airline Guide*, the *OAG Pocket Flight Guide*, or the *OAG Travel Planner and Hotel/Motel Guide* receive updated materials automatically. These publications contain information about all airport locations in North America—their schedules, fares, limousine service, car rental, hotels, and air taxi facilities. Flight information is listed by destination,

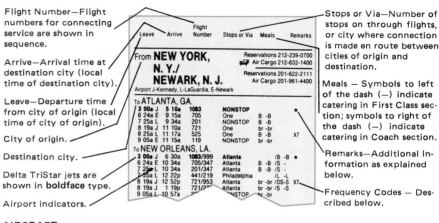

Flight Number—Flight numbers for connecting service are shown in sequence.

Arrive—Arrival time at destination city (local time of destination city).

Leave—Departure time from city of origin (local time of city of origin).

City of origin.

Destination city.

Delta TriStar jets are shown in boldface type.

Airport indicators.

Stops or Via—Number of stops on through flights, or city where connection is made en route between cities of origin and destination.

Meals — Symbols to left of the dash (—) indicate catering in First Class section; symbols to right of the dash (—) indicate catering in Coach section.

Remarks—Additional information as explained below.

Frequency Codes — Described below.

AIRCRAFT:

L10—Lockheed TriStar (L–1011) Fan Jet
    Seating—First Class–32, Coach–261
L-1011-200—Lockheed TriStar Fan Jet
    Seating—First Class–24, Coach/
    Economy–229
D8S—Douglas Super DC-8 Fan Jet
    Seating—First Class–26, Coach–173

DC8—Douglas DC-8 Fan Jet
    Seating—First Class–20, Coach–123
72S—Boeing 727 Super Fan Jet
    Seating—First Class–14, Coach–123
D9S—Douglas Super DC-9 Fan Jet
    Seating—First Class–18, Coach–70

MEALS:
B Breakfast   br Brunch
L Lunch   C Continental Breakfast
D Dinner   DS Deluxe Snack
S Light Snack
(A single meal symbol indicates service to First Class or Deluxe Night Coach only)

FREQUENCY CODES (All flights daily except as noted):
1—Monday   4—Thursday   7—Sunday
2—Tuesday   5—Friday   X—Except
3—Wednesday   6—Saturday

MISCELLANEOUS SYMBOLS:
FY—First Class and Day Coach (Economy when transatlantic) Service

FNYN—Deluxe Night Coach and Night Coach Service

K—Dallas/Ft. Worth—Shreveport Economy Service (no meals)

°Early Bird morning flights or Owly Bird evening flights offering Deluxe Night Coach and Night Coach service, generally at substantial savings over regular daytime service.

/ Separate flights on connecting service.

Printed timetables provided by airlines include instructions on how to read the schedules.

and then by the cities from which flights to the destination are available. Keys to all abbreviations and symbols used in the various schedules are given.

Airline Flight Schedules.   Airline schedules are also available from the various airlines upon request. Although they are not uniform in format, they contain similar information and are easy to read.

Flight schedules are arranged alphabetically in quick reference form. To find the desired service, look for the city in which the trip will originate. There, all destinations are listed alphabetically. In the Delta timetable above, Flight 119 departs from the Newark, New Jersey, airport at 9:05 a.m. and arrives, nonstop, in Atlanta, Georgia, at 11:15 a.m. (Departure time is the local time of the city of origin; arrival time is the local time of the destination city.) Brunch is served in both the first class and coach sections of Flight 119. Flight 1083 is a Lockheed TriStar jet aircraft seating either 32 or 24 first-class passengers and 261 or 229 coach and economy passengers.

Flight Conditions and Rules

Rules and conditions that apply to scheduled flights can be found in the major airline quick-reference schedules. Major considerations are classes of service, fares, reservations and ticketing, baggage, and reconfirmation.

Classes of Service.   Most aircraft used by major airlines have first-class and coach sections. Twin seats in first-class sections are comfortably wide and are spaced to give the passenger generous legroom. Coach seats are usually three across and narrow—somewhat uncomfortable on long trips unless the plane is not full and the middle seat is not occupied.

Economical no-reservation air-shuttle service is available between certain cities such as Washington, New York, Boston, and Newark, and between San Francisco and Los Angeles. Flights usually depart from designated terminals at 60-minute intervals. Backup planes stand by to guarantee everybody a seat no matter how many people arrive. Passengers pay on board with cash, checks, credit cards, and one-way government transportation receipts. Carry-on baggage is accepted on air-shuttle flights.

Fares.   Fares and charges shown in airline schedules are for information only and are subject to change without notice. All domestic fares shown include a federal transportation tax. To verify an air fare, call the airline or a travel agent.

Flight Reservations and Ticketing.   If a company transportation service is not available, the way to make a flight reservation is to telephone or go to the airport terminal, a local airline ticket office, or a travel agency. Through computerized reservation systems, airlines can book and ticket a complete itinerary, including those segments of a trip using routes covered by other carriers.

When the reservation is made in person, the ticket is issued immediately. If the reservation is made by telephone, the ticket is either mailed or held for pickup at the airport. Reservations that are confirmed by an airline agent by phone are, of course, subject to the purchase of a ticket by the time agreed upon by the passenger and the agent, or at the minimum time before flight departure stated in tariff rules.

Executives traveling for business purposes cannot always be sure when they will be ready to return home. In such cases, an *open ticket* can be purchased for them instead of a reserved seat on a scheduled flight. With an open ticket in hand, the traveler merely telephones the airline to reserve space on a particular flight when the desired time of departure is known.

Passengers who are checking in for a boarding pass and seat assignment on a flight on the day of departure are expected to plan their arrival at the airport to allow sufficient check-in time. Passengers may request to be seated in either the smoking or nonsmoking section and may also ask for an aisle or window seat in the fore, aft, or center section of the aircraft, if a choice of seats is available. Most airlines request that passengers be at the airport boarding gate at least five minutes before the scheduled departure time of a domestic flight.

Baggage Allowance.   The term *baggage* includes all articles of luggage—briefcases, typewriters, parcels, and similar articles—whether they are carried in the cabin of the aircraft or checked in the cargo compartment. A coat, umbrella, pocketbook, small camera or binoculars, or reading material is not considered baggage. Identification labels are required on the outside of all checked baggage.

Reconfirmations.   Airlines do not require reconfirmation of continuing or return air reservations on domestic flights. If a stopover is more than 72 hours, however, it is recommended that the airline be advised of the traveler's wish to maintain the continuing or return reservation.

Airport Service Information   An important consideration is the time it will take a traveling executive to get from office or home to the airport, or from the destination airport to a hotel or an appointment. Flight schedules show only actual flying time. Needless to say, if it requires 55 minutes to travel by limousine from a large airport to the downtown area, you would not schedule an executive hosting a noon luncheon meeting on a flight arriving at 11:30.

Ground transportation in the form of airport limousine, bus, taxi, and car rental is available at every airport. Courtesy vehicles are provided by most hotels and motels that are located near the airport.

Buses and limousines operate on regular schedules to and from airports and to and from major downtown hotels or central terminals. Sometimes it is necessary to reserve space on a limousine or to telephone and arrange to be picked up by an airport taxi. Vehicles are also provided to transport travelers between airports serving one city and between airline terminals within an airport. Executives should be reminded that they can get ground transportation guidance from the airline ticket counter at the airport and from their hotel door attendant.

Airline flight schedules indicate the availability of helicopter service between airports, between heliports in the business centers of large cities and airports, and between airports and points beyond that are not adequately served by connecting flights. Helicopter service can save a significant amount of an executive's travel time, but it is more expensive than limousine, taxi, or bus service.

Ground Travel

Some business executives choose to travel by automobile or by train during all or part of a business trip. For long distances, neither mode of travel is likely to be economical because of the time required.

Automobile Travel   Business executives who travel extensively for their companies may be assigned a leased or company-owned car. In some instances, companies negotiate contracts with auto leasing firms, making automobiles available on call to their executives. Either arrangement is practical when the executive's business trips are relatively short and when stops are frequently made en route. You should become familiar with company procedures and policies governing reimbursement for mileage and car-related expenses. The status of the executive's public liability and property damage insurance coverage must also be established.

In most cases, however, executives use their personal cars or those provided by a rental agency for company travel.

Road Information.   When an executive depends on a car for business travel, you should have within reach an up-to-date road atlas, such as those prepared by Rand McNally and Company. State and large-city road maps are also provided by some oil companies and by many company-owned or franchised service stations. On these, you can highlight the roads to be traveled for quick reference by the executive during the trip.

A reliable source of road information for the traveling executive is a motor club such as Allstate or the American Automobile Association (AAA). Members receive all the travel information they need for planning short trips as well as long ones. Custom-made trip plans or "Triptiks" are prepared on request to guide members to their destinations.

Motor clubs keep members posted on road construction—new interstate roads, beltways, and lane expansion—and current toll charges. Other valuable services are provided, such as insurance for drivers; road service for stranded members; hotel, motel, and restaurant ratings; and touring suggestions.

Car Rentals.   Business executives routinely travel by plane and then rent a car to get from the airport to their subsequent destinations and appointments. Airline and railroad timetables indicate the cities with car rental services. A separate subscription guide is published by the Reuben H. Donnelley Corporation of Chicago, which lists all rent-a-car services in the United States and abroad, the locations of rental agency offices and pickup points, daily rates, and mileage charges. The automobile rental companies also publish directories of their rental agencies.

Reservations for a rented car can be made along with the airline travel reservation or with the car rental agency at the point of departure or pickup. Toll-free telephone numbers for out-of-town reservations are listed in the telephone directory by major auto-renting services. In addition to the name, office address, and telephone number of the driver, specify the make and type of car wanted; the date, time, and place of pickup; the probable date and place to which the car will be returned; and the preferred method of payment of charges.

Train Travel   Travel by train has become something of a rarity for many business executives because of the time required to cover long distances, the reduction in service, and the competition from airlines. However, there have been attempts to revive interest in long-distance passenger rail service. Reorganization of railroads with government support has produced Amtrak and Conrail, railway systems that connect cities with large populations and offer improved services. Metroliners connecting Boston, New York, Philadelphia, and Washington, D.C., have reserved seats, fast schedules, and rates that permit them to compete with airlines.

Railway Timetables.   A railway timetable is easy to read. Trains are listed by number, and reference marks and symbols are used to designate available services, special stops, and connecting points. In the partial Conrail timetable illustrated here, express trains between New York City and New Haven, Connecticut, depart from New York at 5:02, 5:20, and 6:07 p.m. each weekday. When consulting a railway timetable, check the date on the cover, since schedules are revised frequently.

Commuter Service.   Commuter train service is available between large cities and their suburbs. Large numbers of business persons living in the suburbs use commuter trains to travel to and from the city. Connecticut, New Jersey, and New York State residents who conduct business in New York City find the commuter trains a suitable and quick way to get to their offices.

NEW YORK TO NEW HAVEN

MONDAY TO FRIDAY, EXCEPT HOLIDAYS

Leave New York	Arrive New Haven	Leave New York	Arrive New Haven	Leave New York	Arrive New Haven
AM	AM	PM	PM	PM	PM
12:35	2:18	2:05	3:45	7:05	8:56
5:40	7:44	3:05	4:45	8:05	9:45
7:05	8:45	4:05	5:48	9:05	10:45
8:05	9:45	4:41	6:25	10:05	11:45
9:05	10:45	4:59	6:53	11:05	12:45
10:05	11:45	X 5:02 E	6:33	12:35	2:18
11:05	12:45	X 5:20	7:08	....	....
12:05	1:45	X 6:07 E	7:46	....	....
1:05	2:45	6:25	8:19	....	....
PM	PM	PM	PM	AM	AM

SATURDAY, SUNDAY & HOLIDAYS
Upper Level

Leave New York	Arrive New Haven	Leave New York	Arrive New Haven	Leave New York	Arrive New Haven
AM	AM	PM	PM	PM	PM
12:35	2:21	2:05	3:45	H 8:05	H 9:45
5:40	7:37	4:05	5:45	9:05	10:45
8:05	9:45	5:05	6:48	11:05	12:48
10:05	11:47	6:05	7:48	12:35	2:18
12:05	1:45	7:05	8:45	....	....
PM	PM	PM	PM	AM	AM

REFERENCE NOTES
Economy off-peak tickets are **not** valid on trains in shaded areas.
Check displays in G.C.T. for departure tracks.
E-Express.
X-Does not stop at 125th Street.
S-Saturdays and Washington's Birthday only.
H-Sundays and Holidays only.
HOLIDAYS- New Year's Day, Washington's Birthday, Memorial, Independence and Labor Day, Thanksgiving and Christmas.

The service shown herein is operated by Consolidated Rail Corporation.

Portion of a railway timetable.

Long-Distance Service.   In some parts of the country, there is still good long-distance passenger train service. Overnight trains connect Chicago with the West Coast and Florida. Similar service connects points on the East Coast with Florida. Nevertheless, the extension of long-distance rail passenger service remains doubtful. Although train travel can be comfortable and convenient, business travelers generally consider it only when there is no other available option. For schedules of all railroads and steamship lines in the United States, Canada, Mexico, and Puerto Rico, consult *The Official Guide of the Railroads*, published by the National Railway Publications Company, New York.

Passenger Accommodations.   There are two classes of rail travel—first class and coach. Coach travel affords the traveler an unreserved standard seat in a coach car. First-class travel includes sleeping accommodations and parlor car and requires a reservation. The least expensive sleeping accommodations are the slumber coach and roomette, in which the bed folds into the wall and serves as a couch during the day. Bedrooms (a room containing an upper and lower berth), compartments (similar to bedrooms but larger), and drawing rooms (compartments with an extra convertible sofa) are also available. Some trains have facilities for transporting passengers' automobiles.

Bus Travel   Bus travel is satisfactory for short business trips where other modes of transportation are limited. High-speed highways and modern, centrally located bus terminals have increased the convenience of bus travel. While reservations are generally not taken, some bus companies with heavily traveled routes do accept them.

International Travel

Although the arrangements for international flights are much the same as those for shorter domestic flights, there are other details that need to be dealt with. The business executive from New York who departs on a flight for Paris at 7 p.m., for example, will cross six time zones before arriving at Orly airport at 1 a.m. New York time, but 7 a.m. local time. Generally, it is advisable not to schedule any business appointments during an executive's first day abroad. When one moves rapidly through a number of time zones, "jet lag" symptoms, including nervous irritability, headaches, and a general feeling of fatigue, may develop.

Business is conducted at a slower pace in most foreign cities. For this reason, executives are advised to limit appointments to two a day. Most major airlines provide special services such as conference rooms, secretarial services, and hotel reservations. You should equip a foreign-bound executive with an ample supply of business cards, because they are customarily presented to each person called on.

Travel Documents   All European countries require a passport for entry. When a traveler enters a foreign country, an immigration officer of that country will stamp the passport with a visa stamp. An embarkation stamp is made when the visitor leaves the country.

Passport Requirements.   A passport is an official document issued by the Department of State granting permission to United States citizens to travel and confirming their right to protection. A valid passport is required for travel in foreign countries except Canada, Mexico, Central American countries, the West Indies, and Bermuda. The business executive who visits countries that do not require a passport should carry documentary evidence of citizenship in case it is requested. A native-born citizen should carry a birth or baptismal certificate, a naturalized citizen, a certificate of naturalization.

Passport application forms can be obtained from travel agents; many major post offices; passport offices in Boston, Chicago, Los Angeles, Miami, New Orleans, New York, San Francisco, Washington; and local federal buildings. To obtain the initial passport, the applicant must appear in person before a clerk of a federal court or state court authorized to naturalize aliens, or an agent of a designated passport office. The following items should be presented:

- The completed application.
- Proof of citizenship (birth certificate, baptismal certificate, or naturalization papers).
- A driver's license bearing the applicant's signature.
- Two identical recent signed photographs, approximately 2½ inches square and taken by a photographer.
- The passport fee.

Business executives may renew their passports by completing Form DSP-82 and mailing it—along with the two signed photographs, the expired passport, and the passport fee—to the nearest passport office.

Passports are valid for five years unless expressly limited to a shorter period. Since it requires about three weeks to process a passport application, executives who engage in foreign travel often should keep their passports in order. When received, the passport should be signed. For the bearer's protection, the names and addresses called for on the inside cover must be filled in. While traveling abroad, a traveler should always keep the passport on his or her person and never carry it in a briefcase or bag or leave it in a hotel room.

Visa Requirements.   A visa is a stamped notation in a passport indicating that the bearer may enter the country for an acceptable purpose and for a specified period of time. A travel agent or the consular officials of the countries the traveling executive plans to visit can inform you of current visa requirements. The *Congressional Directory* can be consulted for the addresses of consular offices.

Vaccination and Inoculation Requirements.   International Certificates of Vaccination or Revaccination are official statements verifying that proper procedures have been followed to immunize a traveler against a disease that could be a threat to the United States and other countries. These certificates can be second in importance only to a passport in permitting uninterrupted international travel.

Overseas Flights

The arrangements for an international flight are similar to those for a domestic flight. There are two classes of service on most flights—first class and economy or tourist class. Meals or refreshments are served during overseas flights. First-class passengers are served special catered meals. Tourist-class meals are not as elaborate as those served in first class. Baggage not considered carry-on or on which the traveler is dependent for health or comfort is figured in the total weight permitted each passenger. First-class passengers are allowed 66 pounds (30 k); tourist-class passengers have a 44-pound (20-k) allowance. An additional charge is made for all baggage over the free allowance.

Fares differ according to the seasons and according to the length of the business executive's stay. Overseas fares change frequently due to the keen

		Daily exc. Tu	Daily	Daily		
		SR 111 747 F Y	SR 101 747 F Y	SR 165 D10 F Y		
Chicago O'Hare	Lv	—	—	17 45 ▼	—	—
Boston	Ar	—	—	21 00	—	—
	Lv	—	—	21 45	—	—
New York J. F. Kennedy	Lv	18 00	21 05		—	—
		next day				
Geneva	Ar	07 20			—	—
			next day	next day		
Zürich Terminal B	Ar	08 55	10 40	10 50	—	—
*Geneva	Ar	—	12 30	12 30	—	—
*Berne	Ar	13 10	13 10	13 10	—	—
*Basel/Mulhouse	Ar	—	12 35	12 35	—	—

		Daily	Daily exc. Tu	Daily		
		SR 100 747 F Y	SR 110 747 F Y	SR 164 D10 F Y		
*Basel/Mulhouse	Lv	10 30	13 10	10 30	—	—
*Berne	Lv	09 00	12 00	09 00	—	—
*Geneva	Lv	10 20	—	10 20	—	—
Zürich Terminal B	Lv	12 00	15 00	11 55	—	—
Geneva	Lv		16 30		—	—
New York J. F. Kennedy	Ar	14 40	19 05		—	—
Boston	Ar	—	—	14 00	—	—
	Lv	—	—	14 40 ▼	—	—
Chicago O'Hare	Ar	—	—	16 15	—	—

A Swissair transatlantic flight schedule.

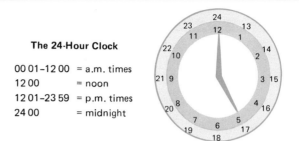

The 24-Hour Clock

00 01–12 00   = a.m. times
12 00   = noon
12 01–23 59   = p.m. times
24 00   = midnight

competition among airlines. When you are making travel arrangements, contact the travel agent or the appropriate airline office for fares.

International Flight Schedules.   Flight schedules of foreign airlines are somewhat different from domestic schedules. The Swissair schedule shown on the opposite page, listing flights from Chicago, Boston, and New York to Zurich, Geneva, Berne, and Basel, illustrates the major differences.

Swissair (SR) flights 111, 101, and 165 depart from New York (daily except Tuesday) at 6 p.m.; from New York (daily) at 9:05 p.m.; and from Chicago at 5:45 p.m. and Boston at 9:45 p.m. Flight 111—first class (F) and coach class (Y)—arrives in Geneva the next day at 7:20 a.m. and in Zurich at 8:55 a.m. A connecting flight (*) to Berne arrives at 1:10 p.m., where bus service is available. The return flights—100, 110, and 164 to New York, Boston, and Chicago—are shown on the bottom half of the schedule.

The 24-hour clock is used in foreign airline timetables. Times shown between 0001 (1 minute after midnight) and 1200 (noon) are a.m. To convert p.m. times back to the 12-hour clock, subtract 12 hours. For example, 1830 hours is 6:30 p.m.

Ship Transportation   Despite drawbacks in terms of both cost and comfort, a business executive may combine business with vacation, traveling one way by plane and then returning home more leisurely by ship. Travel agents can give you full information about available transatlantic crossings and rates. Information about freighter crossings is available for a small fee from TravLtips Freighter Travel Association, 163-09 Depot Road, Flushing, NY 11358 and from Siemer & Hand, Ltd., One Embarcadero Center, San Francisco, CA 94111.

Foreign Train Service   Only two categories of trains are recommended for business travel—first class and second class. In the first group are the reserved accommodations, with four to six persons in a compartment. Second-class accommodations are unreserved, with six to eight persons in a compartment. Extra-fare trains carrying first- and second-class passengers only are available on most important routes.

Transeurop Express.   As its name implies, Transeurop Express trains connect almost 160 of Europe's major cities. These international trains, first class only, vie with each other for service and speed. They have names that identify them, and reservations made well in advance of the trip are recommended. Some popular routes and names are:

Catalan	Barcelona-Avignon-Geneva
Cisalpin	Paris-Milan-Venice
Edelweiss/Iris	Brussels-Zurich
Helvetia	Hamburg-Zurich
Ligure	Avignon-Nice-Milan
Merkur	Copenhagen-Hamburg-Stuttgart
Parsifal	Paris-Düsseldorf-Hamburg
Prinz Eugen	Bremen-Nuremberg-Vienna
Rembrandt	Amsterdam-Munich
Rheingold	Hook of Holland-Cologne-Geneva

Other fast trains run within certain countries as well as on international routes at speeds and with conveniences and comfort often equal to Transeurop Express's. Included in this category are long-distance express and intermediate fast trains and short-haul locals.

Timetables.   If you are planning an executive's train travel, obtain the condensed timetable "The Best Trains in Europe," which is free upon request from any European railroad office in the United States or Canada. Cook's comprehensive European timetable can be purchased by writing to Travel Library, P.O. Box 249, La Canada, CA 91011 or to Thomas Cook Ltd., Timetable Publishing Office, P.O. Box 36, Peterborough PE3 65B, England.

European timetables use a 24-hour clock. Since schedules vary from summer to winter, it is important that you refer to the correct seasonal timetable. From the last week in May to the last week in September the summer schedule is valid, and many more trains run.

Reservations.   The traveling executive who wants to have an uncontested right to a seat, sleeper, or *couchette* must have a reservation. Although in most cases the executive can travel on a European train without a seat reservation, a reserved seat is sometimes desirable.

Everyone must reserve and pay for sleeping accommodations. Sleepers are either first-class compartments, for single or double occupancy, or second-class (tourist class), with two- or three-berth compartments.

Eurailpass.   The Eurailpass allows a business executive unlimited first-class train travel in fifteen countries: Austria, Belgium, Denmark, Finland, France, Germany, Greece, Holland, Italy, Luxembourg, Norway, Portugal, Spain, Sweden, and Switzerland. Available only in the United States, this pass is valid for periods varying from one week to three months. Great Britain has a Britrailpass similar to the Eurailpass.

For the convenience of the passenger, the first-class Eurailpass is issued with open dates. It must be validated by a railroad official before the passenger boards a train for the first time. The initial boarding of a train must occur within six months from the date of issuance stamped on the back of the pass. The pass is valid until arrival at destination by midnight of the last day indicated on the pass.

Car Travel Abroad

For the average two- or three-week foreign business trip, the executive may wish to consider a car rental. Cars are available on an unlimited mileage basis at a set cost per week. The longer the car is rented, the less the weekly cost should be.

To reserve a car in a foreign country, you can call a car-rental office. Airlines and travel agents will also make reservations for you at no charge. Since rental prices vary according to the European city in which the auto is picked up, *The ABCs of European Auto Travel* can be helpful. Obtain this free booklet by writing to Auto Europe, Inc., 1270 Second Avenue, New York, NY 10021. Large car-rental companies also have worldwide directories that list up-to-date prices and regulations.

Although a U.S. driver's license is accepted in most foreign countries, the traveling business executive should obtain an American International Driving Permit. It is obtainable from the American Automobile Association (AAA) here or abroad for a small fee.

Hotel Accommodations Abroad

You can rely on the travel agent or the airline to make hotel reservations for the executive. Since accommodations abroad are not always comparable to those in American hotels, take special care to specify the kind of accommodations desired. It is also recommended that you get a full description of the hotel facilities being reserved.

In England and Holland, the price of a hotel room generally includes breakfast. Other European countries confine their morning meal to the continental breakfast, which consists of coffee and pastry or rolls.

Your Participation in Travel Planning

Whether you are solely responsible for making travel arrangements or work with a company transportation department or a travel agent, there are certain preliminary facts you will want to clarify in discussion with your boss. These include:

- Places to be visited and the dates.
- Preferred modes of transportation.
- Preferred transportation accommodations.
- Preferred hotel accommodations.
- Appointments to be made and events to be attended.

With the necessary preliminary information in mind, you can check transportation schedules and acquire hotel information. Obtain and study current timetables, contact reservation clerks or travel agents, and gather information about hotels and motels from directories such as *Leahy's Hotel Guide and Travel Atlas of the United States, Canada, and Mexico*, published by the American Hotel Register Company, Chicago, or the *Official Hotel Red Book and Directory*, published by the American Hotel Association Directory Corporation, New York.

Contained in these reference books is information such as locations of facilities, number of rooms, rates, names of managers, telephone numbers, and whether the lodging is operated on the European plan (the rate covers the cost of the room only) or the American plan (the rate includes the cost of meals as well as the cost of the room). Check distances between airports and lodging and meeting places to ensure enough time to travel between them.

Begin a trip file into which you can place information collected on available flights and hotel accommodations and papers relating to scheduled meetings and appointments. When it is time to prepare a preliminary itinerary, sort the file into day and time sequence.

Preliminary Trip Plan

When you have as much information as possible, prepare a tentative itinerary for the boss's approval. Indicate choices to be made regarding arrival and departure times, names of airlines with flight numbers, and recommended hotel or motel choices and accommodations. After the executive has indicated preferences, make the necessary transportation and hotel or motel reservations or prepare a statement of these preferences to give to the company transportation department or a travel agent.

Hotel Reservations

When making hotel or motel reservations, check the Yellow Pages of the telephone directory, where toll-free numbers can be found for making out-of-town and worldwide reservations. Most airlines make such reservations for their passengers. American Airlines has an arrangement with Americana hotels, as do TWA with Hilton hotels and United Airlines with Western International hotels. A telephone call to a local Hilton or Sheraton hotel will also assure you a reservation with a member hotel in their communication systems. A worldwide hotel directory can be obtained free of charge from American Express Reservations, Inc., Box G-10, 770 Broadway, New York, NY 10003.

When requesting accommodations (by telephone or teletypewriter or in writing), specify the following items:

* Space—room or suite—and location preferences.
* Accommodations—bed size, tub or shower preference.
* Rate—regular, commercial, or special (convention).
* Number of persons.
* Date and time of arrival—guaranteed arrival if necessary.
* Estimated length of stay.
* Confirmation of reservation.

Final Itinerary

The final itinerary is a comprehensive step-by-step plan of the business trip that tells *when, where* and *how* the executive will proceed. It serves as a daily activities calendar, reminding the executive of things to be done, persons to visit, and problems to be resolved. It should refer to business papers that the executive takes along. An itinerary is shown on pages 399 and 400.

Prepare as many copies of the itinerary as will be needed. The original copy accompanies and guides the executive during the trip. Retain one copy for use in reaching the executive if necessary. Copies are frequently given to other executives in the company who may need them. The executive may ask that a copy be sent to a spouse or another member of the family so that mail sent to the executive's home can be forwarded and communication expedited in the event of a family emergency.

The amount of detail included in the itinerary depends upon the complexity of the travel arrangements and the nature of the business to be transacted.

```
                              ITINERARY

James A. Ward                                      August 14, 19--

          (Indianapolis; Chicago; Pittsburgh; Washington, D.C.)

Sunday, August 16

(St. Louis-Indianapolis)

    4:55 p.m., CDT          Depart St. Louis, Lambert Municipal Airport, Trans
                            World Airlines, Jet Coach (Y) nonstop flight
                            526, DC9.

    6:47 p.m., EDT          Arrive Indianapolis, Weir-Cook Municipal Airport.

                            Accommodation:  Hotel Washington, 14 Washington
                            Street (confirmation attached).  Late arrival
                            expected.
                            SAM speech scheduled for Ballroom on Monday noon.

Monday, August 17

    2:30 p.m.               SAM speech in Ballroom of Hotel Washington.
                            Early dinner with Mr. and Mrs. Charles Haynes
                            at hotel.
                            Check out of hotel before dinner so that you can
                            go directly to airport.

(Indianapolis-Chicago)

    7:30 p.m.               Depart Indianapolis, Delta Air Lines Jet Coach
                            (Y) nonstop flight 730, D9S.

    8:08 p.m., CDT          Arrive Chicago, O'Hare Airport.

                            Accommodation:  Palmer House, State and Monroe
                            Streets (confirmation attached).  Late arrival
                            expected.
                            Regional Sales Conference to be held at Palmer
                            House.  Check for the room numbers of the
                            conference rooms.
                            Frank Somers expects you to call him as soon as
                            you arrive.
```

The first page of an itinerary. Note that confirmations of hotel reservations are attached.

2

Tuesday, August 18

8:30 a.m.	Morning session of Regional Sales Conference.
12 noon	Luncheon presentation scheduled for Empire Room. Notes for your talk are bound in the attached folder.
1:30 p.m.	Afternoon session of Regional Sales Conference.
Reminder	Telephone your sister (412-321-1939). Give her your arrival flight number and time in Pittsburgh.

(Chicago-Pittsburgh)

6:10 p.m.	Depart Chicago, United Airlines Jet Coach (Y) nonstop flight 644, Boeing 737. Dinner served.
8:36 p.m., EDT	Arrive Pittsburgh, Greater Pittsburgh Airport. Pick up Hertz rental car at airport.
Reminder	Purchase flowers.
	Accommodation: Stay at your sister's house.

Wednesday, August 19 — Family reunion.

I will telephone you around 9:30 a.m. regarding office developments during your absence.

Thursday, August 20

(Pittsburgh-Washington, D.C.)

12:30 p.m.	Depart Pittsburgh, United Airlines Jet Coach (Y) nonstop flight 744, Boeing 737. Lunch served.
1:17 p.m., EDT	Arrive Washington, D.C., Dulles Airport.
3:00 p.m.	Appointment with Senator Gomez in his office. Correspondence folder attached.

(Washington, D.C.-St. Louis)

6:00 p.m.	Depart Washington, D.C., Delta Air Lines Jet Coach (Y) nonstop flight 553, DC9. Dinner served.
8:55 p.m., CDT	Arrive St. Louis, Lambert Airport. Use limousine service to city. Your car is parked in company parking lot.

The second page of an itinerary. Note the various reminders and other helpful details.

A complete itinerary includes the following data:

- Day, date, hour, and place of departure.
- Mode of confirmed transportation.
- Day, date, hour, and place of arrival.
- Hotel reservation.
- Appointments and other matters to be attended to.
- Day, date, hour, and place of departure for the return trip.
- Mode of confirmed transportation.
- Day, date, hour, and place of arrival.

An itinerary may be arranged in outline form or in any other way that will present the needed information in a clear and readily understood manner. If the itinerary extends over several days, the days of the week, with their dates, should be displayed prominently, along with the places. Of course, strict chronological order should be used, extending to the events of each day.

Travel Funds and Credit Cards

Since the executive needs funds to cover personal and business expenses while on a business trip, you may be asked to draw a travel advance from the company cashier or from a bank. If international travel is involved, check with the travel agent about any restrictions limiting the amount of foreign currency that can be taken into and out of a country by a foreign traveler.

Traveler's Checks. The traveling executive is advised to carry traveler's checks rather than large sums of cash that can be lost or stolen. American Express, Cook's, and Bank of America are widely known companies that charge only a small fee for traveler's checks. Barclays Bank sells checks in both dollars and pounds to anyone on the way to Europe, without a service charge.

Traveler's checks are issued in numbered denominations of $10, $20, $50, and $100. The executive must personally sign each check when it is purchased and again in sight of the person cashing it. Since it is difficult to forge a signature while under observation, this precaution makes traveler's checks much safer to carry than cash and as acceptable as cash.

Prepare a list of the traveler's check numbers for the executive to carry so that an immediate refund will be possible in the event of loss or theft. Avis will refund up to $100 in lost American Express checks on weekends or holidays when American Express offices are closed.

Credit Cards. Multipurpose credit cards—such as those issued by American Express, Carte Blanche, Diner's Club, VISA, MasterCharge, and International Air Travel—enable the business executive who is traveling abroad to charge goods and services without having to cope with many foreign currency problems. The

Traveler's checks must be signed when purchased and signed again when cashed as a safeguard against theft.

monthly statement of charges that is mailed to the executive can be used to verify expenditures of company advances when preparing the expense report.

Foreign Remittances.   Situations requiring immediate extra funds can arise unexpectedly. In such emergencies, foreign remittance services can send funds safely and quickly to a business traveler.

Funds can be sent abroad easily by such services as American Express or through arrangement with your local bank. To send funds by American Express, for example, you go to an American Express office and state how much you want to send, to whom, and at what address. When you pay that amount and the fee charged for sending it, you are given a receipt. American Express then issues an order to the American Express office nearest to the designated address authorizing payment to the individual named. When that person collects the money, his or her signature is secured to show that the funds were collected.

Remittances may be sent in the currency of a foreign country. That way, the person sending the money knows exactly what the receiver is getting because the currency exchange is made by the sender.

During the Executive's Absence

The executive away on a business trip expects that you will keep the office running smoothly, handling your regular day-to-day tasks and perhaps working on special jobs assigned in advance of the trip.

Make sure you understand clearly who has the authority to handle important business matters during the executive's absence. Depending upon the instructions you received, exercise judgment in handling matters that go beyond your scope of authority. In some offices, such matters are simply referred to the executive's superior or to other authorized company personnel. Many executives make arrangements to telephone their secretaries regularly. If this is your arrangement with the boss, keep notes on matters you want to discuss.

Some executives try to keep up with their correspondence while traveling. They carry a portable dictating machine and mail the tapes back for processing. They may request that copies of reports or correspondence be forwarded during an extended business trip. When this is the case, the copy of the itinerary should contain phone numbers and addresses where mail can be forwarded.

Forwarding Mail   Periodically forward in large envelopes copies, not originals, of any business documents or correspondence that the traveling executive requests. Keep a list of all such material sent, indicating the date on which each item was forwarded. Send copies of forwarded mail to both the executive's current and next locations on the itinerary to allow for slow mail service.

Handling Daily Communications   You are expected to keep a record of all office activities for the traveling executive's review and to arrange the original materials relating to these matters in order of importance. Accumulated materials can be separated into three folders: routine matters already handled, matters requiring attention, and information only.

The first folder should hold those materials that you acknowledge and handle or refer to someone else for appropriate action. Attach carbons or photocopies of the action taken to the original documents in the folder. Place all matters requiring the executive's attention—correspondence, memos, reports, telephone messages, record of office visitors—in another folder, arranged in the order of their importance. Printed matter and other less urgent matters can be placed in an "Information Only" folder.

Posttravel Responsibilities

The day the executive returns to the office following a business trip is likely to be busy, probably hectic. Try to keep the executive's calendar clear of appointments and meetings in order to provide time to clear up the backlog.

Follow-Up Activities

As quickly as possible, brief the executive on all that happened in the office. A *digest of mail* can be used to summarize the executive's business mail and other accumulated matters that require attention. (See page 112.)

A trip generates the need for many follow-up actions. Letters may have to be written to express appreciation for services provided during the trip. Telephone calls may have to be made, and some matters may require referral to other company personnel. Materials may have been promised by the executive, and the necessary arrangements to send them must be made. Files and documents carried by your boss during the trip and new materials must be filed.

Expense Reports

The executive will present you with rough notes on all expenses incurred during the business trip. These notes should be carefully reviewed while the details of

An expense-account form.

Entertainment and Miscellaneous Expense Record					
Date	Place	Misc.—Explain expense Entertainment—List guests & affiliation		Business purpose & Business discussion	Total Expended
11/28	THE WILLOWS	DINNER:	HERMAN ROTH, WHEEL CO.	SALES PLANS	26 75
11/29	HARVEY'S	LUNCH:	ELLEN MALONEY, HARRIS & CO.	SALES PLANS	18 65
12/11	Maguire's	DINNER:	WILLIAM CHU, EASTERN MEETING	ADVERTISING SCHEDULE	31 60
12/13	SHORE COFFEE SHOP	BKFAST:	LOU HEANING, THOMPSON'S	SPECIAL PROMOTION	10 00
12/18	MANOR HOUSE	BKFAST:	LOUISA HOREZ MATOS & CO.	RETURN PROBLEM	7 40
12/21	BEEKMAN'S	LUNCH:	JOE VISCONI NATALI BROS.	DISCOUNT REVISION	11 40

An itemized expense record.

the trip are still fresh in the executive's mind. An accurate record is essential, since an expense report must be submitted and approved periodically. Most companies require receipts for hotel and transportation accommodations and for expenditures above a specified minimum. The executive's statement is generally accepted without receipts for amounts spent on local transportation, personal meals, and tips. Such expenses are usually itemized on the expense-account forms provided by many companies.

Entertainment expenditures are usually entered on the expense-account form in the column marked "Entertainment." An explanation of each entertainment expense is also shown on a separate expense record. Itemized for each entry are the date, the name and location of the establishment, the names of the people entertained, and the business benefit derived.

Reviewing Your Reading

1. What information do you need to know before making a travel reservation for an executive?

2. What are the sources of flight information available to you when a boss's trip is being planned?

3. What precaution should be taken by a business executive who is visiting countries that do not require a passport?

4. Discuss the principle of the 24-hour clock and the way to convert 24-hour-clock time to 12-hour-clock time.

5. When applying for a passport, what items must the traveler present to an agent of a designated passport office?

6. In addition to a passport, what other papers are usually necessary for a trip abroad?

7. Explain how you would forward mail and otherwise keep your boss informed of events while he or she is traveling.

8. What receipts are usually required for preparing an expense report?

9. Explain the advantages of a credit card when an executive is traveling.

10. Discuss the advantage of a Eurailpass to the international traveler and what must be done with it before the traveler boards the first train.

11. Indicate the items you should specify when requesting hotel or motel accommodations.

12. Discuss how much detail should be included in the boss's itinerary.

USING
YOUR
SKILLS

1. Your employer has decided to accept the invitation extended in the letter shown below.

    a. List the things you must do to take care of the details.
    b. Draft a letter of acceptance to the chairperson.
    c. Draft a letter requesting a room reservation at the Royal Palms Hotel.

Dear Ms. Johnson:

The International Engineering Society has selected automation as the theme for its convention.

In view of your tremendous personal knowledge of developments in this field, the committee would like very much to have you serve as a consultant on the panel at the discussion period during the afternoon of the first day of our meeting.

The convention is to be in Chicago at the Royal Palms Hotel, June 21-23. Your panel is scheduled for 2:30 to 4:30 p.m., Monday, June 21. The moderator will be Charles T. Berry, a former associate of yours.

Please let us know at once if you can accept our invitation. Naturally, the Society will be happy to reimburse you for traveling expenses. And if you wish to stay for the entire convention period, by all means plan to do so.

Cordially,
Benjamin C. Rowe
Chairperson, Planning
Committee

2. Draft a memo to your employer describing the advantages traveler's checks offer over cash while on business trips.

3. In selecting a mode of transportation, the relative importance of such factors as expense, time, and general convenience to the traveler must be considered. On a separate piece of paper, indicate the best type of transportation for your employer to take in each of the situations below. If you do not believe the best type of transportation is shown for the situation, decide what you think it should be.

    a. The boss does not want to follow a fixed schedule: plane, auto, train, bus.
    b. The boss wants to attend a meeting Wednesday evening in a city about 400 miles from home and has appointments at home both Wednesday and Thursday mornings: bus, train, plane, auto.

    c. The boss wants to do a little work and think through some plans en route: private compartment on train; coach car seat on train; plane; bus.

    d. The boss wants to move about freely while en route: train, plane, bus.

    e. The boss wants to do some sightseeing: train, plane, bus, auto.

4. Identify the items your boss should have in hand just before departure regardless of the length of the trip, its nature, and the places to be visited.

EXERCISING YOUR JUDGMENT

Wrong Day. Paula Augustine is an easygoing sales executive. You have worked with her for several years and enjoy it. She travels a great deal to keep in touch with branch activities and to conduct product review and training sessions. With the help of the company's efficient travel service, you handle all her trip arrangements. You check out the plane and hotel reservations, arrange for transportation at the destinations (she likes to rent a car), prepare agendas and itineraries, type notes, pack her briefcase, and generally see that travel as well as training session arrangements are complete. You are quite shaken up, therefore, when she storms into your office after returning from a visit to a Northeastern plant and blames you for having goofed up her trip. It seems her ticket home was for the wrong day. She was to return late Friday afternoon, but her ticket was for a Thursday flight. Since Friday flights are usually filled, she was put on standby and had to wait at the airport for five hours before she could board a flight. Even then, she had to be routed in a roundabout way and had to change planes. Although this is Monday morning, she is still quite mad about it and says so. You, on the other hand, can feel your blood pressure rising too because this is the first real mistake you have made and it wasn't really your mistake. It was the company travel service's mistake. You should have caught it, though. What do you say or do? What is your attitude? Why?

APPLYING THE REFERENCE SECTION

The following words are frequently misspelled in business letters and memos. Select the correct spelling from the choices for each word and, on a separate sheet of paper, type one sentence containing each.

1. accomodate, accommodate

2. supercede, supersede

3. occurrence, ocurrence

4. wierd, weird

5. excel, excell

6. mischievious, mischievous

7. liaison, liason

8. facsimile, fascimile

CHAPTER TWENTY-TWO / BANKING PROCEDURES

The scope of your responsibility for performing banking activities will vary, depending upon the size and nature of the business and the preferences of your employer. In large business offices, banking and related activities are usually handled by other designated employees, and your involvement may be limited to tasks such as routing cash remittances and requesting cash disbursements. In small offices, however, you, as executive secretary, may perform many banking duties and keep a variety of financial records for your employer. Many secretaries also assist executives with their personal banking and financial record-keeping.

Whether your banking responsibilities are limited or extensive, you must perform them accurately. And since banking transactions involve privileged information, you must not overlook their importance and confidentiality.

Secretaries should understand thoroughly the services offered by banks and how to make the most effective use of them.

Checking Accounts

Business firms and individuals deposit substantial sums of money in bank accounts for safekeeping and for paying bills with checks drawn against such accounts. With a checking account, a business can maintain necessary control over all cash disbursements, since only certain persons are authorized to sign checks. A carefully written check is a safe way of transferring money.

Signature Cards Banks keep a file of signature cards for each account, which carry the signatures of all those who are authorized to sign or indorse and cash checks.

If you are to sign or cash checks for your employer, the bank must be provided with authorization to honor your signature. A corporation must provide the bank with a copy of its bylaws authorizing the account and specifying the corporate officers authorized to sign checks.

A signature card showing signatures of personnel authorized to sign or cash checks.

Deposit Tickets

A deposit ticket must be prepared for each deposit, listing each item separately. On the ticket are entered the name and address of the depositor, the amount of cash, and an itemized list of all checks. It is considered good practice to identify each check entry by the transit number of the bank on which it is drawn. The transit number is generally printed in the upper right corner of the check. A duplicate copy of the deposit ticket serves as a receipt for the amount deposited. The original is retained by the bank. It serves as the basis for an entry by the bank crediting the depositor's account. In lieu of the duplicate deposit ticket, an entry made by a bank teller in the depositor's passbook is used as a receipt for the amount deposited.

A deposit ticket.

Check with stub for calculating new balance.

The first step in making a bank deposit is to prepare the funds—coins, currency, and checks. Sort coins according to denomination and then, if there are many, count and roll them in coin wrappers supplied by the bank. Write or stamp the name of the depositor on each wrapper for identification. Small numbers of coins may be placed in envelopes on which should be written the value of the coins enclosed. Currency should be sorted by denomination, with each bill facing up and in the same direction. Banks supply special paper bands to use in wrapping bills. Write the account number on each wrapper. Group together all checks drawn on a given bank. Be sure checks and money orders are indorsed before they are deposited.

Checkbook Management

Banks furnish standard checkbooks and registers for a nominal charge or free to depositors. The depositor's name and address and specified advertising data will be printed on checks for a small fee.

Checks are detached from the checkbook as they are written and issued. Before writing the check, however, be sure that you note the information about the check on the stub attached to the check or in the separate checkbook register. This information includes the date, the payee's name, the amount, and the purpose for which the payment is being made. This record is the basis for an entry in the *cash payments journal* for each check written.

If it is your responsibility to handle the checkbook, you should know the bank balance at all times, so that you do not draw a check for an amount greater than that balance. A continuous record of the bank balance can be carried on the check stub or on a separate check register such as the one illustrated below. Note that deposits are added to the balance and checks issued are subtracted, giving the new balance.

CHECK NO.	DATE	CHECK ISSUED TO	AMOUNT OF CHECK	/	DATE OF DEPOSIT	AMOUNT OF DEPOSIT	BALANCE
							12,895 00
198	5/5	Smith & Larson	110 00				12,785 00
					5/7	340 00	13,125 00
199	5/8	Mendoza Shipping Co.	85 75				13,539 25
200	"	Lafarge Manufacturing Co.	297 40				13,241 85
201	"	Delima, Rosa & Cooper	811 00				12,430 85
					5/9	1260 00	13,690 85

A separate checkbook register.

Enter into the check register or the cash payments journal all noncheck payments, such as bank charges and notes payable charged against the account when they fall due. For account balances that fall under a predetermined amount, some banks levy a monthly service charge for accepting and recording deposits, clearing checks deposited, and handling and recording checks. Other bank charges to be debited in the check register include charges for collecting notes and drafts, for writing drafts or cashier's checks, and for handling checks returned by the bank because of insufficient funds in the account of the issuer.

Notes receivable collected by the bank or the proceeds of bank loans (credits other than regular deposits) must be added to the register or cash receipts journal.

A check is a common form of negotiable instrument. It is drawn on a bank by the depositor, who has an account with the bank, to the order of a specified person, or to the bearer. When a check is properly drawn against a credit balance and presented by the person or the company to whose order the check is drawn, the bank must pay the amount. If the maker of a check fails to exercise reasonable care in writing a check, he or she can be held responsible for any financial loss that results. For this reason, it is important to follow these guidelines when typing or writing a check:

1. Bring the checkbook balance up to date on the stub to make sure sufficient funds are in the account to cover the check. The check stub provides space to list the main elements of each check transaction. It not only serves as a record of the check once the check is detached; it is also a source document containing the data needed to post the transaction to an accounting record.
2. Number checks consecutively (unless prenumbered by the bank). The number on the stub must agree with that on the corresponding check.
3. Enter the date on which the check is being drawn. Checks may be dated on Sundays and holidays. "Postdating" a check is permissible but risky. If sufficient funds are not in the bank when the check is written, the payee may cash the check before the depositor can deposit the needed funds. Before the deposit is credited to the account, an overdraft may result. For a check to be returned by the bank to the payee is not only embarrassing to the drawer but a reflection on the financial soundness of the business.
4. On the proper line, enter the payee's name in full, without a title such as Ms., Mr., Dr., or Mrs. To protect against alteration of the name, begin writing at the extreme left and following the name, draw a line from the name to the dollar sign at the right.
5. Write the amount of the check in figures in the space provided following the payee's name. Place the figures close to the dollar sign and close to each other.
6. Write the amount of the check in words. Start at the extreme left of the line so that no additional words can be inserted to increase the amount. This is important since the bank may honor the amount in words if it differs from the amount in figures. Separate the cents amount from the dollar amount by the word *and* and write the cents as a fraction ($\frac{75}{100}$ if written; 75/100 if typewrit-

ten). Fill in the unused space with a line or with dashes. On checks for less than a dollar the figures following the dollar sign should be circled. The word *only* should be written before the amount in words, and the word *cents* should follow, as for example, "Only Seventy-Five Cents." The printed word *dollars* should be crossed out.

7. The purpose of the check payment may be written on the check itself, if space permits.

8. No alterations are permitted in a check. If an error is made in writing a check, mark both the check and the stub "Void." The check thus voided should be filed with the canceled checks so that it is evident that the voided check was not cashed and it is with all the other checks for auditing purposes. Keep checkbooks in a secure place, away from the reach or sight of unauthorized persons.

Voucher Checks.   In addition to the conventional checkbooks and check forms supplied by banks, many business offices make use of printed voucher checks. These are usually unbound and come in assembled packs, with space for itemizing each element in the check transaction. The top portion of the perforated two-part pack is the check itself. Below the perforation is a form on which the details of the payment are written. This form of voucher check does not require a check stub. A copy from the pack is retained as a record of the transaction. Additional copies are often distributed to designated control and accounting centers in the company.

Voucher checks record the details of the transaction.

Check Identification

Banks identify the accounts and checks of depositors by means of account numbers, magnetic ink character recognition (MICR), and check numbers.

Account Numbers.   The account of each depositor is identified by an account number, which appears on all checks and deposit slips supplied by the bank. In the event that the account number is not preprinted, the depositor is expected to record it on the check or deposit ticket before presenting it to a bank clerk.

Transit Numbers.   The fractional number in the upper right corner of a check is the transit number assigned to a bank by the American Bankers Association (ABA). The two top ABA numbers designate the city or state in which the bank is located, followed by the number assigned to that bank. The number below the division line designates the Federal Reserve District, the branch in the district, and the number of days required to clear the check.

Magnetic Ink Numbers.   The American Bankers Association has adopted a system of magnetic ink character recognition (MICR) numbers that are pre-printed in the bottom left corner of all checks. Used in the electronic processing of checks, these characters identify both the bank's transit number and the depositor's account number. When a check is deposited, the date and the amount of the check are recorded in magnetic ink below the MICR numbers. Optical character recognition (OCR) equipment is then used to sort the checks according to issuing banks and to post withdrawals to depositors' accounts.

Stop-Payment Orders

Occasionally, after a check has been drawn and presented to a payee, it becomes necessary to prevent its being cashed. To stop payment on a check, call the bank, and give the name of the drawer of the check, the date and amount, and the name of the payee, and request that the bank stop payment. Confirm this verbal order in writing. Some banks ask the depositor to use a stop-payment form; others accept a confirming letter. In any case, the banks charge a fee for a stop-payment order. Of course, the stop-payment notification must reach the bank on which the check was drawn before the check has been honored. When payment is stopped on a check, write "Stopped Payment" across the stub.

Check Indorsements

Checks and money orders should be indorsed by the payee—that is, the person or company the check is made out to—before they are deposited in a bank. To indorse a check, the payee or the payee's authorized agent writes, types, or stamps his or her name or other pertinent matter on the back of the check.

If the indorser's name appears incorrectly on the face of the check, it should be indorsed twice—first as it appears on the face of the check, and then exactly as it appears on the account signature card. Offices that receive and process large numbers of checks use a rubber stamp or a machine to indorse checks. Three kinds of indorsements are commonly used in business offices: blank, restrictive, and full.

Blank Indorsement.   The most common way of indorsing a check is simply to sign one's name on the back of the check. This is known as a *blank indorsement*.

A check indorsed in blank is payable to the bearer; hence, anyone who has possession of the check can cash it. For this reason a blank indorsement should be used only when the bearer is at the bank and is depositing or cashing the check.

Restrictive Indorsement.   A *restrictive indorsement* is one in which, besides the company name or the indorser's signature, words have been added, such as "For deposit only," which restrict the further indorsement of the check. When deposits are sent to the bank by messenger or by mail, the restrictive indorsement should be used on the accompanying checks. Such checks cannot be used for any purpose other than the one stated.

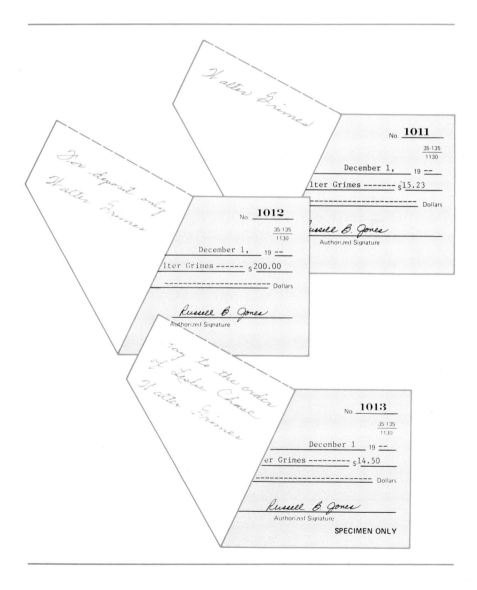

Top to bottom: blank indorsement, restrictive indorsement, and full indorsement.

Full Indorsement. When a check is to be mailed or otherwise transferred to another person or company, the *full indorsement*—sometimes called a special indorsement—should be used. The bearer writes "Pay to the order of," followed by the name of a specified person or company, and signs his or her name. When indorsed in this manner, the check can be cashed only by the payee specified, who must indorse it again before it can be processed further.

Banking by Mail

You can save time by making bank deposits by mail. Banks provide special mail-deposit tickets and envelopes with preprinted account numbers or with space to record them. Indorse the checks "For deposit only" or "For deposit and credit to the account of the depositor [plus account number]" and mail them to the bank along with the itemized deposit ticket. By return mail, the bank sends the depositor a receipt and a replacement mail-deposit ticket and envelope.

After-Hours Deposits

A depositor who receives funds after banking hours may make use of the after-hours depository service of a bank. The deposit is placed into an envelope and dropped through a slot located on the outside of the bank. This can be done at any time when the bank is closed. The following morning the bag under the slot is unlocked by a bank teller, who processes the deposit. The depositor can return to the bank during banking hours to pick up a replacement envelope and a deposit receipt. If the depositor prefers, deposit envelopes will be held unopened until the depositor can get to the bank personally to make the deposit.

Automated Teller Service

A recent innovation in banking services is the 24-hour deposit and cash with-drawal machine. These automated terminals are found in airports, train stations, shopping centers, and supermarkets as well as in banks, as a convenient and fast service to depositors.

Depositors are issued a debit card and a private code number. With the card and the code number the depositor has access to his or her computerized bank account at the automated teller terminal. To make a deposit, the depositor simply

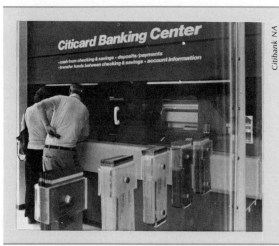

Automated banking terminals enable customers to make deposits or withdrawals at any hour of the day or night.

inserts the debit card into the machine, punches out the code number, places the deposit and deposit ticket into the appropriate slot, and receives a printed record of the transaction. Withdrawals are handled in a similar manner.

Bank Balance Statements Once a month the bank mails each depositor a statement of the account, together with the canceled checks that have been debited from the depositor's account during the month. The statement lists the date and amount of each

THE INDUSTRIAL BANK
Chicago, Illinois 60612

ACCOUNT NUMBER X602-V6048   PERIOD ENDING   11/30/--

Checks	Checks	Deposits	Date	Balance
			11/1	7,311.00
		1,835.00	11/3	9,146.00
600.00			11/5	8,546.00
1,000.00			11/6	7,546.00
400.00			11/9	7,146.00
		600.00	11/11	7,746.00
		1,100.00	11/17	8,846.00
25.00 RI			11/20	8,821.00
300.80			11/29	8,520.20
65.00	4.00 DM		11/30	8,451.20
2.20 SC	497.20	994.20		8,946.00

Beginning Balance	Total Amount of Deposits	Total Amount of Checks Paid	Total Charges	Ending Balance
7,311.00	4,529.20	2,863.00	31.20	8,946.00

Number of Deposits Made	Number of Checks Paid	Number of Other Charges
4	6	3

Codes: CC Certified Check   OD Overdrawn
       DM Debit Memorandum   RI Returned Item
       EC Error Correction   SC Service Charge

Please examine this statement upon receipt and report at once if you find any difference. If no error is reported in ten days, the account will be considered correct. All items are subject to final payment.

A monthly bank statement.

deposit and withdrawal, as well as other items such as service charges, interest credit, and corrections. The balance on the statement and the bank balance in the checkbook stub or register may not agree, and each month the two balances must be reconciled.

Reconciliation Procedure.   It is not difficult to determine why a balance shown in the checkbook differs from that shown on the statement of account. Most banks print a form, such as the one illustrated here, on the reverse side of the depositor's monthly statement. Whether you use the form provided by the bank or another of your choosing, the steps involved in reconciliation are the same:

- Enter on the check stubs and subtract from the checkbook balance any charges and fees appearing on the bank statement. The resulting figure is the *adjusted checkbook balance.*
- On the reconciliation statement record the balance shown as the last figure on the bank statement.
- Compare the amounts of the deposits listed on the bank statement with the amounts of the deposits listed on the check stubs.
- List all deposits in transit—that is, deposits made since the last entry on the bank statement. These have been added on the checkbook stub but do not yet appear on the bank statement.
- Add the total of deposits in transit to the balance taken from the bank statement.
- Compare the amount on each canceled check and any other debit item with the amount listed on the bank statement. Since checks are returned in the order in which they appear on the statement, this step can be completed quickly.

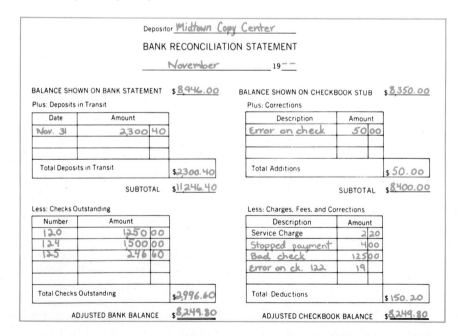

Most banks supply printed forms to help customers reconcile checkbook balances with bank statements.

- Arrange the canceled checks in numerical order.
- Compare each canceled check with the corresponding stub in the checkbook. If the check amount agrees with the stub amount, circle the stub check number to indicate that the check has been paid and is not outstanding.
- List the numbers and the amounts of all checks that are not circled on the stubs. Be sure to include outstanding checks from previous reconciliation statements that still have not been returned.
- From the previous total subtract the total amount of checks outstanding. The resulting figure is the *adjusted bank balance*. The balance shown on the bank statement has now been adjusted by adding any deposits made but not yet recorded and by subtracting any checks issued but not yet paid. Thus, the adjusted bank balance shows the true balance.

The adjusted checkbook balance indicates the actual balance in the account and should be identical with the adjusted bank balance, which also represents the true balance of the account. If the figures agree, the balances are reconciled. If they do not agree, all the details must be rechecked until the error is located.

Balance Differences.   When the adjusted balances for the statement of account and the stub register of the checkbook do not agree, the difference is probably due to one or more of the following reasons:

- A check was omitted in the reconciliation, or one or more of the cleared or outstanding checks were written without a stub record.
- A deposit was omitted in the checkbook stub register. Cross-check the deposits shown on the statement of account with those in the register.
- A deposit sent by mail or left in a night depository was unrecorded in the statement of account.
- A check was drawn for a different sum than that recorded in the stub register.
- There is an arithmetic error in the statement of account or, more likely, in the stub register. Look for a transposition of figures, or an error made when figuring balances in the stub register.

When an error is located, mark the position in the stub register where the error occurred with a reference to the stub number where the correction is made. Enter the correction following the last stub entry, together with a cross-reference to the stub number where the error occurred. Following the last entry in the stub register covered by the statement of account, write "Reconciliation, [date]."

Bank Services   Banks offer many services that may be utilized by your employer. Some of these services are listed below.

Safe-Deposit Boxes.   Executives often need space in a bank's vault for the safekeeping of valuable documents such as contracts, insurance policies, commercial papers, and other items of value. To satisfy such requirements, banks rent *safe-deposit boxes*. These are metal boxes that are locked, by means of two keys, into compartments in the bank's safe-deposit vault. One key is given to the customer and one is retained by the bank.

To gain access to a safe-deposit box, the customer must first register to establish identity. A bank employee then accompanies the customer to the box and opens one of the locks with the bank key and the second lock with the customer's key. The customer carries the box to a private room or booth to inspect or remove items contained in the box or add additional ones.

Certified Checks.   Certain business transactions such as property settlements and large purchases require the guarantee of the person making out the check that sufficient funds are available in the drawer's account to pay the check when it is presented. In such an instance, the business executive writes a personal or company check which you deliver to the bank. A bank officer determines whether there are sufficient funds in the drawer's account to meet payment of the check. If there are, the bank officer immediately charges the account with the amount of the check, writes or stamps "Certified" on the face of the check, and adds an official signature. The drawer of the *certified check* cannot stop payment, and the check will be paid without delay when presented.

Cashier's Checks.   A check drawn by a bank on its own funds and signed by a bank officer is known as a *cashier's check* or *official check*. Anyone can request a cashier's check by paying the bank the amount of the check plus a service charge. Cashier's checks are recommended for transferring large amounts of money. By having these checks made payable to the purchaser of the check, who must then indorse it to the payee, you establish proof of payment.

Bank Drafts.   A bank draft is a check drawn by the bank on another bank in the same or another city in which it has funds on deposit or credit. This form of check is useful when a business executive wishes to transfer a sum of money to another person or company in a distant location.

You can obtain a bank draft for an employer by presenting a personal or company check made payable to the bank for the desired amount. The bank will issue the draft made payable to the specified person or company. The recipient of the draft can then be certain that sufficient funds are available before taking an action such as releasing a shipment of merchandise or beginning work on a contract.

Promise Instruments

Your banking activities may involve handling promise-to-pay instruments such as notes, drafts, and certificates of deposit. They are negotiable and can be transferred to someone else.

Notes   Notes are instruments whereby a person (known as the maker) promises to pay to the order of a second person (called the payee, or bearer) a stated sum of money on demand, sometimes in instalments and sometimes at a stated future date. A note that carries on its face only the promise of the maker is limited to personal

$1,500.00 _____   March 7 *19 --*

Sixty days _____ *after date* I *promise to pay to*

the order of Harriet Kruger--

One Thousand Five Hundred and 00/100------------------------------*Dollars*

at Crestfield National Bank---

Value received with 8% interest   George Markori, Inc.

No. 17   *Due* May 6, 19--   *George Markori*

A promissory note.

security and is known as a promissory note. The personal promise of the maker is often supported by property as collateral security. The payee may require the participation of another person, such as a cosigner or an accommodation party. Notes are often secured by personal property in the form of stock certificates, bonds, and other notes, temporarily placed in control of the payee.

Promissory Notes.   A demand note that carries interest at a stated rate until the amount is paid is a promissory note in its simplest form.

A promissory note may also take the form of a time note, payable at a fixed time following the date of issue, at a stated interest rate. Another type of note is the discount note, which requires the repayment of the amount borrowed plus the interest payable to maturity.

Collateral Notes.   A collateral note is a demand or time note that is secured by the pledge of personal property in the form of a mortgage, another note, a contract, a bank account passbook, or a bill of lading. The collateral is placed with the holder (payee) as security that the note will be paid at maturity. The note gives the payee the right to dispose of the collateral if the maker fails to pay the full amount when it falls due.

Instalment Notes.   An instalment note is an ordinary note in which the principal is payable in a series of payments at specified times, together with interest on the unpaid balance, until the note is paid in full. It contains an acceleration provision, which permits the payee or holder to demand the principal amount and interest immediately upon default by the maker in the payment of any instalment.

Certificate of Deposit   Certificates of deposit are promissory notes issued by banks to depositors. The instrument is payable to the order of the depositor on demand or at a fixed date, and usually with interest. It is, in effect, a negotiable instrument against which checks may not be drawn. Special funds are often deposited in this manner.

Commercial Drafts

A draft is an order instrument through which the drawer or creditor orders the drawee or debtor to pay money to a third party, the payee. Drafts may be either *time*, payable at a specified future date, or *sight*, payable immediately upon presentation of the draft to the payee.

Time Drafts.   A time draft is generally used when a manufacturer is shipping goods to a distributor who requires credit at the time of purchase. Upon receiving a signed acceptance of the debt from the customer, the seller may convert the draft into cash by means of discounting. This means that the seller sells the draft to a bank for its value, less interest and risk charges.

Sight Drafts.   A sight draft is a written order on the drawee to pay on demand the amount named on the draft. It is payable on presentation to the drawee. This instrument is commonly used in connection with c.o.d. shipments, in which case the draft, attached to the bill of lading (receipt from the transportation company for the goods) is sent by the seller's bank to the buyer's bank, where it is presented to the purchaser for payment. The purchaser cannot secure the merchandise until the draft is paid and the bill of lading secured. Drafts of this kind contain no legal obligation until they are accepted by the named drawee.

Trade Acceptances.   A trade acceptance is a draft or bill of exchange drawn by the seller on the purchase of merchandise and accepted by the purchaser. As a rule, the seller of merchandise sends the bill of exchange to the buyer, together with an invoice of the goods sold. The buyer accepts the bill by signing the instrument on its face. The bill, thus signed and accepted, is returned to the seller, who then must ship the merchandise. The seller may discount the trade acceptance at the bank if money is needed immediately.

Electronic Fund Transfer

A new development introduced by the banking community is the electronic fund transfer (EFT) system, which permits a depositor to transfer funds from one account to another without the use of commercial paper or the services of bank personnel.

In some areas the employee's net pay is deposited directly into the employee's bank electronically by means of magnetic tape. This procedure eliminates the need to write employee paychecks. Social security payments are also being made by direct deposit to the bank accounts of those who authorize it.

Routine payments of property taxes, insurance premiums, utility bills, and mortgage payments are also being made by automatic withdrawal from bank customers' checking accounts. Monthly bills are sent to the customer's bank for payment, and the amount is simply subtracted from the depositor's account.

Petty Cash Fund

As an executive secretary you may be responsible for the office petty cash fund. The purpose of a petty cash fund is to allow small payments to be made in cash rather than by check and to provide control over such payments. Typical cash payments are for postage, taxi fares, and incidental office supplies.

PETTY CASH VOUCHER				
CLIENT *Harris Shelf Co*			DATE *1/9/--*	
SHORT TITLE *Bookshelves*			ACCT. NO. *H-4281*	
DETAILS		TELEPHONE	*1*	*90*
Rush delivery of		REPRODUCTION	*4*	*80*
state of plans.		POSTAGE		
Paid photostater		MEALS		
for call and		LOCAL TRANSP.		
confirming		TRAVEL		
wire.		TELEGRAM	*3*	*40*
		OTHER (SPECIFY)		
		TOTAL	*10*	*10*
YOUR SIGNATURE *Joseph Winters*		APPROVED BY *Mary O'Leary*		

When the petty cash fund is set up, a check is written to "Petty Cash" for a specified amount, such as $25. The check is cashed and the currency placed in a drawer or box to be used in making small payments. Expenditures from the fund are carefully controlled, and a record is required for each one. When the fund runs low, it is replenished.

Petty Cash Vouchers

The basic form for control of petty cash is the *petty cash voucher*. This form provides space to record a number, the date, the amount paid, the purpose, and to whom payment is made.

Completing the voucher usually requires two signatures or sets of initials— that of the person authorizing payment, and that of the person receiving payment. When the fund is properly managed, the cash and vouchers on hand total the amount of petty cash provided.

Petty Cash Record

The petty cash record is frequently kept in a standard cash book. Columns are provided for dates, amounts received and expended, and an explanation of expenditures. By adding another column, it is possible to keep a cumulative balance so that you always know the amount in the fund without having to add up the list of expenditures. By including still more columns, you can show the distribution of expenditures so that totals for each particular account may be readily determined.

The petty cash record can be kept in a book or on a distribution sheet, with the cash and the vouchers kept in a locked box. A convenient type of petty cash record consists of a large manila envelope, with the record on the front. The envelope itself serves as a repository for receipts and receipted bills as well as for

PETTY CASH FUND		DATE	EXPLANATION	DISTRIBUTION OF PAYMENTS			
RECEIVED	PAID OUT			ADVERTISING EXPENSE	DONATIONS EXPENSE	MISC. EXPENSES	SUPPLIES EXPENSE
25 00		June 1	To establish fund, check 317				
	6 26	2	Stamps			6 26	
	1 75	2	Messenger service		1 75		
	1 28	4	Felt pens			1 28	
	2 17	8	Express charges	2 17			
	3 30	12	Mailgram				3 30
	2 25	15	Taxi				2 25
	1 10	16	Messenger service		1 10		
	68	17	Postage due	68			
	1 29	20	Stamp pads			1 29	
25 00	20 08		Totals	2 85	2 85	8 83	5 55
	4 92	21	Cash on hand				
25 00	25 00						
4 92		21	Cash on hand				
20 08		21	To replenish fund, check 339				

the cash. This form is especially useful when the petty cash fund is replenished at regular intervals, regardless of the balance on hand. Each envelope represents a definite period, and because the fund is set at a high enough figure so that there is little danger of its running out, there is no need to keep a cumulative balance opposite each item. Whatever type of record is used, the fund and the record should be kept securely in a locked file or desk when not being used.

Part of a petty cash record is shown above.

Replenishment of Petty Cash Fund

When the petty cash fund has been depleted below a predetermined amount, reimbursement is obtained for the amount spent, which will restore the fund to its original amount. Since replenishment covers the exact amount of the expenditures, it is in the nature of a payment for those expenses, and the fund itself is fully restored. If no minimum has been set, you must rely on a judgment of continuing demands on the fund so as not to allow it to become so low that it will be entirely depleted before new funds can be obtained. Sometimes a petty cash fund is replenished at regular intervals, such as weekly or monthly, regardless of the amount of expenditures in the interval.

When replenishment is determined by a depletion minimum or by judgment, the secretary reconciles the petty cash account and arranges for the fund to be replenished.

Follow these steps when reconciling the petty cash account:

- Total the payments according to the vouchers and receipts and enter the total in the petty cash record book.
- Count the cash on hand.
- Check that the total payments plus the cash on hand equals the amount established for the fund.
- Prepare a cash disbursement check for the amount equaling the payments to replenish the fund.
- Cash the check and add the money to the cash fund.

Bank Charges

Much of a bank's income comes from the interest it charges business firms and other customers on money borrowed from the bank. The interest charge depends on the length of time the money is borrowed and the amount.

Interest   When a business executive borrows money, there is a legal obligation to pay interest and to repay the loan. The interest rate is expressed as a percent, such as *12%*. This means that the borrower must pay $12 for each $100 borrowed for a period of one year.

Interest is ordinarily computed on the basis of a 360-day year divided into 12 months of 30 days each. When the time for which interest is to be computed is less than a year, that time is determined in days by figuring its fractional part of 360. The formula or cancellation method used to find the interest is:

$$\text{Interest} = \text{Principal} \times \frac{\text{Rate}}{100} \times \frac{\text{Time}}{360}$$

To find the interest on a $2,800 loan for 90 days at 12 percent, you would make this calculation:

$$\text{Interest} = \$2,800 \times \frac{12}{100} \times \frac{90}{360} = \$84$$

When the banker's year (360 days) is used and the time is given in months, divide the number of months by 12.

The 6 Percent/60-Day Method.   To find the interest on any amount for 60 days at 6 percent, move the decimal point in the principal two places to the left. To figure the interest *on any amount at 6 percent* for *any number of days*, proceed in the following manner:

1. Figure the interest at 6 percent for 60 days.
2. Divide the time in days into sixties and fractions of sixty.
3. Determine interest for each time division by taking the same part of the interest as was taken of the time.
4. Add the interest sums found for the several time divisions to determine the total interest.

The following illustration shows the procedure for figuring the interest on $4,500 for 96 days at 6 percent.

60 days at 6%	$4,500.00 = $45.00
30 days at 6%	1/2 × $45 = 22.50
6 days at 6%	1/10 × $45 = 4.50
(96 days)	Interest = $72.00

Adjusting the 6 Percent/60-Day Method.   To use the 60-day method for rates other than 6 percent, figure the interest on a 6 percent basis and then adjust to the desired rate. Here is an example:

Interest on $775 at 7% for 111 days

$$
\begin{aligned}
\$7.75 &= \text{60 days' interest at 6\% on \$775} \\
3.875 &= \text{30 days' interest at 6\% on \$775} \\
1.937 &= \text{15 days' interest at 6\% on \$775} \\
.775 &= \text{\ \ 6 days' interest at 6\% on \$775} \\
\hline
\$14.337 &= \text{111 days' interest at 6\% on \$775}
\end{aligned}
$$

Convert to the desired rate by using the appropriate fraction to increase or decrease the 6 percent base. For example, 7 percent is 7/6 of 6 percent, or 6 percent plus 1/6. Thus,

$$
\begin{aligned}
\$14.337 &= \text{111 days' interest at 6\% on \$775} \\
+\quad 2.389 &= \text{111 days' interest at 1\% on \$775} \\
\hline
\$16.726 &= \text{111 days' interest at 7\% on \$775}
\end{aligned}
$$

Discounted Notes

A business executive who borrows money from a bank for a short term must sign a note on which the bank collects interest in advance for the term of the note. The interest is referred to as *bank discount*. A promissory note accepted in a business transaction may also be discounted by the holder of the note if cash is needed prior to the maturity date.

At the time the note is discounted, the bank deducts a sum from the amount that is due on the note at maturity. This sum is equal to the interest on the maturity value from the day the note is discounted to the date of maturity.

When a note is discounted at the bank, it is necessary to find the date of maturity and the term of discount in order to determine the amount of bank discount.

Date of Maturity.   To find the date of maturity, count forward from the date of the note the exact number of days, months, or years, after which date the note is to be paid. To find the date of maturity of a 60-day note dated August 27, count forward as follows:

Aug. 28 to Aug. 31	4 days
Sept. 1 to Sept. 30	30 days
Oct. 1 to Oct. 26	26 days
	60 days

60 days from Aug. 27 = Oct. 26, date of maturity

Term of Discount.   The number of days from the day the bank discounts a note to the day a note becomes due is known as the *term of discount*. To find the term of discount, find the date of maturity and the exact number of days from the discount date to the date of maturity. In making this calculation, do not count the first day (discount date), but do count the last day (the date of maturity). To find the term of discount of a 90-day note dated September 8 and discounted October 30, follow these two steps:

1. Date of maturity: 90 days from Sept. 8 = Dec. 7
2. Term of discount: Number of days from Oct. 30 (discount date) to Dec. 7 (due date):

> From Oct. 30 to Oct. 31 =   1 day (excluding Oct. 30)
> From Nov. 1 to Nov. 30 = 30 days
> To Dec. 7   = <u> 7 days</u> (including Dec. 7)
> 38 days, term of discount

Proceeds of an Interest-Bearing Note.   To find the proceeds of an interest-bearing note, first find the date of maturity and the term of discount. Then find the bank discount by figuring the interest on the face of the note for the term of discount at the discount rate. To find the proceeds, subtract the bank discount from the value of the note at maturity. The due-date value of the note is used as a basis for figuring the bank discount and, when applicable, the collection charge.

The following illustrates the procedure for finding the proceeds of a three-month 5 percent note to be discounted at 6 percent on February 18.

1. Face of note: $1,750.00

2. Interest on note:

> $17.50 (6% for 60 days)
> <u> 8.75</u> (6% for 30 days)
> 26.25
> <u>− 4.375</u> (90 days' interest at 1% on $1,750)
> $21.875 = interest at 5% for 90 days on $1,750

3. Interest on note: <u> 21.88</u>

4. Value at maturity: $1,771.88

5. Date of maturity:

> (3 months from Dec. 18) = Mar. 18

6. Term of discount:

> (Number of days from Feb. 18, date of discount, to Mar. 18, date of maturity)
>
> | | |
> |---|---:|
> | From Feb. 18: | 10 days |
> | To Mar. 18: | <u>18 days</u> |
> | Term of discount: | 28 days |

7. Bank discount:

$17.718   (interest at 6% for 60 days on $1,771.88)
$ 5.906   (interest at 6% for 20 days)
  1.771   (interest at 6% for 6 days)
  0.590   (interest at 6% for 2 days)
$ 8.267 = interest at 6% for 28 days on $1,771.88 =   8.27

8. Proceeds: $1,763.61

REVIEWING
YOUR
READING

1. Cite the advantages of using a checking account for making cash disbursements rather than making payments in cash.

2. Explain the purpose of the check stub or checkbook register in the management of a checking account.

3. Describe the reasonable precautions that should be taken when writing the amount of a check in figures and in words.

4. Identify the significance of the preprinted transit numbers in the upper-right corner of a check and the magnetic ink numbers in the bottom-left corner.

5. Explain the recommended procedure for requesting that a bank stop payment on a check that has been mailed.

6. Describe a voucher check and indicate why voucher checks are preferred over regular checks by many companies.

7. Explain why a payee would request payment in the form of a certified check rather than a regular check.

8. Discuss the significance of check indorsement and the reason why a secretary must exercise caution when processing checks with blank indorsements for bank deposit.

9. Discuss the principle involved in verifying the balance between the adjusted bank balance and the adjusted checkbook balance when reconciling a checking account.

10. Discuss four reasons why the adjusted bank balance and the adjusted checkbook balance might not agree after the reconciliation has been completed.

11. Explain the procedure followed to gain access to a safe-deposit box.

12. Explain the nature of each instrument used and the relationship of the parties involved when promissory notes and commercial drafts are negotiated.

13. Discuss the concept of electronic fund transfer and give examples of transactions that are often handled in this manner.

14. Describe the items of information that should be included on a petty cash voucher.

15. Explain the procedure to be followed to replenish a petty cash fund.

USING
YOUR
Skills

1. You are employed by Install, Inc., and receive checks payable to their order from time to time. It is your responsibility to process these checks for deposit to Account 28-41662 at the Liberty National Bank. Indicate the indorsement you would use on these checks, given the following conditions:
   a. The checks are to be mailed to the bank for deposit.
   b. Several of the checks are to be used in payment for services rendered by A & M Pump Company, Inc.
   c. An after-hours bank deposit must be made.
   d. You are depositing checks without indorsement, but one of the checks is from an insurance company in settlement of a claim.
   e. You have been asked to compose an appropriate rubber-stamp indorsement for check deposits.

2. You are about to reconcile a company checkbook balance and a monthly bank statement. The following facts are known: Bank balance, $4,525.10; checks outstanding, #137, $114.69; #141, $22.50; #143, $107.25; uncredited deposit, $179.69; bank service charge, $9.08; check stub balance, $4,469.43. Prepare the reconciliation statement.

3. Your employer holds a $3,500, 120-day, 9 percent promissory note dated February 10 that was accepted in a business transaction. You have been asked to figure the term of discount if the note is presented to the bank for cash on March 12.

4. Find the proceeds of the note in the previous problem if the note is to be discounted by the bank at 10 percent on March 12.

EXERCISING
YOUR
JUDGMENT

The Evening Course. Your employer is a member of a distinguished family in your area, and the proprietor of Nexus Microwave. You have been employed as his administrative and personal assistant for two years. Having had several accounting courses, you have been given the responsibility for managing many of his personal affairs. You keep the records for his investments and for his hobby—the breeding of horses. You maintain expense records on a private plane, a townhouse, and family estate properties. You have a power of attorney and you issue paychecks to employees who maintain your employer's personal properties. You also pay taxes, insurance premiums, utility bills, and general expenses.

You realize that the recordkeeping system in use could be simplified and to some extent automated. You would like to try a punched-card payroll accounting system in which all data required to prepare payroll records and reports would be entered on punched cards. But before approaching your employer, you need to brush up on your knowledge.

In order to keep up to date about processing data by the punched-card system, you take an evening course at the local college in punched-card and integrated data processing systems. What do you do after completing the course? How do you present your recommendations to your employer? What consideration should you give to those affected by the new procedures?

Each of the sentence groups below poses a problem in grammar. On a separate sheet of paper, type each sentence correctly according to the instructions given.

1. **Conjunctions.** A conjunction links words, phrases, clauses, or sentences. Coordinating conjunctions link items of equal rank (*and, or, but, for, so, yet*); subordinating conjunctions introduce subordinate items (*when, though, so that, where*); correlative conjunctions are used in pairs (*not only . . . but also, either . . . or, both . . . and*). Retype the following sentences correctly:

   a. Jessica is neither fast or thorough in her work.

   b. So we will have a holiday Friday, all work must be finished Thursday afternoon.

   c. She is not required to attend meetings, nor bring an excuse when she is absent.

   d. The book was on the top shelf that was hard to reach.

2. **Prepositions.** Prepositions, such as *at, as, of, about, between, from, among, in, into, on, upon,* and *beside,* are easily misused. Retype any of the following sentences that need changing.

   a. Could we divide the expense between the cost centers in our department?

   b. We were so pleased, we could not help and laugh.

   c. Where are you going to send that letter to?

   d. He stood in the doorway, then walked in the room hesitantly.

3. **Pronouns.** The nominative-case forms of the personal pronouns are *I, we, you, he, she,* and *they*. The objective-case forms are *me, us, you, him,* and *them*. For each of the following sentences, identify the pronoun that correctly completes the sentence.

   a. Did you ask Henderson and (them, they) to meet us at three?

   b. Those four people and (him, he) work for our company.

   c. No one saw Hanson and (I, me) depart for the airport.

   d. This is (she, her).

CHAPTER TWENTY-THREE / Office Finance

Understanding basic facts about office finance can give you a clearer view of what business is all about and a more realistic understanding of a secretary's administrative role. The status of an employer's business financial affairs can and often does affect a secretary as well as other office employees. For example, if an investment fails, the employer might begin to look for ways to economize. If a major account is lost, a planned expansion may be canceled. And when an economic recession occurs, pay increases may be reduced or eliminated.

The financial practices and accounts of a business are influenced by the size and nature of its business transactions. Large or small, however, every business must plan and budget to stretch its resources. Cash income must be invested so that it earns money.

To learn more about business finance—forecasting, earnings projections, markets, investments, and the like—you would do well to start reading the financial section of your local newspaper. A paper such as the *Wall Street Journal* gives full coverage of business and financial community news. Subscribe to or seek out a library copy of a business magazine such as *Business Week*, *Forbes*, or *Fortune*. You will see from reading them that there are many forms of assets (that is, things a business possesses that are of value and that must be utilized effectively). Investors and bankers measure the worth of a business by the size of its assets. A business's net sales are also used as a measure of its worth, and so is the number of persons employed.

Financial Reports

When you try to gauge the vitality of a business, you might first wonder, "How much is it worth?" Then you might ask, "How much is it earning or losing?" The first question is answered by the balance sheet; the second, by the income statement. The first tells where the business is; the second, where it is going.

The Balance Sheet

To find out what a business is worth, financial analysts consider all its assets. These include everything the business owns and anything that is owed to it. Then the *liabilities*—that is, everything the business owes to others—are listed. The difference, or balance, is the *net worth* of the business. The sheet on which these figures are listed is referred to as the *balance sheet*, or statement of financial condition.

Note that, as shown in the illustration, a balance sheet represents the situation as it stood on one particular day, here December 31, 19—. The illustrated balance sheet shows assets first, followed by liabilities and *stockholders' equity* (the amount of the interest in the business for which the business is accountable to its stockholders or owners). Assets are always in balance with liabilities plus stockholders' equity. In the assets column you will find listed all the goods and property owned as well as claims against others yet to be collected. Under liabilities are listed all the debts owed.

```
                    CONSOLIDATED TELECOMMUNICATIONS, INC.
                              Balance Sheet
                             December 31, 19--

     ASSETS
     Current Assets:
       Cash                                                  $16,039.00
       Accounts Receivable                       $32,465.00
         Less:  Allowance for Bad Debts              756.45   31,708.55
       Inventories:
         Raw Materials                           $13,000.00
         Work in Process                          10,500.00
         Finished Goods                           20,700.00   44,200.00
       Prepaid Insurance                                       1,525.00
       Supplies on Hand                                          125.00
           Total Current Assets                                            $ 93,597.55
     Fixed Assets:
       Land                                                  $ 5,200.00
       Plant and Equipment                       $41,500.00
         Less:  Allowance for Depreciation        10,560.00   30,940.00
           Total Fixed Assets                                                36,140.00
             Total Assets                                                  $129,737.55


     LIABILITIES
     Current Liabilities:
       Accounts Payable                                      $15,245.00
       Wages Payable                                            450.00
       Payroll Taxes Payable                                  1,190.00
       Income Taxes Payable                                   7,000.00
           Total Liabilities                                                23,885.00


     STOCKHOLDERS' EQUITY
     Capital Stock                                           $60,000.00
     Retained Earnings                                        45,852.55
         Total Stockholders' Equity                                        105,852.55
           Total Liabilities and Stockholders' Equity                      $129,737.55
```

Current Assets.   In general, current assets include cash and those assets that will be converted into cash in the normal course of business, usually within a year from the date of the balance sheet.

Cash is money on deposit in the bank or invested in stocks, bonds, and government securities. *Accounts receivable* represent amounts not yet collected from customers to whom goods were shipped or services rendered prior to payment. Customers are usually given 30 to 90 days in which to pay. Since some customers fail to pay their bills, the total accounts receivable is reduced by a provision for bad (unpaid) debts. The *inventory* of a business may be composed of raw materials to be used in the manufacture of products, partially finished goods, and finished goods ready for shipment to customers. *Prepaid insurance* represents insurance premiums paid in advance for protection in future periods. *Supplies on hand* are those purchased for use in manufacturing and in the office.

Fixed Assets.   Property, plant, and equipment are assets that are not intended for sale and that are used over and over again in making a product, displaying it, warehousing it, and transporting it. Included in this category are land, buildings, machinery, equipment, furniture, and vehicles.

Liabilities.   *Current liabilities* include all debts that fall due within the year. *Accounts payable* represent money owed by the business to its regular business creditors. The business also owes, on any given day, salaries and wages to its employees, interest on funds borrowed from banks, fees for services, insurance premiums, pensions, and similar liabilities. The debt due to the Internal Revenue Service is generally stated separately. The total of the items listed under this classification is the total liabilities of the business.

Stockholders' Equity.   The stockholders' equity or net worth is the proprietary interest that the stockholders have in a business. It is separated for legal and accounting reasons into capital stock and accumulated retained earnings. Shares are evidenced by stock certificates issued by the business to the shareholders. There may be several different types or classes of shares such as preferred stock and common stock.

The retained earnings line on the balance sheet (normally but not always a credit balance) is frequently supported by a separate retained earnings statement. Unless specifically restricted by the board of directors for some future purpose, the retained earnings account is legally available for paying dividends.

Net Working Capital.   The *net working capital* or *net current assets* consists of the difference between the total current assets and the total current liabilities. In the previous illustration of a balance sheet, these figures are:

Current assets	$93,597.55
Minus current liabilities	− 23,885.00
Net working capital	$69,712.55

The net working capital represents assets that would be free and clear if all current debts were paid off. The ability of a business to meet its obligations, expand its volume, and take advantage of opportunities is often determined by its working capital.

Current Ratio.   The *current ratio* is used to judge whether a business has a sound working capital position. Most analysts say that current assets should be at least twice as large as current liabilities. This means that for each $1 of current liabilities, there should be $2 in current assets. In the illustrated balance sheet, the figures are:

$$\frac{\text{Current assets}}{\text{Current liabilities}} = \frac{\$93,597.55}{\$23,885.00} = \frac{3.92}{1} \quad \text{or 3.92 to 1}$$

Therefore, for each $1 of current liability there is $3.92 in current assets.

The Income Statement   The income statement is of great importance, because it shows the record of a company's operating activities (annually or more often). It serves as a guide to the way a business may fare in the future. The income statement matches the amount

CONSOLIDATED TELECOMMUNICATIONS, INC.
Income Statement
Year Ended December 31, 19--

Income:			
Sales		$253,475.00	
Less Sales Returns and Allowances		1,325.00	
Net Sales			$252,150.00
Cost of Goods Sold:			
Finished Goods Inventory, January 1		$ 20,000.00	
Cost of Goods Manufactured (Schedule B)		145,481.00	
Total Available for Sale		$165,481.00	
Less Finished Goods Inventory, December 31		20,700.00	
Cost of Goods Sold			144,781.00
Gross Profit on Sales			$107,369.00
Operating Expenses:			
Selling Expenses:			
Sales Salaries	$12,750.00		
Advertising Expense	31,475.00		
Total Selling Expenses		44,225.00	
Administrative Expenses:			
Officers' Salaries	$28,000.00		
Office Supplies and Expense	11,420.00		
Bad Debts Expense	661.45		
Total Administrative Expenses		40,081.45	
Total Operating Expenses			84,306.45
Net Income Before Income Taxes			$ 23,062.55
Federal Income Tax			11,946.40
Net Income			$ 11,116.15

received from selling goods or services against all the costs incurred in operating the company. The bottom line is a net profit or loss for the year.

Income.   The most important source of revenue always makes up the first item on the income statement. The *net sales figure* is the amount received by a business after taking into consideration returned goods and allowances for reduction in prices.

Secondary sources of revenue are usually referred to as *other income* or *miscellaneous income* and often include such items as income from dividends and interest received from stocks, bonds, or certificates of deposit.

Cost of Sales and Operating Expenses.   *Cost of sales* represents all the costs incurred in order to convert raw materials into finished products. These costs include those of materials, direct labor, rent, electricity, supplies, maintenance, and repairs.

Selling and Administrative Expenses.   Sales representatives' salaries and commissions, advertising and promotion, and travel and entertainment are the major items of *selling expenses*. Managers' salaries, office payroll, rent, and the cost of office supplies are the usual items of *administrative expenses*.

Federal Income Tax.   Income taxes are usually deducted at the bottom of the income statement from the figure entitled "net income before income taxes."

Net Income.   *Net income* is the amount of profit available to pay dividends on the capital stock and to use in the business. From the net income you can judge whether the company is earning money on its investments. However, the historical record for a series of years is generally more reliable than the figure for a single year. Even though a business shows no profit in a particular year, the board of directors may pay a dividend from the accumulation of earnings of previous years.

Analysis of the Income Statement   The total amounts shown on an income statement do not mean much by themselves: a business can have a large amount in net sales and still be unprofitable. An income statement calls for a few detailed comparisons.

Determine the business's *operating margin of profit* (how much it earns for each dollar of sales) and how it has changed over the years. Consolidated Telecommunications had annual sales of $353,475 and showed $23,062.55 as the operating profit. Thus,

$$\frac{\text{Operating profit}}{\text{Sales}} = \frac{\$23,062.55}{\$353,475.00} = 6.5\%$$

means that 6.5 cents remained as a *gross profit* from operations for each dollar of sales. You can compare this operating margin of profit with that produced in previous years. Changes in figures can reflect changes in efficiency. You can also compare the margin-of-profit figure of one company with those of other companies that conduct a similar type of business. If one company's margin of profit is lower than those of other companies in the same field, it may show that the company has not fared very well.

The *net profit ratio* (how much profit is made on every dollar of goods sold) is another guide to indicate how satisfactory the year's activities have been for a business. Consolidated Telecommunications' net profit for the year was $11,116.15. Its net sales for the year amounted to $353,475. Profit was $11,116.15 on $353,475 of sales or

$$\frac{\text{Net profit}}{\text{Sales}} = \frac{\$11,116.15}{\$353,475.00} = 3.14\%$$

This means that for every $1 of goods sold, 3.1 cents in profit ultimately went to the business. By comparing the net profit ratio from year to year for the same company and comparing it with the profit ratio of other companies in the same field, you can judge profit progress.

Budgets

A budget is a plan of financial operations covering a designated period of time, classified according to purpose. The length of the period may vary, but it is usually a complete fiscal year. Every budget provides these elements:

- Forecast of income (net sales).
- Cost of income (cost of goods sold).
- Operating expenses.

A budget provides management with a tool for evaluating projected operating plans and the financial results of those plans. It also offers management information for comparing and evaluating actual operating performance against an approved operating plan.

An effective and useful budget is a composite of the budgets constructed by each person responsible for any part of the overall operating plan. All who have a role in budget construction are thereby able to observe their contribution to a larger operation and measure their performance against a larger projection.

Budget Considerations   Effective budgeting coordinates both planning and control so as to bring about performance that is in harmony with financial results desired by management. The main prerequisites for sound budgeting are:

- Detailed organizational structure with precisely defined authorities, responsibilities, and lines of communication.
- Attainable goals for handling income and expenses.
- Separate elements built from basic data of past results that are modified to reflect trends and prospects.
- Budget period of reasonable length.
- Participation of all those who are responsible for operating results.
- Thorough review of budget proposals at successive management levels.

CONSOLIDATED
TELECOMMUNICATIONS, INC.
Sales Department

STATEMENT OF EXPENSE

MONTH OCT   YEAR 19—

ACCT. NO.	EXPENSE ACCOUNT NAME	CURRENT MONTH			YEAR TO DATE		
		THIS YEAR		LAST YEAR	THIS YEAR		LAST YEAR
		ACTUAL	BUDGET	ACTUAL	ACTUAL	BUDGET	ACTUAL
199	EMPLY FRINGE BENEFITS	1 572	1 500	1 521	15 092	14 200	17 332
202	SALARIES	17 377	15 900	15 218	167 193	158 700	171 394
210	OVERTIME	97			500	200	
211	TEMPORARY HELP		100		262	300	669
219	SLS TRAINING EXPENSES			362	305		1 283
221	TRAV & ENT	1 341	2 000	2 761	19 770	15 000	21 005
312	TEL & TEL FIXED	576	700	449*	5 712	6 600	6 351
314	XEROX CHARGES	540	700	1 063	6 705	6 100	9 390
322	STATIONERY & SUPPLIES	14		20	180	200	205
328	TEL & TEL VARIABLE	921	700	898	8 518	7 000	8 538
329	OFFICE POSTAGE	392	300	340	2 919	2 700	3 014
330	TRANSCRIBING SERVICE	4	100	1 952	815	700	3 318
336	MAGAZINES & BOOKS	83	100	26	644	400	784
339	CONTRIBUTIONS & GIFTS			1 000	400	600	1 000
340	DUES & MEMBERSHIPS			59	39		134
387	ASSMT MESSENGER SVCE	19		2	36		25
399	ALL OTHER EXPENSES	5			193	200	490
451	OCCUP & MAINT EXPENSE	2 052	2 400	2 828	20 521	23 500	28 444
999	NUMBER OF EMPLOYEES				16 000	16 000	
	TOTALS	24 993	24 500	28 499	265 804	252 400	273 376

NOTE: (*) Denotes credit.

A departmental budget.

- Adoption by top management and communication to personnel.
- Frequent reports during the period covered by the budget, comparing actual results with the budget for each budgeted item.

Budget Reports

After it is finally revised and approved, the budget serves as a guide to expenditures during the year. It is not expected that it will work out exactly; in fact, it may need to be revised at periodic intervals. However, expenditures in excess of an authorized budget must be approved, although it is frequently allowable to exceed the specified sum in one item if it is made up in another.

In order to know whether one is keeping within the budget, periodic reports are necessary. The statement of expense shown here is such a report for a departmental budget.

The statement of expense shows at a glance how much has been expended under each expense account number for the current month and for the year to date and the amounts budgeted. In addition, the amounts actually spent the same month and year to date for the previous year are also shown. The difference between the actual and the budgeted totals for the current month reflects a $493 excess in expenditures. The $13,404 excess in authorized expenditures for the year to date can be traced to account numbers 199, 202, and 221.

SECURITIES

Only the corporate form of business organization has the power to issue securities such as bonds (which are, in effect, loans to a business) and shares of stock (which represent part ownership of a business).

Stock

The corporation's charter and bylaws usually provide for the issuance of shares of stock. Holders of one or more shares of voting stock gain certain rights, including the right to participate indirectly in the control of the corporation. Stockholders have the right to share in profits and the right to receive a portion of the corporate assets if the corporation faces liquidation. A stock share is similar to a promissory note of which the corporation is the maker. A stockholder has the right to transfer shares by the indorsement and the delivery of the stock certificates or by a bill of sale. The two major classes of corporate stock are *common stock* and *preferred stock*.

Common Stock.   The corporation that issues common stock is not obligated to pay the value of the stock back to the investor; neither is it obligated to guarantee an annual dividend. Needless to say, common stockholders expect something in return for the risk they run. This may be the expectation of receiving a larger share of the corporation's earnings or perhaps the right to exert an influence in the control of the organization.

Preferred Stock.   Ownership of preferred stock carries certain preferential rights that ownership of common stock does not provide, chiefly the right to share in earnings before the owners of common stock and the right to a priority claim against the assets in the event of dissolution. As a general rule, preferred stock does not carry voting rights.

Preferred stock may be *cumulative* or *noncumulative*. Stocks carrying a cumulative provision require that passed-over cumulative preferred dividends must be paid in full before any dividends can be paid on the common stock. Noncumulative preferred stock does not contain a provision to pay dividends in arrears out of subsequent earnings.

Most preferred stock is *nonparticipating*; that is, the amount or percentage of earnings it can receive as dividends is limited according to prior legal agreement. Stock is *participating* when provision is made for it to participate in earnings in excess of its specified dividend. For example, the specified dividend is first paid on the preferred stock; then a dividend of the same amount, or one figured on the same percentage rate, is paid on the common stock. Finally, any additional earnings are divided between the preferred and common stockholders.

Share Values.   Stock may be *par-value* or *no-par-value* stock. The par value of a share of stock is a nominal, fixed, dollar amount assigned to it by a corporation's charter and bearing no relationship to market value. Its only importance is that the *capital stock account* of the corporation must be credited for the par value of each share issued. The term *no-par-value* means that no fixed dollar amount is assigned to the stock. The market price of no-par-value stock is the price per share at which the stock is currently being traded on the market.

Leverage Factor.   Stock is said to have high leverage if the company issuing it has a large proportion of bonds and preferred stock outstanding in relation to the amount of common stock. For example, consider a company with $5,000,000 of

6 percent bonds outstanding. If the company is earning $375,000 and must pay $300,000 in bond interest, there will be only $75,000 left for the common stock. A decline of 15 percent in earnings would nearly cancel out everything available for the common stock. A greater decline in earnings could wipe out all earnings available for common stock dividends and require the company to dip into accumulated earnings in order to cover full interest on its bonds. This is the danger of high-leverage stocks and a potential weakness of companies that have a disproportionate amount of debt or preferred stock.

Bonds   A bond certificate, like a promissory note, is a written promise by the borrower to pay the lender (bondholder) a sum of money (principal) at a specified future date. Thus, bondholders are creditors of the corporation. Bonds have a specified interest rate that must be paid, usually every six months. They are usually sold in $1,000 denominations and are issued as a rule for a period of 20 to 30 years.

Coupon or Registered Bonds.   Bonds are either *coupon bonds* or *registered bonds*. Coupon bonds have a series of detachable tickets (coupons) that state the amount of interest earned and the date when each payment is due. Coupons are either deposited in banks like cash or exchanged for cash by the corporation. Registered bonds do not have coupons attached, but the interest they earn is mailed to bondholders on specified dates.

Types of Bonds.   *Mortgage bonds* are secured (that is, backed) by a mortgage on the corporation's physical plant and equipment. *Collateral trust bonds* are backed by securities of the corporation. *Debenture bonds* are secured by the corporation's general credit, but they may carry the restriction that no other company assets be pledged as collateral for other purposes. *Convertible bonds* can be exchanged at a stated ratio for common or preferred stock. Once the exchange has been made, it cannot be reversed. *Tax-exempt bonds* are those issued by state, municipality, or other political bodies and are exempt from income tax.

Security   The stocks and bonds of most major corporations are sold throughout the
Transactions   country in stock markets technically referred to as security exchanges. The largest of the national stock exchanges is the New York Stock Exchange, but most large cities have a local stock exchange. The national stock exchanges are made up of individual members, most of whom represent brokerage firms that maintain offices in all major cities.

Other important stock exchanges are the American Stock Exchange (Amex), the Pacific Coast Stock Exchange, the Midwest (Chicago) Stock Exchange, the Philadelphia-Baltimore-Washington Exchange, and the Toronto Stock Exchange. Regional and local exchanges list the securities of local companies and accept buy-and-sell orders for securities listed on the national exchanges.

A corporation must be approved by the Security Exchange Commission (SEC) for listing on a national exchange. The SEC supervises stock exchanges, brokerage firms, and security dealers. It also sees that corporation financial reports and prospectuses (descriptions of businesses) are prepared periodically.

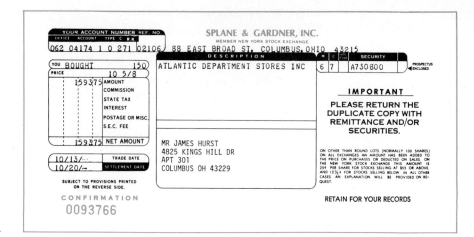

A stock purchase invoice.

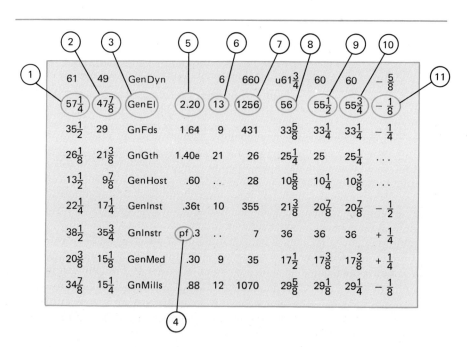

1. High price for year to date: 57¼ points, or $57.25 per share.
2. Low price for year to date: $47,875.
3. Name of stock: General Electric.
4. Preferred stock.
5. Current annual dividend: $2.20 per share.
6. Price-earnings ratio: market price per share divided by earnings per share.
7. Number of shares traded that day (in hundreds): 125,600 shares.

8. High price for day: $56.00 per share.
9. Low price for day: $55.50 per share.
10. Closing price for day: $55.75.
11. Net change from closing price the previous day. Price has dropped 12½ cents. Yesterday's closing price would have been $55.875.

Details of daily stock quotations.

Security Exchange Services. The primary service rendered to investors by stock exchanges is providing a market for the buying and selling of listed securities. Investors always have a purchase price and a selling price available for securities they wish to buy or sell. When an investor instructs a broker to buy or sell shares of stock, that order is carried to the floor of the exchange, where it is transacted by the broker's representative. Brokers charge a commission that usually runs between 1 and 2 percent of the total sale price for each sale or purchase made for a customer. Some states charge a transfer tax on all stock and bond purchases, and the SEC adds a small tax on the sale price.

Security Information. The prices in the securities exchanges are given in daily newspapers. The over-the-counter market consists of public corporations that are not listed with either the main or the regional stock exchanges. Newspaper quotations indicate the prices at which investment bankers or security brokers are willing to purchase or sell a stock.

Daily bond quotations are reported in the newspapers. Included are corporation, foreign, and United States government bonds. Prices are quoted as a ratio of 100 percent of the face value shown on the bond and indicate whether the bond is sold at a premium (above face value) or at a discount (below face value).

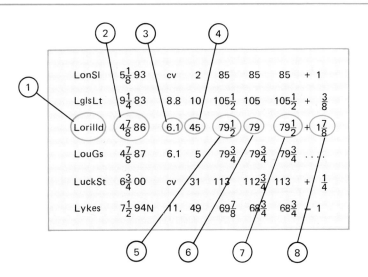

1. Name of company: Lorillard.
2. Description of bond: 4-7/8% bond maturing in 1986.
3. Current yield: annual interest on $1,000 bond divided by today's closing price. $4.875 ÷ $795 = 6.1%.
4. Volume: number of $1,000 bonds traded that day.

5. High price for day: $795.
6. Low price for day: $790.
7. Closing price for day: $795.
8. Net change from closing price the previous day: $18.75. Yesterday's closing price would have been $776.25.

Details of daily bond quotations.

Futures Prices

MONDAY, MAY 21, 19 —

Commodity futures contracts are commitments to buy or sell commodities at a specified time and place in the future. The price is established when the contract is made in open auction on a futures exchange. Only a small percentage of futures trading actually leads to delivery of a commodity, for a contract may change hands or be liquidated before the delivery date. Participants fall into two categories: commercial hedgers who use futures to minimize price risks inherent in their marketing operations and speculators who, employing venture capital, seek profits through price changes. Both purchase contracts with only a small margin payment. Futures prices are an indication of the direction of prices based on current market conditions.

GRAINS & OILS

—Season— High	Low		High	Low	Close	Chg.	Open Interest
WHEAT (CBT) 5,000 bu.; $ per bu.							
3.82½	2.97½	May	3.60½	3.56½	3.58¾	+.02¼	726
3.77½	2.87½	Jul	3.62	3.58	3.60½	+.03¼	13762
3.80	2.90½	Sep	3.65	3.61	3.63½	+.03	9825
3.89½	3.26	Dec	3.76	3.71¾	3.74	+.02	8479
3.98	3.35	Mar	3.84	3.80	3.83	+.03	2165
3.98	3.44½	May	3.83	3.80¼	3.82½	+.02½	328
Sales Fri. 8,293.							
Total open interest Fri. 35,285, up 53 from Thurs.							
WHEAT (KCBT) 5,000 bu.; $ per bu.							
3.69¾	2.90½	May	3.45¼	3.45¼	3.45¼	+.07¾	45
3.64	2.80	Jul	3.47¾	3.43	3.46¾	+.04¾	56805
3.67	3.11¼	Sep	3.52¼	3.48	3.50½	+.04¾	13805
3.73¼	3.22	Dec	3.60¼	3.56½	3.59	+.04	7445
3.75	3.30	Mar	3.64¾	3.63	3.63	+.04	155
Sales Fri: 4,018.							
Total open interest Fri 78,255, up 2,540 from Thu.							
CORN (CBT) 5,000 bu.; $ per bu.							
2.86½	2.30½	May	2.62½	2.59½	2.61	+.01½	884
2.88	2.33	Jul	2.68	2.63¾	2.67½	+.03¼	66778
2.80	2.36	Sep	2.70½	2.66¾	2.70¼	+.03	15886
2.82	2.44	Dec	2.73	2.69¼	2.72¼	+.02¾	55689
2.90	2.54¾	Mar	2.81¼	2.77½	2.80¼	+.02¾	18608
2.95	2.72½	May	2.86¾	2.83½	2.85¾	+.02¾	4006
Sales Fri. 20,604.							
Total open interest Fri. 161,851, up 176 from Thurs.							
OATS (CBT) 5,000 bu.; $ per bu.							
1.72	1.33½	May	1.48¾	1.46½	1.48¾	+.00¾	20
1.62	1.41¾	Jul	1.55	1.52¼	1.54½	+.01¾	3138
1.64	1.48¼	Sep	1.61½	1.58	1.61	+.02¾	828
1.70	1.53¼	Dec	1.67½	1.66¼	1.66¾	+.02¼	608
1.76½	1.63½	Mar	1.73	1.72½	1.73	+.02½	307
Sales Fri. 518.							
Total open interest Fri. 4,901, up 52 from Thurs.							
SOYBEANS (CBT) 5,000 bu.; $ per bu.							
7.97	6.06	May	7.25	7.20½	7.23½	+.03¾	856
8.05½	7.07	Jul	7.41	7.32½	7.40	+.07	40620
7.93	6.08	Aug	7.45½	7.37½	7.44½	+.08	10883
7.43	6.48	Sep	7.37	7.26½	7.37	+.10¼	4920
7.20	6.38½	Nov	7.29	7.16	7.28	+.11½	30669
7.39½	6.55	Jan	7.39½	7.26½	7.38¼	+.11½	10577

FOODS

—Season— High	Low		High	Low	Close	Chg.	Open Interest
COFFEE (NYCSE) 37,500 lb. ¢ per lb.							
163.50	94.00	May	150.50	148.50	150.38	−0.12	131
163.13	92.00	Jul	154.40	151.00	154.01	+1.98	3503
162.30	90.00	Sep	157.90	154.50	157.50	+1.55	3220
161.00	92.50	Dec	155.00	151.75	154.50	+1.48	2057
155.75	111.50	Mar	151.00	148.00	151.00	+0.78	520
155.00	116.00	May	151.00	151.00	151.00	+1.00	326
Est. sales: 1,435 sales Fri. 3,369							
Total open interest Fri. 9,758 off 310 from Thur.							
EGGS, Shell (CME)							
22,500 doz.; ¢ per doz.							
56.30	48.40	May	52.45	51.25	52.40	+ .70	158
56.70	50.30	Jun	52.75	51.50	52.40	+ .70	135
58.10	54.00	Jul	56.00	56.00	56.00	− .50	24
55.00	55.00	Aug			57.05		1
63.25	56.50	Sep	58.40	57.70	58.00	+ .05	349
56.90	56.50	Oct			56.90		3
62.75	59.05	Nov			61.00		26
65.50	59.00	Dec			62.25		84
Est. sales: 169; sales Fri. 135.							
Total open interest Fri. 780, off 71 from Thurs.							
ORANGE JUICE (NYCTN,ca)							
15,000 lb.; ¢ per lb.							
129.50	80.25	Jul	102.90	101.40	101.50	−1.75	2051
130.25	95.55	Sep	103.80	102.50	103.00	−1.45	1454
124.00	98.90	Nov	101.00	100.40	100.70	−1.50	580
118.00	89.50	Jan	99.00	98.30	98.85	−0.85	1036
118.30	93.50	Mar	99.70	99.10	99.50	−0.80	1040
Est. sales: 400 sales Fri. 465							
Total open interest Fri. 7,618 off 35 from Thur.							
SUGAR, World (NYCSE) 112,000 lb.; ¢ per lb.							
10.99	6.87	Jul	7.88	7.75	7.75	−0.13	12674
10.30	7.05	Sep	8.34	8.24	8.25	−0.10	6013
10.38	7.15	Oct	8.54	8.44	8.45	−0.10	7978

A daily commodity listing.

Commodity Exchanges. Commodity exchanges sell merchandise (grains, oil, plywood, cattle, cotton, wool, rubber, hides, potatoes, and metals) rather than stocks and bonds. They buy and sell future contracts for quantities of products that are widely produced and can be stored. They also deal in actual products, or "spot orders." Future trading permits an investor to use these products as a hedge; that is, the investor buys future contracts to offset the cost of actual deliveries of products. In the event that the price of the product drops before the future product is finally sold, the future contract price will decline, offsetting the loss on the spot transaction. Broker members of these exchanges charge a commission for their services in placing orders to buy or sell.

Securities Register. Employers who deal in securities need to have a record of their transactions. When purchased securities are delivered, the information contained in the confirmation letter that accompanies them should be transferred to a securities register. For tax purposes, the register contains the date the investment was purchased, the cost, and the record of income from it.

You can attach the confirmation letter to the security or file it under the name of the broker so that you can retrieve it when the security is to be sold. File the confirmation of the sale of securities with your employer's income tax return.

A separate index card can serve as a security register for each security purchased and sold. Purchase information can be recorded on the front side of the card; sale and dividend data on the reverse side.

Investment and Advisory Services

Financial news and daily stock-bond-commodity trading and futures appear in the newspapers. Data on business conditions and trends is obtained from other specialized publications such as the *Wall Street Journal, Business Week, The*

Stock:	Disney common				
Broker:	Shearson Hayden Stone Inc.				
Where kept:	Union Trust Bank, Safe Deposit Box				
Date	Certificate Number	Transaction	No. of Shares	Share Cost	Total Cost
2/12	R81212	PURCHASED	200	$38\frac{3}{4}$	7,819.75
4/16	R91818	PURCHASED	100	$35\frac{1}{4}$	3,556.72
6/26	R99801	PURCHASED	100	$29\frac{3}{4}$	3,001.78

SECURITY SALE						
Sale Date	Shares Sold	Selling Price	Gross Return	Tax	Commission	Net Return
7/30	100	$31\frac{1}{4}$	3,125	11.25	28.13	3,085.62

A security register card.

Exchange, or the *Commercial and Financial Chronicle*. Reports on specific securities are published by the large brokerage firms.

Several investment advisory services are available to investors. For a fee, they provide information about corporations and stocks to buy, sell, or watch. Organizations such as Standard & Poor's Corporation and Moody's Investors Service, Inc., offer investors diversified services, as does the broker with whom an investor has an account.

Real Estate

Secretaries are sometimes asked to assist an employer in real estate transactions involving the buying and selling of investment property, income property, and occasionally residential property.

Distinguishing Property Types

Investment property generally consists of unimproved real estate held for the purpose of capital growth through increases in prices.

Income property is a broad category of property that produces income directly (rental property) or as a factor in the production of income (commercial property used in one's business). It includes *commercial property*, which is usually zoned for business purposes such as stores and shops, lofts, warehouses, parking lots, and shopping centers. Included too are properties held for income through rental to tenants—apartments, office buildings, and hotels and motels. *Industrial properties* are combinations of land and machinery that are used to assemble, process, and manufacture finished products from raw materials. *Agricultural property* is land suited for the raising of crops or livestock.

Residential property refers to both one-family residences and two- to four-family houses, including condominiums and cooperatives.

Conveyancing Real Estate

Conveyancing real estate is the process of transferring interests (ownership) in property, including land. Ownership in real estate is passed from one person to another in various ways, but most commonly by voluntary sale.

Deed. The method of conveying *title* (evidence of ownership) to real estate is by a formal instrument in writing known as a deed. With it, title to real property is conveyed from one person to another. A deed should be distinguished from a contract of sale or a purchase and sale agreement, which is simply an agreement to convey title in the future. Neither is a will a deed, because it does not require delivery and acceptance.

There are two basic types of deeds—*warranty* and *quitclaim*. Each is sufficient to transfer the interests of the grantor. Warranty deeds are those that contain covenants of warranty and give the grantee (the person to whom the property is conveyed) the greatest degree of protection. Under a quitclaim deed, the grantor makes no warranty as to the condition of the title; that is, the grantor does not warrant possession of any right of title. The quitclaim deed does pass any title the grantor has to the grantee.

Abstract of Title. The buyer of real estate must be satisfied that the seller has good title to the property. This is accomplished by means of a title search. Abstract companies are usually employed to prepare abstracts of the various instruments and court proceedings. The attorney making the search provides the buyer with an abstract of title. This is a summary of the history of the property, including all conveyances, mortgages, liens, unpaid taxes, and other matters important to the security of the buyer. In addition to the abstract of title, the opinion of the attorney is needed regarding any defects, liens (claims against property as security for a debt), or encumbrances disclosed by the abstract.

Title Insurance. The lawyer who presents the abstract of title is merely giving an opinion that the title is good. If the buyer wishes to guard against loss occurring through defects in title to real property, title insurance is obtainable from a title insurance company.

Recording. By statute, no transfer of real estate is valid until the grantor (the person conveying the property) has it properly recorded in the office of record in the county in which the property is located. Recording serves as a notice to the public of one's ownership. It protects both the owner and those who wish to determine the identity of the real property.

Financing Real Estate

Financing a real estate transaction involves taking out a loan in exchange for a *promissory note* and a *mortgage deed*, which is the security pledged for the loan. In signing a promissory note, the buyer promises to repay the lender the money borrowed with interest as stated. This note is evidence of the debt and is written to meet the requirements of a negotiable instrument.

A real estate mortgage deed is an instrument containing the pledge of real estate as security for the repayment of money borrowed. The minimum requirements for the creation of a mortgage deed are that it convey agreement that specific real property shall be security for the payment of an obligation, and that the agreement be in writing in order to guard against fraud.

The mortgage deed contains the conveyance of the property and the *defeasance* clause. The first specifies that upon default by the person who has taken out the mortgage of any of the provisions of the mortgage deed, the person granting the mortgage may sell the mortgaged premises by public auction. The defeasance clause contains conditions relating to principal and interest; taxes, changes, and assessments; fire insurance; and strip or waste of the mortgaged property. Any breach of these conditions would void the mortgage deed.

Keeping Property Records

Secretaries are often called upon to keep records of income and expenses pertaining to investment property. A recommended practice is to establish a file for each income property. The contents of a property income file should include everything pertaining to the unit, including correspondence, leases, bills for repairs and improvements, and a record of income, mortgage payments, and expenses. The banking of investment property revenue and the payment of expense bills must be managed carefully, since all such income and expense must be reported on tax returns.

INSURANCE

A business is considered a person in the eyes of the law and is responsible for actions that affect other persons. It possesses real and personal property assets such as buildings and land (real) and furniture, fixtures, and supplies (personal).

To protect against almost anything that might happen unexpectedly or accidentally and cause a loss or financial burden, a business must buy insurance. The insurance company collects reasonable amounts of money from *policyholders* (purchasers of insurance) and accumulates it in a fund. From this fund, the company pays for the losses suffered by those who are insured.

Types of Insurance   There are various types of insurance available to the business community. The typical business buys liability, property, and personal insurance.

Liability Insurance.   To protect the business from suits that arise from negligent actions committed by owners and employees or caused by products sold, a business requires general liability insurance.

Employers purchase *workers' compensation insurance*, which pays the medical costs and weekly disability benefits of injured workers on behalf of the employer. The amounts paid are specified in the workers' compensation laws of each state or federal jurisdiction. All such benefits are paid in accordance with the schedule set in the law and regardless of fault.

Some businesses require *surety bond* contracts. The insurance company agrees to be responsible for specified obligations of the business. In the construction industry, for example, contracts are frequently awarded only after a surety bond is furnished. The bond guarantees that the company will complete the work specified in the contract. If the company fails to perform, the insuring company must make arrangements to complete the work or pay specified penalties.

Fidelity bonds are also guarantees. The bonding company (insurance company) guarantees to reimburse the employer if an employee steals company assets.

Property Insurance.   Business owners are concerned about direct property losses such as damage to buildings and contents. They are also concerned about indirect losses. After a fire or storm occurs, the business may be prevented from continuing. Earnings are lost or additional expenses incurred to get the business back into operation. To insure against losses, business interruption insurance can be purchased.

Personal Insurance.   Life insurance insures against the uncertainty of the time of death. Its function is to replace income earning ability. There are four types of life insurance coverage: (1) term insurance, (2) whole life insurance, (3) annuities, and (4) endowments.

Term insurance covers the insured for a specified period of time. After the term has expired, there is no more coverage. Term insurance offers maximum protection at low cost, but each year the premium payment increases.

Whole life insurance (ordinary life insurance) covers the insured for life and accumulates savings that can be used in different ways at any time.

The primary purpose of an *annuity* is to provide retirement income. Annual premiums are paid until a predetermined age is reached, in return for a monthly income for life or for a stated number of years. Under the usual arrangements, the employer and employee both make contributions to the plan each payday. If the person who is purchasing the annuity dies before entitlement begins, all contributions (plus interest) are returned to a beneficiary.

The *endowment policy* typically is a combination life insurance and annuity policy. For those who can afford it, an endowment can be ideal for both life insurance and retirement needs. Such policies can provide the insured with a specified amount at the time of retirement plus life insurance so that a beneficiary will have money to live on in the event of death of the insured before retirement age.

Health insurance replaces some of the earning power of the individual by covering loss due to accident or sickness. Health insurance can be purchased two ways—in individual or in group policies. A typical policy provides broad coverage: it pays for medical benefits (hospital charges), physiotherapy (treatments to increase mobility of a body function), miscellaneous charges (diagnostic X rays, anesthetics, lab tests), services of a physician, drugs prescribed by a physician, nursing care in a hospital, braces and artificial limbs, rental of a wheelchair, and emergency transportation. Premiums for individual policies are determined by the age, occupation, benefits received, and physical condition of the applicant. Group insurance premiums are based on benefits, composition of the group, and occupation. The physical condition of each employee is not a factor in determining premiums. The insurance company depends on insuring a group of people who represent an average health risk.

Insurance Records

All correspondence, forms, and documents relating to insurance matters should be filed in a separate insurance folder. Insurance policies and premium payment receipts should be kept in a secure place, such as a safe-deposit box or office safe. When policies are kept in the office, a separate record of each policy should be filed in another location in the event the records are destroyed by fire or other catastrophe.

Claims for losses resulting from fire or theft are expedited when descriptions of lost items are available. A list of office furnishings and equipment should be prepared, kept up to date, and filed with the insurance policy. It should show the cost of each item and the date purchased. If accurate cost information is not readily available, an appraisal should be made by a qualified person.

The recommended way to maintain a record of the executive's personal insurance coverage or that of the company is to prepare an *insurance register*. If one does not exist, you can set one up from the premium notices received during the year. The information called for in the partial listing of a company's insurance policies illustrated on the next page can be found on a premium notice.

A premium distribution card for each policy can help you remember when premiums become due. The policy number and the name and address of both the insurance company and the agent are typed along the top edge of each card.

			COVERAGE		DURATION		PREMIUM	
POLICY NUMBER	COMPANY	AGENT	TYPE	AMOUNT	DATE EFFECTIVE MO. DAY YR.	DATE EXPIRES MO. DAY YR.	RATE	AMOUNT
453289	Great Western	Roberts	Life	20000	2/3/--	2/3/--	A	25000
3025582	Northwestern	Kelly	Life	300000	4/15/--	4/15/--	A	16054
5543322	Equitable	Cooper	Life	500000	7/15/--	1/15/--	S-A	10420
483215	John Hancock	Moore	Life	500000	10/1/--	10/1/--	A	22400
812343	Michigan Mutual	Blake-Stone	Auto	100000 00 / 500000 00	12/15/--	12/15/--	A	14600
H413691	Home Ins. Co.	Kelly	Warehouse	1600000	12/1/--	12/1/--	A	4500
81877XF	Home Ins Co	Kelly	Furniture	500000	12/1/--	6/1/--	S-A	1747

INSURANCE REGISTER — Year Ending Dec. 31, 19—

The abbreviations for the months of the year are typed along the horizontal axis and the current and subsequent years along the left vertical axis of the card. Annual, semiannual, and quarterly premium amounts are entered opposite the correct year and under the appropriate month and annually totaled at the extreme right.

If a premium-distribution card is not sufficient to remind you when premiums are due, use a tickler file. File the card in the tickler file a few days before the expiration date or the premium-payment date. As soon as a renewal or premium payment has been made, advance the card to the next due date.

Payroll and Tax Records

Secretaries have varying responsibilities for payroll records and reports. Some are in complete charge of the payroll, including the processing of salary checks. Others perform only some payroll functions, especially in large businesses where payroll and tax duties are centralized. In still other offices, secretaries may have contact with payroll operations only through the receipt of their own paychecks. You may have responsibilities for some payroll matters, including the need to explain payroll procedures and policies to new employees and to obtain payroll information needed by the payroll department.

Payroll work requires an understanding of the regulations and forms that are legislated by the Federal Insurance Contributions (Social Security) Act (FICA) and the Fair Labor Standards Act, federal and state unemployment compensation acts, and income tax laws.

Social Security

There is no single social security program; there are actually three separate programs, each having a separate fund and a separate tax levied to support it.

The first of the social security programs is the retirement program, or Old Age Survivors Insurance (OASI). This program provides the elderly with retirement benefits and their surviving dependents with survivor's benefits. The second program, Hospital Insurance (HI) or medicare, provides hospitalization insurance for the elderly. The third program is public Disability Insurance (DI), which provides workers with insurance if they become disabled during their working years.

The *Supplemental Medical Insurance* (SMI) program is optional for persons over the age of 65. It is financed jointly by the retired person's contributions and the federal government.

Each of these programs is financed from one payroll tax. See the FICA column on any payroll check.

Social Security Numbers.   Each employed person must obtain a social security number for identification in the government records. To obtain an identification number, file an application with the nearest post office or social security office. You will receive a card stamped with an assigned account number that you retain throughout your life.

Social Security Tax Levels.   To support the social security program, both employers and employees must contribute at the rate specified by law. The present FICA tax rates and those scheduled for the future are listed in the table below.

At the end of each quarter (on March 31, June 30, September 30, and December 31), the employer accumulates the appropriate amounts deducted from each employee's wage, together with the matching company payment, and forwards the amount to the Internal Revenue Service Center for the region.

Self-employed persons such as contractors and farmers pay the FICA tax at a rate that is about three-quarters that paid by employer and employee on the same income. These payments are reported and paid simultaneously with income taxes.

Unemployment Compensation Tax Deductions.   Under the Social Security Act, employers of four or more persons pay a federal tax that is levied to pay the administrative costs of the state unemployment programs. Employers also pay a state unemployment tax from which unemployment compensation is paid to unemployed persons. These payments are reported on special forms and are filed quarterly. Some states levy the unemployment tax on both employees and employers.

FICA TAX RATES				
Year	Tax Rate Employee	Tax Rate Employer	Self-Employed	Taxable Wage Base
1979	6.13%	6.13%	8.10%	$22,900
1980	6.13	6.13	8.10	25,900
1981	6.65	6.65	9.30	29,700
1982	6.70	6.70	9.35	31,800

Income Tax Deductions (Withholding)   Employers are required by the federal government to withhold an advance payment on income taxes on employees' earnings. The amounts are paid to the regional Internal Revenue Service Center at the same time the FICA taxes are paid.

Each employee must file with the employer an Employee's Withholding Allowance Certificate (Form W-4) to indicate the number of personal allowances claimed. Amounts to be withheld are then determined by consulting standard tax tables.

Some states and some cities require state and city income taxes to be withheld from employees' earnings.

Optional Payroll Deductions   Optional payroll deductions such as group insurance premiums, hospitalization insurance, retirement contributions, and stock or savings bond purchases may be made. All such deductions are voluntary and may be canceled by an employee at any time.

Payroll Procedures   Employers usually furnish their employees with an itemized listing of the deductions made from their wages. This information is often found on a stub attached to the paycheck, which an employee must detach before cashing the check.

Employers are required to prepare and file various payroll records for each employee.

Federal Tax Deposits Receipts.   Under social security legislation and the Internal Revenue Code, employers must act as collection agents to gather FICA tax and the income tax due from employees. Taxes withheld that total $200 or more but less than $2,000 must be deposited in a Federal Reserve Bank within 15 days after the close of each of the first 2 months of any calendar quarter. The deposit must be accompanied by a properly filled out punched-card form (Tax Deposit Form 501).

Employer's Quarterly Federal Tax Return.   On or before each April 30, July 31, October 31, and January 31, employers must file an Employer's Quarterly Federal Tax Return (Form 941). The sum of the income tax and the FICA taxes withheld is entered on the front of the form. The net amount payable is determined by deducting the sum of the amounts remitted with the monthly federal Tax Deposits Forms 501 from the total taxes withheld. The balance due must be sent with the Form 941 to the district director of internal revenue for the district in which the office of the employer is located.

Itemized listing of one employee's payroll deductions.

Name Turner, F.												
DETACH AND RETAIN												
REGULAR PAY		OVERTIME PAY		GROSS PAY	DEDUCTIONS				NET PAY	DATE	CHECK NO.	
HOURS	AMOUNT	HOURS	AMOUNT		I.T.W.	F.I.C.A.	GROUP INS.	MISC.				
40	160.00	4	24.00	184.00	24.90	11.28			147.82	4/7	389	

				PAYROLL REGISTER								
For the Week Beginning April 1, 19— and Ending April 7, 19— Paid April, 19—												
EMPLOYEE DATA				EARNINGS				DEDUCTIONS				NET PAY
Name	Marital Status	No. of Allowances	HOURS	Regular	Overtime	Commissions	Total	FICA	Withholding	Other	Total	
TURNER, F.	S	1	44	160 00	24 00		184 00	11.28	24 90		36 18	147 82
WADE, S.	S	1	35	140 00			140 00	8.58	16 20		24 78	115 22
WARREN, B.	S	1	42	200 00	15 00		215 00	13.18	31 20		44 38	170 62
WATANABE, W.	S	1	40	180 00			180 00	11.03	25 90		35 93	144 07
YANCY, D.	S	1	40	160 00			160 00	9.87	20 70		30 57	129 49

Wage and Tax Statement.   By January 31 (or within 30 days after an employee leaves the service of an employer) the employer must furnish a Withholding Tax Statement (Form W-2) to each employee. This form shows the employer's name, address, and identification number and the employee's name, address, and social security number. Also indicated are the FICA taxable wages paid, FICA tax deducted, total wages paid, and federal income tax withheld, if any. Two copies are given to the employee; one copy goes to the Internal Revenue Service (IRS), and one is retained for the employer's records.

Employer's Annual Federal Unemployment Tax Return.   Employers are required to report payments of federal unemployment taxes under the Federal Unemployment Tax Act, using Form 940.

Transmittal of Income and Tax Statements.   Employers must provide a summary that compares the income taxes withheld as reported on all W-2 Forms and the amount of income tax withheld as reported on the four quarterly Forms 941. Form W-3 is used for this report.

Payroll Register and Employee's Earnings Record

Company payroll records vary greatly. Daily time records may be kept for hourly workers and some salaried workers. The time is stamped on time cards as the employees enter and leave their work stations. Other companies give a secretary the responsibility for checking each employee in and out daily on a time sheet.

The Fair Labor Standards Act requires that the payroll records of nonexempt employees be kept on file for a period of four years. An employee's earnings record is usually kept for each employee. If deductions are numerous or require substantial computations, they may be recorded in a separate payroll deductions register. Forms similar to the payroll register illustrated above and the employee's earnings record illustrated at the top of page 450 contain all information required for the quarterly tax reports.

For large payrolls, daily time may be punched into cards for processing on punched-card equipment. Electronic data-processing equipment is also used for computing payrolls and for writing payroll checks.

INCOME TAX RESPONSIBILITIES

Taxes have become so much a part of business operations and personal life that secretaries are expected to be reasonably informed about such matters as

EMPLOYEE EARNINGS RECORD FOR YEAR 19____

Name __TURNER, FRANK__

Address __63 BELMONT ROAD__

__NILES, OHIO 44446__

Telephone No. __555-8214__

Date of Birth __NOVEMBER 16, 19—__

Rate __4.00__

Employee No. __81__

Social Security No. __303-06-1452__

Marital Status __Single__

Withholding Allowances __1__

Position __Stockroom clerk__

Date Employed __November 3, 19—__

| DATE | | HOURS | EARNINGS | | | DEDUCTIONS | | | | | | NET PAY | YEAR-TO-DATE EARNINGS |
PERIOD ENDING	PAID		REGULAR	OVERTIME	TOTAL	INCOME TAX	FICA TAX	INSURANCE PREMIUMS	UNION DUES	OTHER	TOTAL		
JANUARY 7	January 9	40	160 00		160 00	20 70	9 80				30 50	129 50	160 00
14	16	40	160 00		160 00	20 70	9 80				30 50	129 50	320 00
21	23	40	160 00		160 00	20 70	9 80				30 50	129 50	480 00
26	30	40	160 00		160 00	20 70	9 80				30 50	129 50	640 00
FEBRUARY 4	February 6	40	160 00		160 00	20 70	9 80				30 50	129 50	800 00
11	13	42	160 00	12 00	172 00	22 80	10 84				33 64	138 36	972 00
18	20	44	160 00	28 00	188 00	24 90	11 28				36 18	147 82	1156 00
25	27	40	160 00		160 00	20 70	9 80				30 50	129 50	1316 00
MARCH 3	March 5	40	160 00		160 00	20 70	9 80				30 50	129 50	1476 00
10	12	40	160 00		160 00	20 70	9 80				30 50	129 50	1636 00
17	19	40	160 00		160 00	20 70	9 80				30 50	129 50	1796 00
24	26	40	160 00		160 00	20 70	9 80				30 50	129 50	1956 00
31	April 2	40	160 00		160 00	20 70	9 80				30 50	129 50	2116 00
1st Quarter			2080 00	36 00	2116 00	275 40	129 92				405 32	1710 68	
April 7	9	44	160 00	28 00	188 00	24 90	11 28				36 18	147 82	2300 00

income tax forms, taxable income, deduction allowances, and methods of maintaining tax records.

Income Tax Forms

Business operations are conducted by individuals who are proprietors, partners, or corporations. Each uses a different set of tax forms. In addition, the requirements for filing returns and the contents of returns often change from year to year. For these reasons, the following basic requirements and descriptions of required tax forms should be compared with updated instructions when a tax return is being prepared.

Individual Returns. Single, legally separated, or divorced individuals must file a U.S. individual income tax return if their income was at least $2,950. Married persons are required to file a return if their joint income was at least $4,700.

Individuals whose total income is $20,000 or less ($40,000 or less joint income if they are married) and who receive $400 or less in interest or dividends may be able to use a simplified version of the tax return form. Individuals using either version submit their income data and the Form W-2 they received from their employer.

In addition to Form 1040, the individual taxpayer must file a Declaration of Estimated Tax, Form 1040ES, when income from sources not subject to withholding is expected to exceed $500 during the year. The estimated tax may be paid in full with the return or it may be divided into four equal instalments, one paid with the return and one on each of the remaining quarterly payment dates.

Partnership Returns.   Each partnership must file a U.S. Partnership Return of Income, Form 1065. On this form the partners set forth the income earned by the partnership and each partner's share of this income. In addition, partners must report their shares of partnership income on their individual tax returns. Form 1065 must be filed on or before the fifteenth day of the fourth month following the end of the fiscal year. A similar return must be filed for the state.

Corporation Returns.   Corporations file a Corporation Income Tax Return, Form 1120, by March 15 or by the fifteenth of the third month following a taxable year that does not coincide with the calendar year. The tax may be paid in full when the return is filed, or one-half the tax may be paid with the return and the remainder by June 15 of the taxable year. An estimated federal income tax is filed by September of the taxable year by corporations with estimated tax liabilities of $100,000 or more. Fifty percent of the tax in excess of $100,000 is paid with the declaration; another 50 percent by December 15. One-half the remaining tax is due by March 15 of the following year; the remaining tax by June 15.

Information Returns.   Individuals, partnerships, and corporations are required to file an information return, Form 1099, for all business payments made for personal services not reported on Form W-2s; for rents, premiums, annuities, royalties, and interest; and on dividends paid. Included in the information return are business fees paid for professional services to attorneys and accountants.

Withholding Tax Statements.   Every employer must furnish employees with a Withholding Tax Statement, Form W-2, by January 31. This statement includes a total of all wages paid in the taxable year, the federal income tax withheld, the total wages subject to FICA tax, and the total FICA tax withheld. A copy is forwarded to the IRS, and a copy is retained by the employer.

Taxable Income

Income is derived from many sources, and it is received at irregular times during a tax year. All nonexempt (taxable) income, in whatever form it is received, must be included in the income tax return, even though it may be offset by adjustments or deductions. Examples of income that must be reported are wages and salaries, bonuses, commissions, fees, tips, and gratuities; dividends; interest on bank deposits, bonds, notes, and United States savings bonds; profits from business or profession; pensions, annuities, and endowments; profits from the sale or exchange of real estate, securities, or other property; rents and royalties; share of estate or trust income; alimony; prizes and awards.

Tax Deductions and Adjustments

A record of each allowable tax deduction and credit should be kept in a tax file folder for quick reference when the tax return is being prepared.

That part of a person's medical and dental expense that is more than 3 percent of adjusted gross income is deductible. State and local income taxes, real estate taxes, general sales taxes, and state and local taxes on gas used in a car are deductible. Interest expenses such as those on mortgages, general-purpose credit cards, revolving charge accounts, life insurance loans, instalment contracts, debts on investment property, and taxes paid late can all be listed as deductions. Donations made to organizations that are religious, charitable, educational, scientific, or literary in purpose can be deducted. All or part of losses caused by theft, vandalism, fire, storm, and accidents may be deducted.

Miscellaneous amounts, such as expenses for business use of part of a private home, can be deducted if that part is used exclusively and continuously in connection with the business. Some legal contributions to candidates for public office and political committees are deductible. Payments for education required by law or regulation or for maintaining or improving work skills qualify as a deduction. Deductions are also approved for expenses stemming from the production or collection of income, or the management or protection of property held for producing income.

Adjustments to Income.   Employees and self-employed persons (including partners) can deduct certain moving expenses when the move is made in connection with a job or business. Certain business expenses that were not paid by an employer—such as travel, meals, and lodging—can be deducted. Deductions are allowable on contributions to Individual Retirement Accounts (IRAs). Contributions to Keogh Retirement Plans are deductible for sole proprietors, partners, and individuals. Periodic payments of alimony and separate maintenance made under a court decree are also deductible.

Tax Information   Schedules and forms needed to process an income tax return can be obtained from an Internal Revenue Service office, at many banks and post offices, or by using the order blank printed in the general instructions mailed to each person.

IRS publications that contain helpful tax information can be obtained by mail from any district director. Several that should be available to you are *Employer's Tax Guide* (Circular E), *Tax Guide for Small Business*, *Computing Your Tax Under the Income Averaging Method*, *Tax Information on Moving Expenses*, *Tax Information on Disability Payments*, *Income Tax Deductions for Contributions*, *Income Tax Deductions for Interest Expense*, and *Miscellaneous Deductions and Credits*.

Typing and Mailing Tax Returns   Two copies of the income tax form and appropriate supporting schedules should be prepared. One is used as a worksheet and goes into the tax folder, and the other is filed with the regional Internal Revenue Service Center. Tax returns should be mailed as soon as possible after January 1, but not later than April 15. If the executive misses the tax deadline of April 15, a letter on Internal Revenue Service Form 2688 must be sent explaining why the return was not submitted on time. If the reason for missing the deadline is serious illness, loss of essential tax records, or inability to assemble the records in time, an extension of up to 90 days may be given. Persons abroad are given an extension of 2 months.

REVIEWING YOUR READING

1. Explain the three ways used by investors and bankers to measure the worth of a business.

2. Identify the two fundamental questions that must be answered before one can judge whether or not a business is being operated intelligently and successfully.

3. Compare the three classifications of data that make up a balance sheet.

4. Differentiate between current assets and fixed assets.

5. Discuss the significance of the current ratio (current assets divided by current liabilities) and what analysts believe the minimum current assets for a business's safety should be.

6. Identify the primary financial statement that reports income, expenses, and net income or net loss from business operations for a fiscal period.

7. Define a budget, and indicate the elements every budget provides.

8. Discuss the reasons why a budget is a valuable management tool.

9. Explain the two major classes of corporate stock and compare them to corporate bonds.

10. Indicate the primary service rendered to investors by stock exchanges.

11. Explain the function of a deed in real estate transactions and the manner in which warranty deeds and quitclaim deeds differ.

12. Discuss the significance of the abstract of title in the real estate conveyance process.

13. Discuss the relationship that exists between the promissory note and the mortgage deed in financing real estate transactions.

14. Compare the three types of insurance available to the business community.

15. Describe the information contained on a Wage and Tax Statement (Form W-2), which is prepared by employers for distribution to the employee, IRS, and company records.

Using Your Skills

1. Your employer purchased the following stocks and bonds on February 14, 1979:

100 shares	AMF at 16⅝ (closing price)
100 shares	AmAir at 11½
4 bonds	BethSt 8⅜ 01 at 87⅝ (closing price)
300 shares	ContAir at 8⅞
5 bonds	Sears 7⅞ 07 at 87
100 shares	USSteel at 24¼

a. Follow these securities as traded and listed in your daily newspaper. Prepare a report comparing the purchase value of these securities with their market value four weeks and one week before the date of your report.

b. Referring to the illustration of a bond table in this chapter, indicate the year of maturity of the two bond purchases.

2. Obtain a copy of a Wage and Tax Statement (Form W-2) from the Internal Revenue Service and report on the method of completing it.

3. A secretary's responsibilities for income tax records for an executive depend on a number of variables, such as the size of the company, the length of time a

secretary has worked for an executive, and the complexity of company finances. Name five tax documents that all companies must file with the federal government.

4. a. You are a secretary in an insurance agency, and a customer contacts you and asks you to explain the difference between medical coverage and bodily injury liability coverage, and between collision insurance and property damage insurance. How do you answer these questions?

b. It has become popular to buy term life insurance rather than ordinary life insurance. Considering that some people buy life insurance to provide funds for their burial and for their survivors and others buy life insurance to accumulate a fund of money, describe a situation in which term insurance would be the appropriate form of life insurance to purchase, and one in which ordinary life insurance would be appropriate.

ExERCISING
YOUR
JUDGMENT

A Problem in Cooperation.   Paul, a typist, whom you supervise, complains, "I don't see why Ms. Bowman can't make up her mind. This is the third time I've typed this financial report for her. Every time I get it done, she thinks of something else she wants to put in it!" Before you reply to this comment, the following thoughts flash through your mind:

- Ms. Bowman is a meticulously careful person.
- The financial data she handles are very detailed and important.
- New data are coming into Ms. Bowman's office every few days.
- Important company decisions are based on Ms. Bowman's reports.
- Still, you do sympathize with Paul's frustration.

What will you say to Paul? Why? What are you trying to accomplish?

ApplyiNG
THE
REFERENCE
SECTION

1. Type the following sentences correctly, supplying the punctuation that has been omitted:

a. The Safeco Insurance Company in Seattle Washington mailed a pamphlet called Simulated Office Education to the high schools in the northwest

b. His business trip included stops in Omaha Nebraska Rochester New York and Fairfield Connecticut

c. That machine is electric this one is manual

2. Find the punctuation errors in the following sentences and type the sentences correctly:

a. The desk supplies you need at your work station are: blotter, carbon paper, stationery, letterhead, pencils, ball-point pen, and staples.

b. The boss said: "The following security "musts" are to be observed every day: remove everything from the top of your desk and lock it before you leave.

c. The speaker said that Willa Cather's book Shadows on the Rock was one of his favorite stories.

d. "Relent" means "forgive or give in".

e. Have you read Hemingways For Whom the Bell Tolls.

PART
SEVEN / Professional Growth

CHAPTER TWENTY-four

Making Career Choices

"Secretaries wanted, experienced and beginning, high starting salary, liberal benefits program, international division of pharmaceutical company. . . ." "Secretary, marketing research . . . will work with researchers in the field of communications/advertising. . . ." "Secretaries, publishing, looking for more responsibilities, new challenges. . . ." These are the opening words of several advertisements selected from hundreds of ads for secretaries in a large city newspaper. They are an indication of the variety of opportunities available. No doubt one must give careful thought to finding just the right position, but how does one begin?

Exploring Your Opportunities

You can simplify the often perplexing process of choosing the office in which you prefer to work. To do so, you need a plan that will enable you to classify and analyze the great variety of secretarial openings in the business world today.

Size of Organization
Secretaries are employed by large and small companies. In a small organization, the secretary is generally encouraged to become involved in a wide range of office and company activities. Large operations offer a wide assortment of specialized operations, so that a secretary can advance—horizontally or vertically—in order to attain career objectives. You should weigh the advantages and disadvantages of working in large and small operations and decide which is better for you.

Location
A major consideration in focusing on your employment opportunities is location. Do you wish to work for a local business, or are you planning to launch your professional career away from your home community? A secretary often shares

an apartment near the job with one or more roommates rather than commute between distant suburb and city or between city and town. A growing number of young people in our mobile society are seeking career opportunities in the area of their college, in distant states, and in foreign service.

Choice of Field

As soon as you resolve the questions of size and location, you need to think seriously about the kind of business or profession you would like to be identified with. Various kinds of business require competent secretaries. Each has its distinctive characteristics. Each recruits people with special aptitudes and abilities. It is here that you have an opportunity to match your interests and abilities with those of others you will be working with. Determine whether your knowledge of a language, your flair for writing, your facility with math, or your empathy for people might suit you for any of the following fields:

- Finance, insurance, real estate.
- Manufacturing.
- Service.
- Agriculture, mining, construction.
- Transportation.
- Communication and utilities.
- Wholesale, retail trade.
- Education.
- Federal, state, local government.
- Professions.

Type of Office

When you select a field, you will need to narrow your focus further to the type of office in which you would like to work. In the medical field, for example, you might explore the possibility of working for a doctor in a private or group practice; in a hospital; in the medical department of a large corporation; in a pharmaceutical company; or in a public health agency.

Employer

High on the list of important reasons for accepting a secretarial position is the opportunity of working for a dynamic executive. The secretary's expectations of an employer are a reflection of his or her motivation, interests, and qualifications. To the secretary, the employer is the most important person in the company. The employer receives the secretary's first consideration and competent service. In return, the secretary enjoys the recognition given the executive and the opportunities to learn about a special phase of the business. Mutual understanding and a helpful working relationship between secretary and executive help get work done in the most effective way.

Opportunity for Advancement

When you start on a job, you should find out about the opportunities for increased responsibilities and promotion to a higher position, and whether there is a merit system that rewards exceptional work. Although your first concern is to find a job in a field you like and in which you will succeed, you may want to seek a position in a company where you are likely to advance.

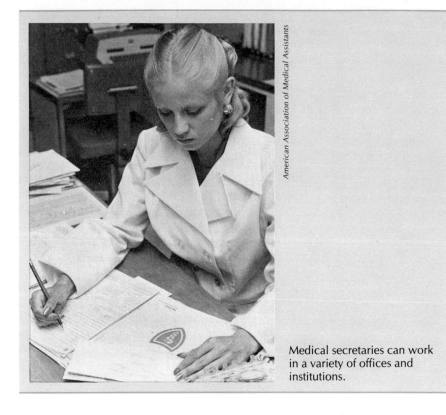

Medical secretaries can work in a variety of offices and institutions.

Medical Secretary

The need for medical secretaries has grown by leaps and bounds in the past few decades. Medicare, medical research, and the general proliferation of related medical services have created an urgent need for secretaries with sharp skills and abilities. Increased numbers of trainees are enrolling in training programs that stress medical office procedures. These trainees seek skills and knowledge that will enable them to attend to the business needs and, in some instances, to the semitechnical activities of the doctor or medical specialist.

Business Duties

Secretarial and related activities performed in medical offices can be divided into these categories:

- Those concerned with the examination and treatment of patients.
- Those indirectly related to the examination and treatment of patients.
- Those concerned with the business affairs of the medical office.

Only the medical specialist can perform the medical activities directly concerned with the examination and treatment of patients. Duties indirectly related to examinations and treatments, however, may be and often are delegated to the medical secretary. Of course, they are performed under the supervision of the medical specialist. Most of the business activities of the medical office—such as making appointments, receiving fees, attending to correspondence, and keeping medical records—are the province of the medical secretary.

A secretary's business-related activities in the medical office may include:

1. Handling the telephone.
2. Transcribing correspondence and medical histories.
3. Processing incoming mail.
4. Filing medical records and correspondence.
5. Receiving patients.
6. Making appointments.
7. Preparing and mailing statements.
8. Writing collection letters.
9. Ordering, handling, paying for and storing medical supplies and drugs.
10. Keeping financial records.
11. Making bank deposits.
12. Completing insurance forms.
13. Quoting fees and arranging payment terms.
14. Making hospital reservations for patients.
15. Using calculating and photocopy machines.
16. Proofreading articles, lectures, manuscripts.
17. Reading medical journals for items of interest.
18. Handling petty cash.
19. Keeping track of renewal of licenses, premiums due, membership fees, subscriptions, and meetings.
20. Making travel arrangements.
21. Gathering material from medical records for use in court.
22. Assisting in the preparation of income tax reports.

Semitechnical Medical Duties

Medical secretaries are occasionally called upon to perform semitechnical medical tasks under the direct or indirect supervision of a medical specialist. By this route, a number of medical secretaries have qualified as full-fledged medical assistants. If properly trained and supervised, a medical secretary may assist in such activities as the following:

- Helping patients understand the physician's instructions.
- Taking a patient's temperature, height, weight, pulse, and part of the medical history.
- Preparing trays for injections.
- Making routine laboratory tests.
- Sterilizing instruments and dressings.
- Preparing patients for physical therapy and supervising treatment, such as diathermy, paraffin bath, whirlpool, and heat lamp.
- Caring for surgical instruments and equipment.
- Replenishing physician's bag and maintaining supplies in examination and treatment rooms.
- Calming and reassuring patients.

The medical secretary fulfills many roles: the receptionist who greets patients and checks their appointments; the accountant who keeps a record of patients' visits and collects fees; the public relations agent who knows all the patients by name, keeps the office running smoothly, and frees the physician to devote more time to professional duties.

Those who wish to strengthen their medical secretarial qualifications can make good use of *Medical Office Procedures*.* Its extensive coverage of medical secretarial duties and responsibilities focuses on meeting and handling patients, processing medical records and forms, managing the medical office, and assisting the physician.

The American Association of Medical Assistants (AAMA) administers a certifying examination to eligible medical secretaries who have had three or more years of employment in a hospital, a clinic, or the office of a doctor. The examination tests knowledge of medical terminology, personal adjustment and human relations, medical law and economics, office skills, and accounting. Those who pass are certified for professional status as medical secretaries.

Medical Terminology   For the novice, becoming familiar with medical terms can be a challenge, but with the correct approach, a little study, and a medical dictionary you can gain a good working knowledge of medical terminology within a fairly short time. You can, for example, learn to pronounce, spell, and know the general meaning of terms such as *dacryocystorhinostenosis* without difficulty. Although unusually long, this is a typical term that describes the narrowing of the passage through which the tears enter the nose. Those familiar with medical terminology would know the spelling, pronunciation, and meaning of the word, even though they had never seen or heard it previously.

Over the years, medical terminology has developed terms that describe the human body, its functions, its normal and abnormal states, diseases and injuries, and the various means, agents, and procedures used to prevent, treat, or cure the many diseases and injuries. Each term must be broken down into its components, each of which carries a meaning.

Prefixes.   Prefixes are used to indicate location, direction, tendency, negation, number, measurement, color, and position. The true prefix is one or more letters or syllables combined at the beginning of a word to further describe, explain, add to, or take away from the meaning of the word. *De-* (away from), *ante-* (before), *com-* (with or together), *em-* (in or within) and *para-* (beside) are examples of prefixes that can alter the meaning of a word.

Suffixes.   A suffix is an element placed after a word, or root, to make a word of different meaning or function. Learning to recognize recurrent suffixes leads to recognition of family resemblances between a new word and words you already know. For example, *-itis* is a suffix that means *inflammation of*. Thus, arth*ritis* is inflammation of the joints, and bronch*itis* is inflammation of the bronchial tubes.

---

* Miriam Bredow, *Medical Office Procedures*, Gregg Division, McGraw-Hill Book Company, New York, 1973.

Stems.   The basic component of any medical word is its stem—the body of the word. The stem provides the basic meaning of the word but lacks descriptive capability without a qualifying suffix or prefix. A sample of the many stem words includes *cardia* (heart), *derma* (skin), *oto* (ear), *phlebo* (vein), *psyche* (mind), *thorax* (chest), and *rhin* (nose).

For a comprehensive classification and presentation of the principal medical combining forms, prefixes, and suffixes, refer to *10,000 Medical Words*.*

Medical History   Much of the medical secretary's day-to-day work is concerned with or related to the patient's medical history. These records are of the greatest importance not only while a patient is under the doctor's care, but also if the patient returns for further care after a span of time.

When a patient comes in for the first time, the doctor obtains all the information needed for diagnosing the condition, prescribing treatment, and forecasting recovery. On subsequent visits the progress of the patient's condition is noted; when the patient is discharged, the date of discharge and the degree of improvement are recorded. This record is called the patient's medical history.

Printed forms are available for keeping patients' histories. These have headings that help one to remember all the questions that must be asked. Some doctors prefer to use plain sheets of 8½- by 11-inch paper so that they can write a patient's history using their own method. In both instances the record is usually typed, either from the doctor's own notes or from dictation, and a clear and readable arrangement is important.

Potential Employers   A wide variety of employers need secretaries trained in medical secretarial procedures and prepared to handle medical terminology.

Doctors and Dentists.   In many cases the medical secretary works for a doctor or a dentist in private practice, handling all the secretarial work. Or the medical secretary may work for a doctor and one or more associates and share the work with another secretary. In group practice, where specialists in different fields occupy a suite of offices or a building together, executive medical secretaries are needed to maintain centralized records and take responsibility for the financial matters of the group.

Hospitals and Clinics.   One of the attractive areas for medical secretarial careers is working in hospitals and clinics. Even the smallest clinic needs secretaries.

Insurance Companies.   All insurance companies have a medical department that examines claims for accident and disability indemnity. Secretaries with a knowledge of medical terminology are in great demand.

---

* Edward E. Byers, *10,000 Medical Words*, Gregg Division, McGraw-Hill Book Company, New York, 1972.

Public Health Departments.   Each state and most municipalities have a health department that deals with, inspects, and maintains standards for public eating places, sanitation facilities, and water supplies and that monitors certain diseases. Trained secretaries are needed in these departments.

Foundations and Institutions.   There are numerous medical research foundations as well as sanatoriums, nursing homes, and convalescent homes, and most need secretaries. Those who have had training in medical secretarial practice are preferred. University medical schools also need secretaries with a medical background.

Business Institutions.   Medical secretaries are needed in the offices of manufacturers and distributors of drugs, pharmaceutical products, surgical instruments, and hospital supplies. In addition, most large corporations have medical departments that provide health services to their employees. Many of these companies give preference to secretaries who are trained in medical terminology and can transcribe medical dictation.

Medicare and Prepaid Medical and Hospitalization Organizations.   There are a large number of prepaid health plan organizations, such as Blue Cross and Blue Shield, whose members pay a monthly fee in return for which their medical bills are paid in part or in full. The operation of any of these plans requires a large amount of secretarial work. The medicare program has created many new secretarial job openings at federal, state, and local levels.

Legal Secretary

Whether you work in a law office or for a corporate officer in the legal department of a company, preparing legal papers is likely to be a large part of your job as a legal secretary. Two helpful references for the legal secretary are the *Legal Secretary's Complete Handbook** and *The Legal Secretary*.† Another source of information about legal secretarial work is *Sletwold's Manual of Documents and Forms for the Legal Secretary*.‡

Many secretaries who qualify for the title legal secretary reach this status through a combination of outside study and on-the-job learning. The National Association of Legal Secretaries (NALS) sponsors a professional legal secretary examination for secretaries who are members of NALS and have five or more years of experience as a legal secretary. The examination covers written communication skill and knowledge, human relations, legal terminology, techniques and procedures, and legal secretarial skills.

---

* Bessie May Miller, *Legal Secretary's Complete Handbook*, 2d ed., Prentice-Hall, Inc., Englewood Cliffs, N.J., 1970.

† Dorothy Adams and Margaret Kurtz, *The Legal Secretary: Terminology and Transcription,* Gregg Division, McGraw-Hill Book Company, New York, 1980.

‡ Evangeline Sletwold, *Sletwold's Manual of Documents and Forms for the Legal Secretary*, Prentice-Hall, Inc., Englewood Cliffs, N.J., 1976.

Martin Bough

Qualified legal secretaries continue to be in great demand.

Legal Documents in Secretarial Work

Although you can get a job in a law office without formal legal secretarial training, you will be one step ahead and earn promotion faster if you first become acquainted with common legal terminology and with the format of various legal documents. Some frequently used ones are discussed below.

Contracts. A contract is a binding agreement to do or to refrain from doing some lawful thing. This definition sounds simple, but its application is not. Contracts are classified in various ways depending upon the elements in them which are emphasized. A contract may be *expressed*, which means that it is stated in words, either oral or written; it may be *implied*, which means it assumes substance by the acts of the parties. Further, a contract may be *formal*, which requires that it be written and under seal, or *simple* and not under seal, in which case it may be oral or written. Contracts are also classified as *executed* when the terms have been carried out by all parties and *executory* when the terms have yet to be performed by one or more parties. Still another way to classify a contract is to designate it as *unilateral*; that is, only one party makes a promise for an act and a contractual relationship is not established until the actual performance of the act. A *bilateral* contract, on the other hand, is one in which each party receives as consideration for the promise made, a promise from the other party to fulfill the conditions of the contract.

Contracts form the basis of many business activities. To be enforceable by law, they must meet five basic requirements.

Agreement. Agreement is achieved when an offer is made by one party, called the *offeror*, and accepted by an unqualified assent of another party, called the *offeree*. It is important that the parties understand each other, for the offer must be definite, must be communicated, and must be made with the intention of entering into an enforceable obligation.

Real Consent.   In any contract it must be apparent that the parties understand each other. If one or more of the parties are led or forced into a contract by mistake, undue influence, duress, fraud, or misrepresentation, the agreement is not genuine and cannot be enforced.

Competent Parties.   Contracts of incompetent persons are voidable. If one of the parties to a contract is a minor or is mentally ill, he or she can void the contract. In actual practice, such contracts are usually carried out by both parties, and it makes little difference that the contract is voidable.

Valid Consideration.   An enforceable contract must be supported by *consideration*—a benefit received by the party making the promise (the *promisor*) or a detriment suffered by the party to whom the promise was made (the *promisee*).

Legal Purpose.   *Legality of purpose* is a basic requirement of every contract. An agreement that requires the performance of an act that is illegal or contrary to the general public interest is not enforceable as a contract.

Power of Attorney.   A *power of attorney* is a legal written authority empowering an adult to act for another in a specified capacity until the instrument is revoked. An executive who wishes the secretary to manage any personal business affairs must execute a power of attorney that specifies the acts the secretary is authorized to perform. The document must be signed by the executive and notarized. A power of attorney may authorize the secretary to sign checks during the employer's absence or to execute a deed or mortgage that must be recorded in a public office. In either case, the authorization may be for a limited period of time or for an indefinite period. That is, it may be a limited or a general power of attorney.

Affidavit and Verification.   An *affidavit* is a separate document attesting to the truth of statements contained in a legal paper. It is a sworn statement by the person making the declaration. It is signed by both the person making the affidavit and the officer administering the oath. A *verification* is a statement made by a person who claims it can be proved as fact. The verification is usually typed on a separate page and always contains a "sworn to" clause. It is usually required in connection with court documents. For example, the complaint filed by a plaintiff is accompanied by a verification, which certifies to the correctness of the content of the complaint.

Acknowledgment.   An acknowledgment is an act by which the party who has executed a legal paper declares, by means of an attached statement, that he or she signed the paper and did so of his or her own free will.

Will and Codicil.   A will is an expression of the wishes of a person concerning the distribution of his or her property after his or her death. A *testator* is a man who makes a will and a *testatrix* is a woman. A will must be in writing if it is to be proved in court, and it should be recorded in the public record. In addition, the will must be signed by the testator or testatrix and by two or more witnesses. An executive's secretary may be asked to sign as one of the witnesses at the end of an *attestation clause*, which validates the will. A *codicil* is an addition to a will and may be added to the original document or recorded on another piece of paper. In either case it must be prepared with all the formalities of the will itself. The *executor* of a will is a person named to carry out the terms of the will as soon as the testator dies.

Preparation of Legal Papers

Material dictated in a legal office is often set up in a style all its own. Legal instruments and court papers are specially arranged and styled to save time and to minimize difficult features that are characteristic of the legal field. (For an example of a typed legal paper, see pages 466–467.)

Number of Copies. The dictator should indicate the number of copies of a legal paper that are needed. As a general rule, the original and the first two copies are signed copies, with the third copy for the file. The number of copies and their distribution are indicated in the upper right corner of the file copy.

Margins. Many legal papers are prepared on printed forms. Where no printed form is available, they are typed on 8½- by 13-inch (215.6 × 338.1 mm) or 1½- by 14-inch (215.6 × 355.6 mm) hard-to-tear white bond paper. The paper has a double rule the length of the sheet 1½ inches (38.1 mm) from the left edge and a single rule ½ inch (12.7 mm) from the right edge. This paper is referred to as "legal cap." You may type within two spaces of the ruled lines, but under no circumstances should the typing touch the rules or go beyond them.

Since legal documents are bound at the top, they are typed with a top margin of 12 blank lines on the first page and a top margin of 9 blank lines on subsequent pages. Allow a bottom margin of at least 9 blank lines.

Page Numbers. On legal documents, pages are numbered 6 blank lines from the bottom, with the number centered between the vertical rulings. At least 2 blank lines separate the page number from the typed material above it. Arabic figures are used for page numbers, and they may have a single hyphen at either side, as -2-. To prevent the insertion of extra pages, the page numbers may be typed as "Page 2 of 4."

Spacing and Paragraphs. Legal documents are generally double-spaced, except for quotations and descriptions, which are single-spaced and indented at both left and right. Each new paragraph is indented 10 spaces. In legal documents, avoid ending a page with the first line of a paragraph. Also avoid beginning a page with the last line of a paragraph.

Punctuation and Form. Legal punctuation is heavier than that in regular business correspondence. Many more commas are used so that the meaning is clear beyond any misinterpretation. Lawsuits have been caused by an omitted or misplaced comma.

Although there are variations in the typing of legal documents, there are some generally accepted rules. The decimal and zeros may be omitted in writing

Start every page at least 1½ in. from top of page to allow for binding. Leave 2 in. on top margin on first page.

Indent 10 spaces for paragraphs.

Keep at least two spaces within the marginal rules.

Spell important numbers, such as sums of money, followed by figures in parentheses.

Number pages as shown here, centered between rules, 3 lines below body.

Allow about 1½ in. space for bottom margin.

CERTIFICATE OF INCORPORATION

of the

MUTUAL REAL ESTATE CO., INC.
(Pursuant to Article Two of the Stock Corporation Law)

We, the undersigned, desiring to form a corporation, pursuant to Article Two of the Stock Corporation Law of the State of New York, all being persons of full age, at least two-thirds of us being citizens of the United States, at least one of us a resident of the State of New York, and at least one of us named as a director being a citizen of the United States and resident of the State of New York, do hereby make, sign, acknowledge, and file this Certificate of Incorporation, as follows:

FIRST: The name of the corporation is to be

MUTUAL REAL ESTATE CO., INC.

SECOND: The purpose for which it is to be formed are to do all the things hereinafter set forth to the same extent as natural persons might or could do, as follows: To buy, sell, mortgage, lease or otherwise obtain, hold and dispose of real estate; build, alter and improve real property; to hold, buy and sell mortgages on real estate, and to do anything necessary or convenient for the accomplishment of such purpose that may lawfully be done.

THIRD: The amount of capital stock is Twenty Thousand Dollars ($20,000).

FOURTH: The number of shares of which this capital stock shall consist is Two Hundred (200), which shall be of the par value of One Hundred Dollars ($100) each, and shall all be common stock.

FIFTH: Its principal office is to be located in the Borough of Brooklyn, County of Kings, City and State of New York.

SIXTH: Its duration shall be perpetual.

SEVENTH: The number of directors shall be three (3) and the directors or officers need not be stockholders.

Page 1 of 2

round sums of money. Titles are centered within the ruled margins. All capitals are used for expressions such as *whereas, in witness,* and *resolved.* Breaking words at the end of a line is avoided. Sums of money are written out and then repeated as figures in parentheses. Abbreviations are avoided if they might cause doubt. Names must be spelled correctly each time they appear in the document.

Get at least 3 lines of body on last page, above signature lines.

Double space text (single space lists and quoted matter).

Use all capitals for such expressions as Whereas, In Witness.

Indicate signature lines by typing an underscore slightly to the right of center of page and extending to right margin.

Acknowledgment is certification that appears at end, showing paper was duly executed and acknowledged.

EIGHTH: The names and post office addresses of the directors until the first annual meeting of the stockholders are as follows:

Names	Post Office Addresses
Francis J. Donnelly	1353 - 78 St., Brooklyn, N.Y.
Louis A. Klos	375 East 26 St., Brooklyn, N.Y.
John W. Clayton	133 Willow St., Brooklyn, N.Y.

NINTH: The names and post office addresses of the subscribers of this certificate, and a statement of the number of shares that each agrees to take in the corporation, are as follows:

Names	Post Office Addresses	No. of Shares
Francis J. Donnelly	1353 - 78 St., Brooklyn, N.Y.	2
Louis A. Klos	375 East 26 St., Brooklyn, N.Y.	2
John W. Clayton	133 Willow St., Brooklyn, N.Y.	1

TENTH: The Secretary of State of the State of New York is designated as the agent of the corporation upon whom process in any action or proceeding against it may be served, and the name, address, and title of the person to whom the Secretary of State shall mail a copy of process against the said corporation which may be served upon him is

Francis J. Donnelly, 1353 - 78 St., Brooklyn, N.Y., director

IN WITNESS WHEREOF, we have made, signed, acknowledged and filed this certificate this 18th day of March 19--.

Francis J Donnelly (L.S.)

Louis A Klos (L.S.)

John W Clayton (L.S.)

State of New York } ss.:
County of Kings

On this eighteenth day of March, 19--, before me did come Francis J. Donnelly, Louis A. Klos, and John W. Clayton, to me known, who did depose and say that they reside in Brooklyn, N.Y.; that they are the parties described in and who executed the foregoing instrument for the purposes therein contained.

In witness whereof, I hereunto set my hand and official seal. *Walter F Fawett*
                                      Notary Public

Page 2 of 2

Signatures and Seal. Signature lines for the names of the parties are provided at the end of legal documents. To prevent the signatures from being attached to some other document, never arrange them to stand alone on a page. At least one or more lines of the typed document must appear on the same page. Use the underscore for typing the lines for the signatures of the principals and for the witnesses. Begin the signature line of the principal four lines below the body of the document, slightly to the right of the center of the page and extending to the right margin. The signature line for witnesses may begin at the left margin and extend slightly to the left of the center of the page, or it may appear below the signature of the principal. When positioned at the left, the first witness line should be preceded by the words *In the Presence of:* and typed one space below the first signature line and seal.

Legal Back.   Typed legal documents are bound in a separate cover called a legal back. It is usually blue paper that is heavier, longer, and sometimes wider than the document itself in order to protect the legal paper from becoming soiled. The cover is attached at the back of the document and is bound at the top. The way to fold the legal back is as follows:

1. Fold the top edge down one inch (25.4 mm).
2. Bring up the bottom edge so that it is even with the top, and fold.
3. Bring up the folded edge to the top, and fold again.

The uppermost surface of the folded legal back is the surface on which the information concerning the contents, referred to as the endorsement, is typed. The endorsement varies with the contents of the legal document, but it generally includes a brief description of the document enclosed and the names of the parties. To prepare the endorsement, partially unfold and insert the legal back into the typewriter with the top of the legal back to the left. Type the endorsement beginning 12 spaces from the top or in the printed panel when one is provided. Finally, insert the legal document in the top fold of the legal back and staple. The document is then folded to match the creases in the legal back.

Corrections.   Most legal documents are first drafted on legal-size paper with the expectation that changes will be made. Note carefully all changes that are

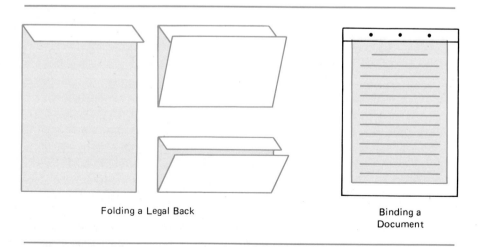

Folding a Legal Back

Binding a
Document

indicated. Erased and corrected words should be kept to a minimum. They are not permitted at all when they involve significant phrases, amounts, or measures. In very important documents, such as wills, there should be no erasing. If an error is made in a document before it has been signed, the entire page should be retyped. If an error requiring a correction by erasing or interlinear addition is found after the document has been signed, the signer of the document should be asked to initial it.

Blank Spaces.   Do not leave blank spaces when completing a printed legal document. If no entry is to be supplied, type spaced hyphens across the blank space. If an insertion is to be made, begin it one space after the preceding printed word; leave no space if the insertion completes the preceding printed word. To prevent unauthorized additions or alterations in larger blank spaces, use a rule and draw an enlarged z in ink to fill the blank space.

Carbon Copies.   Duplicate copies are required of almost all legal documents. Carbons are easily made when the document is typed on plain paper. When typing on legal blanks requiring fill-ins, it is generally better practice to type individual copies and indicate the duplicates of the original by the word *copy* rather than to make carbon duplicates.

If carbon duplicates of fill-in blanks are preferred, take the following precautions:

- Place a folded strip of paper over the top edge of the blanks to prevent slipping.
- Hold the packet to the light to see whether the printed material in one copy lies correctly over the corresponding material in the other copy.
- Loosen the typewriter platen and adjust the edges of the forms if they are not correctly aligned after insertion.

Special Legal Duties   Legal secretaries perform a number of specialized duties that involve legal procedures and legal documents.

Witnessing Signatures.   Legal secretaries are sometimes asked to witness signatures on a legal document, thus attesting to the identity of the signer. Never sign as a witness unless the signatures you are witnessing have been actually written in your presence.

Acting as Notary Public.   You can become a notary public. Notarial commissions are issued by the secretary of state, the governor, or other designated officials in the various states. Application blanks are available upon request, and there is usually a fee, an examination, citizenship qualifications, and bond requirements. Notaries must purchase notary-public seals and rubber stamps to press into the document showing their name, the county in which they are commissioned to act, and the seal of the state. The rubber stamp shows the expiration date of the commission.

As a notary you do not read the document you certify. You give the oath and verify that the signatures are genuine. A notary also witnesses affidavits and signs acknowledgments and verifications that are executed under oath. An acknowledgment is a sworn statement of a person that his or her signature on a document is genuine and made of his or her own free will. A verification is a signer's sworn statement of the truth and correctness of the content of a document.

Procuring Copyrights. In a publisher's office, you may be expected to know about copyrights and the laws pertaining to them. The typical nonpublishing company, however, rarely needs to copyright material.

A copyright is the exclusive right to the publication, production, or sale of the rights to a literary, dramatic, musical, or artistic work. Copyrights run for the life of the creator, plus 50 years. To obtain a copyright on a published work, write to the Register of Copyrights, Library of Congress, Washington, DC 20540, asking for an application form.

Applying for Patents. Patents are often applied for by companies and individuals engaged in research on new products. According to federal patent law, a patent may be obtained by "any person who has invented or discovered any new and useful art, machine, manufacture, or composition of matter, or any new and useful improvements thereof. . . ."

Information concerning patent laws and procedures for obtaining a patent may be had free by writing to the Commissioner of Patents, Washington, DC 20231.

Registering Trademarks. A trademark is any work, name, symbol, or device used to identify a manufacturer's goods and distinguish them from those manufactured or provided by others. A trade name, on the other hand, relates to a business and the goodwill of the business. The Patent Office registers trademarks and trade names for as long as they are in actual use. Information concerning trademarks may be had by writing to the Commissioner of Patents, Washington, DC 20231.

Other Secretarial Specializations

Technical Secretary
In addition to the usual secretarial duties, the work of a technical secretary is likely to include maintaining a technical resource library, gathering materials from other libraries, editing and proofreading papers and reports, and checking specifications, drawings, and standards.

Specialized Skills. The technical secretary must be able to recognize, spell, and use appropriately the technological vocabulary related to the area of research conducted by the company. Words such as *butyrate*, *ribonucleic*, and *ytterbium* should become familiar. A technical secretary should also be able to recognize mathematical or engineering symbols. A knowledge of how to set up statistical tables containing such symbols is necessary. And the technical secretary must be aware of the great need for accuracy in writing or typing research reports. Naturally, an educational background that includes science and mathe-

Engineers Incorporated

Continuing technological development provides many opportunities for technical secretaries.

matics, drafting, statistical typing, and report writing helps a technical secretary. However, a regular secretarial background plus one or two science-oriented courses to learn some technical vocabulary are sufficient for many beginning assignments.

The technical secretary working for a scientist or engineer can serve as an assistant, clearing the path for the employer to spend as much time in the field or the laboratory as possible, free of distractions and interruptions.

A useful reference for a person interested in becoming a technical secretary is *The Technical Secretary.**

If you would like to enter an industry that specializes in research, you might consider training as a technical secretary. Check the help-wanted ads in the newspaper for information about such opportunities. Some of the fields that specialize in technological research and development are the following:

Aerospace.   The most famous organization engaged in aerospace research is, of course, the National Aeronautics and Space Administration (NASA). Aerospace research involves the development of space vehicles and missiles and the investigation of meteorological phenomena.

Electronics and Communications.   The computer has made many changes in the conduct of business. Communications satellites are another product of electronic research.

---

* Dorothy Adams and Margaret Kurtz, *The Technical Secretary: Terminology and Transcription*, Gregg Division, McGraw-Hill Book Company, New York, 1968.

Nucleonics.   Nucleonics is concerned with the uses of atomic energy. The leader in this field is the Atomic Energy Commission (AEC).

Hydrocarbons and Petrochemicals.   Derived from coal, petroleum, and natural gas, hydrocarbons and petrochemicals are used in developing many products such as drugs, cosmetics, and plastics.

Synthetics.   Substitutes for raw material synthetics are used in the manufacture of many products, including clothing, dyes, building materials, and food supplies.

Life Sciences.   Investigations having to do with humans, animals, and plants are an increasingly important category of scientific research. Air pollution and water pollution are two of the many subjects studied by life scientists.

Educational Secretary

The educational secretary may work in a public or private school. There may be only one staff secretary, or each department may have one or more secretaries. The work may be in an elementary school, a high school, an institution of higher education, an educational association, or even a union office.

Public relations is an important aspect of an educational secretary's job. Some work may be done directly for teachers, professors, student groups, or administrators. A skill the educational secretary needs is the ability to meet and talk with different types of people—students, parents, teachers, administrators, board members, business leaders, important visitors, foreigners, and representatives of groups of all kinds.

Public relations is an important aspect of an educational secretary's job.

Variety is another aspect of an educational secretary's job. The duties range from cutting stencils, mimeographing tests, typing speeches and articles or news items for publication to attending rallies and meetings, taking minutes, and preparing state and federal reports. In an elementary or secondary school, the duties may include taking charge of school monies, such as club or sports funds, and ordering and distributing supplies.

There are many advantages to the educational secretary's job, one of which is the stimulating atmosphere of an educational environment.

The National Association of Educational Secretaries (NAES), with offices in Washington, DC, is a department of the National Education Association. The NAES sponsors a professional certificate program for college graduates.

Public Stenographer

For the person who likes to work independently, a job as a public stenographer may be the answer. As the title suggests, a public stenographer works for the public. An office may be set up in a hotel to make secretarial services available to travelers, or space may be rented in a busy commercial center.

The public stenographer, being self-employed, does not have the job security that goes with other types of jobs. The hours are irregular and the income varies from month to month. However, these drawbacks are compensated for by the satisfactions derived from running one's own business. Self-employed secretaries, if they are efficient and know how to manage the business, sometimes make more than highly competent salaried secretaries.

The public stenographer must be able to do all types of secretarial work, know how to operate a variety of business machines, be good at public relations, and be well organized and flexible.

Bilingual Secretary

For most overseas positions with private industry or government, a secretary is expected to exercise all secretarial skills in two languages. Practically every business engages in international trade of one kind or another. Thus, the bilingual secretary is much in demand by companies with international divisions, transportation companies, import-export firms, petroleum companies, banks, and governmental departments and agencies with overseas operations or projects. Also, in urban centers where English is a second language for large segments of the population, bilingual secretaries are employed in government and social service offices and in the school systems.

Communication Skills. The bilingual secretary must be qualified to take dictation in his or her native language and a second language and to transcribe notes into both. You may be called upon to provide hospitality for foreign visitors, and you must therefore be poised and competent and display good judgment. Bilingual secretaries serve as translators of all foreign correspondence for employers as well as for other company officials.

A position with a company involved in international trade usually brings you into contact with many exciting facets of business not routinely encountered by other executive or administrative secretaries—travel, currency transactions, import-export regulations, international relations, Washington lobbies, and political events.

Metric System.   Knowledge of the metric system of measurement is an important additional skill for the bilingual secretary. The system has been adopted by most of the countries of Europe, Great Britain, and South and Central America. In addition, it is a standard system of measurement in science and engineering in the United States. It is expected that the metric system will eventually be used in all fields.

The system is based on a unit of length called a *meter*, which is slightly larger than one yard, being equivalent to approximately 39.37 inches. The names of the linear units larger than the meter, in order of size, are *decameter*, *hectometer*, and *kilometer*. The decameter is ten times the meter, the hectometer is ten times the decameter, and the kilometer is ten times the hectometer. The kilometer is used to measure long distances. It equals approximately 0.6 mile. The metric system also has three units of measure smaller than the meter: one decimeter is 1/10 of a meter, one centimeter is 1/100 of a meter, and one millimeter is 1/1000 of a meter.

In the metric system, not only is each unit 10 times the next smaller unit, but also the name for each measure tells how many units as well as what kind of unit. For example, *deca* means 10, *hecto* means 100, and *kilo* means 1,000. Thus, a *deca*meter is 10 meters; a *hecto*meter is 100 meters; and a *kilo*meter is 1,000 meters. Other units may be obtained by dividing by 10 or powers of 10 to obtain the number of larger units or by multiplying by 10 or powers of 10 to obtain the number of smaller units. Because each unit is 10 times smaller than, or 1/10 as large as, the next larger unit, the metric system is built just like the decimal system with units of tens, hundreds, and thousands. It is thus quite easy to compute in the metric system, since you need only move the decimal point to the right or left to obtain the required unit of measure.

In measuring weights the principal unit is the *gram*. For measuring liquid or dry measure, the unit is the *liter*. The same prefixes apply as for the meter; for example, *decigram*, *centigram*, and *decaliter*.

A table of metric equivalents appears in the Reference Section.

Social Secretary

The social secretary works for either an individual employer or a company and is involved in planning social affairs and maintaining good public relations. The same secretarial skills are necessary as for other positions, but there is an emphasis on getting along with people and on social graces.

The Secretary in Word Processing Centers

In companies having word processing centers, the secretarial functions are divided between two different people—the administrative assistant seated near the executive and the correspondence specialist seated in the word processing center. The correspondence specialist performs the typewriting and transcription functions, while the administrative assistant handles the receptionist, public relations, and other secretarial functions. The administrative assistant may work closely with more than one executive at the midmanagement level or with only one top management executive. This position involves composing routine letters, researching and preparing preliminary drafts of reports, and completing special duties assigned by the executive.

REVIEWING YOUR READING

1. What are six things you should consider when choosing the kind of office in which you prefer to work?

2. Of the business activities performed by medical secretaries, which ones involve communication with patients?

3. Describe each of the word elements that can simplify the acquisition of a medical vocabulary.

4. Describe the variety of positions available to a medical secretary.

5. Explain what is meant by *express* and *implied* contracts.

6. What is meant by *unilateral* and *bilateral* contracts?

7. Identify the five basic requirements of contracts that must be present if they are to be enforceable at law.

8. Compare *affidavit* and *verification*.

9. Explain how punctuation and style in legal documents differ from that used in regular business correspondence.

10. Describe the functions of the two types of secretaries in companies with word processing centers.

USING YOUR SKILLS

1. **Secretarial Specialization.** Assume that you have your choice of being a medical, legal, technical, or educational secretary and all other things, such as salary, working conditions, benefits, and location, are equal. Which career would you choose and why? Type your answer.

2. **Legal Forms.** Visit a lawyer's office and interview the legal secretary. Ask to see blank copies of the various forms that are commonly used in this office; bring examples to class if possible. Each state may have different versions of the same form; therefore, ask for the forms shown in this chapter and compare them.

3. **Typing an Original Legal Document.** Turn to the rough draft for a petition for a voluntary accounting on pages 476–477. Type an original and one carbon, making the necessary changes and corrections.

4. **Technical Terms.** Find the item in Column 2 that matches the Column 1 item by consulting a dictionary or medical and legal references. Type both items on another sheet of paper with the appropriate number.

Column 1	Column 2
a. Medical stems:	
(1) cardia	ear
(2) derma	mind
(3) oto	chest
(4) phlebo	heart
(5) psyche	nose
(6) thorax	skin
(7) rhin	vein

SURROGATE'S COURT : COUNTY OF RARITAN

```
------------------------------------- :
In the Matter of the Judicial Settlement :
of the Account of Proceedings of WEST G. :      PETITION FOR A
THORPE, as Executor of the last Will and :      VOLUNTARY ACCOUNTING
Testament of                             :
                        James A. Linton, :          FILE NO.   001635
                                         :
                             Deceased.   :
------------------------------------- :
```

TO THE SURROGATE'S COURT OF THE COUNTY OF RARITAN:

The petition of West G. Thorpe, Executor of the last Will and Testament

of James A. Linton, deceased, residing at 189 Aberdeen Avenue, Willow

Heights, Raritan County, New York, respectfully shows:

FIRST: The said James A. Linton, deceased, at the time of his death,

resided at Willow Heights, Raritan County, New York and departed this life on the

23d day of November, 1979, leaving a last Will and Testament dated the eighteen

day of March, 1978, a true and correct copy of which is hereto annexed and marked

Exhibit "A."

SECOND: The Last Will and Testament of said party James A. Linton was duly admitted to

probate and Testamentary Letters were granted thereon to your petitioner by

the Surrogate's Court of Raritan County, New York, on the 29th day of December,

1979, and your petitioner is now the duly qualified and acting executor under

the last Will and Testament of said James A. Linton, deceased.

THIRD: Since the issuance of said Letters Testamentary, more than seven

months have elapsed.

FOURTH: The estate herein amounts to more than Five Thousand Dollars ($5,000).

FIFTH: Following are the names and post office addresses of all creditors

or persons claiming to be creditors of decedent (except as shown by the account those who appear to have been paid), of all

legatees, and of all other necessary and proper parties are as follows:

Name	Nature of Interest or Relationship	Post Office Address
James A. Linton, Jr.	Son--1/2 of entire estate	189 Aberdeen Avenue Willow Heights, New York
Susan P. Linton	Daughter--1/2 of entire estate	~~77 Park Avenue New York, New York~~ *189 ABERDEN AVENUE WILLOW HEIGHT. N.Y.*
A. Douglas Randolph	Creditor	14-207 Highland Avenue Jackson Heights, New York 10005
Mrs. P.R. Paine	Creditor	77 Park Avenue New York, New York 10016

There are no other persons other than those above mentioned interested in this proceeding, and all of said above-mentioned persons are of age *full* and *of Soond mind.*

SIXTH: Your petitioner is desirous of rendering to said Surrogate's Court a final account of this proceedings.

WHEREFORE your petitioner prays that his account be judicially settled and that the above-names persons, and all necessary and proper persons, be cited to show just cause why such settlement should not be had, and for such other and further relief as may ~~be~~ deemed just and proper by the court

Dated: August 9, 19--

_____
                                                      Petitioner

Double-space

STATE OF NEW YORK,)
COUNTRY OF RARITAN.) SS.

WEST G. THORPE, the petitioner names in the foregoing petition, being duly sworn, deposes and says that he has read the petition subscribes by him and is familiar with the contents thereof; that the same is true of his own knowledge, and as to those matters he believes it to be true, except as to the matters therin stated to be alleged on information and belief, *foregoing*

SWORN to before me this
10th day of August, 19--

_____
                                                      Petitioner

_____
     Notary Public

	Column 1	**Column 2**

b. Legal terms:

Column 1	Column 2
(1) affidavit	authorization to act for another
(2) codicil	attests to the truth
(3) copyright	addition to a will
(4) executor	carries out the terms of a will
(5) legal back	cover
(6) notary public	verifies signatures
(7) patent	exclusive right to published works
(8) power of attorney	exclusive right to discoveries
(9) trademark	identifies a manufacturer's goods

EXERCISING YOUR JUDGMENT

So You Want To Specialize. You work in a large personnel department in the home office of one of the biggest insurance companies in the country. Most of the personnel records are on punched cards and magnetic tape and are processed by a computer. The emphasis in your department, therefore, is on employee selection, motivation, and development. The head of the department, Dr. Jane Eggertson, is a brilliant psychologist and is highly respected throughout the company. You are the youngest of a team of three secretaries who work for Dr. Eggertson, having been on the job about three months. Although your college specialization was in secretarial and office procedures, you are so impressed by the outstanding job Dr. Eggertson is doing that you decide you want to learn more about psychology and personnel work and perhaps specialize in this field. Should you talk to Dr. Eggertson about it? What are your alternatives? If you talk to her, what will you ask for? How will this affect your relations with your co-workers?

APPLYING THE REFERENCE SECTION

General Review. This exercise is a general one covering business English. It gives you an opportunity to see how much you have improved your command of English grammar, style, spelling, and punctuation during this course.

1. From the choices in parentheses, choose the ones that correctly complete each sentence. Note any other errors and correct them as you retype each sentence on a sheet of paper.
   a. Did he (cite, sight, site) any examples?
   b. The costumes were a colorful (cite, sight, site).
   c. They left early they didnt want to be late for (their, there) meeting.
   d. Many people (dyed, died) in the terrible earthquake in Peru June 1970.
   e. Jane yelled Gus come back as the dog ran between her (flours, flowers).
   f. Mrs. Ashworth attended the (15th, fifteenth) re-union of her class at Vassar college.
   g. She arrived promptly at (9 a.m., nine, 9 p.m.) that morning.
   h. The stamps cost (79 cents, .79, 79¢, $00.79) and Eva was embarassed because she only had 78.

2. Correct any errors you find in the following sentences as you type them on a separate sheet of paper:

a. May 10th is the start of the school systems Fiscal year.

b. He said we cant promise delivery on that order for 12 cases of two inch glass rods.

c. The publishers offered him an eleven per cent royalty.

d. They celabrated there twentyfifth wedding annaversary and she received many gifts but no duplacates.

e. The community centers building will be enlarged.

f. There were three 68s in the list they checked there should have been only 2.

g. It is only a five minutes walk to the Campus.

h. The clubs minutes were read at the meetings end.

CHAPTER TWENTY-five
GETTING THE Right Job

A good job is always available for a capable secretary, but to find the right job for *you* requires preparation and persistence. You need a well-organized plan of action. The object of such a plan is to match your capabilities with the requirements of a specific job—one that will make your years of preparation worthwhile; one that you will be qualified, proud, and happy to accept; one that will give you a feeling of being needed, an opportunity for professional growth, and a sense of financial security.

SOURCES of Job PROSPECTS

Once you have decided upon your secretarial specialization and the type of office and company size that seem best for you, you are ready to begin the steps that can help you get the position you want. Developing a list of job prospects is the first important consideration. Your motto should be "Overlook No Opportunity." You will find that employment opportunities emerge from various recruitment sources: friends and acquaintances, college placement offices, employment agencies, newspaper advertisements, and company personnel offices.

Friends and Acquaintances   You may find the right job through friends and acquaintances. Begin by discussing your employment goals with relatives, neighbors, and other family friends. Ask them to let you know if they hear of an opening in their company for someone with your qualifications.

Many large companies encourage their employees to refer the names of applicants who would be interested in employment. Some even offer a bonus to the referring employee when the person referred is hired.

College Placement Offices

Most colleges and postsecondary schools provide their graduates with placement services. Trained placement counselors seek to match employer needs with student qualifications and expectations. They arrange job interviews for you and then help you evaluate each interview when you report back. Placement officers also invite representatives of large companies to visit schools for personal interviews with interested applicants. In addition, most school placement offices assemble a set of credentials for each graduate—a composite rating of ability and personality, a statement of potential, and recommendations from instructors and previous employers. These credentials are available to employers upon request.

Make sure that your credentials on file with your college placement office are kept up to date after you begin working, so that when inquiries are received for experienced secretaries, placement officers can tell whether you desire a change and what your salary requirements are.

Employment Agencies

Both private and public employment agencies are good sources of leads. Private employment agencies charge a fee for each placement, which is often paid in part or in full by the employer. The fee varies from area to area, but ordinarily it is approximately 10 percent of the first year's salary. In any event, before registering with an agency, be sure you understand the terms of the contract that you are being asked to sign. A directory of agencies that subscribe to a code of ethics can be obtained from the National Association of Personnel Consultants, 1835 K Street, N.W., Washington, DC 20006.

Prepare for an appointment with an employment agency as carefully as you would prepare for an appointment with a personnel officer representing a business firm. Some employers use private employment agency services to avoid having a flood of applications and in order to have someone else do the preliminary screening of applicants.

The United States Employment Service (USES) and state-maintained employment offices list openings in all types of work and, of course, do not charge a fee. By means of counseling and testing, these services try to match applicants to jobs. Civic and religious organizations such as the YMCA frequently offer free employment counseling; in some cities the chamber of commerce provides a similar service. To keep on the active list of any public employment office, you must check in regularly by phone, by mail, or in person.

Newspaper Advertisements

The classified help-wanted ads in your newspaper are an abundant source of leads. Although you should not depend on newspaper ads for all your leads, you should read carefully every issue of the papers you elect to follow. By reading them daily, you can keep up on job opportunities in your community as well as get some idea of prevailing salaries and fringe benefits. Employers who place recruitment ads in the classified columns use either a *signed* advertisement with the name and address of the company or person to contact or a *blind* advertisement. In a blind advertisement a telephone number or box number in place of the company name and address is used.

When you answer a help-wanted ad, mail your letter of application and data sheet the same day the advertisement appears or as soon thereafter as

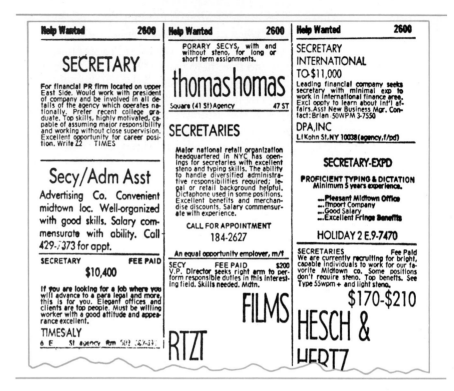

Classified ad sections list a great many secretarial jobs.

possible. Equally important, make certain you have read the ad thoroughly and have furnished all information requested.

A recruitment advertisement will often contain a number of statements that can help you evaluate the position and the company offering it. Look for a reason the position is vacant, for example, a promotion, expansion in the department, or a move to new offices. Pay close attention to descriptions of the job itself: "Handles confidential matters." "Organizes and maintains files." "Disposes of the mail." "Gives information on telephone." "Works for two busy people." "Does varied work, including heavy typing." Watch for items that suggest a company is different or better, such as the mention of a short work week, extra holidays, no time clock, accessibility to transportation, cafeteria facilities, special employee benefits, and promotion policies.

Civil Service Announcements

Opportunities for secretarial positions in civil service are continually available. The civil service secretary may work in some branch of the government, for one of the armed services or the FBI, for a senator or representative, or for one of the many departments or bureaus. The list of opportunities is almost endless and the positions are often attractive. Some offer overseas service. All civil service ratings offer job security.

Before you can be eligible for a secretarial position in the federal service, you must first work as a stenographer in either the GS-3 or GS-4 rating. To qualify as a stenographer, you must pass a shorthand examination (dictated at 80 words a minute) and a typing test (with a minimum speed of 40 words a minute and no more than 3 errors). In addition, each applicant is given a 45-minute general aptitude test covering English, spelling, and current information; a 5-minute alphabetizing test; and a test on computations. Eligibility for the GS-4 rating is achieved with higher scores on all the GS-3 tests plus a year's stenographic or secretarial experience or one year of successful schooling completed beyond high school. Only private secretaries to high-ranking government executives are eligible for GS-5 and GS-6 civil service ratings.

Direct Application

Most companies welcome job applicants. Larger companies maintain their own personnel or employment offices. If you want to work for a particular company, simply walk in or telephone and make an appointment to visit the personnel recruiting officer.

You will be asked to fill out a detailed application blank and discuss your employment expectations. You may be given qualification and screening tests. If there is an opening for a secretary with your qualifications, you may be referred immediately to the executive for an interview. Even if there are no job openings at the time, your credentials will be on file for consideration when a vacancy occurs. Here again, however, it is wise to let the recruiting officer know occasionally that you are still interested in working for that company.

Job Application

Getting the position you want requires a sales campaign, and you should plan one accordingly. You can communicate with a prospective employer in a number of ways: making a personal appearance, placing a telephone call, answering a newspaper ad, or writing a letter of application asking for an appointment and enclosing a data sheet, or résumé. Before you choose what seems most appropriate in a particular case, however, you need to study the job prospects and analyze the qualifications you can offer an employer.

Your Prospects

Obtain as much information as possible about a prospective employer. Inquire about the company from your acquaintances and instructors. Try to find out how old the company is; where its plants, offices, or stores are located; what its products or services are; what its growth has been; and how good its future prospects seem. You can answer some of these questions yourself by examining the company's advertisements in newspapers and magazines and by studying the company's annual report. Information of this kind will furnish you with some insight into the workings of the company; it will also give you something besides yourself to talk about during the interview and will provide material on which to base the questions you should ask.

Your school's placement office is an excellent source for booklets and other material prepared by various firms for recruiting purposes. You can usually obtain a copy of a company's own literature on job opportunities if you send a request directly to the company. Among other publications that can help you find out about a company are the following, most of which can be found in your college or public library:

- *College Placement Directory*, by Zimmerman and Lavine
- *College Placement Annual*, by the College Placement Publications Council
- *Thomas' Register of American Manufacturers*
- *Moody's Manuals*
- *Standard and Poor's Corporation Records*
- *Poor's Register of Directors and Executives*
- *Dun & Bradstreet Reference Book*
- Annual reports of specific companies

The second essential step in preparing to apply for a position is to analyze your strengths and weaknesses in relation to what the job requires. The preparation of your data sheet will enable you to make this analysis.

Data Sheet (Résumé)   Your school placement office may use a standard data sheet that you will be asked to fill in so that it may be used as a résumé of your activities and work experience. However, most schools and a number of companies prefer that job applicants prepare their own data sheets as a supplement to the face-to-face interview. The data sheet that you prepare becomes increasingly important if you change positions in the years after graduation. It is almost indispensable for such uses as application by letter, off-campus interviews, or an intensive job-hunting campaign.

Content and Layout.   A good data sheet helps you make a good impression. Conversely, a poorly prepared, messy-looking data sheet can severely reduce your chances of getting a position even though you may appear to be desirable in every other way. Contents and layouts of data sheets vary as widely as the different individuals who apply for jobs. Interviewers and companies differ as to what they want to see on a data sheet. Most agree, however, that it should be kept simple and contained on one page if possible.

Your data sheet must be typed, preferably on a good-quality bond paper. Multilithed, mimeographed, or otherwise duplicated copies are acceptable if they are done well. The data sheet must be neat. Careless erasures and misspelled words are inexcusable. Be sure to keep a copy on file to save yourself a rewriting job should the original be lost. If you do not have your data sheet duplicated mechanically, it is best to type a new one for each interview. You can then give it the most appropriate emphasis for each job.

Your use of white space is most important in creating an impression of neatness and orderliness. Spacing between all elements creates a clean, pleasing impression, whereas crowding too many details close together results in a cluttered appearance that repels a reader.

Organization.   The way you organize the elements of your data sheet is not as important as the fact that you do organize them in an orderly, meaningful way. It

```
                                        Roxanne Panoff
                                        5425 Sacramento Avenue
                                        Berkeley, California 94700
                                        (213) 555-9271


                        POSITION SOUGHT:  SECRETARIAL

                        I am particularly interested in
                        working in the public service
                        areas of social welfare, education,
                        or health.

        EDUCATION

               Foothills College, Los Altos Hills, California 94022
               Degree:   A.A., 1979
               Major:    Executive Secretarial
               Courses:  Typewriting (65 words a minute); shorthand (110 words a
                         minute); secretarial procedures (correspondence, filing,
                         telephone, financial records, report research and writing,
                         travel arrangements); English; psychology; business law;
                         economics; statistics; business communications.

        SPECIAL INTERESTS AND ACTIVITIES

               Assistant Editor, Pen & Quill, college student literary magazine
               Secretary, Foothills College Student Government
               Member, Volunteers of the Shelters

        BUSINESS EXPERIENCE

               Summer, 1978 - Herrick Memorial Hospital, Berkeley, California,
                              555-6000.
                              Assistant to Director of Volunteers, Mrs. Olive E.
                              Stuart.
                              Registered volunteers, checked assignments, answered
                              telephone, transcribed dictation, acted as relief
                              receptionist.

               Summer, 1977 - State Farm Insurance Company, 222 Lakewood Avenue,
                              Berkeley, California, 555-2121.  Stenographer for
                              three insurance underwriters; reported to Mr. James
                              R. Anderson, Assistant Manager.  Transcribed dictation,
                              processed loss estimates and summaries, answered
                              telephone.
```

A data sheet, or résumé, should be neatly typed.

is best to use a conventional layout with straight lines and conservative paragraphing. Unusually arranged data sheets have occasionally caught the interest of companies, but such formats are best left to the professionals.

A well-presented data sheet is shown above. Note that Roxanne Panoff seeks to highlight her strong points in an honest, straightforward fashion. It is natural for a graduating secretary to emphasize extracurricular activities. If you use a data sheet when you are job-hunting some years after graduation, you will want to highlight your work experience.

Your own circumstances may dictate a different approach to the data sheet. It is important to remember that you must sell your value to a company. To do so, you must appeal to the prospect's interest in what you have to offer.

References.   Most employers prefer that you list references on your data sheet. If you decide to omit them, however, have them readily available so that you can list them on an employer's application form or supply them during the interview. References related to your work experience are preferred to those of social acquaintances. A professor in your field of secretarial training is a good choice. Not all your references should be instructors, however. Include one reference who can attest to your moral and ethical values. Do not use relatives' names. Present the name and title of your school's placement officer and inform the reader that a folder of your credentials is available upon request, if such is the case. Always give the complete name, title, address and telephone number of each reference. Courtesy dictates that you ask your references' permission before using their names.

Work Experience.   List your work experience chronologically, beginning with the last job held and ending with the earliest. Give dates, along with company addresses and a brief description of the work you did. Since any company considering you likes to think that you will be a success, you should note any promotion or recognition that came your way as a result of success in a job. It is better, for instance, to say that you began as a file clerk and were promoted to receptionist than just to list the latter position. Demonstrated ability and progress mean more to an interviewer than the simple fact that you held a certain position. Include minor work experience if it relates in any way to the job you are seeking. You need not state the salary that you earned, but you should be prepared to discuss it if you are interviewed.

Education.   Present your educational background with the most recent training listed first. Give the name and address of each school attended, consecutive years of attendance, dates of graduation, and degrees or diplomas bestowed. Since your major courses in school and your achievements in them indicate your interests and abilities, you should display them. Include typewriting, shorthand, and transcription rates. Some statement of grades or class standing is also appropriate. Frankness is the best approach. Most companies do not limit themselves to seeking only students with the highest grade averages.

Special Interests and Activities.   Don't overlook your special interests and extracurricular activities. Most secretarial jobs are especially appropriate for well-rounded people. The fact that you participate in sports or musical activities or belong to social organizations speaks well for you as a person who gets along with others. If you were recognized by awards or offices, mention those, too. Leadership potential is welcome everywhere. If you had little time for special interests and activities because you worked your way through school and still made good grades, you also have a strong argument in your favor. State what percent of college expenses you earned and how many hours per week you worked.

Application Letter

The primary purpose of an application letter is to obtain an interview. To accomplish this objective, the letter and its accompanying data sheet must function as a sales letter. Together, they must attract the attention of the prospective employer, arouse curiosity about your skills, and suggest that you might be the person for the job so persuasively that an interview is scheduled.

5425 Sacramento Avenue
Berkeley, California 94700
June 7, 19--

Mr. Gerald Owen, Director
San Francisco Neighborhood House
400 Sutter Street
San Francisco, California 94100

Dear Mr. Owen:

At the suggestion of my former employer, Mrs. Olive Stuart, I am writing to inquire whether you have an opening for a secretary on your staff.

As you will see by the enclosed resume, I have recently completed a two-year executive secretarial program at Foothills College in Los Altos Hills.

Last summer I worked with Mrs. Stuart at the Herrick Memorial Hospital, where she is Director of Volunteers. I am also a member of Volunteers of the Shelters, an organization that specializes in working with children and adults served by community institutions such as hospitals, nursing homes, and neighborhood centers.

I feel, therefore, that I am doubly suited for employment in an organization like the San Francisco Neighborhood House, both because of my secretarial training and my volunteer work.

I will telephone you on Wednesday morning to see if you are interested in interviewing me.

Sincerely yours,

(Ms.) Roxanne Panoff

Roxanne Panoff

Enc.

A well-written letter of application can lead to an invitation to come in for an interview.

Appearance.   The first indication the employer has of your qualifications to fill a position is your letter of application. Make sure that this first impression is a favorable one. Use plain, good-quality, business-size stationery. The letter reflects your neatness, your sense of design, and your typewriting ability. No matter how good the content of the letter is, if the letter itself is smudged or poorly typed, you are placing an obstacle in your path. Proofread your letter carefully and type it over as many times as necessary until it is as good as you can make it.

Opening Paragraph.   Your first statements should create a favorable impression. Too many application letters start with vague and wordy statements. For example, "Having seen your advertisement for a secretary in the *Boston Traveler* and feeling that I can qualify for the position, I wish to place my qualifications before you." This opening sentence does not contain anything not already obvious to the employer.

In your opening sentences identify the position (or area) for which you are applying. If the reader is interested and has obtained a good mental image of you from the appearance of the letter, he or she will continue to read. If the opening is weak, awkward, or too general, your entire letter may be disregarded.

Body of the Letter.   Don't write—*talk* to the prospective employer. Use conversational language. Present your major qualifications by stating what you have done or can do. Avoid any tendency to use glittering generalities, which are usually short on facts. Consider this statement: "I am twenty years old, reliable, industrious, and willing to put forth my best efforts to the job that is assigned." Actually, the writer should have stopped after "I am twenty years old." Other examples of meaningless statements are "I am willing and eager to learn" and "I am conscientious and hardworking." This kind of statement should be replaced with convincing details and examples that will enable the employer to conclude that you are in fact a willing, eager, conscientious and hardworking person.

The body of the letter should point out those qualifications or activities that you want to highlight or that you think may be of special importance to the prospective employer.

Closing Statements.   The last sentence or paragraph should motivate the action you desire—the granting of the interview. At this point in your letter, the employer should have decided that you might be the person for the job. It is at this point that you should request that an interview be arranged in writing or by telephone.

Job Interview

The employment interview is one of the most important events in the average person's career experience. The time spent with an employer or an interviewer may determine the entire future course of your life. Yet interviewers often encounter applicants who come without apparent preparation and with only the vaguest idea of what they are going to say. Others, although they undoubtedly do not intend to do so, create an impression of indifference by behaving and

Allied Chemical Corporation

Applicants do best on interviews when they are confident and come prepared.

dressing too casually. At the other extreme, some applicants may think they are being subjected to an inquisition. They are in such a state of nervous fright that they are unable to do much but gulp and respond in monosyllables.

Such mistakes can be avoided by knowing a little of what actually is expected of you and by doing some simple preparation before the interview.

Preparation   Find out the exact place and time of the interview. Write them down and keep the notation with you. Plan to arrive at the designated place at least ten minutes early if you can. Your interviewer may be ahead of schedule. A few extra minutes will also help take care of unexpected emergencies, such as traffic delays. Be certain you have your interviewer's full name and find out how to pronounce it if it looks difficult. Take some kind of notepaper and a pen but keep them out of sight. You may be asked to take something down. If not, make a few notes immediately after you leave the interview. Be prepared to take tests of skills such as dictation, transcription, and typewriting production. A copy of *20,000 Words** can be useful if you must transcribe a letter or memorandum.

Neatness and cleanliness are critically important. Your own good taste in clothing is your best guide. But remember that you are looking for a position, not going to a party. Avoid extremes of style.

Don't become worried over too many details. A genuinely attractive personality and a good school and work record will overcome most small errors.

* Louis A. Leslie, *20,000 Words, Spelled and Divided for Quick Reference*, 7th ed., Gregg Division, McGraw-Hill Book Company, New York, 1977.

The Interview

The interview begins as you approach the company. If you drive to the appointment, park in the designated area. When you enter the reception area (whether it is the main office or the personnel department), approach the receptionist and state the purpose of your visit courteously.

If you do not have an appointment, request one politely. If you do have an appointment, give the time of the appointment, the name of the person you are to see, and your own name. If there is a delay, you will be asked to sit down. If literature about the company or its products is available, you may find it profitable to study it.

Avoid showing impatience at any delay. If you do find it impossible to wait for a long period of time, you may want to approach the receptionist to request an interview at a later time. A better idea is to schedule interviews far enough apart to allow yourself time for delays.

Smoking is prohibited in most public places; therefore, you should not smoke in the reception area, nor during the interview itself.

You cannot rehearse your role before an interview, because you don't know what cues will be given to you. Your best guide, therefore, is to rely on your native courtesy and good sense. Knowing the following basic rules may also help you with most interviews.

It is normal to be a bit apprehensive in an interview. It does help, however, to dry a damp brow or a clammy hand just before meeting your interviewer. Most experienced interviewers discount a certain amount of nervousness. Nevertheless, you should avoid doing things with your hands that might make your state of anxiety obvious.

Greet the interviewer by name as you enter the office. If the interviewer shakes hands with you, use a firm grip. Don't chew gum. Wait until you are offered a chair before you sit down.

A few interviewers like to do most of the talking and judge you by your reactions—the interest, comprehension, and intelligence you show. Others hardly speak at all, and for an inexperienced person these are the most difficult to deal with. Their attitude is that it is up to you to sell yourself. You will have to call on your knowledge of yourself and your interest in the work the company does. In both instances, make sure that your good points get across to the interviewer. Even if the recruiter does much of the talking, remember that you can ask questions that call in turn for a question you want to answer. For example, if you believe you are strong in special interests or activities, simply watch for an opening and ask, "Are you interested in my extracurricular activities?" The interviewer is not likely to say no.

Most interviewers follow a simple question-and-answer pattern. Your ability to answer quickly and intelligently is of great importance. If your answers are confused and contradictory, you will not impress the interviewer. A frank answer, even if it seems a little unfavorable to you, is better than an exaggeration, which not only may tangle you up in the next question but also suggests deception.

Conduct yourself as though you are determined to get the job you are discussing. The recruiter is aware that you may have other job prospects. Never make a disparaging reference about a former employer or about the college you attended. If something went wrong, suggest that at least some of the problem was of your own making. The job interview is not the place for a political or an economic discussion. If you are sounded out about your economic philosophy, try not to say more than is necessary to answer the recruiter's questions. Wherever possible, apply for a specific job. If there is no opening, the way you present your credentials may lead the interviewer to suggest another job, perhaps even better than the position you were seeking. If the company has a training program, you will naturally want to express interest in it.

Ask some specific questions about the company, but don't go off on a tangent in pursuit of irrelevant information. If you get the impression that the interview is not going well and that you have already been rejected, don't let your disappointment show. If you remain confident and determined, there is the chance that the interviewer may reconsider.

Most interviews last between 20 and 30 minutes. Be alert to signs from the interviewer that the session is almost at an end. If you want the job, sum up your interest, tell the recruiter you are interested, and stop.

If you are offered the position and are absolutely sure it is the one you want, accept with a definite yes. If you have the slightest doubt—if you do not want to accept without further thought or further interviews—ask for time. Be courteous and tactful in asking for time to think it over, and try to set a definite date when you can provide an answer. But don't create the impression that you are playing one company off against the other.

More often, a definite offer is not made. The recruiter will probably wish to interview more applicants before making any offers. Thank the recruiter for the time and consideration given to you. In leaving, show as much confidence as you did in arriving. Say something like: "If you have further questions, or if there is anything you want me to do, I hope you will get in touch with me." Then say "Thank you" and depart.

Salary.   Some interviewers do not choose to tell you what the position pays. You may be asked how much you want. The correct procedure in that case is to indicate that you are more interested in a position where you can prove yourself than you are in a specific salary, or that you are willing to accept a beginning salary according to the company schedule. This politely passes the question back to the interviewer, who will generally suggest a figure. In most cases, the offer will be a standard salary for the job level in question. It is in your interest to find out beforehand what the prevailing rate is and the level below which your qualifications will not permit you to go. You can learn what are reasonable beginning salaries for the type of secretarial position you are interested in by referring to help-wanted ads in newspapers or by consulting a salary reference guide published annually by the Administrative Management Society, Maryland Avenue, Willow Grove, PA 19090. Another source of information about salaries is the annual occupational wage survey published by the United States Department of Labor.

Follow-Up.   You do not usually write a thank-you letter following an interview. You should, of course, follow up any further contact suggested during the interview. If the interviewer seemed really interested in you or indicated that you would be contacted—and you aren't—wait about a week after the interview and then write a brief letter to remind the interviewer of your continuing interest in the company.

Factors to Avoid   Seeing ourselves as others see us can bring surprising revelations, for we are usually quite unaware of how our behavior is evaluated by someone else. A job applicant's mannerisms, attitudes, and personality quirks can sometimes create a bad impression and result in the job going to someone else.

The following negative factors noted during employment interviews led to the rejection of job applicants, as reported by 153 companies surveyed by Frank S. Endicott, director of placement at Northwestern University.

- Poor personal appearance.
- Overbearing, overaggressive personality.
- Inability to express oneself clearly.
- Sloppy application blank.
- Indefinite response to questions.
- Failure to ask questions about the job.
- Lack of interest in company.
- Lack of evidence of interest or enthusiasm.
- Lack of courtesy.
- Tactlessness.
- Lack of sense of humor.
- Lack of confidence and poise.
- Lack of purpose or goals.
- Overemphasis on money.
- Unwillingness to start at bottom.
- Evasiveness.
- Condemnation of previous employers.
- Poor handling of personal finances.
- Strong prejudices.
- Narrow interests.

The Application Form   Either before the interview or after it, you may be asked to fill out an application form. Completing the form as directed is a test of your intelligence—your ability to follow printed directions, your accuracy and carefulness, and the legibility of your penmanship. The time you take to complete the form and the neatness you show are also significant.

Legibility.   Your handwriting must be legible. Take particular care that any figures you write are clear. Since the interviewer may use the application form while interviewing, you will begin with one strike against you if your writing is illegible. If the directions request that you type or print, do so.

Accuracy and Carefulness.   Check all the information you have given. Do not leave any blanks. If the information asked for does not apply to you, draw a line through that space or mark it "Does not apply." Otherwise, the interviewer may think you overlooked some items. Misspelled words create a poor impression and also indicate carelessness or lack of basic skills.

Follow directions exactly. An applicant who cannot follow printed directions when given the opportunity to reread carefully will not be able to follow the many oral instructions given on the job and not repeated. If the directions say to print, for example, do so; if they call for last name first, don't put your first name first.

The Right Start

Let us assume that your interview was successful and that you obtained what you believe is a job you will enjoy. Now that you are launched in the new job, what guidelines will help you fulfill your business responsibilities? You will find that the factors that were important in landing the position are even more important in holding it and growing in it.

Accept Existing Methods and Procedures

The slogan "Make haste slowly" is a good one when you begin your new work. As a new employee, be slow to criticize the work methods in the office. Even if the methods and procedures seem inefficient to you, or the results not up to the standard you expected, be open-minded. As you become acquainted with your surroundings and with your co-workers, you may be expected to make suggestions when appropriate. For the time being, however, accept things as they are and do your job the way you are instructed to do it.

Be Friendly

Being friendly to everyone in the office is most important. But there is a significant difference between being friendly and being too eager to form friendships or to socialize. Avoid any tendency to attach yourself to one or two new friends and ignore the rest of the office staff. Lunch with different people and try to make friends with those in other departments as well as in your own. This is an excellent way to learn about other operations in the company.

As a newcomer to an office, let your employer take the initiative in introducing you.

Practice Good Grooming

Use the same care in your everyday grooming as you did when you prepared for the interview. Remember that getting the job is only the first step in your career; you must keep up the good impression. Daily good grooming gives you more confidence and poise.

Set High Performance Standards

You will want to do a particularly good job on your first work assignments. Try to deserve the confidence of your boss from the beginning. The sooner you show that you can turn out good work, the sooner you will be given the increased responsibilities—and salary—you are aiming for.

Be a Good Listener

Your new co-workers will be willing to tell you how they do their jobs and how they fit into the scheme of things. Listen carefully, even though you may not agree with their way of completing assignments. Most important, listen carefully to instructions from experienced workers and from your employer. If you are inclined to be forgetful, or if there are many details to remember, write things down.

Ask Intelligent Questions

Asking intelligent questions when an assignment is first given often helps prevent confusion and mistakes later on. Your employer is so familiar with the work that details can easily be omitted that are necessary to your proper understanding of the job. Be careful, however, not to become a question-asking nuisance. Do not ask pointless questions of busy people when you can easily find the answers yourself. The files or a company manual often can prove extremely helpful.

Learn Names

You will find good human relations easier if you make it a point to remember names. When you are introduced to someone, try to associate the name with something familiar or with some personal characteristic. You may find it helpful to fortify your memory by sketching a floor plan with the names and locations of the people with whom you come in contact.

Learn About the Business

When you receive booklets about the company—personnel policies, office manuals, company history, and so on—read them thoroughly. Soak up all the information you can about the company, its aims, its products, and its policies. Make sure that you begin to learn the vocabulary of the business, especially the vocabulary related to your boss's work. When you have free time, read previous correspondence and advertising materials.

Alertness will help you learn the business. It will also help you be aware of situations that can be improved. An employer wants your suggestions—when given at the proper time—and wants you to take the initiative in assuming responsibilities and in doing what should be done in the best way. Try to anticipate requirements and then be ready for them.

Raises and Promotions

Most often, raises in pay or promotion on the job occur as you earn them. However, you may feel that you have been doing good work and have earned a raise or promotion when your employer has not mentioned one. What should you do?

1. Evaluate your work carefully. List all the duties and responsibilities you had when you started your position and then list all those that have been added since that time. Has the list expanded considerably? Compare your list of tasks with those performed by others in the same job category. Are you doing more or less than they are? Have you performed these tasks more efficiently and more accurately than the others?
2. Evaluate your attitude. Have you been cooperative and done special tasks cheerfully when asked? Have you put in a full day's work? Do you take the initiative in doing your work whether it is assigned or not? Do you plan ahead to avoid last-minute rushes? Do you conserve supplies, or are you wasteful? Are there other questions you might ask yourself?

3. Evaluate your dependability. Are you at work every day? Or do you report sick often (on peak, rush, or slow days)? Do you meet deadlines?

If you can answer all these questions to show that you are doing a *better* job than others in your category, then you may want to consider approaching your supervisor or employer. But go prepared to show that you *deserve* the raise, not that you need it. All of us may feel that we need more money, but an employer will give you a raise only if you contribute more to the team.

Asking for a promotion is similar to asking for a raise. You must show your employer that you have grown to meet the qualifications for a higher position. Use the same strategy of self-evaluation, and add questions about your ability to handle tasks of a more complex nature.

Resignation

Leaving a job in an acceptable manner is important to you and your future. Once you decide to leave your present position, notify your employer and give at least two weeks' notice. It is essential that you stay these two weeks to give the employer an opportunity to find your replacement and to give you time to train the new employee. As you prepare to leave, list the tasks and duties you perform and write out step-by-step procedures for doing each one. During this transition period, continue to be cooperative and cheerful, and work to full capacity.

You may need to ask your present employer to write a recommendation so that you may apply for another position in your own company or another. Also, you may need to ask your employer's permission to use his or her name as a reference on the application blank for the new position. Acquire this permission in advance so your employer knows he or she may be asked for a reference.

Reviewing Your Reading

1. Describe the value of a well-organized plan of action for finding a job.

2. Name three sources of employment opportunities in addition to employment agencies and company personnel offices.

3. Of all the sources of employment leads, which can be the most fruitful in keeping you informed about job opportunities in your area and in giving you some idea of prevailing salaries and fringe benefits?

4. What is a signed advertisement in the classified columns of a newspaper?

5. Why do some companies use blind, or unsigned, help-wanted advertisements?

6. What are the prerequisites for a secretarial position in the federal civil service?

7. What two sources of information about a prospective employer will give you data on products or services, growth, and future prospects?

8. In addition to company annual reports, name three other publications found in college or public libraries that are helpful in finding out about a prospective employer.

9. Explain the significance of the data sheet when preparing to apply for a secretarial position.

10. Although contents and layouts of data sheets vary widely, what basic guidelines can you safely follow?

11. Describe the correct way to list your work experience on a data sheet.

12. What aspect of work experience is of primary importance to an interviewer?

13. What is the main purpose of an application letter? Explain how this purpose is accomplished in conjunction with the data sheet.

14. Explain how completing an application form serves as a test of an applicant's ability.

15. Identify five factors that are important in holding a position and growing in it.

Using Your Skills

1. **Selling Points.** List ten selling points that fit you for the position of administrative secretary. Include your skill in stenography.

2. **Job Sources.** Make a list, complete with addresses and telephone numbers, of as many of the following job sources as are available in your community: federal civil service, state employment office, private employment agencies, office machine companies, state and local civil service offices, and others (such as civic groups, social agencies, and so on).

3. **Preparing a Data Sheet.** Assume that you are applying for a position. Choose the job you would like most to have and prepare a data sheet that will help you put your best foot forward. Make your data sheet distinctive, but keep it in good taste.

4. **Writing Letters of Application.**

   a. Write a letter in answer to the following newspaper advertisement. Assume that you are enclosing the data sheet mentioned above.

   ### Secretary Wanted

   Public Relations Dept. Work for TV and magazine writers. Must be good stenographer. Will take bright beginner if college; 9 to 5, 5 days. Write Box H-8720, including résumé.

   b. Through conversation with Professor Roscoe Santee, with whom you had a college class in music appreciation, you learn of an interesting position as secretary to Dr. Harriet C. Romaine, Dean of the School of Fine Arts in a college in a nearby large city. Professor Santee suggests that you apply for the position. Write the letter.

Exercising Your Judgment

An Interview That Mattered. You have just come from an interview for the job of your dreams. You want the job very much. You had quite a long interview and believe you made a good impression. You talked with Mr. Harold J. Encord, vice president in charge of corporate planning, and to one of his administrative assistants, Mrs. Cora Adair. Mrs. Adair would train you, which means that you would probably work closely with her for at least the first three months. You will eventually specialize in compiling and editing research reports for publication. Your major in college was journalism and you have had some strong college-level office procedures courses as well as some good secretarial experience. You wish there was some way you could make these people understand just how much you want this job. Is there? What would you do in this situation to improve (not jeopardize) your chances of getting this job? Which would you do first? Why?

Applying the Reference Section

Type the following sentences correctly on a separate sheet of paper, supplying any punctuation needed:

1. When you have finished reading this letter fill out the enclosed card and send it to us.
2. Mr. Brown whom you sent to see me explained the situation very well.
3. The man about whom you wrote is not employed here.
4. Your suggestion is of great value however we feel that your plan is not feasible at present.
5. Mrs. Altman's letter which I have already answered mentioned this matter and we shall consider her suggestions at the next meeting.
6. These are the things you should send stationery pens erasers.

CHAPTER TWENTY-SIX

CAREER Mobility

Secretaries have traditionally been viewed as a vital link in the efficient operation of business, industry, government, and the professions. They have earned recognition and respect not only for their mastery of office skills but also for their ability to create, think, and organize. Some highly qualified secretaries work with executives at the policy and operations centers of their companies, and executives view them as catalysts through which company objectives are fulfilled.

Both job entry and advancement opportunities abound for secretaries. The Department of Labor's *Occupational Outlook Handbook* for 1978–1979 projects 295,000 secretarial and stenographic openings for the period 1976–1985, in an occupational group that currently totals 3.5 million. Salaries for qualified secretarial applicants with 1 year of experience usually range between $9,500 and $10,500 a year. Applicants with postsecondary training and some experience can find job offers with salaries that range between $11,000 and $15,000 a year. It is likely that, 5 to 8 years from now, men and women with administrative secretarial skills will earn $20,000 or more a year.

In recent years, the meaning of the word *secretary* has been blurred, owing primarily to dramatic changes affecting office procedures and equipment. And as described in earlier chapters, word processing technology, the need to control costs of office operations, the women's liberation movement, and government affirmative action programs have broadened career paths and opportunities for secretaries. As a result, the image of a secretary's job has changed.

This chapter offers suggestions to help entry-level secretaries realize their potential as important members of an executive's working team and (for those who wish to do so) move upward into management as administrative assistants.

Martin Bough

Secretaries become administrative assistants by acquiring experience, expanding their skills, and assuming greater responsibility.

Professional Growth

Your career as a secretary may be satisfying in itself, or it may lead to an equally challenging postsecretarial position. The direction you take will depend to a large extent on how you manage your strengths and shortcomings and on how sensitive you are to emerging professional developments and needs.

Today the secretarial profession has more potential than it has ever had, but professional growth requires careful planning and self-analysis. In order to create new opportunities for yourself, you must keep adding to your inventory of professional abilities. The way to do this is to become as fully involved as you can in your company's operations. This means putting your latent abilities to work on projects that are assigned to you or for which you volunteer. When you discover useful talents, develop them.

Keep informed about what is going on in the business world. Read the business and financial sections of your newspaper. Read at least one business periodical, such as *Business Week* or *Nation's Business*.

Certified Professional Secretaries

Over 11,000 secretaries are now entitled to use the initials CPS (Certified Professional Secretary) after their names. To a secretary, the designation is comparable in status to the CPA designation for an accountant or to passing the bar examinations for an attorney. You should consider qualifying as a Certified Professional Secretary if you plan to reach the top in the secretarial profession. The certification is widely recognized and respected by management.

A CPS is one who has successfully completed an examination and has met certain secretarial experience requirements. The examination is developed and administered annually by the Institute for Certifying Secretaries, a department of the National Secretaries Association (International).

AT&T Co.

Your career as a secretary may lead to a challenging postsecretarial position.

Various factors are involved in passing the CPS examination. Foremost of these is preparation in the subject matter tested. The amount of preparation required depends upon the background of the candidate and the lapse of time between formal secretarial study and the taking of the examination.

The two-day examination, given in May of each year at a number of colleges and universities throughout the United States and Canada, is divided into six parts: Office Procedures and Administration, Economics and Management, Accounting, Secretarial Skills and Decision Making, Behavioral Science in Business, and Business Law.

1. The office procedures part of the CPS examination covers a secretary's administrative job responsibilities involving business data processing, communications media, office management, office systems, and records management.

2. The major emphasis in the economics and management part is placed on understanding the personnel, finance, production, and marketing functions of business operations.

3. The accounting portion of the examination measures knowledge of the accounting cycle and the ability to analyze financial statements, compute interest and discounts, and summarize and interpret financial data.

4. Another part of the CPS examination is a performance test. Items must be grouped according to priorities and designated items must be completed within a specified time. The production items test dictation and typewriting abilities as well as editing, listening, composing, abstracting, judgment, and follow-up skills.

5. In the behavioral science part of the examination, candidates must examine the principles of human relations and exhibit understanding of themselves and their peers, subordinates, and superiors. This part also examines the fundamentals of needs and motivations, conflict, problem solving, supervision and communication, informal organization, and leadership styles.

6. The final portion of the examination measures the candidate's knowledge of contracts and bailments, law of agency and sales, insurance, negotiable instruments, and real property. Knowledge of regulatory law affecting business is also tested.

Candidates who complete a two-year certificate, diploma, or associate degree program in an accredited school of business, two-year college, technical institute, or four-year college and who pass the CPS examination must in addition complete two years of verified secretarial experience before receiving certification as a CPS. Persons who complete a bachelor's or advanced degree program and pass the CPS examination are required to complete one year of verified secretarial experience before certification as a CPS.

Anyone interested in preparing for the examination can obtain a study outline and bibliography free of charge by writing to NSA Headquarters, 2440 Pershing Road, Suite G-10, Kansas City, MO 64108.

Professional Associations

As management in all types of businesses, professions, and government organizations has given greater responsibility to secretaries, secretaries themselves have increased their efforts to raise their own professional standards and goals. Through membership in secretarial associations and participation in their educational programs, many secretaries have continued their professional training.

Membership in the National Secretaries Association (International) is open to secretaries who have two years' secretarial experience and who meet the other qualifications specified by the association.

In addition to regular membership, two other types of memberships are available: provisional membership for those who have had secretarial experience but do not have the full two years required for regular membership, and associate membership for certified teachers who are actively engaged in teaching business education in a high school, junior or community college, college, university, vocational, or business school and for Certified Professional Secretaries who are employed but are not qualified for regular membership.

Other secretarial associations include the National Association of Educational Secretaries, the National Association of Legal Secretaries, and the American Association of Medical Assistants.

Earning Promotion

Your attitude and activities following initial employment will determine your prospects for career advancement. Learn all you can about the company that employs you. Find out what the other departments in the company are like. Determine whether the position provides for further training and can serve as a springboard to jobs with more responsibility.

There are a number of things you can do from day to day on the job to get ready for a promotion:

Set High Standards.   Your first effort should be to set high performance standards for yourself—standards of excellence. Standards for job performance are generally set with average abilities in mind, but the pursuit of excellence and of job opportunity is a worthy goal for a secretary. Many people have the potential to advance in their careers but waste their resources in uncoordinated, undirected activity. They allow their lives to get out of balance because they do not take a comprehensive look at who they are and where they are going. Excellence and promotions are rarely achieved by chance; they are most likely to result when you look ahead and choose your goals, then work hard and effectively to reach them. First, though, you must decide where you want to go. Next, you must decide how to get there.

Grow Through Efficiency on the Job.   Show those for whom you work that you are worthy of promotion. Improve your work procedures. It is human to make mistakes, but see that you make fewer than when you began. As you become familiar with office routines and the work expected of you, accomplish the tasks with greater speed and efficiency.

To be efficient means to work with intelligence in producing desired results. It has to do with working more intelligently, not necessarily harder. It is actually easier and more productive to work intelligently. Efficient people use their minds. They use knowledge and judgment as well as job skills. They think about

Secretaries who earn promotions have developed efficient work procedures.

their work and foresee benefits to be gained by choosing certain procedures or courses of action over others.

Efficiency is the outcome of clear thinking, self-control, and purposeful study and effort. Find new ways to make yourself more efficient and useful. Then you will require less supervision. Try new methods and discuss new procedures with the boss. If you are aiming for a bigger job, you have to be a better person. You have to grow and earn the right to promotion.

Volunteer for Extra Service.   It is said that a person who wants something done in a hurry turns to the person who is busy. If you are the kind of person whom others in the office feel free to turn to when help is needed, chances are you will be remembered when the time comes for promotion. Don't be afraid to show that you are willing to work; don't be afraid to make yourself known, but not overassertively. Vacation periods, rush periods, and emergencies created by illness all provide opportunities for extra service that will make others notice you and show that you are one who can be counted on. Besides, when you take advantage of opportunities for extra service, you are giving yourself an opportunity to learn more about the business—more than is actually required on your job.

Take Advantage of Training Programs and Workshops.   Many companies offer a variety of training programs to talented employees. Secretaries who wish to develop their professional potential should make their long-range career goals known to their employers. Local colleges and universities offer specialized courses during the evenings. As a fringe benefit, companies often reimburse their employees for tuition expenses when a course improves or adds to the employee's job skills.

Professional organizations offer workshops and seminars for employees who wish to advance into supervisory management positions. The National Secretaries Association (International), the Administrative Management Society, and the American Management Association sponsor training seminars in many major cities across the country. Time off from the job and payment of the registration fee are frequently provided by employers.

Keep Up With Changes.   The changes that are taking place in business methods, policies, and equipment are astounding. Make it your business to keep up with them and with the reasons for them. In your office, changes in procedures may be reported through interoffice memorandums. Read the memorandums carefully. Make sure you understand the new procedures and the reasons for them. If you do, your boss will learn to depend on you to carry out tasks according to recommended procedures.

Try also to keep informed of changes in your employer's field of work. When you see articles in newspapers or magazines that may be of special interest, clip and give them to your employer. Keep up with changes in office supplies and equipment too. When the search is on for better ways of getting things done, you may be able to suggest just the right supplies or equipment, because your knowledge is up to date.

Randall Hagadorn/Allied Chemical Corporation

Management is seeking competent secretaries who have career aspirations.

Develop Assertiveness.   To meet Equal Employment Opportunity Commission affirmative action guidelines, employers are taking positive steps to provide advancement opportunities and to help secretaries, as well as other groups of workers, realize their potential. To develop to your fullest potential, be prepared to identify what you want, be able to tell others about these desires, and be able to work constructively toward your company's goals. Assertiveness can help you develop effective ways of managing yourself, your work, and your person-to-person communications. With the confidence that reflects assertiveness, you can avoid fears that can inhibit your development and even make it difficult for you to ask for more responsibility, to speak up at meetings, and to take steps for further professional development.

The Satisfaction of Work

There is enormous satisfaction in doing work for which you are trained and in which you excel. Add to that the prospect of growth and advancement over the years and you can look forward to a lifetime in which you have options. Few people go through life without working. The wisest of them prepare for work on terms that will provide them with security and fulfillment. The opportunity is yours. Take it.

Reference Section

Abbreviations

Acronyms
Always Acceptable
Government Names
Measurements
Organizations
State Abbreviations
Time and Time Zones
Titles and Academic Degrees

Capitalization

Business Letters
Commercial Products
Days, Months, Holidays, Seasons, Events
Headings and Titles
Initial Words
Laws, Bills, Acts, Treaties
Nouns With Numbers or Letters
Organizations and Government Bodies
Particular Persons, Places, or Things

Compound Words

Compound Adjectives
Compound Nouns
Compound Numbers
Compound Verbs

Envelope Address Placement

Footnotes and Bibliographies

Footnotes
Bibliographies

Forms of Address

Armed Forces Personnel
Education Officials
Government Officials
Religious Dignitaries

Letter and Memorandum Styles

Blocked Letter Style (Modified Block)
Full-Blocked Letter Style (Block)
Semiblocked Letter Style (Modified Block
    With Indented Paragraphs)
Simplified Letter Style
Memorandum Format

Metrication

Metric (SI) Prefixes
Metric (SI) Units
Common Metric (SI) Conversions
    (continued)

Abbreviations

Abbreviations are shortened forms of words and phrases designed to conserve space. They are used frequently in technical writing, statistical data, footnotes, and tables.

In business writing, abbreviations are acceptable in documents such as business forms, catalogs, and routine interoffice memos. In other kinds of business writing, use abbreviations sparingly. The best rule to follow is, when in doubt, spell it out!

Acronyms

Shortened forms derived from the initial letters of words that make up the complete form are appropriately used in business writing.

> PERT (program evaluation and review technique)
> ZIP (Zone Improvement Plan)
> NOW (National Organization for Women)

Always Acceptable

Common abbreviations, such as *Ms., Mr., Mrs., Jr., Sr., Esq., Ph.D.,* and *M.B.A.,* can be used at any time, as can abbreviations that are a part of an organization's legal name, such as *Co., Inc.,* and *Ltd.*

Government Names

Well-known government names are often abbreviated.

> SEC (Securities and Exchange Commission)
> FCC (Federal Communications Commission)
> UN (United Nations)

Measurements

In nontechnical writing, spell out units of measure. In technical writing and in business forms and tables, units of measure may be abbreviated without periods.

oz (ounce, ounces)   rpm (revolutions per minute)
lb (pound, pounds)   mpg (miles per gallon)
yd (yard, yards)   mph (miles per hour)

Organizations

Long organizational names that are commonly identified by their initials are usually abbreviated.

IBM   International Business Machines
AFL-CIO   American Federation of Labor and Congress of Industrial
           Organizations
NAACP   National Association for the Advancement of Colored
           People
NAM   National Association of Manufacturers

State Abbreviations

Use the two-letter state abbreviations in addresses. Use the other abbreviations elsewhere.

State			State		
Alabama	AL	Ala.	Missouri	MO	Mo.
Alaska	AK	. . .	Montana	MT	Mont.
Arizona	AZ	Ariz.	Nebraska	NE	Nebr.
Arkansas	AR	Ark.	Nevada	NV	Nev.
California	CA	Calif.	New Hampshire	NH	N.H.
Canal Zone	CZ	C.Z.	New Jersey	NJ	N.J.
Colorado	CO	Colo.	New Mexico	NM	N. Mex.
Connecticut	CT	Conn.	New York	NY	N.Y.
Delaware	DE	Del.	North Carolina	NC	N.C.
District	DC	D.C.	North Dakota	ND	N. Dak.
of Columbia			Ohio	OH	. . .
Florida	FL	Fla.	Oklahoma	OK	Okla.
Georgia	GA	Ga.	Oregon	OR	Oreg.
Guam	GU	. . .	Pennsylvania	PA	Pa.
Hawaii	HI	. . .	Puerto Rico	PR	P.R.
Idaho	ID	. . .	Rhode Island	RI	R.I.
Illinois	IL	Ill.	South Carolina	SC	S.C.
Indiana	IN	Ind.	South Dakota	SD	S. Dak.
Iowa	IA	. . .	Tennessee	TN	Tenn.
Kansas	KS	Kans.	Texas	TX	Tex.
Kentucky	KY	Ky.	Utah	UT	. . .
Louisiana	LA	La.	Vermont	VT	Vt.
Maine	ME	. . .	Virgin Islands	VI	V.I.
Maryland	MD	Md.	Virginia	VA	Va.
Massachusetts	MA	Mass.	Washington	WA	Wash.
Michigan	MI	Mich.	West Virginia	WV	W. Va.
Minnesota	MN	Minn.	Wisconsin	WI	Wis.
Mississippi	MS	Miss.	Wyoming	WY	Wyo.

Time and Time Zones

The abbreviations *a.m.* and *p.m.*, in expressions of time, are accepted abbreviations.

Standard time zones—*EDT* (eastern daylight time), *CDT* (central daylight time), *MDT* (mountain daylight time), and *PDT* (Pacific daylight time)—and *DST* (daylight savings time) are also accepted abbreviations in business writing.

Titles and Academic Degrees

Abbreviate personal titles when they are used with personal names.

Mr.	Messrs. (plural of Mr.)
Ms.	
Mrs.	
Mme.	
Mses.	Mss. (plural of Ms.)

Neither *Miss* nor *Misses* is an abbreviation.

Spell out all other titles used with personal names, such as *Professor, Senator,* or *President*.

Use periods for abbreviations of academic degrees.

B.A.	Bachelor of Arts
D.D.	Doctor of Divinity
D.D.S.	Doctor of Dental Surgery
Ed.D.	Doctor of Education
LL.D.	Doctor of Laws
M.A.	Master of Arts
M.B.A.	Master of Business Administration
M.D.	Doctor of Medicine
Ph.D.	Doctor of Philosophy
R.N.	Registered Nurse

Capitalization

Capitalizing a word gives it distinction, importance, and emphasis. The modern trend is to use capitalization sparingly. Conventional practice is to capitalize the first word of a sentence and the official names of persons, places, and things. Some words, such as *chairperson*, may or may not be capitalized, depending on whether they serve as proper (capitalized) nouns or as common (lowercased) nouns. The following guidelines are generally accepted.

Business Letters

Capitalize the first word and all nouns in the salutation of a business letter. Capitalize the first word in the complimentary closing.

> My dear Mr. Conroy   To the Heads of Departments   Sincerely yours

Commercial Products

Capitalize trademarks, brand names, proprietary names, names of commercial products, and market grades.

> Prestone   Xerox   Teletype
> Darvon   Coke   Photostat

Capitalize trade names unless they have become common nouns, as shown in a dictionary listing. Note that some manufacturers also capitalize the common-noun element.

> Kitchen Aid dishwasher   Ivory soap   A-C Spark Plugs

But:

> nylon   cellophane   mimeograph

Words may be capitalized in advertising for special emphasis.

> Save money during our annual White Sale.

Days, Months, Holidays, Seasons, Events

Capitalize days, months, holidays, events, periods.

Monday	Yom Kippur
January	Father's Day
Thanksgiving Day	Space Age

Do not capitalize decades and centuries unless they are special expressions.

twenty-first century   the seventies

But:

the Gay Nineties

Capitalize seasons of the year only when they are personified.

Farewell, icy Winter!

Headings and Titles

Capitalize all words in headings and titles except the articles *the, a, an*; the conjunctions *and, as, but, if, or, nor*; and the prepositions *at, for, in, of, off, on, out, to, up*. But capitalize these words when they are first or last.

Accountability and Performance Contracting
Where to Look It Up

Capitalize specific courses but not general subjects, except for proper nouns.

Typewriting I   English Literature II   a course in physics

Capitalize each element of a hyphenated word in a heading, except articles, short prepositions, and short conjunctions. Within a sentence capitalize only that part of a compound that is a proper noun.

Self-Insurance Provisions *(heading)*
These self-insurance provisions include . . . *(within sentence)*
The actress wore Elizabethan-style clothing.

Capitalize the first word following a dash or a colon in a title.

Sweetness and Light—An Eighteenth-Century Life
Shock: The Herald of Death

Initial Words

Capitalize the first word of every sentence.

> Our display was awarded first prize.

Capitalize the first word of an independent question within a sentence.

> The critical problem is, When will the loan be secured?

Capitalize the first word of a quoted sentence.

> He assured her, "The report will be ready tomorrow."

Laws, Bills, Acts, Treaties

Capitalize the exact titles and the shortened forms of laws, bills, acts, and treaties.

> Social Security Act   Taft-Hartley Act   Uniform Commercial Code

Do not capitalize the common-noun part of the title when it is used alone.

> Businesses must comply with the act.

Capitalize the names of contracting parties in legal documents.

> The Lessee will take good care of the property.

Use all capitals for certain words in resolutions and legal documents.

> WHEREAS, the Committee found . . .
> RESOLVED, That a formal . . .

Nouns With Numbers or Letters

Capitalize nouns that are followed by numbers or letters indicating sequence, except *line, note, page, paragraph, size,* and *verse.*

Act III	Check 210	Exercise 18
Figure 4	Flight 51	Invoice 714
Lesson 20	Policy 348910	Track 4
Volume 2		

Note: Do not use the abbreviation for number, *No.,* before a number unless company rules require it. Some insurance companies prefer it for policy numbers (*Policy No. 214685*).

Organizations and Government Bodies

Capitalize the names of companies, associations, societies, political parties, conventions, fraternities, clubs, and religious groups.

University of Connecticut	League of Women Voters
Young Women's Christian Association	Joint Council on Economic Education

Capitalize the names of countries and international organizations as well as national, state, county, and city bodies.

United Nations	Wisconsin Legislature
Supreme Court	State Department

Particular Persons, Places, or Things

Capitalize proper nouns and adjectives derived from them, as well as imaginative names when they designate particular persons, places, or things.

John	Ohio	Liberty Bell
Hoosier	Woman of the Year	First Lady

Nouns that were once proper but are now common are not capitalized.

roman numeral   watt   manila envelope

Capitalize the names of streets, buildings, parks, statues, rivers, oceans, and mountains.

Allegheny River	Pacific Ocean	South Station
Statler Hotel	Stapleton Airport	State Street
Westminster Abbey	Golden Gate Park	Statue of Liberty

Capitalize names of sections of the country when they designate definite regions or pertain to people, but not when they merely indicate direction or general location.

the South	the West Coast	Southern California
out West	the Far East	Southern hospitality

But:

south of Los Angeles

Capitalize *the* only when it is part of the official name of a place or of the legal name of an organization.

The Ohio State University   The Bronx   The Hague

Compound Words

Whether or not to hyphenate certain words is a decision the competent secretary should be able to make, based on a clear understanding of certain general rules. For other words not covered by the basic rules, the secretary should consult an up-to-date dictionary.

The following guidelines can help.

Compound Adjectives

Hyphenate a compound adjective that expresses one idea when it precedes a noun.

> company-managed food service
> never-ending story
> long-range plans
> $20,000-a-year salary

Hyphenate a compound made up of a noun-adjective, noun-participle, adjective-participle, or adjective-noun plus *ed* both before and after the noun.

> tax-exempt, duty-free
> interest-bearing, time-consuming
> soft-spoken, friendly-looking
> high-priced, short-lived

Note: Some noun-adjective combinations, such as *income tax* and *high school*, are easily grasped as units and do not require hyphens.

Do not hyphenate an adverb-participle combination if the adverb ends in *ly*.

> poorly planned program   newly organized staff

Do hyphenate an adverb-participle combination preceding a noun if the adverb does not end in *ly*.

> well-organized department

Hyphenate phrases only when they are used as compound adjectives before a noun.

> a hit-or-miss plan   a life-and-death question

Use a "suspended" hyphen and a space following each adjective when a series of hyphenated adjectives has a common basic element that is used only with the last term.

> right- and left-margin allowance
> one-, two-, and three-inch frames
> pint-, quart-, and gallon-sized measures

Use a hyphen after *self* as a prefix.

> self-confidence   self-evident

Use a hyphen after a prefix to prevent misreading if the prefix ends with *a* or *i* and the base word begins with the same letter.

> ultra-active   semi-independent

Note: Most prefixes ending with *e* or *o* omit the hyphen with base words beginning with the same letter.

> reentry   cooperate
> reemploy   coordinate

The prefix *re* should be followed by a hyphen only to distinguish the word from another word with the same spelling but a different meaning.

> re-count   recount
> re-cover   recover
> re-form   reform
> re-mark   remark

Compound Nouns

Many compound nouns follow no uniform pattern.

> crossroad, cross section, cross-reference
> goodwill, good sense, good-bye
> trademark, trade name, trade-in

Note: If the noun is not listed in an unabridged dictionary, treat the components of a compound noun as separate words.

Hyphenate two nouns when they signify that one thing or one person has two functions.

> secretary-treasurer

Hyphenate *ex* and *elect* in compound titles.

> ex-Governor Dempsey
> Governor-elect Conrad

Compound Numbers

Hyphenate spelled-out numbers between 21 and 99.

> twenty-nine
> one hundred fifty-one
> thirty-four hundred

Separate by a hyphen the numerator and the denominator of a spelled-out fraction.

> two-thirds   nine-sixteenths

Compound Verbs

Compound verbs are usually either hyphenated or solid.

> to double-space   to tape-record
> to proofread   to highlight

Do not confuse a verb-adverb combination with a compound verb.

> to trade in   to follow up

Envelope Address Placement

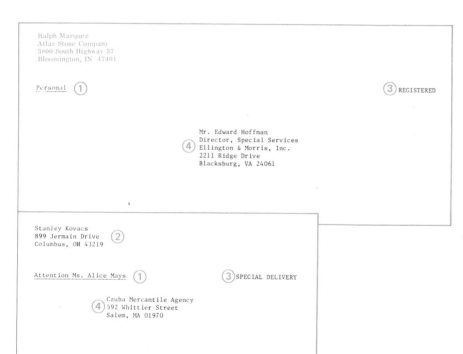

1. Attention lines and special notations are typed in underscored capital and small letters on line 9 (or on the third line below the return address, whichever is lower), aligning with the return address.
2. A typed return address begins on the third line 5 or 6 spaces from the left edge.
3. Notations of special mailing procedures are positioned on line 9, to end 5 or 6 spaces from the right edge of the envelope. They are typed in all-capital letters.
4. Position the name and address on a small envelope on line 12, 2 inches (50 mm) from the left edge; and on a large envelope on line 14, 4 inches (100 mm) from the edge.

Note: The U.S. Postal Service recommends that envelopes or labels be addressed in all capital letters, with no punctuation, and with the two-letter state abbreviations. Use capital letters without punctuation for the addressee. Place the street address or box number on the second line. A box number should precede the name of the post office station. An apartment number should follow the address on the same line. Place the city, state, and ZIP Code and nothing else on the bottom line.

Footnotes and Bibliographies

Footnotes

Indicate footnotes in reports or papers with superior (raised) numbers to the right of words or passages requiring documentation.

Number footnotes consecutively throughout a report or paper or separately for each page. Footnotes may be positioned at the bottom of the page (separated from the text above by a 2-inch-long—24 elite spaces or 20 pica spaces—typed line), between lines in the text proper (separated from the text by rules above and below), or all together at the end of the report or paper.

Indent and single-space footnotes, but double-space between them.

Recommended patterns for constructing reference footnotes are shown below. However, punctuation and styling of footnotes may vary, according to the source consulted.

[1]Author(s), *book title*, publisher, place of publication, year of publication, page number(s).

[2]Ibid., pp. 102–109. (*Ibid.* represents all the elements of the previous footnote except the page numbers.)

[3]Author's surname, op. cit., p. 46. (*Op. cit.* refers to a work previously cited when references to other works have intervened.)

[4]Author's surname, loc. cit. (*Loc. cit.* is used when several footnotes intervene between two references not only to the same work but also to the same page of that work.)

[5]Author (if known), "article title," *name of newspaper*, date, page number, column number.

[6]Author (if known), "article title," *name of magazine*, date, page number.

[7]Author, "article title," *title of journal* (often abbreviated), series number (if given), volume number, issue number (if given), page number, date.

[8]Author (if given), "article title" (if appropriate), *title of bulletin, pamphlet, or monograph*, series title and series number (if appropriate), sponsoring organization, place, date, page number.

[9]Author, "title," identity of unpublished or mimeographed work (dissertation, thesis, or report), name of academic institution, place, date, page number.

Bibliographies

A reference in a bibliography differs from a footnote reference to the same entry in several ways.

1. Entries are not numbered but are listed alphabetically.

2. The surname of the first author appears first. Entries lacking an author are listed by title, disregarding the words *The* or *A* at the beginning of a title.

3. Each entry begins at the left margin, and additional lines within each entry are uniformly indented ten spaces.

Begin a bibliography on a fresh page under the center heading *Bibliography* or *Selected Bibliography*. Type the heading on line 13 and use the same left and right margins as on other pages in the report or paper. Leave two blank lines between the heading and the first entry and one blank line between each single-spaced entry.

When a bibliography contains more than one work by the same author, replace the author's name with a six-hyphen dash in all the entries after the first.

Items of a bibliography may be separated into subgroups and then arranged alphabetically within each subgroup. Subgroups commonly used are the following:

Books	Magazines	Newspapers
Pamphlets	Reports	Unpublished Theses
Audiovisual Materials		

Number the pages of the bibliography consecutively with the appendix, if any.

Forms of Address

The following forms of address and salutation should be used when writing to a person who holds an official position in the military, in education, in government, or in a religious organization. The more formal salutations precede the less formal ones.

Although masculine titles are shown for the sake of simplicity, feminine titles may also be used, as follows:

Substitute	For
Mrs., Miss, or Ms.	Mr.
Madam (title)	Mr. (title)
Madam	Sir

Armed Forces Personnel

Officers and enlisted personnel in the armed forces should be addressed by their titles. All such titles of rank or rating may be abbreviated in addresses before full names and are followed by the appropriate initials USA, USN, etc.

General (Lt. Gen., Maj. Gen., Brig. Gen.)	Colonel (Lt. Col.), Major, Captain
General (or Lt. Gen., Maj. Gen., Brig. Gen.) . . . (full name), USA Address Sir: Dear General . . . (surname):	Colonel . . . (full name), USA or: Major . . . (full name), USA or: Captain . . . (full name), USA Address Sir: Dear . . . (rank) . . . (surname):

Lieutenant (1st Lt., 2d Lt.)

Lieutenant . . . (full name),
USA
Address
Dear Lieutenant . . .
(surname):

Cadet

Cadet . . . (full name), USA
Address
Dear Sir:
Dear Mr. . . . (surname):

Admiral (Fleet Admiral, Vice Admiral, Rear Admiral)

Admiral . . . (full name), USN
or: Vice Admiral . . . (full name),
USN
or: Rear Admiral . . . (full name),
USN
Address
Sir:
Dear Admiral . . . (surname):

Commodore, Captain, Commander, Lt. Comdr.

Commodore . . . (full name),
USN
or: Captain . . . (full name), USN
or: Commander . . . (full name),
USN
Address
Dear . . . (rank) . . . (surname):

Junior Navy Officers (Lieutenant, Lt. jg, Ensign)

Lieutenant . . . (full name),
USN
or: Ensign . . . (full name), USN
Address
Dear Mr. . . . (surname):

Enlisted Personnel

Sergeant . . . (full name), USA
or: Corporal . . . (full name), USA
or: Seaman . . . (full name), USN
Address
Dear . . . (rank) . . . (surname):

Education Officials

The names and addresses of officials in the field of education may be found in the *Education Directory* issued by the U.S. Office of Education.

President or Chancellor of a College or University

Dr. (or Mr.) . . . (full name)
President (or Chancellor), . . .
(name of college)
Address
or: . . . (full name) . . . (highest
degree)
President, . . . (name of
college)
Address
Dear President (or
Chancellor) . . . (surname):
Dear Dr. . . . (surname):

Professor

Professor . . . (full name)
Department of . . .
. . . (name of college)
Address
or: . . . (full name) . . . (highest
degree)
Department of . . .
. . . (name of college)
Address
or: Dr. . . . (full name)
Professor of . . . (subject)
. . . (name of college)
Address

Dear Professor (or Dr.) . . .
(surname):
Dear Mr. . . .

Dean

Dean . . . (full name)
. . . (name of school)
Address
or: Dr. . . . (full name)
Dean, . . . (name of school)
Address
Dear Dean . . . (surname):
Dear Dr. . . . (surname):

Superintendent of Schools

Mr. (or Dr.) . . . (full name)
Superintendent of . . . Schools
Address

Dear Mr. (or Dr.) . . .
(surname):

Principal

Mr. (or Dr.) . . . (full name)
Principal, . . . (name of
school)
Address
Dear Mr. (or Dr.) . . .
(surname):

Member of Board of Education

Mr. . . . (full name)
Member, . . . (name of city)
Board of Education
Address
Dear Mr. . . . (surname):

Government Officials

In routine correspondence with government offices, titles of officials should be used; in official or special correspondence, the personal name is used in the address. Names of U.S. government officials may be found in the current *Congressional Directory* in public libraries. Names of state officials may be found in the state directories; those of city officials may be obtained from the city clerk's office in the city hall.

President of the United States

The President
The White House
Washington, DC 20500
Mr. President:
Dear Mr. President:

Vice President of the United States

The Vice President
The United States Senate
Washington, DC 20510

or: The Honorable . . .
(full name)
The Vice President of the
United States
Washington, DC 20501
Sir:
Dear Mr. Vice President:

Cabinet Member

The Honorable . . .
(full name)
(The) Secretary of . . .
(department)
Washington, DC ZIP Code

or: The Secretary of . . .
(department)
Washington, DC ZIP Code
Sir:
Dear Mr. Secretary:

United States Senator

The Honorable . . .
(full name)
The United States Senate
Washington, DC 20510
or: The Honorable . . .
(full name)
United States Senator
(local address and ZIP Code)
Sir:
Dear Senator . . . (surname):

United States Congressman

The Honorable . . .
(full name)
House of Representatives
Washington, DC 20515
or: The Honorable . . .
(full name)
Representative in Congress
(local address and ZIP Code)
Sir:
Dear Mr. . . . (surname):

Governor, Lieutenant Governor

The Honorable . . .
(full name)
Governor of (or Lt. Governor
of) . . . (state)
State Capital, State ZIP Code
Sir:
Dear Sir:
Dear Governor . . . (surname):

State Senator

The Honorable . . .
(full name)

The State Senate
State Capital, State ZIP Code
Dear Sir:
Dear Senator . . . (surname):

State Representative

The Honorable . . .
(full name)
House of Representatives
(or The State Assembly)
State Capital, State ZIP Code
Dear Sir:
Dear Mr. . . . (surname):

Mayor

The Honorable . . .
(full name)
Mayor of . . . (city)
City, State ZIP Code
Sir:
Dear Mr. Mayor:
Dear Mayor . . . (surname):

Chief Justice of the United States

The Chief Justice of the
United States
Washington, DC 20543
or: The Chief Justice
The Supreme Court
Washington, DC 20543
Sir:
Dear Mr. Chief Justice:

Judge of a Court

The Honorable . . .
(full name)
Judge of . . . (name of court)
City, State ZIP Code
Sir:
Dear Judge . . . (surname):

American Ambassador

The Honorable . . .
(full name)
American Ambassador
City, Country
Sir:
Dear Mr. Ambassador:

American Minister

The Honorable . . .
(full name)
American Minister
City, Country
Sir:
Dear Mr. Minister:

Foreign Ambassador in the United States

His Excellency, . . .
(full name)
Ambassador of . . . (country)
Washington, DC ZIP Code
Excellency:
Dear Mr. Ambassador:

Religious Dignitaries

The names and titles of officials and dignitaries of their respective faiths may be obtained from *The Catholic Directory* and *The Episcopal Church Annual,* which may be found in most public libraries. *Webster's Seventh New Collegiate Dictionary* and *The Gregg Reference Manual* by William A. Sabin also include religious titles in their "Forms of Address" sections.

Examples of forms of address for Roman Catholic, Protestant, and Jewish dignitaries are as follows:

Priest

The Reverend . . .
(full name and initials
of order)
Address
Reverend Father:
Dear Father . . .
(surname)

Protestant Clergy With Doctor's Degree

The Reverend Dr. . . .
(full name)
Address
Reverend Sir:
Dear Dr. . . . (surname)

Rabbi With Doctor's Degree

Rabbi . . .
(full name), D.D.
Address
Dear Rabbi . . .
(surname)

LETTER AND MEMORANDUM STYLES

On the next few pages are illustrated different ways of setting up business letters. They include blocked, full-blocked, semiblocked, and simplified styles. The parts of a letter are identified on the illustration of the blocked letter. The special features of the other letter styles are identified on each illustration.

On occasion, other styles may be adopted for special correspondence (an example is the hanging-indented letter format used mainly for sales promotion letters, in which the first line of each paragraph is typed to a considerably wider measure than the rest of the paragraph). However, most business letters are typed in one of the styles shown on the pages that follow.

An illustration of memorandum format follows the examples of letter styles.

Continuation pages of a letter running more than one page are typed on plain paper, generally of a quality and color matching the letterhead. To type the heading of a continuation page, start seven spaces down from the top of the paper. Leave two blank lines between the heading and the material that follows. Either of the heading styles shown below is acceptable:

> Ms. Carmela Ricciardi
> Page 2
> May 6, 19—

| Ms. Carmela Ricciardi | Page 2 | May 6, 19— |

Continuation pages of an interoffice memo addressed to one or two persons are given a heading like that of a letter. For memos addressed to more than two people, give the subject of the message, underscored, rather than the names of the recipients, as in the example here:

> Spring Conference
> Page 2
> March 15, 19—

Blocked Letter Style (Modified Block)

J. Robert Johnson Co. 246 Maple Avenue Ipswich, MA 01938

(1) August 16, 19--

(2) Blake & Company
Commerce Building
225 South Fremont Street
Portland, Oregon 97212

(3) ATTENTION MR. W. ROSSETTI

(4) Ladies and Gentlemen:

(5) SUBJECT: INVOICE NO. 05123-10

Our salesperson, Vince Tabor, has telephoned us about the missing automotive parts listed on the above invoice but not received by you.

A check of our records indicates that our stock of this item was depleted when your order was filled. It is indeed unfortunate that we neglected to inform you of this fact--please accept our apologies.

(6) You will be glad to know, however, that these items have now been shipped air freight to you and should be received within two days' time.

We are pleased to enclose a copy of our newest catalog, and we look forward to the opportunity of serving you again in the near future.

(7) Sincerely yours,

John Harelson

(8) John Harelson
General Manager

(9) db
Enclosure (10)
(11) cc: Vince Tabor

1. **Date line** is typed on line 15 or 3 lines below letterhead, whichever is lower. It may be started at center or typed to end at the right margin.
2. **Inside address** includes the name and full address of the person or company to whom you are writing.
3. **Attention line** begins at the left margin and may be typed in all-capital letters or underscored and typed in capital and small letters.
4. **Salutation** is an opening greeting. Use a general or company salutation when an attention line is used.
5. **Subject line** may be centered or blocked at left margin and may be typed in all capital letters or underscored with initial caps.
6. **Body of letter** is single-spaced. Paragraphs have a blank line between them and are typed with no indentations.
7. **Complimentary closing** starts at center.
8. **Writer's identification** may include the name and title, just the name, or just the title.
9. **Reference initials** of the signer are omitted when a signer's name is typed.
10. **Enclosure notation** is a reminder that the letter has an enclosure.
11. **Carbon copy notation** is typed at the left margin on the line below the reference initial or the enclosure notation.

Full-Blocked Letter Style (Block)

K ramer ~ Kent 1200 Charles Street, Van Nuys, CA 91409

(1) July 24, 19--

Placement Office
Laurel University
Riverside, Pennsylvania 17868

Attention Placement Director

(2) Dear Sir or Madam

We would like to arrange to visit Laurel University in December to
recruit employees for Kramer-Kent. What do we have to offer? Let me
list some of the reasons your seniors should consider Kramer-Kent.

Kramer-Kent has a liberal hiring policy. We have never discriminated;
your graduates will be considered on merit alone.

Kramer-Kent offers a six-month executive training program open to all
employees. This policy has led to the rapid rise of many young college
graduates to positions of responsibility. We are proud to say that 50
percent of our executives are under thirty-five years of age.

We also offer an excellent benefit program:

(1) 1. Major medical and disability plans cost the employee 25 percent of
         the premium; the remaining 75 percent is paid by Kramer-Kent.

     2. The retirement plan--which an employee may join after one year of
         service--is set up to return the retired employee 80 percent of the
         average salary during the last twenty years of service. Vacations
         are one week after one year of service, two weeks after two years,
         three weeks after three years, and four weeks after ten years.

We hope you will give us the opportunity to explain in detail the
employment possibilities at Kramer-Kent.

(2) Sincerely yours

Roberta J. Fischelman

(3) Ms. Roberta J. Fischelman
     Personnel Director

     aj

1. **All lines** start at left margin except runover lines in numbered list or an indented quotation.
2. **Open punctuation** is used. No colon after salutation, no comma after complimentary closing.
3. **Writer's name** is typed 4 lines below the complimentary closing; writer's title is aligned below it.

Semiblocked Letter Style
(Modified Block With Indented Paragraphs)

Robert & Jones Inc.

134 Apple Lane
Boston, MA 02045

October 8, 19--

Mr. T. E. Powers, President
Pelican Oil & Refining Company
215 Market Street
Shreveport, Louisiana 71101

(2) Dear Mr. Powers:

SUBJECT: FUEL OIL

(1)   Thank you for your letter of October 5, in which you offered to sell us fuel oil.

Mr. J. A. Short, our purchasing agent, has been away from the city, and I have only this morning been able to confer with him about our fuel oil situation.

In going over his commitments, Mr. Short finds that he has purchased as much fuel oil as our storage facilities will take care of. As soon as our stock condition is relieved, he will be glad to discuss our needs with you.

It is likely that I shall be in Shreveport soon, and I hope to have the pleasure of seeing you then.

(2) Very truly yours,

(3) ROBERT & JONES INC.

John E. Taggart

Vice President

(4) JET:sr
(5) cc: Mr. J. A. Short

1. **Paragraphs** are indented 5 or 10 spaces.
2. **Standard punctuation** is used. Colon after salutation, comma after complimentary closing.
3. **Company signature** is typed in all-capital letters 2 lines below complimentary closing.
4. **Reference initials** include signer's initials when name is not typed in signature block.
5. A **carbon copy notation** (cc) is added if someone is to get a copy of the letter.

Simplified Letter Style

New England Products

3904 Windmill Road
Vineyard Haven, MA 02573

(1)   November 1, 19--

       Ms. Kathleen O'Casey
       365 Prospect Street
       Torrington, Connecticut 06790

(2)

(3)   CHRISTMAS SPECIALTIES

(4)   You will be glad to know, Ms. O'Casey, that once more New England
      Products is prepared to help make your family Christmas celebration
      a memorable one.

      In past years, you have ordered evergreen garlands, holly, and
      mistletoe from us, and these perennial favorites are still available.
      In addition, we are featuring an unusual line of Christmas wreaths
      especially designed for our customers by Alicia Baldwin.

      Our assortment of tree ornaments is as beautiful as ever and includes
      new handcrafted miniature toys and dolls from West Germany, Spain, and
      Italy. You will notice that some of the silver ornaments can be
      personalized with initials or first names of family members.

      When you have enjoyed our catalog and made your decision, you will find
      our new simplified order form easy to use. Your order will receive
      prompt personal attention.

(5)   *(Mrs.) Elizabeth Perkins*

(6)   ELIZABETH PERKINS, President

      ab

1. **All lines** begin at left margin.
2. **Salutation** is omitted.
3. **Subject line** in all-capital letters on the third line below inside address.
4. **Body of letter** begins on the third line below the subject line.
5. **Complimentary closing** is omitted.
6. **Writer's identification** is typed on one line in all-capital letters on the fifth line below the body of the letter.

Memorandum Format

FIRST SOUTHERN BANK

(1)

TO All First Southern Bank Staff   **FROM** Helen Certano,
(1)   Personnel Department

SUBJECT Scholarship Fund   **DATE** October 6, 19--

(2) We are pleased to announce the extablishment of a scholarship fund for
children of First Southern Bank employees.

(3) Each year four scholarships of $2,000 each will be awarded to qualified
graduating seniors for study at accredited postsecondary institutions. (3)
The scholarships are not based on financial need.

Application forms and further information are available in the Personnel
Department. The deadline for applying is February 15.

(4) HC

(5) rl
cc: Mr. Marx

1. Align typewritten lines with the bottom of the guide words. Set the left margin two spaces after the longest guide word. Set a tab stop two spaces after longest guide word in right part of heading.
2. Begin message on the third line below the guide words in the heading. Single-space, leaving a blank line between paragraphs.
3. Allow equal left and right margins.
4. Align the writer's initials with the date. No salutation or closing appears.
5. Supply the reference initials of the typist.

METRICATION

Metric (SI) Prefixes

Multiplication Factor	Prefix	Symbol	Meaning
$1\ 000\ 000\ 000\ 000\ 000\ 000 = 10^{18}$	exa	E	one quintillion
$1\ 000\ 000\ 000\ 000\ 000 = 10^{15}$	peta	P	one quadrillion
$1\ 000\ 000\ 000\ 000 = 10^{12}$	tera	T	one trillion
$1\ 000\ 000\ 000 = 10^{9}$	giga	G	one billion
$1\ 000\ 000 = 10^{6}$	mega	M	one million
$1\ 000 = 10^{3}$	kilo	k	one thousand
$100 = 10^{2}$	hecto	h	one hundred
$10 = 10$	deca	da	ten
$0.1 = 10^{-1}$	deci	d	one tenth
$0.01 = 10^{-2}$	centi	c	one hundredth
$0.001 = 10^{-3}$	milli	m	one thousandth
$0.000\ 001 = 10^{-6}$	micro	μ	one millionth
$0.000\ 000\ 001 = 10^{-9}$	nano	n	one billionth
$0.000\ 000\ 000\ 001 = 10^{-12}$	pico	p	one trillionth
$0.000\ 000\ 000\ 000\ 001 = 10^{-15}$	femto	f	one quadrillionth
$0.000\ 000\ 000\ 000\ 000\ 001 = 10^{-18}$	atto	a	one quintillionth

Metric (SI) Units

Quantity	Common Units	Symbol
Length	kilometer	km
	meter	m
	centimeter	cm
	millimeter	mm
	micrometer	μm

Quantity	Common Units	Symbol
Area	square kilometer	km²
	square hectometer	hm²
	square meter	m²
	square centimeter	cm²
	square millimeter	mm²
Volume	cubic meter	m³
	cubic decimeter	dm³ (liter)
	cubic centimeter	cm³ (milliliter)
Velocity	meter per second	m/s
	kilometer per hour	km/h
Frequency	megahertz	MHz
	kilohertz	kHz
	hertz	Hz
Mass	megagram	Mg (metric ton)
	kilogram	kg
	gram	g
	milligram	mg
Density	kilogram per cubic meter	kg/m³ (gram per liter)
Force	kilonewton	kN
	newton	N
Pressure	kilopascal	kPa
Energy, work, quantity of heat	megajoule	MJ
	kilojoule	kJ
	joule	J
	kilowatt-hour	kW • h
Power, heat flow rate	kilowatt	kW
	watt	W
Temperature	kelvin	K
	degree Celsius	°C
Electric current	ampere	A
Quantity of electricity	coulomb	C
	ampere-hour	A • h
Electromotive force	volt	V
Electric resistance	ohm	Ω
Luminous intensity	candela	cd

Common Metric (SI) Conversions

Quantity	Multiply	To Find
Length	inches × 25.4	millimeters
	feet × 0.305	meters
	yards × 0.914	meters
	miles × 1.609	kilometers
Area	square yards × 0.836	square meters
	acres × 0.405	hectares
Volume	quarts × 0.946	liters
	cubic yards × 0.765	cubic meters
Mass	ounces × 28.35	grams
	pounds × 0.454	kilograms
Temperature	degrees Fahrenheit × 5/9 (after subtracting 32)	degrees Celsius
Length	millimeters × 0.039	inches
	meters × 3.281	feet
	meters × 1.094	yards
	kilometers × 0.621	miles
Area	square meters × 1.196	square yards
	hectares × 2.471	acres
Volume	liters × 1.057	quarts
	cubic meters × 1.308	cubic yards
Mass	grams × 0.035	ounces
	kilograms × 2.205	pounds
Temperature	degrees Celsius × 9/5 (then add 32)	degrees Fahrenheit

Numbers

Whether to spell out a number or to express it in figures is a secretarial decision that should be based on a thorough grasp of two generally accepted styles: the *figure style* and the *word style*.

In the figure style figures are used for numbers above 10; in the word style, for numbers above 100. In more formal writing, spelled-out numbers are appropriate. In tabular, technical, or statistical material, figures are appropriate. Between these two extremes lie most of the business communications a secretary handles. In the absence of specific company preferences, choose the figure style for most general correspondence, in which amounts stated in figures are significant quantities. Choose the word style for personal-social letters and invitations and for resolutions and proclamations.

Figure Style

Exact and Approximate Numbers. Spell out numbers 1 through 10; use figures for numbers above 10. For emphasis or quick recognition, numbers 1 through 10 may be expressed in figures.

> Although ten typewriters were ordered, only six were received.
> Research shows that 78 percent of the second letters are vowels.

Related Numbers. If a sentence includes related numbers both below and above ten, use figures.

> She counted 25 primary guides, 8 special guides, 5 individual folders, and 9 miscellaneous folders in the file drawer.

Numbers in the Millions. When numbers *in the millions* or higher consist of a whole number, they may be expressed as combined figures and words.

> 40 million rather than 40,000,000
> 12.6 billion rather than 12,600,000,000
> 2¼ million rather than 2,250,000

General Rules

The following general rules apply whether you are using the figure style or the word style.

Beginning a Sentence. Spell out numbers that begin a sentence. To avoid awkward construction or to aid comprehension, rearrange a sentence so that it does not begin with a number.

> Twenty-five people answered the advertisement.
>
> *Change:* Nineteen hundred and thirty-three was the year Franklin D. Roosevelt was first inaugurated.
>
> *To:* Franklin D. Roosevelt was first inaugurated in 1933.

Indefinite Numbers and Amounts. Spell out approximations and indefinite amounts.

> It happened about fifty years ago.
>
> The mistake cost the company almost a million dollars.

Ordinals. Spell out ordinals that can be expressed in one or two words.

> the Eighteenth Amendment
> the ninety-third session
> in the twentieth century

Ordinal figures are expressed as *1st, 2d* or *2nd, 3d* or *3rd, 4th, 5th, 6th,* and so on in certain expressions of dates and in numbered street names above 10.

> We expect him on the 7th.

For clarity, use ordinal figures with numbered street names above 10 when a word such as *East* or *West* does not separate the building number from the street number.

> 118 12th Street

Dates. Complete dates are expressed in month-day-year sequence.

> November 22, 1972.

In military correspondence and in letters from foreign countries, the sequence is day-month-year.

> 8 June 1972

Use cardinal figures (1, 21, 31) when the day follows the month.

> Pay your income tax before April 15.

Use ordinal words (*third, eleventh*) in word style or ordinal figures (*1st, 16th*) in figure style for the day when it precedes the month or when the month is omitted.

> He flew to Miami on the twenty-sixth of July. (*or* 26th)
> The convention programs were mailed on the 15th. (*or* fifteenth)

Spell out dates in formal correspondence, legal documents, and proclamations.

> January twenty-sixth, nineteen hundred and seventy-two.
> The twenty-sixth of January, one thousand nine hundred and seventy-two.
> This twenty-sixth day of January, in the year one thousand nine hundred and seventy-two.

Centuries and decades may be expressed in words or figures.

> fifteenth century   15th century
> 1500s   the 1980s
> the nineteen-eighties   the eighties, the '80s

Measurements.   Use figures for measurements that have technical significance (such as weights and measures). Abbreviate units of measure (or use symbols) only in technical matter or in tabulations. Do not use a comma between the parts of a measurement.

> The room measured 4 by 8 meters.
> The carton weighed 4 pounds 12 ounces.
> Order two tables, each 4'6" x 6'8".
> The package weighs 2 kilograms.

Spell out measurements that are not emphasized or that lack technical significance.

> She drank three cups of coffee.

Money.   Use figures to express amounts of money, except in legal documents.

> $14.32   approximately $5,000 $1,058.75   over $20

In legal documents, amounts of money are expressed first in words and then in figures within parentheses.

> Three Thousand Forty-five and 75/100 Dollars ($3,045.75)
> Five Hundred Dollars ($500)

Use a decimal point and zeros with whole dollar amounts only when other figures in the same column are so expressed.

> He spent $12 on food and $24.75 on entertainment.
> Food $12.00
> Entertainment   24.75
> Tips   1.80
> $38.55

Rounded amounts of money of a million or more may be expressed partly in words, except when the amount contains a whole number and something more than a simple fraction.

> $14 million   *or*   14 million dollars
> $2.5 billion   *or*   2.5 billion dollars
> $15¼ million *or*   15¼ million dollars

But:

> $12,475,000

Related amounts of money may be expressed partly in words, but the word "million" or "billion" is used with each figure.

> $5 million to $10 million

For amounts under a dollar, use figures and the word *cents*. Spell out amounts under a dollar only when they are not significant or emphatic.

> The refill cartridge cost 78 cents.
> The clerk was surprised to find a silver fifty-cent piece in the cash drawer.

The cents sign and the dollar sign are repeated with each amount in a series of amounts or a price range.

> A comparison of prices charged by different stores for the same item revealed the following amounts: 19¢, 21¢, 23¢, and 25¢.
> 20¢ to 60¢
> $100,000 to $300,000

Fractions.   Use figures for mixed numbers except at the beginning of a sentence.

The picture was enlarged 2½ times its original size.
Two and one-half inches of asphalt was placed on the driveway.

Do not mix typewriter keyboard fractions (½, ¼) with constructed fractions (9/16, 3/8) in the same sequence. With constructed fractions, use the diagonal (/) and separate a whole number from a fraction by a space.

The frame measured 8 1/2 x 16 3/8. (*Not* 8½ x 16 3/8)

Spell out fractions that stand alone unless the fraction is long and awkward or unless the fraction is used in technial matter.

Each employee received a refund at one-half the tuition.
The workers installed half-inch copper tubing. (½-inch copper tubing *in technical matter*)

If an *of* phrase follows the fraction, spell out the fraction.

one-third of the employees
three thirty-seconds of an inch

Decimals. Use figures for all decimals. Do not use commas in the part of a number to the right of the decimal.

2.1825   10,250.50634

Place a zero before the decimal point when a decimal is not preceded by a whole number unless the decimal begins with a zero.

0.29   .028   1.28

Percentages, Ratios, and Proportions. Use figures for percentages and spell out *percent* except in tabulations.

The carriers were seeking 20 percent annual wage increases.

Fractional percentages under 1 percent should be spelled out or expressed as decimal figures.

one-quarter of 1 percent   0.25 percent

Where a range of percentages is given, the word *percent* follows the last figure only. When the symbol % is used, it is needed after each figure to avoid misunderstanding.

10 to 20 percent   10% to 20%

Use figures for ratios and proportions.

> 8 to 1 ratio, 8:1 ratio
> odds of 50 to 1
> a 50-50 chance
> a proportion of 7 to 3

Time.   Use figures with *a.m.* and *p.m.*

> The plane departs at 8:30 a.m.
> The meeting is scheduled for 1:30 p.m.

Do not add zeros to denote minutes when time is expressed on the hour, except in tables where other times are given in hours and minutes.

> His dental appointment was at 1 p.m.
> Trains leave for Chicago at 8:05 a.m., 1 p.m., and 4:40 p.m.

Leave	Arrive
5:55	7:00
7:25	8:30
10:00	11:05

Noon and *midnight* may be expressed in words alone, except when used in connection with other times expressed in figures.

> The clock struck the hour of midnight.
> From 12 midnight until 3 a.m. he lay restless, unable to sleep.

When expressing time on the hour without *a.m., p.m.,* or *o'clock,* spell out the hour.

> His appointment was at two in the afternoon.

When expressing time in hours and minutes without *a.m., p.m.,* or *o'clock,* either spell out the number or use figures.

> They sat down to dinner at six forty-five in the evening.
> The bus departed at 9:56 in the morning.

In nontechnical writing, spell out periods of time unless they are used as significant statistics or require more than two words.

> fourteen days from today
> during the previous twelve months
> a 35-hour week
> a 20-year mortgage
> 250 years ago

Ages.   Spell out a person's age and numbers designating anniversaries in nontechnical correspondence.

> Tomorrow he will be eighteen years old.
> They planned to celebrate their twentieth wedding anniversary.

Use figures to express ages in personal data sheets; in matters pertaining to employment, retirement, and insurance; and when the number requires more than two words if spelled out.

> At age 62 he will be eligible for retirement benefits.
> The antique chest is 275 years old.
> She worked for me for 2 years 4 months. (*No comma between the elements.*)

Numbered Items.   Use figures to express serial numbers of invoices, telephone numbers, house or room numbers, and model numbers.

> Invoice 1062   (203) 321-4648   Room 201   Figure 12

Use figures following *Chapter, page,* and *Volume.*

> Chapter 20   page 126   Volume 12

Use commas to separate numbers that do not represent a continuous sequence; use a hyphen to link two figures that represent a continuous sequence.

> pages 14, 34, and 54
> records for the years 1952, 1962, and 1972
> read pages 212–224
> in Volumes 8–10

When sequences of years or of page numbers occur often, the second figure may be shortened, as shown below. Note that if the word *from* is used, the word *to* or *through* must also be used.

> 1965–70 *or*   1965–1970
> 1971–2 *or*   1971–1972
> 1900–1950 (*not* 1900–50)
> 1840–1920 (*not* 1840–20)

But:

> from 1960 to 1980

Roman numerals are used for main topics in outlines and for divisions of literary and legislative materials. Pages in the front section of a book, preceding the actual text, are usually numbered in small roman numerals.

Volume XXIII   Chapter V   page iii   MCMLXXII (1972)

Always use figures with abbreviations and symbols.

$74   23%   9:30 p.m.   9 ft or 9′

Note: Repeat the symbol with each number in a range; do not repeat a word or an abbreviation.

9′ x 12′   9 by 12 ft or 9 x 12 ft
20%–23%   20 to 23 percent

Word Style

Two-Word Numbers. Spell out all numbers that can be expressed in one or two words. (Hyphenated compound numbers, such as *twenty-one*, count as one word.)

Six hundred people attended.
twenty-one million

Related Numbers. Spell out all related numbers even if some are above 100 and some are below.

We sent our five hundred survey forms and subsequently received one hundred responses.

Large Round Numbers. Use the fewest words possible when spelling out large round numbers.

We received over sixteen hundred telephone calls about the fare increase. (*Not* one thousand six hundred)

Numbers in the Millions. Numbers in the millions or higher that require more than two words when spelled out may be expressed as combined figures and words.

450 million *rather than* 450,000,000
6½ billion *rather than* 6,500,000,000
255.8 million *rather than* 255,800,000

Proofreader's Marks

Symbol in Margin	Mark in Text	Meaning
℘	money**s**	Take out, delete.
℘	ac**c**ademic	Take out and close up space.
⌒	al together	Close up horizontal space.
#	two**or** three	Add space.
¶	asset. The balance	Start a new paragraph.
No ¶	asset. ⟋ The balance	Run in with preceding paragraph.
[	today's order	Move to left.
]	today's order	Move to right.
⊔	The office	Lower.
⊓	The office	Raise.
tr	A meeting regular	Transpose.
sp	the ④ items	Spell out.
stet	the great majority	Restore word or words crossed out.
many	there are types	Insert marginal word or words.
cap	february 10	Capitalize lowercase letter.
lc	Spring	Lowercase capital letter.
sc	44 B.C.	Change to small caps.
wf	the (last) analysis	Wrong font.
rom	the (last) analysis	Set in roman type.
bf	the last analysis	Set in boldface type.
ital	The word word is	Set in italic type.
⊙	Mr	Insert period.
⅄/⅄	white blue and green	Insert commas. (The diagonal indicates the end of one correction.)
⌃	trade that is,	Insert semicolon.
⊙	these items	Insert colon.
ⱽ	its important	Insert apostrophe.
ⱽ/ⱽ	Casey at the Bat	Insert quotation marks.
=/	dry clean	Insert hyphen.
?/	"How" she asked.	Insert question mark.
⸨/⸩	on July 6	Insert parentheses.
[/]	at 8 p.m.	Insert brackets.
!	Hurrah	Insert exclamation point.
⊢M⊣	these people the ones who	Insert em dash.
⊢N⊣	pages 1 4	Insert en dash.

Punctuation

Carefully placed punctuation marks signal the proper relationship of words, phrases, and clauses. Punctuation, wisely used, clarifies the meaning of a sentence when word order alone is not sufficient.

Guidelines for punctuation are briefly reviewed below. For a full treatment of punctuation, consult a standard handbook of English, such as *The Gregg Reference Manual* (5th ed., by William A. Sabin, Gregg Division, McGraw-Hill Book Company, New York, 1977).

Apostrophe

Use an apostrophe to form the possessive of nouns: (1) add *'s* to *singular* nouns, (2) add *'s* to *singular* nouns ending in *s* unless the addition of an *s* makes the word difficult to pronounce, (3) add *'* to *plural* nouns ending with *s*, (4) add *'s* to *plural* nouns that do not end in *s*.

(1) John's	Helen and Mary's	girl's
(2) boss's	Charles's	Dawkins'
(3) boys'	ladies'	instructors'
(4) women's	freshmen's	children's

Insert an apostrophe at the exact point where a letter or letters are omitted to form contractions.

they're *for* they are
can't *for* cannot
nat'l *for* national

Use an apostrophe for plurals of lowercase letters and figures.

b's   3's

Use an apostrophe to indicate the omission of figures in dates.

the class of '74   the '60s

Asterisk

Use an asterisk to refer the reader to a footnote at the bottom of a page.

> These fashions are from the '40s.*
> _____
> *A simple *s* is usually added to a contracted year, to avoid two apostrophes.

Brackets

Use brackets to enclose a correction or an insertion in quoted matter.

> "Ladies and Gentlemen: I did not expect such a large turnout [at the Coliseum]. This must be a record attendance."

Colon

Use a colon between a clause and a series when the clause contains an anticipatory phrase or word, such as *the following, as follows, thus, these,* and leads to a series of explanatory or implied explanatory words, phrases, or clauses.

> Several points were made, especially these: accuracy, promptness, and clarity.
> A number of matters were discussed, including the following: production speedup, overtime compensation, and pension plan.

Use a colon between two independent clauses when the second clause explains or illustrates the first clause and there is no coordinating conjunction or transitional expression linking the two clauses.

> The report I have been asked to prepare sounds challenging: it will require extensive research, and I can utilize the note-taking techniques I have learned.

Use a colon before such transitional expressions as *for example, namely,* and *that is* when they introduce words, phrases, or a series of clauses anticipated earlier in the sentence.

> When you get up from a chair three important moves are required: namely, pulling one foot back so that the heel is even with the front edge of the seat, pulling the other foot a little farther back, and leaning forward slightly as you push with both legs.

Use a colon following short introductory words, such as *Note, Caution,* or *Exception*.

> *Note:* This stretch of the road is closed from November through March.

Use a colon after the salutation in a business letter (unless you are using open punctuation or a comma with a social-business letter) and between the dictator's and the transcriber's initials.

Gentlemen: Dear Mr. Drewry: RJY:csr

Use a colon to separate the figures in hours and minutes.

8:30 a.m.   10:30 p.m.

Use a colon to represent the word *to* in statements of proportions.

2:1   5:7

Comma

Use a comma before a coordinating conjunction (*and, but, or, nor*) that separates two independent clauses in a compound sentence.

Comparison with last year's figures reveals a rise in executive travel expenses, but further study is needed to find the reason.

When no coordinating conjunction is used between two independent clauses, use a semicolon (or a colon or a dash if appropriate).

When a dependent clause precedes a main clause, use a comma to separate them. Such introductory clauses may be elliptical (words omitted). But if the introductory dependent clause is the subject of the sentence, do not use a comma.

If you purchase these brackets in lots of 500, you are eligible for a 5 percent trade discount.

But:

What happens at the committee meeting today will determine when the announcement will be made.

Use a comma to separate a dependent clause when it interrupts or follows the main clause only if the dependent clause is not essential to the sense of the sentence. Such a clause is called a *nonrestrictive* clause; one that is essential to the meaning is called a *restrictive* clause.

Mr. Johnson, who recently joined the firm, is on the committee. (*nonessential*)
The taxi arrived before I was ready to leave. (*essential*)

Use a comma after introductory participial phrases, prepositional phrases, and infinitive phrases introduced by the word *to*.

Gesturing with his hands, he attempted to attract attention.

To maintain good customer relations, she answered the complaint letter immediately.

Use commas to set off parenthetical, transitional, or introductory expressions that are not necessary to the grammatical completeness of the sentence or to its meaning.

As a rule, the holiday schedule is distributed by February 1.

His opening remarks, in my opinion, were unnecessary.

Such expressions include the following:

as a result	however	of course
as a rule	in addition	on the other hand
at any rate	in other words	otherwise
consequently	meanwhile	respectively
finally	moreover	that is
first	namely	therefore
for example	nevertheless	yes

Note: After a short introductory prepositional phrase, no comma is required, unless its omission will lead to misunderstanding.

In 1980 she graduated from college.

In 1980, 546 students graduated.

Use a comma before the conjunctions *and, or,* or *nor* and between other words or phrases used in series.

The mail had been opened, date-stamped, and sorted before he arrived.

Note: When *and, or,* or *nor* is used to connect all items in a series, do not separate the items by commas.

Use a comma to separate two or more consecutive adjectives modifying the same noun.

The job description called for an experienced, productive manager.

Use commas to set off words, phrases, and clauses that identify or explain other terms. This use is called *appositive.*

Mr. Franklin, your local representative, has written me regarding your recommendation.

Use a comma to indicate the omission of a word (usually a verb).

The balance on January 10 was $14.50; on February 10, $54.10; and on March 10, $67.80.

Use a comma to ensure clarity.

He arrived yesterday afternoon; soon after, he completed the assignment.

Use commas to set off names and titles used in direct address.

Your analysis of the report, Ms. Phillips, was excellent.

Use commas before and after the year when it follows the month and day.

He began work on November 29, 1972, under the terms of the contract.

Use commas to separate the name of a city from the name of a state or a country and to denote a person's residence or business affiliation.

Write to the manufacturer in St. Louis, Missouri, for information.
Mr. Croft, of National Industries in Hartford, Connecticut, will attend the conference.

Use commas to separate thousands, hundreds of thousands, millions, and so on in large numbers.

1,874,210 $250,450

A comma usually precedes the opening quotation mark of a quoted statement when it occurs at the end of a sentence.

Mr. Canfield stated, "Proceed with the plan you described to me."

DASH

A dash should not be used indiscriminately in place of the comma, the semicolon, the colon, or parentheses. It should be used only when special forcefulness is desired and other punctuation would be inadequate. Overuse destroys its effectiveness and conveys the impression of jumpy, disorganized thinking.

The dash is constructed by striking the hyphen key twice, with no space before, between, or after the hyphen. Do not begin a new line with a hyphen.

Use a dash in place of commas or parentheses to set off parenthetical expressions.

The work is exciting—see for yourself—and well worth your time.

Use a dash in place of a semicolon between relatively brief, closely related independent clauses.

Only one thing is lacking—we need your name on the dotted line.

Use a dash in place of a colon to introduce explanatory expressions.

The office has several extra features—indirect lighting, carpet, drapes, and a supply closet.

Use a dash to show an abrupt change in thought or an afterthought.

She researched the material thoroughly—did we ever recognize her contribution?

Use a dash before such words as *these, they,* and *all* when they are used to summarize a preceding list.

Checks, paper currency, and coins—these should be itemized on a bank deposit slip.

Diagonal

The diagonal without space before or after is used in certain abbreviations and symbols.

c/o, care of   B/L, bill of lading

Use the diagonal in writing fractions and in some serial numbers.

4/5   5/8   3H/24617

Ellipsis

Use three ellipsis points (spaced periods) for an omission *within* a sentence.

The data on all the different methods . . . were presented by the chairperson.

Use four ellipsis points to show omission at the *end* of a sentence.

The plan outlined was adopted unanimously. . . . Mr. Norton was asked to head the study group.

Exclamation Point

Use an exclamation point at the end of a sentence to express surprise or other strong emotions.

You did a remarkable job!

Use an exclamation point after a word or phrase that expresses strong feelings.

Oh!   Wait!   Congratulations!   What a day!

Note: When exclamations are mild, a comma or a period is sufficient.

Oh, what's the use.

Parentheses

Parentheses are used to set off nonessential elements in a sentence. They serve to deemphasize rather than emphasize.

Use parentheses to enclose explanatory material that is independent of the main thought of the sentence.

The manager made it clear that for the remainder of the year (there are four fiscal periods) expenses must be cut substantially.

Use parentheses to set off parenthetical elements when dashes or commas would be too emphatic.

James Taylor (our sales representative in Portland, Oregon) will handle your account.

Use parentheses to set off references and directions.

Our interpretation of the ruling (page 27, first paragraph) is not the same as his.

Use parentheses to enclose dates and numbers or letters that separate enumerated items within a sentence.

At the time of the acquisition (1969) both managements agreed to the new location.
Do these things: (1) read; (2) sort; (3) open.

Period

Use a period at the end of sentences that make a statement or express a command.

She checked her coat and briefcase.
Congratulations on your promotion.

Use a period at the end of requests or demands that are phrased as a question out of politeness, where the writer expects action rather than a yes or no answer.

> Will you let me know the type of paper you prefer.
> Would you send your check to the address shown on the invoice.

Note: If a period seems presumptuous, use a question mark instead, or rephrase the question in statement form.

> Please send your check to the address shown on the invoice.

Use a period at the end of elliptical expressions that appear as complete statements or commands.

> Yes.   No.   Certainly.

In a separate-line listing, use periods after the items if they are independent clauses, dependent clauses, or long phrases. Do not use a period after short items unless they are essential to the grammatical completeness of the introductory statement.

> Divide a word·
> 1. After a prefix; before a suffix.
> 2. Between the elements of a compound.
> 3. After a one-letter syllable within the root of a word.
> Let me know which of the following is convenient for you:
> August 1
> August 8
> September 3

Use a period to separate a whole number from a decimal fraction.

> 7.5 percent $12.45

Use a period at the end of single-word abbreviations, after each initial of small-letter abbreviations, and after initials in a person's name.

> pp.   Inc.   Dr.   a.m.   p.m.   R. L. Jones

QUESTION MARK

Use a question mark at the end of a direct question.

> Who should I say is calling?

Use a question mark at the end of an elliptical word or phrase that represents a complete question.

> She didn't agree with the report. Why?

Use a question mark at the end of statements that are intended as questions or that express uncertainty.

> He didn't contribute to the discussion?
> He joined the staff in 1966(?).

Use a question mark after each question in a series (for emphasis).

> Have you finished trimming the hedge? cutting the lawn? and weeding the garden?

Quotation Marks

Quotation marks are used to (1) enclose someone else's exact words, (2) set off words and phrases, and (3) indicate titles of literary and artistic works.
Use quotation marks to enclose the exact words of a speaker or writer.

> He said, "The return on investment is not satisfactory."

Note: For quotations of more than one paragraph, use quotation marks at the beginning of each paragraph and at the end of the last paragraph. Omit quotation marks, however, when long quotations are indented or single spaced in double-spaced material.

Use quotation marks to enclose technical or trade terms when they are first introduced, slang, or words out of context.

> Capital letters are often referred to as "upper case."

Use quotation marks around titles that represent part of a complete published work—such as chapters and sections within a book; articles in magazines; or short works such as essays, lectures, or poems.

> He placed special emphasis on the chapter entitled "Inventories" in *Advanced Accounting* by Johnson.
> Please read "A Call for Total Commitment," by Howard Day, in this month's *American Vocational Journal*.

Use quotation marks around the titles of unpublished works, such as manuscripts, dissertations, and reports.

A summary of the study entitled "Qualifications of the Administrative Secretary, with Implications for the Collegiate Curriculum" by Harry P. Graham, appeared in last month's *Business Education Forum*.

Use single quotation marks around a quotation within a quotation. To type a single quotation mark, use the apostrophe key.

He replied angrily, "That 'jerk' is my brother."

The order of punctuation marks in relation to closing quotation marks is as follows: commas and periods are placed inside the closing quotation marks; semicolons and colons go outside; question marks and exclamation marks go inside when they apply only to the quoted matter and outside when they apply to the entire sentence containing the quotation.

Jane submitted her article, "Next Year's Profit Outlook."

Jane submitted her article, "Next Year's Profit Outlook"; she is waiting for the magazine's decision.

Jane submitted her article, "What Is Next Year's Profit Outlook?"

Have you read Jane's article, "Next Year's Profit Outlook"?

Semicolon

Use a semicolon to separate two independent clauses when the coordinating conjunction (*and, but, or,* or *nor*) is omitted.

The sales staff came at three; the office staff came at four.

Use a semicolon to indicate a stronger break than a comma between two independent clauses joined by the coordinating conjunction *and, but, or,* or *nor*.

Normal Break: Our recruitment program for secretaries was to feature local high school career days, but these must now be postponed until after we move to our new plant.

Stronger Break: Our recruitment program for secretaries was to feature local high school career days; but these must now be postponed until after we move to our new plant.

Use a semicolon between independent clauses linked by such transitional words as *accordingly, consequently, for example, hence, however, namely, nevertheless, so, that is, therefore, thus*.

The position had been filled; therefore, he was not interviewed.

Note: A comma is not needed after a transitional expression of only one syllable.

The meeting adjourned at 4:30; then each manager departed for dinner.

Use a semicolon to separate items in a series or a series of parallel subordinate clauses that already contain commas or other punctuation.

Attending the seminar were Elaine Richardson, president of Sommers, Inc.; Roberta Newman, director of Research Associates, Inc.; and Jack Orcutt, consultant.

Underscore

A word that is referred to as a word and a word that is being defined are usually underscored for emphasis.

The words adapt, adept, and adopt are often confused.
The term trespass is defined as a wrongful injury to or interference with the property of a third person.

Underscore titles of complete works that are published—such as books, pamphlets, magazines, newspapers, movies, plays, and musicals.

A subscription to Administrative Management is recommended for every career-minded secretary.

Punctuation Styles for Letters

The two commonly accepted punctuation styles for letters, *standard* and *open*, are shown below. Note that open punctuation omits the colon after the salutation and the comma after the complimentary closing.

Open Punctuation

November 18, 19—

Mr. Isaac Klempner
Sales Manager
The Weekly News Inc.
1011 Fairfield Avenue
Westport, CT 06880

Dear Mr. Klempner

Sincerely

WESTVALE COMPANY

Fred Tilski

Research Director

FT:mh
Enclosure
cc Ms. Moran

Standard Punctuation

November 18, 19—

Mr. Isaac Klempner
Sales Manager
The Weekly News Inc.
1011 Fairfield Avenue
Westport, CT 06880

Dear Mr. Klempner:

Sincerely,

WESTVALE COMPANY

Fred Tilski

Research Director

FT:mh
Enclosure
cc Ms. Moran

Spelling Guidelines

This part of the Reference Section is designed to help you recognize and avoid errors caused by failure to apply the rules of spelling and errors caused by carelessness.

Webster's New Collegiate Dictionary and *Webster's Third New International Dictionary* serve as the authorities for the spelling rules presented here.

Doubling a Final Consonant

In words of one syllable (*ship*) that end in a single consonant (*ship*) preceded by a single vowel (*ship*), double the final consonant before a suffix beginning with a vowel (*ship*per).

drop	dropped	bag	baggage
plan	planning	slip	slippage
occur	occurred	glad	gladden

(*Exceptions:* bus, buses; fix, fixed; tax, taxing)

When a one-syllable word ends in a single consonant (*ship*) preceded by a single vowel (*ship*) before a suffix beginning with a consonant (*ship*ment), do not double the final consonant.

drop	droplet
bad	badly
glad	gladness

When a word of more than one syllable ends in a single consonant (*credit*) preceded by a single vowel (*credit*) and the accent does not fall on the last syllable of the word root (*credit*), do not double the final consonant before a suffix beginning with a vowel (*credit*ed).

defer	deferred	control	controller
concur	concurrent	transfer	transferred

(*Exceptions:* program, programmed, programming)

In words of one or more syllables that end with more than one consonant, do not double the final consonant of the root word.

| depend | dependable | persist | persistence |
| perform | performance | confirm | confirming |

For words ending in a single consonant preceded by more than one vowel, do not double the final consonant of the root word.

| equal | equalize | appear | appearance |
| obtain | obtainable | need | needy |

Final Y to I

In words ending in *y* preceded by a consonant, change the *y* to *i* before adding any suffix except one beginning with *i*.

| modify | modifier | likely | likelihood |
| defy | defiant | ordinary | ordinarily |

Words ending in *y* preceded by a vowel usually retain the *y* before any suffix.

| betray | betrayal | obey | obeying |
| annoy | annoyance | delay | delayed |

(*Exceptions:* pay, paid; lay, laid; day, daily)

Homonyms

The words that follow are commonly confused homonyms—words similar in sound but different in spelling and meaning. The definitions given are limited to those that illustrate the essential differences in meaning. For more detailed definitions, consult a dictionary.

If you habitually confuse certain words, make your own card file of them for frequent review.

accept to receive, agree
except to exclude, leave out; but

adapt to change
adopt to take as one's own

addition increase
edition publication (from edit)

adverse opposed to
averse unwilling

advice an opinion (noun)
advise to give an opinion (verb)

affect to act upon
effect to accomplish

all ready prepared (adj.)
already by this time (adv.)

all together in the same place
altogether entirely

all ways all means
always all the time

altar used in worship (noun)
alter to change (verb)

any one any single or individual thing or person *Example:* Is any one of you willing to come?

anyone any person *Example:* Has anyone heard this?

bases foundations (plural)

basis foundation (singular)

biannual twice a year

biennial every two years

capital principal, head, assets

capitol building occupied by a state legislature

cite to quote

sight vision

site location

complement to complete

compliment praise

confidant one to whom a secret is told

confident certain or sure

consul foreign representative

council assembly

counsel advice

decent proper

descent ancestry; downward slope

dissent disagreement

decree law

degree grade

desert to abandon (verb), barren place (noun)

dessert the last course of a meal

device a plan or scheme (noun)

devise to scheme (verb)

dual double

duel combat

emigrant one who leaves a country

immigrant one who enters a country

eminent prominent, high in rank

imminent threatening, likely to occur immediately

farther at a greater distance

further in addition to, moreover

formally ceremoniously

formerly before

forth forward

fourth number 4

hoard to save

horde vast number

holy sacred

wholly entirely

incite arouse

insight understanding

ingenious clever

ingenuous frank

it's it is

its possessive pronoun

lean thin

lien legal claim on property

lightening making lighter

lightning discharge of electricity from clouds

load quantity

lode mineral deposit

loan something lent

lone alone, solitary

loath unwilling (adjective)

loathe to detest (verb)

loose to set free

lose to miss

pair two of a kind

pare to peel

pear a fruit

passed past tense of *pass* (verb)

past time gone by (noun)

pore to gaze intently

pour to flow

precede to go before in time or importance

proceed to go forward, to carry on

principal chief, main

principle rule

prophecy prediction (noun)

prophesy to predict (verb)

rain falling water

reign to rule

rein to check or control

raise lift up

raze destroy

right correct, straight

rite a formal ceremony

wright workman (combining form, as in *playwright*)

write to express on paper, compose

role a part in a play

roll a list

shear to cut (verb)

sheer thin (adjective)

shone past tense of *shine*

shown past participle of *show*

stationary stable, fixed, standing

stationery letters, paper

than used in comparisons

then at that time, therefore

their belonging to them

there in that place

they're they are

waive to give up a right

wave to signal

ware goods

wear to carry on the person

where at what place

who's who is

whose possessive of *who*

you're you are

your possessive of *you*

IE and EI Words

Position *i* before e except after c or when the sound is a long a as in *freight*.

I Before E

achieve	relief	yield	anxiety
believe	brief	view	variety

(*Exceptions:* either, neither, height, forfeit, foreign)

After C

deceive	receipt	receive	conceive

(*Exceptions:* science, efficient, financier)

Sounded Like A

eight	heir	weight	vein
freight	neighbor	their	veil

ING After IE and Y

In words ending in *ie*, change the *ie* to *y* before adding *ing*.

die	dying	tie	tying
lie	lying	vie	vying

Add *ing* after *y* without change.

deny	denying
study	studying
vary	varying

Silent Final E

Drop the silent final *e* before a suffix beginning with a vowel.

advise	advisory	enclose	enclosure
argue	arguing	desire	desirous
base	basic	sale	salable

(*Exceptions:* agree, agreeing; mile, mileage)

Retain the silent final *e* before a suffix beginning with a consonant.

encourage	encouragement	nine	ninety
manage	management	trouble	troublesome

(*Exceptions:* acknowledge, acknowledgment; argue, argument)

Word Demons

Certain words in the English language represent unique spelling problems or exceptions to common rules. Some frequently encountered "word demons" are listed here:

accommodate	changeable	eligible	miscellaneous
acquiesce	commitment	embarrass	pamphlet
aisle	concede	emphasize	panicky
alleged	conscious	exaggerate	preceding
apparently	consensus	exorbitant	pursue
auxiliary	corroborate	facsimile	questionnaire
bankruptcy	describe	forfeit	relevant
benefited	dilemma	innocuous	resume
calendar	eighth	liaison	supersede

Word Division

Dividing a word at the end of a line should be avoided if possible, so as not to distract or confuse the reader. In any typewritten material that is to be read aloud, for example, it is best not to divide any words.

If a word must be divided, the break is made between syllables and then according to the basic rules reviewed below. If you are not sure of the syllabication after pronouncing the word carefully, then consult the dictionary.

The rules of this section apply to typewritten material.

Basic Rules

Do not divide one-syllable words.

> judge   bridge   passed   raced

Do not divide any word with fewer than six letters. Leave a syllable of at least three characters (two letters and hyphen) on the upper line and a syllable of at least three characters (one of which may be punctuation) on the next line.

> re- port   plat- en   bill- ing

Do not separate a beginning or an ending syllable of one letter.

> alone (*not:* a- lone)
> many (*not:* man- y)
> ideal (*not:* i- deal)

Do not divide abbreviations and contractions.

Divide a hyphenated compound word at the hyphen; divide a solid compound word between the elements of the compound.

> self- control   father- in-law   business- persons   time- table

Divide a word after a prefix.

> pre- test   mis- spell   con- tract   dis- place

Note: *Avoid* divisions of prefixes that can confuse a reader, such as *am-, in-,* and *super-.*

Divide a word before a suffix.

collect- ible   loca- tion   substan- tial   consign- ment

Divide after a syllable of one letter that occurs within the word rather than before it.

navi- gate   regu- late   sepa- rate   criti- cal

Divide between two separately sounded vowels that come together in a word rather than before or after them.

sci- ence   re- iterate   valu- able   propri- etary

Do not separate word groups that should be read together, such as title and surname, month and day or year, or number and abbreviation or unit of measure.

Dr. Luttinger   Frank Harris III   December 2
66 Janes Lane $14,210

Note: If you must: (a) divide dates between the day and year; (b) divide street addresses between the name of the street and the word *Street, Avenue,* and so on; (c) divide places between the city and the state; (d) divide names of persons between the given name and surname and between the title and the name; (e) divide extremely long numbers after a comma.

Never begin a new line with a hyphen.
No more than two consecutive lines should end with hyphens.
Never divide the last word on a page or at the end of the last full line in a paragraph.
Divide *after* a double consonant before a suffix is added when a word ends in a double consonant.

staff- ing   sell- ers

Divide *between* double consonants when a final consonant is doubled because a suffix is added.

ship- ping   refer- ral

Divide between double consonants *within* the base word.

mil- lion   suc- cess   recom- mend   neces- sary

Index